Microeconomic Theory
An Integrated Approach

Stephen Mathis
Shippensburg University

Janet Koscianski
Shippensburg University

Prentice
Hall

Upper Saddle River, New Jersey 07458

Library of Congress Cataloging-in-Publication Data

Mathis, Stephen.
   Microeconomic theory : an integrated approach / Stephen A. Mathis,
Janet Koscianski.
      p. cm.
   Includes index.
   ISBN 0-13-011418-9
   1. Microeconomics. 2. Economics, Mathematical. I. Koscianski, Janet. II. Title.

   HB172 .M377 2002
   338.5—dc21

                                                        2001055417

AVP/Executive Editor: Rod Banister
Editor-in Chief: P. J. Boardman
Managing Editor (Editorial): Gladys Soto
Assistant Editor: Marie McHale
Editorial Assistant: Lisa Amato
Media Project Manager: Victoria Anderson
Marketing Manager: Kathleen McLellan
Marketing Assistant: Christopher Bath
Managing Editor (Production): John Roberts
Production Editor: Maureen Wilson
Production Assistant: Dianne Falcone
Production Coordinator: Suzanne Grappi
Associate Director, Manufacturing: Vincent Scelta
Production Manager: Arnold Vila
Manufacturing Buyer: Michelle Klein
Cover Design: Jayne Conte, Art Director
Cover Illustration/Photo: Mick Tarel/Artville
Full-Service Project Management and Composition: UG / GGS Information Services,
Inc.
Printer/Binder: Courier-Westford

Credits and acknowledgments borrowed from other sources and reproduced, with
permission, in this textbook appear on appropriate page within text.

Pearson Education LTD.
Pearson Education Australia PTY, Limited
Pearson Education Singapore, Pte. Ltd
Pearson Education North Asia Ltd
Pearson Education Canada, Ltd
Pearson Educación de Mexico, S.A. de C.V.
Pearson Education–Japan
Pearson Education Malaysia, Pte. Ltd

10 9 8 7 6 5 4 3 2 1
ISBN 0-13-011418-9

Brief Contents

Contents

Preface

Microeconomic theory is one of the most important courses taken by economics and business students. We base this contention on the fact that microeconomics consists of analyzing the rational decision-making processes of many types of agents, including consumers, entrepreneurs, suppliers of resources, investors, and even government policy makers. This broad applicability of microeconomics to many types of decision-making problems endows this subject with special significance. Although many of the details associated with specific problems are supplied by other subject areas, microeconomics provides the framework and techniques for solving these problems. For this reason, the approach we use to present microeconomics focuses on constructing and analyzing fundamental models. By emphasizing broad-based underlying principles, students can analyze a wider variety of real-world problems than is possible by using an approach that dwells on overly specific microeconomic problem or puzzles.

A full and broad understanding of microeconomics is greatly facilitated by applying several tools of analysis. Accordingly, we develop concepts using verbal intuition, graphics, and calculus, carefully integrating these facets of microeconomic analysis throughout our text. Both the focus on fundamental principles and the integration of basic calculus throughout the text distinguish our approach from so many others. We bring in the calculus, not to complicate the analysis, but rather to simplify it. Using basic tools of calculus, we are able to demonstrate to students how to solve many models and problems by generating actual numerical solutions. We believe this approach is much more effective than merely presenting concepts in a survey manner. Furthermore, we demonstrate how calculus reinforces the graphical analysis, and in so doing, we can help students understand what the graphical solutions actually represent. It has been our experience that, without the underlying mathematics, students often view graphs as mere pictures to be memorized.

Students need only a basic understanding of differential calculus in order to use this text. As we have observed over the years, most students have little difficulty performing basic calculus operations. Rather, their difficulty often lies in synchronizing not only the calculus, but also the graphics, with specific microeconomic concepts. We believe we have solved this problem by integrating calculus throughout the text, directly connecting it with each microeconomic concept, rather than presenting it in detached appendices or footnotes.

AUDIENCE

The basic concepts covered in this text are central both to a course in intermediate microeconomics and to first-year graduate courses for MBA or master's-level economics programs. To give professors some flexibility regarding the level at which some material is covered, we have placed the dagger symbol, †, before those sections that contain advanced analyses. Students should already be familiar with many of the basic principles covered in our text, for they are common to all levels of microeconomic theory. In this text, we often ask readers to recall certain material from their principles of microeconomics course, with the expressed intent to remind students of key concepts covered in their introductory microeconomics course which we examine at a higher analytical level in this book.

AN INTEGRATED APPROACH

We have subtitled our book "An Integrated Approach" to signal our extraordinary attention to presenting theoretical microeconomic concepts with words, graphs, mathematics, and real-world examples. Each method of presentation is carefully and closely coordinated with the others. By its very nature, mathematics is a very succinct and precise means of expressing economic concepts. Accordingly, we have made extensive use of calculus throughout this text in order to demonstrate to students that mathematics can actually simplify the way they express microeconomic theories and solve economic problems. To ensure that students truly comprehend the topics in our text, we include several numerical examples in each chapter and solve them step by step. Our book encourages students to get "down and dirty" with microeconomic theory by motivating them to sit down with pencil and paper and solve real microeconomic problems. Through these problems students can immediately test their understanding of key topics, since they can check their answers with the solutions appearing in the text. We also include numerous real-world applications in an effort to relate the microeconomic concepts we cover in the text to actual events. These applications are based on articles published in a variety of well-known business and economics publications such as *The Wall Street Journal*, *The Economist*, *Business Week*, and *Fortune*.

Finally, throughout this text we make frequent references to topics we covered in previous sections or chapters. By doing so, we establish cross-references of important, interrelated topics as they are developed. We believe this process helps the reader to get the "big picture" and thereby avoid seeing the chapters as separate, unrelated entities. These cross-references also facilitate the student's ability to return to specific sections and review prerequisite concepts when necessary. Throughout this book, key terms are presented in bold when they are first introduced. They are also listed with their page references at the end of each chapter, as well as in the Glossary at the end of the book.

ORGANIZATION

We have broadly divided the topics covered in this text into six major areas: preliminary mathematical techniques, theory of the consumer, theory of the firm, market structures, input markets, and general equilibrium analysis. Specifically, in Chapters 1 and 2 we develop the essential mathematical tools used throughout this book. In Chapter 1 we review the rules of derivatives for both univariate and multivariate functions, and we develop the method for optimizing univariate functions. In Chapter 2 we expand our discussion of optimization, focusing on unconstrained and constrained optimization of multivariate functions. We also carefully develop the Lagrangian multiplier method and demonstrate its use in modeling rational decision making by consumers and firms in the presence of constraints.

Following this mathematical review, the next five chapters concentrate on the economic behavior of consumers. In Chapter 3 we establish the foundations of consumer choice by developing utility functions and the related concepts of marginal utility and indifference curves. In an appendix to Chapter 3 (available at the website for this text at www.prenhall.com/mathis), we modify the traditional consumer choice model to incorporate the effect of risk on the consumer's decision-making process. In Chapter 4 we extend our analysis of consumer theory by introducing the concept of a budget constraint. Using the Lagrangian multiplier method introduced in Chapter 2, we demonstrate how to solve the consumer's constrained utility maximization problem both mathematically and graphically. In Chapter 5 we use the results of this process to establish relationships between the quantity demanded of a good and key economic variables such as the own-price of the good, the price of a related good, and the consumer's level of income. We further analyze these relationships in Chapter 6 where we derive the market demand curve for a good by aggregating the individual demand curves developed in Chapter 5. In Chapter 7 we examine the concept of elasticity and apply it to the market demand function in terms of own-price, cross-price, and income elasticities of demand. In addition to discussing the theoretical, graphical, and mathematical analyses of elasticity, we also explore a variety of real-world applications of elasticity measures.

A major change in topics occurs in Chapter 8; in this and the following four chapters, we develop the theory of the firm. Initially, we examine the behavior of the firm from a short-run perspective by introducing a production function containing only one variable input. In Chapter 9 we relax this assumption by allowing all inputs used by the firm in the production of its output to vary, thereby shifting the analysis of firm behavior from a short-run to a long-run perspective. In Chapter 10 we apply the Lagrangian multiplier method to the theory of the firm to demonstrate how constrained optimization techniques can be applied to various production decisions faced by profit-maximizing firms. The concepts comprising production theory, in both the short run and the long run, provide the foundation for analyzing firm's costs of production in these distinct time periods. After we establish the critical connections between production theory and cost theory in Chapter 11, we direct our attention to the graphical and mathematical analysis of various types of cost functions for firms operating in the long run. In Chapter 12, we derive several short-run costs of production and analyze the various interrelationships among these costs both within and across time periods.

Beginning in Chapter 13 and continuing through Chapter 19, our attention shifts from the pure theory of the firm to the behavior of firms operating within various types of market structures. Specifically, in Chapter 13 we discuss the characteristics of perfectly competitive market structures and develop short-run models of perfectly competitive firm behavior. In Chapter 14 we direct our analysis to the behavior of perfectly competitive firms in the long run. We also analyze the performance results obtained from these models, regarding output, price, cost, and profit, for the individual firm and the market as a whole, and from a broader social perspective. In Chapter 15 we similarly analyze monopolistic market structures. This analysis is followed in Chapter 16 by our comparison of the economic performance results regarding price, output, cost, and profit associated with a monopolistic market to those obtained under perfectly competitive market conditions. In Chapter 17 we discuss oligopolistic market structures in terms of their specific firm and market characteristics, as well as their economic performance. We also analyze the traditional models of oligopoly using game theory in Chapter 18. We conclude our study of market structures in Chapter 19 with our analysis of monopolistic competition.

After examining the behavior of firms within four distinct market structures, Chapters 20, 21, and 22 discuss input markets. Specifically, we analyze labor and capital markets, focusing on the derivation of market supply and demand curves for both inputs, and the determination of input prices in these markets. Finally, we devote Chapters 23 and 24 to the topic of general equilibrium analysis. In many ways, Chapters 23 and 24 may be regarded as capstone chapters inasmuch as they incorporate information regarding consumer equilibrium which we developed in Chapters 3 and 4 with concepts related to producer equilibrium which we discussed in Chapters 9 and 10. We also examine issues regarding the efficiency of perfectly competitive markets, along with the inefficiency of monopolized markets using a general equilibrium framework.

ANCILLARIES

Accompanying our text is an ancillary package containing an Instructor's Manual and Study Guide. The Instructor's Manual includes chapter summaries, solutions to end-of-chapter exercises appearing in the text, and additional problems to assist professors in creating their exams. Students can access answers to selected exercises at the website for this text at www.prenhall.com/mathis. The Study Guide contains chapter summaries, key terms, and additional exercises, along with their solutions. We have written all of the ancillary items ourselves, thus ensuring accuracy and a very close coordination between these materials and our textbook.

ACKNOWLEDGMENTS

We are indebted to the many individuals who reviewed various drafts of the manuscript and whose comments we have incorporated into our text. Our special thanks go to: Ronald Deiter, Iowa State University; David Eaton, Murray State University; Thomas Garrett, Kansas State University; Barnali Gupta, Miami University of Ohio; Claire Hammond, Wake Forest University; Thomas Jeitschko, Texas A&M University; Val Lambson, Brigham Young University; Nancy Lutz, Virginia Tech; John Mukum Mbaku, Weber State University; L. W. Murray, University of San Francisco; Philip Roe Murray, Webber College; Thomas Nechyba, Duke University; Thomas d. VanderVeen, Skidmore College.

We also extend our very special thanks to Vickie Shaak who accurately and tirelessly typed the many drafts of our manuscript. Vickie not only is an excellent secretary, but also managed to maintain a pleasant and encouraging attitude throughout this process, despite the enormous demands we placed on her.

In addition, we would like to thank the numerous individuals at Prentice Hall for their many contributions leading to the publication of our text. In particular, we are grateful to Rod Banister, Executive Editor for Economics at Prentice Hall, for his steadfast guidance. We would also like to thank Marie McHale, Assistant Editor, and Lisa Amato, Editorial Assistant, for their efforts in coordinating our work with the reviewers, and Maureen Wilson, Production Editor, for her assistance in preparing our manuscript for publication. Finally, we extend our appreciation to Denise May of UG / GGS Information Services, Inc. for her assistance in coordinating our work with the production team.

Stephen Mathis and Janet Koscianski

CHAPTER 1

Review of Basic Calculus Techniques

1.1   INTRODUCTION

Economics is the social science concerned with how scarce resources are allocated across unlimited alternative uses. This process of resource allocation involves the amounts of goods and services produced, the combinations of inputs used in their production, and the distribution of these goods and services across different consumers. The theoretical basis of this resource allocation is the focus of microeconomics. More specifically, microeconomics is the analysis of rational decisions made by individual economic agents, such as consumers, firms, and owners of resources, that are intended to achieve some goal where the process of making these decisions is more formally known as optimization. Individual consumers make decisions regarding the kinds and amounts of specific goods and services they choose to purchase and consume with the intent of maximizing their satisfaction. As an example, the simple process of an individual maximizing her satisfaction at lunch by deciding the amounts of goods, such as hotdogs and soda pop, to consume constitutes an optimization problem. Firms determine the types and levels of outputs they desire to produce, while simultaneously determining the combinations of inputs they will employ to produce these outputs. For example, if a firm produces an output using machines and laborers as inputs, it will decide the amounts of each input that will minimize its costs of production. Owners of resources, such as capital and labor, also make decisions regarding the amounts of these inputs they wish to make available to firms for use in producing goods and services. In this case, laborers will determine the amounts of leisure time and income from working that correspond to a maximum level of their satisfaction. Ultimately, by analyzing these types of decisions, we can provide the basis for understanding how markets for various goods and services perform in allocating or distributing resources.

The general approach to analyzing optimization problems by economic agents consists of constructing models that accurately represent their rational decision-making processes. A **model** is *a formal framework that expresses relationships among certain facts.* We can construct models to explain and/or predict the behavior of a variable, or a group of variables, on the basis of another variable or group of variables. The first step in this process is to determine which variables to explain and which to use to provide the explanation. The variables labeled as **dependent, or objective, variables** are those *designated to be explained and/or predicted.* The variables identified as **independent, or decision, variables** are those *that provide the basis for explanation and/or*

1

prediction. For example, a firm's profit is affected by its level of production. Therefore, profit represents the dependent variable, and output is the independent variable.

In a general sense, making rational choices is a matter of choosing the amount(s) of some decision, or independent, variable(s) such that the extra benefit received from the last unit chosen is just equal to its extra cost. In economics, the process of measuring and comparing the extra benefits and extra costs associated with a rational decision is known as marginal analysis. Marginal functions are used to represent the rates of change of corresponding total functions. For example, a marginal revenue function measures the rate of change of a firm's total revenue (sales) function or, alternatively stated, the change in a firm's total revenue due to a change in its sales of output. Similarly, a marginal cost function represents the rate of change in a firm's total cost function or the change in a firm's total cost resulting from a change in the amount of output it produces. Economic analysis employs many marginal functions, and if the changes in the variables are measured in infinitesimally small amounts, we can represent marginal functions with derivatives. Thus, differential calculus plays an extremely important role in microeconomic analysis, a fact we will demonstrate throughout this book. This chapter reviews those basic calculus techniques used most often in solving microeconomic problems and provides some examples of how they apply to microeconomic theory.

1.2   DERIVATIVES OF UNIVARIATE FUNCTIONS

The derivative is perhaps one of the most important mathematical concepts developed in calculus. In this section we will discuss the notion of a derivative and illustrate it graphically as it applies to functions that contain only one independent variable, also known as univariate functions. Afterward, we will outline the rules used for computing derivatives of univariate functions and demonstrate each rule with a numerical example. Finally, we will discuss how derivatives can be applied to economic functions to convey important information.

1.2.1   Concept of a Derivative

We mentioned previously that a function that contains only one independent variable is also known as a univariate function. Specifically, *if some dependent variable, y, is a function of a single independent variable, x, then y is said to be a* **univariate function** *of x*. We can express this concept mathematically as

$$y = f(x),$$

illustrated graphically in panels (A) and (B) of Figure 1.1, where the independent variable, x, is plotted on the horizontal axis and the dependent variable, y, is plotted on the vertical axis.

The two univariate functions in Figure 1.1 differ from one another. The one in panel (A) is linear, whereas its counterpart in panel (B) is nonlinear. Using the Greek letter delta Δ to denote the change in a variable, recall that the slope of a univariate

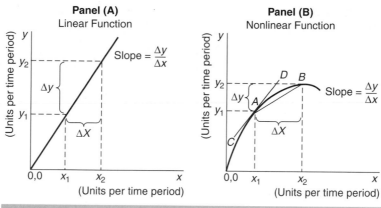

FIGURE 1.1 Univariate Functions

function is the change in the variable measured on the vertical axis, Δy, divided by the change in the variable measured on the horizontal axis, Δx:

$$\text{slope of } f(x) = \frac{\Delta y}{\Delta x}.$$

In this case, the change in x and the corresponding change in y are discrete, meaning that these changes occur over distinct, measurable intervals. For a linear function such as the one in panel (A), the magnitude of the changes in x and y has no impact on the value of the slope of the function. This result occurs because the slope of a linear function is constant. However, for nonlinear functions, such as the one appearing in panel (B), the slope varies along the function, and as a result, the magnitude of the changes in x and y will affect the value of the slope. Therefore, when evaluating the slope of a nonlinear function, it is necessary to distinguish between an average slope and an instantaneous one. In panel (B) of Figure 1.1, we can find the average slope of the function between points (x_1, y_1) and (x_2, y_2) by using the formula $\Delta y/\Delta x$. This actually measures the slope of the secant, or line segment connecting points A and B, which lie on the function, not the slope of the function at either point A or point B. However, if the change in x becomes smaller and smaller, then the average slope between two points lying on a nonlinear function better approximates the value of the slope of a line drawn tangent to a nonlinear function at a particular point.

A precise mathematical measure exists to evaluate the slope of a function when the change in x is an infinitesimally small value and thus approaches, but does not equal, zero. This instantaneous slope measure is a derivative. Specifically, the derivative of $y = f(x)$, denoted dy/dx or $f'(x)$, is mathematically stated as

$$\frac{dy}{dx} = f'(x) = \lim_{\Delta x \to 0} \frac{\Delta y}{\Delta x} = \lim_{\Delta x \to 0} \frac{f(x + \Delta x) - f(x)}{\Delta x},$$

where $\lim_{\Delta x \to 0}$ indicates that the change in x is some infinitesimally small value that approaches but does not equal zero. Since $y = f(x)$, then $\Delta y = f(x + \Delta x) - f(x)$. Therefore, when this limit exists, dy/dx measures the limit of the slope of a secant joining

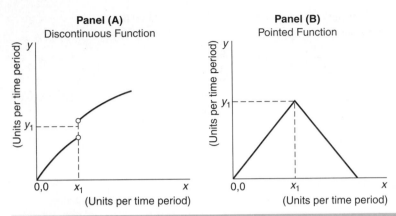

FIGURE 1.2 Examples of Univariate Functions Where dy/dx Does Not Exist at (x_1, y_1)

two infinitesimally close points lying on a function as the change in x approaches zero, as well as the slope of a line drawn tangent to a function at the same point.

Note that a necessary, but not a sufficient, condition for a derivative to exist at a particular point on a function is that the function must be continuous at that point, or, alternatively stated, it must be an unbroken curve. Specifically, a function $f(x)$ is continuous at a particular point in its domain, say c, if: (1) the function possesses a definite value at c, (2) the function has a limit as x approaches c, and (3) the limit is equal to the value of the function at c. If any one of these three conditions fails to hold, then the function is not continuous. For example, a limit will not exist at a missing point in a function, since as the value of x approaches the missing point, the value of $f(x)$ fails to exist, as does its derivative at this point. Such a situation appears in panel (A) of Figure 1.2.

Earlier we stated that continuity was a necessary condition for the differentiability of a function but that it was not sufficient. Specifically, for a derivative to exist at a particular point on a function, the function must also be smooth, meaning that it does not contain any sharp points or corners. Why? The reason is that we could draw an infinite number of lines, all with different slopes, tangent to a function that comes to a sharp point. Therefore, a unique value for the derivative will not exist at this point. Panel (B) of Figure 1.2 illustrates a continuous, but nondifferentiable, function.

1.2.2   Rules for Differentiating Univariate Functions

Given a univariate function that is both continuous and smooth throughout, it is possible to determine its derivative by applying one or more of the specific rules of differentiation outlined in the following.

1. *Constant Function Rule.* The derivative of a constant function is zero. Let $y = f(x) = c$, where c is a constant value; then,

$$\frac{dy}{dx} = \frac{df(x)}{dx} = \frac{dc}{dx} = 0.$$

If $y = f(x)$ is equal to some constant value c, then regardless of the value of x, a change in x would have no impact on the value of y; hence $dy/dx = 0$.

Example:

Let
$$y = f(x) = 6,$$
then
$$\frac{dy}{dx} = \frac{d6}{dx} = 0.$$

2. *Constant Multiplied by a Function Rule.* Let y be equal to the product of a constant c and some function $f(x)$, such that $y = cf(x)$. Then the derivative of y with respect to x will be equal to the constant multiplied by the derivative of $f(x)$. Stated mathematically,

$$y = cf(x)$$
then
$$\frac{dy}{dx} = \frac{d(cf(x))}{dx} = c\frac{df(x)}{dx}.$$

Example:

Let
$$y = 12x,$$
then
$$\frac{dy}{dx} = 12\frac{dx}{dx} = 12(1) = 12.$$

3. *Power Rule.* Let $y = f(x) = x^n$, where the dependent variable x is raised to a constant value, the power n,

then
$$\frac{dy}{dx} = \frac{d(x^n)}{dx} = nx^{n-1}.$$

Example:

Let
$$y = f(x) = x^3,$$
then
$$\frac{dy}{dx} = \frac{d(x^3)}{dx} = (3)x^{3-1} = 3x^2.$$

4. *Sum (Difference) Rule.* Let y be equal to the sum (difference) of two functions $f(x)$ and $g(x)$. Then the derivative dy/dx is equal to the sum (difference) of the derivative of $f(x)$, $df(x)/dx$, and the derivative of $g(x)$, $dg(x)/dx$. We can state this rule mathematically as follows:

Let
$$y = f(x) \pm g(x),$$
then
$$\frac{dy}{dx} = \frac{d[f(x) \pm g(x)]}{dx} = \frac{df(x)}{dx} \pm \frac{dg(x)}{dx}.$$

Example:

Let $y = f(x) + g(x)$ where $f(x) = 6x^2$ and $g(x) = 9x$,

then
$$y = f(x) + g(x) = 6x^2 + 9x,$$

Therefore, by the sum rule,

$$\frac{dy}{dx} = \frac{d[f(x) + g(x)]}{dx} = \frac{d(6x^2)}{dx} + \frac{d(9x)}{dx}.$$

We can compute the final result for dy/dx by applying the power rule and the constant multiplied by a function rule to obtain,

$$\frac{dy}{dx} = \frac{d(6x^2)}{dx} + \frac{d(9x)}{dx} = 12x + 9.$$

5. *Product Rule.* The derivative of a function, that is, the product of two functions, will be equal to the first function multiplied by the derivative of the second, plus the second function multiplied by the derivative of the first. For example, if $y = f(x) \cdot g(x)$, where $f(x)$ and $g(x)$ are two functions of the variable x,

then $$\frac{dy}{dx} = \frac{d[f(x) \cdot g(x)]}{dx} = f(x)\frac{dg(x)}{dx} + g(x)\frac{df(x)}{dx}.$$

Example:

Let $y = x^2 (10 - 4x)$; therefore, $f(x) = x^2$ and $g(x) = 10 - 4x$, then by the product rule,

$$\frac{dy}{dx} = x^2 \frac{d(10 - 4x)}{dx} + (10 - 4x) \frac{dx^2}{dx},$$

and by applying prior rules of differentiation,

$$\frac{dy}{dx} = x^2 (-4) + (10 - 4x)2x = -4x^2 + 20x - 8x^2 = -12x^2 + 20x.$$

6. *Quotient Rule.* The derivative of a function that is the quotient of two other functions, such as $y = f(x)/g(x)$, is equal to the denominator multiplied by the derivative of the numerator, minus the numerator multiplied by the derivative of the denominator, all divided by the denominator squared. Mathematically stated, given $y = f(x)/g(x)$, where $g(x) \neq 0$, then its derivative, dy/dx, is

$$\frac{dy}{dx} = \frac{g(x)\frac{df(x)}{dx} - f(x)\frac{dg(x)}{dx}}{[g(x)]^2}.$$

Example:

Let $y = \frac{2x^3}{4 - 5x^2}$; therefore, $f(x) = 2x^3$ and $g(x) = 4 - 5x^2$.

We can compute the derivative, dy/dx, by applying the quotient rule as follows:

$$\frac{dy}{dx} = \frac{(4 - 5x^2) \frac{d(2x^3)}{dx} - 2x^3 \frac{d(4 - 5x^2)}{dx}}{(4 - 5x^2)^2}.$$

We can simplify this result by applying the sum (difference), product, power, and constant rules as follows:

$$\frac{dy}{dx} = \frac{(4 - 5x^2)(6x^2) - 2x^3\,(-10x)}{(4 - 5x^2)^2}$$

$$= \frac{24x^2 - 30x^4 + 20x^4}{(4 - 5x^2)^2}.$$

$$= \frac{24x^2 - 10x^4}{(4 - 5x^2)^2}.$$

7. *Chain Rule.* The derivative, dy/dx, of a function $y = f(z)$, which is a function of another function, $z = g(x)$, is equal to the derivative of the first function, $y = f(z)$, with respect to z, multiplied by the derivative of the second function, $z = g(x)$, with respect to x. Mathematically,

$$y = f(z), \text{where } z = g(x),$$

then

$$\frac{dy}{dx} = \frac{dy}{dz} \cdot \frac{dz}{dx} = \frac{df(z)}{dz} \cdot \frac{dg(x)}{dx}.$$

Example:

Let $y = z^3$ where $z = 8x^2$,

then

$$\frac{dy}{dx} = \frac{dz^3}{dz} \cdot \frac{d(8x^2)}{dx} = (3z^2)(16x).$$

Substituting $z = 8x^2$ into the right-hand side of the preceding equation yields

$$\frac{dy}{dx} = 3(8x^2)^2\,(16x) = 3(64x^4)(16x) = 3072x^5.$$

†8. *Natural Logarithmic Rule.* The natural logarithmic function rule is used when y is a natural logarithmic function of x of the form $y = \ln f(x)$.[1] In such a case, the derivative of y with respect to x is equal to

$$\frac{dy}{dx} = \frac{1}{f(x)} \frac{df(x)}{dx}.$$

Example:

Let $y = \ln 3x$,

then

$$\frac{dy}{dx} = \frac{1}{3x} \cdot \frac{d3x}{dx}$$

$$= \frac{1}{3x}\,(3)$$

$$= \frac{1}{x}.$$

---

† Indicates optional material.

[1] A natural logarithmic function is defined as the definite integral of some term, $1/t$, for which t ranges from zero to x. Mathematically, this is expressed as

$$\ln x = \int_1^x \frac{1}{t}\, dt \text{ for all } x > 0.$$

†9. *Natural Exponential Function Rule.* The natural exponential function rule is used when the natural base, e, is raised to a power that is some function of the independent variable x, such as $y = e^{f(x)}$.[2] In this case, the derivative is equal to the original exponential function multiplied by the derivative of the exponent. Thus, if $y = e^{f(x)}$

then

$$\frac{dy}{dx} = e^{f(x)}\frac{df(x)}{dx}.$$

Example:

Let $y = e^{6x^3}$,

then

$$\frac{dy}{dx} = e^{6x^3}\frac{d6x^3}{dx} = 18x^2\, e^{6x^3}.$$

1.2.3 Derivatives as Marginal Functions

Now that we have established the basic rules for differentiating a univariate function, we will show how to apply derivatives to microeconomic concepts. In economic theory, it is conventional to refer to *the first derivative of a total function as a* **marginal function**. Applications of marginal functions abound throughout microeconomic analysis. For example, a firm's total cost function expresses its cost, TC, in terms of its level of production, q. In this case, the first derivative of this total cost function measures the firm's marginal cost function, which we can state mathematically as

$$MC = \frac{dTC}{dq} = \frac{df(q)}{dq}.$$

This function measures the rate at which a firm's total cost changes as the firm changes its level of production. The following numerical example should help to clarify this concept.

Example:

Let's assume we can mathematically express a firm's total cost associated with the production of a good as

$$TC = q^3 - 4q^2 + 6q.$$

We determine the firm's marginal cost function by taking the first derivative of this total cost function as follows:

$$MC = \frac{dTC}{dq} = \frac{d(q^3 - 4q^2 + 6q)}{dq} = 3q^2 - 8q + 6.$$

Similarly, a firm's total revenue function, TR, expresses its revenue in terms of its level of sales, q. Thus, the marginal revenue function measures the change in a firm's total revenue due to a change in the firm's level of sales. We compute the firm's mar-

---

† Indicates optional material.
[2]A natural exponential function has as its base, e, where $e = \lim_{n \to \infty} [1 + 1/n]^n \approx 2.7817281228$. Therefore, if x is any real number, and assuming $y = e^x$, then $\ln y = x$.

ginal revenue function by taking the first derivative of the firm's total revenue function as $MR = dTR(q)/dq$.

Example:

Assume a firm's total revenue associated with the sale of a good is

$$TR = 125q - 3q^2.$$

We can compute the firm's marginal revenue function as follows:

$$MR = \frac{dTR}{dq} = \frac{d(125q - 3q^2)}{dq} = 125 - 6q.$$

These numerical examples illustrate some of the ways we can apply derivatives of univariate functions in microeconomics.

1.2.4   Higher-Order Derivatives of Univariate Functions

Once we have determined the derivative of a function, it is also possible to take its derivative. This concept of *the derivative of a derivative is generally known as a* **higher-order derivative**. Specifically, if $y = f(x)$, then dy/dx, also denoted $f'(x)$, is known as the first-order derivative of y. The derivative of the first-order derivative, $df'(x)/dx$, also denoted d^2y/dx^2, $d(dy/dx)/dx$, or $f''(x)$, is known as the second-order derivative. Since dy/dx measures the rate of change in the function $y = f(x)$, then it follows that the second-order derivative, d^2y/dx^2, measures the rate of change of the rate of change of that function. We can also think of the second-order derivative as measuring the slope of the marginal function. Other higher-order derivatives such as third, $f'''(x)$, and fourth, $f''''(x)$, order derivatives are computed in a similar manner. For example, if $y = x^3 + 4x^2 - 6x + 9$, then using various rules of differentiation outlined in the previous section, we compute the first-order derivative as

$$\frac{dy}{dx} = f'(x) = \frac{d(x^3 + 4x^2 - 6x + 9)}{dx} = 3x^2 + 8x - 6,$$

and the second-order derivative is equal to

$$\frac{d^2y}{dx^2} = f''(x) = \frac{d\left(\frac{dy}{dx}\right)}{dx} = \frac{d(3x^2 + 8x - 6)}{dx} = 6x + 8.$$

Later in this chapter, we will demonstrate that second-order derivatives play a critical role in establishing the criteria necessary for determining whether an extreme value of a function is a maximum, a minimum, or an inflection point of the function.

1.3   OPTIMIZATION OF UNIVARIATE FUNCTIONS

When conducting economic analysis, we typically assume that economic agents, such as producers and consumers, make rational decisions that will lead to the best possible outcomes for their particular objectives. Recall from your principles of microeconomics course that a consumer's goal is typically to maximize the utility, or satisfaction, he receives from consuming goods and services. A firm's goal may be to maximize either its profit or, in a simplified example assuming zero production costs, the total revenue it earns from selling a good.

We know that it is possible to express many economic phenomena using univariate functions of the form $y = f(x)$. Now we will focus our attention on finding the solution value of an independent variable, also known as a decision variable, that corresponds to an optimum value for some univariate function. We will assume that this function represents the objective, or goal, of some economic agent, and thus it is called an objective function. Note that the term *optimum* is rather general, since it is applied to either a maximum or a minimum value. For example, an individual's objective function may represent the satisfaction or utility she receives from consuming goods and services. Thus, her goal will be to maximize this objective function. As another example, a firm's objective function may be represented by its cost function. Therefore, in this case, the firm's goal is to minimize its objective function. However, before discussing the specific criteria needed to determine whether a particular value of a decision variable maximizes or minimizes a function, it is first necessary to define an important related term.

A **critical value** *in the domain of a function will exist if at this value the first derivative of the function is equal to zero.* Therefore, given the generalized univariate function,

$$y = f(x),$$

if

$$\frac{dy}{dx}\bigg|_{x=x_0} = f'(x_0) = 0.$$

then x_0 will be a critical value of the decision variable x for this function. Note that the vertical line to the right of dy/dx indicates that the derivative of y with respect to x is evaluated where $x = x_0$. We have demonstrated this concept graphically in Figure 1.3.

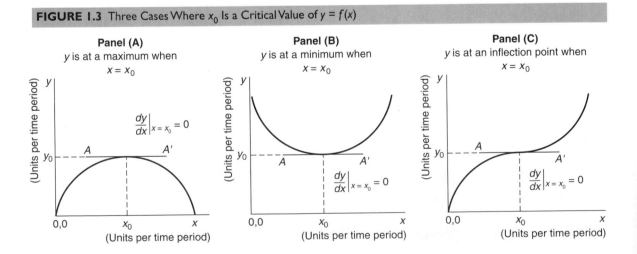

FIGURE 1.3 Three Cases Where x_0 Is a Critical Value of $y = f(x)$

Clearly, the first derivative of each of the three functions is equal to zero at the critical value x_0 since the line AA', drawn tangent to each function at the point (x_0, y_0), has a slope of zero. However, when the decision variable is equal to x_0, the corresponding value of the function y_0 is at a maximum in panel (A), a minimum in panel (B), and at a point of inflection where the function changes its curvature, from concave to convex, at that point in panel (C). Therefore, it is obvious that merely taking the first derivative of a function and setting it equal to zero will not guarantee that the corresponding value of the function represents a maximum at that point, since it could also represent either a minimum or an inflection point.

To determine whether a critical value of a decision variable yields a maximum, a minimum, or an inflection point of that function, it is necessary to evaluate the second-order derivative of the function at this particular point. Recall that the second-order derivative of a function measures the rate of change of the slope of a total function. We can also think of the second-order derivative as measuring the slope of a marginal function. For example, if the second-order derivative is positive, this indicates that the associated marginal function is positively sloped. It also means that the slope of the total function is increasing, given some infinitesimally small increase in the independent, or decision, variable beyond its critical value. Therefore, the total function will be at a minimum at this critical value of the decision variable. Conversely, if the second-order derivative is negative, the associated marginal function will be negatively sloped. Therefore, the slope of the total function will be decreasing, given some infinitesimally small increase in the independent variable beyond its critical value. Finally, an inflection point of a function will exist if at the critical value of the decision variable, the second-order derivative is equal to zero and the third-order derivative does not equal zero.[3] We can mathematically state both the necessary and sufficient conditions for a maximum, a minimum, and an inflection point for a generalized univariate function of the form $y = f(x)$, assuming that this function is both continuous and twice differentiable at the critical value x_0.

For y to be maximized at x_0 :

First-Order Condition (Necessary Condition)

$$\frac{dy}{dx}\bigg|_{x=x_0} = f'(x_0) = 0.$$

Second-Order Condition (Sufficient Condition)

$$\frac{d^2y}{dx^2}\bigg|_{x=x_0} = f''(x_0) < 0.$$

---

[3]It is also possible to have inflection points in functions where $dy/dx \neq 0$ at the point of inflection. However, since the focus of this section is on critical values of functions where $dy/dx = 0$, we have intentionally omitted any discussion of this type of inflection point.

For y to be minimized at x_0 :

First-Order Condition (Necessary Condition)

$$\frac{dy}{dx}\bigg|_{x=x_0} = f'(x_0) = 0.$$

Second-Order Condition (Sufficient Condition)

$$\frac{d^2y}{dx^2}\bigg|_{x=x_0} = f''(x_0) > 0.$$

The following mathematical examples demonstrate the methodology we use in solving a maximization problem, a minimization problem, and a problem containing an inflection point.

Maximization example:

Assume the total revenue function for a firm is $TR = 240q - 4q^2$. To determine the level of output, q, that will optimize (maximize) the firm's total revenue, examine both the first-order and second-order conditions for maximizing a function.

Step 1: First-Order Condition Compute the first derivative of TR, set it equal to zero, and solve for the critical value of the decision variable, q_0, as follows:

$$\frac{dTR}{dq} = \frac{d(240q - 4q^2)}{dq} = 240 - 8q = 0.$$

Therefore,

$$8q = 240$$
$$q_0 = 30 \text{ units.}$$

To determine the value of total revenue at the critical value of the decision variable, simply substitute $q = 30$ into the total revenue function as follows:

$$TR = 240(30) - 4(30)^2 = 7200 - 3600 = \$3600.$$

Step 2: Second-Order Condition To determine whether total revenue is at a maximum when $q = 30$ units, evaluate the second derivative of the total revenue function as follows:

$$\frac{d^2TR}{dq^2} = \frac{d\left(\frac{dTR}{dq}\right)}{dq} = \frac{d(240 - 8q)}{dq} = -8 < 0.$$

Since the second derivative of the total revenue function is a negative value, we are assured that total revenue achieves a maximum value of \$3600 when $q = 30$ units.

We can demonstrate this problem graphically in Figure 1.4 where the total revenue function is plotted in panel (A). Note that when $q = 30$ units, total revenue reaches its maximum value of \$3600. Panel (B) illustrates the associated marginal revenue function, which graphically demonstrates the first-order condition, indicating that when the total revenue function reaches a maximum value of \$3600 at $q = 30$ units, marginal revenue, dTR/dq, equals zero. Also note that the marginal revenue function is negatively sloped, indicating that the slope of the total revenue function decreases as q increases. It is also true that the value of marginal revenue is positive until q reaches 30, since the total revenue function is positively sloped until that level of sales. When q is equal to 30 units, total revenue is at a maximum. Thus, the slope of the total revenue function, which is the value of marginal revenue, at that point is equal to zero. If the firm should choose to produce more than 30 units of output, its total revenue will fall. Also, the slope of the total revenue function, and hence the value of marginal revenue, will be negative. The second-order condition for a maximum is illustrated in panel (C). Note that regardless of the value of q, d^2TR/dq^2, is equal to a negative value, specifically –8, thus ensuring that total revenue is at a maximum when $q = 30$ units.

Minimization example:

Assume that the average, or per unit, cost function for a firm is $AC = q^2 - 8q + 24$. To determine the level of output, q, at which average cost is minimized, we must examine both the first-order and second-order conditions for a minimum.

Step 1: First-Order Condition   Compute the first-order derivative of average cost, dAC/dq, and set it equal to zero. Thus,

$$\frac{dAC}{dq} = 2q - 8 = 0.$$

Solve for the critical value of the decision variable, q_0, as follows:

$$2q = 8$$

$$q_0 = \frac{8}{2} = 4 \text{ units.}$$

Substitute $q = 4$ units into the average cost function to determine the value of average cost at the critical value:

$$AC = 4^2 - 8(4) + 24 = 16 - 32 + 24 = \$8.$$

Step 2: Second-Order Condition   To confirm that the firm's average cost function is minimized at the critical value of the decision variable, $q_0 = 4$ units, the second-order derivative of the average cost function, d^2AC/dq^2, must be a positive value when $q_0 = 4$ units. In this case,

$$\frac{d^2AC}{dq^2} = \frac{d\left(\dfrac{dAC}{dq}\right)}{dq} = \frac{d(2q - 8)}{dq} = 2 > 0,$$

which indicates that this average cost function achieves a minimum value of \$8 when $q = 4$ units.

  We can also apply graphical analysis to this optimization problem by plotting the average cost function in panel (A) of Figure 1.5. Note that average cost is minimized at the value of \$8 when q is equal to 4 units.

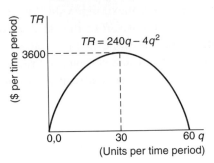

Panel (A)
Total Revenue Function

$TR = 240q - 4q^2$

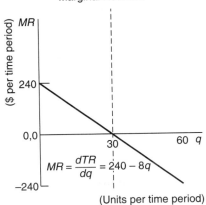

Panel (B)
Marginal Revenue

$MR = \dfrac{dTR}{dq} = 240 - 8q$

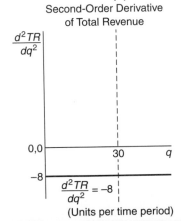

Panel (C)
Second-Order Derivative
of Total Revenue

$\dfrac{d^2 TR}{dq^2} = -8$

FIGURE 1.4 Total Revenue, Marginal Revenue, and the Second-Order Derivative for the Function $TR = 240q - 4q^2$

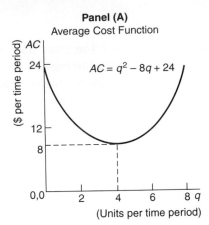

Panel (A)
Average Cost Function

$AC = q^2 - 8q + 24$

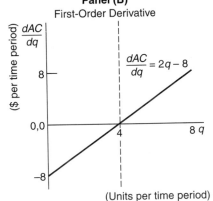

Panel (B)
First-Order Derivative

$\dfrac{dAC}{dq} = 2q - 8$

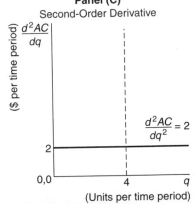

Panel (C)
Second-Order Derivative

$\dfrac{d^2 AC}{dq^2} = 2$

FIGURE 1.5 Average Cost, the First-Order Derivative, and the Second-Order Derivative for the Function $AC = q^2 - 8q + 24$

The associated first-order derivative function, dAC/dq, plotted in panel (B), is equal to zero when average cost is minimized at $q = 4$ units, thus illustrating the first-order condition. Finally, in panel (C), we can observe that the second-order condition for a minimum is satisfied since the value of the second-order derivative of the average cost function, d^2AC/dq^2, is a positive value, 2, at the critical value, $q = 4$.

Inflection point example:

Let $y = f(x) = 1/3x^3 - 4x^2 + 16x + 10$. We can determine the critical value of the decision variable for this function by examining the first-order and second-order conditions.

Step 1: First-Order Condition   Compute the first-order derivative of the function, set it equal to zero:

$$\frac{dy}{dx} = x^2 - 8x + 16 = 0,$$

and solve for the critical value of x, x_0, by factoring the quadratic function as follows:

$$x^2 - 8x + 16 = 0$$
$$(x - 4)(x - 4) = 0$$
$$x - 4 = 0.$$

Therefore,

$$x_0 = 4.$$

Substitute the critical value, $x_0 = 4$, into the original function to determine the value of y when $x = 4$; thus,

$$y = 1/3(4)^3 - 4(4)^2 + 16(4) + 10 = 31.33.$$

Step 2: Second-Order Condition   To determine whether the function is at a maximum, a minimum, or at an inflection point when $x = 4$, we must examine the value of the second-order derivative. Thus,

$$\frac{d^2y}{dx^2} = 2x - 8,$$

and substituting $x = 4$ into the second-order derivative yields

$$2(4) - 8 = 8 - 8 = 0.$$

Since the second-order derivative is equal to zero, the critical value, x_0, may be an inflection point. We can verify this by examining the third-order derivative, d^3y/dx^3. If the value of d^3y/dx^3 is not equal to zero, then an inflection point is guaranteed at the critical value of the function. Therefore, since

$$\frac{d^3y}{dx^3} = 2 \neq 0,$$

we are assured that the function is at an inflection point when $x = 4$.

1.4 DERIVATIVES OF MULTIVARIATE FUNCTIONS

We will now expand our analysis of optimization by examining **multivariate functions**, or *functions that contain more than one independent variable*. After developing various mathematical techniques related to multivariate functions, we will show how these concepts can be applied to microeconomic analysis.

1.4.1 Concept of a Partial Derivative

Many of the functions we use in analyzing consumer and firm behavior are multivariate in nature. For example, a firm may use two inputs, capital, K, and labor, L, to produce its output, Q. Therefore, its production function will be a multivariate function, expressed generally as $Q = f(K,L)$. We will now extend the concept of a derivative to make it applicable to these types of functions. In the case of multivariate functions, we must distinguish two categories of derivatives: partial derivatives and total derivatives. Let's discuss partial derivatives first.

In general, a multivariate function is of the form,

$$y = f(x, w, \dots, z),$$

where y is the dependent variable and $x, w, \dots, z$, represent some number of independent variables. A functional relationship exists because for each set of admissible values for the independent variables, $x, w, \dots, z$, there exists only one corresponding value for the dependent variable, y. However, if we wish to express y as a function of any one of the independent variables, such as x, we must specify, or hold constant, the values of the remaining independent variables, $w, \dots, z$, at particular levels. Otherwise, a different y value will correspond to each value of x when we allow any of the remaining independent variables to vary. For example, we can modify the equation, $y = f(x, w, \dots, z)$, to express a functional relationship between y and x as

$$y = f(x, \overline{w}_1, \dots, \overline{z}_1),$$

where $\overline{w}_1, \dots, \overline{z}_1$, represent the specified, or constant, levels of the other independent variables, $w, \dots, z$ respectively. Similarly, we can express y as a function of w as

$$y = f(\overline{x}_1, w, \dots, \overline{z}_1).$$

In this case, we are holding the remaining independent variables constant at specified levels, denoted $\overline{x}_1, \dots, \overline{z}_1$. In fact, we could express y as a function of z or any one of these independent variables.

It is now possible to introduce the concept of a **partial slope**, which represents *the change in the dependent variable in a function due to a change in any one of the independent variables, while holding all remaining independent variables constant*. We express the partial slope relating y to x as

$$\left.\frac{\Delta y}{\Delta x}\right|_{\overline{w}_1, \dots, \overline{z}_1,} \quad \text{or} \quad \frac{\Delta f(x, \overline{w}_1, \dots, \overline{z}_1)}{\Delta x},$$

where the vertical slash indicates that the variables listed after it are being held constant at specified levels. Similarly, the partial slope relating y to w is

$$\left. \frac{\Delta y}{\Delta w} \right|_{\bar{x}_1, \ldots, \bar{z}_1,} \quad \text{or} \quad \frac{\Delta f(\bar{x}_1, w, \ldots, \bar{z}_1)}{\Delta w}.$$

In general, by using this procedure, we can derive a partial slope relating the dependent variable, y, to each of the independent variables.

So far we have based the discussion of partial slopes on discrete changes in the independent variables. It is a small step to extend the concept of a partial slope to an instantaneous partial slope. We achieve this by allowing for infinitesimally small changes in the independent variable under focus and applying the concept of a limit discussed in Section 1.2.1. The result of this procedure is called a **partial derivative**, defined as *the change in a dependent variable in a function resulting from an infinitesimally small change in an independent variable, while holding all other independent variables constant.* The partial derivatives associated with a multivariate function represent the instantaneous partial slopes of the function, where there exist as many partial derivatives as there are independent variables. Again, we emphasize that what distinguishes a partial derivative from the broader derivative concept, known as a total derivative, is that all independent variables, except the one under analysis, are held constant. For the multivariate function,

$$y = f(x, w, \ldots, z),$$

the set of corresponding partial derivatives are:

$$\frac{\partial y}{\partial x} = \lim_{\Delta x \to 0} \left. \frac{\Delta y}{\Delta x} \right|_{\bar{w}_1, \ldots, \bar{z}_1}$$

$$\frac{\partial y}{\partial w} = \lim_{\Delta w \to 0} \left. \frac{\Delta y}{\Delta w} \right|_{\bar{x}_1, \ldots, \bar{z}_1}$$

$$\vdots \qquad \vdots \qquad \vdots$$

$$\frac{\partial y}{\partial z} = \lim_{\Delta z \to 0} \left. \frac{\Delta y}{\Delta z} \right|_{\bar{x}_1, \ldots, \bar{w}_1}.$$

The ∂ symbol, rather than the d used earlier, indicates that we are taking a partial derivative. Also, note that for many functions each partial derivative will be a function of some or all of the independent variables listed in the original function. We can use the generalized multivariate production $Q = f(K, L)$, introduced earlier, to demonstrate how partial derivatives are used in microeconomics. Since the dependent variable Q is a function of two independent variables, L and K, there will be two partial derivatives for this function, $\partial Q / \partial L$ and $\partial Q / \partial K$.

The first partial derivative, $\partial Q / \partial L$, measures the change in a firm's output resulting from an infinitesimally small change in its use of labor, while holding its capital input constant. Similarly, $\partial Q / \partial K$ measures the change in the firm's output resulting from an infinitesimally small change in its use of capital, while holding its labor input constant. Later in this section, we will develop this microeconomic application of partial derivatives even further, using a numerical example of a specific multivariate production function.

Some clarification is needed to reconcile this discussion regarding partial derivatives with that pertaining to derivatives of univariate functions. By definition, univariate functions contain only one independent variable; as a result, when we take a derivative with respect to that independent variable, there are no other variables to hold constant. Therefore, in the univariate case, there is no difference between a partial derivative and the broader total derivative for which none of the independent variables are held constant. However, for multivariate functions this distinction is very important, and we will discuss it in detail in the next section.

It is possible to illustrate the partial derivative graphically. As an example, assume the multivariate function,

$$y = f(x, z),$$

which contains two independent variables, x and z, and one dependent variable, y. We can represent this function by the three-dimensional diagrams shown in panels (A) and (B) of Figure 1.6. When finding the partial derivative of y with respect to x, we must hold the value of the variable z constant at some level such as $\bar{z}_1$. Thus, the term,

$$\frac{\partial y}{\partial x} = \frac{\partial f(x, \bar{z}_1)}{\partial x},$$

represents an instantaneous partial slope, or more specifically, the instantaneous slope of the two-dimensional curve AA' we create by taking the cross-section at $\bar{z}_1$. This is shown in panel (A) of Figure 1.6. We can demonstrate the changing values of the partial derivative, $\partial y/\partial x$, by the changing slopes of lines drawn tangent to the curve AA' at different values for the variable x. The values of $\partial y/\partial x$ are positive but decreasing for increasing values of x up to x_2, at which point the value is zero. For increases in x beyond x_2, $\partial y/\partial x$ becomes negative. If z is held constant at some

FIGURE 1.6 Panel (A) Cross-Section and Tangents Demonstrating Partial Slopes for a Multivariate Function, While Holding z Constant; Panel (B) Cross-Section and Tangents Demonstrating Partial Slopes for a Multivariate Function, While Holding x Constant

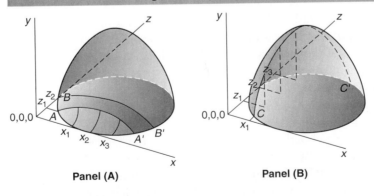

Panel (A)

Panel (B)

other value, such as $\bar{z}_2$, where $\bar{z}_2 > \bar{z}_1$, then the partial derivative of y with respect to x is

$$\frac{\partial y}{\partial x} = \frac{\partial f(x, \bar{z}_2)}{\partial x}.$$

This partial derivative represents the slope of the two-dimensional curve or cross-section BB', also illustrated in panel (A). Thus, for most functions, the values of the computed partial derivative, $\partial y/\partial x$, depend not only on the value of x but also on the level at which z is held constant.

Using the same function, $y = f(x, z)$, we can also find the partial derivative of y with respect to z, expressed as

$$\frac{\partial y}{\partial z} = \frac{\partial f(\bar{x}_1, z)}{\partial z}.$$

In this case we hold the value of x constant at some level such as $\bar{x}_1$, and $\partial y/\partial z$ represents the instantaneous slope of the cross-section CC' in panel (B) of Figure 1.6. Similar to the previous analysis, different levels of x will result in different cross-sections, so once again, as is the case for many multivariate functions, the value of the partial derivative, $\partial y/\partial z$, depends on the values of both x and z.

Analysis of some specific functions should help to clarify the computation of partial derivatives. Assume a multivariate function is of the form,

$$y = x^2 z^3.$$

We can compute the partial derivative of y with respect to x by treating z, and as a result z^3, as constant, and then by applying the ordinary rules for differentiation discussed in Section 1.2.2. The result of such a procedure is

$$\frac{\partial y}{\partial x} = 2x^{2-1}z^3 = 2xz^3.$$

Now suppose the value at which z has been held constant is known—say $z = 4$. The partial derivative then becomes

$$\frac{\partial y}{\partial x} = 2xz^3 = 2x(4)^3 = 128x.$$

Finally, we can evaluate this derivative for a specific value of x—say $x = 3$—as follows:

$$\frac{\partial y}{\partial x} = 128x = 128(3) = 384.$$

Similarly, we compute the partial derivative of y with respect to z from the original function, $y = x^2 z^3$, as

$$\frac{\partial y}{\partial z} = 3x^2 z^{3-1} = 3x^2 z^2,$$

where in this case we are treating x as a constant. We can evaluate the partial derivative, $\partial y/\partial z$, for particular values of x and z—for example, $x = 3$ and $z = 4$, yielding

$$\frac{\partial y}{\partial z} = 3x^2z^2 = 3(3)^2z^2 = 27z^2 = 27(4)^2 = 432.$$

As another example, assume a function is of the form

$$y = x^2 + xz + z^2,$$

where the goal is to find and evaluate $\partial y/\partial x$ and $\partial y/\partial z$ for the values $x = 1$ and $z = 2$. Then

$$\frac{\partial y}{\partial x} = 2x + z = 2(1) + 2 = 4$$

and

$$\frac{\partial y}{\partial z} = x + 2z = 1 + 2(2) = 5.$$

Many functions we use in economic analysis are multivariate, and as a result, partial derivatives are used rather extensively in determining associated marginal functions. For example, we might represent a consumer's level of satisfaction by a utility function of the form

$$U = x^{1/2}y^{1/2},$$

where U is some index representing the consumer's level of utility, and x and y represent amounts of two goods consumed by the individual. The marginal utility associated with a good measures the change in utility resulting from a change in the individual's consumption level of that good, while holding her consumption of all other goods constant. Thus, in this example, we can compute the marginal utility functions MU_x and MU_y, for goods x and y, respectively, by taking the partial derivatives of the utility function as follows:

$$MU_x = \frac{\partial U}{\partial x} = 1/2x^{-1/2}y^{1/2} = 1/2\left(\frac{y}{x}\right)^{1/2},$$

and

$$MU_y = \frac{\partial U}{\partial y} = 1/2x^{1/2}y^{-1/2} = 1/2\left(\frac{x}{y}\right)^{1/2}.$$

We can evaluate these functions for particular quantities of the goods x and y. For example, if $x = 1$ and $y = 4$, then,

$$MU_x = 1/2\left(\frac{y}{x}\right)^{1/2} = 1/2\left(\frac{4}{1}\right)^{1/2} = 1,$$

and

$$MU_y = 1/2\left(\frac{x}{y}\right)^{1/2} = 1/2\left(\frac{1}{4}\right)^{1/2} = 1/4 = 0.25.$$

Another application of partial derivatives is in the analysis of production theory. Earlier we discussed the concept of a production function which shows the maximum amount of output that a firm can produce from various combinations of inputs. Suppose such a production function is of the form,

$$Q = K^{1/4}L^{3/4},$$

where, once again, Q represents units of a firm's output and K and L denote units of the inputs capital and labor, respectively. Recall from your principles of microeconomics course that the marginal product of an input measures the change in output produced by a firm resulting from a change in that input, while holding all other inputs constant. The marginal product functions, MP_K and MP_L, for the K and L inputs, respectively, can be computed as

$$MP_K = \frac{\partial Q}{\partial K} = 1/4K^{-3/4}L^{3/4} = 1/4\left(\frac{L}{K}\right)^{3/4},$$

and

$$MP_L = \frac{\partial Q}{\partial L} = 3/4K^{1/4}L^{-1/4} = 3/4\left(\frac{K}{L}\right)^{1/4}.$$

If $K = 16$ and $L = 81$, then we evaluate these marginal product functions as

$$MP_K = 1/4\left(\frac{L}{K}\right)^{3/4} = 1/4\left(\frac{81}{16}\right)^{3/4} = 0.84,$$

and

$$MP_L = 3/4\left(\frac{16}{81}\right)^{1/4} = 1/2 = 0.50.$$

In future chapters we will demonstrate the usefulness of partial derivatives in solving many other types of problems in microeconomics. Perhaps the most important application of partial derivatives is the role they play in solving optimization problems involving multivariate functions, which is the focus of Chapter 2. Before discussing this application, however, it is useful to define the concept of a total derivative.

1.4.2   Concept of a Total Derivative

A **total derivative** represents *the change in the dependent variable in a function due to an infinitesimally small change in an independent variable, where all independent variables are allowed to vary.* This type of derivative becomes particularly useful when interdependencies exist between or among the independent variables in a function, or between the independent variable(s) and some other variable with respect to which we are taking the derivative. As a consequence, a total derivative measures indirect, or interaction, effects as well as direct effects of one variable on another. As an example, suppose that for the multivariate function

$$y = f(x, z),$$

there exists some relationship between the independent variables, x and z, represented as

$$z = z(x).$$

When taking the derivative of y with respect to x, a total derivative will allow not only for the direct effect that a change in x has on y, but also for the indirect effect that a change in x has on y through its impact on z. Therefore, the total derivative of y with respect to x, denoted dy/dx, is

$$\frac{dy}{dx} = \frac{\partial f(x,z)}{\partial x}\frac{dx}{dx} + \frac{\partial f(x,z)}{\partial z}\frac{dz}{dx},$$

or since $\dfrac{dx}{dx} = 1$,

$$\frac{dy}{dx} = \frac{\partial f(x,z)}{\partial x} + \frac{\partial f(x,z)}{\partial z}\frac{dz}{dx}.$$

Finally, since $y = f(x,z)$, we can write the expression more concisely as

$$\frac{dy}{dx} = \frac{\partial y}{\partial x} + \frac{\partial y}{\partial z}\frac{dz}{dx}.$$

This expression is similar to the results generated using the chain rule in Section 1.2.2. The first term in the above equation, $\partial y/\partial x$, records the direct effect of a change in x on y, while the other independent variable, z, is held constant. The second term, $\partial y/\partial z$ dz/dx indicates the indirect effect of a change in x on the variable y. Note that this term has two components. The first, $\partial y/\partial z$, measures the change in y due strictly to a change in z. However, for this total derivative, dy/dx, any change in z is due to a change in x, and this effect is indicated by the second term, dz/dx.

We can use a numerical example of a total derivative to provide further clarification. Recall the function, used in an earlier example:

$$y = x^2 z^3.$$

Now, however, assume that there exists a relationship between the independent variables x and z expressed as

$$z = 2x.$$

We compute the total derivative of y with respect to x as

$$\frac{dy}{dx} = \frac{\partial y}{\partial x} + \frac{\partial y}{\partial z}\frac{dz}{dx} = \frac{\partial(x^2 z^3)}{\partial x} + \frac{\partial(x^2 z^3)}{\partial z}\frac{d(2x)}{dx},$$

or

$$\frac{dy}{dx} = 2xz^3 + 3x^2 z^2(2) = 2xz^3 + 6x^2 z^2.$$

Let's use an example pertaining to a monopolist's marginal revenue to demonstrate how the total derivative can be applied to microeconomics. Assume that the demand curve faced by a monopolist for its output is

$$Q = 1000 - 10P.$$

Since the monopolist is the only provider of a good in a market, it affects the market price of the good, P, when it changes its level of output, Q. Therefore, the price in the market is a function of the monopolist's output. This relationship between P and Q can be derived by solving the above demand curve for P as follows:

$$10P = 1000 - Q$$

$$P = 100 - \frac{1}{10}Q.$$

Recall from your principles of microeconomics course that a firm's total revenue, TR, is computed as

$$TR = P \cdot Q,$$

and its marginal revenue is computed as

$$MR = \frac{dTR}{dQ}.$$

Therefore, we can express the monopolist's total revenue in this case as

$$TR = P \cdot Q,$$

where

$$P = 100 - \frac{1}{10}Q.$$

By taking the total derivative of the monopolist's total revenue function, we can determine its marginal revenue as follows:

$$MR = \frac{dTR}{dQ} = \frac{\partial TR}{\partial Q} + \frac{\partial TR}{\partial P} \cdot \frac{dP}{dQ}$$

$$MR = \frac{dTR}{dQ} = P + (Q)\left(-\frac{1}{10}\right)$$

and substituting $P = 100 - 1/10Q$ into the above equation, we find

$$MR = \frac{dTR}{dQ} = 100 - \frac{1}{10}Q - \frac{1}{10}Q = 100 - \frac{1}{5}Q.$$

We have now demonstrated how we can use derivatives of univariate and multivariate functions in microeconomics to compute various types of marginal functions. In addition, we have also shown how we can use univariate derivatives to solve univariate optimization problems. In the next chapter, we will demonstrate how derivatives of multivariate functions can be used to solve even more complex multivariate optimization problems.

1.5   SUMMARY

This chapter provides a thorough review of those calculus techniques most frequently encountered in microeconomic theory. The concept of a derivative was discussed, along with the most commonly used rules of differentiation. In addition, we distinguished between total and partial derivatives. We also presented the necessary and sufficient conditions for optimizing univariate functions. A summary of the most important topics covered in this chapter are outlined as follows.

- A univariate function contains only one independent variable, $y = f(x)$, and its average slope is equal to $\Delta y/\Delta x$, where Δy and Δx represent discrete changes in the variables y and x, respectively.
- The instantaneous slope of the univariate function $y = f(x)$ is equal to its derivative, $dy/dx = f'(x)$.
- One of the most useful economic applications of the derivative is in solving optimization (maximization or minimization) problems. An optimization problem for a univariate function means finding the solution value for the decision variable that corresponds to an optimum value (maximum or minimum) for the dependent, or objective, variable.
- A critical value for the independent variable, x, in a univariate function, $y = f(x)$, exists if at this value the first derivative of the function is equal to zero—that is, $dy/dx = 0$. This is also known as a first-order condition for an optimum.
- A multivariate function contains more than one independent variable. As a result, we must distinguish between partial and total derivatives for this type of function.
- A partial derivative represents the change in the dependent variable in a function resulting from an infinitesimally small change in one of the independent variables, while holding all others constant.
- A total derivative measures the change in the dependent variable in a function due to an infinitesimally small change in an independent variable, when all independent variables are allowed to vary.

KEY TERMS

- critical value, page 10
- dependent, or objective, variables, page 1
- higher-order derivative, page 9
- independent, or decision, variables, page 1
- marginal function, page 8
- model, page 1
- multivariate function, page 16
- partial derivative, page 17
- partial slope, page 16
- total derivative, page 21
- univariate function, page 2

EXERCISES

1.1 Find dy/dx for each of the functions:
   a. $y = 3x^3 - 2x^2 + 9x + 4$
   b. $y = 13x^0$
   c. $y = (4x^2 + 2)(3x^3 + 12x)$
   d. $y = 100/x^2$
   e. $y = (2x^2 - 3x)/(6x + 2)$

†1.2 Find dy/dx for each of the functions:

    a. $y = 2 \ln 2x$

    b. $y = \ln e^{2x}$

    c. $y = 100e^{.5x}$

1.3 Find $f'(x), f''(x)$, and $f'''(x)$ for each of the following functions:

    a. $y = 4x^4 + 3x^3 + 2x^2 + x + 1$

    b. $y = (2x^3 + x^2)(x^2 - 5x)$

    c. $y = 1/x^3$

1.4 Determine the marginal revenue function for a firm, given its total revenue function is $TR = 120\,q - 2q^2$.

Next, find the level of output, q, that will maximize the total revenue for this firm. Also compute the maximum amount of total revenue received by the firm. (*Hint*: Examine the first-order and second-order conditions for a maximum.)

1.5 A total cost function for a firm is $TC = 1/3q^3 - 2q^2 + 6q + 10$. Find its associated marginal cost function and the level of output where marginal cost is at a minimum. Also determine the minimum value of marginal cost. (*Hint*: Examine the first-order and second-order conditions for a minimum.)

1.6 Given the function,

$$y = 5x^2z^3,$$

    a. Find $\partial y/\partial x$ and $\partial y/\partial z$.

    b. Evaluate the partial derivatives in part a for $x = 2$ and $z = 3$.

    c. Now assume that a relationship exists between x and z such that

$$z = 4x^2.$$

    Find dy/dx and evaluate it for $x = 2$ and $z = 3$.

1.7 Given the function,

$$y = 8x^2z^2 - 2x^3z^3,$$

    a. Determine the functions for $\partial y/\partial x$ and $\partial y/\partial z$.

    b. Find the functions for dy/dx and dy/dz.

1.8 A consumer's utility function is given as

$$U = f(x,y) = 200\,x^{.5}\,y^{.5}$$

where U denotes his level of utility received from consuming goods x and y.

    a. Determine the functions for the consumer's marginal utility of good x, MU_x, and his marginal utility of good y, MU_y.

    b. Compute the values of MU_x and MU_y when the individual is consuming 16 units of good x and 4 units of good y.

CHAPTER 2

Unconstrained and Constrained Optimization of Multivariate Functions

2.1 INTRODUCTION

In Chapter 1, we demonstrated how derivatives of univariate functions are used to determine the value of a single independent, or decision, variable that corresponds to an optimum value of some dependent, or objective, variable. Depending on the particular problem, and hence function, we are analyzing, this optimum value for the objective variable may represent either a maximum or a minimum. However, many concepts used in economic analysis involve multivariate functions, or functions containing more than one independent variable. In this chapter, we will extend and apply the optimization process to these multivariate functions. In addition, note that the optimization process demonstrated in Chapter 1 was conducted without imposing any restrictions, or constraints, on the decision variable. However, within the context of most economic analysis, there exists a scarcity of resources, which ultimately leads to some type of restriction, or constraint, on the amount(s) of the decision variable(s) that can be selected in an optimization problem. As a result, such a constraint also limits the optimized value of the objective variable. In general, this type of problem consists of determining the values of the decision variable(s) that correspond to an optimal value for the objective variable given some predetermined constraining factors. Appropriately, we designate this process as constrained optimization.

As an example, suppose an individual goes to lunch with the intent of deriving satisfaction, or utility, from consuming two goods, hotdogs and soda pop. Thus, the individual's level of utility constitutes the objective variable to be maximized, and the amounts of the two goods represent the decision variables. Now, assume that the individual has a limited amount of money to spend on lunch and must pay prices for the hotdogs and soda pop. This being the case, the total amounts of these two goods the individual can purchase and consume are constrained by these factors, as is the maximum level of utility she can achieve. The "problem" faced by this individual is to select the combination of the two goods, hotdogs and soda pop, that maximize her level of satisfaction, or utility, given the constraining factors of the prices she must pay for the goods and the amount of money she has to buy them.

More generally, in this chapter, we will demonstrate the process of both constrained and unconstrained optimization of multivariate functions. By so doing, we can once again show the important role played by differential calculus in solving microeconomic problems.

2.2   UNCONSTRAINED OPTIMIZATION OF MULTIVARIATE FUNCTIONS

Perhaps the most useful application of partial derivatives to economic analysis is in solving optimization problems involving multivariate functions. The process of optimizing—either maximizing or minimizing—a multivariate function is similar to what we discussed in Section 1.3 of Chapter 1 for a univariate function. The difference is that multivariate functions have more than one decision (independent) variable. Thus, optimizing such a function means finding the solution values for the n number of decision variables that will yield an optimum value for the objective (dependent) variable.

2.2.1   First-Order Conditions

We can demonstrate the optimization procedure for a multivariate function by once again using the multivariate function $y = f(x,z)$ (see Chapter 1, Figure 1.6). Recall that the partial derivative, $\partial y/\partial x$, represents the instantaneous partial slope of the function, or the change in y with respect to x, holding z constant. In other words, $\partial y/\partial x$ represents the slope of each two-dimensional cross-section of the multivariate function, where each cross-section occurs at some fixed value of z. These cross-sections appear in panel (A), where you can see that the value of x that maximizes the value of y for each cross-section occurs where $\partial y/\partial x = 0$ in each case. Thus, we can determine an entire set of values for x that optimize—in this case maximize—the value of y for different levels of z.

Similarly, the partial derivative, $\partial y/\partial z$, represents the partial slope of the function, or the change in y with respect to z, holding x constant. Thus, $\partial y/\partial z$, measures the slope of each two-dimensional cross-section established at fixed values for x, which we demonstrated previously in panel (B) of Figure 1.6. We can determine the values of z that correspond to an optimum (maximum) value for y where $\partial y/\partial z = 0$ for each cross-section. As a result, a set of values for z are determined that maximize the value of y for different levels of x.

The goal of an optimization problem is to find the solution values of the independent (decision) variables—in this case x and z—that correspond to an optimum for the entire multivariate function, represented by the variable, y. Thus we must optimize the objective variable, y, with respect to each independent variable, x and z, where we have established the first-order conditions for such an optimum to be

$$\frac{\partial y}{\partial x} = 0 \quad \text{and} \quad \frac{\partial y}{\partial z} = 0.$$

Note that we can extend the logic for multivariate functions containing more than two independent variables—for example, $y = f(x,w, \ldots, z)$—such that the first-order conditions for an optimum are

$$\frac{\partial y}{\partial x} = \frac{\partial y}{\partial w} = \cdots = \frac{\partial y}{\partial z} = 0.$$

Returning to the more limited function, $y = f(x,z)$, we have shown that each of the first-order conditions for an optimum,

$$\frac{\partial y}{\partial x} = 0 \quad \text{and} \quad \frac{\partial y}{\partial z} = 0,$$

represents two sets of local extremes. This is true because each first-order condition maximizes the objective variable, y, with respect to one of the decision variables for different levels of the other. Although the independent variables x and z are not related to each other in the original function, they are related to each other in the first-order conditions since each partial is set equal to the common value of zero. These first-order conditions represent a system of two equations in two variables, which we can solve simultaneously to yield the solution values for x and z that correspond to the optimum value for y. We have demonstrated this process in Figure 2.1, where the solution values for the independent variables are designated as x^* and z^*, and the optimum, or in this case maximum, value for the dependent variable is y^*. These values correspond to the peak of the function, where the two lines, AA' and BB', drawn tangent to the surface at this point are horizontal. That the two tangents are horizontal indicates that the two partial slopes, $\partial y/\partial x$ and $\partial y/\partial z$, are simultaneously equal to zero, which is simply a graphical representation of the first-order conditions for an optimum.

A specific example should help to clarify this procedure. Assume that the goal is to determine the values for the variables x and z that maximize the multivariate function

$$y = 28x + 4xz - 2x^2 - 4z^2.$$

The first-order conditions for a maximum are

$$\frac{\partial y}{\partial x} = 28 + 4z - 4x = 0,$$

and

$$\frac{\partial y}{\partial z} = 4x - 8z = 0.$$

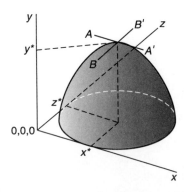

FIGURE 2.1 Solution Values Pertaining to an Unconstrained Maximum for a Multivariate Function

A relationship now exists between the variables x and z since each partial derivative is set equal to zero. Thus, it is possible to solve for one variable in terms of the other in either of the two equations. Selecting the equation, $\partial y/\partial z = 4x - 8z = 0$, and solving for x yields

$$4x = 8z,$$

or

$$x = 2z.$$

Substituting the term $2z$ for x in the equation for $\partial y/\partial x$ generates the result,

$$28 + 4z - 4(2z) = 0,$$
$$28 - 4z = 0,$$

or

$$z^* = 7.$$

We can then substitute this value for z into the equation for $\partial y/\partial z$ to yield

$$4x - 8(7) = 0,$$

or

$$x^* = 14.$$

Finally, we can determine the maximum value for y by substituting the solution values for x and z into the original function as

$$y = 28(14) + 4(14)(7) - 2(14)^2 - 4(7)^2,$$

or

$$y^* = 196.$$

In some situations, the goal may be to find solution values for the decision variables that will minimize the value of the objective variable. For example, a firm may seek to combine the inputs it uses in its production process in a manner that will correspond to a minimum level of cost. In this situation, the amounts of inputs represent the firm's decision variables, and the firm's cost constitutes its objective variable. This is still an optimization problem but with a different goal. Again, assume the general multivariate function is

$$y = f(x,z)$$

but has the form shown in Figure 2.2. The minimum value for y is y^*, and the values for x and z corresponding to this minimum are x^* and z^*. Note that the two lines, CC' and DD', drawn tangent to the surface at the minimum value of y are horizontal, indicating that the partial slopes of y with respect to both x and z must be equal to zero. Thus, the first-order conditions for a minimum are

$$\frac{\partial y}{\partial x} = 0 \quad \text{and} \quad \frac{\partial y}{\partial z} = 0.$$

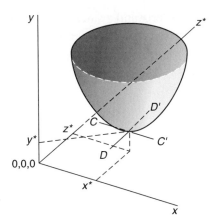

FIGURE 2.2 Solution Values Pertaining to an Unconstrained Minimum for a Multivariate Function

For a broader multivariate function such as

$$y = f(x, w, \ldots, z),$$

the first-order conditions for a minimum are simply

$$\frac{\partial y}{\partial x} = \frac{\partial y}{\partial w} = \cdots = \frac{\partial y}{\partial z} = 0.$$

The point is that the first-order conditions for a minimum are exactly the same as those for a maximum. Therefore, solving a minimization problem is procedurally the same as before: Find the partial derivatives, set them equal to zero, and solve the resulting system of equations simultaneously to find the solution values for all the variables. The question is, how do we determine whether the solution values correspond to a maximum or a minimum for the objective variable? The answer to this question, as with univariate functions, lies in the process of determining and evaluating the second-order conditions associated with the original function.

†2.2.2 Second-Order Conditions

Before beginning the discussion of second-order conditions for optimizing multivariate functions, let's define the mathematical notation that we will use to express these conditions. Given the multivariate function $y = f(x, z)$, we have shown that the two corresponding first-order partial derivatives are denoted as $\partial y / \partial x$ and $\partial y / \partial z$. However, an alternative and more compact means of expressing these partials is f_x and f_z, respectively. Similarly, we can also express the second-order derivatives in this compact manner as

$$f_{xx} = \frac{\partial^2 y}{\partial x^2} = \frac{\partial\left(\frac{\partial y}{\partial x}\right)}{\partial x}, \quad f_{zz} = \frac{\partial^2 y}{\partial z^2} = \frac{\partial\left(\frac{\partial y}{\partial z}\right)}{\partial z}, \quad f_{xz} = \frac{\partial^2 y}{\partial x \partial z} = \frac{\partial\left(\frac{\partial y}{\partial x}\right)}{\partial z}, \quad \text{and}$$

$$f_{zx} = \frac{\partial^2 y}{\partial z \partial x} = \frac{\partial\left(\frac{\partial y}{\partial z}\right)}{\partial x},$$

where f_{xx} represents the partial derivative of $\partial y/\partial x$, taken with respect to x, and f_{zz} denotes the partial derivative of $\partial y/\partial z$, taken with respect to z. The last two second-order partial derivatives, $\partial^2 y/\partial x \partial z$ and $\partial^2 y/\partial z \partial x$, represent the cross-partial derivatives of the function, y. In the case of the cross-partial derivative, $\partial^2 y/\partial x \partial z = f_{xz}$ measures the partial derivative of the partial derivative, $\partial y/\partial x$, taken with respect to the variable z, while $\partial^2 y/\partial z \partial x = f_{zx}$ denotes the partial derivative of $\partial y/\partial z$ taken with respect to x.

Using this notation, we find that the second-order conditions for an unconstrained maximum are as follows:

$$f_{xx} < 0, \quad f_{zz} < 0,$$

and

$$[f_{xx} f_{zz} - (f_{xz})^2] > 0,$$

while the second-order conditions for an unconstrained minimum are

$$f_{xx} > 0, \quad f_{zz} > 0,$$

and

$$[f_{xx} f_{zz} - (f_{xz})^2] > 0.$$

In the case of an unconstrained maximum, the conditions that both f_{xx} and f_{zz} are negative imply that the slope of a plane drawn tangent to the three-dimensional function will decrease if either the value of x is increased beyond its critical value or the value of z is increased beyond its critical value. Similarly, for a constrained minimum to exist, f_{xx} and f_{zz} must both be positive, indicating that the slope of a plane drawn tangent to the function will increase if the value of either x or z is increased beyond its optimizing level.

Note that the term $[f_{xx} f_{zz} - (f_{xz})^2] > 0$ is common to the second-order conditions for both a maximum and a minimum. This term is the condition for a saddle point, and it prevents the function from being at a maximum when viewed from the axis of one of the independent variables while simultaneously achieving a minimum when viewed from the axis of the other independent variable. The phrase "saddle point" is appropriate here. Think of a saddle on a horse. When we view the saddle from the side of the horse, it appears that the saddle is at a minimum at its center. However, when viewed from the rear of the horse, the saddle appears to achieve a maximum at its center. Thus, the saddle point condition ensures that when we view the function at its critical values from both the x and z axes, the function is either at a maximum or at a minimum, but it never achieves both simultaneously.

The following numerical example may provide some additional insight into the process of computing and interpreting the second-order conditions for an unconstrained multivariate optimization problem. Recall the multivariate function, $y = 28x + 4xz - 2x^2 - 4z^2$ analyzed in the previous section. We determined that the function was optimized at $y^* = 196$ when $x^* = 14$ and $z^* = 7$. To determine whether the value of $y^* = 196$ represents a minimum or maximum value for y, we must analyze the second-order conditions for this function as follows.

Step 1: Determine the first-order conditions

$$f_x = \frac{\partial y}{\partial x} = 28 + 4z - 4x = 0,$$

and

$$f_z = \frac{\partial y}{\partial z} = 4x - 8z = 0.$$

Step 2: Determine the second-order partial derivatives

$$f_{xx} = \frac{\partial\left(\frac{\partial y}{\partial x}\right)}{\partial x} = -4,$$

$$f_{xz} = \frac{\partial\left(\frac{\partial y}{\partial x}\right)}{\partial z} = 4,$$

$$f_{zz} = \frac{\partial\left(\frac{\partial y}{\partial z}\right)}{\partial z} = -8,$$

and

$$f_{zx} = \frac{\partial\left(\frac{\partial y}{\partial z}\right)}{\partial x} = 4.$$

Step 3: Evaluate the second-order conditions

$$f_{xx} = -4 < 0, \quad f_{zz} = -8 < 0,$$

and

$$[f_{xx}f_{zz} - (f_{xz})^2] = (-4)(-8) - (4)^2 = 32 - 16 = 16 > 0.$$

Therefore, we can conclude that the function $y = 28x + 4xz - 2x^2 - 4z^2$ achieves a maximum value of 196 when $x^* = 14$ and $z^* = 7$.

2.3 CONSTRAINED OPTIMIZATION

As we have mentioned, microeconomics consists largely of analyzing the processes by which economic agents, such as consumers or firms, make rational choices. In most cases the decisions of economic agents are generally limited or constrained by some predetermined factors. For example, a problem confronting an individual consumer is that of finding the combination of goods to maximize her utility. However, the individual will be limited, or constrained, in the amounts of goods she can afford to buy and consume, by such factors as her income and the prices she must pay for the goods. Thus, the maximum level of utility she can achieve is constrained as well. This problem is a matter of constrained optimization or, more specifically, constrained utility maximization. In general, **constrained optimization** is *the process of maximizing or minimizing some objective function subject to the limitations imposed by some predetermined factors affecting the values of the decision variables.*

We can solve constrained optimization problems by incorporating the limiting factors, along with the decision variables, into an equation known as a constraint and then solving it simultaneously with the first-order conditions for an optimum. This process generates solution values for the decision variables that correspond to a constrained optimum for the objective function.

There are two methods for solving constrained optimization problems: the substitution method and the method of Lagrangian multipliers. First we will briefly describe the substitution method. In this method, we compute the total derivative of the objective function with respect to one of the decision variables and set it equal to zero. Since the relationship between the two decision variables is represented by some constraint, we can determine the derivative of one decision variable with respect to the other and substitute this term into the total derivative for the objective function. We then solve this resulting expression to determine the solution value for the remaining decision variable. Subsequently, we can find the solution value(s) for the other decision variable(s) and the objective variable by substituting the appropriate solved values back into the original function.

We can illustrate this process using general notation. Assume the goal is to optimize (maximize or minimize) some objective function,

$$y = f(x,z),$$

subject to some constraint, which specifies a predetermined relationship between the decision variables as

$$g(x,z) = \bar{c}_1,$$

where $\bar{c}_1$ represents some constant value. We can solve this constraint to express one variable in terms of the other such as

$$z = z(x).$$

Using this constraint with the objective function, we can determine the solution values for the corresponding constrained optimum as shown in Figure 2.3. The vertical plane represents the constraint $z = z(x)$ and cuts the surface of the objective function, $y = f(x,z)$, producing the arc, AA'. As a result, the solution values for the constrained optimum, x^{**}, z^{**}, and y^{**}, are different—in this case smaller—than those pertaining to the unconstrained optimum, x^*, z^*, and y^*. When these results differ, we say the constraint is binding since incorporating it into the optimization problem produces results different from those associated with an unconstrained optimum. Also, it is important to note that, in general, the solution values for the decision variables obtained for

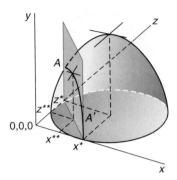

FIGURE 2.3 Comparison of Solution Values for an Unconstrained and Constrained Maximum

the constrained maximization problem will not merely be proportional reductions of the solution values for the unconstrained problem.

For example, a constrained optimization problem faced by a business firm is to determine the amounts of inputs it uses to produce some predetermined level of output in the least costly manner. Suppose the firm is in the business of painting buildings. The inputs it uses are capital, consisting of hydraulic lifts, spray painting machines, ladders, and brushes, and labor. If the amount of output—the square footage to be painted—is very high, it will most likely use more capital compared to labor, as it would be efficient to do so. The firm will likely use several hydraulic lifts as well as high-powered spray painting machines. However, if the firm produces less output, painting less square footage, isn't it logical that it will probably do so with fewer complex machines and more painters using just brushes and ladders? In other words, as the predetermined level of output is altered, the ratio by which the firm combines its inputs changes. Therefore, in general, if we know that a constraining relationship exists among a group of decision variables, it is imperative that we always include this relationship in the initial construction of the optimization problem in order to determine the solution.

2.3.1 Lagrangian Multiplier Method

The most common method for solving constrained optimization problems is the method of Lagrangian multipliers. We use this method more frequently than the substitution method because it is generally less cumbersome for more complex problems, and both methods produce the same results. In general, the method of Lagrangian multipliers incorporates the objective function that is to be optimized, along with the constraint, into one function defined as a Lagrangian function, that we will designate as $\mathcal{L}$. Throughout this text, we will examine problems with only one constraint, although we can use the method to incorporate additional constraints. What makes this method less cumbersome than the substitution method is that it allows for the use of partial, rather than total, derivatives in the maximization process.

Specifically, the **Lagrangian function**, $\mathcal{L}$, *consists of the objective function plus a created variable*, λ, *multiplied by the constraint expressed in standard form*. We create the variable, λ, to serve as a tool in solving a constrained optimization problem. In addition, when we express an equation in standard form, we arrange it so that it is equal to zero. Thus, the constraint in standard form, multiplied by λ, is also equal to zero, and including this term in the Lagrangian function leaves the original objective function unchanged. As a result, optimizing the Lagrangian function is the same as optimizing the objective function. When solving a constrained optimization problem using the Lagrangian multiplier method, we first take the partial derivative of $\mathscr{L}$ with respect to each independent variable, including all of the decision variables and λ. We then set the partial derivatives equal to zero, creating a system of equations known as first-order conditions. Each equation represents a set of local extremes because each represents an optimum for the Lagrangian function with respect to one of the independent variables. As a result, we can determine the value for that independent variable corresponding to an optimum for $\mathscr{L}$, given specified values for the others. However, since we can specify these other independent variables at many different values, any one of the equations comprising the first-order conditions represents an entire set of local optima.

We can solve the system of first-order conditions simultaneously to determine solution values for the decision variables and the created variable λ, which together correspond to an overall optimum value for the objective function. We define this situation as a global optimum since we have determined it from the entire system of local optimums. Finally, by substituting the appropriate solution values for the decision variables into the objective function, we can obtain the constrained optimum (maximum or minimum) value for the objective variable.

We will first demonstrate this process using general notation. Assume that the goal is to optimize the objective function

$$y = f(x,z)$$

subject to some constraint,

$$g(x,z) = \bar{c}_1,$$

where $\bar{c}_1$ represents some constant value. We can express this constraint in standard form as

$$\bar{c}_1 - g(x,z) = 0.$$

After multiplying the constraint in standard form by the created variable λ, we construct the generalized Lagrangian function, $\mathscr{L}$, as

$$\mathscr{L} = y + \lambda \, [\bar{c}_1 - g(x,z)],$$

or

$$\mathscr{L} = f(x,z) + \lambda \, [\bar{c}_1 - g(x,z)].$$

This function contains the objective function and the Lagrangian multiplier, λ, multiplied by the constraint in standard form. Note that we have solved the constraint such that it is equal to zero; therefore, optimizing the Lagrangian function will produce a constrained optimum for the objective function, $f(x,z)$.

The first-order conditions for optimizing the Lagrangian function are

$$\frac{\partial \mathcal{L}}{\partial x} = \frac{\partial f(x,z)}{\partial x} - \lambda \frac{\partial g(x,z)}{\partial x} = 0$$

$$\frac{\partial \mathcal{L}}{\partial z} = \frac{\partial f(x,z)}{\partial z} - \lambda \frac{\partial g(x,z)}{\partial z} = 0$$

$$\frac{\partial \mathcal{L}}{\partial \lambda} = \bar{c}_1 - g(x,z) = 0.$$

Note that we have computed the equation representing $\partial \mathcal{L} / \partial \lambda$ to be the original constraint in standard form. This is not a matter of chance. We have carefully designed the Lagrangian function for this outcome to occur; as a result, solving the system of partial derivatives, or local extremes, generates solution values pertaining to an optimum for the Lagrangian function and a constrained optimum for the objective function, $y = f(x,z)$. We can now solve this system of three equations in three independent variables, x, z, and λ, simultaneously to obtain solution values corresponding to a constrained optimum value for y. There is some additional interpretation associated with the term λ, which represents the change in $\mathcal{L}$ with respect to a one-unit change in the value of the constraint $\bar{c}_1$. Since the optimum for $\mathcal{L}$ is also the constrained optimum for the objective function, $y = f(x,z)$, then λ also represents the change in y with respect to a one-unit change in the value of the constraint. Alternatively stated, λ indicates the marginal effect on the objective function due to a change in the constraint.

Let's further examine the process of constrained optimization and the method of the Lagrangian multiplier by returning to the specific objective function, $y = 28x + 4xz - 2x^2 - 4z^2$, used in the unconstrained optimization example solved earlier. However, in this situation, assume we impose some type of constraining relationship on the two decision variables x and z, such that $x + z = 6$. As a result, the Lagrangian function in this example is

$$\mathcal{L} = y + \lambda\,(6 - x - z).$$

Substituting $y = 28x + 4xz - 2x^2 - 4z^2$ into the function above yields

$$\mathcal{L} = 28x + 4xz - 2x^2 - 4z^2 + \lambda\,(6 - x - z),$$

or

$$\mathcal{L} = 28x + 4xz - 2x^2 - 4z^2 + \lambda 6 - \lambda x - \lambda z.$$

Accordingly, the first-order conditions for an optimum are

$$\frac{\partial \mathcal{L}}{\partial x} = 28 + 4z - 4x - \lambda = 0$$

$$\frac{\partial \mathcal{L}}{\partial z} = 4x - 8z - \lambda = 0$$

$$\frac{\partial \mathcal{L}}{\partial \lambda} = 6 - x - z = 0.$$

We can solve these three equations representing local extremes, or an optimal value for $\mathscr{L}$ with respect to x, z, and λ, respectively, simultaneously to obtain solution values for the decision variables and λ. There are many ways to accomplish this objective. One of the most efficient approaches is to solve each of the first two equations in terms of λ and then divide one of the resulting equations by the other to eliminate λ. Thus,

$$28 + 4z - 4x = \lambda$$

and

$$4x - 8z = \lambda,$$

and dividing the first of these equations by the second yields

$$\frac{28 + 4z - 4x}{4x - 8z} = \frac{\lambda}{\lambda} = 1,$$

or

$$28 + 4z - 4x = 4x - 8\,z.$$

We can solve either of the decision variables in terms of the other. In this case, solving for x in terms of z yields

$$8x = 28 + 12z,$$

or

$$x = \frac{28 + 12z}{8} = \frac{7 + 3z}{2}.$$

We have now reduced the problem from three equations in three variables to two equations in two variables, represented by the above equation and the equation for $\partial \mathscr{L}/\partial \lambda$, which by construction is the constraint in standard form. Substituting the equation for x expressed in terms of z into the constraint yields

$$6 - \left(\frac{7 + 3z}{2}\right) - z = 0,$$

or

$$12 - 7 - 3z - 2z = 0,$$
$$5z = 5,$$
$$z^* = 1.$$

By substituting this solution value for z back into the equation for x, we obtain

$$x^* = \frac{7 + 3(1)}{2} = 5.$$

Next, the value for λ* can be found by substituting the values for x^* and z^* into the equation for either $\partial\mathcal{L}/\partial x$ or $\partial\mathcal{L}/\partial z$ from the first-order conditions. Using the equation for $\partial\mathcal{L}/\partial z$,

$$4x - 8z - \lambda = 0,$$
$$4x - 8z = \lambda,$$
$$4(5) - 8(1) = \lambda,$$
$$\lambda^* = 12.$$

Finally, we obtain the optimized, in this case maximized, value for y by substituting the solution values of $x^* = 5$ and $z^* = 1$ into the objective function as

$$y^* = 28(5) + 4(5)(1) - 2(5)^2 - 4(1)^2$$
$$= 140 + 20 - 50 - 4 = 106.$$

We can interpret the result of $\lambda^* = 12$ as indicating that if the constraint is relaxed by one unit, from $x + z = 6$ to $x + z = 7$, then the optimal value of the objective variable, y^*, will increase by 12 units. Alternatively, should the constraint be decreased by one unit from $x + z = 6$ to $x + z = 5$, then y^* will decrease by 12 units. You can verify these results by solving the constrained optimization problem using the altered constraints.

The application of the optimization problem, both unconstrained and constrained, to a simple conceptual example should provide additional insight. Assume that the familiar objective function $y = 28x + 4xz - 2x^2 - 4z^2$ represents the utility function for a child, where y measures his level of utility in terms of some index representing a ranking of preferences, and x and z represent units of candy and soda pop, respectively, consumed daily by the child. Note that a utility function reflects the satisfaction an individual receives from consuming amounts of goods, and thus it also reflects that individual's tastes for these goods. In Section 2.2.1, we maximized this function in the absence of a constraint. In the current context, we can interpret those solutions to indicate that the child would select $x^* = 14$ pieces of candy and $z^* = 7$ bottles of soda pop per day, achieving a maximum level of utility of 196.

Now suppose that for either health or budgetary reasons the child's mother imposes a constraint, or limitation, on the child's total daily consumption of the two goods represented by

$$x + z = 6.$$

In this case, the mother is assuming the two goods are equally expensive and equally "healthy." The constraint states that the total amount consumed of x and z, or candy and soda pop, must equal 6 units per day. The choice of dispersing the 6 total units of x and z is left to the child. We can interpret this situation as a constrained utility maximization problem for which we obtained the solutions earlier in this section to be $x^* = 5$ pieces of candy and $z^* = 1$ bottle of soda pop per day, or exactly 6 units of x and z per day. In this case, the child's utility is at a level of 106, which is less than the 196 level of utility for the unconstrained case. Notice that if the mother had specified the choices for the child as, say, $x = 4$ pieces of candy and $z = 2$ bottles of soda pop, where $x + z$ still equals 6 units in total, the child's utility would be

$$U = 28(4) + 4(4)\,(2) - 2(4)^2 - 4(2)^2,$$

or $$U = 112 + 32 - 32 - 16 = 96.$$

The maximum amount of utility is less in this case because the child has not been given the opportunity to optimize his utility function. Of course, most of the constrained optimization problems encountered by consumers and firms tend to be considerably more complex than this example. However, the basic principle associated with the constrained optimization process is the same.

†2.3.2   Primal and Dual Analyses

The generalized constrained optimization problem described earlier can be stated as:

$$\text{Maximize (Minimize) } y = f(x,z)$$
$$\text{subject to} \qquad g(x,z) = \bar{c}_1,$$

where $y = f(x,z)$ represents the objective function to be maximized or minimized, $g(x,z) = \bar{c}_1$, represents the constraint, and x and z are the decision variables. We demonstrated that the corresponding Lagrangian function for this problem is formulated by substituting the objective function and the constraint, in standard form, into the Lagrangian expression yielding

$$\mathcal{L} = f(x,z) + \lambda\,[\bar{c}_1 - g(x,z)].$$

It is convention in economics to refer to the original optimization problem under analysis as the primal, which can represent either a maximization or a minimization problem. Using the Lagrangian multiplier method outlined earlier in this chapter, we derived and then simultaneously solved the first-order conditions for the primal problem to obtain values of the decision variables, x and z, which optimize the objective function $y = f(x,z)$, subject to the constraint.

An alternative approach for solving this problem, known as the dual, yields the same solution values for x^* and z^* because it uses the same fundamental information as the primal problem. Specifically, if the primal is a maximization problem, then its corresponding dual will be a minimization problem. Conversely, if the primal is a minimization problem, then its dual will be a maximization problem. These problems are very closely related because the objective function of one acts as the constraint of the other. Therefore, the objective function for the primal, $y = f(x,z)$, becomes the constraint in the dual problem, where the value of y will be set at a predetermined level, $\bar{y}_1$. As a result, the constraint for the dual is $f(x,z) = \bar{y}_1$. Furthermore, the constraint used in the primal problem, $g(x,z) = \bar{c}_1$, becomes the objective function in the dual, and c will no longer be a specified value since it represents the value of the objective function to be optimized, specifically, $c = g(x,z)$. Given the previously stated generalized primal problem, we can state its associated dual as:

$$\text{Minimize (Maximize) } \quad c = g(x,z)$$
$$\text{subject to} \qquad f(x,z) = \bar{y}_1.$$

After expressing the constraint in standard form, as $\bar{y}_1 - f(x,z) = 0$, we can construct the Lagrangian function for the dual problem, denoted $\mathcal{L}^D$, as

$$\mathcal{L}^D = g(x,z) + \lambda^D \left[\bar{y}_1 - f(x,z)\right].$$

Once again, after determining and solving the system of first-order conditions, we can find the solution values for x^*, z^*, and λ^{D*} that optimize the value of the objective function, $g(x,z)$.

Using a numerical example, we will show that the values of x^* and z^* will be identical given either approach, provided that the optimal value for the objective function in the primal is specified as the constraining value in the dual. However, the value of λ^{D*}, the Lagrangian multiplier for the dual, will be equal to the reciprocal of λ^*, the Lagrangian multiplier for the primal. Returning once again to the constrained optimization problem solved earlier in this chapter, recall that the original, thus primal, problem was

$$\text{Maximize} \quad y = 28x + 4xz - 2x^2 - 4z^2$$
$$\text{subject to} \quad x + z = 6.$$

Therefore, the Lagrangian function in this example was

$$\mathcal{L} = 28x + 4xz - 2x^2 - 4z^2 + \lambda\,(6 - x - z),$$

or

$$\mathcal{L} = 28x + 4xz - 2x^2 - 4z^2 + \lambda 6 - \lambda x - \lambda z,$$

and the associated first-order conditions were

$$\frac{\partial \mathcal{L}}{\partial x} = 28 + 4z - 4x - \lambda = 0$$

$$\frac{\partial \mathcal{L}}{\partial z} = 4x - 8z - \lambda = 0$$

$$\frac{\partial \mathcal{L}}{\partial \lambda} = 6 - x - z = 0.$$

Solving the first-order conditions simultaneously, we find that the values of x, z, and λ that maximize the objective function are $x^* = 5$, $z^* = 1$, $\lambda^* = 12$, and, subsequently, $y^* = 106$.

Now, using the information contained in the primal problem, we can formulate the associated dual problem as

$$\text{Minimize} \quad c = x + z$$
$$\text{subject to} \quad 28x + 4xz - 2x^2 - 4z^2 = 106.$$

The Lagrangian function for the dual is, therefore,

$$\mathcal{L}^D = x + z + \lambda^D \,(106 - 28x - 4xz + 2x^2 + 4z^2),$$

or

$$\mathcal{L}^D = x + z + \lambda^D 106 - \lambda^D 28x - \lambda^D 4xz + \lambda^D 2x^2 + \lambda^D 4z^2,$$

where we derive the first-order conditions as

$$\frac{\partial \mathscr{L}^D}{\partial x} = 1 - 28\lambda^D - 4\lambda^D z + 4\lambda^D x = 0$$

$$\frac{\partial \mathscr{L}^D}{\partial z} = 1 - 4\lambda^D x + 8\lambda^D z = 0$$

$$\frac{\partial \mathscr{L}^D}{\partial \lambda^D} = 106 - 28x - 4xz + 2x^2 + 4z^2 = 0.$$

We can determine the values of x, z, and λ^D that minimize the value of the objective function by solving the first two equations in the set of first-order conditions for λ^D and then dividing one of the resulting equations by the other to eliminate λ^D.

Rearranging the terms in $\partial \mathscr{L}^D/\partial x$ yields

$$1 = 28\,\lambda^D + 4\,\lambda^D z - 4\,\lambda^D x$$
$$1 = \lambda^D\,(28 + 4z - 4x)$$
$$\lambda^D = \frac{1}{28 + 4z - 4x}$$

Similarly, rearranging terms in $\partial \mathscr{L}^D/\partial z$ yields

$$1 = 4\,\lambda^D x - 8\,\lambda^D z$$
$$1 = \lambda^D\,(4x - 8z)$$
$$\lambda^D = \frac{1}{4x - 8z}.$$

Combining the above results for λ^D yields

$$\frac{1}{28 + 4z - 4x} = \frac{1}{4x - 8z},$$

or

$$28 + 4z - 4x = 4x - 8z.$$

Solving for x in terms of z results in the following:

$$-8x = -12z - 28,$$

or

$$x = \frac{12z + 28}{8} = \frac{3z + 7}{2}.$$

Substituting the above equation for x, expressed in terms of z, into the equation for $\partial \mathscr{L}^D/\partial \lambda^D$ yields

$$106 - 28\left(\frac{3z + 7}{2}\right) - 4\left(\frac{3z + 7}{2}\right)z + 2\left(\frac{3z + 7}{2}\right)^2 + 4z^2 = 0,$$

which we can simplify as

$$32.5 - 35z + 2.5z^2 = 0,$$

or

$$13 - 14z + z^2 = 0.$$

We can factor and solve the above quadratic equation for its two roots as

$$(z - 13)(z - 1) = 0.$$

Therefore,

$$z^* = 13 \quad \text{or} \quad z^* = 1.$$

Checking both roots for z indicates that when $z = 1$, then

$$x^* = \frac{3z + 7}{2} = \frac{3(1) + 7}{2} = \frac{10}{2} = 5.$$

Thus,

$$c = x + z = 5 + 1 = 6.$$

If $z = 13$, then

$$x^* = \frac{3z + 7}{2} = \frac{3(13) + 7}{2} = \frac{46}{2} = 23,$$

and

$$c = x + z = 13 + 23 = 36.$$

Clearly, we minimize the value of the objective function, c, at a value of 6 when $x^* = 5$ and $z^* = 1$.

Finally, by using either of the first-order conditions, $\partial \mathcal{L}^D / \partial x$ or $\partial \mathcal{L}^D / \partial z$, we can determine the optimal value of λ^D. Using the first-order condition,

$$\frac{\partial \mathcal{L}^D}{\partial z} = 1 - 4\lambda^D x + 8\lambda^D z = 0,$$

and substituting $x^* = 5$ and $z^* = 1$ into the above equation yields

$$1 - 4\lambda^D (5) + 8\lambda^D (1) = 0$$
$$1 - 20\lambda^D + 8\lambda^D = 0$$
$$1 - 12\lambda^D = 0$$
$$-12\lambda^D = -1$$
$$\lambda^{D^*} = \frac{1}{12}.$$

Recall that in the primal problem $\lambda^* = 12$. The value of λ^{D^*} for this dual problem is equal to the reciprocal of λ^*, or 1/12. We may interpret this value of $\lambda^{D^*} = 1/12$ to indicate that if we decrease the constraint, y, by one unit from $28x + 4xz - 2x^2 - 4x^2 = 106$ to $28x + 4xz - 2x^2 - 4z^2 = 105$, then the optimal value of the objective function, z, will decrease by 1/12 unit, from 6 to 5 11/12 units. Alternatively, should we increase the right-hand side variable of the constraint by one unit from 106 to 107, then the optimal value of z will increase from 6 to 6 1/12 units.

2.4   SUMMARY

This chapter focused on developing the necessary conditions for optimizing multivariate functions. We discussed the concepts of both constrained and unconstrained optimization of these functions, with a particular emphasis on constrained optimization. Specifically, constrained optimization is the process of maximizing or minimizing some objective function subject to the limitations imposed by predetermined factors affecting the values of the decision variables. The most common technique for solving such constrained optimization problems is the method of Lagrangian multipliers.

KEY TERMS

- constrained optimization, page 33
- Lagrangian function, page 34

EXERCISES

2.1 Suppose a function is

$$y = 14x + 2xz - x^2 - 2z^2.$$

Determine the values of the independent variables, x and z, that correspond to a maximum value for the dependent variable, y. What is this maximum value of y?

2.2 Using the same function given in Exercise 2.1, assume there is a constraining relationship between the independent variables represented as

$$x + z = 11.$$

Find the values of x and z that maximize the objective function subject to this constraint. Also, determine the constrained maximum value for y. Compare these results for x, z, and y to those computed in Exercise 2.1.

2.3 Assume a function is

$$y = 2x^{1/4} z^{3/4},$$

and a constraining relationship exists between the independent variables as

$$100x + 10z = 100,000.$$

Find the values of x and z that maximize the value of y using the Lagrangian multiplier method. Also, compute and interpret the value of the Lagrangian multiplier, λ.

2.4 Using the Lagrangian multiplier method, determine the values of x and y that maximize the value of the function

$$f(x,y) = 2xy,$$

subject to the constraining relationship between the independent variables x and y specified as

$$x + 2y = 4.$$

2.5 Using the Lagrangian multiplier method, determine the values of x and y that optimize the following constrained minimization problem:

$$\text{Minimize} \quad z = x + 4y$$
$$\text{subject to} \quad x^{1/2} y^{1/2} = 100.$$

Also determine the minimum value of z.

2.6 Given the function,

$$y = 2x^{1/4} z^{3/4},$$

where the relationship between x and z is

$$100x + 10z = w,$$

assume that the value of w is unknown, but the value of y is specified as $y = 6410$. Find the optimal values for $x, z, w,$ and λ for which the value of w is minimized.

2.7 Explain the relationship between the procedures used in Exercises 2.3 and 2.6. Also compare the values for λ computed in both exercises and determine the relationship between these two values.

2.8 What is implied by the fact that a constraint is binding? If a constraint is not binding, what is the difference between the unconstrained and constrained optimization solutions? Why?

CHAPTER 3

Utility Theory

3.1 INTRODUCTION

Economics is the science of analyzing how relatively scarce resources are allocated across virtually unlimited human wants. In most economies, this allocation process occurs in markets that involve the interaction of buyers and sellers of goods and services. Therefore, when analyzing these markets we must focus on both the supply of and the demand for goods and services. The concept of supply involves how these goods and services are produced. This topic, broadly defined as the theory of the firm, will be our focus in Chapters 8–12. Demand, however, reflects the tastes and preferences of individuals for various goods and services, as well as their ability to obtain such goods and services. This topic is known broadly as the theory of the consumer, and it will be our focus in Chapters 3–7.

Our primary goal in this chapter is to establish a foundation for consumer choice problems by developing a formal framework for representing a consumer's preferences for different combinations of goods. For example, isn't it logical that as an individual consumes less of one good, say clothing, she must have additional amounts of another, such as food, in order to maintain a constant level of satisfaction? Ultimately, by analyzing these problems of consumer choice we can develop various functions and curves relating the quantity demanded of a good to underlying determinants, such as a consumer's income and the prices of goods and services. Keeping these goals in mind, we will cover several specific topics in this chapter, including the development of utility functions and curves, the various assumptions underlying utility analysis, and two approaches for indicating utility. Afterward, we will extend our analysis to develop related concepts such as marginal utility curves, indifference curves, and marginal rates of substitution. These concepts provide much of the basis for solving consumer optimization problems, which will be our focus in Chapters 4 and 5.

3.2 UTILITY AND UTILITY FUNCTIONS

Economists use the term **utility** to refer to the *satisfaction an individual receives from consuming goods and services.* Thus, we can express the level of utility that an individual derives from consuming various combinations of goods and services in terms of a relationship known as a **utility function**, defined as *a function that expresses a consumer's level of utility in terms of the amounts of goods and services she consumes.* Mathematically, we can express a utility function as

$$U = U(X, Y, W, \ldots, Z),$$

where U represents some measure of a consumer's utility and $X, Y, W, \ldots, Z$, represent her consumption levels of various goods and services. For the sake of clarity, we will demonstrate most utility analysis with only two goods, and we will therefore use a more simplified utility function, expressed mathematically as

$$U = U(X, Y).$$

This function, containing three variables, U, X, and Y, is illustrated in Figure 3.1, where the level utility, U, is plotted on the vertical axis and the amounts of the two goods, X and Y, are plotted on the two base axes established at right angles to each other.

This three-dimensional diagram illustrates the relationship between the dependent variable in the utility function, U, and the two independent variables, the consumption levels of the two goods, X and Y. For example, observe in this diagram that if the consumer chooses X_1 amount of good X and Y_1 amount of good Y, then her corresponding level of utility is U_1. If her consumption level of good X increases to X_2, while still consuming Y_1 amount of good Y, then her corresponding level of utility is U_2, where in this case $U_2 > U_1$. In general, we can represent this three-dimensional utility function by the surface illustrated in Figure 3.1, comprising an infinite number of combinations of goods X and Y. Since we have not yet assumed a specific functional form, the surface shown represents only one of many possibilities. For example, not all utility functions possess a unique maximum or peak, as shown by the one illustrated in Figure 3.1.[1] Nevertheless, this particular surface still demonstrates many properties associated with utility functions, and it will be very useful to us in subsequent analysis.

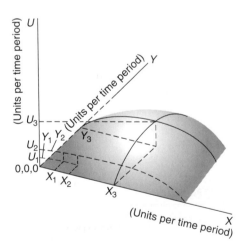

FIGURE 3.1 Three-Dimensional Utility Function with Bliss Point

---

[1]We refer to the unique maximum for this type of utility function, occurring at goods combination (X_3, Y_3), as a bliss point, because any change in the consumption levels of either good from this combination leads to a decrease in the consumer's utility. We should emphasize that for this type of utility function, this implication holds true for increases, as well as decreases, in X and Y from the combination (X_3, Y_3).

Our next step in developing the theory of the consumer is to define the notion of a rational consumer. Specifically, a **rational consumer** *uses all prevailing information available to choose among various goods and services with the explicit goal of maximizing her utility*. Therefore, when faced with two or more alternative sets of goods and services, the rational consumer chooses to consume that particular combination of goods and services which she perceives will yield the highest level of utility.

3.2.1   Assumptions Underlying Consumer Behavior

To ensure that an individual is consuming amounts of goods and services that are perceived to maximize her utility, we must make the following set of assumptions regarding a consumer's preferences.

i) *Completeness.* Given two consumption bundles, or combinations of goods, A and B, one and only one of the following statements must be true.

1. The consumer prefers bundle A to bundle B.
2. The consumer prefers bundle B to bundle A.
3. The consumer likes bundles A and B equally and, therefore, is said to be indifferent between the two bundles.

   The assumption of completeness ensures that the rational consumer is capable of comparing alternative consumption bundles and determining which is preferred, or if she finds them to be equally desirable.

ii) *Transitivity.* Given three bundles, A, B, and C, if bundle A is preferred to bundle B and bundle B is preferred to bundle C, then bundle A must be preferred to bundle C. We will use the assumption of transitivity of consumer preferences in Section 3.5.2 to prove that indifference curves cannot intersect.

iii) *Continuity.* If bundle A is preferred to bundle B, then bundle A will also be preferred to any other bundle that is very similar to bundle B. The assumption of continuity allows us to use continuous mathematical functions, to which calculus techniques can be applied, in modeling consumer behavior.

An additional assumption, that we often use in consumer theory is that of *nonsatiation*, which simply states that an individual prefers consuming more of a good than less of a good. This assumption is reflected in many utility functions such as the one illustrated in Figure 3.2, where we can observe that an individual's utility always rises with increases in her consumption level of either good X or Y. However, note that for utility functions, such as that shown in Figure 3.1, an individual can achieve points of satiation for amounts of either good consumed. In addition, for this type of utility function there exists a point of global satiation, defined as a bliss point, shown as goods combination (X_3, Y_3) in Figure 3.1. Observe in this figure that increases in the individual's consumption of either of the two goods beyond levels X_3 and Y_3 will cause her utility to decline.

Since the concept of consumer satisfaction, or utility, is abstract and varies across individuals, we will refer to both types of utility functions, illustrated in Figures 3.1 and 3.2, in much of our subsequent consumer theory analysis.

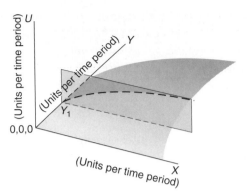

FIGURE 3.2 Three-Dimensional Utility Function Reflecting Nonsatiation

3.2.2 Cardinal and Ordinal Utility

Two distinct approaches to utility analysis have evolved in economic theory. The first of these approaches involves the concept of **cardinal utility**, which is based on the assumption that *a consumer has the ability to accurately evaluate the amount of utility he derives from consuming a particular combination of goods and services, and assign an actual (cardinal) number to it*. In other words, this approach assumes that utility can actually be measured in terms of some unit of satisfaction. Recall from your principles of microeconomics course that this unit is known as the concept of a **util**, defined as *a unit of measure for the amount of satisfaction an individual receives from consuming goods and services*. The second approach to utility analysis involves a less restrictive way of indicating consumer satisfaction, known as **ordinal utility**. Applying this concept, we find that *individuals are only required to rank consumption bundles from best to worst, on the basis of the amount of utility received*, rather than assign specific numerical utility values to particular combinations of goods and services.

We can demonstrate these concepts of cardinal and ordinal utility by assuming a specific form of utility function. As an example, let's suppose that an individual's utility function is expressed mathematically as

$$U = U(X,Y) = X^{1/2} Y^{1/2},$$

where U represents the level of utility that the individual receives from consuming good X, say, soda pop, and good Y, hotdogs. Note that this type of utility function adheres to the assumption of nonsatiation that we illustrated in Figure 3.2. Now that we know the particular utility function, it is easy to compute the level of satisfaction, in utils, that this individual receives from consuming goods X and Y. For example, if the consumer drinks one bottle of soda pop and eats one hotdog, as represented by combination A in Table 3.1, then we can compute his resulting level of cardinal utility as follows:

$$U = U(X,Y) = X^{1/2} Y^{1/2} = (1)^{1/2} (1)^{1/2} = 1 \text{ util.}$$

TABLE 3.1   Utility Values Computed for the Utility Function, $U = U(X,Y) = X^{1/2}Y^{1/2}$

Combinations of Goods X and Y	Units of Good X	Units of Good Y	Cardinal Value of Utility (utils/period of time)	Ordinal Utility Ranking
A	1	1	1	1(worst)
B	2	2	2	2
C	4	9	6	3
D	16	25	20	4(best)

If he chooses to increase his consumption to two units of each good, as represented by combination B, then his level of satisfaction rises in accordance with the assumption of nonsatiation. We compute this new value of cardinal utility as

$$U = U(X,Y) = X^{1/2}\,Y^{1/2} = (2)^{1/2}\,(2)^{1/2} = 2^1 = 2 \text{ utils,}$$

which is higher than that associated with the consumption of just one bottle of soda pop and one hotdog. We can compute alternative levels of cardinal utility for this individual by substituting other values for the variables X and Y into the utility function, $U = U(X,Y) = X^{1/2}\,Y^{1/2}$, as shown in Table 3.1.

The concept of ordinal utility is also illustrated in this table. By examining these utility values, we can also rank the alternative consumption combinations from best to worst, thus employing the economic concept of ordinal utility. Once again, the principle of nonsatiation still applies, as you can observe from the table that the consumer will rate the combination containing 16 units of good X and 25 units of good Y as preferred to any of the other combinations containing smaller quantities of both goods. More generally, the ranking of (X,Y) combinations A through D is D > C > B > A, which we can demonstrate by assigning the respective rankings of 4 > 3 > 2 > 1. Note that in the ordinal case, the magnitudes of the actual numbers are not important because they do not represent specific units of measurement. What is important is the ordering of the numbers as they are assigned to the different combinations of goods. Also, note that this ordinal ranking of 4 > 3 > 2 > 1 is consistent with the rankings associated with the cardinal measurements of utility for bundles D, C, B, and A, which were 20 utils > 6 utils > 2 utils > 1 util, respectively. In the utility analysis which follows, we will apply the cardinal approach because it provides for a rather clear introduction to consumer theory. However, we will base the majority of the consumer theory analysis in the remainder of this chapter, as well as in future chapters, on the less restrictive ordinal approach.

3.3   UTILITY CURVES

In some instances, it is desirable to focus on the relationship between utility and the consumption levels of only one of the goods, say X. However, for many utility functions, such as those illustrated in Figures 3.1 and 3.2, given any value of good X there will be different values for U, depending on the level at which the other good, Y, is held constant. For example, in Figure 3.1, when $X = X_1$, the corresponding value for U is U_1 if $Y = Y_1$, U_2 if $Y = Y_2$, and so forth. Similarly, for any value of good Y, there are different corresponding values for U, depending on the level at which good X is held constant. These relationships reflect the multivariate nature of the utility function expressed earlier. Thus, as discussed in Chapter 2, in order to focus on a functional relationship between two of the variables, we must hold the remaining variable(s) constant at some level(s). For example, we can express the relationship between U and X once we have specified Y at some level such as $\overline{Y}_1$. As a result, we can now express the utility function as

$$U = U(X,\overline{Y}_1),$$

where for each value of X there exists a unique value for U. This relationship is known as a **utility curve** defined as *a curve that expresses a consumer's utility in terms of his consumption level of a good, while holding his consumption levels of all other goods constant.* We have illustrated the graphical derivation of this utility curve for good X in Figure 3.3 by cutting the three-dimensional surface with a vertical plane established at $\overline{Y}_1$. By doing this, we have eliminated the third (Y) axis, enabling us to establish the resulting two-dimensional graph demonstrating the relationship between U and X, as illustrated in Figure 3.4.

If the individual consumes X_1 units of good X, along with the specified $\overline{Y}_1$ amount of good Y, the corresponding utility level is U_1. As the amount of good X he consumes increases to X_2 and then X_3, while he continues to consume $\overline{Y}_1$, his utility increases to U_2 and U_3, respectively. Should the amount of good X he consumes increase beyond X_3 to say X_4, while still holding Y constant at $\overline{Y}_1$, his level of utility will decrease, in this case to U_4. This result reflects the fact that the nonsatiation assumption breaks down at $(X_3,\overline{Y}_1)$ for this particular utility function. For this reason we represent the

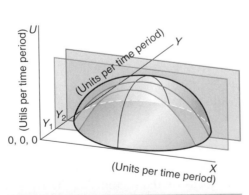

FIGURE 3.3 Derivation of Utility Curves from Three-Dimensional Utility Function with Bliss Point

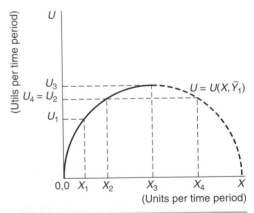

FIGURE 3.4 Utility Curve for Good X Reflecting Satiation

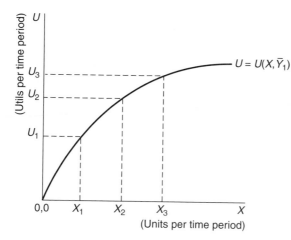

FIGURE 3.5 Utility Curve with Nonsatiation

declining portion of the utility function as a dotted curve in Figure 3.4. Although this range exists in theory, it makes no sense for a rational consumer to increase his consumption of good X beyond X_3, as long as his consumption of good Y is held constant at $\overline{Y}_1$, because such increases in good X result in decreases in the individual's level of utility. Such actions clearly violate the assumption of rational consumer behavior we discussed earlier.

We can also derive a utility curve from the utility function shown in Figure 3.2, for which the nonsatiation assumption always holds true. We derive this utility curve for good X by once again cutting the three-dimensional surface with a vertical plane established at Y_1, the predetermined consumption level of good Y. The resulting two-dimensional utility curve is illustrated in Figure 3.5, which demonstrates a direct relationship between utility and consumption levels of good X over the entire curve. Note that this utility curve is similar to the one shown in Figure 3.4 except that it never achieves a maximum; therefore, utility never declines with increases in consumption levels of good X. An example in which this situation arguably holds true is for income. Isn't it reasonable to believe that for most individuals, increases in their income will never cause their level of utility to decline?

We have established utility curves demonstrating the relationship between utility and good X on the assumption that the individual's consumption of good Y is held constant at $\overline{Y}_1$. What will happen if Y is specified at a different level, such as $\overline{Y}_2$, where $\overline{Y}_2 > \overline{Y}_1$? Returning to Figure 3.3, we will now construct a new vertical plane at $\overline{Y}_2$, cutting a new cross-section of the utility surface. Mathematically, we can express this new univariate function as

$$U' = U(X, \overline{Y}_2),$$

and plot it along with $U = U(X, \overline{Y}_1)$ as shown in Figure 3.6. The new utility curve, $U' = U'(X, \overline{Y}_2)$, lies above the original, $U = U(X, \overline{Y}_1)$, indicating that at any chosen level of good X, the corresponding level of U is higher than that for the original curve.

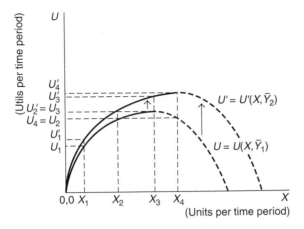

FIGURE 3.6 Utility Curves for Good x with $Y = \overline{Y}_1$ and $Y = \overline{Y}_2$

This result occurs because the individual now has more units of good Y to combine with the amounts of good X that are consumed. For example, at X_1, $U_1' > U_1$, at X_2, $U_2' > U_2$, at X_3, $U_3' > U_3$ and so forth. In economic jargon, this result is known as an upward shift in the utility curve relating U to X, caused by the increase in consumption of good Y from $\overline{Y}_1$ to $\overline{Y}_2$.

In a broader sense, $U' = U(X,\overline{Y}_2)$ simply represents a new cross-section that we have taken further up the utility surface as shown in Figure 3.3. In this particular representation, the utility curve has not only shifted up, but is also skewed further to the right, generating a maximum utility level, U_4', at a higher level of good X, X_4, than for the original utility curve that achieved a maximum at X_3. This result depends on the shape of the underlying utility surface that has been assumed for this demonstration. Note that we could explore many other surfaces that would yield different results. However, this particular utility function, or surface, exhibits many relevant economic properties. As a result, it is quite common in consumer theory. Specifically, the property in question is based on the assumption that the utility a consumer receives from consuming amounts of one good is positively affected by the consumption levels of the other good included in the utility function.

For example, suppose good X represents bottles of soda pop and good Y denotes hotdogs. If the number of hotdogs he consumes is set at $\overline{Y}_1 = 1$ hotdog, then as the individual consumes additional bottles of soda pop, good X, his utility rises up to the point X_3, at which his maximum attainable level of utility associated with consuming good X along with one hotdog is achieved at U_3. If the number of units of good Y he consumes increases to $\overline{Y}_2 = 2$ hotdogs, then the utility curve shifts up, and each level of soda pop consumption, X, yields a higher level of utility than before, when he consumed $\overline{Y}_1 = 1$ hotdog. By now, it should be apparent that we can construct a different utility curve relating U to consumption of good X for each preset level of good Y, generating an entire set of such curves as shown in Figure 3.7.

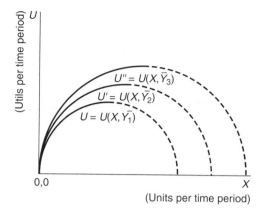

FIGURE 3.7 Set of Utility Curves for Good X

Our analysis has focused on the relationship between utility and good X. Note, however, that we can also establish a set of utility curves relating utility to alternative quantities of good Y in a similar manner by holding consumption of good X at specified levels.

3.3.1   Marginal Utility and the Concept of Diminishing Marginal Utility

When we analyzed the initial utility curve, $U = U(X,\overline{Y}_1)$ illustrated in Figure 3.4, we showed that as X increased from 0 to X_1 to X_2 to X_3, U increased correspondingly from 0 to U_1 to U_2 to U_3. Since the utility curve is continuous, an infinite number of points lie between those selected for discussion. If we examine Figure 3.4 more closely, we can observe that while the successive increments in good X, $(X_1 - 0)$, $(X_2 - X_1)$, and $(X_3 - X_2)$, are of equal size, the corresponding increments in utility, $(U_1 - 0)$, $(U_2 - U_1)$, and $(U_3 - U_2)$ are of different magnitudes. Specifically, $(U_3 - U_2) < (U_2 - U_1) < (U_1 - 0)$, indicating that utility rises at a decreasing rate with respect to increases in the consumption levels of good X, until X_3. After X_3 utility actually begins to decline with any further increases in X. In mathematical terms, we can state that the slope of this utility curve, $\Delta U/\Delta X$, is diminishing up to X_3. If changes in the independent variable, good X, can be reduced to infinitesimally small amounts, and the other independent variable, good Y, is held constant, this slope can be interpreted as the partial derivative, $\partial U/\partial X$. More broadly, this term represents the partial slope associated with each cross-section of the utility function $U = U(X,Y)$, established at different fixed values of Y, or specifically in this case, the slope of the utility curve $U = U(X,\overline{Y}_1)$. Similarly, $\partial U/\partial Y$ represents the slope of the cross-sections of $U = U(X,Y)$, letting good Y vary and holding consumption of good X constant.

We stated in Chapter 1 that slopes and derivatives can often provide a considerable amount of economic information, and they can be interpreted as marginal functions. Within the current context, these slopes and derivatives represent marginal utility functions where the **marginal utility** *of a good is the change in utility resulting from a change in the amount of the good consumed, while holding consumption of all other goods constant.* If the changes in consumption are infinitesimally small, we can express this definition mathematically as

$$MU_{good} = \lim_{\Delta good \to 0} \frac{\Delta U}{\Delta \, good}\bigg|_{\text{other goods held constant}} = \frac{\partial U}{\partial \, good}.$$

Since the utility function under analysis contains only two goods, X and Y, we can compute the marginal utilities associated with each good as

$$MU_X = \lim_{\Delta X \to 0} \frac{\Delta U}{\Delta X}\bigg|_{Y_1} = \frac{\partial U}{\partial X}$$

and

$$MU_Y = \lim_{\Delta Y \to 0} \frac{\Delta U}{\Delta Y}\bigg|_{X_1} = \frac{\partial U}{\partial Y}.$$

As an example, suppose an individual has the utility function,

$$U = X^{1/2} Y^{1/2},$$

where in the present analysis, we assume that utility is measured in utils. This particular utility function exhibits the nonsatiation assumption and is characterized by a curve such as that illustrated in Figure 3.5. We compute the marginal utility functions for goods X and Y for this utility function as

$$MU_X = \frac{\partial U}{\partial X} = \frac{1}{2} X^{-1/2} Y^{1/2} = \frac{1}{2} \left(\frac{Y}{X} \right)^{1/2}$$

and

$$MU_Y = \frac{\partial U}{\partial Y} = \frac{1}{2} X^{1/2} Y^{-1/2} = \frac{1}{2} \left(\frac{X}{Y} \right)^{1/2}.$$

If the consumption levels of X and Y are specified at particular levels, say $X = 4$ units and $Y = 9$ units, then we can evaluate marginal utility for this combination of goods as

$$MU_X = \frac{1}{2} \left(\frac{9}{4} \right)^{1/2} = \frac{1}{2} \left(\frac{3}{2} \right) = \frac{3}{4} \text{ util}$$

and

$$MU_Y = \frac{1}{2} \left(\frac{4}{9} \right)^{1/2} = \frac{1}{2} \left(\frac{2}{3} \right) = \frac{1}{3} \text{ util}.$$

We can interpret the result $MU_X = \frac{3}{4}$ util to indicate that at the chosen combination of goods, $X = 4$ and $Y = 9$, an infinitesimally small increase (decrease) in the amount of good X consumed, while holding consumption of good Y constant at 9 units, results in an increase (decrease) in the consumer's utility of $\frac{3}{4}$ util. Similarly, $MU_Y = \frac{1}{3}$ util indicates that at the chosen combination of goods, an infinitesimally small increase (decrease) in the amount of good Y consumed, while holding consumption of good X constant at 4 units, results in an increase (decrease) in utility of $\frac{1}{3}$ util.

Now let's assume that the individual's consumption of good Y increases to 16 units, while holding his consumption of good X constant at 4 units. The marginal utility values now become

$$MU_X = \frac{1}{2}\left(\frac{16}{4}\right)^{1/2} = \frac{1}{2}\left(\frac{4}{2}\right) = 1 \text{ util}$$

and

$$MU_Y = \frac{1}{2}\left(\frac{4}{16}\right)^{1/2} = \frac{1}{2}\left(\frac{2}{4}\right) = \frac{1}{4} \text{ util.}$$

Note that, for this function, altering the consumption level of good Y affects not only the marginal utility value of good Y, decreasing it from $\frac{1}{3}$ util to $\frac{1}{4}$ util, but also the marginal utility value of good X, increasing it from $\frac{3}{4}$ util to 1util. We can generate similar results by changing the quantity of good X consumed, while holding consumption of good Y constant.

As we stated earlier, these marginal utilities represent the partial slopes associated with a utility function, or the slopes of the cross-sections derived from such a function. We can demonstrate this point graphically by returning to the utility curve $U = U(X, \overline{Y}_1)$ depicted in Figure 3.4 and graphing its associated slope. This relationship is shown in Figure 3.8, where the two curves are linked by their common horizontal axes, since the utility curve, $U = U(X, \overline{Y}_1)$ is a function of X, as is its derivative, or slope, $\partial U / \partial X$.

We can derive the marginal utility curve for good X, shown in panel (B) of this figure, from the utility curve shown in panel (A) by drawing lines tangent to the utility curve at various values for good X and then plotting the slopes of these tangents in the graph in panel (B). The slopes of these tangents are the instantaneous slopes of the utility curve, or $\partial U / \partial X$.

Observe that as the consumption of good X increases from X_1 to X_2 to X_3, the tangents become flatter, indicating a declining slope at each successive value of X. Thus at X_1, the value of the marginal utility of X is $MU_{X,1}$. At X_2, MU_X declines to $MU_{X,2}$, and at X_3, the tangent to the utility curve is horizontal, indicating that its slope, or $MU_{X,3}$, is equal to zero. At this point, where $X = X_3$ and $MU_{X,3} = 0$, the utility curve in panel (A) achieves a maximum. You may recall from Chapter 1 that a function is at a critical value when its derivative is equal to zero. Finally, at any value of X greater than X_3, a tangent to the utility curve is negatively sloped, indicating a negative value for marginal utility. For example, at X_4, $MU_{X,4} < 0$, it therefore, makes no sense for a rational consumer to choose any amount of good X greater than X_3, provided he is also consuming the fixed level of good $Y, \overline{Y}_1$. A negative marginal utility reflects the fact that increases in the consumption of good X will actually reduce a consumer's utility. In this case, an increase in X from X_3 to X_4 reduces utility from U_3 to U_4. Intuitively, this result reflects the old adage that it is possible to get "too much of a good thing."

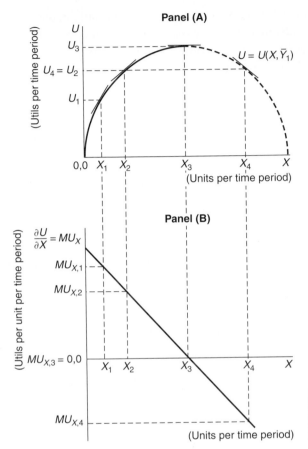

FIGURE 3.8 Derivation of Marginal Utility Function from Utility Curve

The actual shape of the marginal utility curve depends on the underlying utility function. In this case, as with many others, we can observe that the level of MU_X diminishes over the entire consumption range of good X. In a broader sense, there exist utility functions and curves for which the marginal utility from consuming additional units of a good may be constant, or in some cases, may actually increase. However, the property of diminishing marginal utility is so prevalent in consumer theory that it is known as the **law of diminishing marginal utility**. This law states that *as additional units of a good are consumed, while holding the consumption of all other goods constant, the resulting increments in utility will diminish.* We should emphasize that for the relevant range of the consumption of good X, in this case from 0 to X_3, although MU_X is diminishing, total utility is still increasing. Specifically, it is increasing at a decreasing rate.

The intuition underlying this concept is quite basic, as we can illustrate by returning to the example where X represented bottles of soda pop, Y represented hotdogs, and the value of good Y is again held constant at $\overline{Y}_1 = 1$ hotdog. We would expect that for most consumers the increase in utility from consuming the first bottle of soda pop

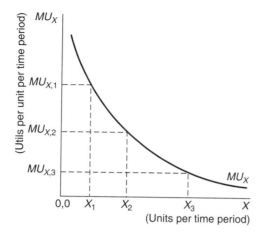

FIGURE 3.9 Marginal Utility Function Reflecting Nonsatiation

would be the greatest. If the individual consumes a second bottle of soda pop, combined with one hotdog, the increase in his utility is likely smaller than for the first bottle. As additional bottles of soda pop are consumed, we expect that the increases in his utility, MU_X, will continue to diminish until he achieves a maximum level of utility, U_3, corresponding to X_3 bottles. He will not rationally wish to consume any additional soda pop beyond, say $X_3 = 3$ bottles, because additional units of good X result in decreases in his utility, or negative marginal utility.

We can also derive a marginal utility function for the utility curve reflecting nonsatiation, shown in Figure 3.5. Recall in this case that utility increases with increases in the amount of good X consumed over the entire range of X. However, observe that these increases in utility become successively smaller with increases in X, reflecting diminishing marginal utility of good X, as illustrated in Figure 3.9. For this case of nonsatiation, the marginal utility curve is similar to the one we derived earlier in Figure 3.8, the difference being that in the nonsatiation case it never achieves a value equal to or less than zero.

We need to establish one final point. Just as an increase in the consumption level of the good that we hold constant causes the utility curve for the variable good to shift up to the right, as in the case illustrated in Figure 3.6, such an increase also causes the marginal utility curve to similarly shift. In our previous example, an increase in good Y from $\overline{Y}_1 = 1$ hotdog to $\overline{Y}_2 = 2$ hotdogs, causes the marginal utility of soda pop, MU_X, to increase. Furthermore, this result holds true for each level of good X selected. This case is illustrated in Figure 3.10 where we can observe that both the utility curve and the marginal utility curve associated with good X shift up and to the right as Y increases from $\overline{Y}_1$ to $\overline{Y}_2$.

Also observe in this figure that $MU_X' = 0$ utils at X_4, corresponding to the higher maximum value for utility, U_4', attained when consumption of good Y increases from $\overline{Y}_1$ to $\overline{Y}_2$. The important point is that for this utility function, as is frequently the case, the marginal utility derived from consuming one good is affected by the consumption levels of the other good.

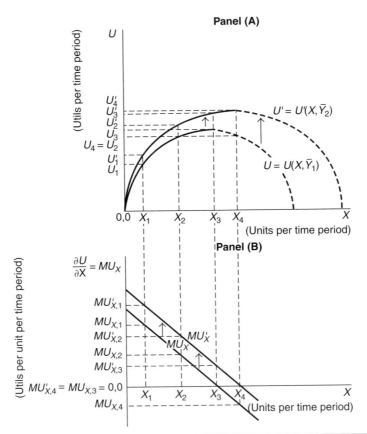

FIGURE 3.10 Utility and Marginal Utility Curves for Good X When $Y = \bar{Y}_1$ and $Y = \bar{Y}_2$

3.4 INDIFFERENCE CURVES

In a cardinal utility analysis, the concepts of marginal utility and diminishing marginal utility play important roles in the process of rational consumer decision making. However, in order to model this process more fully, we must make some modifications to the previous discussion. Rational decision making, from a consumer's perspective, involves choosing the amounts of goods that maximize her level of utility, given certain considerations or limitations. These limitations will be discussed in Chapter 4 and incorporated into our analysis at that time. At this point, our essential modification is to allow both goods in the utility function to vary simultaneously. In this way, we allow the consumer to choose from various combinations of the two goods. However, from the perspective of graphical clarity, it is desirable to hold one of the variables in the utility function, $U = U(X,Y)$, constant. This will enable our analysis to be conducted using two-dimensional graphs. Thus, we will hold utility constant at some specified

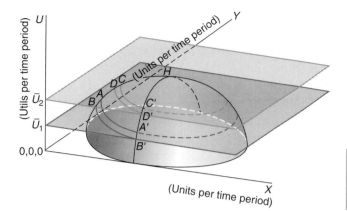

FIGURE 3.11 Derivation of Indifference Curves from Three-Dimensional Utility Function

level, say $\overline{U}_1$, while allowing the consumption levels of goods X and Y to vary. As a result, we can represent the utility function as

$$\overline{U}_1 = U(X,Y).$$

This process is demonstrated in Figure 3.11, where the utility surface has been cut horizontally by a plane constructed at $\overline{U}_1$ on the vertical axis. This plane has cut out an oval, of which the segment AA', between the solid lines of the utility surface, is one part. Since the third dimension, U, has now been fixed at $\overline{U}_1$, we can project the oval containing the segment AA' into the X–Y plane. This projection is represented by the oval containing the segment BB'. With the third dimension eliminated, we can imagine grasping the Y-axis and rotating the X–Y plane upright until it is vertical, producing the two-dimensional graph shown in Figure 3.12.

The resulting oval is actually a contour. However, as we will show in subsequent discussion, the relevant segment for utility analysis is the solid portion, BB'. This contour is known as an **indifference curve**, an example of which is represented by the

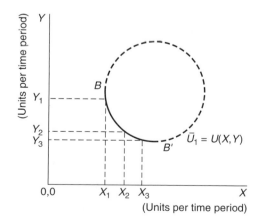

FIGURE 3.12 Indifference Curve Reflecting Satiation

function $\overline{U}_1 = U(X,Y)$, illustrated in Figure 3.12. This curve is defined as a *set of combinations of two goods that yield the same level of utility*. By observing the contour in Figure 3.12, we can see that the consumer is able to derive the same level of utility, $\overline{U}_1$, by choosing goods combinations (X_1,Y_1), (X_2,Y_2), (X_3,Y_3), or more generally, any one of the infinite number of (X,Y) combinations that lie on the indifference curve. The name of this curve is quite appropriate, since logically a consumer would be indifferent as to which (X,Y) combination on the curve she selects because they all yield the same level of utility. If a consumer chooses to move down the segment BB', from combination (X_1,Y_1) to (X_2,Y_2), she is choosing to consume fewer units of good Y, while substituting more units of good X in their place in order to maintain her utility constant at the level $\overline{U}_1$. Of course, the converse is also true if she chooses to move up the segment BB' by selecting more Y and less X.

The indifference curve we have presented in Figure 3.12 pertains to only one level of utility, $\overline{U}_1$. Referring back to Figure 3.11, it is possible to specify U at a different level, such as $\overline{U}_2$, where $\overline{U}_2 > \overline{U}_1$. In this case, we can construct another plane at $\overline{U}_2$ which cuts the utility surface, thus generating another indifference curve, or contour, containing the segment CC'. By projecting this indifference curve into the X–Y plane, we can produce a second indifference curve, containing the segment DD', shown in the two-dimensional graph illustrated in Figure 3.13.

More generally, we can derive an entire map of indifference curves where each pertains to a different fixed level of utility, U, on the vertical axis in Figure 3.11. Referring to the solid portions, BB', DD', and so forth, observe that those indifference curves lying further to the "northeast" in the two-dimensional indifference curve map correspond to increasingly higher levels of utility, since they also refer to higher U values on the vertical axis in the three-dimensional diagram in Figure 3.11. However, for this particular utility function, these results hold true only up to the bliss point, designated point H in Figure 3.13. This point corresponds to the global maximum for the utility function, also designated point H in Figure 3.11.

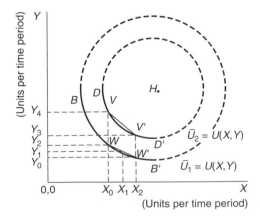

FIGURE 3.13 Indifference Curve Mapping

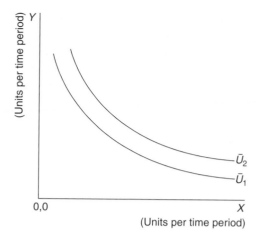

FIGURE 3.14 Indifference Curves Reflecting Nonsatiation

Similarly, indifference curves can be derived for the utility function exhibiting nonsatiation shown in Figure 3.2. By cutting the utility surface horizontally with planes established at different constant levels of utility, we can construct a map of corresponding indifference curves such as those illustrated in Figure 3.14. In this situation, observe that the indifference curves are not ovals, but instead possess negative slopes throughout the X–Y plane.

3.4.1   Marginal Rate of Substitution

Once we understand the concept of an indifference curve and an indifference curve map, we can focus on the movement along any one indifference curve. Recall that all (X,Y) goods combinations lying on a particular indifference curve yield the same level of utility. As a result, any movement along such a curve generally reflects some degree of tradeoff or substitutability between the goods, while holding utility constant. This tradeoff is measured by the slope of the indifference curve, specifically in this case, dY/dX. We can compute the formula for this derivative, dY/dX, from the utility function, $U = U(X,Y)$, by taking the total derivative of U with respect to X and setting it equal to zero. A total derivative is appropriate in this situation, because both X and Y are treated as variable, and the result, dU/dX, is set equal to zero, because utility, U, is held constant along an indifference curve. As a result, given the utility function,

$$U = U(X,Y),$$

the total derivative is

$$\frac{dU}{dX} = \frac{\partial U(X,Y)}{\partial X}\frac{dX}{dX} + \frac{\partial U(X,Y)}{\partial Y}\frac{dY}{dX} = 0,$$

and since $dX/dX = 1$ and $U = U(X,Y)$, then

$$\frac{\partial U}{\partial X} + \frac{\partial U}{\partial Y}\frac{dY}{dX} = 0.$$

Solving for the slope of the indifference curve yields

$$\frac{dY}{dX} = \frac{-\frac{\partial U}{\partial X}}{\frac{\partial U}{\partial Y}}.$$

We can see that the term on the right-hand side of this equation is the ratio of the marginal utility functions for goods X and Y, respectively. Therefore, we can express this equation as

$$\frac{dY}{dX} = \frac{-MU_X}{MU_Y},$$

or

$$-\frac{dY}{dX} = \frac{MU_X}{MU_Y}.$$

The economic interpretation associated with the negative of this slope of an indifference curve is referred to as the **marginal rate of substitution**, or **MRS**, which is defined as *the rate at which a consumer is willing to substitute one good for the other within her utility function, while receiving the same level of utility*. More specifically, should consumption of one good decrease (increase) by some amount, the *MRS* represents the amount by which the other good must increase (decrease) in order to hold utility constant. Note that this rationale pertains to only the solid portions of an indifference curve, such as BB' and DD' shown in Figure 3.13. However, for the indifference curves illustrated in Figure 3.14 the above reasoning applies to the entire curves. In either case, for any movement along an indifference curve, one of the changes, dX or dY, will be negative since one good is being substituted for the other in order to hold utility constant. As a result, the derivative dY/dX is negative. For this reason, according to convention we define the *MRS* as the negative of the slope of an indifference curve. Thus, for the relevant range of an indifference curve, the *MRS* is forced to be a positive number, which is mathematically defined as

$$-\frac{dY}{dX} = MRS = \frac{MU_X}{MU_Y}.$$

In an effort to clarify the notions of an indifference curve and its associated marginal rate of substitution, we will apply these concepts to the particular utility function presented in Section 3.2.2. Recall that the specific utility function we analyzed previously was $U = X^{1/2} Y^{1/2}$, and the marginal utility functions were computed as

$$MU_X = \frac{\partial U}{\partial X} = \frac{1}{2}X^{-1/2}Y^{1/2} = \frac{1}{2}\left(\frac{Y}{X}\right)^{1/2}$$

and

$$MU_Y = \frac{\partial U}{\partial Y} = \frac{1}{2}X^{1/2}Y^{-1/2} = \frac{1}{2}\left(\frac{X}{Y}\right)^{1/2}.$$

Recall that we derived an indifference curve from a utility function by holding utility constant at some level such as $\overline{U}_1$. Thus, the indifference curve in this case is simply

$$\overline{U}_1 = X^{1/2}Y^{1/2},$$

or since Y is measured on the vertical axis, we can express it as

$$Y^{1/2} = \frac{\overline{U}_1}{X^{1/2}}$$

$$\left(Y^{1/2}\right)^2 = \left(\frac{\overline{U}_1}{X^{1/2}}\right)^2$$

or

$$Y = \frac{\overline{U}_1^2}{X}.$$

As an example, we can let $\overline{U}_1 = 6$ utils; then the indifference curve is

$$Y = \frac{6^2}{X} = \frac{36}{X}.$$

Should the consumer choose $X = 4$ units, then she must select $Y = 36/4 = 9$ units, in order to maintain $\overline{U}_1 = 6$ utils. If we specify U at a different level, say $\overline{U}_2 = 8$ utils, then the relevant indifference curve is

$$Y = \frac{8^2}{X} = \frac{64}{X}.$$

We can generate an entire map of indifference curves, one for each specified level of U, and the MRS can be computed for each combination of goods that lie on any such curve. Returning to the specific indifference curve,

$$Y = \frac{36}{X} = 36X^{-1},$$

we can compute the marginal rate of substitution by first determining the derivative of this equation with respect to X as

$$\frac{dY}{dX} = -36X^{-2}.$$

Therefore,

$$MRS = -\frac{dY}{dX} = 36X^{-2} = \frac{36}{X^2},$$

and if $X = 4$ units, then

$$MRS = \frac{36}{4^2} = \frac{36}{16} = 2.25.$$

A common method for computing the *MRS* is to use the formula derived earlier which expresses it as the ratio of marginal utilities. Thus,

$$MRS = \frac{MU_X}{MU_Y} = \frac{\frac{1}{2}\left(\frac{Y}{X}\right)^{1/2}}{\frac{1}{2}\left(\frac{X}{Y}\right)^{1/2}} = \frac{Y}{X},$$

and if the (X,Y) combination is $X = 4$ and $Y = 9$, then

$$MRS = \frac{Y}{X} = \frac{9}{4} = 2.25.$$

This method yields the same result that we obtained earlier by computing the *MRS* directly as the negative of the slope of the indifference curve, $-dY/dX$. How can we interpret this result? When the individual is consuming 4 units of good X and 9 units of good Y, she is willing to substitute 1 unit of good X for 2.25 units of good Y in order to maintain a constant utility level of $\bar{U}_1 = 6$ utils.[2] Alternatively, the consumer is willing to substitute 2.25 units of good Y for 1 unit of good X while maintaining utility constant at 6 utils.

3.4.2 Monotonic Transformations and Ordinal Utility

Our preceding discussion of marginal utility and the marginal rate of substitution was conducted using cardinal utility analysis, where we assumed that utility can be measured in terms of a unit known as the util. Most economists, however, believe that the concept of cardinal utility is unnecessarily unrealistic and that its application to the analysis of consumer behavior is overly restrictive. This latter contention is based on the fact that it is possible to generate similar results regarding consumer behavior with the application of ordinal utility analysis, which is based on the less restrictive assumption that consumer preferences need only be ranked rather than actually measured. Thus, in the case of ordinal utility analysis, any numbers representing values of utility simply represent indices that indicate the ordered ranking that a consumer places on various combinations of goods. The actual magnitudes assigned to the utility indices associated with consuming various combinations of goods and services, as well as the magnitudes of the differences between these indices, are of no particular relevance. For example, a consumer may prefer a combination of goods, say, four tacos and two drinks, over a combination that includes two tacos and one drink. However, it is impossible to actually measure the amount by which one combination is preferred over the other.

Using ordinal utility analysis, we can demonstrate that identical consumer preferences can be represented by different utility functions. To do so, however, it is neces-

---

[2]Since we are using a derivative, dY/dX, in this analysis, there is a 2.25-unit reduction in good Y to have an infinitesimally small increase in good X. However, for expository purposes, it is convenient for us to refer to one-unit changes in the independent variable.

sary that these utility functions constitute positive monotonic transformations of each other. *A function such as V(U) is a* **positive monotonic transformation** *of another function U provided V(U₁) > V(U₀) whenever U₁ > U₀.* In other words, the transformed function, $V(U)$, preserves the ordering associated with the original function, U. The relevance of a positive monotonic transformation in consumer theory relates to the fact that an individual's consumption choice between two goods depends on the rate at which he is willing to substitute one good for the other at various combinations of the two goods. This concept is the consumer's marginal rate of substitution, or *MRS*, which we discussed previously. For particular combinations of goods, the *MRS* will be identical for different utility functions that are monotonic transformations of each other.

For the utility function, $U = U(X,Y)$, recall that for any indifference curve associated with this utility function, the marginal rate of substitution between the two goods X and Y is

$$\frac{-dY}{dX} = MRS = \frac{MU_X}{MU_Y}.$$

Now assume that another utility function, V, is a monotonic transformation of the utility function $U = U(X,Y)$ or

$$V = V(U) = V[U(X,Y)],$$

where both U and V represent some utility indices. We can compute the formula for the slope, and hence *MRS*, for an indifference curve for a particular fixed value of V as

$$\frac{dV}{dX} = \frac{dV(U)}{dX} = \frac{dV}{dU}\left(\frac{\partial U(X,Y)}{\partial X}\frac{dX}{dX} + \frac{\partial U(X,Y)}{\partial Y}\frac{dY}{dX}\right) = 0.$$

After dividing by dV/dU and since $dX/dX = 1$. this equation becomes

$$\frac{\partial U(X,Y)}{\partial X} + \frac{\partial U(X,Y)}{\partial Y}\frac{dY}{dX} = 0.$$

Solving for dY/dX, yields the following:

$$\frac{dY}{dX} = \frac{\dfrac{-\partial U(X,Y)}{\partial X}}{\dfrac{\partial U(X,Y)}{\partial Y}} = \frac{\dfrac{-\partial U}{\partial X}}{\dfrac{\partial U}{\partial Y}} = \frac{-MU_X}{MU_Y}.$$

Finally, since $MRS = MU_X/MU_Y$, then

$$\frac{-dY}{dX} = MRS = \frac{MU_X}{MU_Y},$$

which is the same result that we computed for the utility function $U = U(X,Y)$ in Section 3.4.1.

As an example, assume two specific utility functions are represented as $U = X^{1/2}Y^{1/2}$ and $V = U^2 = (X^{1/2}Y^{1/2})^2$. Earlier we demonstrated that the MRS associated with any indifference curve pertaining to the utility function $U = X^{1/2} Y^{1/2}$ is derived as

$$-\frac{dY}{dX} = MRS = \frac{MU_X}{MU_Y} = \frac{Y}{X},$$

and thus for particular values of X and Y, say $X = 4$ units and $Y = 9$ units, the value of the MRS is computed as

$$MRS = \frac{9}{4} = 2.25.$$

For the utility function $V = (X^{1/2}Y^{1/2})^2$, we derive the MRS by using the product rule, along with other rules for differentiation as

$$\frac{dV}{dX} = \frac{d(X^{1/2}Y^{1/2})^2}{dX} = 2\left[\frac{1}{2}X^{1/2}Y^{-1/2}\frac{dY}{dX} + \frac{1}{2}X^{-1/2}Y^{1/2}\frac{dX}{dX}\right] = 0$$

$$= X^{1/2}Y^{-1/2}\frac{dY}{dX} + X^{-1/2}Y^{1/2} = 0$$

$$\frac{dY}{dX} = \frac{-X^{-1/2}Y^{1/2}}{X^{1/2}Y^{-1/2}} = -\frac{Y}{X},$$

and therefore,

$$-\frac{dY}{dX} = MRS = \frac{Y}{X}.$$

For the particular goods combination $X = 4$ units and $Y = 9$ units we used earlier, the MRS of the monotonic transformation $V = (X^{1/2}Y^{1/2})^2$ is computed as

$$MRS = \frac{Y}{X} = \frac{9}{4} = 2.25,$$

which is the same value we computed for the utility function, $U = X^{1/2} Y^{1/2}$.

The important point of this discussion is that when we analyze a consumer's decision-making process it is the rate at which the consumer is willing to substitute one good for the other, or MRS, that plays the key role in determining the amounts of goods that an individual chooses to consume. In Chapter 4, we will include some constraining factors in this process of consumer choice and demonstrate how we can compute particular values of these goods. However, at this point it is only important to note that we can represent a consumer's preferences regarding one good as opposed to another by a family of utility functions and associated indifference curves. We define these utility functions as positive monotonic transformations of each other. Conceptually, these functions maintain the order of the computed utility indices, U, and the relative magnitudes of the exponents pertaining to the levels of the goods comprising the utility functions. For example, $U = X^{1/2} Y^{1/2}, U = XY, U = X^2Y^2, U = AX^{1/2}Y^{1/2}$, and $U = A + X^{1/2} Y^{1/2}$ are all positive monotonic transformations of each other, where for the latter two functions the term A represents some positive constant value. In each case the MRS is identical, and although the particular values of U vary across these functions for common (X,Y) combinations the ordering will be the same. As a result, the particular magnitudes of the various U values are irrelevant.

Note that not all functions are monotonic transformations of each other. For example, $U = X^{1/2} Y^{1/2}$ and $U = X^{1/4} Y^{3/4}$ are not such transformations, for the intensity of the consumer's preference of one good over the other differs across the two utility functions. This fact is reflected by the different relative magnitudes of the X and Y exponents in the two functions. As another example, $U = X^{1/2} Y^{1/2}$ and $U = - X^{1/2} Y^{1/2}$ do not constitute positive monotonic transformations of each other, as the directionality of the computed U values associated with the two functions differ for common (X,Y) combinations. In summary, we can conduct the theory of consumer choice within the context of an ordinal utility analysis, for which a consumer's preference for one good over another can be represented by a family of utility functions, each constituting a monotonic transformation of another. Also note that the important concept underlying consumer choice for this type of analysis is the marginal rate of substitution of one good for another rather than the concepts of individual marginal utilities per se.

We can use utility functions, along with their related indifference curves and marginal rates of substitution, to demonstrate the intensity of a consumer's preferences for one good relative to another. Any such underlying preference is embedded in the consumer's utility function. As a result, it plays an important role in determining the shape of the indifference curves derived from such a utility function. As an example, suppose goods X and Y are defined as a consumer's leisure time and income, respectively, where income represents the other goods that the consumer may enjoy due to not choosing leisure—namely, goods she can obtain indirectly by working. The consumer is confronted with a rational tradeoff between the two goods, where this tradeoff is reflected by the shape of the indifference curves shown in Figure 3.15.

In panels (A) and (B) of this figure, we have illustrated indifference curves for two consumers, each possessing a different attitude toward income and leisure time. In panel (A), the indifference curves tend to have steeper slopes, indicating a preference bias toward leisure over income. Observe that this consumer is willing to sacrifice a large amount of income, $Y_2 - Y_1$, in order to increase her leisure time by a very small amount, $X_2 - X_1$. Intuitively, these indifference curves describe an individual who has a more relaxed and less materialistic attitude. In panel (B), note that the indifference curves tend to be flatter than in the preceding case, representing an individual with a preference bias toward income over leisure time. In this situation, the consumer needs to receive a larger increase in leisure time, $X_3 - X_1$ in order to sacrifice the same amount of income, $Y_2 - Y_1$. The indifference curves for this individual describe someone who is more ambitious and materialistic. This example is part of the income–leisure model that we will develop in detail in Chapter 21. At this point, it simply serves to demonstrate how we can illustrate different consumer preferences and biases using indifference curve analysis.

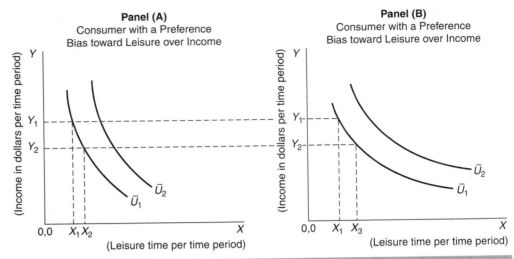

FIGURE 3.15 Indifference Curve Maps Revealing Different Preferences toward Goods

3.5 CHARACTERISTICS OF INDIFFERENCE CURVES

Before we can incorporate indifference curves into more complex analysis of consumer behavior, it is necessary to discuss some characteristics associated with these curves. Many of these characteristics follow, in part, from the assumptions underlying consumer behavior that we outlined in Section 3.2.1. These characteristics are that indifference curves have maps that are everywhere dense, cannot intersect, generally possess negative slopes, and are generally strictly convex.

3.5.1 Indifference Curve Maps Are Everywhere Dense

This characteristic, which follows from the continuity and completeness assumptions, indicates that all combinations of goods lie on some indifference curve plotted in X–Y space. Thus, for any two combinations of goods, a consumer either prefers one combination to the other or is indifferent between the two combinations. In the first instance, one combination lies on a higher indifference curve than the other, and in the second case the two combinations must lie on the same indifference curve.

3.5.2 Indifference Curves Cannot Intersect

The second characteristic associated with indifference curves is that they cannot intersect. The rationale for this characteristic is that intersecting indifference curves violate either the assumption of transitivity or the assumption of nonsatiation stated in Section 3.2.1. These two assumptions provide part of the basis for utility analysis; therefore, we must expect them to hold true simultaneously. We can establish the logic of nonintersecting indifference curves by showing the inconsistency of consumer preferences associated with intersecting curves. Referring to Figure 3.16, combinations A

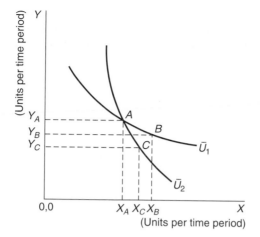

FIGURE 3.16 Illogic of Intersecting Indifference Curves

and B lie on a common indifference curve, $\overline{U}_1$, as a result, the consumer should be indifferent between them.

Similarly, combinations A and C lie on another common indifference curve, $\overline{U}_2$, and thus the consumer should be indifferent between these two combinations. Because of the assumption of transitivity stated in Section 3.2.1, since the consumer is indifferent between combinations A and B, and combinations A and C, he should also be indifferent between combinations B and C. However, by observing Figure 3.16, it is clear that combination B contains greater amounts of both goods X and Y than does combination C, specifically $X_B > X_C$ and $Y_B > Y_C$. By the assumption of nonsatiation, combination B should be preferred to C; however, this assumption will be violated if transitivity is maintained. Conversely, if the assumption of nonsatiation is maintained, then the transitivity assumption will be violated. Clearly, they both cannot hold true simultaneously, and as a result, we must reject the possibility of intersecting indifference curves.

3.5.3 Indifference Curves Generally Possess Negative Slopes

The third characteristic of indifference curves is that, generally, they have negative slopes. This characteristic is reflected in the solid portions BB' and DD' of the contours presented in Figure 3.13, or in the entire indifference curve mapping illustrated in Figure 3.14. Typically, a negative slope reflects some degree of substitutability between the two goods within the consumer's utility function. If consumption of one good decreases, then some amount of the other good must be substituted in its place in order to keep the consumer's utility constant. As we discussed earlier, this slope is $dY/dX = -MU_X/MU_Y$, and therefore it is negative provided both marginal utilities are positive.

There are some exceptions to this characteristic of negatively sloped indifference curves. The first is for those situations in which one of the marginal utilities possesses a negative value. This occurs with utility functions such as that shown in Figure 3.1, for the range where the nonsatiation assumption breaks down. Although this outcome exists in theory, we can show that it generally does not fall into the realm of rational consumer behavior. As a result, we can use the phenomenon of negative marginal utility to separate the portions of indifference curves that are generally relevant to consumer theory from those portions that are not applicable. Observe from the formula for the slope of an indifference curve that if one of the marginal utilities acquires a negative value, the slope, dY/dX, becomes positive. Thus either

$$\frac{dY}{dX} = -\left(\frac{-MU_X}{MU_Y}\right) > 0$$

or

$$\frac{dY}{dX} = -\left(\frac{MU_X}{-MU_Y}\right) > 0.$$

Alternatively stated, since $MRS = -dY/dX$, then in either of the above cases, $MRS < 0$.

Intuitively, this result indicates that if the amount of the good possessing a negative marginal utility increases, then the amount of the other good, possessing a positive marginal utility, will also have to increase in order to hold utility constant. In this case, the consumer is not substituting one good for the other but instead is compensating himself in order to keep utility constant. In simpler language, a good possessing a negative marginal utility is detrimental to the consumer, and we sometimes aptly refer to it as a "bad" rather than a good. If the consumer receives more of the "bad," then he must simultaneously consume more of the "good" in order to maintain a constant level of utility. The question that arises, however, is: why would a rational consumer voluntarily choose to consume more units of a detrimental good or "bad"? In most instances, a rational consumer will not make this choice. Therefore, we can rule out as irrational behavior a consumer selecting more units of a good possessing a negative marginal utility and thus operating on a positively sloped portion of an indifference curve. We will continue this discussion in greater detail in the appendix to this chapter, which focuses on some exceptions to negatively sloped indifference curves.

3.5.4 Indifference Curves Are Generally Strictly Convex

The final characteristic related to indifference curves is that they are generally strictly convex toward the origin as shown in Figure 3.13. A function is strictly convex if a line segment drawn between two points on the function lies strictly above the function, exclusive of the two endpoints. The indifference curves depicted in Figure 3.13 are strictly convex since the line segment WW' connecting the goods combinations (X_0,Y_2) and (X_2,Y_0) on the $\overline{U}_1$ indifference curve, and the line segment VV' between the goods combinations (X_0,Y_4) and (X_2,Y_3) on the $\overline{U}_2$ indifference curve, both lie strictly above the respective indifference curves, exclusive of their endpoints. Also note that any combination of goods that lies on a line segment joining two combinations of goods on a strictly convex indifference curve, exclusive of its endpoints, represents a goods combination that yields a higher level of utility than any combination on the indifference curve. Referring once again to Figure 3.13, we find that the goods combination (X_1, Y_1) that lies on the WW' line segment would be on a higher indifference curve and therefore yield a higher level of utility than either (X_0, Y_2) or (X_2, Y_0), the endpoints of this line segment on the $\overline{U}_1$ indifference curve. The intuition for these results is as follows. Any goods combination lying on a line segment joining two points on an indifference curve represents some type of averaged combination of the two goods combinations constituting the endpoints of the line segment. Therefore, given strictly convex indifference curves, a rational consumer will prefer a more balanced combination of goods relative to combinations containing extreme amounts of the same goods.

For example, consider an individual whose utility function is expressed as $U = X^{1/2}Y^{1/2}$. If this individual consumes the goods combination $X_1 = 4$ units and $Y_1 = 9$ units, then

$$U = (4)^{1/2}(9)^{1/2} = 6.$$

Alternatively, if she consumes the goods combination $X_2 = 9$ units and $Y_2 = 4$ units, once again,

$$U = (9)^{1/2}(4)^{1/2} = 6,$$

thereby indicating that both of these goods combinations lie on the $U = 6$ indifference curve. However, an averaged goods combination, which we determine by taking the average value of X and the average value of Y, yields an even higher level of utility. In this case the average value of good X, denoted X_M, is

$$X_M = \frac{4+9}{2} = \frac{13}{2} = 6.5 \text{ units},$$

while the average value of good Y, Y_M, is

$$X_M = \frac{9+4}{2} = 6.5 \text{ units}$$

Substituting the values $X_M = 6.5$ units and $Y_M = 6.5$ units into the individual's utility function indicates that the associated level of utility, U_M, is

$$U_M = (6.5)^{1/2}(6.5)^{1/2} = 6.5.$$

This amount is clearly greater than the level of utility attained when the individual consumes either of the less balanced combinations, (X_1, Y_1) or (X_2, Y_2).

The distinctive shape of convex indifference curves also reflects the fact that, as a consumer moves down to the right along an indifference curve, choosing to consume fewer units of good Y and more units of good X, the slope of the indifference curve, dY/dX, becomes less negative. This result indicates that as her consumption of good X increases by constant increments, the amounts by which her consumption of good Y must decrease, in order to maintain the same level of utility, become successively smaller. Alternatively, we can state that the negative of the slope of the indifference curve, which measures the marginal rate of substitution of good X for good Y, diminishes as X increases and Y decreases. Recall that $MRS = MU_X/MU_Y$; thus, a diminishing

MRS reflects the fact that the ratio of marginal utilities must be declining as more units of good *X* are substituted for good *Y*. It is tempting for us to state that this result reflects the law of diminishing marginal utility stated earlier. However, technically speaking, the law of diminishing marginal utility is neither necessary nor sufficient for this result to occur. For example, assume a utility function of the form, $U = X^2 Y^2$, for which the marginal utilities of good *X* and good *Y*, respectively, are

$$MU_X = 2XY^2,$$

and

$$MU_Y = 2X^2Y.$$

Provided the consumption levels of the two goods are both positive, then increases in the consumption levels of goods *X* and *Y* cause the respective marginal utilities to rise, demonstrating increasing, rather than diminishing, marginal utilities. Note that this implication also operates in reverse in that decreases in either *X* or *Y* cause the respective marginal utilities to decrease. Generally, we can state that these marginal utility functions reflect a direct, rather than an inverse, relationship between the amount of a good consumed and its marginal utility. For example, if $X = 1$ unit and $Y = 2$ units, then

$$U = (1)^2 (2)^2 = 4$$
$$MU_X = 2(1)(2)^2 = 8$$
$$MU_Y = 2(1)^2 (2) = 4,$$

and therefore,

$$MRS = \frac{MU_X}{MU_Y} = \frac{8}{4} = 2.$$

If we increased the amount of good *X* consumed to $X = 2$ units, while holding consumption of good *Y* constant at $Y = 2$ units, then the marginal utility of good *X* would increase from 8 to 16, computed as

$$MU_X = 2(2)(2)^2 = 16.$$

This result clearly defies the law of diminishing marginal utility. However, is it still possible to have a diminishing marginal rate of substitution in this case? The answer is yes, and we can demonstrate this result by moving along one indifference curve, thus holding the consumer's utility constant. Suppose the consumption level of good *X* increases to $X = 2$ and *Y* decreases to $Y = 1$ unit, so that we can hold utility constant at $U = 4$, computed as

$$U = (2)^2(1)^2 = 4.$$

The values of the marginal utilities are now

$$MU_X = 2(2)(1)^2 = 4$$
$$MU_Y = 2(2)^2(1) = 8,$$

and thus the marginal rate of substitution is computed as

$$MRS = \frac{MU_X}{MU_Y} = \frac{4}{8} = \frac{1}{2}.$$

In summary, with this example we have demonstrated that it is possible to achieve a diminishing MRS as good X is substituted for good Y, even though the two marginal utilities are increasing, rather than diminishing, given increases in the consumption levels of the respective goods.

We can also analyze the characteristic of convexity and a diminishing MRS with respect to the more common case of diminishing marginal utilities for both goods. This implication is associated with the general utility functions we have been using throughout most of this chapter. However, even in these cases, it is necessary to reemphasize the earlier assumption that increases in the consumption level of one good enhances the marginal utility associated with the other, *ceteris paribus*. Once we understand these assumptions, then moving down to the right along an indifference curve, reflecting the consumption of less Y and more X, the marginal utility of good X decreases, reflecting both the law of diminishing marginal utility and the fact that the consumption of less Y reduces the marginal utility of good X. Simultaneously, the marginal utility of good Y increases because of the law of diminishing marginal utility operating in reverse and also the fact that consuming more of good X enhances the marginal utility of good Y. The phrase, "the law of diminishing marginal utility operating in reverse," simply means that consuming less of a good, while holding the other constant, makes it more scarce and therefore increases its marginal utility. Since $MRS = MU_X/MU_Y$, a falling MU_X combined with an increasing MU_Y causes the MRS to diminish.

We can demonstrate this result by reanalyzing the utility function $U = X^{1/2} Y^{1/2}$ presented earlier. Recall that we generated a specific indifference curve in Section 3.4.1 by setting $U = 6$, derived as

$$Y = \frac{U^2}{X} = \frac{6^2}{X} = \frac{36}{X}.$$

Further, the marginal utility functions were

$$MU_X = \frac{1}{2}\left(\frac{Y}{X}\right)^{1/2}$$

and

$$MU_Y = \frac{1}{2}\left(\frac{X}{Y}\right)^{1/2}.$$

Finally,

$$MRS = \frac{MU_X}{MU_Y} = \frac{\frac{1}{2}\left(\frac{Y}{X}\right)^{1/2}}{\frac{1}{2}\left(\frac{X}{Y}\right)^{1/2}} = \frac{Y}{X}.$$

If $X = 4$ units and $Y = 9$ units, then

$$MRS = \frac{Y}{X} = \frac{9}{4} = 2.25.$$

Moving down to the right along this indifference curve for $U = 6$, we see that a decrease in Y to $Y = 4$ units indicates that X must be increased to

$$X = \frac{36}{Y} = \frac{36}{4} = 9 \text{ units}$$

in order to hold utility constant at $U = 6$. At this new combination, the MRS is

$$MRS = \frac{MU_X}{MU_Y} = \frac{Y}{X} = \frac{4}{9} = 0.44.$$

Clearly, the MRS of X for Y has diminished due to consuming fewer units of good Y and more units of good X. Intuitively, this result indicates that the rate at which an individual is willing to substitute one good for another is dependent on how many units of each good he is currently consuming.

This characteristic of strict convexity of a consumer's preferences does have some exceptions. One particularly noteworthy exception occurs when a consumer perceives two goods as perfect substitutes. For example, some individuals may perceive coffee and tea as perfectly substitutable beverages. In this case, the two goods can be used interchangeably; therefore, the consumption of one good does not affect the marginal utility of the other. Similarly, consuming more units of one good while holding the consumption level of the other constant, will not cause the marginal utility of that good to diminish. These results follow from the fact that the use of one good neither enhances nor detracts from the level of satisfaction generated by the other good. Thus, movement along an indifference curve does not cause the marginal utilities to change. Since the MRS is defined as the ratio of the two marginal utilities, it remains a con-

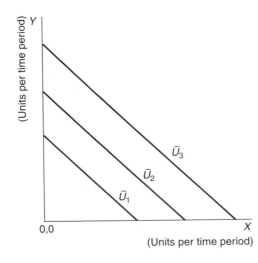

FIGURE 3.17 Indifference Curve Map for Perfect Substitutes

stant value for all combinations of goods on such an indifference curve. This result also implies that the slope of the indifference curve in this case will also be constant since $dY/dX = -MRS$, and thus an associated indifference curve will be linear rather than strictly convex.[3] A set of indifference curves for this case of perfect substitutes is shown in Figure 3.17.

3.6   SUMMARY

In this chapter we identified the goal of the rational consumer along with the critical assumptions underlying consumer preferences. We subsequently used this information to develop utility functions and indifference curves, as well as to analyze the related topics of marginal utility, diminishing marginal utility, and the marginal rate of substitution. The key topics we discussed in this chapter are as follows.

- A utility function expresses the level of satisfaction received by an individual in terms of the amounts of goods and services she consumes.
- In developing consumer theory, we assume that a rational consumer's preferences abide by the axioms of completeness, transitivity, continuity, and, in some cases, nonsatiation.
- Cardinal utility assumes that the consumer has the ability to accurately measure the level of utility he derives from consuming a particular combination of goods. By contrast, ordinal utility is a less restrictive means of indicating consumer satisfaction since an individual is only required to rank his consumption bundles.
- The marginal utility of a good measures the change in utility resulting from an infinitesimally small change in the consumption level of that good, holding consumption levels of other goods constant.
- The law of diminishing marginal utility states that as additional units of a good are consumed, while holding the consumption of all other goods constant, the resulting increments to utility will diminish.
- An indifference curve is a set of combinations of two goods which yield the same level of utility.
- The negative of the slope of an indifference curve measures the marginal rate of substitution (MRS), defined as the rate at which a consumer is willing to substitute units of one good for another while maintaining the same level of utility.
- Indifference curves possess the following characteristics: they are everywhere dense, nonintersecting, typically negatively sloped, and usually strictly convex toward the origin.
- An exception to the general characteristic that indifference curves are negatively sloped occurs when one of the two goods is an economic "bad."
- An exception to the strict convexity characteristic of indifference curves occurs when the two goods are perfect substitutes.

---

[3]Technically speaking, these indifference curves are still convex but not strictly convex.

KEY TERMS

- cardinal utility, page 48
- indifference curve, page 59
- law of diminishing marginal utility, page 56
- marginal rate of substitution, page 62

- marginal utility, page 54
- ordinal utility, page 48
- positive monotonic transformation, page 65
- rational consumer, page 47

- ridge lines for an indifference curve mapping, page, 79
- util, page 48
- utility, page 45
- utility curve, page 50
- utility function, page 45

EXERCISES

3.1 Economists assume that consumer preference relations follow three important properties. Discuss these properties and the economic significance of each.

3.2 Distinguish between the economic concepts of diminishing marginal utility and diminishing marginal rate of substitution.

3.3 Donna consumes goods X and Y according to the following utility function,

$$U(X,Y) = 2X + 4XY + Y.$$

Compute Donna's marginal rate of substitution of good X for good Y for two points on the indifference curve where $U = 10$. Does her *MRS* diminish?

3.4 Assume a consumer's utility function is

$$U = f(X, Y) = 10X^{.5}Y^{.5},$$

where X and Y represent the quantities of two goods the individual consumes. Plot the individual's indifference curve when his utility is held constant at $U = 40$. [*Hint*: In this case, it may be easier to plot the indifference curve for U^2.]

3.5 Refer to the utility function given in the previous exercise. Determine whether the marginal utility of good X diminishes as the consumer purchases additional units of the good, *ceteris paribus*. Similarly, determine if the marginal utility of good Y diminishes as additional units of this good are consumed, *ceteris paribus*.

3.6 Again, refer to the utility function given in Exercise 3.4.
   a. Assume the individual is consuming 1 unit of good X and 9 units of good Y. What is the value of the marginal utility of good X? What is the value of the marginal utility of good Y? What is the value of the utility index for this individual at this consumption combination?
   b. Determine the rate at which good X can be substituted for good Y when the individual is consuming 16 units of good X and 64 units of good Y.

3.7 Ziggy consumes three goods, $X, Y,$ and Z. His utility function is specified as

$$U(X,Y,Z) = 6X + 3Y - 0.5Z.$$

Assume that Ziggy's mother makes him always consume 20 units of good Z.
   a. Plot Ziggy's indifference curve when his utility level is held constant at 50.
   b. Determine Ziggy's marginal rate of substitution of good X for good Y and

provide an interpretation of this value.

   c. Does his marginal rate of substitution diminish?

3.8 Refer to the utility function given in Exercise 3.7.

   a. How many units of good X must Ziggy consume when he is consuming 8 units of good Y and 20 units of good Z in order to receive a utility level of 20?

   b. Briefly describe the type of goods X, Y, and Z must logically represent to Ziggy given his utility function.

Appendix

3A.1 INDIFFERENCE CURVES WITH POSITIVE SLOPES

Although we typically assume that indifference curves possess negative slopes, some exceptions to this assumption prevail in traditional microeconomic theory. For example, consider the indifference curve map shown in Figure 3A.1.

In this figure, observe that combination (X_2,Y_2) lies on the indifference curve, or contour, for the fixed utility level $\overline{U}_3$. If consumption of good Y decreases to Y_1 and consumption of good X increases to X_3, utility remains constant at $\overline{U}_3$ since the adjustment is along the same indifference curve. This movement is within the negatively sloped range of the curve and the $MRS > 0$, indicating substitutability between the goods. At combination (X_3,Y_1), note that a line drawn tangent to the indifference curve is horizontal indicating a slope, dY/dX, of zero. Since $dY/dX = -(MU_X/MU_Y)$, we can deduce that for dY/dX to be zero, the numerator in the formula, MU_X, must be equal to zero. This is also the same result shown in Figure 3.8, where at X_3, for the utility curve $U = U(X,\overline{Y}_1)$, $MU_X = 0$ and $U = \overline{U}_3$. Also, observe in this figure that increasing X from X_3 to X_4 yields a

negative value for MU_X. This same result is shown in Figure 3A.1 where an increase in the amount of good X consumed, from X_3 to X_4, necessitates an increase in the consumption of good Y, from Y_1 to Y_2, in order to maintain utility at $\overline{U}_3$. The indifference curve for this range of X is positively sloped, reflecting the fact that good X has become detrimental, or $MU_X < 0$. Another way for us to view this result is that if consumption of good X increases from X_3 to X_4 and good Y is held constant at $\overline{Y}_1$, then the consumer will receive a lower level of utility, $\overline{U}_2$, represented by the outer contour in Figure 3A.1. Referring back to Figure 3.8, we can again observe this reduction in utility to U_2 as X increases from X_3 to X_4 and good Y is held constant at $\overline{Y}_1$.

We can present a similar discussion if consumption of good Y increases until MU_Y becomes negative. At combination (X_1,Y_3), a line drawn tangent to the indifference curve representing $\overline{U}_3$ is vertical, indicating an undefined value for the slope, dY/dX. Since $dY/dX = -MRS = -(MU_X/MU_Y)$, we can deduce that for this result to occur, $MU_Y = 0$. If consumption of good Y increases to Y_4, then utility level $\overline{U}_3$ can only be maintained by increasing consumption of good X. In this case, good Y has become detrimental, or $MU_Y < 0$, and the indifference curve again acquires a positive slope. As we stated earlier, these portions of an indifference curve for which $MU_X < 0$ or $MU_Y < 0$ correspond to combinations of goods that a rational individual will not choose to consume. However, our preceding analysis is useful in determining the boundaries within which the relevant range of an indifference curve is located. For the indifference curve representing $\overline{U}_3$, these boundaries are located at combinations (X_3,Y_1) and (X_1,Y_3). Similarly, the boundaries

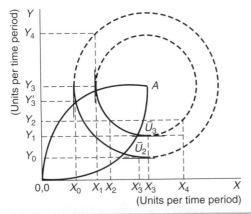

FIGURE 3A.1 Economically Relevant Ranges of Indifference Curve Mapping for Case of Satiation

78

defining the relevant range of the indifference curve representing $\overline{U}_2$ occur at combinations (X_3',Y_0) and (X_0,Y_3'). We can apply this line of reasoning to the entire set of indifference curves generated from this type of utility function, thus establishing a set of boundaries known as **ridge lines for an indifference curve mapping**. We define these lines as *sets of combinations of goods, such as X and Y, corresponding to the conditions where $MU_X = 0$ or $MU_Y = 0$. Since the $MRS = MU_X/MU_Y$, we can also express the ridge line corresponding to the combinations of goods X and Y for which $MU_X = 0$ as those combinations of goods for which the *MRS*, or negative of the slope of each indifference curve, is equal to zero. For the type of utility function we have used throughout much of this chapter, the ridge line we defined above is illustrated in Figure 3A.1 as the lower of the two curves designated *OA*. Similarly, we can express the ridge line associated with the combination of goods X and Y for which $MU_Y = 0$ as those combinations of goods X and Y for which the *MRS*, or the negative of the slope of each indifference curve, is undefined. This ridge line is illustrated in Figure 3A.1 as the upper of the two curves OA. Together these ridge lines define the relevant range of the indifference curve

map for which the marginal utilities of both goods X and Y are both nonnegative.

We have shown that for the utility function underlying the majority of the analysis in this chapter, the positively sloped portions of an indifference curve can be ruled out as containing combinations of goods that will not be selected by a rational consumer. However, there are some situations for which this result can still be useful. For example, suppose two goods are defined as attributes that are related to each other, where one of the attributes is considered desirable and the other is undesirable. As an example, let good X represent the return from an investment and good Y be the associated risk. In this case X represents a "good" with $MU_X > 0$, and Y represents a "bad" with $MU_Y < 0$. In this type of example it is generally the case that in order to obtain more of the desirable good, X, the rate of return, the consumer must be willing to accept more of the undesirable "bad," Y, the associated risk. Alternatively stated, if the consumer is willing to accept more risk, Y, then he must receive a higher rate of return, X, in order to maintain a constant level of utility. In this case, the indifference curve has a positive slope, and the *MRS* will be negative. This application is very useful in the field of finance, when analyzing investment portfolio theory.

3A.2   RIGHT-ANGLE INDIFFERENCE CURVES

Another exception to the characteristic of negatively sloped indifference curves is the case for which two goods represent perfect complements. In general, we consider two goods as complements if they are used in conjunction with each other. Specifically, the consumption of one good enhances the utility derived from consuming the other. Traditional examples of complementary goods are such combinations as bread and butter, peanut butter and jelly, or beer and pretzels. Two goods that represent perfect complements take this relationship to the

extreme in that the goods must be consumed together according to some fixed proportion in order for the consumer to derive any given level of utility. Technically, we can represent this relationship by a fixed coefficient utility function of the form

$$U = \text{minimum}\left(\frac{X}{a},\frac{Y}{b}\right).$$

The terms a and b are the positive fixed coefficients that define the proportion in which the two goods, X and Y, must be consumed in order to generate levels of utility, U. The term *minimum* preceding the right-hand side of the function indicates that the level of utility received by the consumer is restricted to the smaller of the two ratios, X/a or Y/b, included in the utility function.

As an example, assume the two goods are X = autos and Y = tires, and utility is generated by consuming the service of functional automobiles. The two goods represent perfect complements in that they must be consumed together in a ratio of 4 tires to 1 automobile for any utility to be generated. In this case, the fixed coefficient utility function is,

$$U = \text{minimum}\left(\frac{X}{1},\frac{Y}{4}\right),$$

where $a = 1$ and $b = 4$. If $X = 1$ auto and $Y = 4$ tires, then

$$U_1 = \text{minimum}\left(\frac{1}{1},\frac{4}{4}\right) = 1,$$

where U_1 represents an index of the level of utility attained from consuming the services from one functional auto. This combination of X and Y is shown in Figure 3A.2 as occurring at the corner of the indifference curve for utility level $\overline{U}_1$. If the value of X increases to $X = 2$ autos, while the individual still consumes $Y = 4$ tires, his level of utility would remain at U_1 because the second auto is useless when only 4 tires are still being consumed. Mathematically, we demonstrate this result as

$$U_1 = \text{minimum}\left(\frac{2}{1},\frac{4}{4}\right) = 1,$$

where the value of U_1 is still 1 because the ratio 4/4, is the constraining factor. This result also holds true if the consumption of good X increases to $X = 3$, $X = 4$, etc., autos while holding Y constant at $Y = 4$ tires. Using this process, we can produce the horizontal portion of the indifference curve for the utility level U_1. Similarly, if Y increases to $Y = 5$, $Y = 6$, etc., tires, while holding X constant at $X = 1$ auto, the level of utility again remains constant at U_1. For example, if $Y = 5$ and $X = 1$, the utility function is,

$$U_1 = \text{minimum}\left(\frac{1}{1},\frac{5}{4}\right) = 1,$$

where the term 1/1 becomes the constraining factor. For the value of utility to increase to $U_2 = 2$, the consumption of X and Y would have to increase to $X = 2$ autos and $Y = 8$ tires, in accordance with the tire/auto ratio of 4/1 prescribed by the utility function. Thus,

$$U_2 = \text{minimum}\left(\frac{2}{1},\frac{8}{4}\right) = 2,$$

where the optimal combination lies on the higher indifference curve representing $\overline{U}_2 = 2$ level of utility. In summary, if two goods are perfect complements, the associated indifference curves assume the shape of right angles such as those shown in Figure 3A.2. Note that the relevant points on these curves are the corners, while the remaining horizontal and vertical portions correspond to combinations containing extraneous amounts of the goods X and Y, respectively.

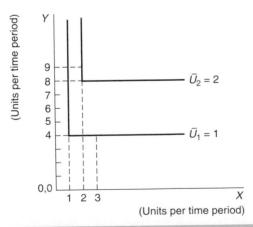

FIGURE 3A.2 Indifference Curves for Perfect Complements

CHAPTER 4

Consumer Optimization

4.1 INTRODUCTION

The concepts of utility, marginal utility, indifference curves, and marginal rates of substitution, which we developed in the previous chapter, establish an analytical framework for examining consumer preferences. Recall that we defined a rational consumer as an individual who seeks to consume goods and services in amounts that correspond to a maximum level for his utility. However, we need to reconcile this goal of utility maximization with some constraining economic factors to which all consumers, to various degrees, are subjected. Since an individual's utility is dependent on the amounts of goods he consumes, isn't it logical that any factors that restrict, or constrain, the amounts of these goods he can obtain will also constrain the amount of utility he receives? Of course, the answer to this question is yes, where the relevant constraining factors are essentially of two types. First, the goods and services desired by a consumer are relatively scarce, and as a result, he must pay prices for them. Second, since most microeconomic analysis is static, meaning it is conducted at a single point in time, the amount of money income the consumer can use to purchase the goods and services he consumes is fixed at some finite value. Formally, we can now express this concept of consumer choice as a constrained optimization problem. Our goal is to determine the solution values for decision variables representing the consumption levels of goods and services that correspond to an optimum value for some objective variable, such as utility or expenditure, subject to some constraining factors.

There are different approaches to the problem of constrained optimization for the consumer. However, our primary focus in this chapter will be on constrained utility maximization, where, in this case, the goal of the rational consumer is to maximize her utility subject to predetermined prices of the goods and her money income. For example, consider a teenager who earns $100 per week from her part-time job. She goes to a mall each week to shop for two of her favorite things: CDs, which cost $12.50 each, and videos, each of which costs $20. In this case, the goal of the teenager is to select the number of CDs and videos that will maximize her utility, yet not have her expenditures on these two goods exceed her weekly income of $100. In order to solve such a problem, we will show how these predetermined factors can be used to develop a budget equation, which in many cases of consumer optimization acts as a constraint that limits the consumer's choices. Once we have established the budget equation, the remainder of this chapter is devoted to solving the consumer's constrained optimization problems, both graphically and mathematically. The solutions to these problems provide the optimal levels of goods that an individual chooses to consume. More broadly, they provide the foundation for the development of individual demand functions, which we will analyze in the next chapter.

4.2 BUDGET EQUATION

Our discussion of consumer choice in Chapter 3 made no mention of any factors that could limit an individual's consumption choices. Realistically, however, a number of such limitations act to constrain a consumer's choices. What are some of these limiting factors? Even in a simple model of consumer choice, we would expect that the amounts of goods consumed, and the subsequent utility received, by an individual will be constrained by the prices she must pay for the goods and by the money income she has available for purchasing these goods.

Initially, we will assume that the individual can choose to purchase and consume a number of goods denoted $X, Y, \ldots, Z$, where each good is assumed to have a positive price. Also, we will assume that the consumer has no control over these prices because they are determined through the interaction of all buyers and sellers of each good in the market. As a result, the individual treats the prices of goods $X, Y, \ldots, Z$, denoted $\overline{P}_{X,1}, \overline{P}_{Y,1}, \ldots, \overline{P}_{Z,1}$, respectively, as predetermined. In addition, we will also assume that the consumer possesses a finite amount of money income, denoted $\overline{I}_1$, that she can spend to acquire these goods. Using this price and income information, we can now formulate the consumer's budget equation. Intuitively, you can think of this equation as an expression that equates the consumer's expenditure on various goods and services to her money income. More formally, the **budget equation** is *the set of combinations of goods and services an individual is able to purchase, given a predetermined level of money income and predetermined levels of prices of the goods, where her expenditure on these goods exactly equals her income.* Mathematically, we can express the budget equation as

$$\underbrace{\overline{P}_{X,1}X + \overline{P}_{Y,1}Y + \ldots + \overline{P}_{Z,1}Z}_{\text{Expenditure on goods and services}} = \underset{\text{Income,}}{\overline{I}_1}$$

where the terms $\overline{P}_{X,1}X, \overline{P}_{Y,1}Y, \ldots, \overline{P}_{Z,1}Z$, represent the consumer's expenditures on goods $X, Y, \ldots, Z$, respectively.

As in the previous chapter, we will assume for the sake of clarity that the consumer chooses between just two goods, X and Y; therefore, her simplified budget equation becomes

$$\overline{P}_{X,1}X + \overline{P}_{Y,1}Y = \overline{I}_1. \tag{4.1}$$

By inspecting equation (4.1), it is evident that this budget equation is linear, where the two variables, X and Y, represent the quantities of the two goods that can be purchased, given predetermined values of $\overline{P}_{X,1}, \overline{P}_{Y,1}$, and $\overline{I}_1$. We can plot the budget equation, like the indifference curves introduced in Chapter 3, in goods space where the quantity of good X is measured on the horizontal axis and the quantity of good Y is plotted on the vertical axis. Since the budget constraint is linear, this is easily accomplished by solving for the X- and Y-intercepts and plotting these results as illustrated in Figure 4.1.

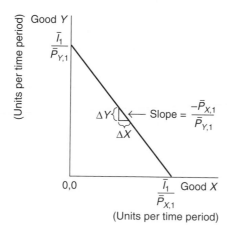

FIGURE 4.1 Consumer's Budget Equation, $\bar{P}_{X,1}X + \bar{P}_{Y,1}Y = \bar{I}_1$

Solving equation (4.1) for Y yields

$$\bar{P}_{X,1}X + \bar{P}_{Y,1}Y = \bar{I}_1$$

$$\bar{P}_{Y,1}Y = \bar{I}_1 - \bar{P}_{X,1}X$$

$$Y = \frac{\bar{I}_1}{\bar{P}_{Y,1}} - \frac{\bar{P}_{X,1}}{\bar{P}_{Y,1}}X.$$

(4.2)

We can determine the value of the Y-intercept by substituting $X = 0$ into equation (4.2) yielding, $Y = \bar{I}_1/\bar{P}_{Y,1}$, or the predetermined value of the individual's income divided by the unit price of good Y. Intuitively, the value of this vertical intercept measures the maximum number of units of good Y that the consumer could purchase if she spent her entire income on good Y. Similarly, we can compute the value of the X-intercept by setting the value of Y equal to zero in either equation (4.1) or equation (4.2) and solving for the subsequent value of X as $X = \bar{I}_1/\bar{P}_{X,1}$. This value measures the maximum number of units of good X the consumer can purchase if she devoted her entire income solely to purchasing this good.

For example, if a consumer has $100 of income to spend on either good X or good Y, and if the price of good X is $10 per unit while the price of good Y is $20 per unit, then if the individual chooses only to purchase good Y, she could obtain a maximum amount of good Y of

$$\frac{\bar{I}_1}{\bar{P}_{Y,1}} = \frac{\$100}{\$20} = 5 \text{ units.}$$

Alternatively, if she wishes to consume only good X, then the maximum amount of good X she could purchase is

$$\frac{\bar{I}_1}{\bar{P}_{Y,1}} = \frac{\$100}{\$10} = 10 \text{ units.}$$

Note that the consumer could also choose to purchase positive amounts of both goods, say, four units of good X and three units of good Y, while exactly exhausting her income.

The budget constraint also embodies the concept of opportunity cost since if an individual purchases additional units of one good, she must reduce her purchases of the other in order to remain within her budget. We can represent the opportunity cost of one good in terms of the other by the slope of the budget equation, $\Delta Y/\Delta X$. This slope value can be read directly from equation (4.2) as the coefficient, $-P_{X,1}/P_{Y,1}$, associated with the variable X. Alternatively, we can compute this value by taking the derivative of Y with respect to X as

$$\frac{dY}{dX} = \frac{d\left(\dfrac{\bar{I}_1}{\bar{P}_{Y,1}}\right)}{dX} - \frac{d\left(\dfrac{\bar{P}_{X,1}}{\bar{P}_{Y,1}}\right)}{dX} = \frac{-\bar{P}_{X,1}}{\bar{P}_{Y,1}}.$$

Since this slope is equal to the negative of the ratio of the unit price of good X to the unit price of good Y, it measures the rate in the market at which goods X and Y can be substituted for one another. For example, if the unit prices of goods X and Y are \$10 and \$20, respectively, then the slope of the budget equation is

$$\frac{dY}{dX} = \frac{-\bar{P}_{X,1}}{\bar{P}_{Y,1}} = \frac{-\$10}{\$20} = -\frac{1}{2}.$$

This value indicates that in the marketplace, where goods are exchanged on the basis of their relative prices, the consumer could exchange 1 unit of good Y for 2 units of good X, or alternatively, 1 unit of good X for 1/2 unit of good Y.

In the preceding analysis, we assumed that an individual receives utility from consuming goods and services, not from merely holding income, and thus she spends all of this income on the two goods, X and Y. However, if this assumption is relaxed, it is possible to construct a **budget set**, defined as *the set of combinations of goods that are affordable to a consumer, given predetermined levels of the prices of the goods and income*. Using the same terms from the earlier analysis, we can express the budget set as

$$\bar{P}_{X,1}X + \bar{P}_{Y,1}Y \leq \bar{I}_1.$$

This set includes all combinations of goods X and Y which satisfy this inequality, including those that satisfy the budget constraint, $\bar{P}_{X,1}X + \bar{P}_{Y,1}Y = \bar{I}_1$. Referring once again to Figure 4.1, we see that a consumer's budget set is represented by the triangular area which is bounded by, and inclusive of, the budget constraint and the X and Y axes. However, we must emphasize that in the analysis of consumer behavior developed in this chapter, we assume that the consumer's goal is to maximize the utility she receives from consuming goods and services. As a result, the consumer will not choose a combination that does not fully exhaust her available income; thus, all combinations of goods selected will always lie on the budget constraint, $\bar{P}_{X,1}X + \bar{P}_{Y,1}Y = \bar{I}_1$.

4.2.1 Effects of Changes in Income on the Budget Equation

What happens to the budget equation if the consumer's income changes, say increases, *ceteris paribus*? Intuitively, it should be clear that if the consumer's income increases while the prices of all goods and services remain unchanged, she could acquire additional units of these goods. Graphically, such a situation is shown in Figure 4.2 for an increase in income from $\bar{I}_1$, to $\bar{I}_2$.

Observe that the budget equation shifts to the right in a parallel manner, where the original is represented as $\bar{P}_{X,1}X + \bar{P}_{Y,1}Y = \bar{I}_1$ and the new budget equation as $\bar{P}_{X,1}X + \bar{P}_{Y,1}Y = \bar{I}_2$. This is a parallel shift because the slope of the budget equation, $-\bar{P}_{X,1}/\bar{P}_{Y,1}$, does not change since the price of each good has remained constant. However, as income rises from $\bar{I}_1$ to $\bar{I}_2$ the values of the X- and Y-intercepts increase, yielding the higher X- and Y-intercept values of $\bar{I}_2/\bar{P}_{X,1}$ and $\bar{I}_2/\bar{P}_{Y,1}$, respectively. For example, assume the prices of goods X and Y are, respectively, $\bar{P}_{X,1} = \$10$ and $\bar{P}_{Y,1} = \$20$, and the consumer's initial level of income is $\bar{I}_1 = \$100$. Thus, we represent the consumer's budget constraint as

$$10X + 20Y = 100.$$

We compute the slope of this budget constraint as

$$\frac{-\bar{P}_{X,1}}{\bar{P}_{Y,1}} = \frac{-\$10}{\$20} = -\frac{1}{2},$$

the value of the Y-intercept as

$$\frac{\bar{I}_1}{\bar{P}_{Y,1}} = \frac{\$100}{\$20} = 5,$$

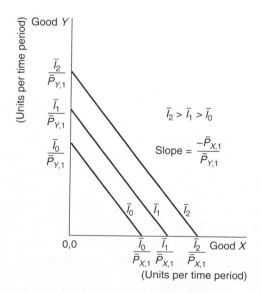

FIGURE 4.2 Effect of a Change in Income, *Ceteris Paribus*, on the Budget Equation

and the value of the X-intercept as

$$\frac{\bar{I}_1}{\bar{P}_{X,1}} = \frac{\$100}{\$10} = 10.$$

If the consumer's income rises from $\bar{I}_1 = \$100$ to $\bar{I}_2 = \$200$, *ceteris paribus*, then the consumer's new budget equation is

$$10X + 20Y = 200.$$

The slope of this new budget equation remains unchanged since neither P_X nor P_Y has changed. However, the value of each of the intercepts is altered. The new Y-intercept value is

$$\frac{\bar{I}_2}{\bar{P}_{Y,1}} = \frac{\$200}{\$20} = 10$$

and the new X-intercept is

$$\frac{\bar{I}_2}{\bar{P}_{X,1}} = \frac{\$200}{\$10} = 20.$$

Therefore, this increase in income, *ceteris paribus*, results in a rightward parallel shift in the budget equation.

Conversely, if the consumer's income falls, holding $\bar{P}_{X,1}$ and $\bar{P}_{Y,1}$ constant, she must purchase fewer units of goods X and Y. A reduction in consumer income from $\bar{I}_1$ to $\bar{I}_0$, *ceteris paribus*, has no impact on the slope of the budget equation since $dY/dX = -\bar{P}_{X,1}/\bar{P}_{Y,1}$. However, the values of the X- and Y-intercepts are both reduced to $\bar{I}_0/\bar{P}_{X,1}$ and $\bar{I}_0/\bar{P}_{Y,1}$, respectively, for the new budget equation $\bar{P}_{X,1}X + \bar{P}_{Y,1}Y = \bar{I}_0$. We have illustrated this scenario in Figure 4.2 demonstrating the parallel leftward shift of the budget equation.

4.2.2   Effects of a Change in the Price of a Good on the Budget Equation

The position of the budget equation in goods space is also affected by the prices of goods X and Y. Therefore, a change in the price of either good, *ceteris paribus*, affects this position. As an example, assume that the price of good X rises from $\bar{P}_{X,1}$ to $\bar{P}_{X,2}$, while holding the price of good Y and income constant at $\bar{P}_{Y,1}$ and $\bar{I}_1$, respectively. The new budget equation is $\bar{P}_{X,2}X + \bar{P}_{Y,1}Y = \bar{I}_1$. Since the slope of the budget equation is equal to the negative of the ratio of the price of good X to the price of good Y or, $dY/dX = -\bar{P}_{X,2}/\bar{P}_{Y,1}$, a change in the price of one of the goods, *ceteris paribus*, causes the slope of the budget equation to change. In this case, where we assume that the price of good X increases to $\bar{P}_{X,2}$, the slope of the budget equation increases, in absolute value terms, to $\bar{P}_{X,2}/\bar{P}_{Y,1}$, and thus the new budget equation appears steeper relative to the original as illustrated in Figure 4.3.

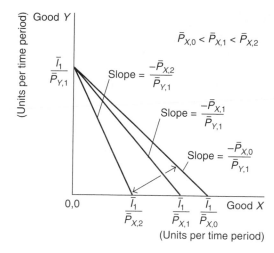

$\bar{P}_{X,0} < \bar{P}_{X,1} < \bar{P}_{X,2}$

Slope = $\dfrac{-\bar{P}_{X,2}}{\bar{P}_{Y,1}}$

Slope = $\dfrac{-\bar{P}_{X,1}}{\bar{P}_{Y,1}}$

Slope = $\dfrac{-\bar{P}_{X,0}}{\bar{P}_{Y,1}}$

FIGURE 4.3 Effects of Changes in Price of Good X, *Ceteris Paribus*, on the Budget Equation

The value of the X-intercept, which was previously $\bar{I}_1/\bar{P}_{X,1}$, is also affected by an increase in the price of good X to $\bar{P}_{X,2}$. Specifically, the value of the X-intercept now decreases to $\bar{I}_1/\bar{P}_{X,2}$ and thus moves leftward closer to the origin, indicating that for any positive level of good Y, the consumer has to purchase fewer units of good X than before the price increase. Note that the Y-intercept of the budget equation, $\bar{I}_1/\bar{P}_{Y,1}$, remains unaltered since neither of the two components defining this intercept changes. Recall that this Y-intercept represents the maximum amount of good Y the consumer is able to purchase if she chooses to spend all of her money income on good Y. As a result, a change in P_X has no impact on the value of this term. Therefore, the new budget equation resulting from the increase in the price of good X has the same vertical intercept as the original budget equation, where we have shown it to be pivoting clockwise upon this common point in Figure 4.3.

We can further demonstrate the effect of a change in the price of one good, *ceteris paribus*, with the following numerical example. Assume once again, that initially the price of good X is $\bar{P}_{X,1} = \$10$, the price of good Y is $\bar{P}_{Y,1} = \$20$ and the consumer's level of income is $\bar{I}_1 = \$100$. Therefore, the budget equation is

$$10X + 20Y = 100.$$

We compute the value of the slope of the budget equation as

$$\frac{-\bar{P}_{X,1}}{\bar{P}_{Y,1}} = \frac{-\$10}{\$20} = -\frac{1}{2}.$$

The value of the Y-intercept is

$$\frac{\bar{I}_1}{\bar{P}_{Y,1}} = \frac{\$100}{\$20} = 5,$$

while the value of the X-intercept is

$$\frac{\overline{I}_1}{\overline{P}_{X,1}} = \frac{\$100}{\$10} = 10.$$

Now if we assume that the price of good X increases from $\overline{P}_{X,1} = \$10$ to $\overline{P}_{X,1} = \$20$, *ceteris paribus*, the new budget equation is

$$20X + 20Y = 100.$$

The slope of this budget equation changes since the price of one of these goods has changed, where the new slope is

$$\frac{-\overline{P}_{X,2}}{\overline{P}_{Y,1}} = \frac{-\$20}{\$20} = -1,$$

which is larger, in absolute value terms, than the initial slope of -1/2. The increase in the price of good X also decreases the value of the X-intercept to

$$\frac{\overline{I}_1}{\overline{P}_{X,2}} = \frac{\$100}{\$20} = 5.$$

However, the value of the Y-intercept, $\overline{I}_1/\overline{P}_{Y,1} = \$100/\$20 = 5$, remains unaltered since neither of the two components that define this intercept has changed.

Alternatively, if the price of good X falls, *ceteris paribus*, from its original level, $\overline{P}_{X,1}$, to a new level, say $\overline{P}_{X,0}$, then the slope of this budget equation is $-\overline{P}_{X,0}/\overline{P}_{Y,1}$, which is smaller, in absolute value terms, than the initial slope, $-\overline{P}_{X,1}/\overline{P}_{Y,1}$. Therefore, as illustrated in Figure 4.3, this new budget equation, $\overline{P}_{X,0}X + \overline{P}_{Y,1}Y = \overline{I}_1$, appears flatter than the original. Once again, only the value of the X-intercept of the budget equation changes, increasing from $\overline{I}_1/\overline{P}_{X,1}$ to $\overline{I}_1/\overline{P}_{X,0}$, while the value of the Y-intercept remains unchanged at $\overline{I}_1/\overline{P}_{Y,1}$. In Figure 4.3, we have illustrated this decrease in the price of good X as causing a counterclockwise pivot of the budget equation on its Y-intercept.

We can also analyze a change in the price of good Y, *ceteris paribus*, in a similar manner. For example, if the price of good Y rises from $\overline{P}_{Y,1}$ to $\overline{P}_{Y,2}$, the slope of the budget equation decreases in absolute value terms to $\overline{P}_{X,1}/\overline{P}_{Y,2}$ and the new budget equation is flatter than the original, as shown in Figure 4.4.

In addition, the value of the Y-intercept of this equation decreases from its original value, $\overline{I}_1/\overline{P}_{Y,1}$, to the lower value, $\overline{I}_1/\overline{P}_{Y,2}$. However, the value of the X-intercept remains as $\overline{I}_1/\overline{P}_{X,1}$, since neither income nor the price of good X has been altered. In Figure 4.4, we have illustrated the effect of this increase in the price of good Y, *ceteris paribus*, on the budget equation, where this equation is shown as pivoting counterclockwise on its X-intercept.

Conversely, if the price of good Y decreases from $\overline{P}_{Y,1}$ to $\overline{P}_{Y,0}$, *ceteris paribus*, the slope of the budget equation increases, in absolute value terms, from $\overline{P}_{X,1}/\overline{P}_{Y,1}$ to $\overline{P}_{X,1}/\overline{P}_{Y,0}$ and thus the new budget equation appears steeper than the original, as shown in Figure 4.4. In this scenario, the value of the Y-intercept of the budget equa-

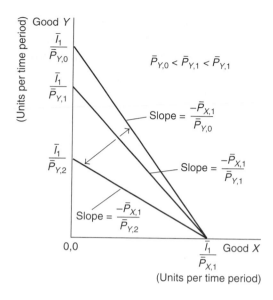

$$\bar{P}_{Y,0} < \bar{P}_{Y,1} < \bar{P}_{Y,1}$$

$$\text{Slope} = \frac{-\bar{P}_{X,1}}{\bar{P}_{Y,0}}$$

$$\text{Slope} = \frac{-\bar{P}_{X,1}}{\bar{P}_{Y,1}}$$

$$\text{Slope} = \frac{-\bar{P}_{X,1}}{\bar{P}_{Y,2}}$$

FIGURE 4.4 Effects of Changes in Price of Good Y, *Ceteris Paribus*, on the Budget Equation

tion increases from $\bar{I}_1/\bar{P}_{Y,1}$ to $\bar{I}_1/\bar{P}_{Y,0}$ while the value of its X-intercept remains unchanged at $\bar{I}_1/\bar{P}_{X,1}$. Therefore, following the reduction in the price of good Y, the new budget equation pivots clockwise on its X-intercept as shown in Figure 4.4.

4.3   CONSTRAINED UTILITY MAXIMIZATION

Earlier, we stated that the goal of the consumer is to choose that combination of goods and services that maximizes his utility. In this chapter, our focus thus far has been on the budget equation $\bar{P}_{X,1}X + \bar{P}_{Y,1}Y = \bar{I}_1$. Once we specify income at some level, such as $\bar{I}_1$, this equation limits the number of units of goods the consumer can purchase and ultimately consume. In this section, we will simultaneously analyze the concepts of a consumer purchasing and consuming goods and services. By doing so, we can develop the constrained utility maximization problem for the consumer.

In this problem, we assume that the individual is able to purchase and consume only two goods, X and Y, and the prices that he must pay for these goods, $\bar{P}_{X,1}$ and $\bar{P}_{Y,1}$, are determined in perfectly competitive output markets. Therefore, these prices are treated as fixed from the consumer's perspective. In addition, we assume that the level of income that the consumer has to spend on goods and services is also fixed at some predetermined level, $\bar{I}_1$. Since the budget equation acts as a limiting, or constraining, mechanism in the consumer's constrained utility maximization problem, we may now consider it as a budget constraint. However, it is important to note that this is not always the case. In fact, we will demonstrate in Section 4.4 that the budget equation is treated as the objective function to be optimized (minimized) in the consumer's constrained expenditure minimization problem.

In the constrained utility maximization problem presently under analysis, we represent the utility that the individual receives from consuming alternative combinations of goods X and Y using the indifference curves we developed in Chapter 3. Recall that the consumer's indifference curves and his budget constraint are plotted in goods space; therefore, we can graph them simultaneously, as shown in Figure 4.5.

This figure contains an indifference curve mapping indicating three alternative levels of utility, U_0, U_1^*, and U_2, where $U_2 > U_1^* > U_0$. Also contained in this figure is a budget constraint, labeled $\bar{I}_1$, reflecting the maximum amount of income available to the consumer for purchasing goods X and Y. Our objective in this analysis is to determine the values of the decision variables, goods X and Y, for which the consumer will receive the maximum amount of utility given the predetermined prices of the goods and level of income that he can spend on these goods.

Graphically, we solve the constrained utility maximization problem by determining the (X,Y) goods combination that is common to both the highest attainable indifference curve and the budget constraint. Recall that the budget constraint separates the set of affordable combinations of goods X and Y from those that are unaffordable. Therefore, any indifference curve that lies strictly above the budget constraint represents a level of utility associated with combinations of goods X and Y that are unattainable to the consumer since they lie outside of his budget set. In Figure 4.5 this situation applies to indifference curve U_2 since it lies strictly above the budget constraint.

Referring once again to this figure, we can see that the consumer can afford to purchase goods combinations (X_0,Y_0), (X_1^*,Y_1^*), or (X_2,Y_2), and that he exactly exhausts his income with any of these consumption choices since they all lie on the budget constraint, $\bar{P}_{X,1}X + \bar{P}_{Y,1}Y = \bar{I}_1$. However, the consumption combinations (X_0,Y_0) and (X_2,Y_2) yield a utility level of U_0, which clearly is not the highest level of utility the individual is capable of attaining in this situation. How can the consumer allocate

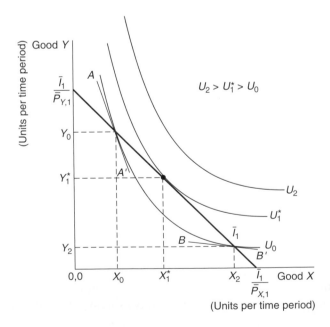

FIGURE 4.5 Constrained Utility Maximization

his income differently to purchase and consume combinations of goods X and Y that will make him happier?

First, let's focus on goods combination (X_0, Y_0). If the individual simultaneously reduces his consumption of good Y from Y_0 to Y_1^* and increases his consumption of good X from X_0 to X_1^*, then he is able to increase his level of utility. Specifically, his level of satisfaction from purchasing and consuming combination (X_1^*, Y_1^*) rather than combination (X_0, Y_0), is the higher utility level U_1^* rather than U_0. Note that he is still spending the same level of income, $\bar{I}_1$. We can similarly analyze the effect on this consumer's utility if he alters his consumption combination from (X_2, Y_2). If the individual reduces his purchases of good X from X_2 to X_1^*, and increases his consumption of good Y from Y_2 to Y_1^*, then his utility level again rises from U_0 to U_1^*. Once again the consumer is still choosing a consumption combination that lies on his budget constraint. Intuitively, the higher level of utility associated with consumption combination (X_1^*, Y_1^*), relative to combinations (X_0, Y_0) and (X_2, Y_2), makes logical sense. Typically, most individuals prefer to purchase and consume a more balanced combination of goods rather than a combination that is skewed toward either of the two goods. For example, if good X is assumed to represent bottles of soda pop, and Y is hotdogs, then typically an individual is more satisfied if he consumes a relatively more "balanced diet" of soda pop and hotdogs, rather than eating either one of these foods in excess.

4.3.1 Necessary Condition for Constrained Utility Maximum

The consumption combination (X_1^*, Y_1^*) shown in Figure 4.5 is known as the optimal combination of goods X and Y. We use asterisks to designate the notion of optimality, in this case, a constrained utility maximum for the consumer. Note that the indifference curves plotted in this figure are strictly convex. As a result, the optimal combination of goods, (X_1^*, Y_1^*), is unique since there is only one point at which a strictly convex indifference curve is tangent to the budget constraint.

This tangency implies that at the optimal goods combination, (X_1^*, Y_1^*), the slope of the indifference curve is equal to the slope of the budget constraint. Recall from Chapter 3 that the slope of the indifference curve, dY/dX, is equal to the negative of the marginal rate of substitution of good X for good Y, which in turn is equal to the negative of the ratio of the marginal utility of good X to the marginal utility of good Y, or, mathematically stated $dY/dX = -MRS = -MU_X/MU_Y$. In addition, earlier in this chapter we demonstrated that the slope of the budget constraint is $dY/dX = -\bar{P}_{X,1}/\bar{P}_{Y,1}$. Therefore, in general, at the optimal consumption combination, (X_1^*, Y_1^*),

$$\underbrace{\text{slope of indifference curve}} = \underbrace{\text{slope of budget constraint}}$$

$$-MRS = \frac{-MU_X}{MU_Y} \quad = \quad \frac{-\bar{P}_{X,1}}{\bar{P}_{Y,1}}$$

or, after multiplying both sides of this equation by –1, we obtain,

$$MRS = \frac{MU_X}{MU_Y} = \frac{\bar{P}_{X,1}}{\bar{P}_{Y,1}}. \tag{4.3}$$

Equation (4.3) is known as the necessary condition for a constrained utility maximum that must be satisfied in order for the consumer to be maximizing his utility subject to his budget constraint.

What does this necessary condition mean? Recall that the marginal rate of substitution measures the rate at which the consumer is willing to substitute units of one good for units of another while maintaining the same level of utility. Also recall that the slope of the budget constraint measures the rate in the market at which goods X and Y are exchanged on the basis of their relative prices. Therefore, we can interpret the constrained utility maximization process as the individual adjusting his consumption of goods X and Y to the point where the rate at which he is willing to substitute one good for the other, while receiving the same level of utility, equals the rate at which he can substitute purchases of these goods for each other in the market, while spending the same amount of income.

Referring once again to Figure 4.5, if the individual consumes goods combination (X_0, Y_0), then the necessary condition for a constrained utility maximum will not be met. We can demonstrate this by constructing a line, AA', drawn tangent to the indifference curve at this point, and observing that it is steeper than the budget constraint. From an economic perspective, this situation implies that since the slope of the indifference curve is equal to $-MRS = -MU_X/MU_Y$, and the slope of the budget constraint is $-\overline{P}_{X,1}/\overline{P}_{Y,1}$, then at the goods combination (X_0, Y_0), $-MRS = -MU_X/MU_Y < -\overline{P}_{X,1}/\overline{P}_{Y,1}$. After multiplying both sides by -1 to eliminate the negative signs, $MRS = MU_X/MU_Y > \overline{P}_{X,1}/\overline{P}_{Y,1}$. As we discussed earlier, the consumer can increase his utility by purchasing and consuming fewer units of good Y and more units of good X. By making this adjustment, his marginal rate of substitution will fall, due to the earlier assumption of strict convexity and the associated diminishing MRS. This substitution of good X for good Y will continue until the $MRS = MU_X/MU_Y = \overline{P}_{X,1}/\overline{P}_{Y,1}$, thereby satisfying the necessary condition for a constrained utility maximum. Using a similar analysis, you can verify that the necessary condition does not hold true for goods combination (X_2, Y_2). Observe, in Figure 4.5, that $MRS < \overline{P}_{X,1}/\overline{P}_{Y,1}$. As an exercise, it is left to you to develop a different consumption plan for the individual which would achieve a constrained utility maximum.

There is an alternative way for us to analyze the necessary condition for a constrained utility maximum. This approach entails rearranging equation (4.3) by dividing both sides of equation (4.3) by $\overline{P}_{X,1}$ and multiplying both sides by MU_Y to express the relationship as

$$\frac{MU_X}{\overline{P}_{X,1}} = \frac{MU_Y}{\overline{P}_{Y,1}}. \tag{4.4}$$

This equation contains the same information as equation (4.3); however, it allows us to use a somewhat different interpretation, based on cardinal utility analysis. Specifically, this condition, $MU_X/\overline{P}_{X,1} = MU_Y/\overline{P}_{Y,1}$, indicates that at the optimal combination of goods, (X_1^*, Y_1^*), the marginal utility the consumer receives from the last dollar he spends on good X equals the marginal utility he receives from the last dollar he spends on good Y. For example, if goods X and Y again represent bottles of soda pop and hotdogs, respectively, and if $MU_X/\overline{P}_{X,1} = 10$ utils for the last dollar spent on soda pop while $MU_Y/\overline{P}_{Y,1} = 2$ utils for the last dollar spent on hotdogs, then a rational consumer benefits by purchasing fewer hotdogs and more soda pop. By spending one less dollar on hotdogs, he sacrifices 2 utils of satisfaction. However, if this dollar is used to purchase additional bottles of soda pop, the consumer gains 10 utils of satisfaction, thus experiencing a net gain in utility of 8 utils. As long as the consumer can increase his utility, he will continue this substitution process, causing the marginal utilities of each good to change, until he achieves equality between $MU_X/\overline{P}_{X,1}$ and $MU_Y/\overline{P}_{Y,1}$. Note that since the consumer takes the prices of the goods as given, the only way for him to establish equality between $MU_X/\overline{P}_{X,1}$ and $MU_Y/\overline{P}_{Y,1}$ is to change his consumption of the goods, which in turn, alters the marginal utility he receives from each good.

4.3.2 Corner Solutions

Note that in our previous analysis of the necessary condition for a constrained utility maximum, the optimal consumption combination contains positive amounts of both goods X and Y. We refer to this type of result as an interior solution. However, it is also possible for a consumer to maximize her utility, given the predetermined values for income and the prices of both goods, by spending all of her income on only one of the two goods. This type of outcome is known as a corner solution, since graphically the constrained utility-maximizing combination of goods, (X_1^*,Y_1^*), is located on one of the outer corners of the budget set. More specifically, if (X_1^*,Y_1^*) is a corner solution, then it lies on either of the intercepts of the budget equation with the X- or Y-axis.

Will the necessary condition for a constrained utility maximum hold true when (X_1^*,Y_1^*) is a corner solution? The answer to this question is, sometimes. If the indifference curve and the budget constraint are tangent at one of the two outer corners of the budget set, then the necessary condition, $MRS = MU_X/MU_Y = \overline{P}_{X,1}/\overline{P}_{Y,1}$, is satisfied. However, it is more likely that, rather than being tangent at the corner solution, the indifference curve and the budget equation will actually cross each other. In such a situation, the tangency of the individual's indifference curve with the budget equation occurs where consumption of one of the two goods is negative and thus lies outside of the economically relevant range of goods space.

Figure 4.6 depicts a corner solution in which the necessary condition for a constrained utility maximum is not being met. At the optimal consumption combination, (X_1^*,Y_1^*), the slope of the line AA', drawn tangent to the indifference curve at this point, is steeper than the slope of the budget equation and therefore, $MRS = MU_X/MU_Y > \overline{P}_{X,1}/\overline{P}_{Y,1}$. Intuitively, such a situation arises when the individual strongly prefers good X relative to good Y, and good Y is relatively more expensive than good X. For the consumer to move from this corner solution, where he is choosing to exhaust his income solely on good X, to an interior solution where positive amounts of both goods are purchased, either the price of good X has to increase or the price of good Y has to decrease. Either of these scenarios, provided the prices change sufficiently,

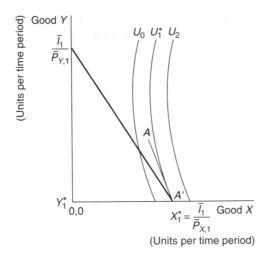

FIGURE 4.6 Corner Solution for Constrained Utility Maximum

results in an increase in the absolute value of the slope of the budget equation such that the necessary condition for a constrained utility maximum occurs at an interior solution.

4.3.3 Constrained Utility Maximization: Lagrangian Multiplier Method

We can also analyze the necessary condition for a constrained utility maximum mathematically. Specifically, we will use the Lagrangian multiplier method introduced in Chapter 2 to generate the necessary condition for a constrained utility maximum. In addition, we will demonstrate how to determine the optimal values of the consumer's decision variables, the consumption levels of goods X and Y, the maximized value of the objective variable, utility, U, and the value of the Lagrangian multiplier, λ. Mathematically, we can express the constrained utility maximization problem of the consumer as

$$\text{Maximize} \quad U = U(X,Y)$$
$$\text{subject to} \quad \bar{I}_1 = \bar{P}_{X,1}X + \bar{P}_{Y,1}Y$$

where $U = U(X,Y)$ denotes the consumer's utility function, which in this problem represents the objective function to be maximized, and $\bar{I}_1 = \bar{P}_{X,1}X + \bar{P}_{Y,1}Y$ is the consumer's budget equation, which is treated as the constraint. We will solve this constrained optimization problem using the Lagrangian multiplier method, which is comprised of the following three steps:

Step 1   Set up the Lagrangian function, $\mathscr{L} = \mathscr{L}(X,Y,\lambda)$.

$$\mathscr{L} = \mathscr{L}(X,Y,\lambda) = U + \lambda(\bar{I}_1 - \bar{P}_{X,1}X - \bar{P}_{Y,1}Y),$$

or since $U = U(X,Y)$,

$$\mathscr{L} = \mathscr{L}(X,Y,\lambda) = U(X,Y) + \lambda(\bar{I}_1 - \bar{P}_{X,1}X - \bar{P}_{Y,1}Y).$$

The Lagrangian function embodies the objective function, in this case, the utility function, the Lagrangian multiplier, λ, and the constraint, which in this problem is the consumer's budget equation. Note that we have rearranged the terms of the budget equation so that it is equal to zero before entering it into the Lagrangian function. We have done this so that its inclusion into the Lagrangian function does not affect the value of the objective function, U. As a result, maximizing $\mathcal{L}$ is mathematically equivalent to maximizing U, while still incorporating all of the information embodied in the budget constraint.

Step 2   Determine the first-order conditions by partially differentiating the Lagrangian function with respect to X, Y, and λ and setting each of these partial derivatives equal to zero. Thus

$$\frac{\partial \mathcal{L}}{\partial X} = \frac{\partial U(X,Y)}{\partial X} - \lambda \overline{P}_{X,1} = 0 \tag{4.5}$$

$$\frac{\partial \mathcal{L}}{\partial Y} = \frac{\partial U(X,Y)}{\partial Y} - \lambda \overline{P}_{Y,1} = 0 \tag{4.6}$$

$$\frac{\partial \mathcal{L}}{\partial \lambda} = \overline{I}_1 - \overline{P}_{X,1} X - \overline{P}_{Y,1} Y = 0. \tag{4.7}$$

Step 3   Solve the first-order conditions simultaneously for the unique values of X, Y, and λ that maximize the consumer's utility, U. We can solve this system of first order-conditions in numerous ways. One of the easiest is for us to first add $\lambda \overline{P}_{X,1}$ to both sides of equation (4.5) and add $\lambda \overline{P}_{Y,1}$ to both sides of equation (4.6). Next, we divide the altered version of equation (4.5) by the altered version of equation (4.6) to obtain

$$\frac{\partial U(X,Y)}{\partial X} \bigg/ \frac{\partial U(X,Y)}{\partial Y} = \frac{\lambda \overline{P}_{X,1}}{\lambda \overline{P}_{Y,1}},$$

or since $U = U(X,Y)$,

$$\frac{\partial U}{\partial X} \bigg/ \frac{\partial U}{\partial Y} = \frac{\lambda \overline{P}_{X,1}}{\lambda \overline{P}_{Y,1}}.$$

After canceling the λ terms and recognizing the terms $\partial U/\partial X$ and $\partial U/\partial Y$ as the marginal utilities of goods X and Y, respectively, we obtain the familiar necessary condition for a constrained utility maximum,

$$MRS = \frac{MU_X}{MU_Y} = \frac{\overline{P}_{X,1}}{\overline{P}_{Y,1}}.$$

Note that this is the same result we obtained graphically in Section 4.3.1. In addition to generating the necessary condition for a constrained utility maximum, the Lagrangian multiplier method also yields optimal values for X, Y, λ, and U, once we introduce a specific utility function and values for the predetermined factors P_X, P_Y, and I.[1] We will demonstrate this process with the following numerical example.

Numerical Example 1: Constrained Utility Maximization Problem

$$\text{Maximize} \quad U = U(X,Y) = X^{.5}\,Y^{.5}$$

$$\text{subject to } \bar{I}_1 = \bar{P}_{X,1}X + \bar{P}_{Y,1}Y,$$

where the predetermined level of income is $\bar{I}_1 = \$800$ and the predetermined prices of goods X and Y are $\bar{P}_{X,1} = \$4$ and $\bar{P}_{Y,1} = \$1$, respectively.

Step 1 Set up the Lagrangian function.

$$\mathcal{L} = \mathcal{L}(X,Y,\lambda) = X^{.5}Y^{.5} + \lambda\,(\bar{I}_1 - \bar{P}_{X,1}X - \bar{P}_{Y,1}Y).$$

Step 2 Determine the first-order conditions.

$$\frac{\partial \mathcal{L}}{\partial X} = 0.5X^{-.5}Y^{.5} - \lambda\bar{P}_{X,1} = 0 \tag{4.8}$$

$$\frac{\partial \mathcal{L}}{\partial Y} = 0.5X^{.5}Y^{-.5} - \lambda\bar{P}_{Y,1} = 0 \tag{4.9}$$

$$\frac{\partial \mathcal{L}}{\partial \lambda} = \bar{I}_1 - \bar{P}_{X,1}X - \bar{P}_{Y,1}Y = 0 \tag{4.10}$$

Step 3 Solve the first-order conditions simultaneously for the unique values of X, Y, and λ that maximize utility, U. Thus, rewrite equations (4.8) and (4.9), respectively, as

$$0.5X^{-.5}Y^{.5} = \lambda\bar{P}_{X,1} \tag{4.8$'$}$$

and

$$0.5X^{.5}Y^{-.5} = \lambda\bar{P}_{Y,1}. \tag{4.9$'$}$$

Divide equation (4.8$'$) by equation (4.9$'$) to generate the necessary condition for a constrained utility maximum as

$$\frac{0.5X^{-.5}Y^{.5}}{0.5X^{.5}Y^{-.5}} = \frac{\lambda\bar{P}_{X,1}}{\lambda\bar{P}_{Y,1}}$$

or

$$\frac{Y}{X} = \frac{\bar{P}_{X,1}}{\bar{P}_{Y,1}}.$$

---

[1] The necessary condition for a constrained utility maximum, $MRS = MU_X/MU_Y = \bar{P}_{X,1}/\bar{P}_{Y,1}$ also represents the necessary condition for a constrained utility minimum. Since the goal of the rational consumer is the former, in order for us to ensure that any solutions are consistent with this goal, the second-order conditions for a constrained utility maximum must also be examined. However, due to the mathematical complexities associated with computing these conditions, we will assume throughout this text that these second-order conditions are being fulfilled by virtue of the functions we have chosen for analysis.

We can identify the term Y/X as the *MRS*, since it represents MU_X/MU_Y. After rearranging the terms in the necessary condition, we can now solve for Y as

$$Y = \frac{\overline{P}_{X,1}X}{\overline{P}_{Y,1}}.$$ **(4.11)**

Substituting the right-hand side of equation (4.11) into the constraint, equation (4.10), yields

$$\overline{I}_1 - \overline{P}_{X,1}X - \overline{P}_{Y,1}\left(\frac{\overline{P}_{X,1}X}{\overline{P}_{Y,1}}\right) = 0$$

$$\overline{I}_1 - \overline{P}_{X,1}X - \overline{P}_{X,1}X = 0$$

$$\overline{I}_1 - 2\overline{P}_{X,1}X = 0$$

$$X_1^* = \frac{\overline{I}_1}{2\overline{P}_{X,1}}.$$ **(4.12)**

We now substitute the predetermined values of $\overline{I}_1$ and $\overline{P}_{X,1}$ into equation (4.12) to determine the optimal level of consumption for good X as

$$X_1^* = \frac{800}{2(4)} = 100 \text{ units.}$$

This optimal value, $X_1^* = 100$, along with the predetermined values of $\overline{P}_{X,1} = \$4$ and $\overline{P}_{Y,1} = \$1$, can be substituted into equation (4.11) to solve for the optimal consumption level of good Y as

$$Y_1^* = \frac{\overline{P}_{X,1}X_1^*}{\overline{P}_{Y,1}} = \frac{4(100)}{1} \quad 400 \text{ units.}$$

We determine the maximum level of utility the consumer receives by substituting the optimal values of the goods, 100 units of good X and 400 units of good Y, into the objective (utility) function as

$$U_1^* = U(X_1^*, Y_1^*) = (100)^{.5}(400)^{.5} = 200.$$

Finally, we determine the value of λ^*, the Lagrangian multiplier, by substituting the optimal values of X and Y into either equation (4.8) or (4.9). Using equation (4.8), we compute the value of λ^* as

$$0.5(100)^{-.5}(400)^{.5} - \lambda(4) = 0$$

$$0.5\left(\frac{1}{10}\right)(20) = \lambda(4)$$

$$1 = \lambda(4)$$

$$\lambda^* = \frac{1}{4}.$$

Recall from Chapter 2 that we may interpret the value of λ^* as measuring the effect on the objective function when the value of the constraint is changed by one unit.

Free Choice and Utility Maximization

Throughout this chapter we have shown that a rational consumer achieves a constrained utility maximum by choosing to purchase and consume amounts of goods and services for which the marginal rate of substitution is equal to the ratio of their prices. However, an individual's ability to attain a constrained utility maximum is based on the assumption that he is free to make the choices necessary to consume optimal combinations of goods and services. Therefore, it follows that the more a consumer's choice process is restricted, the less utility he receives. Recently, economists Bruno Frey and Alois Stutzer of the University of Zurich conducted a study designed to analyze the effect on consumers' utility attributed to the degree of choice associated with various political institutions. A summary of their results, published in *The Economist*, is detailed as follows.

> "Until recently nobody had conducted a systematic survey of the effect of political institutions on happiness. You would expect people in democracies to be happier than people living in authoritarian states. Even among democracies, you might expect different sorts of constitutional arrangements to be more or less conducive to human flourishing. You might expect citizens to be happier in systems that gave them a greater sense of control over what their politicians do, for instance, or in systems that gave them a fuller role as participants.

> *Devil in the data*

> Which is where Switzerland—one country with many political systems—comes in. Switzerland has a federal structure that reserves major powers to the 26 cantons, and the cantons themselves vary in the ease with which citizens participate. Cantons use assorted instruments of "direct democracy:", notably "initiatives" to change the canton's constitution, and referendums to stop new laws, change existing ones, or prevent new public spending. The rules controlling these instruments (the number of sig-

natures required to start an initiative, the time allowed to gather signatures, and so on) differ from place to place.

Bruno Frey and Alois Stutzer of the University of Zurich have studied a survey of 6,000 Swiss residents that asked "How satisfied are you with your life as a whole these days?", with answers on a scale of one ("completely dissatisfied") to ten ("completely satisfied"). These answers were then compared, first with conventional economic and demographic information, and then with the "direct democracy" data for the relevant cantons.

The extent of democracy in the cantons is captured on a scale running from one to six. Messrs Frey and Stutzer find that a one-point increase in this democracy index, after stripping out the effects of the other variables, increases the share of people who say they are very happy by 2.7 percentage points. What this means is that the marginal effect of direct democracy on happiness is nearly half as big as the effect of moving from the lowest monthly income band (SFr980–1,285, or $660–865) to the highest (SFr4,501 and above).

There is an interesting further wrinkle. You might ask, which aspect of direct democracy is it that makes people happier—the outcome (better government, as one might suppose) or the process? Turning again to their wonderful data, Messrs Frey and Stutzer answer this question as well. Participation in initiatives and referendums is restricted to Swiss nationals. Foreigners living in Switzerland enjoy the better results, if there are any, but only nationals get the benefit of taking part. In fact, it turns out that direct democracy improves the happiness of foreigners and Swiss nationals alike—but the increase for foreigners is smaller, only about one-third of the increase for nationals. A happy country, it seems, is one where politics is not just a spectator sport."[2]

[2]Frey, Bruno, and Stutzer, Alois, "Happiness and Institutions," Working Paper, University of Zurich, quoted in *The Economist*, "Happiness is a Warm Vote," April 17, 1999, p. 82.

Since the constraint in this problem is the consumer's budget equation, a change in the constraint by one unit generally implies that the amount of income is changed by one dollar in the budget equation. By employing this viewpoint in the constrained utility maximization problem, we can interpret λ^* as effectively measuring the change in utility due to a one dollar change in the consumer's income, $\partial U/\partial I$; hence, it can also be thought of as measuring the marginal utility of income. In this particular problem we found the value of λ^* to be 0.25. Therefore, a one dollar increase in the consumer's income leads to a 0.25 increase in his maximum level of satisfaction, from 200 to 200.25. Conversely, a one dollar decrease in the individual's income results in a reduction in his maximum attainable utility by 0.25, from 200 to 199.75. For additional practice, we have included another numerical example of constrained utility maximization in the appendix to this chapter.

†4.4 CONSTRAINED EXPENDITURE MINIMIZATION

It is convention in microeconomics to label the constrained utility maximization problem that we analyzed in the preceding section as the primal problem of the consumer. However, recall from Chapter 2 that there exists an alternative approach to formulating constrained optimization problems known as the dual. This approach yields the same solution values for the decision variables, in this case X and Y, provided the dual problem embodies the same fundamental information as the primal. Sometimes the dual is the preferred approach when solving constrained optimization problems because we can derive alternative economic interpretations directly related to marginal analysis from its results. The most important result of such interpretations is that of a compensated demand function, which we will develop in the next chapter.

The dual to the constrained utility maximization problem is known as the constrained expenditure minimization problem, whereas in the case of its primal counterpart, we will once again assume that the consumer takes the prices of goods X and Y as given, since they are determined in competitive goods markets. However, in the dual problem it is assumed that the utility attained by the individual is predetermined at some level, say $\overline{U}_1$, whereas the consumer's expenditure on goods X and Y is a variable that the individual seeks to minimize by his selection of the decision variables X and Y. In contrast, recall that in the primal, constrained utility maximization problem, we treated the consumer's utility as variable, while his expenditure on goods X and Y was set equal to his predetermined level of income. In the dual problem, we also assume that the consumer's expenditure on goods X and Y is exactly equal to his income, but using this approach we no longer treat it as predetermined. Therefore, the budget equation, $I = \overline{P}_{X,1}X + \overline{P}_{Y,1}Y$, we used in the primal problem is renamed the expenditure equation, $E = \overline{P}_{X,1}X + \overline{P}_{Y,1}Y$, and acts as the objective function in the dual, where E is the variable to be minimized. In summary, the primal and dual problems are very closely related because the objective function of one problem acts as the constraint in the other, and vice versa.

†4.4.1 Necessary Condition for a Constrained Expenditure Minimum

The constrained expenditure minimization problem of the consumer is depicted graphically in Figure 4.7, where the objective function to be minimized is represented by the expenditure equation $E = \overline{P}_{X,1}X + \overline{P}_{Y,1}Y$. In Figure 4.7, we have plotted three different expenditure equations, each of which represents a set of combinations of goods X and Y for which the consumer's expenditure on these goods equals, in ascending value, E_0, E_1^*, or E_2 dollars. The constraint in this problem is represented by the indifference curve $\overline{U}_1$, demonstrating alternative combinations of goods X and Y that yield the predetermined level of utility that the consumer seeks to acquire, $\overline{U}_1$, via his consumption of goods X and Y.

Figure 4.7 shows that any one of the three indicated combinations of goods X and Y, (X_0,Y_0), $(X_1'^*,Y_1'^*)$ or (X_2,Y_2), is capable of yielding the predetermined level of utility $\overline{U}_1$, since all three combinations lie on the $\overline{U}_1$ indifference curve. However, goods combination (X_0,Y_0), which lies on the $\overline{E}_2$ expenditure equation, is clearly not the best choice for the expenditure-minimizing consumer. By substituting more units of good X for units of good Y until he is consuming the goods combination $(X_1'^*,Y_1'^*)$, the individual can still achieve the desired predetermined level of utility, $\overline{U}_1$, while incurring a lower level of expenditure, E_1^*, than the expenditure level E_2 associated with purchasing goods combination (X_0,Y_0). Similarly, goods combination (X_2,Y_2) also does not constitute the optimal consumption choice for the consumer since he can attain the same predetermined level of utility, $\overline{U}_1$, with the lower level of expenditure, E_1^*, by reducing his consumption of good X, from X_2 to $X_1'^*$, and increasing his consumption

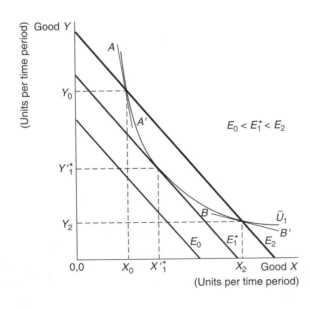

FIGURE 4.7 Constrained Expenditure Minimization

of good Y, from Y_2 to $Y_1'^*$. It should also be apparent that while any combination of goods lying on the E_0 expenditure equation is less expensive than combinations (X_0,Y_0), $(X_1'^*,Y_1'^*)$, or (X_2,Y_2), none of the (X,Y) combinations on E_0 satisfies the utility requirement of $\overline{U}_1$ implied by the constraint. We can observe this fact in Figure 4.7 by noting the lack of any (X,Y) combinations common to both the indifference curve $\overline{U}_1$ and the expenditure equation E_0.

As was the case in the primal constrained utility maximum problem, the necessary condition for an optimal solution in the dual calls for the indifference curve to be tangent to the expenditure equation. In Figure 4.7 we can observe that this tangency condition only holds true at goods combination $(X_1'^*,Y_1'^*)$ where the slope of the indifference curve, $dY/dX = -MRS = -MU_X/MU_Y$, is equal to the slope of the expenditure equation, $dY/dX = -\overline{P}_{X,1}/\overline{P}_{Y,1}$. Thus, at $(X_1'^*,Y_1'^*)$,

$$\underbrace{\text{slope of indifference cure}}_{} = \underbrace{\text{slope of expenditure equation}}_{}$$

$$-MRS = \frac{-MU_X}{MU_Y} = \frac{-\overline{P}_{X,1}}{\overline{P}_{Y,1}} \tag{4.13}$$

or, after we multiply both sides of equation (4.13) by -1, we obtain the familiar necessary condition for a constrained optimum

$$MRS = \frac{MU_X}{MU_Y} = \frac{\overline{P}_{X,1}}{\overline{P}_{Y,1}}.$$

This equality represents the necessary condition for a constrained expenditure minimum, which is the same condition we obtained earlier for a constrained utility maximum.

We can reaffirm the fact that the goods combinations (X_0,Y_0) and (X_2,Y_2) do not represent constrained expenditure minimization solutions for utility level $\overline{U}_1$ by observing that the necessary condition does not hold true at these combinations. Once again referring to Figure 4.7, we can see that the line AA', drawn tangent to the indifference curve at goods combination (X_0,Y_0), possesses a greater slope, in absolute value terms, than the expenditure equation, thereby indicating that the $MRS = MU_X/MU_Y > \overline{P}_{X,1}/\overline{P}_{Y,1}$ at this combination of goods. The consumer can reduce his expenditure by altering his consumption of goods X and Y to consume fewer units of good Y and more units of good X while still maintaining the specified level of utility, $\overline{U}_1$. By making this change, his MRS decreases due to our earlier assumption of strict convexity of the indifference curve. This substitution of good X for good Y continues until $MRS = MU_X/MU_Y = \overline{P}_{X,1}/\overline{P}_{Y,1}$, which occurs when the individual is consuming $(X_1'^*,Y_1'^*)$. This combination of goods minimizes his expenditure and yet still yields the predetermined level of utility, $\overline{U}_1$. As an exercise, you can verify that the necessary condition for a constrained expenditure minimization also does not hold true at consumption combination (X_2,Y_2).

†4.4.2 Constrained Expenditure Minimization: Lagrangian Multiplier Method

We can also analyze the process of constrained expenditure minimization from a mathematical perspective. To do so, we will use the same Lagrangian multiplier method that we applied to the primal constrained utility maximization problem solved earlier in this chapter. Recall from Chapter 2 that when we formulate the dual problem the constraint from the primal problem acts as the objective function in the dual, while the objective function for the primal serves as the constraint for the dual. In the case of the dual expenditure minimization problem, the objective function is the consumer's budget equation, $\overline{P}_{X,1}X + \overline{P}_{Y,1}Y = I$, that we treated as the constraint in the primal. The constraint in the dual is the individual's utility function, $U = U(X,Y)$, which we treated as the objective function in the primal. Since we assume that the consumer spends all of his income on the two goods, X and Y, the income variable, I, represents the consumer's total expenditure, E. Therefore, we can express the budget equation as an expenditure equation, or

$$E = \overline{P}_{X,1}X + \overline{P}_{Y,1}Y,$$

where E represents the objective variable to be minimized. We can think of this dual approach to the consumer optimization problem as a constrained expenditure minimization problem. Using this approach, the consumer seeks to determine the optimal values for the consumption levels of the two goods, X and Y, that correspond to a minimum value for his expenditure, E^*, subject to attaining a predetermined level of utility, $\overline{U}_1$.

We express this constrained expenditure minimization problem mathematically as

$$\text{Minimize} \quad E = \overline{P}_{X,1}X + \overline{P}_{Y,1}Y$$
$$\text{subject to} \quad \overline{U}_1 = U(X,Y).$$

We will use the Lagrangian multiplier method to solve this problem as outlined in the following three steps.

Step 1 Set up the Lagrangian function.

$$\mathscr{L}^D = \mathscr{L}^D(X,Y,\lambda) = E + \lambda[\overline{U}_1 - U(X,Y)]$$

or since $E = \overline{P}_{X,1}X + \overline{P}_{Y,1}Y$,

$$\mathscr{L}^D = \mathscr{L}^D(X,Y,\lambda) = \overline{P}_{X,1}X + \overline{P}_{Y,1}Y + \lambda[\overline{U}_1 - U(X,Y)].$$

The Lagrangian function for this problem, $\mathscr{L}^D$, embodies the objective function, which in this case is the consumer's expenditure equation, the Lagrangian multiplier for this dual problem, λ^D, and the constraint. In this case, the constraint consists of the predetermined level of utility, $\overline{U}_1$, minus the individual's utility function, $U = U(X,Y)$. Note that once again we have solved the constraint such that it is equal to zero; thus, its presence in the Lagrangian function does not affect the value of the objective variable, E. As a result, minimizing $\mathscr{L}^D$ is mathematically equivalent to minimizing E while incorporating all of the information contained in the constraint.

Step 2   Determine the first-order conditions by partially differentiating the Lagrangian function with respect to X, Y, and λ^D and setting each of these partial derivatives equal to zero as follows:

$$\frac{\partial \mathscr{L}^D}{\partial X} = \overline{P}_{X,1} - \lambda^D \frac{\partial U(X,Y)}{\partial X} = 0 \tag{4.14}$$

$$\frac{\partial \mathscr{L}^D}{\partial Y} = \overline{P}_{Y,1} - \lambda^D \frac{\partial U(X,Y)}{\partial Y} = 0 \tag{4.15}$$

$$\frac{\partial \mathscr{L}^D}{\partial Y} = \overline{U}_1 - U(X,Y) = 0. \tag{4.16}$$

Step 3   Solve the first-order conditions simultaneously to determine the unique values of X, Y, and λ^D that minimize the consumer's expenditure on goods X and Y, while still yielding the predetermined level of utility, $\overline{U}_1$. One way for us to proceed with this solution process is to add $\lambda^D \partial U(X,Y)/\partial X$ to both sides of equation (4.14) and $\lambda^D \partial U(X,Y)/\partial Y$ to both sides of equation (4.15). Afterward, we divide the altered version of equation (4.14) by the altered version of equation (4.15) as

$$\frac{\overline{P}_{X,1}}{\overline{P}_{Y,1}} = \frac{\lambda^D \dfrac{\partial U(X,Y)}{\partial X}}{\lambda^D \dfrac{\partial U(X,Y)}{\partial Y}},$$

where employing the reflexive property to the above equation yields

$$\frac{\lambda^D \dfrac{\partial U(X,Y)}{\partial X}}{\lambda^D \dfrac{\partial U(X,Y)}{\partial Y}} = \frac{\overline{P}_{X,1}}{\overline{P}_{Y,1}}. \tag{4.17}$$

After canceling the λ^D terms and substituting MU_X for $\partial U(X,Y)/\partial X$ and MU_Y for $\partial U(X,Y)/\partial Y$ in equation (4.17), we obtain the familiar necessary condition for a constrained consumer expenditure minimum

$$MRS = \frac{MU_X}{MU_Y} = \frac{\overline{P}_{X,1}}{\overline{P}_{Y,1}}.$$

Once a specific utility function and predetermined values for U, P_X, and P_Y are introduced, we can use this constrained expenditure minimization approach to solve for the optimal values of the consumption levels of the goods X and Y, the minimized value of expenditure, E^*, and the Lagrangian multiplier, λ^D. In the following numerical example, we will solve a constrained expenditure minimization problem for the same utility function and price levels used in the primal constrained utility maximization problem solved earlier in Numerical Example 1. However, in this case, it is the level of utility that is predetermined rather than the level of expenditure. In order to demonstrate the relationship between the two approaches, we have predetermined the level of utility at $\overline{U}_1 = 200$, which corresponds to the solution value obtained when we solved the earlier primal problem.

Numerical Example 2: Constrained Expenditure Minimization

$$\text{Minimize } E = \overline{P}_{X,1}X + \overline{P}_{Y,1}Y$$
$$\text{subject to } \overline{U}_1 = X^{.5}Y^{.5}$$

where the predetermined prices of goods X and Y are $\overline{P}_{X,1} = \$4$ and $\overline{P}_{Y,1} = \$1$, and the predetermined level of utility is $\overline{U}_1 = 200$.

Step 1 Set up the Lagrangian function.

$$\mathcal{L}^D(X,Y,\lambda^D) = \overline{P}_{X,1}X + \overline{P}_{Y,1}Y + \lambda^D(\overline{U}_1 - X^{.5}Y^{.5})$$

Step 2 Determine the first-order conditions.

$$\frac{\partial \mathcal{L}^D}{\partial X} = \overline{P}_{X,1} - 0.5\lambda^D X^{-.5}Y^{.5} = 0 \tag{4.18}$$

$$\frac{\partial \mathcal{L}^D}{\partial Y} = \overline{P}_{Y,1} - 0.5\lambda^D X^{.5}Y^{-.5} = 0 \tag{4.19}$$

$$\frac{\partial \mathcal{L}^D}{\partial \lambda^D} = \overline{U}_1 - X^{.5}Y^{.5} = 0 \tag{4.20}$$

Step 3 Solve the first-order conditions simultaneously for the unique values of X, Y, and λ^D which minimize the consumer's expenditure, E, while yielding the predetermined level of utility, $\overline{U}_1$. We can rewrite equations (4.18) and (4.19) respectively, as

$$\overline{P}_{X,1} = 0.5\lambda^D X^{-.5}Y^{.5} \tag{4.18$'$}$$
$$\overline{P}_{Y,1} = 0.5\lambda^D X^{.5}Y^{-.5} \tag{4.19$'$}$$

Dividing equation (4.18$'$) by equation (4.19$'$), we obtain the necessary condition for a constrained expenditure minimum as

$$\frac{\overline{P}_{X,1}}{\overline{P}_{Y,1}} = \frac{0.5\lambda^D X^{-.5}Y^{.5}}{0.5\lambda^D X^{.5}Y^{-.5}}$$

or, after simplifying the above equation and applying the reflexive property,

$$\frac{Y}{X} = \frac{\overline{P}_{X,1}}{\overline{P}_{Y,1}}. \tag{4.21}$$

Recognize, the term Y/X in equation (4.21) is the *MRS* since it represents MU_X/MU_Y. After rearranging terms in the necessary condition, we solve for the value of Y as

$$Y = \frac{\overline{P}_{X,1}X}{\overline{P}_{Y,1}}. \tag{4.22}$$

Substituting the results in equation (4.22) into equation (4.20), the constraint, yields the following:

$$\overline{U}_1 - X^{.5}\left(\frac{\overline{P}_{X,1}X}{\overline{P}_{Y,1}}\right)^{.5} = 0$$

$$\overline{U}_1 - X\left(\frac{\overline{P}_{X,1}}{\overline{P}_{Y,1}}\right)^{.5} = 0$$

$$\overline{U}_1 = X\left(\frac{\overline{P}_{X,1}}{\overline{P}_{Y,1}}\right)^{.5}$$

$$X_1'^* = \overline{U}_1\left(\frac{\overline{P}_{Y,1}}{\overline{P}_{X,1}}\right)^{.5}. \tag{4.23}$$

By substituting the predetermined values of $\overline{P}_{X,1} = \$4$, $\overline{P}_{Y,1} = \$1$, and $\overline{U}_1 = 200$ into equation (4.23), we compute the optimal level of consumption for good X as

$$X_1'^* = (200)\left(\frac{1}{4}\right)^{.5} = 100 \text{ units.}$$

Substituting the predetermined values of $\overline{P}_{X,1}$ and $\overline{P}_{Y,1}$, along with the optimal value of X, into equation (4.22) yields the optimal value of Y as

$$Y_1'^* = \frac{\overline{P}_{X,1}X}{\overline{P}_{Y,1}} = \frac{(4)(100)}{(1)} = 400 \text{ units.}$$

We can compute the minimum expenditure on goods X and Y, E^*, by substituting the predetermined prices of these goods, $\overline{P}_{X,1} = \$4$ and $\overline{P}_{Y,1} = \$1$, along with the optimal consumption levels of goods X and Y, $X_1'^* = 100$ units and $Y_1'^* = 400$ units, into the expenditure function. Accordingly

$$E^* = \overline{P}_{X,1}X_1'^* + \overline{P}_{Y,1}Y_1'^*,$$
$$E^* = \$4.00(100) + \$1.00(400) = \$800.00.$$

Note that the optimal value of expenditure, E^*, obtained in this constrained expenditure minimization problem is the same as the predetermined value of income we used in the primal constrained utility maximization problem in Numerical Example 1.

Finally, using equation (4.18), we determine the value of λ^D as

$$\overline{P}_{X,1} - 0.5\,\lambda^D X^{-.5}Y^{.5} = 0$$
$$4 - 0.5\,\lambda^D(100)^{-.5}(400)^{.5} = 0$$
$$4 = 0.5\,\lambda^D\frac{1}{10}(20)$$
$$\lambda^{D*} = 4.$$

We interpret the value of λ^{D*} in this constrained expenditure minimization problem as measuring the effect on the minimum value of the consumer's expenditure function due to a one-unit change in the predetermined level of utility. In the present numerical example, $\lambda^{D*} = 4$, indicating that if the level of utility is increased from 200 to 201, then the minimum expenditure needed to achieve this higher level of utility rises by $4 from $800 to $804. Conversely, if the level of utility falls by 1 from 200 to 199, then the minimum level of expenditure necessary to obtain this lower level of utility decreases from $800 to $796. Note that while the solution values for goods X and Y in this dual constrained expenditure minimization problem are the same as those we obtained for the primal constrained utility maximization problem solved in Numerical Example 1, the optimal values of λ and λ^D are not identical. In general, the value of λ^{D*} computed for the dual problem equals the reciprocal of the optimal value of λ computed for the primal. We have demonstrated this relationship in the present example where the optimal value of λ^D computed for the dual is equal to 4, while the optimal value of λ computed in Numerical Example 1 for the primal was equal to 1/4.

4.5 SUMMARY

Our primary focus in this chapter has been on developing and solving constrained optimization problems for a rational consumer. The solutions to these problems not only generate the optimal amounts of goods consumed by an individual, but also provide the foundation for developing both individual ordinary and compensated demand functions, which will be our focus in the next chapter. The major concepts we covered in this chapter are as follows.

- The budget equation represents the set of combinations of goods and services an individual is able to purchase, given predetermined prices of the goods and money income, where the individual's expenditure on these goods is exactly equal to her income.
- An increase (decrease) in the consumer's income, *ceteris paribus*, causes the budget equation to shift to the right (left) in a parallel fashion, thereby increasing (decreasing) the consumer's budget set.
- A change in the price of one of the two goods, *ceteris paribus*, alters the slope of the budget equation, $-\overline{P}_{X,1}/\overline{P}_{Y,1}$, as well as one of its two intercept values.
- In the primal constrained optimization problem of the consumer, the goal of the consumer is to determine the consumption levels of goods that yield the maximum amount of utility while exhausting her predetermined money income, given predetermined prices of the goods.
- The necessary condition that must be satisfied at the optimal goods combination, (X^*, Y^*), states that the marginal rate of substitution for these goods must equal the ratio of their prices.

KEY TERMS

- budget equation, page 82
- budget set, page 84

EXERCISES

4.1 Eddie has $10 to spend on meatball sandwiches, good X, and root beer sodas, good Y.

   a. If the price of a meatball sandwich is $5 and the price of a root beer soda is $2, formulate and plot Eddie's budget equation in goods space.

   b. Assume that the price of a root beer soda decreases to $1, *ceteris paribus*. Once again, formulate Eddie's budget equation and plot it in goods space.

   c. Suppose Eddie's income doubles to $20 and the prices of the goods are the same as those reported in part a. What is the effect on Eddie's budget equation relative to the one plotted in part a?

4.2 Mr. D'Kay loves to eat candy. His utility function is specified as

$$U = U(L,C) = LC + L + 2C$$

where C = chocolate truffles (in pounds)

L = lollipops (in pounds)

The price of a pound of chocolate truffles is $5, and the price of a pound of lollipops is $2. Mr. D'Kay's daily income is $51.

   a. Determine Mr. D'Kay's daily utility-maximizing consumption combination of truffles and lollipops.

   b. Determine the maximum amount of utility he can achieve.

   c. Determine the value of λ^* and provide a written interpretation of this value as it specifically applies to Mr. D'Kay.

4.3 Lyle derives utility from consuming neckties (X) and hair mousse (Y). His utility function is specified as

$$U = U(X,Y) = 8X^{.5}Y^{.5}.$$

Lyle must pay $20 for a necktie and $15 for a can of hair mousse. His monthly income is $6000.

   a. Determine the optimal quantities of neckties and hair mousse that Lyle should purchase.

   b. Determine the maximum amount of utility he will receive.

   c. Determine the value of λ^* and provide a written interpretation of this value as it specifically applies to Lyle.

   d. Plot in goods space the budget constraint and the indifference curve representing the maximum utility attained in this problem. Also indicate the optimal consumption combination, as well as the values of the slope and intercepts associated with the budget constraint.

†4.4 Formulate the dual constrained expenditure minimization problem associated with Exercise 4.3.

   a. Determine the optimal quantities of neckties and hair mousse that Lyle should purchase.

b. Determine the minimum amount of expenditure made by Lyle.

c. Determine the value of λ^{D*} and provide a written interpretation of this value as it specifically applies to Lyle.

†4.5 Ivana derives utility from consuming caviar (C) and champagne (W). Her utility function is given as

$$U = U(C,W) = 10C^{.5}W^{.5}.$$

The price of a tin of caviar is $100, while the price of a bottle of champagne is $16.

a. Determine the quantities of caviar and champagne Ivana must purchase in order to receive a utility level of 200.

b. Determine the minimum expenditure Ivana must make in order to achieve a level of utility equal to 200.

c. Compute the value of λ^* for this problem and interpret its value as it specifically applies to Ivana.

4.6 A consumer's utility function is given as

$$U = U(X,Y) = 3X + 3Y$$

where X and Y represent the quantities of the two goods consumed. Assume the consumer's income is $1200, the unit price of good X is $4, and the unit price of good Y is $3.

a. Graph the consumer's budget constraint.

b. Refer to the consumer's utility function. What type of relationship is implied for goods X and Y?

c. On the same graph used for part a, plot the consumer's indifference curve that corresponds to the highest level of utility she can attain.

d. Indicate the utility-maximizing consumption combination on the graph. [*Hint*: Do not use the Lagrangian multiplier method to solve this problem.]

4.7 Assume that an individual derives utility, U, from consuming razors, R, and razor blades, B, and he desires to have several functional razors—specifically, each razor must contain one razor blade. Also, assume that the prices of razors and razor blades are $P_R = \$5$ and $P_B = \$0.50$, respectively, and the individual has allotted $16.50 for purchasing these items.

a. Describe the nature of the relationship between the two goods in this case, and construct an appropriate indifference curve.

b. What are the optimal levels of the two goods the individual chooses to consume?

c. Compute the associated level of utility received by this individual.

d. After the purchases of the two goods have been made, suppose the same individual is given yet another razor, free of charge. Will his utility increase as a result of this extra razor? Why or why not?

4.8 Are there some people for whom the economic concept of a budget constraint does not apply? Defend your response.

4.9 What role does strict convexity of indifference curves play in the consumer's constrained optimization problem?

Appendix

4A CONSTRAINED UTILITY MAXIMIZATION PROBLEM USING AN ADDITIVE UTILITY FUNCTION

In this section, we solve another constrained utility maximization problem. This problem is similar to the one we solved in the chapter, but it involves a somewhat different type of utility function.

Maximize $\quad U = U(X,Y) = 10X^{.5} + 20Y^{.5}$

subject to $\quad \bar{I}_1 = \bar{P}_{X,1}X + \bar{P}_{Y,1}Y$,

where the predetermined level of income is $\bar{I}_1 = \$300$, and the predetermined prices of goods X and Y are $\bar{P}_{X,1} = \$1$ and $\bar{P}_{Y,1} = \$2$, respectively.

Step 1   Set up the Lagrangian function.

$$\mathcal{L} = \mathcal{L}(X,Y,\lambda) = 10X^{.5} + 20Y^{.5} + \lambda(\bar{I}_1 - \bar{P}_{X,1}X - \bar{P}_{Y,1}Y).$$

Step 2   Determine the first-order conditions.

$$\frac{\partial \mathcal{L}}{\partial X} = 5X^{-.5} - \lambda\bar{P}_{X,1} = 0 \quad \textbf{(4A.1)}$$

$$\frac{\partial \mathcal{L}}{\partial Y} = 10Y^{-.5} - \lambda\bar{P}_{Y,1} = 0 \quad \textbf{(4A.2)}$$

$$\frac{\partial \mathcal{L}}{\partial \lambda} = \bar{I}_1 - \bar{P}_{X,1}X - \bar{P}_{Y,1}Y = 0 \quad \textbf{(4A.3)}$$

Step 3   Solve the first-order conditions simultaneously for the unique values of X, Y, and λ that maximize utility, U. Thus, rewrite equations (4A.1) and (4A.2), respectively, as

$$5X^{-.5} = \lambda\bar{P}_{X,1} \quad \textbf{(4A.1')}$$

$$10Y^{-.5} = \lambda\bar{P}_{Y,1} \quad \textbf{(4A.2')}$$

Divide equation (4A.1') by equation (4A.2') to obtain the necessary condition for a constrained utility maximum as

$$\frac{5X^{-.5}}{10Y^{-.5}} = \frac{\lambda\bar{P}_{X,1}}{\lambda\bar{P}_{Y,1}}$$

or

$$\frac{Y^{.5}}{2X^{.5}} = \frac{\bar{P}_{X,1}}{\bar{P}_{Y,1}}$$

The term $Y^{.5}/2X^{.5}$ is the marginal rate of substitution since it measures the ratio of the marginal utility of good X to the marginal utility of good Y. We can rearrange the terms in the necessary condition to solve for Y as

$$Y^{.5} = 2X^{.5}\frac{\bar{P}_{X,1}}{\bar{P}_{Y,1}}$$

$$(Y^{.5})^2 = \left[2X^{.5}\frac{\bar{P}_{X,1}}{\bar{P}_{Y,1}}\right]^2$$

$$Y = 4X\frac{\bar{P}_{X,1}^2}{\bar{P}_{Y,1}^2}. \quad \textbf{(4A.4)}$$

Substituting the results from equation (4A.4) along with the predetermined values of $\bar{I}_1 = \$300$, $\bar{P}_{X,1} = \$1$, and $\bar{P}_{Y,1} = \$2$ into equation (4A.3), the budget constraint, yields

$$\bar{I}_1 - \bar{P}_{X,1}X - \bar{P}_{Y,1}\left(4X\frac{\bar{P}_{X,1}^2}{\bar{P}_{Y,1}^2}\right) = 0$$

$$\bar{I}_1 - \bar{P}_{X,1}X - 4X\frac{\bar{P}_{X,1}^2}{\bar{P}_{Y,1}} = 0$$

$$\frac{\bar{P}_{X,1}\bar{P}_{Y,1}X + 4X\bar{P}_{X,1}^2}{\bar{P}_{Y,1}} = \bar{I}_1$$

$$X\frac{\left(\bar{P}_{X,1}\bar{P}_{Y,1} + 4\bar{P}_{X,1}^2\right)}{\bar{P}_{Y,1}} = \bar{I}_1$$

$$X = \frac{\bar{P}_{Y,1}\bar{I}_1}{\bar{P}_{X,1}\bar{P}_{Y,1} + 4\bar{P}_{X,1}^2}$$

$$X_1^* = \frac{2(300)}{(1)(2) + 4(1)^2} = \frac{600}{6} = 100 \text{ units.}$$

By substituting the optimal value of X, $X_1^* = 100$, along with the predetermined values of $\overline{P}_{X,1}$ and $\overline{P}_{Y,1}$ into equation (4A.4), we determine the optimal consumption level for good Y as

$$Y_1^* = 4X_1^* \frac{\overline{P}_{X,1}^{\,2}}{\overline{P}_{Y,1}^{\,2}}$$

or

$$Y_1^* = 4(100) \frac{(1)^2}{(2)^2} = 100 \text{ units.}$$

Substituting the optimal consumption values for goods X and Y into the objective (utility) function, we compute the maximum level of utility the consumer can achieve as

$$U_1^* = U(X_1^*, Y_1^*) = 10(100)^{.5} + 20(100)^{.5} = 300.$$

Finally, we determine the value of λ^*, the Lagrangian multiplier, by substituting the optimal consumption values for X and Y into either

equation (4A.1) or (4A.2). Using equation (4A.1), we determine the value of λ^* as

$$5X^{-.5} - \lambda P_{X,1} = 0$$
$$5(100)^{-.5} = \lambda(1)$$
$$\lambda^* = 0.50.$$

We interpret the value of λ^* as measuring the effect on the objective function of a one-unit change in the constraint. The objective function in this problem is the individual's utility function, and since a one-unit change in the value of the constraint represents a one dollar change in income, then we can also interpret λ^* as measuring the marginal utility of income, $\partial U / \partial I$. In this particular problem, since $\lambda^* = 0.50$, then a one dollar increase in the consumer's income, from \$300 to \$301, results in a 0.50 increase in his maximum attainable level of utility from 300 to 300.50. Conversely, a one dollar decrease in his income leads to a 0.50 decrease in the consumer's maximum attainable level of utility from 300 to 299.50.

CHAPTER 5

Individual Demand Functions and Related Topics

5.1 INTRODUCTION

In the previous chapter we demonstrated how we can model and solve a rational consumer's constrained utility maximization decision-making process. This process consists of determining the combination of goods that corresponds to a maximum level of utility for the individual, subject to a set of predetermined constraining factors. These constraining factors include the prices the individual must pay for the goods he consumes and the level of money income he has available for purchasing those goods. Logically, if any of these predetermined factors change, we will generally expect a subsequent change in the optimal amounts of goods the consumer chooses. As a result, it is possible for us to establish some very useful relationships between the optimal consumption level of a good, also known as the quantity demanded of a good, and each of the underlying variables contained in the constrained utility maximization process. More specifically, the broad outcome associated with this process is known as an individual's demand function, an expression that relates the optimal consumption levels of a particular good to its own price, the prices of other goods, and the consumer's money income.

For example, recall our previous example in which an individual chooses to purchase and consume hotdogs and soda pop. In this case, we can show that the consumer's demand function for hotdogs relates the optimal quantity demanded of hotdogs to the underlying determinants in the constrained utility maximization problem, specifically, the price of hotdogs, the price of soda pop, and his money income. Similarly, his demand function for soda pop relates the optimal quantity demanded of soda pop to the price of soda pop, the price of hotdogs , and his money income. In general, we can derive various relationships from a demand function by holding all but one of the determinants of the demand function constant, *ceteris paribus*, where these relationships are known as Engel curves, own-price demand curves, and cross-price demand curves. By analyzing each of these curves, we will be able to draw some important conclusions regarding the responsiveness of the quantity demanded of a good to changes in each of its underlying determinants.

5.2 INDIVIDUAL DEMAND FUNCTIONS

In Chapter 4 we demonstrated how both the primal and dual approaches can be used to solve constrained consumer choice problems. Although both approaches provide valuable information, it is the primal approach that is generally our main focus in consumer theory. Specifically, recall that for the two-good case, the goal of the rational consumer in the primal problem is to determine the consumption levels of goods X and Y that correspond to a maximum value of utility for the objective function $U = U(X,Y)$, subject to the budget constraint $P_X X + P_Y Y = I$. For the numerical examples we solved in Chapter 4, the values of the prices of the two goods, P_X and P_Y, and money income, I, were set at the predetermined values $\overline{P}_{X,1}$, $\overline{P}_{Y,1}$, and $\overline{I}_1$, respectively. By solving the constrained utility maximization problems, we obtained specific optimal consumption values for the two goods, X and Y. However, should the values of any of these predetermined factors change, we expect the solutions to those problems to yield different optimal consumption levels for goods X and Y.

Using general notation, we can express the derived equations for the optimal consumption values of X and Y as

$$X = X(P_X, P_Y, I)$$

and

$$Y = Y(P_Y, P_X, I),$$

where the solution values for X and Y depend on the nature of the consumer's utility function and on the specific values of the determinants in the demand functions, P_X, P_Y, and I. We can also apply this process to a constrained utility maximization problem that is extended to the multi-good case, where the utility function to be maximized is

$$U = U(X, Y, W, \ldots, Z),$$

and the corresponding budget constraint is

$$\overline{P}_{X,1} X + \overline{P}_{Y,1} Y + \overline{P}_{W,1} W + \ldots + \overline{P}_{Z,1} Z = \overline{I}_1.$$

The terms, $\overline{P}_{X,1}, \overline{P}_{Y,1}, \overline{P}_{W,1}, \ldots, \overline{P}_{Z,1}$, represent the predetermined prices for the goods $X, Y, W, \ldots, Z$, respectively, and $\overline{I}_1$ represents the predetermined level of consumer income. By solving the constrained utility maximization problem, we derive a set of equations for the optimal consumption levels of the goods as

$$X = X(P_X, P_Y, P_W, \ldots, P_Z, I)$$
$$Y = Y(P_X, P_Y, P_W, \ldots, P_Z, I)$$
$$W = W(P_X, P_Y, P_W, \ldots, P_Z, I)$$
$$\vdots \qquad \vdots$$
$$Z = Z(P_X, P_Y, P_W, \ldots, P_Z, I).$$

What exactly have we derived? Each of the functions shown above for the multi-good case, as well as each of the functions presented earlier for the two good cases, represents an individual's **demand function**, defined as a *function that expresses the optimal consumption level of a good, usually called the quantity demanded of a good, in terms of the prices of all the goods and money income in the constrained utility maxi-*

mization problem. For the sake of clarity, we will conduct the following analysis for the two-good case described earlier. In the remainder of this chapter, we will focus on how changes in the determinants in a demand function affect the solution values for X and Y, generated by the constrained utility maximization process. By doing so, we can establish various relationships between the optimal quantity of a good a consumer chooses and each of these underlying determinants, *ceteris paribus.* Our analysis will focus only on the optimal amounts of good X, or the quantity demanded of good X, with the understanding that we can conduct a similar analysis for the optimal amounts of good Y.

5.3   INDIVIDUAL ENGEL CURVES

The first relationship we will examine is between the optimal quantities of good X chosen by the consumer and different levels of her money income, I. Assume that money income increases from $\bar{I}_1$ to $\bar{I}_2$, and then again to $\bar{I}_3$, while holding the prices of goods X and Y constant. Recall that in Chapter 4 we showed that increases in money income cause the consumer's budget constraint to shift out to the right, allowing the consumer to purchase greater combinations of the two goods X and Y. However, although the consumer is spending more income, the net impact on her choices regarding either good depends on the nature of that good, a point we will discuss in detail later in this section. The shifts in the budget constraint are demonstrated in Figure 5.1, where the values of both the X- and Y-intercepts increase by equal amounts. Also, note that the slopes of the budget constraints have the same value, $-\bar{P}_{X,1}/\bar{P}_{Y,1}$, indicating that we have held the prices of the two goods constant in this analysis.

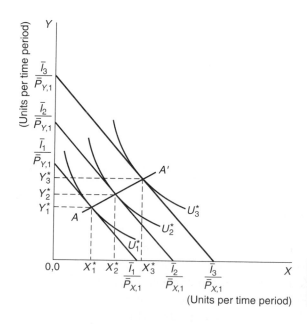

FIGURE 5.1 Income Consumption Curve, with Good X as Normal

We can solve the consumer's constrained utility maximization problem for each level of money income, I, generating different optimal combinations, (X^*, Y^*), for the two goods. By doing so, the necessary condition for a constrained utility maximum, $MRS = \overline{P}_{X,1}/\overline{P}_{Y,1}$, is satisfied at each of these combinations of goods. These results appear in Figure 5.1, where at each optimal (X, Y) combination three indifference curves are constructed tangent to each of three budget constraints representing the different income levels, $\overline{I}_1$, $\overline{I}_2$, and $\overline{I}_3$. Higher levels of money income enable the consumer to purchase and consume more expensive combinations of the two goods. Therefore, we expect that these higher levels of income correspond to optimal combinations of goods lying on indifference curves representing higher levels of utility. Accordingly, the income levels $\overline{I}_1$, $\overline{I}_2$, and $\overline{I}_3$ generate constrained utility maximization solutions for goods X and Y of (X_1^*, Y_1^*), (X_2^*, Y_2^*), and (X_3^*, Y_3^*), respectively, which directly correspond to utility levels U_1^*, U_2^*, and U_3^*, where $U_3^* > U_2^* > U_1^*$. We can also establish a relationship between the optimal consumption levels of goods X and Y and the levels of money income. This relationship is represented by the curve AA', passing through each of the optimal (X, Y) combinations shown in Figure 5.1. We define this curve, known as an **income consumption curve**, as *a set of combinations of goods corresponding to constrained utility maximum solutions for different levels of money income, while holding the prices of the goods constant*. More concisely, it is a set of optimal combinations of goods corresponding to different levels of money income.

Using the information conveyed by the income consumption curve, we can focus on the relationship between the optimal consumption levels of one of the goods, say X, and money income. In reality, we have already demonstrated this relationship by the income consumption curve. However, we have presented the income variable, I, corresponding to this curve in a rather inconvenient location. Specifically, it is located in the numerators of the X- and Y-intercepts. We can create a clearer presentation of this relationship by generating another graph that measures the optimal consumption levels of good X on the vertical axis and money income on the horizontal axis. This relationship is known as an **Engel curve** and is defined as *a function that expresses the optimal consumption levels of a good for different levels of income, while holding the prices of all goods constant*. Mathematically, we can express the Engel curve for good X as

$$X = X(\overline{P}_{X,1}, \overline{P}_{Y,1}, I),$$

where I denotes the consumer's money income, and $\overline{P}_{X,1}$ and $\overline{P}_{Y,1}$ represent the prices of the two goods held constant at some specified levels. We derive the Engel curve for good X, illustrated in Figure 5.2, from the income consumption curve shown in Figure 5.1.

In both of these figures, observe that as income increases from I_1 to I_2 to I_3, the individual's consumption level of good X correspondingly increases from X_1^* to X_2^* to X_3^*, respectively. This direct relationship between optimal consumption levels of good X and levels of money income, I, is reflected by the positive slope of the Engel curve shown in Figure 5.2. The case we have illustrated in this figure pertains to a **normal**

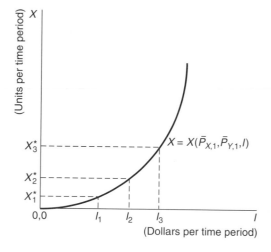

FIGURE 5.2 Engel Curve for Good X, with Good X as a Luxury

good, defined as *a good for which the optimal consumption level varies directly with money income.* The slope of the Engel curve associated with a normal good may increase as income increases, as shown in Figure 5.2, but in some instances it may decrease with increases in *I*, as demonstrated in Figure 5.3. Logically, these results have something to do with the nature of the good.

Normal goods can be subdivided into two categories: luxuries and necessities. For a normal good that is a luxury, such as fine jewelry, increases in the consumer's income cause her optimal consumption level of the good to increase by increasing amounts. Thus, for a normal good that is a luxury the slope of the Engel curve, dX/dI, increases as income increases. However, for a normal good that is deemed a necessity, such as socks, increases in the consumer's income cause her optimal consumption level of the good to increase but by decreasing amounts. In this case, the slope of the Engel curve, dX/dI, is still positive, but it decreases as income increases. Intuitively, we expect that the percentage of a consumer's income spent on a luxury good increases as income

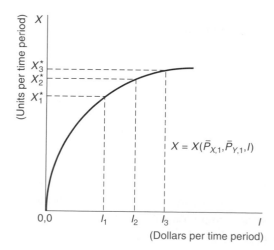

FIGURE 5.3 Engel Curve for Good X, with Good X as a Necessity

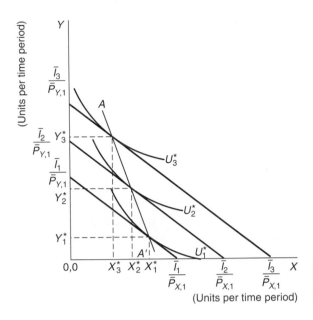

FIGURE 5.4 Income Consumption Curve, with Good X as Inferior

increases. However, for a necessity, such as socks, we expect that the percentage of a consumer's income spent on this type of good decreases as her income increases. In the case of a necessity, it is common sense to believe that a consumer will not buy many more pairs of socks simply because her income increases. We will examine this topic in greater detail in the next chapter using a concept known as income elasticity.

We define a second broad type of good as an **inferior good**, or *a good for which the optimal consumption level varies inversely with income*. This is a good that the consumer perceives to be of lower quality, such as canned spaghetti and used clothing. When the consumer's income rises, she tends to substitute better quality products such as steak or new clothing, respectively, in these cases, in place of the inferior goods. An income consumption curve for a case in which one of the goods, X, is inferior while the other good, Y, is normal is shown in Figure 5.4. Once again, as the consumer's money income increases from $\bar{I}_1$ to $\bar{I}_2$, to $\bar{I}_3$, her budget constraint shifts out to the right in a parallel fashion. However, in this case, because of the increases in income, the individual chooses to consume smaller amounts of the inferior good, X, and greater amounts of the normal good, Y. Figure 5.4 shows that the optimal (X,Y) combinations corresponding to income levels of $\bar{I}_1, \bar{I}_2$, and $\bar{I}_3$, are (X_1^*,Y_1^*), (X_2^*,Y_2^*), and (X_3^*,Y_3^*), respectively, where $X_3^* < X_2^* < X_1^*$, and $Y_3^* > Y_2^* > Y_1^*$. These decreases in the optimal consumption levels of good X corresponding to increases in money income yield an income consumption curve, designated AA' in Figure 5.4, that is negatively sloped. We can also use this information to derive an Engel curve for the inferior good, X, as illustrated in Figure 5.5. This figure demonstrates that for the case of an inferior good, the Engel curve has a negative slope, again indicating that higher levels of money income result in lower optimal consumption levels of the good.

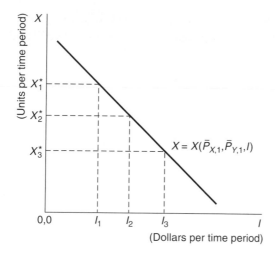

FIGURE 5.5 Engel Curve for Good X, with Good X as Inferior

The mathematical derivation of an Engel curve is a simple process once we understand the constrained utility maximization procedure. Recall Numerical Example 1, discussed in Chapter 4. In that example we specified the utility function as $U = X^{.5}Y^{.5}$ and the consumer's budget constraint as $\overline{P}_{X,1}X + \overline{P}_{Y,1}Y = \overline{I}_1$, where $\overline{P}_{X,1} = \$4$, $\overline{P}_{X,1} = \$1$, and $\overline{I}_1 = \$800$. Our solutions to that constrained utility maximization problem yielded optimal consumption levels for goods X and Y as

$$X_1^* = \frac{\overline{I}_1}{2\overline{P}_{X,1}} = \frac{800}{2(4)} = 100 \text{ units,}$$

and

$$Y_1^* = \frac{\overline{I}_1}{2\overline{P}_{Y,1}} = \frac{800}{2(1)} = 400 \text{ units}$$

Since the Engel curve expresses the optimal consumption level of a good in terms of money income, we can generate such a curve for each of the goods by treating income as variable while holding the prices of the goods constant. Thus, the Engel curves for goods X and Y are, respectively,

$$X = \frac{I}{2\overline{P}_{X,1}} = \frac{I}{2(4)} = \frac{1}{8}I$$

and

$$Y = \frac{I}{2\overline{P}_{Y,1}} = \frac{I}{2(1)} = \frac{1}{2}I.$$

In this case, the Engel curve for each good has a positive slope, indicating that both X and Y are normal goods. Specifically, the slope of the Engel curve for good X is $\partial X/\partial I = 1/8$, indicating that for a one dollar change in money income, the optimal consumption level of good X changes by 1/8 unit in the same direction. Similarly, the slope of the Engel curve for good Y is $\partial Y/\partial I = 1/2$, indicating that a one dollar change in money income causes the optimal consumption level of good Y to change by 1/2 unit in the same direction.

5.4 INDIVIDUAL OWN-PRICE DEMAND CURVES

The consumer's constrained utility maximization procedure provides us with the basis for defining yet another relationship between the optimal consumption level of a good and another one of the factors underlying the process. Specifically, we can develop a relationship between the optimal consumption level, or quantity demanded, of a good and its own price, while holding the prices of other goods and money income constant. First we will develop this relationship graphically. Assume that the price of good X increases from $\overline{P}_{X,1}$ to $\overline{P}_{X,2}$ to $\overline{P}_{X,3}$, while holding money income, I, and the price of good Y, P_Y, constant. In Chapter 4 we showed that increases in the price of good X, *ceteris paribus*, cause the consumer's budget constraint to rotate clockwise, decreasing the X-intercept values. These results are illustrated in panel (A) of Figure 5.6 where the X-intercept values of the budget constraints decrease from $\overline{I}_1/\overline{P}_{X,1}$ to $\overline{I}_1/\overline{P}_{X,2}$ to $\overline{I}_1/\overline{P}_{X,3}$, as the price of good X successively increases from $\overline{P}_{X,1}$ to $\overline{P}_{X,2}$ to $\overline{P}_{X,3}$. These results indicate that if the consumer spends all of his income on good X, then clearly he must purchase fewer units of this good as its price increases.

Note that the intercept value for good Y, $\overline{I}_1/\overline{P}_{Y,1}$, remains unaffected, since neither the value of I nor the value of P_Y has changed. This result is logical since this value represents the maximum amount of good Y the consumer can purchase if he spends all of his income on good Y. Finally, the slope of the budget constraint, $-P_X/P_Y$, becomes steeper, or higher in absolute value terms, increasing from $|-\overline{P}_{X,1}/\overline{P}_{Y,1}|$ to $|-\overline{P}_{X,2}/\overline{P}_{Y,1}|$ to $|-\overline{P}_{X,3}/\overline{P}_{Y,1}|$, indicating that the rate at which the consumer is able to purchase more units of good Y due to purchasing fewer units of good X increases as P_X increases. Generally, an increase in P_X worsens the consumer's position because for any amount of income spent on good X, fewer units of that good can now be purchased. The only exception to this result occurs when the consumer has already chosen an optimal combination of goods that lies on the Y-intercept, where he is purchasing no units of good X.

Returning to the more general case illustrated in panel (A) of Figure 5.6, assume that the consumer has solved the constrained utility maximization problem by choosing the optimal combination of goods, X_1^* and Y_1^*, where both are positive values. This result is based on the specified levels for income, $\overline{I}_1$, and prices, $\overline{P}_{X,1}$ and $\overline{P}_{Y,1}$, and it corresponds to a maximum attainable utility level of U_1^*. The optimal combination of goods X and Y occurs where the indifference curve for U_1^* is tangent to the budget constraint $\overline{P}_{X,1}X + \overline{P}_{Y,1}Y = \overline{I}_1$. At this combination of goods, the necessary condition for a constrained utility maximum, $MRS = \overline{P}_{X,1}/\overline{P}_{Y,1}$, is satisfied. As the price of good X increases from $\overline{P}_{X,1}$ to $\overline{P}_{X,2}$ to $\overline{P}_{X,3}$, the budget constraint rotates clockwise yielding new optimal solution values for goods X and Y of (X_2^*, Y_2^*) and (X_3^*, Y_3^*), corresponding to the successively lower levels of utility U_2^* and U_3^*, respectively. The curve con-

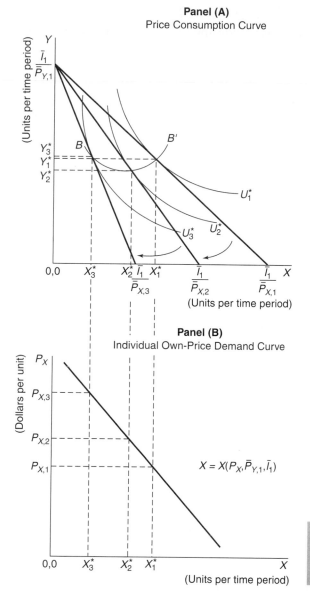

Panel (A)
Price Consumption Curve

Panel (B)
Individual Own-Price Demand Curve

FIGURE 5.6 Derivation of Own-Price Demand Curve for Good X from Price Consumption Curve

necting these optimal (X,Y) combinations, known as a **price consumption curve**, is *a set of combinations of two goods corresponding to constrained utility maximization solutions for different prices for one good, while holding the price of the other good and money income constant.* More concisely, it is a set of optimal combinations of goods corresponding to different levels of prices for one of the goods. The price consumption curve, labeled BB' in panel (A) of Figure 5.6, indicates the optimal consumption levels of good X, where $X_1^* > X_2^* > X_3^*$, for price levels of $\overline{P}_{X,1} < \overline{P}_{X,2} < \overline{P}_{X,3}$, respectively. The implications for good Y in this case are somewhat less consistent as $Y_1^* > Y_2^*$, but

$Y_3^* > Y_2^*$, corresponding to $\overline{P}_{X,1}, \overline{P}_{X,2}$, and $\overline{P}_{X,3}$, respectively. Ultimately, the effect on purchases of good Y depends on how the total expenditure on good X, $P_X X$, changes as P_X changes. This, in turn, depends on the magnitude of the response of the change in the quantity demanded of good X due to the change in its own price, P_X. We will conduct this analysis more formally in Chapter 7 after we establish the concept of an elasticity.

Our main focus at this point is on how the optimal consumption level of good X changes due to a change in its own price, P_X. We have already demonstrated this relationship with the price consumption curve. However, in that analysis P_X was presented in an inconvenient location, specifically, in the denominator of the X-intercept, I/P_X. We can observe the relationship between X and P_X more clearly by generating another graph, where X and P_X are plotted on the horizontal and vertical axes, respectively. The resulting curve should be familiar from your principles of microeconomics course. It is known as the **individual's own-price demand curve**, defined as *a curve that expresses the optimal consumption level, or quantity demanded, of a good in terms of its own price, while holding other prices and money income constant.*

We express this curve mathematically as

$$X = X(P_X, \overline{P}_{Y,1}, \overline{I}_1),$$

where the price of good Y and money income are held constant at some specified levels. The graphical derivation of this curve is shown in Figure 5.6 where we can observe the linkage between the price consumption curve in panel (A) and the own-price demand curve in panel (B) by their common horizontal axes representing good X. The own-price demand curve has a negative slope reflecting the fact that higher P_X values correspond to lower optimal consumption levels, or quantities demanded, of good X. Generally, this inverse relationship between the quantity demanded of a good and its own price follows the well-known law of demand. However, there is a notable exception, known as Giffen's Paradox, that we will discuss in Section 5.4.1. There is another point that we should note for the purpose of technical clarification. The dependent variable in an own-price demand curve is the quantity demanded of the good, X in this case, while its own price, P_X, is represented as one of the independent variables. This being the case, we ordinarily expect to plot the dependent variable, X, on the vertical axis and the independent variable, P_X, on the horizontal. However, it is convention in economic analysis to plot these variables as shown in panel (B) of Figure 5.6, with P_X and X plotted on the vertical and horizontal axes, respectively. This representation is known as an inverse own-price demand curve, and we can express it mathematically as

$$P_X = X^{-1}(X, \overline{P}_{Y,1}, \overline{I}_1).[1]$$

We should keep this point in mind when interpreting slopes and intercepts of both own-price demand and inverse own-price demand curves.

---

[1] For example, given the linear demand curve for good X, $X = X(P_X) = b_0 - b_1 P_X$, the corresponding inverse demand function is $P_X = X^{-1}(X) = b_0/b_1 - 1/b_1 X$.

As with the Engel curve, the derivation of an own-price demand curve is simply an extension of the constrained utility maximization procedure. Returning to our specific utility function, $U = X^{1/2} Y^{1/2}$, we can demonstrate this procedure mathematically. In Chapter 4 we used the primal approach to maximize this utility function subject to the budget constraint, $\overline{P}_{X,1} X + \overline{P}_{Y,1} Y = \overline{I}_1$, given $\overline{I}_1 = \$800$, $\overline{P}_{X,1} = \$4$, and $\overline{P}_{Y,1} = \$1$. We computed the optimal consumption levels for goods X and Y as

$$X_1^* = \frac{\overline{I}_1}{2\overline{P}_{X,1}} = \frac{800}{2(4)} = 100 \text{ units}$$

and

$$Y_1^* = \frac{\overline{I}_1}{2\overline{P}_{Y,1}} = \frac{800}{2(1)} = 400 \text{ units}$$

If the price of good X increases to $\overline{P}_{X,2} = \$8$, then

$$X_2^* = \frac{\overline{I}_1}{2\overline{P}_{Y,2}} = \frac{800}{2(8)} = 50 \text{ units,}$$

indicating that the increase in P_X causes a decrease in the optimal consumption level, or quantity demanded, of good X. By allowing the price of good X to vary, we can generate an infinite number of X and P_X combinations from this equation. Therefore, the own-price demand curve is

$$X = \frac{\overline{I}_1}{2P_X} = \frac{800}{2P_X} = \frac{400}{P_X} = 400 P_X^{-1},$$

where income is held constant at $\overline{I}_1 = 800$. Implicitly, we have also held the price of good Y constant at $\overline{P}_{Y,1} = \$1$, although this term has been mathematically canceled out of the formula in this simple case. Finally, note that the relationship between the quantity demanded of good X and its own price, P_X, is inverse since, in this case, P_X appears in the denominator of the function. Similarly, we can derive the own-price demand curve for good Y as

$$Y = \frac{\overline{I}_1}{2P_Y} = \frac{800}{2P_Y} = \frac{400}{P_Y} = 400 P_Y^{-1},$$

where in this case the demand for good Y is a function of its own price, P_Y, income, which is held constant at $\overline{I}_1 = \$800$, and implicitly the price of good X, which has been held constant at $\overline{P}_{X,1} = \$4$.

5.4.1   Substitution and Income Effects

Returning our focus to good X, we can use the own-price demand curve to determine the total effect that a change in the price of good X has on the quantity demanded of that good. In panel (B) of Figure 5.6 we demonstrated that when the price of good X increases from $\overline{P}_{X,1}$ to $\overline{P}_{X,2}$ to $\overline{P}_{X,3}$, the optimal consumption level, or quantity demanded, of good X falls from X_1^* to X_2^* to X_3^*, respectively. Although this result must seem obvious, it is more complicated than it initially appears. More broadly, it raises the following question: What are the underlying reasons for a response, if any, in the quantity demanded of a good due to a change in its own price?

Economists have defined two underlying reasons for this response. The first is the **substitution effect**, defined as *the impact that a change in the price of a good has on the quantity demanded of that good, which is due to the resulting change in relative prices while holding utility constant*. The relative prices of two goods are measured as the ratio of their prices, in this case, P_X/P_Y. This ratio changes if either of the two prices changes. The substitution effect reflects the tendency for a rational consumer to substitute away from the good that becomes increasingly expensive relative to the other and toward the good that becomes increasingly cheaper in a relative sense. Thus, if the price of good X increases, say from $\overline{P}_{X,1}$ to $\overline{P}_{X,2}$, while holding the price of good Y constant at $\overline{P}_{Y,1}$, the relative price increases from $\overline{P}_{X,1}/\overline{P}_{Y,1}$ to $\overline{P}_{X,2}/\overline{P}_{Y,1}$, and the consumer substitutes away from good X toward good Y. For example, consider a situation where the consumer chooses to spend his limited income on either pizza or hamburgers, where the price of a piece of pizza is $1.50 and the price of a hamburger is $2.50. If the price of a slice of pizza rises to $2.00, then the price of a slice of pizza relative to the price of a hamburger increases from $1.50/$2.50 to $2.00/$2.50. This increase in relative prices causes the consumer to substitute away from pizza and toward more hamburgers.

The second underlying reason for a change in the quantity demanded of a good due to a change in its own price is the **income effect**, defined as *the impact that a change in the price of a good has on the quantity demanded of that good due strictly to the resulting change in real income, or purchasing power*. If the price of a good changes, holding money income and the price of the other good constant, then the number of units of that good the consumer is able to purchase will be affected. For example, if the price of good X rises, the consumer's real income, or purchasing power, decreases, thus affecting the amount of good X demanded.

The directionality of this income effect, however, depends on the nature of the good. Recall from Section 5.3 that we classified goods as either normal or inferior. In the case of a normal good, a change in a consumer's income has a direct impact on his optimal consumption level, or quantity demanded, of the good. In the current context, the change is in real income caused by a price change rather than a change in money income, yet the impact is similar. Specifically, if the price of a good increases, causing a reduction in the consumer's real income, the income effect causes him to demand fewer units of the good, provided the good is normal. Conversely, if the price of a good decreases, the consumer's real income rises, and provided the good is normal, he demands more units of the good.

An inferior good, on the other hand, is one for which a change in income yields an inverse effect on the quantity demanded of that good. Therefore, an increase in the price of an inferior good, which subsequently results in a decrease in the consumer's real income, causes him to demand more units of that good. Conversely, a decrease in its price causes his real income to rise, and provided the good is inferior, the consumer demands fewer units of the good. We should emphasize that these results pertain strictly to the income effect that is independent of the substitution effect discussed earlier. We compute the total effect of a change in the price of a good on the quantity demanded of that good as the summation of the substitution and income effects, or

$$\text{total effect} = \text{substitution effect} + \text{income effect}.$$

We can graphically demonstrate the substitution, income, and total effects of a price change for the case of an increase in the price of good X, say from $\overline{P}_{X,1}$ to $\overline{P}_{X,2}$. Note that once again, we are holding money income, I, and the price of the other good, P_Y, constant. Initially, the consumer's budget constraint is $\overline{P}_{X,1}X + \overline{P}_{Y,1}Y = \overline{I}_1$, as shown in panel (A) of Figure 5.7, yielding an X-intercept value of $\overline{I}_1/\overline{P}_{X,1}$ and a slope value of $-\overline{P}_{X,1}/\overline{P}_{Y,1}$.

The optimal consumption levels for goods X and Y are X_1^* and Y_1^*, respectively, corresponding to a constrained utility maximum of U_1^*. This optimal combination of goods occurs where the indifference curve representing U_1^* is tangent to the initial budget constraint, $\overline{P}_{X,1}X + \overline{P}_{Y,1}Y = \overline{I}_1$. As we described earlier, an increase in the price of good X from $\overline{P}_{X,1}$ to $\overline{P}_{X,2}$ causes the consumer's budget constraint to rotate clockwise, reducing the X-intercept value to $\overline{I}_1/\overline{P}_{X,2}$ and increasing the slope, in absolute value terms, to $\overline{P}_{X,2}/\overline{P}_{Y,1}$.

Our goal in this analysis is to separately demonstrate the substitution and income effects resulting from this increase in P_X, where the summation of these two effects equals the total effect on X. Recall that the substitution effect is the impact of a change in the price of a good on the optimal consumption level of that good, due strictly to the resulting change in the relative prices of the goods. In this case, good X has become relatively more expensive as compared to good Y. We can isolate the substitution effect associated with this price increase and show it graphically by applying a tool known as a compensated, or fictitious, budget constraint. This constraint is shown in panel (A) of Figure 5.7 as the dotted line CC'. For us to demonstrate only the substitution effect, we must construct this compensated budget constraint so that it embodies two essential properties. First, it must be parallel to the new actual budget constraint, which in this case is $\overline{P}_{X,2}X + \overline{P}_{Y,1}Y = \overline{I}_1$. Since parallel lines possess common slopes, the slope for both the compensated budget constraint and the new actual budget constraint is $-\overline{P}_{X,2}/\overline{P}_{Y,1}$, reflecting the higher set of relative prices resulting from the increase in P_X.

The second property associated with the compensated budget constraint is that it must be tangent to the original indifference curve, in this case, representing utility level, U_1^*. This indicates that we have theoretically adjusted the consumer's real income, which has been affected by the price change, to keep his utility constant at its original level. By constructing the compensated constraint in this way. we have eliminated any income effect from the analysis; therefore, any change in the optimal consumption level of good X only reflects the substitution effect. In this case, because the increase in P_X causes real income to fall, the consumer is theoretically being compensated for this loss in his real income. The combination of goods X and Y corresponding

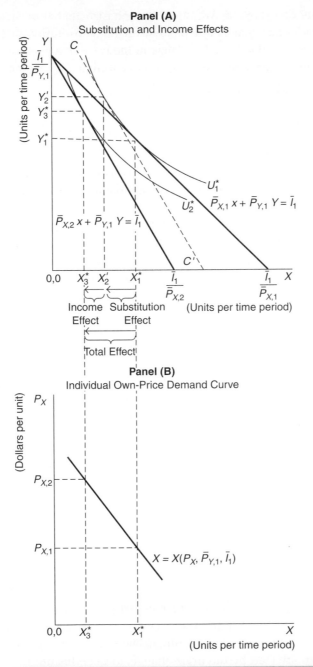

Panel (A)
Substitution and Income Effects

Panel (B)
Individual Own-Price Demand Curve

FIGURE 5.7 Substitution and Income Effects for an Increase in the Price of Good X, with Good X as Normal, and Associated Individual Own-Price Demand Curve

to the point of tangency between the compensated budget constraint and the original indifference curve is (X_2', Y_2'), where $X_2' < X_1^*$ and $Y_2' > Y_1^*$. To emphasize the impact on the consumption level of a good resulting from a change in its own price, we will continue to use the "*" notation to denote the optimal consumption levels, and we will use the "'" notation to represent adjusted consumption levels resulting only from the substitution effect. Since through this procedure we have eliminated the income effect, the decrease in the consumption of good X, or $(X_2' - X_1^*) < 0$, represents the consumer's substitution away from good X caused by the increase in its own price, P_X. This substitution is toward good Y, where you can observe in panel (A) of Figure 5.7 that the individual's consumption level of good Y increases by the amount $(Y_2' - Y_1^*) > 0$.

An example of isolating the substitution effect associated with a price change was a tax and rebate plan proposed by the U.S. Congress in the early 1990s to reduce consumption of gasoline. Although never passed into law, it was proposed that the federal tax on gasoline be increased by 7.5 cents per gallon. At the same time, the government would offer consumers a cash rebate, generated from the revenue collected from the higher gasoline tax. By doing so, the government would cushion the impact of the tax on low-income consumers by effectively removing the income effect associated with the increase in the price of gasoline. However, the remaining substitution effect caused by the higher, after-tax, price of gasoline would have resulted in a decrease in the quantity demanded of this good, which was the intent of the plan.

Now that we have isolated the substitution effect, we can reintroduce the income effect into the analysis and establish the total effect we described earlier. Recall that the income effect measures the impact that a change in the price of a good has on the optimal consumption level, or quantity demanded, of a good due strictly to the resulting change in the consumer's real income. In this case, the increase in P_X causes the consumer's real income to fall. However, the directionality of this result on the optimal consumption level of good X depends on whether the consumer considers this good as normal or inferior. If a good is normal, the optimal consumption level of that good varies directly with the consumer's income. Therefore, in this case, the decrease in real income brought about by the increase in P_X causes the individual's optimal consumption level of good X to decrease.

This result is illustrated in panel (A) of Figure 5.7 by the further decrease in consumption of good X from X_2' to X_3^*, or $(X_3^* - X_2') < 0$. The new optimal combination of goods, (X_3^*, Y_3^*), occurs at the point of tangency between the lower indifference curve representing U_2^*, where $U_2^* < U_1^*$, and the new actual budget constraint, $\overline{P}_{X,2}X + \overline{P}_{Y,1}Y = \overline{I}_1$. The decrease in the optimal consumption level of good X, $(X_3^* - X_1^*)$, is the total effect on the consumption of good X due to the increase in its price. Since $(X_2' - X_1^*)$ represents the substitution effect, the remainder of the impact on X, $(X_3^* - X_2')$, indicates the income effect. Note that in the case of a normal good, the income effect reinforces the substitution effect, meaning that they both operate in the same direction. In this case, an increase in P_X causes a decrease in the optimal consumption level of good X due to both the substitution and income effects. As a result, the associated total effect is a large reduction in the quantity demanded of good X. This result is also demonstrated in panel (B) of Figure 5.7 where the individual's own-price demand curve for this case has been derived.

Alternatively, we can assume that good X is inferior rather than normal, and as a result, the individual's optimal consumption level of the good varies inversely with her real income. We have illustrated this situation in panel (A) of Figure 5.8 for, once again, an increase in P_X.

The substitution effect is identical to the previous case and is shown as, $(X_2' - X_1^*) < 0$, demonstrating the decrease in the quantity demanded of good X due to the increase in relative goods prices, P_X/P_Y. Again, the increase in P_X results in a decrease in real income, but in this case of an inferior good, the result causes the consumer to increase her consumption of good X. This increase is due strictly to the income effect, and it runs counter to the substitution effect, which causes the consumer to decrease her consumption level of the good. Therefore, when summed together, these two effects offset each other, at least in part, and the total effect is measured as the net difference between the substitution and income effects.

In the case of a normal good, the substitution and income effects reinforce each other, since they operate in the same direction. As a result, the total effect of an increase in P_X is unambiguously a decrease in the optimal consumption level of good X. However, for the inferior good case, the directionality of the total effect depends on the relative magnitudes of the counteracting substitution and income effects. Therefore, we cannot determine the directionality of the total effect for an inferior good on the basis of pure economic theory. Instead, we must rely on statistical tests of consumer behavior to estimate the magnitudes of the substitution and income effects. Available statistical evidence suggests that, for virtually all inferior goods, the substitution effect dominates the income effect. As a result, the total effect on the optimal consumption level of such a good is inversely related to its price.

Referring again to panel (A) of Figure 5.8, the income effect is $(X_4^* - X_2') > 0$, which partially offsets the substitution effect of $(X_2' - X_1^*) < 0$, yielding a total effect of $(X_4^* - X_1^*) < 0$. Thus, in this case, the total effect of an increase in P_X still reflects a decrease in the optimal consumption level of the good, as illustrated by the corresponding individual own-price demand curve shown in panel (B) of Figure 5.8. We can compare this result to that which we obtained earlier for the normal good, shown in panels (A) and (B) of Figure 5.7. As we might expect, the total effect for the inferior good, $(X_4^* - X_1^*)$, is smaller, in absolute value terms, than that for the normal good, $(X_3^* - X_1^*)$, due to the partially offsetting, rather than reinforcing, income effect.

There is a notable exception to the statistical evidence that the substitution effect usually dominates the income effect for the case of inferior goods. This is the case of a Giffen good, named after economist Robert Giffen, who became rather famous for his study of the effect of rising potato prices on the quantity demanded of potatoes in Ireland during the 1860s. In general, a **Giffen good** is *an inferior good for which the income effect dominates the substitution effect*. This type of good is extremely rare in the real world, but it does provide an interesting theoretical exercise. We have

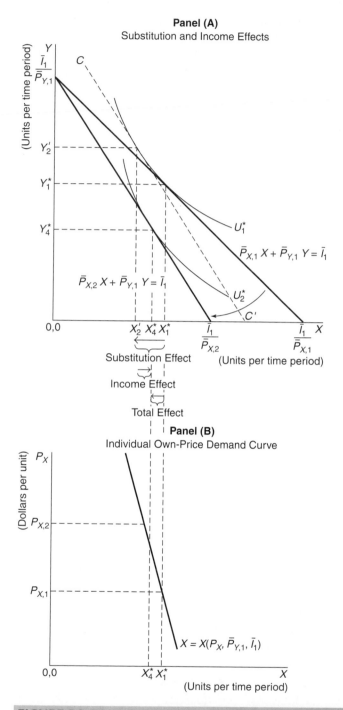

FIGURE 5.8 Substitution and Income Effects for an Increase in the Price of Good X, with Good X as Inferior, But Not Giffen, and Associated Individual Own-Price Demand Curve

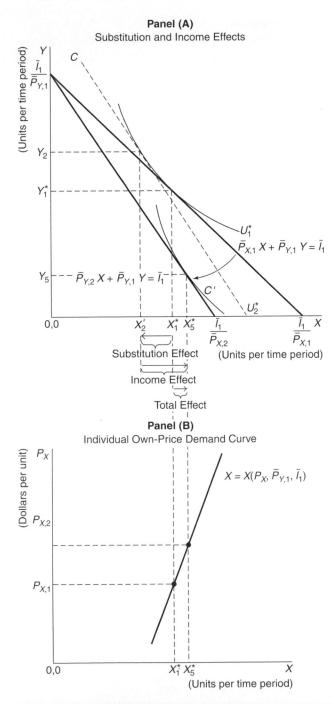

FIGURE 5.9 Substitution and Income Effects for an Increase in the Price of Good X, with Good X as a Giffen Good, and Associated Individual Own-Price Demand Curve

demonstrated the case of a Giffen good in panel (A) of Figure 5.9 for an increase in the price of good X. Observe that the income effect, $(X_5^* - X_2') > 0$, is greater than the substitution effect, $(X_2' - X_1^*) < 0$, and as a result, the total effect is

$$(X_5^* - X_1^*) = [(X_2' - X_1^*) + (X_5^* - X_2')] > 0.$$

This result is very rare since it requires that an increase in P_X causes an increase in the quantity demanded of good X. For such an outcome to occur, the percentage of a consumer's income spent on good X must be very large. Therefore, an increase in P_X results in a very large decrease in real income, causing the consumer to demand lesser amounts of other more highly priced goods. Even after the increase in P_X, he substitutes more of the still relatively cheaper good X for the other goods. As a result, the associated own-price demand curve for this individual is positively sloped, as illustrated in panel (B) of Figure 5.9.

We can use the preceding analysis of substitution and income effects for the cases of normal, inferior but non-Giffen goods, and Giffen goods to provide additional insight into the slopes of the corresponding own-price demand curves. The possible outcomes for the own-price demand curves corresponding to each of these three cases are shown together in Figure 5.10.

In each of the cases, the price of good X is initially $P_{X,1}$ and the corresponding quantity demanded is X_1^*. As P_X increases to $P_{X,2}$, the resulting total effect on the optimal consumption level, or quantity demanded, of good X varies, depending on the type of good. At $P_{X,2}$, if good X is normal, the quantity demanded is X_3^*, indicating a large decrease in the quantity demanded of good X due to the increase in its price. This result produces the comparatively flatter own-price demand curve D_1. If good X is inferior, but not a Giffen good, then at $P_{X,2}$ the quantity demanded of good X is X_4^*, indicating a smaller decrease in X than for the normal good; therefore, the own-price demand curve is steeper than in the preceding case. Finally, if good X is a Giffen good,

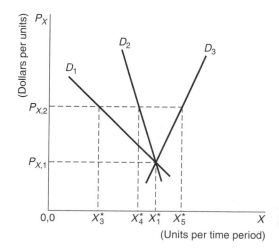

FIGURE 5.10 Own-Price Demand Curves for Good X as Either Normal, D_1, Inferior But not Giffen, D_2, or Giffen, D_3

then at $P_{X,2}$ the quantity demanded is X_5^*, reflecting an increase in the quantity demanded of good X due to an increase in its price. As a result, in the case of a Giffen good, the own-price demand curve actually has a positive slope, a situation that is extremely rare. We have derived price consumption curves and own-price demand curves for the case of an increase in the price of a good. The opposite situation, the case of a decrease in the price of a good, is left to you as an exercise.

†5.4.2 Compensated Demand Functions

We have shown graphically how the total effect of a change in the price of a good on the optimal consumption level of that good can be decomposed into the associated substitution and income effects. We can also demonstrate these substitution and income effects using a mathematical approach. To do so, we will return to the dual constrained optimization problem discussed in Chapter 4. The dual approach treats the consumer's optimization problem as a constrained expenditure minimization problem. So when we use this approach, the goal of the rational consumer is to determine the optimal values for the decision variables, goods X and Y, that correspond to a minimum value for the objective function, $E = \overline{P}_{X,1}X + \overline{P}_{Y,1}Y$, subject to a predetermined level of utility, $\overline{U}_1 = U(X,Y)$. Recall that expenditure, E, is the same value as income, I, spent on the two goods. As a result, we can interpret the budget equation, $\overline{P}_{X,1}X + \overline{P}_{Y,1}Y = I$, as the expenditure equation, $\overline{P}_{X,1}X + \overline{P}_{Y,1}Y = E$. In Section 4.4.2 of Chapter 4, we demonstrated how to use the constrained expenditure minimization procedure to determine the optimal values of the consumption levels of the goods, X^* and Y^*, and the constrained expenditure minimum value, E^*. We solved a constrained minimization problem using the specific utility function, $\overline{U}_1 = X^{1/2} Y^{1/2}$, assuming prices for the goods X and Y of $\overline{P}_{X,1} = \$4$ and $\overline{P}_{Y,1} = \$1$ respectively, and a predetermined level of utility, $\overline{U}_1 = 200$. We obtained the following solutions to this problem as

$$X_1'^* = \left(\frac{\overline{P}_{Y,1}}{\overline{P}_{X,1}}\right)^{1/2} \overline{U}_1 = \left(\frac{1}{4}\right)^{1/2} 200 = \frac{1}{2}(200) = 100 \text{ units}$$

and

$$Y_1'^* = \frac{\overline{P}_{X,1}}{\overline{P}_{Y,1}} X_1'^* = \frac{4}{1}(100) = 400 \text{ units.}$$

The optimal consumption levels for the two goods are denoted as $X_1'^*$ and $Y_1'^*$, so that we can differentiate the manner in which we compute these values from those we determine using the primal, or constrained utility maximization, approach. In this dual problem, the computed optimal values for X and Y are the same as those we computed earlier by solving the primal problem. However, note that this result occurs only because we predetermined the level of expenditure, $\overline{E}_1$, specified for the primal problem, as that value necessary to obtain the level of utility $\overline{U}_1$, predetermined for the dual problem.

Our focus now is on the derived equations for the optimal consumption values of the two goods, X' and Y'. Without specifying any particular values for P_X, P_Y, and U, we can express these equations as

$$X' = \left(\frac{P_Y}{P_X}\right)^{1/2} U,$$

and since, $Y' = \dfrac{P_X}{P_Y}X'$;

$$Y' = \frac{P_X}{P_Y}\left(\frac{P_Y}{P_X}\right)^{1/2} U = \frac{P_X}{P_Y}\left(\frac{P_X}{P_Y}\right)^{-1/2} U = \left(\frac{P_X}{P_Y}\right)^{1/2} U.$$

More generally, for the two goods case, these functions for goods X and Y can be written as

$$X' = X(P_X, P_Y, U)$$

and

$$Y' = Y(P_Y, P_X, U).$$

We refer to each of these equations for X' and Y' as a **compensated demand function**, defined as *a function that expresses the optimal consumption level, or quantity demanded, of a good in terms of its own price, the prices of other goods, and utility*. Note that the optimal consumption levels, X' and Y', for the compensated demand functions are generally not the same as those for the ordinary demand functions we developed in Section 5.2, as

$$X = X(P_X, P_Y, I),$$

and

$$Y = Y(P_X, P_Y, I).$$

The difference arises because the compensated demand functions are derived from the dual, or the constrained expenditure minimization, process, while the ordinary demand functions are derived from the primal, or constrained utility maximization, process. As a result, the compensated demand functions contain utility, U, as one of the independent variables, while the ordinary demand functions contain money income, I. There is one exception, mentioned earlier, for which $X' = X$ and $Y' = Y$. This occurs when the predetermined level of money income for the primal problem is exactly equal to the amount of money necessary to purchase the amounts of goods X and Y that yield the same predetermined level of utility as in the dual problem.

Returning to the compensated demand functions for goods X and Y, we can focus on the relationship between the compensated quantity demanded of a good and its own price, by holding the prices of other goods and utility constant at some specified levels. Thus,

$$X' = X(P_X, \overline{P}_{Y,1}, \overline{U}_1)$$

and

$$Y' = Y(P_Y, \overline{P}_{X,1}, \overline{U}_1).$$

Each of these equations is known as a **compensated demand curve**, defined as *a curve that expresses the optimal consumption level, or quantity demanded, of a good in terms of its own price while holding the prices of other goods and utility constant.* Returning to the specific example, recall that the compensated demand functions for goods X and Y are, respectively,

$$X' = \left(\frac{P_Y}{P_X}\right)^{1/2} U,$$

and

$$Y' = \left(\frac{P_X}{P_Y}\right)^{1/2} U.$$

Thus, if $\overline{P}_{X,1} = \$4, \overline{P}_{Y,1} = \$1$ and $\overline{U}_1 = 200$, as specified earlier in the constrained expenditure minimization problem, we compute the compensated demand curves for goods X and Y as

$$X' = \left(\frac{1}{P_X}\right)^{1/2} 200 = \frac{200}{P_X^{1/2}} = 200 P_X^{-1/2},$$

and

$$Y' = \left(\frac{4}{P_Y}\right)^{1/2} 200 = \frac{400}{P_Y^{1/2}} = 400 P_Y^{-1/2}.$$

†5.4.3 Expenditure Function

We can extend our analysis of compensated demand curves to derive another closely related concept defined as an **expenditure function**, *which expresses a consumer's expenditure in terms of the prices of goods and his level of utility*, or

$$E = E(P_X, P_Y, U).$$

More specifically, for a given set of prices, say $\overline{P}_{X,1}$ and $\overline{P}_{Y,1}$, E represents the level of expenditure necessary to obtain some desired level of utility, U, expressed as

$$E = E(\overline{P}_{X,1}, \overline{P}_{Y,1}, U).$$

Returning to our previous example, the budget equation (also known as the expenditure equation), was $E = P_X X + P_Y Y$, and our constrained expenditure minimization procedure yielded optimal values for goods X and Y as

$$X' = \left(\frac{P_Y}{P_X}\right)^{1/2} U,$$

and

$$Y' = \left(\frac{P_X}{P_Y}\right)^{1/2} U.$$

By substituting these equations for X' and Y' into the expenditure equation, we can obtain the expenditure function as follows:

$$E = P_X X' + P_Y Y'$$

$$E = P_X \left(\frac{P_Y}{P_X}\right)^{1/2} U + P_Y \left(\frac{P_X}{P_Y}\right)^{1/2} U$$

$$E = P_X^{1/2} P_Y^{1/2} U + P_X^{1/2} P_Y^{1/2} U$$

or

$$E = 2P_X^{1/2} P_Y^{1/2} U.$$

If $P_X = \$4$ and $P_Y = \$1$, then we express the consumer's expenditure function as

$$E = 2(4)^{1/2}(1)^{1/2} U = 4U.$$

We can solve this equation for any desired level of utility to obtain the level of expenditure necessary to purchase the quantities of the two goods that correspond to that desired value of U. For example, if the desired level of utility is 200, then

$$E = 4(200) = \$800,$$

and therefore \$800 is the minimum level of expenditure necessary to purchase the optimal quantities of the two goods, $X'^* = 100$ and $Y'^* = 400$, that correspond to the utility level $U = 200$. We determined these optimal values for X' and Y' previously in Chapter 4 by solving the constrained expenditure minimization problem. In the next section we will demonstrate how the expenditure function plays a key role in mathematically analyzing substitution and income effects through an expression known as the Slutsky equation.

†5.4.4 Slutsky Equation

Our broader purpose for developing compensated demand equations and expenditure functions is to provide a framework within which we can mathematically demonstrate the substitution and income effects that were developed conceptually and graphically earlier. Our focus here will be on good X, for which we have demonstrated the compensated demand curve as

$$X' = X(P_X, \overline{P}_{Y,1}, \overline{U}_1).$$

This curve expresses the optimal consumption level of good X in terms of its own price, P_X, while holding the price of the other good, P_Y, and utility, U, constant at predetermined levels. We can provide additional insight by deriving this curve graphically as shown in Figure 5.11.

In panel (A), the original budget equation is $\overline{P}_{X,1} X + \overline{P}_{Y,1} Y = \overline{I}_1$, corresponding to optimal levels of goods X and Y at $(X_1'^*, Y_1'^*)$ and utility level $\overline{U}_1$. If the price of good X increases from $\overline{P}_{X,1}$ to $\overline{P}_{X,2}$ to $\overline{P}_{X,3}$, the budget equation rotates clockwise. We derive the compensated demand curve for good X by holding utility constant at $\overline{U}_1$, thereby theoretically removing the subsequent decreases in real income caused by the

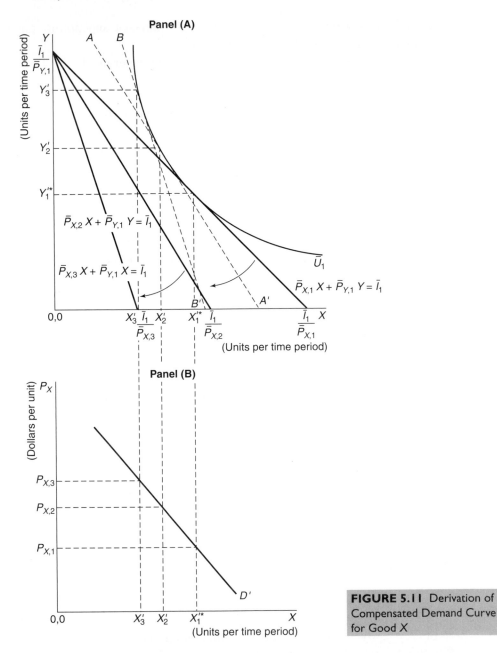

FIGURE 5.11 Derivation of Compensated Demand Curve for Good X

increases in the price of good X. As discussed earlier, this procedure eliminates the income effect, and we can demonstrate this result by constructing the compensated budget constraints AA' and BB', shown in panel (A) of Figure 5.11. We construct these compensated constraints so that they are parallel to the new actual budget equations $\overline{P}_{X,2}X + \overline{P}_{Y,1}Y = \overline{I}_1$ and $\overline{P}_{X,3}X + \overline{P}_{Y,1}Y = \overline{I}_1$, respectively, and tangent to the original indifference curve representing $\overline{U}_1$. The resulting decreases in the consumption level of good X from to $X_1'^*$ to X_2', and from X_2' to X_3' represent the substitution effects we described in Section 5.4.1.

We can also use this analysis to graphically generate the compensated demand curve shown in panel (B) of Figure 5.11. This curve reflects only the substitution effects regarding the quantity demanded of a good due to changes in its own price. Mathematically, we represent these substitution effects by the partial derivative $\partial X'/\partial P_X$, which measures the change in the optimal consumption level of good X due to a change in its own price, while holding P_Y and U constant.[2] This partial derivative, $\partial X'/\partial P_X$, is the slope of the compensated demand curve for good X, or the reciprocal of the slope of the inverse compensated demand curve plotted in panel (B) of Figure 5.11.

We demonstrated earlier that the total effect of a change in the price of a good on the optimal consumption level, or quantity demanded, of that good can be decomposed into the substitution and income effects, where we have just shown that the substitution effect is the slope of the compensated demand curve, $\partial X'/\partial P_X$. Once the income effect has been established, we can demonstrate a mathematical representation of the above relationship. The result of this entire process is known as the **Slutsky equation**, which *represents the mathematical decomposition of the total effect of a change in the price of a good on the quantity demanded of that good, into the summation of the subsequent substitution and income effects.* To derive the Slutsky equation, it is first necessary to establish a starting point at which the quantity demanded of a good pertaining to the ordinary demand curve is equal to the quantity demanded of that good corresponding to its compensated demand curve. In Figure 5.11 this quantity is consumption level $X_1'^*$, where the ordinary quantity demanded, X_1^*, is equal to the compensated quantity demanded, X_1'. This result occurs because at this value of X, the level of expenditure, E, is just sufficient to purchase amounts of goods X and Y that yield the predetermined level of utility, $\overline{U}_1$. Therefore, if P_X changes, while holding P_Y and U constant, the resulting change in X' is the substitution effect and any other change in X must be due to the income effect. The compensated and ordinary demand functions for good X are, respectively,

$$X' = X'(P_X, P_Y, U)$$

and

$$X = X(P_X, P_Y, E).$$

Therefore, if initially $X' = X$, then

$$X'(P_X, P_Y, U) = X(P_X, P_Y, E).$$

---

[2]Technically, the slope of the compensated demand curve, $\partial X'/\partial P_X$, which is also defined as the substitution effect, is an instantaneous slope in that it represents the change in the quantity demanded of good X due to an infinitesimally small change in its own price, P_X. As a result, any values generated by this term will be somewhat different from the finite changes that we have shown graphically in the figures that represent the results of the substitution effects. They are not quite the same, but it has become convention to use one definition to approximate the other. We will also apply this same type of approximation to the partial derivatives used to define the income effect discussed later in this section.

The expenditure function represents the minimum level of expenditure, for a given set of prices, necessary to obtain a desired level of utility. Earlier, we derived this function as

$$E = E(P_X, P_Y, U).$$

Substituting this expenditure function into the ordinary demand function yields

$$X'(P_X, P_Y, U) = X[P_X, P_Y, E(P_X, P_Y, U)]. \tag{5.1}$$

Our objective here is to determine how the compensated quantity demanded, X', and the ordinary quantity demanded of a good, X, respond to changes in its own price, P_X. We can demonstrate these responses by taking the partial derivative of both sides of equation (5.1) with respect to P_X, thus holding P_Y and U constant. By applying the chain rule discussed in Chapter 1, we compute this derivative as

$$\frac{\partial X'}{\partial P_X} = \frac{\partial X}{\partial P_X} + \frac{\partial X}{\partial E}\frac{\partial E}{\partial P_X},$$

or after rearranging terms,

$$\frac{\partial X}{\partial P_X} = \frac{\partial X'}{\partial P_X} - \frac{\partial X}{\partial E}\frac{\partial E}{\partial P_X}. \tag{5.2}$$

We define this result as the Slutsky equation, which contains several recognizable terms. The term on the left-hand side, $\partial X/\partial P_X$, represents the change in the quantity demanded of good X resulting from a change in its own price, while holding other prices and money income constant. We can also identify it as the slope of the ordinary demand curve for good X. The right-hand side contains two components. We recognize the first term, $\partial X'/\partial P_X$, as the substitution effect, which is also the slope of the compensated demand curve. This term is always negative, reflecting the inverse nature of the substitution effect. This result follows from the fact that if P_X increases, thus increasing the relative prices of goods X and Y, P_X/P_Y, the consumer will substitute away from good X and toward good Y, and therefore X' will decrease. By the process of elimination, we can deduce that the remaining term, $(\partial X/\partial E)(\partial E/\partial P_X)$, must represent the income effect. Earlier, in deriving the ordinary demand function, we assumed that the consumer spends all of his money income on goods X and Y, and therefore his expenditure, E, must equal his income, I, in this function. The second component of this term, $\partial E/\partial P_X$, represents the change in expenditure resulting from a change in P_X, while holding all other terms constant. In other words, it measures the change in expenditure necessary to purchase amounts of goods X and Y that maintain a desired utility level, given a change in the price of good X. Note that this change in expenditure is only hypothetical since expenditure is equal to money income, which is being held constant. As a result, the change in the price of good X is manifested through a change in the quantities demanded of goods X and Y, thereby causing a change in utility. Consequently, this term, $\partial E/\partial P_X$, accounts for the change in purchasing power, or real income, resulting from a change in P_X. The first component of the term $\partial X/\partial E$ $\partial E/\partial P_X$, or $\partial X/\partial E$, indicates the consumer's change in the quantity demanded of good

X due to a change in his real income. Thus, the whole term, $\partial X/\partial E \ \partial E/\partial P_X$, indicates the change in the quantity demanded of good X due to the change in his real income, or purchasing power, caused by the change in P_X. This result is the income effect we discussed in Section 5.4.1, which may have a direct or an inverse impact on the consumption level of good X depending on whether the good is normal or inferior.

The Slutsky equation, which we have expressed in equation (5.2), is frequently presented in a slightly modified form. Since the substitution effect, $\partial X'/\partial P_X$, represents the change in the quantity demanded of good X resulting from a change in its own price, while holding utility constant, we can express this term as $\partial X/\partial P_X|_{\overline{U}_1}$, where the vertical slash indicates that we are holding the term on the right-hand side, utility, constant at the level $\overline{U}_1$. In addition, since expenditure, E, is equal to income, I, in the ordinary demand function, we can use these terms interchangeably. Finally, since $E = P_X X + P_Y Y$, then $\partial E/\partial P_X = X$, which simply represents the change in expenditure resulting from a change in P_X, while holding P_Y, X, and Y constant. Based on the above interpretations, we can rewrite the Slutsky equation as

$$\frac{\partial X}{\partial P_X} = \frac{\partial X}{\partial P_X}\Big|_{\overline{U}_1} - \frac{\partial X}{\partial I}X,$$

where the term $\partial X/\partial P_X|_{\overline{U}_1}$ is the substitution effect and the term $(\partial X/\partial I)X$ represents the income effect.

We can demonstrate the results embodied in the Slutsky equation by further analyzing the numerical example we used throughout this chapter. The version of the Slutsky equation presented in equation (5.2) is best suited for this analysis. Focusing on good X, recall that the ordinary demand function for good X is

$$X = \frac{E}{2P_X} = \frac{1}{2}E\,P_X^{-1}.$$

Thus, the total effect of a change in P_X on the quantity demanded of good X is

$$\frac{\partial X}{\partial P_X} = -\frac{1}{2}E\,P_X^{-2} = -\frac{E}{2P_X^2},$$

and if $I = E = \$800$ and $P_X = \$4$, then

$$\frac{\partial X}{\partial P_X} = -\frac{800}{2(4)^2} = -25 \text{ units.}$$

Note that this slope is negative, indicating an inverse relationship between the quantity demanded of good X and its own price, P_X. Technically, this partial derivative represents an instantaneous slope that measures the change in quantity demanded of good X due to an infinitesimally small change in its own price, P_X. However, we often find it useful to consider this result as an approximation of the response in the quantity demanded of good X due to a one-unit change in its own price. When we use this approximation, a slope value of -25 indicates that a one-unit change in P_X results in a 25-unit response in the quantity demanded of good X, in the opposite direction. For example, if P_X increases by \$1, then the consumer will demand 25 fewer units of good X.

We can decompose this total effect, $\partial X/\partial P_X$, by analyzing the Slutsky equation in the form

$$\frac{\partial X}{\partial P_X} = \frac{\partial X'}{\partial P_X} - \frac{\partial X}{\partial E}\frac{\partial E}{\partial P_X}.$$

Earlier, we derived the compensated demand function for this problem as

$$X' = \left(\frac{P_Y}{P_X}\right)^{1/2} U = P_X^{-1/2} P_X^{1/2} U,$$

Therefore, the slope of this compensated demand function, which is also the substitution effect, is, $\partial X'/\partial P_X$, or

$$\frac{\partial X'}{\partial P_X} = -\frac{1}{2}P_X^{-3/2} P_Y^{1/2} U,$$

Recall in Section 5.4.3 we derived the expenditure function for this problem yielding

$$E = 2P_X^{1/2} P_Y^{1/2} U,$$

and therefore we can solve this function for utility, U, as

$$U = \frac{E}{2P_X^{1/2} P_Y^{1/2}}.$$

Substituting this result for U into the equation for the slope of the compensated demand function, $\partial X'/\partial P_X$, yields the substitution effect as

$$\frac{\partial X'}{\partial P_X} = -\frac{1}{2}P_X^{-3/2} P_Y^{1/2}\left(\frac{E}{2P_X^{1/2} P_Y^{1/2}}\right) = -\frac{1}{4}P_X^{-2} E = -\frac{E}{4P_X^2}. \tag{5.3}$$

The remaining term in the Slutsky equation, $\partial X/\partial E \; \partial E/\partial P_X$ is the income effect, which is computed by determining its component partial derivatives, $\partial X/\partial E$ and $\partial E/\partial P_X$. We compute the term $\partial X/\partial E$, directly from the ordinary demand function, $X = E/2P_X$, as

$$\frac{\partial X}{\partial E} = \frac{1}{2}P_X^{-1},$$

and the term $\partial E/\partial P_X$ from the budget or expenditure equation, $E = P_X X + P_Y Y$, as

$$\frac{\partial E}{\partial P_X} = X.$$

The income effect, $\partial X/\partial E \; \partial E/\partial P_X$, is therefore,

$$\frac{\partial X}{\partial E}\frac{\partial E}{\partial P_X} = \frac{1}{2}P_X^{-1} X = \frac{X}{2P_X},$$

or since, $X = E/2P_X$, we can also express it as,

$$\frac{\partial X}{\partial E}\frac{\partial E}{\partial P_X} = \frac{1}{2P_X}\left(\frac{E}{2P_X}\right) = \frac{E}{4P_X^2}. \tag{5.4}$$

Recall that the Slutsky equation expresses the total effect, $\partial X/\partial P_X$, in terms of the substitution and income effects as

$$\frac{\partial X}{\partial P_X} = \frac{\partial X'}{\partial P_X} - \frac{\partial X}{\partial E}\frac{\partial E}{\partial P_X}.$$

Substituting the computed terms from equations (5.3) and (5.4) representing the substitution and income effects, respectively, into the Slutsky equation yields

$$\frac{\partial X}{\partial P_X} = -\left(\frac{E}{4P_X{}^2}\right) - \left(\frac{E}{4P_X{}^2}\right) = -\frac{2E}{4P_X{}^2} = -\frac{E}{2P_X{}^2},$$

which is the same result we obtained earlier by computing $\partial X/\partial P_X$ directly from the ordinary demand function. Since in this problem we assumed that $E = \$800$ and $P_X = \$4$, we calculate the numerical value for $\partial X/\partial P_X$ from the Slutsky equation as

$$\frac{\partial X}{\partial P_X} = -\left(\frac{800}{4(4)^2}\right) - \left(\frac{800}{4(4)^2}\right)$$

$$= -12.5 \text{ units} - 12.5 \text{ units} = -25 \text{ units},$$

which is the same value for $\partial X/\partial P_X$ we obtained earlier. The first term, -12.5 units, represents the value of the substitution effect, and the second term, -12.5 units, is the value of the income effect. Note that, in this case, the substitution and income effects reinforce each other to produce a large inverse relationship between X and P_X, reflecting the fact that good X is normal.

5.5   CROSS-PRICE DEMAND CURVES

We can generate yet another relationship from the ordinary demand function. This relationship is the **cross-price demand curve**, defined as *a function that expresses the quantity demanded of a good in terms of the price of another good, while holding its own price and money income constant*. In the two goods case, we can develop a cross-price demand curve for good X and for good Y. However, the focus of our analysis shall once again be on good X for which the cross-price demand curve is represented as

$$X = X(\overline{P}_{X,1}, P_Y, \overline{I}_1).$$

Note that now we have held the own price of good X, P_X, and money income, I, constant at specified levels; thus, we are focusing on the relationship between the quantity demanded of good X and the price of good Y, P_Y. We will first develop this relationship graphically by returning to the consumer's constrained utility maximization problem demonstrated in panel (A) of Figure 5.12. As with our earlier cases, the initial budget constraint is, $\overline{P}_{X,1}X + \overline{P}_{Y,1}Y = \overline{I}_1$, and the optimal consumption combination of goods X and Y is (X_1^*, Y_1^*), which is the combination corresponding to the point of tangency between this initial budget constraint and the indifference curve representing utility level U_1^*. Therefore, at this goods combination, the necessary condition for a

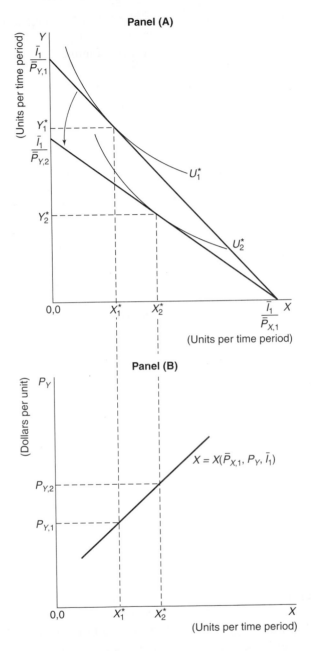

Panel (A)

Panel (B)

FIGURE 5.12 Derivation of Cross-Price Demand Curve for Substitutes

constrained utility maximum is satisfied or, $MRS = P_X/P_Y$. Now suppose the price of good Y increases from $\overline{P}_{Y,1}$ to $\overline{P}_{Y,2}$, while holding the price of good X and money income constant at $\overline{P}_{Y,1}$ and $\overline{I}_1$, respectively. As a result, the budget constraint rotates counterclockwise, the Y-intercept, I/P_Y, decreases in value from $\overline{I}_1/\overline{P}_{Y,1}$ to $\overline{I}_1/\overline{P}_{Y,2}$, and the slope, in absolute value terms, P_X/P_Y, decreases from $\overline{P}_{X,1}/\overline{P}_{Y,1}$ to $\overline{P}_{X,1}/\overline{P}_{Y,2}$.

This change in P_Y affects the optimal consumption levels of both goods X and Y. However, the focus of our analysis is on the impact of such a price change on the quantity demanded of good X, which is affected for two familiar reasons. First, the increase in P_Y causes good X to become relatively less expensive. As a result, the consumer substitutes toward good X and away from good Y, reflecting the substitution effect we described earlier. In addition, the increase in P_Y causes a reduction in real income, or purchasing power, affecting the consumption levels of both goods X and Y. This result is the now familiar income effect, where the directionality of the impact on good X depends on whether good X is normal or inferior.

In the example shown in panel (A) of Figure 5.12, as the price of good Y increases, the optimal consumption level of good X increases from X_1^* to X_2^*. At this point the new budget constraint, $\overline{P}_{X,1}X + \overline{P}_{Y,2}Y = \overline{I}_1$, is tangent to the indifference curve representing U_2^*, where $U_2^* < U_1^*$. This increase in the consumption level of good X is the total effect on good X due to the increase in P_Y, representing the summation of the substitution and income effects. Thus, we have established a relationship between the quantity demanded of good X and the price of good Y. This relationship is the cross-price demand curve, shown in panel (B) of Figure 5.12. Note that in panel (B) the price of good Y is plotted on the vertical axis rather than the consumption level of good Y, as is the case in panel (A). In this case, the cross-price demand curve for good X has a positive slope, or $\partial X / \partial P_Y > 0$, reflecting the fact that an increase in P_Y causes the quantity demanded of good X to increase.

5.5.1 Gross Substitutes and Gross Complements

We can distinguish several characteristics associated with good X when the total effect of a change in P_Y on the optimal consumption level of this good is direct. First, an increase in P_Y causes the consumer to substitute away from good Y and toward good X. This result indicates a direct substitution effect. In our two-goods example, this result is very simplistic since if a consumer substitutes away from one good following an increase in its price, then she has no alternative but to spend more of her income on the other good. However, the increase in P_Y also produces an income effect due to the associated decrease in real income. Provided good X is normal, this decrease in real income has an inverse effect on the consumption of good X. However, in this example, since the total effect is ultimately direct, this inverse income effect must be smaller in magnitude than the direct substitution effect.

Alternatively, if good X is inferior, then the income effect is direct, and the substitution and income effects reinforce each other to create a large direct total effect. We have shown the positively sloped cross-price demand curve, in inverse form, derived from this analysis in panel (B) of Figure 5.12. This curve reflects the ultimate nature of the relationship between the two goods, X and Y. Generally, we classify two goods as **gross substitutes** if *the quantity demanded of one good varies directly with the price of the other good, while holding its own price and money income constant.* We include the word "gross" in this term to indicate that the directionality of the relationship between the quantity demanded of a good and the price of another good reflects both the substitution and income effects.[3]

Not all cross-price demand curves have positive slopes, indicating that two goods may not be gross substitutes for each other. Once again we will analyze the impact of an increase in the price of good Y on the quantity demanded of good X. However, the results in this case, illustrated in panels (A) and (B) of Figure 5.13, are vastly different from those we derived in the preceding analysis. As before, the initial optimal combination of goods is (X_1^*, Y_1^*) occurring at the point of tangency between the budget constraint, $\overline{P}_{X,1}X + \overline{P}_{Y,1}Y = \overline{I}_1$, and the indifference curve representing utility level U_1^*. When the price of good Y increases to $\overline{P}_{Y,2}$, the budget constraint pivots counterclockwise, indicating a lower Y-intercept value, $\overline{I}_1/\overline{P}_{Y,2}$, and a smaller slope value in absolute value terms, $\overline{P}_{X,1}/\overline{P}_{Y,2}$. However, unlike our earlier analysis, the total effect on the quantity demanded of good X is a decrease from X_1^* to X_2^*, which we can observe in both panels (A) and (B) of Figure 5.13. As a result, the cross-price demand curve illustrated in panel (B) possesses a negative slope, or $\partial X/\partial P_Y < 0$, indicating an inverse relationship between P_Y and the quantity demanded of good X. Since this is a two-goods example, the substitution effect must still be direct, reflecting the tendency for the consumer to substitute away from the increasingly expensive good, Y, and toward the relatively cheaper good, X. For the total effect to be inverse, this direct substitution effect must be more than offset by a large inverse income effect. The increase in P_Y causes real income to decrease, where this income effect is inverse provided good X is normal. However, if good X is inferior, both the income and substitution effects are direct, and thus we can rule out the possibility of an inverse total effect in this case.

In summary, for a cross-price demand curve to have a negative slope, the good in question, which in this case is good X, must be normal and the income effect must be greater than the substitution effect. When this result occurs, we describe the two goods as gross complements. More generally, we define two goods as **gross complements** if *the quantity demanded of one good varies inversely with the price of the other good, while holding its own price and money income constant.* We can analyze goods that are deemed gross substitutes or gross complements more technically using the Slutsky equation, as demonstrated in the appendix to this chapter.

A numerical example should help us to understand the above concepts. In the appendix to Chapter 4, we solved a constrained utility maximization problem for the

---

[3]One good is a substitute for another if the relationship between the quantity demanded of that good and the price of another is direct. In the case we are discussing here, we can state that if $\partial X/\partial P_Y > 0$, then good X is a gross substitute for good Y. However, this is not necessarily a two-way street in that good Y may not be a gross substitute for good X. This seemingly contradictory result reflects the fact that changes in the price levels of either of the two goods may produce vastly different income effects depending in part on how heavily the two goods are consumed. For example, assuming the two goods are normal, a change in P_Y may produce a small inverse income effect that fails to counteract the direct substitution effect. Thus, the total effect is direct, or $\partial X/\partial P_Y > 0$, and we can say that good X is a gross substitute for good Y. However, a change in P_X may produce a very large inverse income effect that more than offsets the direct substitution effect. In this case, $\partial Y/\partial P_X < 0$, and we say that good Y constitutes a gross complement for good X.

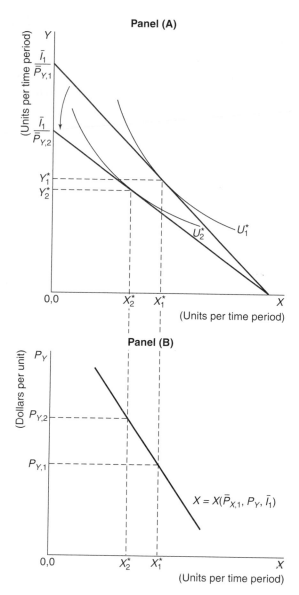

FIGURE 5.13 Derivation of Cross-Price Demand Curve for Complements

specific utility function, $U = 10X^{.5} + 20Y^{.5}$. The predetermined values for the prices of the goods and money income were $\overline{P}_{X,1} = \$1$, $\overline{P}_{Y,1} = \$2$, and $\overline{I}_1 = \$300$, respectively. Our solution to that problem yielded an optimal consumption level for good X as

$$X^* = \frac{\overline{I}_1 \overline{P}_{Y,1}}{\overline{P}_{X,1}\overline{P}_{Y,1} + 4\overline{P}_{X,1}^2} = \frac{300(2)}{1(2) + 4(1)^2} = 100 \text{ units.}$$

However, prior to substituting the specific values for P_X, P_Y, and I into the above equation, recognize that the term $IP_Y/P_X P_Y + 4P_X^2$ is the ordinary demand function for good X. This is the function from which we can derive the Engel, own-price demand, and cross-price demand curves. However, our focus here is on the cross-price demand curve. Recall that this is a curve that expresses the quantity demanded of a good, in this case good X, in terms of the price of another good, specifically the price of good Y, P_Y. Note that we are holding the own price, P_X, and money income, I, constant at specified levels. For this example, the expression

$$X = \frac{\bar{I}_1 P_Y}{\bar{P}_{X,1} P_Y + 4\bar{P}_{X,1}^2} = \frac{300 P_Y}{(1)P_Y + 4(1)^2} = \frac{300 P_Y}{P_Y + 4},$$

represents the cross-price demand curve for good X. We can classify goods X and Y as either gross substitutes or gross complements by evaluating the slope, $\partial X/\partial P_Y$, of this cross-price demand curve. Employing the quotient rule,

$$\frac{\partial X}{\partial P_Y} = \frac{(P_Y + 4)\dfrac{\partial 300 P_Y}{\partial P_Y} - 300 P_Y \dfrac{\partial (P_Y + 4)}{\partial P_Y}}{(P_Y + 4)^2}$$

$$= \frac{(P_Y + 4)300 - 300 P_Y(1)}{(P_Y + 4)^2} = \frac{1200}{(P_Y + 4)^2} > 0.$$

Since the denominator is raised to the second power, this value must always be positive, indicating that goods X and Y are gross substitutes. If we specify P_Y at some particular value such as $\bar{P}_{Y,1} = \$2$, then

$$\frac{\partial X}{\partial P_Y} = \frac{1200}{(2 + 4)^2} = \frac{1200}{36} = 33\tfrac{1}{3} > 0.$$

This value indicates that for an infinitesimally small change in the value of P_Y, at this point on the cross-price demand curve, the consumer changes her quantity demanded of good X by $33\tfrac{1}{3}$ units in the same direction.

5.5 SUMMARY

In this chapter, we have extended the analysis of individual consumer behavior, introduced in Chapter 4, by using the consumer's constrained utility maximization problem to determine his ordinary demand functions. These functions provide our basis for examining particular relationships between the quantity demanded of a good and each of its determining factors: money income, the own price of the good, and the price of another good. We have defined these relationships as the Engel curve, the own-price demand curve, and the cross-price demand curve, respectively. These important concepts, as well as other related topics we have developed in this chapter, are as follows.

- A consumer's demand function expresses his optimal level of consumption of a good, referred to as the quantity demanded of a good, in terms of the prices of all the goods in the constrained utility maximization problem, and money income.

- An income consumption curve represents a set of combinations of goods corresponding to constrained utility maximum solutions for alternative levels of income, while holding the prices of the goods constant.

- An Engel curve is a function that expresses an individual's optimal consumption of a good in terms of her money income while holding the prices of the goods constant.

- A price consumption curve represents a set of optimal combinations of goods corresponding to alternative levels of the price of one of the two goods, while holding the price of the other good and the level of money income constant.

- An individual's own-price demand curve relates the quantity demanded of a good as a function of its own price, while holding the prices of other goods and money income constant.

- The total effect of a change in the price of a good can be separated into its two subcomponents, the substitution effect and the income effect. The substitution effect measures the impact that a change in the own price of a good has on the quantity demanded of that good due solely to the resulting change in the relative prices of the goods.

- The income effect measures the impact that a change in the own price of a good has on the quantity demanded of that good due to the resulting change in real income.

- A good that is exceptionally inferior is known as a Giffen good. In this rare case, the income effect dominates the substitution effect.

- A cross-price demand curve relates the quantity demanded of a good to the price of another good, while holding the own price of the good and money income constant.

- Two goods are gross substitutes (complements) if the quantity demanded of one good is directly (inversely) related to the price of the other good, while holding its own price and money income constant.

KEY TERMS

- compensated demand curve, page 132
- compensated demand function, page 131
- cross-price demand curve, page 139
- demand function, page 112
- Engel curve, page 114
- expenditure function, page 132

- Giffen good, page 126
- gross complements, page 142
- gross substitutes, page 141
- income consumption curve, page 114
- income effect, page 122
- individual's own-price demand curve, page 120

- inferior good, page 116
- net complements, page 149
- net substitutes, page 149
- normal good, page 114
- price consumption curve, page 119
- Slutsky equation, page 135
- substitution effect, page 122

EXERCISES

5.1 Given the information provided in Exercise 4.5 in Chapter 4, what are the equations for Ivana's compensated demand curves for caviar and champagne?

5.2 Assume an individual's own-price demand function for good X is

$$X = X(P_X, P_Y, I) = 50 - 3P_X + 0.5P_Y + 0.0005I$$

where P_X = unit price of good X
  P_Y = unit price of good Y
   I = individual's income

a. Compute the individual's own-price demand curve when P_Y = $2.00 and I = $30,000.

b. Compute the individual's cross-price demand curve when P_X = $4.00 and I = $30,000.

c. Determine whether goods X and Y are gross substitutes or gross complements.

5.3 Refer to the own-price demand function for good X in Exercise 5.2.

a. Compute the individual's Engel curve when P_X = $4.00 and P_Y = $2.00.

b. Determine whether good X is a normal good or an inferior good.

5.4 Using strictly convex indifference curves and linear budget constraints, construct graphs to illustrate the substitution, income, and total effects of a decrease in the price of good X for each of the following three cases.

a. X is a normal good.

b. X is an inferior but not a Giffen good.

c. X is a Giffen good.

5.5 Using the graphs constructed for Exercise 5.4, derive the corresponding individual own-price demand curves.

5.6 Assume that an individual has the utility function

$$U = X^{1/2}Y^{1/2},$$

where X and Y represent units of goods X and Y, respectively, and U is some index of utility. This individual spends all of her money income, I, on the two goods where the unit prices of goods X and Y are, P_X and P_Y, respectively. If I = $100, P_X = $2, and P_Y = $2, the individual maximizes her utility by consuming 25 units of each good and receives an amount of utility reflected by the index, U = 25.

a. Verify the results presented above.

b. Suppose the government decides to assist this individual by subsidizing her purchases of good X so that the effective price is now P_X = $1 for this consumer. Compute the utility-maximizing levels of goods X and Y, along with the associated level of utility received by this individual. What is the total amount of the subsidy?

5.7 Refer to the information in the previous exercise. Using the amount of the subsidy provided by the government to the individual, computed in part b in Exercise 5.6, now assume that the government decides to simply pay the consumer this sum directly, thereby effectively increasing her money income, I, by this amount. Under these circumstances, compute the utility-maximizing levels of goods X and Y along with the level of utility received by this individual.

5.8 Compare the results computed in the previous two exercises for the levels of X, Y, and U. In which case does the consumer receive the higher level of utility? Since the government is effectively paying the same amount in either case, why is the individual's maximum level of utility different for the two cases?

Appendix

5A.1 GROSS SUBSTITUTES AND GROSS COMPLEMENTS USING THE SLUTSKY EQUATION

We are able to classify two goods as either gross substitutes or gross complements for one another by examining the Slutsky equation developed in Section 5.4.4. We derived this equation by partially differentiating the compensated and ordinary demand functions for good X with respect to its own price, P_X, at an (X,Y) combination common to both functions. It is also possible for us to partially differentiate these functions with respect to P_Y, where this procedure enables us to determine the impact of a change in P_Y on the quantity demanded of good X. Thus,

$$X'(P_X,P_Y,U) = X(P_X,P_Y,E),$$

or since,

$$E = E(P_X,P_Y,U),$$
$$X'(P_X,P_Y,U) = X[P_X,P_Y,E(P_X,P_Y,U)].$$

Therefore,

$$\frac{\partial X'}{\partial P_Y} = \frac{\partial X}{\partial P_Y} + \frac{\partial X}{\partial E}\frac{\partial E}{\partial P_Y},$$

or

$$\frac{\partial X}{\partial P_Y} = \frac{\partial X'}{\partial P_Y} - \frac{\partial X}{\partial E}\frac{\partial E}{\partial P_Y}. \qquad \textbf{(5A.1)}$$

The terms in this version of the Slutsky equation should be familiar to us because they are very similar to those in equation (5.2). The difference is that in equation (5A.1) the compensated and ordinary demand functions have been differentiated with respect to P_Y rather than P_X. The term on the left-hand side of equation (5A.1), $\partial X/\partial P_Y$, measures the change in the quantity demanded of good X, with respect to a change in the price of good Y. The first term on the right-hand side of this equation, $\partial X'/\partial P_Y$, represents the change in the

compensated quantity demanded of good X due to a change in P_Y. Alternatively, it measures the change in the quantity demanded of good X while holding utility constant, due to a change in P_Y, and therefore also represents the substitution effect. Finally, the remaining term, $\partial X/\partial E$ $\partial E/\partial P_Y$, measures the change in the quantity demanded of good X due to the change in P_Y, operating through the resulting change in real income. Accordingly, this term represents the income effect. We can also express this version of the Slutsky equation as

$$\frac{\partial X}{\partial P_Y} = \left.\frac{\partial X}{\partial P_Y}\right|_{\bar{U}_1} - X\frac{\partial X}{\partial I},$$

where this slight modification follows the same procedures we discussed in Section 5.4.4. The first term on the right-hand side of the above equation represents the substitution effect, and the second term is the income effect.

We classify two goods, X and Y, as either gross substitutes or gross complements by observing the sign associated with $\partial X/\partial P_Y$. If $\partial X/\partial P_Y > 0$, then we classify the two goods as gross substitutes, since this result indicates a direct relationship between the quantity demanded of good X and the price of good Y. In such a case, the related cross-price demand curve has a positive slope. Conversely, if $\partial X/\partial P_Y < 0$, then we classify the two goods as gross complements, since the relationship between the quantity demanded of good X and the price of good Y is inverse. In this case, the related cross-price demand curve will have a negative slope. The term *gross* is appropriate when evaluating $\partial X/\partial P_Y$ because it embodies both the substitution and income effects as we can observe from the Slutsky equation.

5A.2   NET SUBSTITUTES AND NET COMPLEMENTS

There is an alternative method for evaluating two goods as either substitutes or complements. Using this approach, we classify goods as either net substitutes or net complements on the basis of the sign associated with only the substitution effect, or alternatively stated, the slope of the compensated demand curve. Specifically, we say two goods are **net substitutes** if *the quantity demanded of one good varies directly with the price of the other good, while holding its own price and utility constant.* Conversely, two goods are **net complements** if *the quantity demanded of one good varies inversely with the price of the other good, while holding its own price and utility constant.* Many economists contend that these "net" terms represent more theoretically pure definitions of substitutes and complements than their gross counterparts. This contention is based on the fact that the income effect brought about by a price change has been eliminated, allowing us to focus only on the substitution effects. As a result, this approach provides us with a classification scheme for substitutes and complements more in line with traditional opinion, such as beef versus pork and bread versus butter, respectively. However, a problem arises when we use these net definitions of substitutes and complements in that it is very difficult to separate substitution and income effects using real-world data. Therefore, for practical reasons, most relationships between quantities demanded and prices of goods that we actually observe represent gross relationships.

From a theoretical perspective, our discussion of net substitutes and net complements becomes somewhat more complicated because it requires an expansion of our analysis beyond the two-goods case. Clearly, in the two-goods model that we have used extensively throughout this chapter, the goods must always be classified as net substitutes, or $\partial X'/\partial P_Y > 0$. The theoretical analysis of net complements and net substitutes is trivial in this case since an increase in the price of good Y always causes the consumer to buy fewer units of good Y. Clearly, he has to substitute toward good X since there are no other alternative goods available.

To demonstrate a meaningful analysis of net substitutes and net complements, we must extend the analysis to three or more goods. Thus, we expand the Slutsky equation by initially including $X, Y, W, \ldots, Z$ goods along with their respective prices, $P_X, P_Y, P_W, \ldots, P_Z$, in the constrained consumer optimization problem. Afterward, we can partially differentiate the quantity demanded of any one of the goods, such as X, with respect to each of the prices yielding

$$\frac{\partial X}{\partial P_X} = \frac{\partial X'}{\partial P_X} - \frac{\partial X}{\partial E}\frac{\partial E}{\partial P_X}$$

$$\frac{\partial X}{\partial P_Y} = \frac{\partial X'}{\partial P_Y} - \frac{\partial X}{\partial E}\frac{\partial E}{\partial P_Y}$$

$$\frac{\partial X}{\partial P_W} = \frac{\partial X'}{\partial P_W} - \frac{\partial X}{\partial E}\frac{\partial E}{\partial P_W}$$

$$\vdots \qquad \vdots \qquad \vdots$$

$$\frac{\partial X}{\partial P_Z} = \frac{\partial X'}{\partial P_Z} - \frac{\partial X}{\partial E}\frac{\partial E}{\partial P_Z}.$$

It is now possible for us to classify goods X and Y, X and $W, \ldots, X$ and Z, as net substitutes or net complements by simply evaluating the signs associated with $\partial X'/\partial P_Y$, $\partial X'/\partial P_W, \ldots,$ $\partial X'/\partial P_Z$, respectively.

CHAPTER 6

Market Demand Curves

6.1 INTRODUCTION

In Chapter 5 we constructed own-price demand curves, Engel curves, and cross-price demand curves for an individual consumer. We derived these curves by solving the consumer's constrained utility maximization problem and then applying appropriate interpretations to the results. While analyzing these curves enhances our understanding of consumer theory, we need to obtain broader versions of these curves before we can analyze how markets perform. Accordingly, our purpose in this chapter is to demonstrate how to aggregate, or sum, these individual own-price demand, Engel, and cross-price demand curves across all consumers of a good to obtain their corresponding market counterparts. We will also show how the construction of these market curves is affected by interdependencies among consumers' purchasing choices often represented in the form of trends or fads.

6.2 CONSTRUCTION OF MARKET OWN-PRICE DEMAND CURVES

In Chapter 5 we solved the consumer's constrained utility maximization problem to derive the broad individual demand function as

$$X = X(P_X, P_Y, I),$$

where X is the quantity demanded of good X, P_X represents the price of good X, P_Y is the price of the alternative good Y, and I represents the individual's money income. We also demonstrated in Chapter 5 that we can focus explicitly on the relationship between the quantity demanded of good X and its own price, P_X, if we hold the price of the alternative good, P_Y, and the individual consumer's money income, I, constant at some specified levels denoted $\overline{P}_{Y,1}$ and $\overline{I}_1$, respectively. The resulting relationship is the individual's own-price demand curve that we represent as

$$X = X(P_X, \overline{P}_{Y,1}, \overline{I}_1).$$

Alternatively, we can focus on the relationship between the quantity demanded of good X and a consumer's money income, I, by specifying the prices of the two goods at particular levels, such as $\overline{P}_{X,1}$ and $\overline{P}_{Y,1}$. This relationship is the individual's Engel curve represented as

$$X = X(\overline{P}_{X,1}, \overline{P}_{Y,1}, I).$$

Finally, we obtain the individual's cross-price demand curve for good X

$$X = X(\overline{P}_{X,1}, P_{Y,1}, \overline{I}_1),$$

by specifying values for the own-price and money income variables, represented as $\overline{P}_{X,1}$ and $\overline{I}_1$, respectively. This curve explicitly indicates the relationship between the quantity demanded of good X and the price of the alternative good, P_Y.

The own-price demand, Engel, and cross-price demand curves are all closely related. In general, once we solve the consumer optimization problem and derive the broad demand function, $X = X(P_X, P_Y, I)$, we can obtain any one of these three curves by simply specifying which factor, either P_X, P_Y or I, to treat as explicitly variable and which factors to hold constant. Keep in mind that the values for X in this demand function, as well as the associated own-price demand curve, Engel curve, and cross-price demand curve, represent optimal consumption levels of this good.

We can demonstrate the relationships among the demand function and its various associated curves with a numerical example. Assume that the constrained utility maximization process generates the demand function

$$X = -2P_X + 4P_Y + 0.5I,$$

and we specify the independent variables as $\overline{P}_{X,1} = \$2, \overline{P}_{Y,1} = \$1$, and $\overline{I}_1 = \$12$ (in thousands), as deemed appropriate. We derive the own-price demand curve by leaving P_X as variable and substituting the values for P_Y and I as

$$X = X(P_X, \overline{P}_{Y,1}, \overline{I}_1) = -2P_X + 4(1) + 0.5(12)$$

or

$$X = 10 - 2P_X.$$

We derive the Engel curve by allowing I to vary and specifying values for P_X and P_Y yielding

$$X = X_I(\overline{P}_{X,1}, \overline{P}_{Y,1}, I) = -2(2) + 4(1) + 0.5I,$$

or

$$X = 0.5I.$$

Finally, we construct the cross-price demand curve by allowing P_Y to vary and specifying values for P_X and I as

$$X = X_Y(\overline{P}_{X,1}, P_Y, \overline{I}_1) = -2(2) + 4P_Y + 0.5(12)$$

or

$$X = 2 + 4P_Y.$$

The three types of curves presented above, both in general notation and in this example, pertain to an individual consumer. However, it is possible for us to return to the consumer optimization problem and solve it for a second consumer. In the absence of price discrimination, consumers pay the same prices for the two goods X and Y, but as a rule, they have different preferences and incomes. As a result, the overall demand function for the second consumer is most likely somewhat different than that for the first consumer. We can repeat this process for additional consumers, ultimately generating $1, 2, \ldots, n$ broad individual demand functions as

$$X_1 = X_1(P_X, P_Y, I_1)$$
$$X_2 = X_2(P_X, P_Y, I_2)$$
$$\vdots \qquad \vdots$$
$$X_n = X_n(P_X, P_Y, I_n),$$

where the subscripts pertaining to the X and I variables denote the number of the consumer. We can apply our previous interpretations to each of these n number of demand functions to construct n number of own-price demand, Engel, and cross-price demand curves.

We develop market curves by aggregating these n number of individual curves. Our present focus will be on the market own-price demand curve, although we can also construct market Engel and cross-price demand curves using similar procedures. Our first step is to modify the broad individual demand functions into own-price demand curves by specifying the price of good Y and the money income levels for each of the n individual consumers who collectively constitute the market for good X. Thus,

$$X_1 = X_1(P_X, \overline{P}_{Y,1}, \overline{I}_{1,1})$$
$$X_2 = X_2(P_X, \overline{P}_{Y,1}, \overline{I}_{2,1})$$
$$\vdots \qquad \vdots$$
$$X_n = X_n(P_X, \overline{P}_{Y,1}, \overline{I}_{n,1}).$$

Note that the first subscript for income, I, pertains to the number of the consumer, and the second subscript refers to the particular level at which we specify each consumer's income. Thus, $\overline{I}_{1,1}, \overline{I}_{2,1} \ldots \overline{I}_{n,1}$, most likely represent different values, since we would not expect all individuals to have the same level of income.

The **market own-price demand curve**, X_m, represents *the aggregation of n number of individual own-price demand curves*. We construct the market own-price demand curve by selecting specific prices for good X, such as $P_{X,1}$ and $P_{X,2}$, and substituting them into each individual own-price demand curve to obtain the amount of good X demanded by each consumer at each of these prices. For example, at $P_{X,1}$, the individual consumers $1, 2, \ldots, n$ demand $X_{1,1}, X_{2,1}, \ldots, X_{n,1}$ quantities of good X, respectively. In terms of notation, the first subscript represents the number of the particular consumer, and the second refers to the corresponding price of good X. We compute the amount of good X demanded in the market at the price $P_{X,1}$ by summing the amount of good X consumed by each individual as

$$X_{m,1} = X_{1,1} + X_{2,1} + \ldots + X_{n,1},$$

where $X_{m,1}$ represents the market quantity demanded for good X at the price $P_{X,1}$. When the price of good X is $P_{X,2}$, the individual consumers demand $X_{1,2}, X_{2,2}, \ldots, X_{n,2}$ units of this good, respectively, and we compute the market quantity demanded for good X, $X_{m,2}$, at $P_{X,2}$ as

$$X_{m,2} = X_{1,2} + X_{2,2} + \ldots + X_{n,2}.$$

In general, the market own-price demand curve, X_m, is equal to the summation of the individual own-price demand curves or

$$X_m = X_1 + X_2 + \ldots + X_n.$$

We demonstrate this procedure in Figure 6.1, where the individual demand curves, $X_1, X_2, \ldots, X_n$, and the market demand curve, X_m, are labeled $D_1, D_2, \ldots, D_n$, and D_m, respectively. Theoretically, we can select $1, 2, \ldots, j$ prices, denoted $P_{X,1}, P_{X,2}, \ldots$ $P_{X,j}$, and generate j number of market quantities demanded. For the sake of clarity, assume that all of the individual demand curves are linear and, as a result, we can establish the market demand curve by connecting the two points $(X_{m,1}, P_{X,1})$ and $(X_{m,2}, P_{X,2})$ in Figure 6.1. This process is quite simple and is known as a horizontal summation since we can link the own-price demand curves horizontally, due to their common vertical axes representing the price of good X.

An extension of the numerical example we presented earlier may help to further clarify this procedure. Assume the demand function for consumer 1 is

$$X_1 = -2P_X + 4P_Y + 0.5I_1.$$

For $P_Y = \$1$ and $I_1 = \$12$ (in thousands), the own-price demand curve for consumer 1 is

$$X_1 = 10 - 2P_X. \tag{6.1}$$

For the sake of simplicity, we will assume there is only one other consumer, consumer 2, and his demand function for good X is

$$X_2 = -P_X + 3P_Y + 0.4I_2.$$

FIGURE 6.1 Horizontal Summation of Individual Own-Price Demand Curves

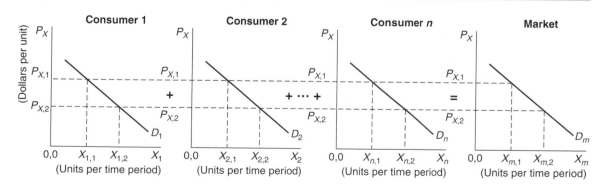

Since all consumers pay the same prices for both goods X and Y, we specify the price of good Y as $\overline{P}_{Y,1} = \$1$ for consumer 2, the same value as for consumer 1. However, the income for consumer 2 is likely to be different from that of consumer 1, say $\overline{I}_{2,1} = \$5$ (in thousands). Thus, the own-price demand curve for consumer 2 is

$$X_2 = -P_X + 3(1) + 0.4(5)$$

or

$$X_2 = 5 - P_X. \tag{6.2}$$

The market own-price demand curve is the summation of the individual demand curves or

$$X_m = X_1 + X_2.$$

Thus, after substituting the expressions for X_1 and X_2 from equations (6.1) and (6.2), respectively, into the above equation, we compute the market own-price demand curve as

$$X_m = (10 - 2P_X) + (5 - P_X)$$

or

$$X_m = 15 - 3P_X. \tag{6.3}$$

By substituting particular values for P_X into the individual own-price demand curves, we can determine the (X_m, P_X) coordinates that lie on the market own-price demand curve. For example, if $P_X = \$1$, then

$$X_{1,1} = 10 - 2(1) = 8$$

and

$$X_{2,1} = 5 - 1 = 4.$$

Thus, by summing the quantities demanded of good X by individuals 1 and 2, we compute the market quantity demanded at $P_X = \$1$ *as*

$$X_{m,1} = X_{1,1} + X_{2,1} = 8 + 4 = 12.$$

Alternatively, we can determine this value for $X_{m,1}$ by substituting $P_X = \$1$ directly into the market demand curve as

$$X_{m,1} = 15 - 3(1) = 12.$$

Similarly, if $P_X = \$2$, then

$$X_{1,2} = 10 - 2(2) = 6$$

and

$$X_{2,2} = 5 - 2 = 3,$$

and as a result,

$$X_{m,2} = 6 + 3 = 9.$$

Alternatively, we can compute $X_{m,2}$ directly from the market own-price demand curve as

$$X_{m,2} = 15 - 3(2) = 9.$$

6.3 BANDWAGON EFFECTS

We typically demonstrate market own-price demand curves as the result of a horizontal summation process such as we described in Section 6.2. However, we have based this rather straightforward process on the critical assumption that individual consumers' utility functions, and hence demand functions, are independent of one another. This assumption implies that each consumer is a true individualist, meaning that his consumption of a good is not dependent on any other consumer's purchases of that same good. However, for many goods, such as clothing, food, and beverages, this may not always be the case. Many consumers follow a leader, thus establishing some type of trend or **bandwagon effect** regarding the consumption of some goods. A bandwagon effect occurs when *some individuals' quantities demanded of a good are directly dependent on other individuals' consumption levels of that good.*[1] When a bandwagon effect exists, we must modify the horizontal summation process to take into account this interdependency when we construct a market own-price demand curve.

Assume the market for good X consists of two consumers, where only the first person is a pure individualist. As a result, the quantity of good X demanded by consumer 1 is a function of the prices she must pay for the two goods, X and Y, and her money income. Thus, the demand function for consumer 1 is the same as in the earlier case, represented as

$$X_1 = X_1(P_X, P_Y, I_1).$$

Similarly, the own-price demand curve for consumer 1 is the same as we demonstrated earlier, or

$$X_1 = X_1(P_X, \overline{P}_{Y,1}, \overline{I}_{1,1}). \tag{6.4}$$

However, assume the second consumer bases her demand for good X partly on the quantity of good X demanded by consumer 1. As a result, we represent her demand function for good X as

$$X_2 = X_2(P_X, P_Y, I_2, X_1). \tag{6.5}$$

The difference between this situation and our earlier analysis is the inclusion of the amount of good X demanded by consumer 1, X_1, in the second consumer's demand function. In addition, if this modification is to represent a bandwagon effect, we must

---

[1]In a broader sense, the bandwagon effect and the snob effect, discussed in the next section, are types of network externalities. This relatively recent term, refers to any situation where some consumers' demand for a good is dependent on the number of other consumers purchasing the good. In some cases, this externality may result from the fact that the effectiveness associated with a particular good is enhanced as more people use it, such as the case with communication devices.

assume that $\partial X_2 / \partial X_1 > 0$, indicating that as consumer 1 increases (decreases) her consumption of good X, consumer 2 responds by increasing (decreasing) her consumption of that good as well. We obtain the own-price demand curve for consumer 2 by substituting the expression for consumer 1's demand function, X_1, represented in equation (6.4), into equation (6.5) and specifying values for P_Y, I_1, and I_2, yielding

$$X_2 = X_2[P_X, \overline{P}_{Y,1}, \overline{I}_{2,1}, X_1(P_X, \overline{P}_{Y,1}, \overline{I}_{1,1})].$$

There is an important methodological point we must note regarding how the inclusion of a bandwagon effect influences the aggregation process. A change in P_X, P_Y, or I_2 produces an immediate effect on X_2. Specifically, a change in P_X causes a movement along the own-price demand curve for consumer 2, while a change in P_Y or I_2 results in a shift in this curve. The quantity of good X demanded by consumer 1, X_1, depends on P_X, P_Y, and I_1. Thus, any change in P_Y or I_1 causes the own-price demand curve for consumer 1 to shift, resulting in a change in X_1, which in turn causes the own-price demand curve for consumer 2 to shift. Since $\partial X_2 / \partial X_1 > 0$, an increase (decrease) in X_1 causes the own-price demand curve for consumer 2 to shift to the right (left), indicating that she demands greater (lesser) amounts of good X at each price, P_X. However, the slope of the own-price demand curve for consumer 2 remains unaffected because the ultimate cause of this shift is due to a change in some autonomous factor such as P_Y or I_1. Unlike P_X, we are not treating these factors as explicitly variable in this own-price demand curve for good X.

A change in P_X also affects X_1, which in turn influences X_2. However, in this case, we treat P_X as explicitly variable and plot it on the vertical axes of the own-price demand curves. Provided X is not a Giffen good, if P_X decreases, both X_1 and X_2 increase. However, the increase in X_1 causes an additional increase in X_2 due to the bandwagon effect. In this situation, the bandwagon effect provides an additional channel by which a change in P_X affects X_2, and as a result, the slope of the own-price demand curve for consumer 2, $\partial X_2 / \partial P_X$, increases. Since we usually plot demand curves in their inverse form, such as $P_X = X_2^{-1}(X_2, \overline{P}_{Y,1}, \overline{I}_{2,1}, X_1)$, the reciprocal of the slope of the own-price demand curve for consumer 2, $\partial P_X / \partial X_2$, becomes less negative or smaller in absolute value terms.

We demonstrate this result in Figure 6.2, where you can observe that after the bandwagon effect is taken into account, the own-price demand curve for consumer 2 becomes the flatter curve D_2'. At $P_{X,1}$, both consumers demand zero amounts of good X; thus, the market quantity demanded is also zero, since it is the summation of X_1 and X_2. At the lower price, $P_{X,2}$, consumer 1 demands $X_{1,2}$, and with no bandwagon effect, consumer 2 demands $X_{2,2}$, simply because of the lower price. Therefore, at $P_{X,2}$, in the absence of a bandwagon effect, the market quantity demanded is $X_{1,2} + X_{2,2} = X_{m,2}$, and we represent the market demand curve as D_m. However, with a bandwagon effect present, the increase in X_1 from zero to $X_{1,2}$, causes X_2 to increase from $X_{2,2}$ to $X_{2,2}'$ and we represent the own-price demand curve for consumer 2 as the flatter curve D_2'. As a result, the market quantity demanded is $X_{1,2} + X_{2,2}' = X_{m,2}'$ and the market own-price demand curve is the flatter curve D_m'. In summary, the bandwagon effect

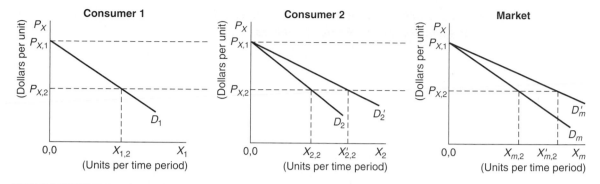

FIGURE 6.2 Construction of Market Own-Price Demand Curve with a Bandwagon Effect

compounds the price effect, making the market own-price demand curve more quantity-price responsive.

Returning to the previous numerical example, we can demonstrate the bandwagon effect mathematically. Recall, the demand function for consumer 1 is

$$X_1 = -2P_X + 4P_Y + 0.5I_1,$$

and thus when $P_Y = \$1$ and $I_1 = \$12$ (in thousands), we compute the own-price demand curve for consumer 1 as

$$X_1 = 10 - 2P_X.$$

These results are the same as in the earlier example because the behavior of consumer 1 is independent of the behavior of consumer 2. However, now assume that the demand function for consumer 2 is represented as

$$X_2' = -P_X + 3P_Y + 0.4I_2 + X_1,$$

where the inclusion of the term X_1 represents the dependence of the quantity of good X demanded by consumer 2, now denoted as X_2', on the amount of good X demanded by consumer 1. When $P_Y = \$1$ and $I_2 = \$5$ (in thousands), this function becomes

$$X_2' = -P_X + 3(1) + 0.4(5) + X_1$$

or

$$X_2' = 5 - P_X + X_1.$$

Substituting the own-price demand curve for consumer 1, $10 - 2P_X$, for X_1 we obtain

$$X_2' = 5 - P_X + (10 - 2P_X)$$

or

$$X_2' = 15 - 3 P_X.$$

The slope of this own-price demand curve is $\partial X_2'/\partial P_X = -3$, which is greater in absolute value terms than $\partial X_2/\partial P_X = -1$, the slope associated with the own-price demand curve for consumer 2 containing no bandwagon effect, represented in equation (6.2). We determine the market own-price demand curve, now denoted X'_m, by summing the two individual demand curves in this example as

$$X'_m = X_1 + X'_2 = (10 - 2P_X) + (15 - 3P_X)$$

or

$$X'_m = 25 - 5P_X.$$

Note that this market own-price demand curve also possesses a slope value, $\partial X'_m/\partial P_X = -5$, that is greater, in absolute value terms, than $\partial X_m/\partial P_X = -3$, the slope value of the market own-price demand curve containing no bandwagon effect, represented in equation (6.3). This result indicates that the introduction of a bandwagon effect into the aggregation process produces a market own-price demand curve that is more quantity-price responsive.

We have illustrated the results of this numerical example in Figure 6.3, demonstrating the comparison between the two aggregation processes. At $P_{X,1} = \$4$, the quantity of X demanded by consumer 1 is

$$X_{1,1} = 10 - 2(4) = 2.$$

With no bandwagon effect, the own-price demand curve for consumer 2 is D_2, and we compute her quantity demanded at the price of \$4 as

$$X_{2,1} = 5 - (1)4 = 1.$$

Thus, the market quantity demanded at this price is

$$X_{m,1} = X_{1,1} + X_{2,1} = 2 + 1 = 3.$$

Alternatively, we can compute $X_{m,1}$ directly from the market demand curve as

$$X_{m,1} = 15 - 3(4) = 3,$$

where this curve, D_m, does not include the bandwagon effect.

With the introduction of a bandwagon effect, the own-price demand curve for consumer 2 is D'_2, and her quantity demanded at $P_{X,1} = \$4$ is

$$X'_{2,1} = 15 - 3(4) = 3.$$

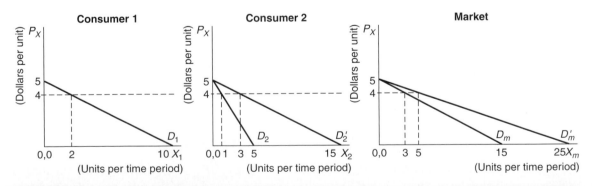

FIGURE 6.3 Numerical Example of Bandwagon Effect

By summing the two individual own-price demand curves, we determine the market quantity demanded, given the existence of a bandwagon effect, as

$$X'_{m,1} = X_{1,1} + X'_{2,1} = 2 + 3 = 5.$$

Alternatively, by substituting $P_{X,1} = \$4$ directly into the market own-price demand curve containing the bandwagon effect, we can compute this same value as

$$X'_{m,1} = 25 - 5(4) = 5,$$

where we determine $X'_{m,1}$ using the flatter or more quantity-price responsive market demand curve, D'_m

---

REAL-WORLD APPLICATION 6.1

The Bandwagon Effect as It Relates to Marketing

Concepts developed in microeconomic theory often provide the basis for many other business disciplines. The bandwagon effect, which we analyzed in Section 6.3, is one such example. It is easy to see how this concept relates to the processes of adoption and diffusion studied in the field of marketing. Specifically, the diffusion process refers to when different segments of a market, representing groups of consumers, are likely to purchase a product. The first consumers of a product, or the leaders, are described as innovators, while the remaining groups of consumers are categorized in succession as early adopters, early majority, late majority, and laggards. Although the diffusion process is often considered as dynamic, the fundamental principle of interdependence among consumers associated with the static bandwagon effect still holds true. Therefore, as the price of a product is reduced and the innovators increase their purchases, the remaining groups increase their purchases of the product, not only because of the lower price, but also because the innovators have increased their consumption of the product. As a result, the own-price market demand curve for the product becomes more own-price sensitive as this process continues.

We can observe this process in the demand for personal computers. From the time they were first introduced in 1977 until 1981, personal computers recorded small sales: U.S. households purchased only 1.1 million PCs during this time period. By 1984, however, sales increased to 7.5 million units, and in 1995, U.S. households owned approximately 40 million personal computers.[2] Some of this increase in personal computer sales was due to technological improvements, such as speed and storage capacity associated with the product, and undoubtedly a substantial amount of the increase was the result of reductions in price from several thousand dollars per unit to less than one thousand dollars for some models. However, it is also logical for us to attribute some of the increase in personal computer sales to the bandwagon effect, since successive market segments have observed and followed the purchasing habits of the innovative, or leading, consumers.

---

[2]Joel R. Evans and Barry Berman, *Marketing* (Upper Saddle River, NJ: Prentice Hall, 1997), pp. 371–372.

6.4 SNOB EFFECTS

Another phenomenon that can influence the aggregation process is known as the **snob effect**. Procedurally, it is similar to the bandwagon effect we just discussed, but in this case the impact on the market quantity demanded of a good is just the opposite. Specifically, it is possible that some consumers want to avoid being identified with the tastes, and hence purchases, of other consumers. As a result, we say a snob effect exists if *some individuals' quantities demanded of a good are inversely related to other individuals' consumption levels of that good* .

We can demonstrate this effect using the two-consumer example, where we assume that consumer 1 behaves independently, and consumer 2, once again, is influenced by the quantities demanded by consumer 1. Thus, as before, X_1 is introduced as a factor in the demand function for consumer 2. However, since this inclusion represents a snob effect, $\partial X_2/\partial X_1 < 0$, indicating that as X_1 increases, X_2 decreases. Further, if the increase in X_1 is caused by a reduction in P_X, then the slope of consumer 2's own-price demand curve becomes smaller in absolute value terms, and the plotted inverse own-price demand curve becomes steeper than the curve constructed in the absence of a snob effect. As a result, once we complete the aggregation process, the market own-price demand curve is steeper, or less quantity-price responsive as compared to an own-price market demand curve containing no snob effect. Intuitively, this result occurs because the snob effect counteracts some of the price effect associated with an own-price demand curve.

We are likely to find examples of the snob effect in the world of high fashion, where many newly introduced lines of clothing command a very high price. Therefore, many of these products are purchased by consumers who are considered to be among the more elite and affluent members of society. As the production techniques associated with these goods improve, their prices often tend to decline, causing additional consumers to enter the market. As this occurs, many of the elite and affluent consumers, who initially purchased the product at the higher prices, reduce their purchases in order to avoid being identified with a product that is becoming more commonplace. Ultimately, this behavior causes the market own-price demand for the good to be less sensitive to changes in its own price. We include a further analysis of the snob effect in Exercise 6.4.

6.5 SUMMARY

In this chapter we developed the market own-price, Engel, and cross-price demand curves both mathematically and graphically. In addition, we demonstrated how the construction of a market own-price demand curve is affected by the introduction of consumer interdependence in the form of either bandwagon or snob effects. The key topics we covered in this chapter are as follows.

- We derive the market own-price demand curve for a good by summing the quantities demanded by all consumers of the good at alternative prices.

- If some individuals' quantities demanded of a good are directly related to other individuals' consumption levels of that good, then a bandwagon effect exists.
- The introduction of a bandwagon effect generates a flatter market own-price demand curve than one that exists in its absence.
- In contrast, a snob effect exists if some individuals' quantities demanded of a good are inversely related to other individuals' consumption levels of that good.
- The introduction of a snob effect produces a steeper market own-price demand curve than one occurring in its absence.

KEY TERMS

- bandwagon effect, page 155
- market own-price demand curve, page 152
- snob effect, page 160

EXERCISES

6.1 The market for good X consists of two consumers possessing the own-price demand curves

$$X_1 = 20 - 5P_X$$

and

$$X_2 = 12 - 3P_X,$$

where X_1 and X_2 represent the quantities of good X demanded by consumers 1 and 2, respectively, and P_X is the price of good X.

a. Compute the market own-price demand curve for good X.

b. Graphically demonstrate the horizontal summation process by which we construct the market own-price demand curve.

6.2 Refer to the individual own-price demand curves in Exercise 6.1. However, now alter the own-price demand curve for consumer 2 to be

$$X_2 = 12 - 3P_X + 2X_1.$$

What type of effect have we introduced into the aggregation process? Compute the market own-price demand curve in this situation. Also, compare the slopes of this curve and the market own-price curve you computed in Exercise 6.1.

6.3 Assume a market demand function of the form,

$$X = 20 - 0.2P_X + 0.4P_Y + 0.1\, I,$$

where P_X and P_Y are the prices of goods X and Y, respectively, and I is consumers' income. Assume $P_X = \$10$, $P_Y = \$20$, and $I = \$30$ (in thousands) where appropriate.

a. Compute the own-price demand curve for good X.

b. Compute the Engel curve for good X and determine if good X is normal or inferior.

c. Compute the cross-price demand curve for good X and determine if goods X and Y are gross substitutes or gross complements.

6.4 Suppose that some consumers of a rather fashionable, but highly priced, good do not desire to be associated with goods that are more commonly consumed. Assume that for some reason the price of this good decreases, and accordingly more individuals choose to purchase and consume it. How would you describe the own-price demand curves pertaining to these initial, rather elite, consumers? Describe what type of effect is taking place in this situation. What is the impact of this particular effect on the market own-price demand curve for the good?

6.5 Assume that good X is not a Giffen good, and as a result, all individual own-price demand curves for good X possess negative slopes. We have demonstrated that market own-price demand curves are constructed essentially by horizontally summing the individual own-price demand curves comprising the market for a good. Is there a situation for which the market own-price demand curve for good X might possess a positive slope? If so, explain what conditions must underlie such a phenomenon.

CHAPTER 7

Demand-Related Elasticities

7.1 INTRODUCTION

In the preceding chapter we showed how individual own-price demand curves for a good can be aggregated to construct the market own-price demand curve for that good. We also implied that similar procedures can be applied to individual Engel curves and cross-price demand curves to generate their market counterparts as well. The slope and intercept coefficients associated with these curves are of considerable interest to us. In particular, the slope coefficients indicate both the directionality and magnitudes of responses in the market quantity demanded of a good to changes in such independent variables as the own-price of the good, consumer income, and the prices of other goods. In this chapter, we will use these slope coefficients to create elasticities, or indicators of responsiveness, that are independent of the units in which the variables are measured. Because they are unitless, we can use these elasticities to make comparisons of responsiveness across markets for different goods. Specifically, we will develop several types of elasticities, the own-price, income, and cross-price elasticities of demand, relating to the market own-price demand, Engel, and cross-price demand curves, respectively.

These elasticity measures are used extensively in the business world. One of the most important applications is found in analyzing changes in the value of consumers' expenditures on a good in response to changes in the price of that good. For example, if a fast-food restaurant raises the price of its hamburgers, will there be an increase in the amount of revenue it receives from hamburger sales? Or will the higher price result in consumers drastically reducing their purchases of these hamburgers, thus causing the dollar value of the restaurant's hamburger sales to decline? The answer to this question, as well as many others regarding the responsiveness of the quantity demanded of a good to changes in own-price, income, or cross prices, depends on the value of the appropriate elasticity.

7.2 THE CONCEPT OF AN ELASTICITY

In Chapter 6, we demonstrated that the aggregation of individual demand functions for a good, such as X, yields the broad market demand function

$$X_m = X_m(P_X, P_Y, I_m).$$

In this function, the term X_m represents the market quantity demanded of good X, P_X and P_Y denote the prices of good X and the alternative good Y, respectively, and I_m

represents the summation of individual money incomes for the consumers of good X. The market own-price demand curve is

$$X_m = X_m(P_X, \overline{P}_{Y,1}, \overline{I}_{m,1}),$$

where we have specified the price of the alternative good, Y, and the aggregate money income variable, I_m, at the levels $\overline{P}_{Y,1}$ and $\overline{I}_{m,1}$, respectively. Similarly, the market Engel curve is

$$X_I = X_I(\overline{P}_{X,1}, \overline{P}_{Y,1}, I_m),$$

where we have specified the price of good X at $\overline{P}_{X,1}$ and the price of good Y at $\overline{P}_{Y,1}$. Finally, the market cross-price demand curve is

$$X_Y = X_Y(\overline{P}_{X,1}, P_Y, \overline{I}_{m,1}),$$

where the own-price and money income levels are specified at $\overline{P}_{X,1}$ and $\overline{I}_{m,1}$, respectively.

We have derived these market curves from the consumer optimization process discussed in Chapter 4, which includes just two goods as decision variables. In addition, we are treating the associated prices and the individual's money income as the only potential determinants of the quantity demanded of either of these goods. More broadly, we can extend the interpretation of market demand functions to include additional determinants of the quantity demanded of a good, such as X_m. For example, we might express a more comprehensive market demand function as

$$X_m = X_m(P_X, P_Y, P_W, \ldots, P_Z, I_m, T_m, N),$$

where the additional factors, $P_W, \ldots, P_Z$, represent the prices of more alternative goods, $W, \ldots, Z$, respectively, T_m represents some measure of consumer tastes, and N represents the number of consumers demanding good X. This list of determinants is by no means comprehensive, but it should closely resemble the list of familiar determinants of market demand you have encountered in most principles of microeconomics textbooks.

We can derive the associated market own-price demand curve, as we did in the simpler case, by specifying values for all independent variables other than P_X. This curve may be represented by any one of a number of functional forms, depending on the underlying consumer utility functions and the type of aggregation process. For example, one type of market own-price demand curve is the linear form

$$X_m = b_0 - b_1 P_X,$$

where b_0 and b_1 represent the X_m intercept and slope coefficients, respectively. What do b_0 and b_1 measure? Specifically, b_0 indicates the quantity demanded of X_m when the price of good X, P_X, is equal to zero. Thus, in the two goods case, b_0 represents the influence on X_m resulting from changes in factors other than P_X, such as P_Y or I_m. In this linear case the slope coefficient, b_1, is constant and indicates $\partial X_m / \partial P_X$, or the change in X_m resulting from a change in P_X. An alternative type of market own-price demand curve is the form

$$X_m = b_1 P_X^c,$$

where $b_1 > 0$ and c is generally < 0. In this case the coefficients b_1 and c affect the slope, since $\partial X_m / \partial P_X = c b_1 P_X^{c-1}$. Note, however, that for this own-price market demand curve there is no X_m intercept, and the specified factors, such as P_Y or I, affect the value of its slope. Also observe that the slope for this form of market own-price demand curve varies along the curve since it is a function of P_X.

The sign of a slope indicates the directionality of the relationship between two variables, and its magnitude indicates the degree of responsiveness associated with such a relationship. Therefore, we can extract a considerable amount of useful information by analyzing slope coefficients. There is a major difficulty, however, in attempting to use slope values to compare the responsiveness between two variables across different functions. Slope values are dependent on the units in which the variables are measured. For example, the slope of an own-price demand curve indicates the change in the quantity demanded of a good, measured in units of that good, resulting from a change in its price, usually measured in dollars per unit. However, the units of measurement logically vary across different types of goods. As examples, gravel is usually measured in tons, gasoline in gallons, cloth in yards, and so forth. What we need is a measure of quantity-price responsiveness that is independent of the units of measurement, so that we can make meaningful comparisons of such responsiveness across different own-price demand curves.

The measure that meets this objective is known as an **elasticity**, which is generally defined as a *number that indicates the degree of responsiveness between two variables, regardless of the units of measurement*. More specifically, it is a ratio of the percentage changes in two variables. Since the percent terms cancel each other out, the resulting number has no dimensions, and it thus provides a measure that we can use to compare responsiveness across different functions containing similar variables but different units of measurement. We can apply the elasticity concept to virtually any two variables. Our focus in this chapter, however, is on market demand functions and the related own-price demand, Engel, and cross-price demand curves. Therefore, we will develop and analyze three specific types of elasticities—own-price elasticity of demand, income elasticity, and cross-price elasticity of demand. In the following sections, we will distinguish these different elasticities on the basis of which variables we choose to analyze.

7.3 OWN-PRICE ELASTICITY OF DEMAND

The first elasticity we will discuss is the **own-price elasticity of demand**, where our focus, in this case, is on the relationship between the quantity demanded of a good, say X, and its own price, P_X. This elasticity is *the ratio of the percentage change* *in the quantity demanded of a good to the percentage change in the price of that good* or

$$E_{X,P_X} = \frac{\%\Delta X}{\%\Delta P_X},\qquad(7.1)$$

In this case, E represents an elasticity, and the subscripts indicate the variables we are measuring. Therefore, we can interpret the term E_{X,P_X} as the own-price elasticity of demand for good X. The term, ΔP_X, represents a change in the variable P_X, while ΔX signifies the subsequent change in the variable X. Observe, in this elasticity formula, that we can cancel out the percentage terms in both the numerator and denominator, leaving a unitless value for E_{X,P_X}.

We can expand this expression for an elasticity into a working formula by substituting definitions of percentage changes into the numerator and denominator as

$$E_{X,P_X} = \frac{\%\Delta X}{\%\Delta P_X} = \frac{\dfrac{\Delta X}{X}}{\dfrac{\Delta P_X}{P_X}},$$

or, more concisely,

$$E_{X,P_X} = \frac{\Delta X}{\Delta P_X}\frac{P_X}{X}.$$

Observe that the first term in this expression, $\Delta X/\Delta P_X$, is the slope of the own-price demand curve, indicating that the own-price elasticity of demand is simply a modification of this slope.

We can determine the most precise measure of this slope by allowing for only an infinitesimally small change in the variable P_X. As a result, we replace the term $\Delta X/\Delta P_X$ by the partial derivative of X with respect to P_X, and we express the working formula for own-price elasticity of demand as

$$E_{X,P_X} = \frac{\partial X}{\partial P_X}\frac{P_X}{X}.$$

We interpret this formula as a point elasticity because it pertains to a particular point on the own-price demand curve. Also note that for virtually all own-price demand curves, $\partial X/\partial P_X \le 0$, and as a consequence $E_{X,P_X} \le 0$ as well. Convention varies across economics textbooks about what to do with the negative sign generally associated with this elasticity. The convention we have adopted here is to use the absolute value of the computed values for E_{X,P_X}, or

$$E_{X,P_X} = \left|\frac{\partial X}{\partial P_X}\frac{P_X}{X}\right|,$$

and as a result, the computed values for E_{X,P_X} are nonnegative.

The computed value of E_{X,P_X} may fall into one of three categories. The first category contains values where $E_{X,P_X} > 1$. In this case, we define own-price demand as **elastic**, indicating that *for some percentage change in the price of a good, there is a greater percentage change in the opposite direction of the quantity demanded of that good*. For example, $E_{X,P_X} = 2$, indicates that a 1 percent increase in price results in a 2 percent decrease in quantity demanded, or conversely, a 1 percent decrease in price results in a 2 percent increase in quantity demanded. In general, if own-price demand is elastic, the degree of quantity response is relatively high, reflecting a disproportionately large percentage change in quantity demanded of a good in response to some percentage change in its price. Further, the greater the value of E_{X,P_X}, the more elastic the own-price demand. For example, if $E_{X,P_X} = 10$, then a 1 percent change in P_X causes a 10 percent change in X, in the opposite direction. The extreme case of an elastic own-price demand occurs when $E_{X,P_X} \to \infty$, where in this situation, we say that own-price demand is infinitely, or perfectly, elastic, indicating that any change in P_X results in an infinite response in the quantity demanded of good X.

The second category of own-price elasticity of demand corresponds to those situations where $E_{X,P_X} = 1$. In this case, own-price demand is defined as **unit elastic**, indicating *that some percentage change in the price of a good results in an equivalent percentage change in the quantity demanded of that good in the opposite direction*. For example, a 1 percent rise in P_X generates a 1 percent decrease in quantity demanded of good X.

The third category of own-price elasticity of demand pertains to values where $E_{X,P_X} < 1$. In this case, own-price demand is defined as **inelastic**, indicating that *for some percentage change in the price of a good there is a smaller corresponding percentage change in the quantity demanded of that good in the opposite direction*. For example, if $E_{X,P_X} = 0.5$, then a 1 percent increase in P_X results in a 0.5 percent decrease in the quantity demanded of good X. In general, if own-price demand is inelastic, the degree of quantity response is relatively low, indicating that the percentage change in quantity demanded is disproportionately lower than the percentage change in price. Therefore, the smaller the computed value of E_{X,P_X} the more inelastic is own-price demand. The extreme case of inelastic own-price demand occurs when $E_{X,P_X} = 0$. In this situation, we describe own-price demand as perfectly inelastic, indicating that for any percentage change in P_X, there is no change at all in the quantity demanded of good X.

7.3.1 Own-Price Demand Curves with Variable Elasticities

The actual computation of own-price elasticity of demand is quite simple. It should be clear from the preceding analysis that this elasticity relates to the own-price demand curve, for which the most common form is a linear demand curve with a negative slope represented as

$$X = b_0 - b_1 P_X.$$

We compute the own-price elasticity for any point on this curve as

$$E_{X,P_X} = \left| \frac{\partial X}{\partial P_X} \frac{P_X}{X} \right| = \left| -\frac{b_1 P_X}{X} \right| = \frac{b_1 P_X}{X}.$$

Although the slope of this own-price demand curve is a constant, $-b_1$, the value of the elasticity varies along the curve as P_X and X vary. More specifically, moving down a negatively sloped linear demand curve, decreasing P_X and increasing X, causes the P_X/X ratio to decrease and therefore decreases the E_{X,P_X} value as well. For example, assume an own-price demand curve of the form

$$X = 10 - P_X.$$

Using this curve, we have selected several values for P_X and computed the corresponding values for X, as shown in Table 7.1. In addition, we have plotted this own-price demand curve in panel (A) of Figure 7.1. For this demand curve, $\partial X/\partial P_X = -1$, and therefore

$$E_{X,P_X} = \left| \frac{(-1)P_X}{X} \right| = \frac{P_X}{X}.$$

Using this result, we have computed elasticity values for selected points on the own-price market demand curve and have presented them in the third column of Table 7.1. Reading down the table, as P_X decreases and X increases, is identical to moving down the plotted own-price market demand curve. As we expect, the computed own-price elasticity values in this table become successively lower as the price of good X decreases. For this negatively sloped linear demand curve, the values of E_{X,P_X} cover the entire range of elasticity categories discussed above. At the midpoint of the curve, $(5,5)$, $E_{X,P_X} = 1$, or own-price demand is unit elastic. For values of P_X and

TABLE 7.1 Values of P_X, X, E_{X,P_X}, TR_X, and MR_X for Market Own-Price Demand Curve, $X = 10 - P_X$

P_X (dollars per unit)	X (units per time period)	E_{X,P_X}	TR_X (dollars per time period)	MR_X (dollars per unit)
10	0	—	0	—
9	1	9	9	9
8	2	4	16	7
7	3	$\frac{7}{3}$	21	5
6	4	$\frac{3}{2}$	24	3
5	5	1	25	1
4	6	$\frac{2}{3}$	24	-1
3	7	$\frac{3}{7}$	21	-3
2	8	$\frac{1}{4}$	16	-5
1	9	$\frac{1}{9}$	9	-7
0	10	0	0	-9

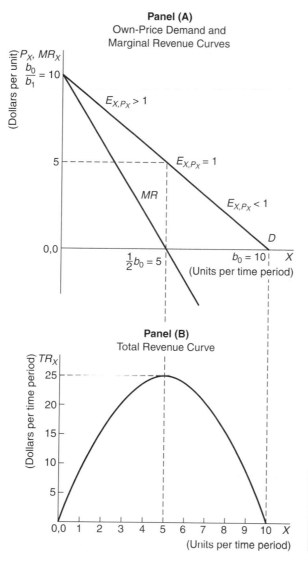

FIGURE 7.1 Relationships among Own-Price Elasticity, and Own-Price Demand, Total Revenue, and Marginal Revenue Curves

X that lie above the midpoint, or where $P_X > 5$ and $X < 5$, $E_{X,P_X} > 1$, or own-price demand is elastic. Finally, for values of P_X and X that lie below the midpoint, or where $P_X < 5$ and $X > 5$, $E_{X,P_X} < 1$, or own-price demand is inelastic. This breakdown for the ranges of elasticity holds true for all negatively sloped, linear own-price demand curves. Thus, in order to compute E_{X,P_X} for this type of curve, first we must always specify the point on the curve at which we are evaluating E_{X,P_X}.

It should be clear from our previous discussion that it is impossible to describe a negatively sloped linear own-price demand curve as either an elastic or inelastic curve, because it contains all ranges of elasticity. We are emphasizing this point because there is often a tendency to describe a relatively flat own-price demand curve as being elastic or a relatively steep own-price demand curve as inelastic. Any statement of this nature actually involves an implicit comparison between two curves of different slopes and intercepts. For example, it is correct for us to say that a relatively flat own-price demand curve is more elastic than a relatively steep own-price demand curve, for some common point or range of quantity-price coordinates. In absolute value terms, a relatively flat curve possesses a smaller slope value for its inverse form, $\partial P_X/\partial X$, than that for a relatively steep curve. Thus, the slope of the own-price demand curve, $\partial X/\partial P_X$, for the flatter case is greater than that for the steeper case. As a result, for any common P_X and X values, the flatter demand curve yields a greater value for E_{X,P_X} and we say that it is more elastic than the steeper own-price demand curve at that point of comparison.

7.3.2 Total and Marginal Revenue

One of our most useful applications of own-price elasticity is as an indicator of the change in the value of total consumer expenditures on a good, resulting from a change in its price. From the seller's perspective, this amount is defined as **total revenue** or *the total value of consumers' expenditures associated with the sale of a good*. We denote this term TR and compute it by multiplying the price of a good, measured in \$/unit, by the total number of units of the good sold. Thus, TR is expressed in dollars, and for some good X is represented as

$$TR_X = P_X X.$$

Using the own-price demand curve

$$X = 10 - P_X,$$

we have computed several values for TR_X corresponding to different quantity-price combinations, where these TR_X values are shown in the fourth column of Table 7.1. Note that in this case our computed TR_X values vary across different points on the demand curve.

A broader question is, how does TR vary as P varies? If the price of a good decreases, and if the market quantity demanded of that good remains constant, then clearly TR decreases. Generally, however, the market quantity demanded of a good is inversely related to its price. We have demonstrated this fact in Table 7.1 by the own-price demand curve,

$$X = 10 - P_X,$$

which shows that as P_X decreases X correspondingly increases. Therefore, the effect on TR_X is a matter of which variable, P_X or X, changes more, where this information is embodied in the concept of own-price elasticity. For example, if own-price demand is elastic, or $E_{X,P_X} > 1$, some percentage change in P_X causes a greater percentage change in the quantity demanded of good X in the opposite direction. Thus, if P_X decreases, X increases more on a percentage basis, causing TR_X to subsequently increase. This reasoning is demonstrated in Table 7.1, where we can observe that for the elastic range of own-price demand, or where $E_{X,P_X} > 1$, a reduction in the price of good X results in an increase in total revenue. However, when own-price demand is elastic, an increase in P_X causes a greater percentage decline in the quantity demanded of good X, and TR_X falls.

Alternatively, for the inelastic range of the own-price demand curve, or where $E_{X,P_X} < 1$, a decrease in P_X causes a disproportionately smaller percentage increase in X, and TR_X subsequently declines. If P_X increases in this case, X decreases by a smaller percentage amount, and TR_X increases. Finally, if own-price demand is unit elastic, or where $E_{X,P_X} = 1$, a percentage change in P_X in either direction causes an equivalent percentage change in X in the opposite direction, and TR_X remains constant. You can verify all of these outcomes by observing the results in Table 7.1. Specifically, if $P_X = \$10$, $X = 0$ because no units of the good are purchased at this price, and as a result, $TR_X = \$0$. As P_X is reduced throughout the elastic range of the own-price demand curve, TR_X increases and achieves a maximum value of \$25 at the midpoint of the demand curve, (5,5), where $E_{X,P_X} = 1$. As P_X is reduced further, moving down through the inelastic range of the demand curve, TR_X declines until ultimately $TR_X = 0$ when $P_X = \$0$.

We can also demonstrate the relationship between TR_X and the own-price demand curve graphically. Before doing so, however, we must first introduce another concept known as **marginal revenue**, denoted MR. The marginal revenue associated with the sale of a good, such as X, measures *the change in total revenue resulting from a change in the quantity of that good sold*. Technically, this definition pertains to infinitesimally small changes in good X, and as a consequence, we can represent it as the derivative dTR_X/dX. In many instances, however, MR_X is considered as the extra revenue associated with selling an extra unit of a good; thus, in this situation we can represent it as $\Delta TR_X/\Delta X$. We can also interpret the marginal revenue associated with the sales of good X as measuring the slope of the corresponding total revenue curve, TR_X. Both representations of MR_X are essentially the same; the only difference is whether the change in X is finite, ΔX, or infinitesimally small, dX. For the example we presented in Table 7.1, the increments in X are finite, specifically, $\Delta X = 1$, and we computed the MR_X values in the last column of the table as $\Delta TR_X/\Delta X$. Thus, for the first unit of good X sold

$$MR_X = \frac{\Delta TR_X}{\Delta X} = \frac{9-0}{1-0} = 9.$$

For the second unit

$$MR_X = \frac{\Delta TR_X}{\Delta X} = \frac{16-9}{2-1} = 7,$$

and by repeating this procedure we have generated the column of MR_X values in Table 7.1 for one-unit increments in X. Note that the values of MR_X are positive for the elastic range of the own-price demand curve and negative for the inelastic range.

We can derive the marginal revenue function from the associated total revenue function. If we take infinitesimally small changes in X, rather than one-unit changes, then $MR_X = dTR_X/dX$. Since

$$TR_X = P_X X,$$

then by applying the product rule we determine the marginal revenue function as

$$MR_X = \frac{dTR_X}{dX} = P_X \frac{dX}{dX} + X \frac{dP_X}{dX}$$

or

$$MR_X = P_X + X \frac{dP_X}{dX} \tag{7.2}$$

Note that we have taken the derivative with respect to X, since the amount of the good sold is treated as the decision variable. We apply the product rule in this case since P_X is a function of X, as represented by the inverse form of the own-price demand curve. Finally, since virtually all market own-price demand curves reflect an inverse relationship between price and quantity demanded, generally $dP_X/dX < 0$, and therefore the term $X dP_X/dX$ is negative. As a result, $MR_X < P_X$, and the MR_X curve lies beneath the own-price demand curve. In part, this relationship is based on the absence of any price discrimination, meaning that once a market price is established, all units of the good are sold at that same price. Since price and quantity demanded are inversely related, price must be decreased in order to sell an additional unit of a good. However, in the absence of price discrimination, the price is reduced for all units sold, including those units that could have been sold at higher prices.

Returning to finite changes in X, specifically $\Delta X = 1$, we can use equation (7.2) to provide a somewhat more insightful calculation of the marginal revenue values in Table 7.1. Decreasing the value of P_X from $P_{X,1}$ to $P_{X,2}$ in order to increase sales of good X by one unit yields a value for MR_X equal to the new lower price, $P_{X,2}$, multiplied by the additional unit sold, $\Delta X = 1$, plus the number of units of the good, X_1, that were previously sold at the original higher price, $P_{X,1}$, multiplied by the reduction in price, ΔP_X. Thus, we can rewrite equation (7.2) for finite changes in X and P_X as

$$MR_X = P_X + X \frac{\Delta P_X}{\Delta X}. \tag{7.3}$$

After substituting the particular values for P_X and X into equation (7.3) and noting that $\Delta X = 1$, we obtain

$$MR_X = P_{X,2} + X_1(P_{X,2} - P_{X,1}),$$

where $(P_{X,2} - P_{X,1}) < 0$. Using the data in Table 7.1, we compute the value of MR for the first unit sold as

$$MR_X = 9 + 0(9 - 10) = 9$$

and for the second unit as

$$MR_X = 8 + 1(8 - 9) = 7.$$

These are the same results we computed earlier using $MR_X = \Delta TR_X / \Delta X$. However, this latter approach provides us with somewhat more insight into the concept of marginal revenue.

Given our previous analysis, it should be clear that both the total revenue and the associated marginal revenue functions are derived from the own-price demand curve. We can further demonstrate these derivatives using the general linear own-price demand curve,

$$X = b_0 - b_1 P_X,$$

for which the inverse own-price demand curve is

$$P_X = \frac{b_0}{b_1} - \frac{1}{b_1}X.$$

Thus,

$$TR_X = P_X X = \left(\frac{b_0}{b_1} - \frac{1}{b_1}X\right)X$$

or

$$TR_X = \frac{b_0}{b_1}X - \frac{1}{b_1}X^2$$

and

$$MR_X = \frac{dTR_X}{dX} = \frac{b_0}{b_1} - \frac{2}{b_1}X.$$

In this case, the TR_X function is quadratic, while the MR_X function and own-price demand curve are linear. Comparing the intercept and slope values for the inverse own-price demand curve and the marginal revenue function, observe that the P_X- and MR_X-intercepts, b_0/b_1, are equal and that the slope of the MR_X function, $-2/b_1$, is twice as large in absolute value terms, compared to the slope of the inverse own-price demand curve, $-1/b_1$. Finally, the X-intercept for the inverse own-price demand curve is b_0, whereas the X-intercept for the MR_X function is $b_0/2$. We compute this MR-intercept by setting MR_X equal to zero and solving for X as

$$MR_X = \frac{b_0}{b_1} - \frac{2}{b_1}X = 0$$

$$\frac{2}{b_1}X = \frac{b_0}{b_1}$$

$$X = \frac{b_0}{2}.$$

Returning to the specific example, for which the own-price demand curve is

$$X = 10 - P_X,$$

we compute the inverse own-price demand curve as

$$P_X = 10 - X.$$

Thus,

$$TR_X = P_X X = (10 - X)(X) = 10X - X^2$$

and

$$MR_X = \frac{dTR_X}{dX} = 10 - 2X.$$

We have plotted these curves in panels (A) and (B) of Figure 7.1, where we can demonstrate the various relationships among the own-price demand, total revenue, and marginal revenue curves. We can also link these relationships to the different ranges for own-price elasticity of demand. The MR_X curve lies beneath the market own-price demand curve, and thus for any positive value of X, $MR_X < P_X$. In the elastic range of the own-price demand curve, or where $E_{X,P_X} > 1$, $MR_X > 0$, and a percentage decrease in P_X, that subsequently causes a larger percentage increase in X (moving left to right), causes TR_X to increase. In the inelastic range, or where $E_{X,P_X} < 1$, $MR_X < 0$, and a percentage decrease in P_X, results in a disproportionately smaller percentage increase in X, causing TR_X to decrease. Finally, observe that TR_X reaches its maximum level where the market own-price demand curve is unit elastic, or where $E_{X,P_X} = 1$, and $MR_X = 0$. We must make a point of clarification about this result. Observe in Table 7.1 that $MR_X = 1$ rather than 0, at what appears to be the midpoint of the own-price demand curve, where $E_{X,P_X} = 1$. This apparent discrepancy is the slight difference in results we generate from using discrete one-unit changes in X as the basis for computing MR_X, as opposed to using infinitesimally small changes in X for the same purpose. In Table 7.1, we have computed MR_X using one-unit increments in X or

$$MR_X = \frac{\Delta TR_X}{\Delta X},$$

where $\Delta X = 1$. Thus, the value of $MR_X = 1$, actually pertains to the interval from $X = 4$ to $X = 5$. However, we derived the MR_X curve shown in panel (A) of Figure 7.1, using infinitesimally small increments in X, or dTR_X/dX, and thus $MR_X = 0$ pertains to the point where $X = 5$.

We have also demonstrated the relationship between marginal revenue and own-price elasticity of demand in Figure 7.1. However, we can express this relationship more formally with a direct formula. As noted earlier,

$$TR_X = P_X X$$

and

$$MR_X = \frac{dTR_X}{dX} = P_X + X\frac{dP_X}{dX}.$$

We can rearrange this equation by factoring out P_X as

$$MR_X = P_X\left(1 + \frac{X}{P_X}\frac{dP_X}{dX}\right).$$

Since own-price demand curves are univariate, containing only the variables X and P_X, then $dP_X/dX = \partial P_X/\partial X$, therefore

$$MR_X = P_X\left(1 + \frac{X}{P_X}\frac{\partial P_X}{\partial X}\right).$$

We can recognize the term $X/P_X\,(\partial P_X/\partial X)$ as the negative of the reciprocal of the own-price elasticity, so we can now express MR_X as

$$MR_X = P_X\left(1 - \frac{1}{E_{X,P_X}}\right). \tag{7.4}$$

Equation (7.4) is a concise representation of the relationship between MR_X and E_{X,P_X}.[1] At the point of unit elasticity $E_{X,P_X} = 1$; therefore,

$$MR_X = P_X\left(1 - \frac{1}{1}\right) = 0.$$

If own-price demand is elastic, $E_{X,P_X} > 1$, then

$$MR_X = P_X\left(1 - \frac{1}{E_{X,P_X}}\right) > 0.$$

Finally, if own-price demand is inelastic, $E_{X,P_X} < 1$, and

$$MR_X = P_X\left(1 - \frac{1}{E_{X,P_X}}\right) < 0.$$

All of these results are consistent with the graphical relationships between E_{X,P_X} and MR_X shown in panel (Λ) of Figure 7.1.

7.3.3 Own-Price Demand Curves with Constant Elasticities

We have shown that for negatively sloped linear demand curves, the computed own-price elasticity of demand varies along the curve. There is another familiar type of own-price demand curve, for which the own-price elasticity remains constant across

---

[1]Earlier, we defined the own-price elasticity of demand as $E_{X,P_X} = |\partial X/\partial P_X \cdot P_X/X|$. Note that we arbitrarily expressed this elasticity as an absolute value in order to force the computed elasticity values to be nonnegative. The term $\partial X/\partial P_X \cdot P_X/X$ is typically negative since generally $\partial X/\partial P_X < 0$, and as a result, $\partial X/\partial P_X \cdot P_X/X = -E_{X,P_X}$. This is the result included in equation (7.4) that expresses MR_X in terms of E_{X,P_X}.

different points on the curve. These curves are of the form we briefly mentioned earlier

$$X = b_1 P_X^c,$$

where b_1 is some positive constant. We can demonstrate that for this type of own-price demand curve, the absolute value of the constant exponent, c, represents the own-price elasticity of demand. The slope of this own-price demand curve is

$$\frac{\partial X}{\partial P_X} = cb_1 P_X^{c-1}$$

and therefore

$$E_{X,P_X} = \left| \frac{\partial X}{\partial P_X} \frac{P_X}{X} \right| = \left| (cb_1 P_X^{c-1}) \frac{P_X}{X} \right|.$$

After substituting $b_1 P_X^c$ for X, this expression is

$$E_{X,P_X} = \left| (cb_1 P_X^{c-1}) \left(\frac{P_X}{b_1 P_X^c} \right) \right| = \left| (cP_X^c) \left(\frac{1}{P_X^c} \right) \right| = |c|.$$

In this case, the own-price elasticity is a constant value and is therefore independent of the values of P_X and X. Since most own-price demand curves exhibit an inverse relationship between quantity demanded and price, the value of c is generally less than zero. However, by taking the absolute value of c, we can eliminate the negative sign and thus apply the usual interpretations regarding the value of the own-price elasticity of demand. For example, assume the own-price demand curve is

$$X = 4P_X^{-1/2}.$$

Therefore,

$$\frac{\partial X}{\partial P_X} = (-\tfrac{1}{2})(4)P_X^{-1/2-1} = -2P_X^{-3/2}$$

and

$$E_{X,P_X} = \left| (-2P_X^{-3/2}) \left(\frac{P_X}{X} \right) \right| = \left| (-2P_X^{-3/2}) \left(\frac{P_X}{4\,P_X^{-1/2}} \right) \right| = \left| -\tfrac{1}{2} \right| = \tfrac{1}{2}.$$

Alternatively, since $c = -\tfrac{1}{2}$, we can obtain this same result by simply taking the absolute value of the exponent, $\left| -\tfrac{1}{2} \right| = \tfrac{1}{2}$. In this case, we interpret the own-price elasticity as inelastic, since $E_{X,P_X} < 1$.

We have illustrated a general form for a constant elasticity demand curve in Figure 7.2. Observe that this curve has neither an X nor a P_X intercept, and that the slope varies along the curve. Moving down the curve, the absolute value of the slope of the inverse demand curve, $\partial P_X/\partial X$, decreases, and therefore its reciprocal, $\partial X/\partial P_X$, increases in absolute value terms. More importantly, the increases in the absolute value of the slope, $|\partial X/\partial P_X|$, precisely offset the decreases in the P_X/X ratio. As a result, the elasticity remains constant along such an own-price demand curve.

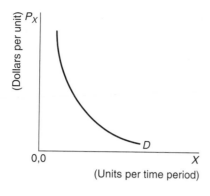

FIGURE 7.2 Constant Elasticity Own-Price Demand Curve

Finally, there are two extreme types of own-price demand curves that we should mention before closing the discussion of own-price elasticity of demand. The first type applies to the own-price demand curve

$$X = b_0 - b_1 P_X,$$

where $b_1 = 0$, and therefore

$$X = b_0.$$

In this case, the quantity demanded of good X, b_0, does not vary at all with P_X. The corresponding own-price demand curve, shown in panel (A) of Figure 7.3, is vertical since there exists only one value of X for an infinite number of P_X values. The change in X with respect to a change in P_X, $\partial X/\partial P_X$, is equal to b_1 which is equal to zero. As a result, $E_{X,P_X} = 0$, and we describe the own-price demand as perfectly inelastic.[2]

FIGURE 7.3 Two Extreme Types of Own-Price Demand Curves with Constant Elasticities

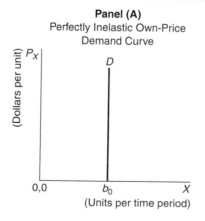
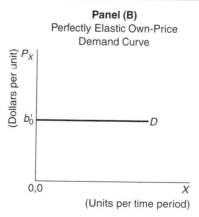

Panel (A)
Perfectly Inelastic Own-Price Demand Curve

Panel (B)
Perfectly Elastic Own-Price Demand Curve

---

[2]Realistically, completely vertical demand curves do not exist. However, there may exist certain ranges of prices for which a vertical approximation may be appropriate.

The other extreme case occurs if, for some value of the price of good X, P_X, there exist an infinite number of values for the quantity demanded of good X. In this case, we cannot define X as a function of P_X because for any value of P_X there exists no unique value for X. However, the inverse own-price demand function, or curve, does exist in the form

$$P_X = b_0' - b_1'X,$$

where $b_1' = 0$, and therefore

$$P_X = b_0'.$$

Specifically, P_X is equal to some constant value, and the plotted inverse own-price demand curve is horizontal, as we have shown in panel (B) of Figure 7.3, with the slope, $\partial P_X/\partial X = b_1' = 0$. Since there are an infinite number of possible values of X for which $P_X = b_0'$, or any other constant value, the own-price elasticity of demand is infinite as well, or $E_{X,P_X} = \infty$, and we define the own-price demand as perfectly elastic.

An example of a perfectly elastic own-price demand curve is that for a perfectly competitive firm. You may recall from your principles of microeconomics course that in this case, the price of good X, P_X, is determined in the market and the individual firm takes this price as predetermined. The firm can theoretically sell any amount of good X at that price, and the own-price demand curve for the typical perfectly competitive firm is horizontal, or perfectly elastic. Conceptually, this result reflects the fact that a perfectly competitive firm faces many perfect substitutes for its product. Therefore, if such a firm attempts to raise the price of its output above the market-determined price, consumers will choose to purchase the many lower priced perfect substitutes instead. In the next section we will discuss in greater detail how the number and closeness of substitutes for a good impacts the value of its own-price elasticity of demand.

7.3.4 Determinants and Applications of Own-Price Elasticity of Demand

It is possible for us to make meaningful comparisons of the quantity-price responsiveness across own-price demand curves for different goods and services using own-price elasticity estimates. In Section 7.3.1 we demonstrated that the value of an own-price elasticity varies over a negatively sloped linear own-price demand curve for a particular good or service. Specifically, E_{X,P_X} changes from elastic to unit elastic to inelastic values, as the price decreases and, correspondingly, as the quantity demanded of the good increases. However, we also showed in the previous section that there are some own-price demand curves for which the own-price elasticity does not vary along the curve. In general, we can use these constant own-price elasticities to compare the responsiveness of the quantity demanded of a good to changes in its own-price, across many diverse products. Before making such comparisons, however, it is important that you first understand the underlying determinants that affect own-price elasticity of demand.

Research has revealed a variety of factors known to affect consumers' responsiveness between the quantity demanded of a good and changes in its price. Economists typically categorize these underlying factors in terms of the availability and closeness of substitutes for the good or service being analyzed, the length of the time period under analysis, and the percentage of a household's total expenditures attributable to a particular good or service.

Availability and Closeness of Substitutes

The number and perceived closeness of substitutes for a particular good or service affects consumers' responsiveness to a change in the own-price of a good. Logically, the more substitutes that exist for a good and the closer are these substitutes, the more elastic is the own-price elasticity of demand. If consumers perceive that there are many close substitutes for a good or service, they will not be as compelled to continue purchasing a good for which the price increases as they would be in the absence of many close substitutes. Conversely, if the price of this good decreases, consumers will be inclined to increase their consumption of the good significantly, since they tend to switch to this product in place of other substitute goods. However, if a good has no close substitutes and its price increases, then consumers are likely to still purchase significant amounts of the product at the higher price.

The number and closeness of substitutes for a good, and hence the associated value of own-price elasticity, are partly determined by how broadly we define the product under analysis. Specifically, if the good or service is very broadly defined, then the number of substitutes available is much smaller because many potential substitutes become part of the product definition. For example, a consumer may observe that there are many substitutes for a narrowly defined product such as Ford Mustangs. However, as we define the product under analysis in successively broader terms, as say Fords, domestic automobiles, automobiles, or passenger vehicles, the number of substitute goods becomes successively smaller, and as a result, so do the corresponding own-price elasticities of demand.

For example, in Table 7.2, where we have reported the estimated own-price elasticities of demand for several goods and services, observe that this value for automobiles is 2.4. In contrast, the own-price elasticity of demand for a particular model of automobiles, specifically Ford Mustangs, is much larger, measuring 8.4. This disparity in elasticities is undoubtedly due to the fact that while there exist some substitutes for automobiles in general, such as trucks, vans, or motorcycles, far more substitutes are available for the more specifically defined product, Mustangs. These substitutes include Corvettes, Miatas, and Toyota MR2s, as well as many other models of automobiles. Also note in Table 7.2 that the own-price elasticity of demand for specific soft drinks, such as Coca-Cola and Pepsi-Cola, exceeds the value of one, indicating elastic demand for these products. We also expect these elasticity values to exceed that associated with the more broadly defined product, soft drinks.

Another related issue affecting the own-price elasticity of demand is whether the good is perceived as a necessity or as a luxury item. Clearly, if consumers perceive a

TABLE 7.2 Estimated Own-Price Elasticities in the Short and Long Run for Selected Goods and Services

Good or Service	Short Run E_{X,P_X}	Long Run E_{X,P_X}
Cigarettes[a]	0.4	0.8
Residential electricity[b]	0.1	1.9
Magazines & newspapers[b]	0.4	—
China and glassware[b]	1.6	2.6
Funerals and burials[b]	0.4	—
Automobiles[b]	1.2	2.4
Ford Mustang[c]	—	8.4
Coca-Cola[d]	—	1.7
Pepsi-Cola[d]	—	2.0
U.K. lottery tickets[e]	—	1.8

[a]Gary Becker, Michael Grossman, and Kevin Murphy, "An Empirical Analysis of Cigarette Addiction," *American Economic Review* 84, June 1994, pp. 396–418.

[b]Hendrick S. Houthakker and Lester D. Taylor, *Consumer Demand in the United States: Analyses and Projections*, 2nd ed. (Cambridge, MA: Harvard University Press, 1970), pp. 166–167.

[c]F. Owen Irvine, Jr., "Demand Equations for Individual New Car Models Estimated Using Transaction Prices with Implications for Regulatory Issues," *Southern Economic Journal*, January 1983, p 776.

[d]F. Gasmi, J.J. Laffont, and Q. Vuong, "Econometric Analysis of Collusive Behavior in a Soft-Drink Market," *Journal of Management Strategy* 1, Summer 1992, p. 296.

[e]Lisa Farrell and Ian Walker, "The Welfare Effects of Lotto: Evidence from the U.K.," *Journal of Public Economics* 72, 1999, p. 113.

good as a necessity, they believe there are no close substitutes for this particular product. An example of such a good is some specific, life-sustaining prescription medicine for which no substitute drugs exist. Should the price of this medicine either rise or fall, there will be virtually no change in purchases of the drug. Clearly, not all goods and services are viewed as necessities by consumers. Some goods are perceived as luxury items, where the distinction between luxury and necessity goods is largely determined by consumers' tastes and preferences. For a luxury good, consumers can typically postpone their purchases without incurring any dire repercussions, and as a result, many other goods are viewed, at least indirectly, as substitutes. Since it is not imperative that consumers purchase a particular luxury item, the own-price elasticity of demand is much higher for these goods and services than for necessities.

Elasticity measures are used extensively in the business world. If firms possess knowledge regarding the responsiveness of consumer demand to changes in the price of a good, these firms can manipulate this price to increase revenue. Thus, the impact of a change in the price of a good on the value of a firm's sales, or total revenue, is reflected by the corresponding own-price elasticity of demand. As an example, we can observe this type of pricing behavior in the commercial airline industry. When reducing airfares, the major carriers do not cut all of their fares by the same amount. Rather, they often reduce those fares associated with vacation destinations, such as Orlando or San Francisco, because they believe these trips to be luxury goods for which the own-price demand is highly elastic. In contrast, business travel is perceived as a necessity for which there are few good substitutes. As a result, airfares for business travel are seldom discounted since air carriers know that they will not generate many additional ticket sales between, say, St. Louis and Des Moines, by reducing the price of such a ticket.

We can observe another application of own-price elasticity of demand in the failed attempt by the U.S. Congress in 1990 to raise tax revenue by placing a very high tax on yachts priced at over $100,000, as well as on other luxury goods such as private planes, jewelry, and furs.[3] This luxury tax raised little tax revenue because consumers avoided it by purchasing yachts and planes in the secondary (used) market where the tax did not apply, or by purchasing other luxury goods that were not affected by the tax, such as powerboats. A far more effective tax, in terms of revenue collected, is that levied on cigarettes. Whether due to addiction or habit, smokers have a relatively inelastic demand for cigarettes, and as a result, they do not substantially decrease their consumption of cigarettes when the price increases. Therefore, when the government seeks to raise a significant amount of revenue by means of an excise tax, it has greater success levying a tax on a good or service characterized by inelastic own-price demand.

Time Period under Analysis

When analyzing own-price elasticity of demand for a good or service, economists collect data for the sales of a product and its price over a specified time period. By adjusting the duration of their analysis, they can estimate own-price elasticities for both short and longer periods of time. From a consumer's perspective, the length of time under analysis is of utmost importance. Recall that when many close substitutes exist for a good or service, the own-price elasticity of demand is larger than when only a few substitutes are available. However, a consumer typically needs time to search for these alternative goods. Therefore, the longer the time period under consideration, the more price responsive is consumers' demand for a product. For example, commercial airlines are aware that travelers who purchase their tickets well in advance of their departure date have a more elastic demand than those individuals who purchase their tickets a few hours before a flight is scheduled to depart. As a result, airlines charge much less for advance purchase tickets, knowing that consumers have sufficient time to look for alternative means of getting to their destination. However, those individuals buying their tickets just prior to departure do not have enough time to seek other

---

[3]Rick Wartzman and David Rogers. "Luxury Tax Repeal Won't be Blocked by Administration," *Wall Street Journal*, March 2, 1993, p. A-2.

The Relevance of Own-Price Elasticity of Demand for Tobacco Products to the Tobacco Resolution of 1998

In 1998, an agreement known as the Tobacco Resolution was reached between a group of U.S. states and the tobacco industry, resulting in a settlement that, among other concessions, required the tobacco companies to pay a sum to the states totaling $246 billion over a period of 25 years. At the outset, this agreement appeared to be devastating to the tobacco industry in that their cumulative annual pretax operating profits as of 1997 were only $8.4 billion. Clearly, the tobacco companies had to increase the price of tobacco products significantly in order to defray the costs of the settlement. Yet, because of the law of demand, such a price increase would cause a reduction in the quantity of the product sold. As a result, the effect of a price increase on the tobacco companies' revenues and profits ultimately depends on the own-price elasticity associated with the demand for tobacco products.

Most estimates of this own-price elasticity have indicated that the demand for tobacco products is highly inelastic. This implies that the tobacco industry has been able to pass along most of the higher costs associated with the Tobacco Resolution in the form of higher product prices without experiencing a substantial reduction in the quantity of their product sold. Although based on predictions associated with an earlier, but similar, proposed agreement, the reasons and estimates supporting this contention have been succinctly summarized in an article by Michael M. Phillips and Suein L. Hwang published in the *Wall Street Journal*. Some important excerpts from this article are given below.

Tobacco demand is inelastic. Smokers don't cut their intake much even when prices rise. Frank J. Chaloupka, associate professor of economics at the University of Illinois in Chicago, figures adult cigarette-smoking declines only about 4% for every 10% cigarette-price increase (half from reduced intake, half from people quitting).

There aren't obvious substitutes. If orange juice prices soar, consumers can buy lemonade. Smokers have no such easy choice.

Prices will pick up the slack. Because every major producer has agreed to settle—tiny Liggett settled separately—it is unlikely any one company would undercut the others.

Both [Jeffrey E. Harris, an economics professor at the Massachusetts Institute of Technology] and W. Kip Viscusi, a Harvard Law School economist and expert witness for the tobacco industry, believe the price of a pack of cigarettes will rise 62 cents on average within five years to provide the companies with enough revenue to pay off the plaintiffs."[4]

---

[4]Michael M. Phillips and Suein L. Hwang, "Why Tobacco Pact Won't Hurt Industry," *Wall Street Journal*, September 12, 1997, pp. A1, A10.

forms of transportation, and thus airlines charge much higher prices to these customers. Table 7.2 provides short- and long-run own-price elasticities that have been estimated for several goods. These results are consistent with the theoretical discussion we presented earlier, since the long-run elasticities are greater than their short-run counterparts in every case.

Percentage of Consumers' Total Expenditures Spent on a Good

Another factor greatly influencing the responsiveness of consumers' purchases of a good to changes in its price is the percentage of their household budgets spent on the product. The demand for goods constituting a large fraction of consumers' total expenditures tends to have larger own-price elasticities than those comprising a smaller portion. This conclusion follows because some percentage change in the price of a big ticket item has a much larger impact on consumers' budgets than does an equivalent percentage change in the price of a relatively cheaper good. We can observe this economic phenomenon in Table 7.2 where the own-price elasticity of demand for automobiles is much greater than that for magazines and newspapers.

7.4 INCOME ELASTICITY AND ITS APPLICATION

We have devoted a great amount of time discussing own-price elasticity of demand, largely because this particular elasticity is so frequently encountered in business and economic analysis. However, two other elasticities related to consumer theory are also quite useful. These are the income elasticity and the cross-price elasticity, where both of these elasticities also relate to the broad market demand function we derived in the previous chapter.

Income elasticity is *the percentage change in the quantity demanded of a good resulting from a percentage change in money income*. Mathematically, we express the income elasticity for a good, such as X, as

$$E_{X,I} = \frac{\%\Delta X}{\%\Delta I} = \frac{\frac{\Delta X}{X}}{\frac{\Delta I}{I}} = \frac{\Delta X}{\Delta I}\frac{I}{X} = \frac{\partial X}{\partial I}\frac{I}{X}.$$

As with own-price elasticity of demand, the term E represents elasticity, where the subscripts indicate the variables under focus, in this case, the quantity demanded of a good, X, and money income, I, both measured in market terms. The term $\partial X/\partial I$ represents the change in X due to an infinitesimally small change in I, or the slope of an Engel curve. In the previous chapter we specified the Engel curve as

$$X = X_I(\overline{P}_{X,1}, \overline{P}_{Y,1}, I),$$

or, if we include additional determinants, as

$$X = X_I(\overline{P}_{X,1}, \overline{P}_{Y,1}, \overline{P}_{W,1}, \ldots, \overline{P}_{Z,1}, I, \overline{T}_1, \overline{N}_1).$$

What distinguishes these equations as Engel curves is that we are holding all of the determinants of X other than I, constant at specific levels. Engel curves may have positive or negative slope values, depending on the nature of the relationship between the consumption of good X and consumer income. Furthermore, since the I/X term included in $E_{X,I}$ is always positive, the sign of the slope of an Engel curve, $\partial X/\partial I$, determines the sign of an income elasticity. Both the sign and the magnitude of this income elasticity value indicate how the quantity demanded of a good responds to a change in consumers' money income, and thus provide some insight into the nature of the good.

Goods may fall into one of two broad categories, based on the computed value of $E_{X,I}$. First, if $E_{X,I} \geq 0$, we classify the good as normal. Recall from Chapter 5 that a normal good is one for which the optimal consumption level, generally, varies directly with income. Thus in the current context, we can state that a normal good is one for which some percentage change in money income causes some percentage change in quantity demanded, in the same direction. For example, if $E_{X,I} = 0.5$, then a 1 percent increase in I results in a 0.5 percent increase in X, or conversely, a 1 percent decrease in I causes a 0.5 percent decrease in X. We can further categorize normal goods according to their income elasticity values. Specifically, if $0 \leq E_{X,I} \leq 1$, we consider the good, X, to be a necessity, such as basic clothing and food, because some percentage change in money income causes a disproportionately smaller change in the quantity demanded of the good. The previous example, for which $E_{X,I} = 0.5$, is just such a case. Alternatively, if $E_{X,I} > 1$, then we consider the good as a luxury, such as jewelry or fine wines, since a percentage change in I results in a disproportionately larger percentage change in consumption of good X. For example, if $E_{X,I} = 4.0$, a 1 percent increase in I causes a 4 percent increase in X.

We can also demonstrate that the percentage of consumers' incomes spent on a good either rises or falls, as income increases, on the basis of whether the good is a luxury or a necessity, respectively. For a necessity, the percentage of consumers' incomes spent on good X, $\overline{P}_{X,1}X/I$, decreases as income increases, and conversely, for a luxury, $\overline{P}_{X,1}X/I$ increases as income increases. We can prove this by evaluating the sign of the derivative of $\overline{P}_{X,1}X/I$ with respect to I. Thus, applying the quotient rule, we obtain

$$\frac{d\left(\dfrac{\overline{P}_{X,1}X}{I}\right)}{dI} = \frac{I\left(\dfrac{d(\overline{P}_{X,1}X)}{dI}\right) - \overline{P}_{X,1}X\dfrac{dI}{dI}}{I^2},$$

or

$$\frac{d\left(\dfrac{\overline{P}_{X,1}X}{I}\right)}{dI} = \frac{I\overline{P}_{X,1}\dfrac{dX}{dI} - \overline{P}_{X,1}X}{I^2}.$$

Factoring out the term $\overline{P}_{X,1}X$ from the right-hand side of this equation yields

$$\frac{d\left(\dfrac{\overline{P}_{X,1}X}{I}\right)}{dI} = \frac{\overline{P}_{X,1}X\left(\dfrac{I}{X}\dfrac{dX}{dI} - 1\right)}{I^2}.$$

Since for an Engel curve, we hold constant all determinants of X, other than I, then

$$\frac{dX}{dI} = \frac{\partial X}{\partial I}.$$

Therefore,

$$\frac{d\left(\frac{\overline{P}_{X,1}X}{I}\right)}{dI} = \frac{\overline{P}_{X,1}X(E_{X,I}-1)}{I^2}, \tag{7.5}$$

and we can evaluate the change in the percentage of consumers' incomes spent on good X with respect to a change in income, $d(\overline{P}_{X,1}X/I)/dI$, on the basis of the value of $E_{X,I}$. As noted earlier, if a good, such as X, is a normal good that is also a necessity, $0 \leq E_{X,I} \leq 1$, and the term $E_{X,I} - 1$ in equation (7.5) is less than zero. As a result, $d(\overline{P}_{X,1}X/I)/dI < 0$, indicating that the percentage of consumers' incomes spent on good X varies inversely with income. If $E_{X,I} = 1$, then $E_{X,I} - 1 = 0$, and $d(\overline{P}_{X,1}X/I)/dI = 0$. This result indicates that the percentage of consumers' incomes spent on good X does not vary with income but instead remains constant as income changes. On the other hand, if a good such as X is a luxury, $E_{X,I} > 1$ and $d(\overline{P}_{X,1}X/I)/dI > 0$, indicating that the percentage of consumers' incomes spent on good X varies directly with income.

The other broad category of goods based on values of $E_{X,I}$ is for $E_{X,I} < 0$, where in this case, we classify the good as inferior. Recall in Chapter 5 we defined an inferior good as one for which the optimal consumption level varies inversely with income. In this context, an inferior good is one for which some percentage change in money income causes some percentage change in the quantity demanded of the good in the opposite direction. For example, if $E_{X,I} = -2.0$, a 1 percent increase in I causes a 2 percent decrease in X, or conversely, a 1 percent decrease in I causes a 2 percent increase in X. Some examples of inferior goods are items such as beans and hot dogs. Many consumers decrease their quantity demanded of these goods as their incomes rise, substituting toward better quality goods, such as steak or seafood. The percentage of consumers' incomes spent on an inferior good varies inversely with income since the absolute amount of the good demanded also varies in such a manner. In Figure 7.4 we

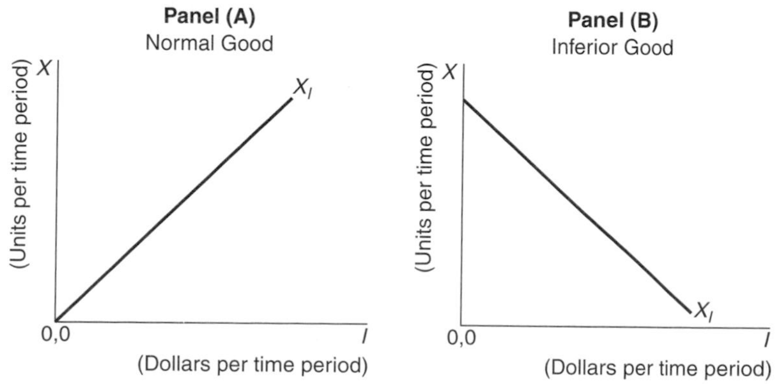

FIGURE 7.4 Examples of Engel Curves for Two Different Types of Goods

present two examples of hypothetical Engel curves for a good such as X. In panel (A) the Engel curve possesses a positive slope on the assumption that good X is normal. Alternatively, if we assume that good X is inferior, then it is characterized by the negatively sloped Engel curve shown in panel (B).

The actual computation of an income elasticity is quite simple, where it is dependent on the nature of the Engel curve. For Engel curves possessing no intercept, the income elasticity is constant and therefore independent of the X and I values. In this case, for an income value of zero, the quantity demanded of the good is zero. Specifically, this type of Engel curve is of the form

$$X = B_1 I^\alpha.$$

Therefore,

$$\frac{\partial X}{\partial I} = \alpha B_1 I^{\alpha-1}$$

and

$$E_{X,I} = \frac{\partial X}{\partial I} \frac{I}{X} = (\alpha B_1 I^{\alpha-1})\left(\frac{I}{X}\right) = (\alpha B_1 I^{\alpha-1})\left(\frac{I}{B_1 I^\alpha}\right),$$

or

$$E_{X,I} = \frac{\alpha I^\alpha}{I^\alpha} = \alpha.$$

For example, if we assume an Engel curve as

$$X = 4I^2,$$

then

$$E_{X,I} = (8I)\left(\frac{I}{4\,I^2}\right) = 2.$$

In this case, the good is normal since $E_{X,I} > 0$, indicating that a 1 percent increase in I causes a 2 percent increase in X. We can also classify the good as a luxury item since $E_{X,I} > 1$.

For Engel curves with a positive X-intercept, the income elasticity varies along the curve. In this case, consumers purchase some of the good even when their incomes are zero. In this situation, the Engel curve is of the form

$$X = B_0 + B_1 I^\alpha,$$

where the intercept of the Engel curve is some positive value B_0, indicating that consumers purchase B_0 amount of good X when $I = 0$. The slope of this Engel curve is

$$\frac{\partial X}{\partial I} = \alpha B_1 I^{\alpha-1}$$

and therefore,

$$E_{X,I} = \frac{\partial X}{\partial I} \frac{I}{X} = (\alpha B_1 I^{\alpha-1})\left(\frac{I}{X}\right),$$

or

$$E_{X,I} = (\alpha B_1 I^{\alpha-1})\left(\frac{I}{B_0 + B_1 I^\alpha}\right) = \frac{\alpha B_1 I^\alpha}{B_0 + B_1 I^\alpha}. \qquad (7.6)$$

In this case, $E_{X,I}$ depends on the value of I and therefore varies along the Engel curve. Specifically, since an increase in I causes the numerator in equation (7.6) to increase more than the denominator, our computed $E_{X,I}$ value increases, in absolute value terms, as I increases.

As an example, assume the Engel curve is

$$X = 10 + 4I^{1/2},$$

then

$$E_{X,I} = (2I^{-1/2})\left(\frac{I}{10 + 4I^{1/2}}\right) = \frac{2I^{1/2}}{10 + 4I^{1/2}}.$$

Thus, if $I = \$4$ (in thousands of dollars)

$$E_{X,I} = \frac{2(4)^{1/2}}{10 + 4(4)^{1/2}} = \frac{4}{10 + 8} = \frac{4}{18} = \frac{2}{9} = 0.22,$$

However, if $I = \$9$ (in thousands of dollars)

$$E_{X,I} = \frac{2(9)^{1/2}}{10 + 4(9)^{1/2}} = \frac{2(3)}{10 + 4(3)} = \frac{6}{22} = \frac{3}{11} = 0.27.$$

These results indicate that the computed income elasticity increases as income increases. Further, we characterize this good as normal since $E_{X,I} > 0$, and more specifically, as a necessity since $E_{X,P_I} < 1$.

In Table 7.3, we report estimated income elasticities for several goods. Observe that in the short run, the different goods fall into different income elasticity categories. Based on these income elasticity values, we can say that furniture is a luxury good, physicians' services are a necessity, and potatoes constitute an inferior good.

An interesting application of income elasticity information is in the field of marketing. After acquiring information about the relationships between consumers' expenditures on various goods and their incomes, firms can more precisely target their advertising to customers in those income groups that will be most responsive. For example, Jaguar advertises its automobile in the *Wall Street Journal*, a publication with a readership of much higher than average income, whereas advertisements for Chevy trucks often appear in the pages of *TV Guide*, whose readership has a comparatively lower average income.

TABLE 7.3	Estimated Income Elasticities in the Short and Long Run for Various Goods and Services	
Good or Service	**Short Run** $E_{X,I}$	**Long Run** $E_{X,I}$
Furniture[a]	2.60	0.53
Physicians' services[a]	0.28	1.15
Jewelry and watches[a]	1.00	1.60
Foreign travel[a]	0.24	3.09
Potatoes[a]	−0.20	−0.81
Coca-Cola[b]	—	0.68
Pepsi-Cola[b]	—	1.70
U.K. lottery tickets[c]	—	0.27

[a]Hendrick S. Houthakker and Lester D. Taylor, *Consumer Demand in the United States: Analyses and Projections*, 2nd. ed. (Cambridge, MA: Harvard University Press, 1970), pp. 166–167.

[b]F. Gasmi, J.J. Laffont, and Q. Vuong, "Econometric Analysis of Collusive Behavior in a Soft-Drink Market," *Journal of Management Strategy* 1, Summer 1992, p. 296.

[c]Lisa Farrell and Ian Walker, "The Welfare Effects of Lotto: Evidence from the UK," *Journal of Public Economics* 72, 1999, p. 113.

7.5 CROSS-PRICE ELASTICITY OF DEMAND AND ITS APPLICATIONS

The final elasticity related to consumer theory that we will discuss is the **cross-price elasticity of demand**, defined as *the percentage change in the quantity demanded of a good resulting from a percentage change in the price of another good.* Thus, for two goods, X and Y, the formula for the cross-price elasticity of demand for good X is

$$E_{X,P_Y} = \frac{\%\Delta X}{\%\Delta P_Y} = \frac{\dfrac{\Delta X}{X}}{\dfrac{\Delta P_Y}{P_Y}} = \frac{\Delta X}{\Delta P_Y}\frac{P_Y}{X} = \frac{\partial X}{\partial P_Y}\frac{P_Y}{X}.$$

The term $\partial X/\partial P_Y$ represents the change in the quantity demanded of good X due to an infinitesimally small change in the price of good Y, and represents the slope of the cross-price demand curve

$$X = X_Y(\overline{P}_{X,1}, P_Y, \overline{P}_{W,1}, \dots, \overline{P}_{Z,1}, \overline{I}_1, \overline{T}_1, \overline{N}_1).$$

Since the term P_Y/X is always positive, the sign of $\partial X/\partial P_Y$ determines the sign of the cross-price elasticity.

Both the sign and the magnitude of the cross-price elasticity reveal a considerable amount of information about the nature of the relationship between two goods. If $E_{X,P_Y} > 0$, we classify goods X and Y as gross substitutes. Recall in Chapter 5 we defined gross substitutes as two goods for which the quantity demanded of one good varies directly with the price of the other good, holding its own price and money income constant. In this context, we characterize such goods as those for which some percentage change in the price of one good causes some percentage change in the quantity demanded of the other, in the same direction. In this case, an increase in the price of good Y causes consumers to purchase less of good Y and to substitute more units of good X in its place. We use the term *gross substitutes* because the effects on the quantities demanded of goods X and Y caused by a price change embody both the income and substitution effects discussed in Chapter 5. For example, $E_{X,P_Y} = 5.0$ indicates that a 1 percent increase (decrease) in the price of good Y generates a 5 percent increase (decrease) in the quantity demanded of good X. Finally, the greater the value of E_{X,P_Y}, the closer are goods X and Y as constituting substitutes for each other.

If $E_{X,P_Y} < 0$, we classify goods X and Y as gross complements. Recall in Chapter 5 we defined gross complements as two goods for which the quantity demanded of one good varies inversely with the price of the other, holding its own price and money income constant. In this context we characterize such goods as those for which some percentage change in the price of one good causes some percentage change in the quantity demanded of the other, in the opposite direction. Complements are goods that are used in conjunction with each other, and as a result, an increase in the price of one good causes a decrease in the quantity demanded of both goods. For example, if $E_{X,P_Y} = -3.0$, a 1 percent increase in the price of good Y results in a 3 percent decrease in the quantity demanded of good X, as well as causing some decrease in the quantity demanded of good Y. Generally, we can say that the greater the value of E_{X,P_Y}, in absolute value terms, or the more negative the value of E_{X,P_Y}, the more closely related are the two goods as complements. Finally, a value of $E_{X,P_Y} = 0$ indicates no relationship between goods X and Y, and in this case, a change in P_Y has no effect on the quantity demanded of good X.

We mentioned earlier that cross-price elasticities are related to cross-price demand curves. Two examples of cross-price demand curves are shown in Figure 7.5,

FIGURE 7.5 Examples of Cross-Price Demand Curves for Two Different Relationships Between Goods X and Y

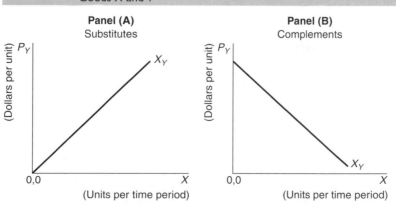

Panel (A)
Substitutes

Panel (B)
Complements

where P_Y and X are plotted on the vertical and horizontal axes, respectively. In panel (A) we assume that goods X and Y are gross substitutes; therefore, the cross-price demand curve possesses a positive slope. In panel (B), we assume that goods X and Y are gross complements; thus, the cross-price demand curve has a negative slope. The computed cross-price elasticities can be either constant or variable, depending on the nature of the underlying cross-price demand curve. For curves of the form

$$X = a_1 P_Y^\delta,$$

we compute the cross-price elasticity by first determining the slope of the cross-price demand curve as

$$\frac{\partial X}{\partial P_Y} = \delta a_1 P_Y^{\delta-1}.$$

Therefore,

$$E_{X,P_Y} = (\delta a_1 P_Y^{\delta-1})\left(\frac{P_Y}{X}\right),$$

or

$$E_{X,P_Y} = (\delta a_1 P_Y^{\delta-1})\left(\frac{P_Y}{a_1 P_Y^\delta}\right) = \delta.$$

In this case, the value of the cross-price elasticity is a constant, δ, and therefore it is independent of the values of P_Y and X. For example, assume the cross-price demand curve is

$$X = 10 P_Y^3.$$

Then

$$E_{X,P_Y} = (30 P_Y^2)\left(\frac{P_Y}{10\ P_Y^3}\right) = 3,$$

indicating that a 1 percent increase in P_Y causes a 3 percent increase in the quantity demanded of good X. In this case we classify the two goods, X and Y, as gross substitutes.

For cross-price demand curves of the form

$$X = a_0 + a_1 P_Y^\delta,$$

we compute the cross-price elasticity in the following manner. Since,

$$\frac{\partial X}{\partial P_Y} = \delta a_1 P_Y^{\delta-1},$$

$$E_{X,P_Y} = (\delta a_1 P_Y^{\delta-1})\left(\frac{P_Y}{a_0 + a_1\ P_Y^\delta}\right),$$

or

$$E_{X,P_Y} = \frac{\delta a_1 P_Y^\delta}{a_0 + a_1 P_Y^\delta}.$$

In this case, the value of E_{X,P_Y} depends on the value of P_Y, and thus its value varies along the cross-price demand curve. As an example, assume the cross-price demand curve is

$$X = 10 - 2P_Y,$$

Therefore,

$$\frac{\partial X}{\partial P_Y} = -2,$$

and hence

$$E_{X,P_Y} = (-2)\left(\frac{P_Y}{10 - 2\,P_Y}\right) = \frac{-2\,P_Y}{10 - 2\,P_Y}.$$

If $P_Y = \$1$, then

$$E_{X,P_Y} = \frac{-2(1)}{10 - 2(1)} = \frac{-2}{8} = -0.25,$$

and if $P_Y = \$2$ then

$$E_{X,P_Y} = \frac{-2(2)}{10 - 2(2)} = \frac{-4}{10 - 4} = \frac{-4}{6} = -0.67.$$

These computed values for E_{X,P_Y} are negative, indicating that the two goods are gross complements.

In Table 7.4 we have reported the estimated cross-price elasticities for various goods and services. Based on these cross-price elasticities, we interpret all pairs of goods listed in the table as substitutes, with the exception of subcompact cars and full-size cars. Also, these cross-price elasticity values indicate that the degree of substitutability within each pair of goods varies greatly across the various combinations. For example, the cross-price elasticity between Coca-Cola and Pepsi-Cola is estimated to be 0.61, indicating that these goods are indeed substitutes for each other. More specifically, we can interpret this elasticity value as indicating that a 1 percent increase (decrease) in the price of Pepsi-Cola results in a 0.61 percent increase (decrease) in the quantity demanded of Coca-Cola.

A common application of cross-price elasticity information is in the area of retailing. An entrepreneur who knows that the cross-price elasticity between two goods is a negative value can use this information as justification for reducing the price of one good to increase sales of the complementary good. For example, an audio specialty store may elect to reduce the price of stereo receivers in an effort to boost stereo speaker sales. Another application of cross-price elasticity information is found in the microeconomic field of industrial organization. This field of economics focuses on the characteristics of various types of market structures, such as perfect competition, monopolistic competition, oligopoly, and monopoly. According to economic theory, a firm is considered to possess monopoly power in a market if it is the sole producer of a

TABLE 7.4 Estimated Cross-Price Elasticities for Various Goods and Services

Quantity of Good X	Price of Good Y	E_{X,P_Y}
Electricity	Natural gas	0.20[a]
Margarine	Butter	1.50[b]
Pork	Beef	0.40[b]
Coffee	Tea	0.15[c]
Subcompact Volkswagon	Full-size cars	0.00[d]
Coca-Cola	Pepsi-Cola	0.61[e]

[a]Robert Halvorsen, "Energy Substitution in U.S. Manufacturing," *Review of Economics and Statistics,* November 1977, p. 386.

[b]Dale M. Heien, "The Structure of Food Demand: Interrelatedness and Duality," *American Journal of Agricultural Economics,* May 1982, p. 220.

[c]J. Huang, J.J. Siegfried, and F. Zardoshty, "The Demand for Coffee in the United States 1963–77," *Quarterly Journal of Business and Economics,* Summer 1980, p. 44.

[d]F. Owen Irvine, Jr., "Demand Equations for Individual New Car Models Estimated Using Transaction Prices with Implications for Regulatory Issues," *Southern Economic Journal,* January 1983, p. 775.

[e]F. Gasmi, J.J. Laffont, and Q. Vuong, "Econometric Analysis of Collusive Behavior in a Soft-Drink Market," *Journal of Management Strategy* 1, Summer 1992, p. 296.

product for which there exist no close substitutes. For example, in 1956, E.I. du Pont was the sole producer of cellophane, a product used largely to wrap food. The U.S. Justice Department challenged du Pont's monopoly power, contending that du Pont was in a unique position to control output and raise the price of this food wrap. Du Pont countered this accusation with statistical estimates of cross-price elasticities between cellophane and other food-wrapping materials, such as waxed paper and aluminum foil. The cross-price elasticities were found to be large positive values, indicating that close substitutes for cellophane existed at that time. Therefore, Du Pont was not found guilty of maintaining extraordinary monopoly power in this market.

7.6 SUMMARY

In this chapter, our primary focus was on various measurements of the responsiveness of the quantity demanded of a good to changes in key variables comprising the market own-price, Engel, and cross-price demand curves. Specifically, by modifying the slopes of each of these curves, we developed and analyzed own-price, income, and cross-price elasticities. We also showed how business analysts can use each of these elasticity measures in the real world. The key topics we covered in this chapter are as follows.

- Own-price elasticity of demand, E_{X,P_X}, measures the percentage change in quantity demanded of a good resulting from a percentage change in the price of that good.

- If $E_{X,P_X} > 1$, $E_{X,P_X} = 1$, or $E_{X,P_X} < 1$, we classify the own-price elasticity of demand as being elastic, unit elastic, or inelastic, respectively.
- Total revenue, TR, is the value of consumers' expenditures associated with the sale of a good.
- Marginal revenue, MR, measures the change in total revenue resulting from a change in the quantity of that good sold.
- Own-price elasticity of demand for a good or service is affected by the availability and closeness of substitutes for the product, the length of the time period under analysis, and the percentage of households' total expenditures attributable to that particular good or service.
- Income elasticity, $E_{X,I}$, measures the percentage change in quantity demanded of a good resulting from a percentage change in consumers' money income.
- If $E_{X,I} \geq 0$, we categorize the good as normal, where for a subcategory of normal goods, known as luxury goods, $E_{X,I} > 1$. The other subcategory of a normal good pertains to $0 \leq E_{X,I} \leq 1$, where we characterize the good as a necessity. Finally, if $E_{X,I} < 0$, then we classify the good as inferior.
- The cross-price elasticity of demand, E_{X,P_Y}, measures the change in the quantity demanded of a good resulting from a percentage change in the price of another good.
- If $E_{X,P_Y} > 0$, then we classify goods X and Y as gross substitutes. Conversely, if $E_{X,P_Y} < 0$, then we classify goods X and Y as gross complements.

KEY TERMS

- cross-price elasticity of demand, page 188
- elastic, page 167
- elasticity, page 165
- income elasticity, page 183

- inelastic, page 167
- marginal revenue, page 171
- own-price elasticity of demand, page 165

- total revenue, page 170
- unit elastic, page 167

EXERCISES

7.1 For each pair of goods or services listed here, identify the one for which own-price elasticity of demand is greater and provide a brief rationale for your choice.
   a. diet soda; Diet Coke
   b. tuition at a public university; tuition at a private university
   c. emergency room medical services; annual medical physical examination
   d. refrigerator; milk
   e. long-distance telephone service Monday through Friday from 8:00 A.M. to 5:00 P.M.; long-distance telephone service Monday through Friday from 5:00 P.M. to 11:00 P.M.
   f. prescription medicines; vitamins

7.2 The market demand curve for good Z is given as

$$Z = 8P_Z^{-2},$$

where

Z = market quantity demanded for good Z in units per time period
P_Z = price of good Z in dollars per unit.

a. Determine the value of the own-price elasticity of demand for good Z.
b. Provide a written interpretation of the own-price elasticity value you computed in part a.
c. Compute the marginal revenue function using equation (7.4).
d. Determine the value of marginal revenue when the price of good Z is $30.
e. At what price will marginal revenue equal $1.00?

7.3 Assume the market own-price demand curve for good Y is given as

$$Y = 100P_Y^{-1},$$

where

Y = market quantity demanded for good Y in units per time period
P_Y = price of good Y in dollars per unit.

a. Determine the value of the own-price elasticity of demand for good Y.
b. Provide a written interpretation of the own-price elasticity value you computed in part a.
c. Compute the value of marginal revenue using equation (7.4).
d. Will the value of marginal revenue vary as the price of good Y varies? Explain why, or why not.
e. Compute total revenue and relate your answer to your response to part d.

7.4 Annual market own-price demand for widgets has been estimated as

$$W = 200 - 4P_W + 5I + 0.5P_G,$$

where

W = quantity demanded of widgets in units/year
P_W = price of a widget in dollars/unit
I = per capita income in thousands of dollars/year
P_G = price of a gadget in dollars/unit

a. Calculate the own-price demand curve for $I = 20$ and $P_G = 4$.
b. Using your result from part a, calculate the quantity of widgets demanded when $P_W = 3$.
c. Calculate the own-price elasticity of demand for widgets when $P_W = 3$, $I = 20$, and $P_G = 4$. Provide a written interpretation of your answer.
d. In light of your answer to part c, is it a rational business decision for a revenue-maximizing entrepreneur to raise the price of widgets? Explain your response.

7.5 Refer to the market own-price demand curve for widgets in Exercise 7.4.

  a. Calculate the cross-price elasticity of demand for widgets assuming once again that $P_W = 3$, $I = 20$, and $P_G = 4$. Provide a written interpretation of your result.

  b. In light of your answer to part a, how is the quantity demanded of widgets affected if the price of gadgets increases?

  c. Calculate the income elasticity for $P_W = 3$, $I = 20$, and $P_G = 4$, and provide a written interpretation of your result.

  d. How could an entrepreneur use the information you computed in part c?

7.6 The annual market demand function for good X has been estimated as

$$X = 115 - 2P_X - 2.5I - 1.5P_Y,$$

where

$$X = \text{quantity demanded of good } X \text{ in units/year}$$
$$P_X = \text{price of good } X \text{ in dollars/unit}$$
$$I = \text{per capita income in thousands of dollars/year}$$
$$P_Y = \text{price of good } Y \text{ in dollars/unit}$$

  a. Calculate the own-price demand curve for $I = 30$ and $P_Y = 10$.

  b. Using your result from part a, determine the quantity demanded of good X when $P_X = 8$.

  c. Assuming $P_X = 8$, $I = 30$, and $P_Y = 10$, compute the own-price elasticity of demand for good X. Provide a written interpretation of your result.

  d. In light of your response to part c, suggest a rational business strategy for an entrepreneur selling good X. Explain your response.

7.7 Refer to the market demand function in Exercise 7.6.

  a. Assuming $P_X = 8$, $I = 30$, and $P_Y = 10$, calculate the cross-price elasticity of demand for good X. Provide a written interpretation of your result.

  b. Provide a real-world example of two goods or services that have a relationship corresponding to the cross-price elasticity value you computed in part a.

  c. Calculate the value of income elasticity when $P_X = 8$, $I = 30$, and $P_Y = 10$.

  d. Provide a real-world example of a good or service that appropriately represents good X, given your response to part c.

7.8 A producer of upscale coffee makers and coffee brewing accessories has estimated the cross-price elasticity for some of its products, which appear in the following table.

Quantity of Good X	Price of Good Y	E_{X,P_Y}
Coffee bean grinder	Coffee maker	−0.04
Gold mesh coffee filter	Coffee maker	−2.70

Develop a rational marketing strategy for a store with very limited floor space that sells all of these goods. Incorporate the estimated cross-price elasticities in your analysis.

CHAPTER 8

Production in the Short Run

8.1 INTRODUCTION

Generally, firms engage in the business of using inputs such as labor, raw materials, and capital to produce goods and services that are then sold to consumers. Logically, a typical firm pursues this activity for the purpose of earning a profit, or the difference between its revenue and cost. Producing and selling goods and services involve many decisions on the part of a firm, such as how much output to sell and how to combine various inputs in its production process. In this chapter, as well as in the next five, our focus will be on a topic known as the theory of firm, which essentially consists of analyzing a firm's production process and its related costs. However, it is important that we remember that the goal of profit maximization underlies these concepts. After all, doesn't it make sense that, in order for a firm to earn a maximum profit, it must produce its output in the most efficient manner?

Our initial focus in this chapter is on describing the process of production and relating it to the concept of a production function. Within this context, we will also discuss the notion of how economists divide time into two distinct periods, the short run and the long run. In the remainder of this chapter, we will discuss production in the short run, where we assume that at least one of a firm's inputs is treated as fixed. Included in this discussion are such topics as a firm's total, marginal, and average product functions, along with their associated interrelationships. Finally, we will conclude the chapter by analyzing these functions to define concepts known as the Stage I, II, and III areas of production, and we will subsequently demonstrate which of these stages is relevant to rational firm behavior.

8.2 PRODUCTION FUNCTIONS

The production of a good or service by a firm involves combining resources, or inputs, in accordance with some technologically defined process. An **input** is simply *a resource that a firm uses in its production process for the purpose of creating a good or service.* Recall from your principles of economics courses that economists separate resources into the categories of land, labor, and capital. More specifically, the term *land* refers to natural resources such as minerals and raw materials, *labor* refers to human efforts, and *capital* is the created means of production such as machinery and factory buildings. Also playing an important role in a production process is the **state of technology**, defined as *society's pool of knowledge concerning the industrial arts.* It is important that we recognize that, within the context of production theory, the term *technology* refers to ideas and concepts rather than to tangible items. For example, we consider a computer as a capital input, whereas we classify the knowledge necessary to build it as representing technology. Although the prevailing state of technology plays a very important role in defining a production process, we generally do not treat it as an explicit variable when analyzing firm behavior. This is, in part, due to the fact that changes in technology often occur independent of firm behavior. Thus, the typical firm is frequently in the position of reacting to these changes rather than initiating them as a consequence of its own decision-making process. As a result, our assumption that treats technology as a predetermined factor underlying a production process enables us to focus our analysis of firm behavior strictly on the selection of different input combinations.

We can describe the production process used by a firm more specifically in terms of a **production function**. This is *a function that shows the maximum quantity of output of a good or service that can be produced from various combinations of inputs, while holding technology constant at some predetermined state.* Mathematically, we represent a firm's production function as

$$Q = f(K_A, K_B, \ldots, K_Z, L_A, L_B, \ldots, L_Z),$$

where Q denotes the maximum quantity of output produced. The terms K_A, K_B, $\ldots$, K_Z, represent the amounts of different types of capital inputs used in the firm's production process. Examples of capital inputs are items such as tools and factory buildings, which are measured in machine hours. The terms L_A, L_B, $\ldots$, L_Z denote the amounts of different types of labor inputs employed, such as skilled versus unskilled labor, all measured in labor hours. We generally consider the third major category of resources, land, as being part of the capital inputs. In addition, we have omitted technology as an explicit argument in the production function for reasons discussed earlier.

For the sake of clarity, we will reduce the number of independent variables in the production function by grouping the different types of capital inputs, K_A, K_B, $\ldots$, K_Z, and labor inputs, L_A, L_B, $\ldots$, L_Z, into just two broad categories, K and L, respectively. Thus, we can express the more simplified general production function as

$$Q = f(K, L),$$

where K and L represent all capital and labor type inputs, respectively, used by the firm in the process of producing output, Q. This simplified production function containing three variables, Q, K, and L, is illustrated as a three-dimensional production surface in Figure 8.1. We have plotted the dependent variable, Q, on the vertical axis and the two independent variables, K and L, on the base axes established perpendicular to each other. The particular surface, or function, shown in Figure 8.1 represents only one of many possible surfaces, or functional forms, associated with a production function. However, the particular function in this figure exhibits many properties commonly associated with production processes, and thus we often use it in the discussion of production theory. Of particular note is that in many production processes, the use

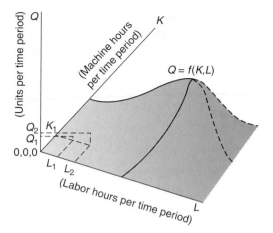

FIGURE 8.1 Production Function

of one input affects the productivity of the other. In this figure we have demonstrated the relationship between the quantity of output produced, Q, and the various combinations of inputs, K and L. For example, observe that if the firm uses K_1 amount of capital and L_1 amount of labor, then the corresponding maximum level of output produced is Q_1. If the firm increases the level of labor it uses in its production process to L_2, while still using K_1 amount of capital, the corresponding maximum level of output produced rises to Q_2. More generally, this production surface contains an infinite number of capital and labor combinations and an infinite number of corresponding output values.

8.2.1   Short Run vs. Long Run

Depending on the length of time under consideration, a firm is not always able to change the amounts of all inputs that it uses in its production process. As a result, we can divide the inputs used by a firm into two broad categories: fixed inputs and variable inputs. A **fixed input** is *an input for which the quantity used cannot be changed during the time period under consideration*. Alternatively, a **variable input** is *an input for which the quantity used can be changed during the time period under consideration*. The time period under consideration is the determining factor in distinguishing these two categories of inputs.

For relatively short periods of time, it is conventional for us to consider capital-type resources, such as plant and equipment, as examples of fixed inputs and labor-type resources as examples of variable inputs. However, in the real world the distinction of a resource as being either fixed or variable is not as easy as it might first appear. This distinction depends on the length of time we choose for analysis and on how quickly the amounts of the different types of inputs can be altered. Generally, we expect that the longer the time period we choose to consider, the greater are the number of inputs we can treat as variable. Thus, it has become convention in economic analysis to divide lengths of time into two periods—the short run and the long run—where the distinction between these two periods is on the basis of whether we treat any inputs as fixed. Specifically, the **short run** is *a period of time during which at least one of a firm's inputs is treated as fixed*, whereas the **long run** is *a period of time during which none of a firm's inputs remain fixed, or alternatively, all of a firm's inputs are treated as variable.*

We distinguish these two time periods on the basis of whether a firm has any fixed inputs because it is virtually impossible to define the short and long run in terms of some absolute lengths of time and then consistently apply these definitions to different firms in different types of industries. For example, suppose we choose a period of one year for consideration and apply this period to two firms—a hotdog stand and an automobile manufacturer. For the hotdog stand, the one-year period most likely constitutes the long run, since we would expect all of its inputs to be variable. In this case, it should be easy for the firm to vary, not only its use of labor, but also the amount of capital it employs, since it is not difficult to alter the size of the stand and the relatively simple machinery used in the preparation of hotdogs. In contrast, the automobile manufacturer uses large plants, covering millions of square feet and containing quite complex machinery, in its production process. It is unlikely that a period of one year constitutes enough time for this firm to make complete adjustments in all of its inputs, especially its capital. Thus, a one-year period represents a short-run situation for this firm, whereas the long run probably consists of a period of several years. As this example demonstrates, a particular time period that represents the long run for one firm may constitute the short run for another. Therefore, these two time periods are distinguished simply on the basis of whether any inputs are treated as fixed, regardless of the absolute length of time involved. We will reserve our analysis of firm production behavior in the long run for Chapters 9 and 10, and devote the remainder of this chapter to analyzing production in the short run.

8.3   TOTAL PRODUCT CURVES

A special short-run situation is the **market period or immediate run**, defined as *a period of time during which all of a firm's inputs remain fixed*. In this case, provided we treat technology as constant, the firm's output is also fixed at some specified level. Generally, this situation applies to an extremely short period of time, and since we treat everything pertaining to a firm's production process as fixed, it does not lend itself to any meaningful analysis from the perspective of production theory. Therefore, it is more useful for us to examine the broader short-run situations for which at least one input remains fixed and at least one input is treated as variable. By doing so, we can focus on the relationship between the quantity of output produced by a firm and any one of the inputs in the production function. After we set all but one of the inputs at some specified values, the modified production function becomes a short-run production curve, often referred to as a total product curve for the variable input. Specifically, a **total product curve** is *a curve that expresses the maximum quantity of output, or total product, produced by a firm explicitly as a function of one input, while holding all other inputs and technology constant at some specified levels.*

We can apply this concept to the simplified production function containing just two inputs, capital, K, and labor, L, represented as

$$Q = f(K,L).$$

Our choice as to which input to treat as fixed as opposed to variable, is a matter of how we choose to focus our analysis, although it is usually convention to fix capital and treat labor as variable. The reason for this approach is that generally, it takes a firm more time to make adjustments to capital inputs such as plant and machinery than it does to make adjustments to the amount of labor it employs. Therefore, we modify the production function as

$$TP_L = Q = f(\overline{K}_1,L),$$

where we have fixed the amount of capital used in the production process at $K = \overline{K}_1$ units. Conceptually, this function now represents a short-run production curve, also known as the total product of labor curve, TP_L, relating the quantity of output produced to various amounts of labor combined with a fixed level of capital.

We have illustrated the derivation of this curve in Figure 8.2. Observe that we have "cut" the three-dimensional production surface with a vertical plane constructed at the fixed level of capital $\overline{K}_1$ on the K-axis. This process creates the two-dimensional cross-section containing the curve TP_L, which we then plot in Q-L space. As we have illustrated in Figure 8.3, this curve represents the total product of labor curve, TP_L, indicating the various levels of output produced, Q, that correspond to different amounts of labor combined with a fixed level of capital.

We can observe that if the firm employs L_1 units of labor, combined with the specified $\overline{K}_1$ units of capital, the corresponding amount of output produced is $TP_{L,1}$. If the firm successively increases the amount of labor it uses to L_2, L_3, and L_4, while still using $\overline{K}_1$ units of capital, then output increases to $TP_{L,2}$, $TP_{L,3}$, and $TP_{L,4}$, respectively. Note that for levels of labor use beyond L_4 units, the TP_L curve in Figure 8.3 is illustrated as a dotted line. We have done this because increases in labor beyond L_4, when combined with $\overline{K}_1$ units of capital, cause the amount of output produced by the firm to

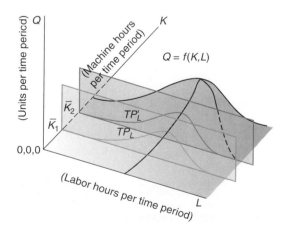

FIGURE 8.2 Derivation of TP_L Curves from Production Function

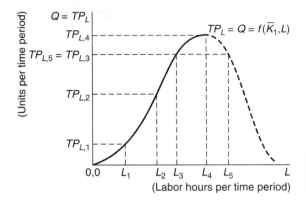

FIGURE 8.3 TP_L Curve for $K = \overline{K}_1$

decrease. Observe, that if labor is increased from L_4 to L_5 units, the corresponding level of output produced by the firm decreases from $TP_{L,4}$ to $TP_{L,5}$ units. Since we assume that firms behave rationally, this increase in labor from L_4 to L_5, or to any level beyond L_4, does not make economic sense, even if the labor input is costless.

We have derived the particular total product of labor curve, TP_L, shown in Figure 8.3, for the fixed level of capital, $\overline{K}_1$ units. Suppose we fix capital at a greater level, such as $\overline{K}_2$ units. Returning to Figure 8.2, observe that the production surface is now cut by a plane established at $\overline{K}_2$ on the K-axis, where this process creates a new cross-section containing the curve TP_L' lying further up the production surface than TP_L. We have now generated a new total product of labor curve, TP_L', which we have illustrated in Figure 8.4, along with the original total product curve, TP_L.

The difference between these two TP_L curves is that we derived TP_L' for $K = \overline{K}_2$, while TP_L was derived for $K = \overline{K}_1$. In two-dimensional space, the total product of labor curve appears to have shifted up and to the right. In addition, observe in Figure 8.4 that

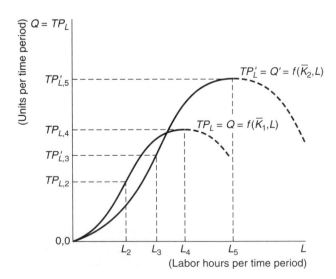

FIGURE 8.4 TP_L Curve for $K = \overline{K}_1$ and TP_L' Curve for $K = \overline{K}_2$

the TP'_L curve achieves a maximum at a higher level of output, or total product, $TP_{L,5}$, corresponding to a greater amount of labor employed, L_5, than does the curve TP_L, which reaches its maximum at $TP_{L,4}$ corresponding to L_4 units of labor. It is also interesting for us to note that, for this particular underlying production function, $TP'_L < TP_L$ for lower levels of labor. However, as additional units of labor are employed, TP'_L rises above TP_L, eventually achieving the higher maximum value, $TP_{L,5}$.

We can intuitively explain the relationship between the two total product curves shown in Figure 8.4. If a firm produces a very small amount of output, thus using a very small amount of the variable input, L, it is logically more efficient to combine this low level of labor with a small amount of capital, K. If the firm uses a larger amount of fixed capital, such as plant and equipment, this small amount of labor may actually be less productive than when combined with the smaller amount of capital. For example, imagine a few laborers having to move around in a very large factory building during some production process. A smaller building enables the few laborers to be closer to the machinery and other types of capital they are using and, therefore, to be more productive at this low level of output. Of course, if the firm chooses to produce more output by increasing the amount of labor it uses, then a greater amount of capital, such as a larger factory building containing more equipment, ultimately allows the workers to become more productive at these higher levels of output. The particular shapes of the TP_L curves depend on the production function from which we have derived them. However, it should be evident that, in this case, we can generate an entire family of TP_L curves from the underlying production function, one for each level at which we have fixed capital, K.

8.4   MARGINAL PRODUCT CURVES

By focusing on any one of the TP_L curves, we can observe that as the amount of labor employed increases, while holding capital constant at some level, the quantity of output produced, or TP_L, increases at an increasing rate up to the inflection point of the TP_L function. Beyond this point, further increases in labor cause TP_L to increase, but at a decreasing rate, until finally the TP_L curve achieves a maximum, a point beyond which any further increases in the amount of labor employed cause TP_L to decrease. For example, return to Figure 8.3 which contains a total product of labor curve, TP_L, established for $K = \overline{K}_1$ units of capital. Note that TP_L increases at an increasing rate as labor is increased from zero to L_2, then increases at a decreasing rate from L_2 to L_4, and decreases for any increases in L thereafter. Mathematically, we can describe these rates of change in TP_L with respect to changes in L in terms of the slope of the TP_L curve, dTP_L/dL or $\partial Q/\partial L$. Since $TP_L = Q$, once we have fixed the level of capital at some value, we can compute either version of this derivative, dTP_L/dL or $\partial Q/\partial L$, from the total product of labor curve. Alternatively, since $\partial Q/\partial L$ is a partial derivative, we can compute it directly from the production function, $Q = f(K,L)$.

Recall from Chapter 1 that within the context of economic theory, we can interpret slopes of functions as representing marginal functions. Applying this interpretation to our current analysis, we find that the slope of the total product curve for an input represents the marginal product curve for that input. Specifically, the **marginal product of an input** is *the change in the production of output, or total product, due to a change in the amount of that input used in a production process, while holding all other inputs constant.* Notationally, we represent this definition of a marginal product as

$$MP_{input} = \frac{\partial Q}{\partial\ input} = \frac{d\ TP_{input}}{d\ input}.$$

Since the production function we have used throughout this chapter contains only two inputs, labor and capital, we define the marginal product curve associated with each input as

$$MP_L = \frac{\partial Q}{\partial L} = \frac{d\ TP_L}{dL}$$

and

$$MP_K = \frac{\partial Q}{\partial K} = \frac{d\ TP_K}{dK},$$

respectively.

Since our primary focus in this chapter is on production in the short run when capital is fixed, our following discussion will center on the marginal product of the labor input.

As we stated earlier, a marginal product curve simply represents the slope of the corresponding total product curve. We have demonstrated this fact in Figure 8.5, where the TP_L curve is shown in panel (A) and its associated MP_L curve is shown in panel (B). Since the MP_L curve is the slope, or derivative, of the TP_L curve, it is necessarily a function of the same independent variable, L. Thus, we can link the two curves, TP_L and MP_L, by common horizontal axes representing L. For each level of labor employed by the firm, we can demonstrate the corresponding marginal product of labor value by constructing a line tangent to the TP_L curve and determining its slope. We have plotted the values of these slopes in panel (B) of Figure 8.5 to construct the MP_L curve. Note that the tangents to the TP_L curve possess positive slopes at L_1, L_2, and L_3, or for any level of labor up to L_4. However, comparing the slopes of these tangents, observe that the tangent constructed to the TP_L curve at L_2 is steeper than the one constructed at L_1, thus indicating a higher slope, or MP_L, value at L_2 than at L_1. The line we have drawn tangent to the TP_L curve at L_3 is flatter than the one constructed at L_2, thus yielding a lower slope and MP_L value. At L_4, where TP_L is maximized, the tangent to the TP_L curve is horizontal, indicating a slope, or MP_L, value of zero. Finally, if the firm increases the amount of labor it employs to L_5, the corresponding tangent possesses a negative slope, or MP_L, value. These results are shown in panel (B) of Figure 8.5, where we can observe that the MP_L curve rises up to L_2, where it achieves its maximum value, and then diminishes thereafter, achieving a value of zero at L_4, and becoming negative for any subsequent increases in L.

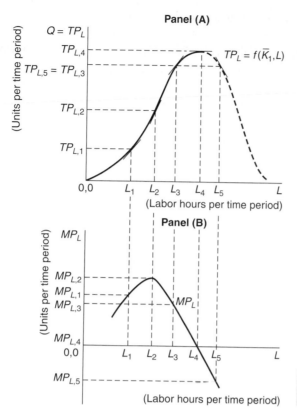

FIGURE 8.5 Derivation of MP_L Curve from TP_L Curve

We can explain the shape of this particular MP_L curve intuitively. Essentially, whether the MP_L rises or falls with increases in labor use is a consequence of the amount of this variable input, labor, that is used relative to the fixed input, capital. The fact that the MP_L rises as labor is increased from zero to L_2 units reflects a situation where the firm is using too little labor relative to the amount of fixed capital, such as factory space or machinery. Thus, by increasing the amount of labor employed, not only does the production of output rise, but it rises at an increasing rate. If the amount of labor is increased beyond L_2, then the MP_L diminishes, eventually reaching a value of zero at L_4, then becoming negative for additional increases in L. For the range between L_2 and L_4, note that the production of output increases with increases in labor, but it does so at a decreasing rate. Beyond L_4, increases in labor actually cause a reduction in output. This characteristic of a diminishing marginal product is so prevalent in production theory that we describe it as the **law of diminishing marginal productivity of an input**. This law states that *as additional units of an input are used in a production process, while holding all other inputs constant, the resulting increments to output, or total product, begin to diminish beyond some point.* The rationale for this result is that as more units of an input, such as labor, are added to a production process, they are still working with the same amount of the fixed input, which in our analysis is capital. As a result, these additional amounts of labor are less productive than those that preceded them.

As an example, suppose a firm is in the business of paving a road, where the output is measured by the amount of square footage of road paved per hour. The capital inputs are fixed, consisting of one paving machine, one truck for hauling cement, and some hand tools such as shovels and rakes used in finishing the road bed. If one laborer is added to the production process, output rises from zero to some positive level. However, given that the laborer must drive and unload the truck, operate the paving machine, and work on finishing the road bed, it is unlikely that the level of output will be very high.

Now assume a second laborer is employed, who continuously operates the truck. As a result, the level of output rises due to the addition of the second laborer, but more importantly, it will likely rise at an increasing rate, meaning that the extra output produced after adding a second laborer exceeds the extra output that resulted from employing the first laborer. It is not that the second laborer is a more productive human being than the first, per se, but rather that two laborers can use the fixed amount of capital more efficiently than just one. In terms of marginal product, the second laborer's marginal product exceeds that of the first, and thus the marginal product of labor is increasing as these successive units of labor are employed. This trend may continue as a third laborer is employed to use the hand tools in finishing the road bed, and thus the marginal product of the third laborer may exceed that of the previous two.

Eventually, however, as additional laborers are employed, the situation is going to change. The addition of a fourth, fifth, and other, laborers, probably increases output, but with a fixed amount of capital with which to work, their extra contributions to the production of output will likely be smaller than for those laborers preceding them. For example, the fourth laborer employed may ride along in the truck and perform some minor tasks, and the fifth laborer may do some limited work with the hand tools. As a result, the level of output rises as these successive laborers are employed, but by smaller and smaller increments. Thus, we can state that, in this example, the marginal product of labor diminishes as more than three laborers are employed.

To demonstrate a negative marginal product for labor, the firm would have to employ so many laborers relative to the fixed amount of capital that additional laborers would actually reduce the level of output produced. We can describe this result through a rather ridiculous situation in which the laborers are literally getting in each other's way or slowing down the paving machine. The old adage "too many cooks in the kitchen spoil the broth" is an appropriate description of this result. Note that no rational firm will employ additional units of an input if its marginal product becomes negative. Rather, once the marginal product of an input reaches a value of zero, and provided technology is held constant, the only way a firm can increase its level of output is by increasing the amount of the fixed input used in its production process. Technically, this result is impossible to accomplish in the short run if only two inputs are included in the production function, since by definition, we treat one of the inputs as fixed. However, it is useful for us to analyze different short-run scenarios for which the fixed input, usually capital, is specified at different levels.

We derived the TP_L and MP_L curves illustrated in Figure 8.5 while holding capital constant at $\overline{K}_1$ units. As we demonstrated earlier, an increase in the level of this fixed capital input, from $\overline{K}_1$ to $\overline{K}_2$ units, results in a rightward shift in the TP_L curve in the manner shown in Figure 8.4. It follows that, since we derive the MP_L curve from the TP_L curve, an increase in the fixed amount of capital also causes the MP_L curve to shift. The exact nature of the shift depends on the underlying production function and its associated TP_L curve. However, the production function we are using in this analysis is quite common, and as a result, so is the type of shift in the MP_L curve illustrated in panel (B) of Figure 8.6.

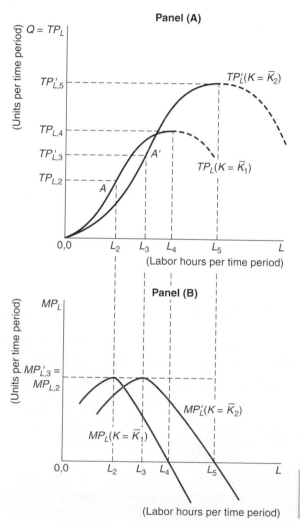

FIGURE 8.6 Derivation of MP_L and MP_L' Curves from TP_L and TP_L' Curves

Observe that an increase in capital from $\overline{K}_1$ to $\overline{K}_2$ units causes the MP_L curve to shift to the right, where we designate the new curve as MP'_L. This curve achieves the same maximum value as that for the initial MP_L curve pertaining to $K = \overline{K}_1$. However, this MP'_L curve reaches its maximum value at a higher level of labor use, specifically at L_3 rather than L_2, as is the case for the original curve labeled MP_L. Note that these values of L correspond to the inflection points A and A', on the respective total product of labor curves, TP_L and TP'_L, shown in panel (A). Also observe that MP'_L is equal to zero at a higher level of labor use, L_5, than is MP_L, that equals zero at L_4 units of labor. These L_4 and L_5 values of labor correspond to the maximum values for the respective total product of labor curves, TP_L and TP'_L.

Mathematically, the derivation of total and marginal product of labor curves is an easy process. As an example, let's assume a production function of the form

$$Q = f(K,L) = 8K^{1/2}L^{1/2}.$$

We establish the total product of labor curve by fixing capital at some specified level, say $\overline{K}_1 = 1$ unit. In this case, the TP_L curve is

$$TP_L = Q = f(\overline{K}_1,L) = 8(1)^{1/2}L^{1/2} = 8L^{1/2}.$$

Note that this curve applies to a short-run situation, since we are treating one of the inputs as fixed. Recall that the corresponding marginal product of labor curve is the slope, or derivative, of this total product curve, and thus,

$$MP_L = \frac{dTP_L}{dL} = \frac{dQ}{dL} = 4L^{-1/2} = \frac{4}{L^{1/2}}.$$

Alternatively, we can derive the MP_L curve directly from the production function, $Q = 8K^{1/2}L^{1/2}$, by taking the partial derivative of Q with respect to L as

$$MP_L = \frac{\partial Q}{\partial L} = 4K^{1/2}L^{-1/2} = 4\left(\frac{K}{L}\right)^{1/2}.$$

Since we have fixed capital at $\overline{K}_1 = 1$ unit, then

$$MP_L = 4\left(\frac{1}{L}\right)^{1/2} = \frac{4}{L^{1/2}},$$

which is the same result we obtained earlier. We can evaluate both the TP_L and MP_L curves for different levels of labor, L. For example, if $L = 1$ unit then

$$TP_{L,1} = 8(1)^{1/2} = 8 \text{ units of output}$$

and

$$MP_{L,1} = \frac{4}{L^{1/2}} = \frac{4}{(1)^{1/2}} = 4 \text{ units of output.}$$

If L increases to $L = 4$ units, then

$$TP_{L,2} = 8(4)^{1/2} = 16 \text{ units of output}$$

and

$$MP_{L,2} = \frac{4}{L^{1/2}} = \frac{4}{(4)^{1/2}} = \frac{4}{2} = 2 \text{ units of output.}$$

Note that the underlying production function we are using in this example is somewhat different from the one we used in the earlier graphical analysis. In particular, this total product of labor curve, depicted in panel (A) of Figure 8.7, increases at a decreasing rate throughout the entire range of labor values, never achieving a maximum. In addition, the associated marginal product of labor curve in this mathematical example exhibits diminishing marginal productivity for labor over the entire range of labor use, as illustrated in panel (B) of Figure 8.7. You can verify this result by substituting

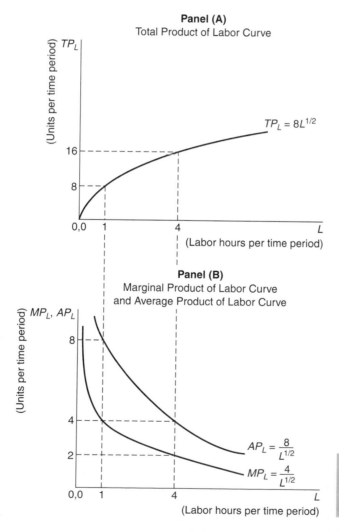

FIGURE 8.7 TP_L, MP_L, and AP_L Curves for the Production Function $Q = 8K^{1/2} L^{1/2}$ where $\overline{K}_1 = 1$

increasing values of labor, L, into the MP_L curve, $MP_L = 4/L^{1/2}$, and observing the successively smaller values.

If we set capital at a higher value in this example, say $\overline{K}_2 = 4$ units, both the total product and marginal product of labor curves are altered as

$$TP'_L = Q' = 8(4)^{1/2}L^{1/2} = 16L^{1/2}$$

and

$$MP'_L = \frac{dTP'_L}{dL} = \frac{\partial Q'}{\partial L} = 8L^{-1/2} = \frac{8}{L^{1/2}}.$$

Thus, if $L_1 = 1$ and $L_2 = 4$ units of labor, then we evaluate the TP'_L and MP'_L curves as

$$TP'_{L,1} = 16(1)^{1/2} = 16 \text{ units of output,}$$
$$TP'_{L,2} = 16(4)^{1/2} = 32 \text{ units of output,}$$
$$MP'_{L,1} = \frac{8}{(1)^{1/2}} = 8 \text{ units of output,}$$

and

$$MP'_{L,2} = \frac{8}{(4)^{1/2}} = 4 \text{ units of output.}$$

This increase in capital from 1 unit to 4 units causes both the total product and marginal product of labor curves in this example to shift up, reflecting the fact that labor has become more productive since it has more capital with which to work. As a result, $TP'_L > TP_L$ and $MP'_L > MP_L$ at each value of L.

Finally, although our primary focus in this chapter is on treating capital as the fixed input and labor as the variable input, it is certainly possible for us to reverse these roles. Suppose we fix labor at $\overline{L}_1 = 1$ unit and treat capital as the variable input. In this case we can establish a total product curve for capital, TP_K, and its associated marginal product curve, MP_K, as

$$TP_K = Q = f(K, \overline{L}_1) = 8K^{1/2}(1)^{1/2} = 8K^{1/2}$$

and

$$MP_K = \frac{dTP_K}{dK} = \frac{\partial Q}{\partial K} = 4K^{-1/2} = \frac{4}{K^{1/2}}.$$

If $K_1 = 1$ and $K_2 = 4$ units, then we evaluate these curves as

$$TP_{K,1} = 8(1)^{1/2} = 8 \text{ units of output,}$$
$$TP_{K,2} = 8(4)^{1/2} = 16 \text{ units of output,}$$
$$MP_{K,1} = \frac{4}{(1)^{1/2}} = 4 \text{ units of output,}$$

and

$$MP_{K,2} = \frac{4}{(4)^{1/2}} = 2 \text{ units of output.}$$

In this situation, a change in the amount of the fixed input, labor, causes the TP_K and MP_K curves to shift in a manner similar to the shifts in the TP_L and MP_L curves we discussed previously.

8.5   AVERAGE PRODUCT CURVES

There is another important economic concept and related curve that we can derive from the production function or the total product curve. This concept is known as the **average product of an input**, defined as *the amount of output produced per unit of an input used in a production process, while holding all other inputs constant.* In notational terms, we represent an average product as

$$AP_{\text{input}} = \frac{Q}{\text{input}} \bigg|_{\text{other inputs}_1} = \frac{TP \text{ input}}{\text{input}} \bigg|_{\text{other inputs}_1}.$$

Specifically, since the simplified production function we are using throughout this chapter contains only two inputs, K and L, we will focus on the average products of capital and labor, computed, respectively, as

$$AP_K = \frac{Q}{K} \bigg|_{\overline{L}_1} = \frac{TP_K}{K} \bigg|_{\overline{L}_1},$$

and

$$AP_L = \frac{Q}{L} \bigg|_{\overline{K}_1} = \frac{TP_L}{L} \bigg|_{\overline{K}_1}.$$

We can derive average product curves both graphically and mathematically. Since the mathematical derivation of these curves is quite simple, we will demonstrate this approach first by returning to our earlier numerical example. As noted earlier, the specific production function was

$$Q = f(K,L) = 8K^{1/2}L^{1/2}.$$

Thus, we compute the average product of labor function, AP_L, as

$$AP_L = \frac{Q}{L} = \frac{8K^{1/2}L^{1/2}}{L} = 8K^{1/2}L^{-1/2} = 8\left(\frac{K}{L}\right)^{1/2}.$$

If we fix capital at $\overline{K}_1 = 1$ unit, then the AP_L curve is

$$AP_L = 8\left(\frac{1}{L}\right)^{1/2} = \frac{8}{L^{1/2}}.$$

Alternatively, we can obtain the same result from the TP_L curve for $\overline{K}_1 = 1$ unit. This curve was

$$TP_L = Q = f(\overline{K}_1, L) = 8L^{1/2},$$

and therefore,

$$AP_L = \frac{TP_L}{L} = \frac{Q}{L} = \frac{8L^{1/2}}{L} = \frac{8}{L^{1/2}}.$$

We can evaluate this average product of labor curve for different levels of labor, say $L_1 = 1$ unit and $L_2 = 4$ units, as

$$AP_{L,1} = \frac{8}{(1)^{1/2}} = 8 \text{ units of output per labor hour}$$

and

$$AP_{L,2} = \frac{8}{(4)^{1/2}} = 4 \text{ units of output per labor hour.}$$

In this example we see that AP_L decreases with increases in the amount of labor employed, where we have illustrated this result in panel (B) of Figure 8.7.

If we fix the amount of capital at a higher level such as $\overline{K}_2 = 4$ units, then the new average product of labor curve is

$$AP'_L = 8\left(\frac{4}{L}\right)^{1/2} = \frac{16}{L^{1/2}},$$

and if $L_1 = 1$ unit and $L_2 = 4$ units, we evaluate AP'_L as

$$AP'_{L,1} = \frac{16}{(1)^{1/2}} = 16 \text{ units of output per labor hour,}$$

and

$$AP'_{L,2} = \frac{16}{(4)^{1/2}} = 8 \text{ units of output per labor hour.}$$

In general, the increase in capital from $\overline{K}_1 = 1$ unit to $\overline{K}_2 = 4$ units enhances the average product of labor at each value of labor use. As an exercise, it is left to you to derive the average product curve for capital by specifying some fixed level of the labor input.

We can also derive the average product of labor curve, AP_L, graphically by returning to the original production surface and the associated total product of labor curve, TP_L, that we established for $\overline{K}_1$ units of capital. We have again illustrated this TP_L curve in panel (A) of Figure 8.8, where we have also demonstrated its associated average product of labor curve, AP_L, in panel (B). Since both the total and average product of labor are functions of the labor input, we can link the two graphs by their common horizontal axes. Observe in panel (A), that if the firm uses L_1 units of labor, the corresponding level of output produced is $TP_{L,1}$. We can demonstrate the value of

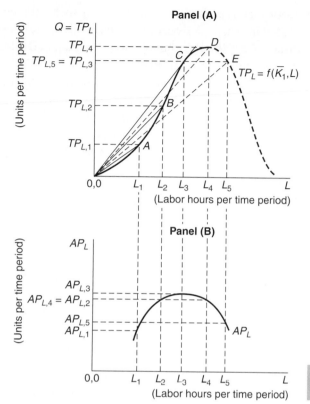

FIGURE 8.8 Derivation of AP_L Curve from TP_L Curve

the average product of labor at this level of labor use, L_1, by constructing a ray, designated OA, from the origin to the point $(L_1, TP_{L,1})$ on the TP_L curve and determining the slope of this ray. In general, the slope of any such ray is Δrise/Δrun, or, more specifically in this case, $\Delta TP_L/\Delta L$. The slope of the particular ray OA is therefore, $(TP_{L,1} - 0)/(L_1 - 0)$, where the numerator of this term is the vertical distance between $TP_{L,1}$ and the origin, and the denominator is the horizontal distance between L_1 and the origin. If the amount of labor employed is increased to L_2 and consequently TP_L rises to $TP_{L,2}$, we can determine the corresponding value of AP_L by constructing another ray, OB, from the origin to the TP_L curve at the point $(L_2, TP_{L,2})$, and computing its slope as $(TP_{L,2} - 0)/(L_2 - 0)$. We can continue this process, constructing rays from the origin to the TP_L curve at $(L_3, TP_{L,3})$, $(L_4, TP_{L,4})$, $(L_5, TP_{L,5})$, and so forth.

By plotting the values of the slopes of these rays in panel (B), we construct the AP_L curve. Note that all of the rays possess positive slopes, and thus the AP_L values are all positive. However, also observe that the slopes of these rays, and thus the AP_L values, vary as the amount of labor is altered. As the level of labor employed increases from L_1 to L_2 to L_3 units, the corresponding rays, OA, OB, and OC become successively steeper, indicating successively higher slope values. As a result, the AP_L curve shown in panel (B) rises as the amount of labor employed increases from L_1 to L_2 to

L_3. As the amount of labor increases further from L_3 to L_4 to L_5, the corresponding rays OD and OE, illustrated in panel (A), become successively flatter, indicating successively lower slope values. Thus, the AP_L curve shown in panel (B) declines correspondingly. The ray, OC, we have drawn from the origin to the TP_L curve at (L_3, $TP_{L,3}$), is of particular interest because it is also tangent to the TP_L curve. This ray, OC, is steeper than the rays preceding it, OA and OB, and it is also steeper than the rays following it, OD and OE. In short, it is the steepest of all the rays and thus indicates the level of labor use, L_3, at which the AP_L achieves a maximum. The position of the particular AP_L curve we have illustrated in this analysis is dependent on the level

---

REAL-WORLD APPLICATION 8.1

Capital Deepening and Productivity in the United States

Macroeconomic theory, which involves the analysis of economic aggregates, or economy-wide totals, of such variables as national output, employment, and productivity, is ultimately based on microeconomic principles. In most static macroeconomic models, we treat the amount of capital available in a given time period as fixed, since we consider the level of this input to be the result of investment undertaken in previous time periods. This fixed amount of capital in a particular time period, along with the given state of technology, affects the productivity of the variable input, labor, used in firms' production processes, and therefore the amount of output produced.

Analysis of macroeconomic data for the United States indicates that productivity, measured as the annual percentage growth rate in real output, has risen in recent years, achieving a level of 3.5 percent per annum by 1991 with a significant acceleration in this figure after 1995. A study by the economic forecasting firm, Macroeconomic Advisers, determined that potential productivity in the U.S. economy increased by 2.6 percent between 1995 and 1998.[2] Since macroeconomic data consist of economywide totals, analytical conclusions regarding specific sectors of the economy and the determination of the sources of productivity changes are often subject to debate. The study by Macroeconomic Advisers attempted to eliminate the influences of temporary and cyclical factors, thus concentrating on permanent structural changes in the economy. According to their results, nearly one-third of the increase in potential productivity can be attributed to technological improvements in computer manufacturing. In addition, they concluded that there has been a structural increase in the productivity of those laborers that use computers. Specifically, they estimate that one-third of the increase in potential productivity is the result of capital deepening, which largely reflects the investment and use of computer hardware and software by various components of the labor force. From a microeconomic perspective, this result is consistent with our assumption that increases in the amount of capital used in a production process enhance the productivity of labor, thus shifting the total, marginal, and average product of labor curves up and to the right.

---

[2] "Readjusting the Lens," *The Economist*, November 20, 1999, pp. 29–30.

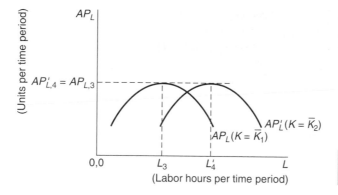

FIGURE 8.9 AP_L Curves for $K = \overline{K}_1$ and $K = \overline{K}_2$

at which we fixed capital, K. We demonstrated earlier that, if capital is fixed at a different level, both the total and marginal product of labor curves shift to new positions. Specifically, if we fix capital at a higher level, say $\overline{K}_2$, rather than $\overline{K}_1$ units, these curves shift to the right in the manner shown in Figures 8.4 and 8.6, respectively. Similarly, such an increase in capital from $\overline{K}_1$ to $\overline{K}_2$ also causes the average product of labor curve to shift to the right. We have illustrated this result in Figure 8.9 where you can observe that, for the particular production function used in this analysis, the two average product of labor curves, AP_L and AP'_L, corresponding to $\overline{K}_1$ and $\overline{K}_2$, respectively, achieve equal maximum values, $AP_{L,3} = AP'_{L,4}$. However, the AP'_L curve reaches its maximum value at a higher level of labor use, L'_4, than does the AP_L curve, which achieves its maximum value at L_3 units of labor.

8.6   RELATIONSHIPS AMONG TOTAL, MARGINAL, AND AVERAGE PRODUCTS

It is important that we understand the relationships among the total, marginal, and average product of labor curves. Since all of these curves are functions of the amount of labor employed, we can plot them with common horizontal axes as shown in panels (A) and (B) of Figure 8.10. Observe that the MP_L and AP_L curves intersect, and thus $MP_L = AP_L$ at L_3 units of labor, corresponding to the maximum value for AP_L. Graphically, we have demonstrated the rationale for this result in panel (A), where at L_3 units of labor, the ray we have drawn from the origin to the TP_L curve is also tangent to this curve. Since the slope of a ray from the origin to the TP_L curve yields the AP_L value, and the slope of a tangent to the TP_L curve yields the MP_L value, then the AP_L and MP_L must be equal at this level of labor use, L_3, at which the AP_L achieves a maximum.

We can also prove this result mathematically by maximizing the AP_L curve with respect to L. Recall from Chapter 1 that the necessary condition for a curve to reach a maximum value is that its slope must be equal to zero.[1] Thus, the procedure for

---

[1]We are assuming in this proof that the second-order condition for a maximum is fulfilled, or $d^2 AP_L/dL^2 < 0$.

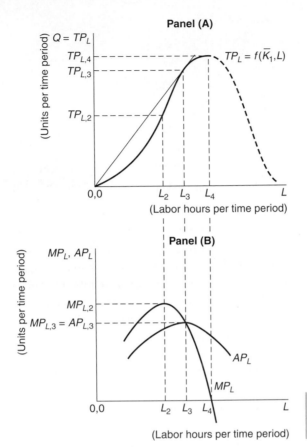

FIGURE 8.10 Relationships among TP_L, MP_L, and AP_L Curves

maximizing the AP_L curve involves us taking the derivative of AP_L with respect to L and setting it equal to zero. As mentioned earlier, $AP_L = Q/L$, where $Q = TP_L = f(\overline{K}_1, L)$, or

$$AP_L = \frac{TP_L}{L} = TP_L L^{-1}.$$

By employing the product rule

$$\frac{dAP_L}{dL} = TP_L \frac{dL^{-1}}{dL} + L^{-1} \frac{dTP_L}{dL} = 0$$

or

$$\frac{dAP_L}{dL} = -TP_L L^{-2} + L^{-1} \frac{dTP_L}{dL} = 0.$$

Dividing by L^{-1} yields

$$-TP_L L^{-1} + \frac{dTP_L}{dL} = 0,$$

or

$$\frac{dTP_L}{dL} = \frac{TP_L}{L}.$$

Since we can recognize dTP_L/dL as the MP_L and TP_L/L as the AP_L, then $MP_L = AP_L$ when the AP_L curve is at a maximum.

To complete the rationale underlying the relationship between the MP_L and AP_L curves demonstrated in Figure 8.10, we need some additional explanation. Note that for levels of labor use less than L_3, $MP_L > AP_L$, and also for this range of L, the AP_L increases with increases in L up to L_3 units. Intuitively, this result is quite straightforward. The marginal product curve, MP_L, represents the increments to TP_L, or Q, associated with increases in L. Thus, if $MP_L > AP_L$, then for increases in L, we expect a rise in the average, or per unit, function, $AP_L = TP_L/L$. We can explain this result further with a simple example demonstrating the general relationship between marginal and average values. Assume a baseball player has compiled a batting average of .300, up to some game in July, in which he achieves four hits out of five times at bat. On this day his batting performance is $\frac{4}{5}$ or .800, which represents his marginal performance. Since this marginal performance of .800 exceeds his overall season average of .300, his batting average consequently rises.

Returning to Figure 8.10, observe that for levels of labor use greater than L_3, $MP_L < AP_L$, and as L increases beyond L_3, the AP_L decreases. Based on our earlier rationale, we expect this result because, if $MP_L < AP_L$, then the increments to TP_L associated with increases in L are less than the average, and as a result the AP_L declines. In terms of the baseball player example, again assume a hitter has a .300 season batting average prior to some game in July. If he gets only one hit out of five times at bat in this game, then his marginal performance is $\frac{1}{5}$, or .200, and his season batting average declines as a result.

8.7 STAGES OF PRODUCTION

We can use the relationships between marginal and average products to define the range of an input use over which a rational firm chooses to operate, or alternatively, to define those ranges where a rational firm will not choose to operate. Formally, these ranges are known as the Stage I, II, and III areas of production. In Figure 8.11 we have reproduced the marginal and average product curves for labor that were shown in panel (B) of Figure 8.10 and we have also designated the stages of production. We have derived these MP_L and AP_L curves for a fixed level of capital, $\overline{K}_1$.

The **Stage I area of production** is *the range of production for which increases in the use of a variable input cause increases in its average product.* As we have shown in Figure 8.11, Stage I refers to the range of labor use from zero units up to, but not including, L_3 units. Over this range of L, $MP_L > AP_L$ and thus AP_L rises with increases in L. The **Stage II area of production** is *that range for which increases in the use of a variable input cause decreases in its average product, while values of its associated marginal*

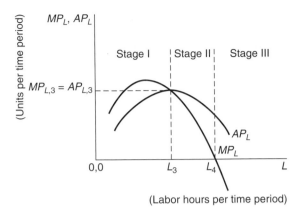

FIGURE 8.11 Stages of Production

product remain nonnegative. Referring again to Figure 8.11, we see that Stage II pertains to the range of labor use from L_3 to L_4 units inclusively, over which $MP_L \geq 0$, but for which $MP_L < AP_L$. We can also observe that AP_L decreases with increases in L. Finally, the **Stage III area of production** is *that range for which the use of a variable input corresponds to negative values for its marginal product.* For this stage of production, increases in the variable input cause decreases in its total product. In Figure 8.11, observe that Stage III begins after L_4 units of labor and continues indefinitely as labor use increases.

Because of our rather restrictive assumption of having only one variable input associated with these stages of production, any inferences we draw from this analysis regarding production theory are quite limited. However, we can use the stages of production to provide a rationale for establishing the range of a variable input use over which a rational firm chooses to operate. By using the process of elimination, we can deduce that this range of operation applies to the Stage II area of production. We can dismiss Stage III quite easily as representing a nonviable range of labor use since MP_L is negative over this stage. We demonstrated earlier that a negative marginal product of an input indicates that increases in its use cause decreases in the production of output, an action no rational firm will undertake. Conversely, a negative marginal product of an input also implies that by decreasing its use, a firm can increase its production of output. As a result, a rational firm will never choose to operate in the Stage III area of production.

Eliminating Stage I as a viable range of variable input use, however, is somewhat more difficult. As shown in Figure 8.11, within this stage increases in the amount of labor employed, while holding the amount of capital constant, cause the average product of labor, AP_L, to rise. Thus, on the basis of production efficiency, a firm has an incentive to continue employing additional amounts of labor up to L_3 units, since by so doing, it is able to increase the amount of output produced per labor hour. As a result, the firm will employ additional units of labor until it moves out of the Stage I area of production. This argument, however, is an insufficient explanation for dismissing Stage I because we can also apply this same argument to virtually all of Stage II. Wouldn't a firm operating in any area of Stage II beyond L_3, have an incentive to reduce the amount of labor it employs, because by doing so, it can achieve a higher AP_L? For example, if a firm employs L_4 units of labor, it can increase the AP_L by decreasing its labor use to L_3 units. In fact, by this line of reasoning, the only viable level of labor use is L_3 units, at which the AP_L achieves a maximum. Since this is an overly restrictive conclusion, we need to expand our rationale for eliminating Stage I. This is a difficult process, and unfortunately we cannot clearly demonstrate it by simply observing the MP_L and AP_L curves shown in Figure 8.11.

The critical fact, which we cannot directly illustrate in this figure, is that for the Stage I area of the variable input, labor, the values for the marginal product of the fixed input, capital, are negative. This fact follows from the particular production function we are using in this analysis. At first glance, it seems a contradiction in terms to discuss the marginal product of a fixed input. However, we demonstrated earlier that for the production function underlying this analysis, the use of one input affects the marginal productivity of the other. Therefore, even when the amount of capital is fixed, the values for the marginal product of capital are affected by the amount of labor employed. This being the case, the Stage I area of production refers to situations for which the amount of labor used is so low relative to the fixed amount of capital that it causes the marginal product of capital to be negative. As mentioned earlier, imagine a very large factory building with only a few laborers using it. Logically, the few laborers would be more productive in a smaller building where they didn't have to cover so much area. However, as more labor is employed, the marginal productivity of the factory building rises as the larger number of laborers utilize the space more efficiently. The relevant point is that within Stage I, $MP_K < 0$, and thus a rational firm chooses not to operate in this range of labor use.

Once Stages I and III have been eliminated, we can reason that a rational firm chooses to operate in Stage II because the marginal products of both inputs are nonnegative in this stage. We should emphasize that we apply these stages of production to define the relevant range of the use of an input based purely on the grounds of production efficiency. Furthermore, in the absence of any additional information regarding such important factors as the prices of inputs, the amount of money a firm can afford to spend on purchasing inputs, or the amount of output it desires to produce, it is impossible for us to determine a specific level of variable input use within Stage II that a firm will select. However, this analysis does enable us to narrow our focus of production theory to include only relevant levels of input use.

8.8 SUMMARY

As the first of five chapters devoted to the theory of the firm, our primary focus in this chapter has been on production issues in the short run. After introducing the concept of a production function, we fixed the amount of capital used by a firm, enabling us to derive the total, marginal, and average product of labor curves. We subsequently analyzed these curves and used them to demonstrate the economic concepts of the law of diminishing marginal productivity of an input, and the stages of production. The major topics we discussed in this chapter are summarized as follows.

- A production function expresses the maximum quantity of output that can be produced when employing various combinations of inputs, given the prevailing state of technology.
- The short run is a time period during which at least one of a firm's inputs remains fixed, while the long run is a sufficiently long enough period of time for all inputs used by the firm to be treated as variable.
- A total product curve expresses the maximum level of output, or total product, that can be produced as a function of one variable input while holding all other inputs and the state of technology constant.
- The marginal product of an input measures the change in the production of output, or total product, due to a change in the use of that input, while holding all other inputs and technology constant.
- The law of diminishing marginal productivity of an input states that as additional units of an input are employed in a production process, holding all other inputs and technology constant, the resulting increments to output, or total product, begin to diminish beyond some point.
- The average product of an input measures the amount of output produced per unit of that input employed in a production process, holding all other inputs constant.
- The Stage I area of production includes that range of production for which increases in the use of a variable input cause increases in its average product. The Stage II area of production constitutes that range of production for which increases in the use of a variable input result in decreases in its average product, but for which the corresponding marginal product remains nonnegative. Finally, the Stage III area of production constitutes that range for which the use of a variable input corresponds to negative values for its marginal product.

KEY TERMS

- average product of an input, page 211
- fixed input, page 199
- input, page 197
- law of diminishing marginal productivity of an input, page 205
- long run, page 200

- marginal product of an input, page 204
- market period or immediate run, page 200
- production function, page 198
- short run, page 200
- Stage I area of production, page 217

- Stage II area of production, page 217
- Stage III area of production, page 218
- state of technology, page 197
- total product curve, page 200
- variable input, page 199

EXERCISES

8.1 Explain the economic concept of the law of diminishing marginal productivity of an input. Does this phenomenon occur only in the short run, only in the long run, or in both the short run and the long run? Use an appropriate graph to illustrate this concept.

8.2 A compact disc manufacturer's production function is specified as

$$Q = f(K,L) = 64\ K^{1/2}L^{1/2}.$$

In the short run, the compact disc producer fixes its capital at 400 units.
a. Determine the firm's total product of labor curve.
b. Determine the firm's marginal product of labor curve.
c. Determine the firm's average product of labor curve.

8.3 Use the results that you obtained in Exercise 8.2 to answer the following questions.
a. If the firm has an output quota of 512,000 compact discs, how many laborers must it employ in the short run to achieve this level of production?
b. Does the marginal product of labor diminish as the compact disc producer hires additional workers? Demonstrate your conclusion both mathematically and graphically.

8.4 A mechanical pencil producer uses both labor and capital to produce its output. In the short run, its use of capital is fixed at some level, say $\overline{K}_1$, while it can vary its use of labor, L, in order to affect its level of production. Thus, we can generally state the firm's short-run production function as

$$Q = f(\overline{K}_1,L),$$

and we can express the firm's marginal product of labor, MP_L, as $MP_L = \partial Q/\partial L$. In addition, assume we know the following information with regard to the mechanical pencil manufacturer's production:

$$\text{when } L = 0;\ Q = 0,\ MP_L = 0,\ \text{and } \frac{\partial MP_L}{\partial L} > 0.$$

$$\text{when } 0 < L < 15;\ Q > 0,\ MP_L > 0,\ \text{and } \frac{\partial MP_L}{\partial L} > 0.$$

$$\text{when } L = 15;\ Q > 0,\ MP_L > 0,\ \text{and } \frac{\partial MP_L}{\partial L} = 0.$$

$$\text{when } 15 < L < 25;\ Q > 0,\ MP_L > 0,\ \text{and } \frac{\partial MP_L}{\partial L} < 0.$$

$$\text{when } L = 25;\ Q > 0,\ MP_L = 0,\ \text{and } \frac{\partial MP_L}{\partial L} < 0.$$

$$\text{when } L > 25;\ Q > 0,\ MP_L < 0,\ \text{and } \frac{\partial MP_L}{\partial L} < 0.$$

Using the above information, complete the following exercises.

  a. Sketch the firm's total product of labor curve and identify those segments that are concave, those that are convex, and any inflection points.
  b. Determine the level of labor use that maximizes the firm's output.
  c. In a separate graph, sketch the firm's marginal product of labor curve beneath the total product of labor curve.
  d. Determine the level of labor use that maximizes the marginal product of labor.
  e. Beyond what level of labor use do diminishing marginal returns to labor begin?

8.5 Is the length of the time period known as the short run identical for firms operating in different industries? Provide a real-world example to support your response.

8.6 A yacht builder uses labor and capital to produce yachts as described by the following production function:

$$Q = f(K,L) = 120K^2L^2 - K^3L^3.$$

In the short run, the firm's capital is fixed at 10 units.

  a. Determine the firm's total product of labor curve.
  b. Determine the firm's average product of labor curve.
  c. Determine the firm's marginal product of labor curve.
  d. At what level of labor use do diminishing returns set in for the yacht builder?

8.7 Use the results you obtained in Exercise 8.6 to answer the following questions.

  a. At what level of labor use is average product of labor maximized?
  b. At what level of labor use is the yacht producer's output maximized in the short run?
  c. What is the maximum number of yachts the firm can produce in the short run?

8.8 Assume a production function for which you treat labor as fixed and capital as variable. Using this scenario, define the stages of production. Intuitively explain why a firm will not operate in Stage I in this case.

CHAPTER 9

Production in the Long Run

9.1 INTRODUCTION

In Chapter 8, we introduced the concept of a production function and analyzed it while holding one of the inputs constant. As a result, our analysis related to only short-run situations. Alternatively, if we treat all inputs, such as capital and labor, as variable, the production function pertains to the long run. In this case, our analysis of the production process becomes somewhat more complex because a firm now faces more decision variables. Furthermore, depending on the type of production process, or "recipe," used by a firm in producing its output, the manner in which it combines its inputs to produce a given level of output will vary widely. For example, some goods can be produced solely according to processes that allow a firm to efficiently use only a limited, or finite, number of input combinations to produce a particular level of output. In these situations, the degree of substitutability between the inputs is limited, where for extreme cases, there may be no substitution at all. As an example, in the process of baking a cake, we cannot substitute sugar for flour or vice versa. However, for many other production processes an unlimited number of input combinations can be used to efficiently produce a given level of output. In these situations, there exists a great degree of substitutability between the inputs.

In this chapter, we will discuss these different types of production processes, after which we will develop the concept of an isoquant, or a set of capital and labor combinations that yield a particular level of output. In addition, for those appropriate production processes, we will develop a measure for the degree of substitutability between inputs, known as the marginal rate of technical substitution. Finally, the important characteristics associated with isoquants will be discussed. Many of the graphical and mathematical methods used in this chapter closely parallel those we used previously in the development of consumer theory. However, be sure to keep in mind that the decision variables are now the amounts of the variable inputs, usually capital and labor, employed by the firm in the long run.

9.2 CONDITIONS UNDERLYING PRODUCTION

Since a firm has the ability to vary all of its inputs in the long run, it logically alters its input use to achieve some particular goal which, ultimately, is consistent with maximizing its profit. However, underlying a firm's long-run decision-making behavior are two basic conditions that define two different types of production processes. The first is the **condition of variable proportions**, which refers to *those processes for which it is possible to produce a given level of output from an infinite number of input ratios*. In these situations, a firm can use an infinite number of input proportions, usually consisting of capital and labor, to produce some desired level of output. The important implication of this condition is that some degree of substitutability always exists between the inputs used in a production process, where this condition underlies the vast majority of our analysis in this chapter.

The second condition defining a production process is the **condition of fixed proportions**, which refers to *those processes for which it is possible to produce a given level of output from a finite number of input ratios.* The extreme case for this condition occurs when a given level of output can be efficiently produced from only one input ratio. In this case, there exists no substitutability between the inputs used in producing the output. In other words, the inputs represent perfect complements in the production process because it is impossible to change output without changing both inputs in a manner that maintains the specific input ratio necessary for production to take place.

Mathematically, we represent this condition by a production function of the form

$$Q = \text{minimum} \left(\frac{K}{a}, \frac{L}{b} \right),$$

where $a > 0$ and $b > 0$.

In this function, Q represents units of output, and K and L denote units of the inputs capital and labor, respectively. The coefficients a and b define the proportion by which the inputs, K and L, must be combined to produce the output, Q, and the term "minimum" means that the level of output produced is restricted to the smaller of the two ratios included in the function. For example, if a production process mandates that capital and labor must be combined in a capital/labor ratio of 1/2, then $a = 1$ and $b = 2$, and we specify the production function as

$$Q = \text{minimum} \left(\frac{K}{1}, \frac{L}{2} \right).$$

If 2 units of K and 2 units of L are available, then

$$Q = \text{minimum} \left(\frac{2}{1}, \frac{2}{2} \right),$$

and only 2/2, or 1, unit of output can be produced, since the restricting input is labor. In this case, the second unit of capital is useless. As another example, if 2 units of capital and 5 units of labor are available, then

$$Q = \text{minimum} \left(\frac{2}{1}, \frac{5}{2} \right),$$

and 2/1 or 2 units of output can be produced, where in this case, the restricting input is capital.

9.3   ISOQUANTS

Since the condition of variable proportions is far more prevalent in the real world, we will assume that it underlies the following production analysis, unless otherwise stated. Thus, we can express the production function in the form

$$Q = f(K,L),$$

as discussed in Chapter 8. We have illustrated this function in three-dimensional space in Figure 9.1. Although we have shown the entire function in this figure, only the section bounded by the solid lines *IJ* and *HJ* is relevant to the following analysis. This conclusion follows from our reasoning presented in Chapter 8. If we hold one of the inputs constant, for example K, at some value, such as $\overline{K}_1$, Q increases as L increases up to the point where L corresponds to the solid line *IJ*. Beyond this point, increases in L cause decreases in Q. Using our terminology from Chapter 8, we find that as additional units of labor are used in a production process, holding the capital input constant, a point is reached at which the marginal product of labor equals zero and becomes negative thereafter. Similarly, if we hold labor constant at some value, such as $\overline{L}_1$, and increase capital, K, Q increases up to a value of K corresponding to the other solid line in Figure 9.1, *HJ*. Beyond this line, increases in K cause decreases in Q, or, alternatively stated, the marginal product of capital becomes negative.

Rational firms will not knowingly continue to employ additional units of an input after its marginal product achieves a value equal to zero since doing so decreases their production of output. Thus, rational firms only utilize inputs that have marginal products that are greater than or equal to zero, thereby confining themselves to the region *HJI*. As noted earlier, this region corresponds to the Stage II area of production we described in Chapter 8. In Figure 9.1, we have illustrated the boundaries that delineate the area within which a rational firm produces its output, with the solid lines *IJ* and *HJ*. These lines provide the basis for boundaries known as **ridge lines for an isoquant**

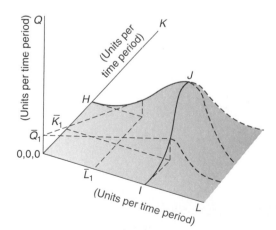

FIGURE 9.1 Production Function Assuming Variable Proportions

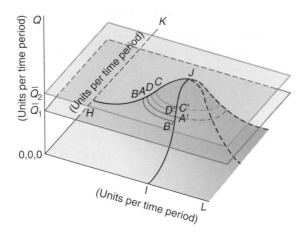

FIGURE 9.2 Derivation of Isoquants from Three-Dimensional Production Function

mapping, defined as *sets of input combinations for which the marginal product of one of the inputs is equal to zero.* Although we conventionally plot ridge lines in two-dimensional K–L space, the line IJ, shown in the three-dimensional graph, Figure 9.1, represents the set of (L,K) combinations for which $MP_L = 0$, and the line HJ represents the set of (L,K) combinations for which $MP_K = 0$.

We can create a clearer graphical analysis by generating a two-dimensional curve that explicitly allows both inputs to vary, while still containing the information represented in the three-dimensional graph in Figure 9.1. We accomplish this by holding the quantity of output constant at some level, such as $\overline{Q}_1$, and by taking a two-dimensional cross-section of the broader function, as shown in Figure 9.2. We have cut the three-dimensional graph with a plane constructed at $\overline{Q}_1$, producing the curve AA' within the relevant region, HJI. Since we have now fixed the value of the third dimension, Q, at $\overline{Q}_1$, we can project the curve AA' into the K–L plane where it is represented by the curve BB'. With the third dimension eliminated, imagine grasping the K-axis and rotating the K–L plane upright until it is vertical, thus producing the two-dimensional graph shown in Figure 9.3. The resulting curve, BB', is known as an **isoquant,** or a *set*

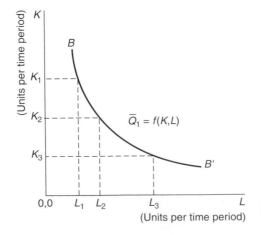

FIGURE 9.3 Isoquant

of input combinations that can be used to produce a given level of output. We can demonstrate the implications associated with an isoquant by examining the curve shown in Figure 9.3. This curve indicates that a firm can produce the specified level of output, $\overline{Q}_1$, from input combinations (L_1,K_1), (L_2,K_2), (L_3,K_3), or more generally, from an infinite number of K–L combinations that lie on the isoquant. By moving down the isoquant from input combination (L_1,K_1) to combination (L_2,K_2), it should be clear that if the firm uses less capital, K_2, rather than K_1, it must use more labor, L_2, as opposed to L_1, to still produce the given level of output, $\overline{Q}_1$.

The isoquant shown in Figure 9.3 pertains to only one level of output, $\overline{Q}_1$. Referring back to Figure 9.2, we can fix Q at a different level, such as $\overline{Q}_2$, where $\overline{Q}_2 > \overline{Q}_1$. In

---

REAL-WORLD APPLICATION 9.1

Transforming an Outdated Plant

Occasionally it takes something as drastic as the closing of a plant to force necessary changes in a firm's outdated production process. Such was the case for the Owens-Corning Fiberglass Corporation's plant in Jackson, Tennessee.[1] At the height of its production in 1986, the plant employed 700 workers, far too many for its outdated capital. By 1987, the year the plant closed its doors, it employed 540 workers who were led by four layers of management. In addition, the capital employed was 30 years old and grossly outdated. In its final year of operation, prior to massive restructuring, the Jackson plant produced 130 million pounds of fiberglass.

The following year, Owens-Corning management declared a production hiatus for the Jackson plant. Over the next seven years sweeping changes were invoked affecting the use of both capital and labor in the plant's fiberglass production process. Greater automation and a "new glass-making recipe" were key elements in bringing the defunct plant back on-line. In addition, by using a new blend of raw materials and an updated production technology, all waste generated by the refurbished plant could be recycled, thereby eliminating the need for any additional resources to bring the plant into compliance with prevailing environmental laws.

Overall employment at the plant decreased substantially. By the time of its reopening in 1994, only 80 laborers, guided by a single layer of management, were needed to generate 130 million pounds of fiberglass, the same amount of output produced in 1987 when it used substantially more labor and less capital. Part of Owens-Corning Jackson's adjustment to its production process has been the technological improvement in the capital input it uses. However, from a theoretical perspective, another type of adjustment made to this plant typifies the long-run economic concept of movement along an isoquant. Between 1987 and 1994, the plant chose to substitute capital for labor in its production process, while holding its output constant at 130 million pounds of fiberglass. This case study also exemplifies how the appropriate combination of long-run production adjustments can transform an inefficient and environmentally harmful plant into an industry standout.

---
[1]Fred R. Bleakley, "How an Outdated Plant Was Made New," *Wall Street Journal*, October 21, 1994, p. B-1.

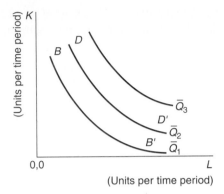

FIGURE 9.4 Isoquant Mapping

this situation, we use another plane, created at the higher output level, $\overline{Q}_2$, to cut the surface, thus generating another curve, CC'. In two-dimensional space, projecting CC' into the K–L plane yields the curve DD', representing a second isoquant. We have shown this curve, DD', along with the original isoquant, BB', in Figure 9.4. The isoquant DD' represents a set of input combinations that can be used to produce the higher level of output, $\overline{Q}_2$. We can use a similar procedure to generate the isoquant for output level $\overline{Q}_3$, where note that $\overline{Q}_3 > \overline{Q}_2 > \overline{Q}_1$. More generally, we can derive an entire map of isoquants where each pertains to a fixed level of Q measured along the vertical axis in Figure 9.2. Thus, isoquants indicate successively higher levels of output as they lie further to the northeast since they correspond to higher levels of output, Q, on the vertical axis for the three-dimensional graph shown in Figure 9.2.

9.4 MARGINAL RATE OF TECHNICAL SUBSTITUTION

Movement along any one isoquant provides us with considerable information regarding the substitutability between the inputs used in a firm's production process. In general, rates of change along a curve are represented by its slope. Specifically, for an isoquant, we can determine the rate at which one input can be substituted for the other in the process of producing a given level of output. Since the rise variable is capital, K, and the run variable is labor, L, the slope of an isoquant is measured as the derivative, dK/dL. We compute this term from the production function by taking the total derivative of Q with respect to L and setting the result equal to zero because by definition, Q remains constant as movement occurs along an isoquant. Hence, given the production function

$$Q = f(K,L),$$

$$\frac{dQ}{dL} = \frac{\partial f(K,L)}{\partial K}\frac{dK}{dL} + \frac{\partial f(K,L)}{\partial L}\frac{dL}{dL} = 0,$$

or

$$= \frac{\partial Q}{\partial K}\frac{dK}{dL} + \frac{\partial Q}{\partial L} = 0.$$

Thus, we can express the slope of the isoquant as

$$\frac{dK}{dL} = \frac{\dfrac{-\partial Q}{\partial L}}{\dfrac{\partial Q}{\partial K}}.$$

The term $\partial Q/\partial L$ represents the change in output resulting from a change in the labor input, while holding capital constant, or the marginal product of labor, MP_L. Similarly, we can identify $\partial Q/\partial K$ as the marginal product of capital, MP_K. Accordingly, the slope of an isoquant is

$$\frac{dK}{dL} = \frac{-MP_L}{MP_K},$$

or alternatively

$$\frac{-dK}{dL} = \frac{MP_L}{MP_K}.$$

Our economic interpretation associated with the negative of this slope is known as the **marginal rate of technical substitution**, or **MRTS**, defined as *the rate at which one input can be substituted for the other in a production process, while producing some constant level of output.* Since we generally measure K on the vertical axis, the *MRTS* represents the amount of capital that must be sacrificed in order to substitute more labor in the production process, while producing the same level of output. Alternatively, we can interpret it as the amount of capital that must be substituted for labor while producing a constant level of output. Depending on whether the firm is substituting L for K, or K for L, either dK or dL, respectively, will be negative. As a result, in order to express the *MRTS* as a positive value, we define it as the negative of the slope of an isoquant, or

$$-\frac{dK}{dL} = MRTS = \frac{MP_L}{MP_K}.$$

We can use a specific production function to provide a numerical example, which should help clarify the concept of an isoquant and its associated *MRTS*. Assume the production function is

$$Q = 3K^{1/3}L^{2/3},$$

where the marginal product functions are

$$MP_L = \frac{\partial Q}{\partial L} = 2K^{1/3}L^{-1/3} = 2\left(\frac{K}{L}\right)^{1/3}$$

and

$$MP_K = \frac{\partial Q}{\partial K} = (1)K^{-2/3}L^{2/3} = \left(\frac{L}{K}\right)^{2/3}.$$

We derive an isoquant by holding the quantity of output constant at some specified value, such as $\overline{Q}_1$, and therefore in this case, it is represented as

$$\overline{Q}_1 = 3K^{1/3}L^{2/3}.$$

Since K is measured on the vertical axis, we can express this isoquant as

$$K^{1/3} = \frac{\overline{Q}_1}{3L^{2/3}}$$

$$(K^{1/3})^3 = \left(\frac{\overline{Q}_1}{3L^{2/3}}\right)^3,$$

or

$$K = \frac{\overline{Q}_1^3}{27L^2}.$$

If we specify the level of output as $\overline{Q}_1 = 9$ units and the firm uses $L_1 = 1$ unit of labor, then the amount of capital used is

$$K_1 = \frac{9^3}{27(1)^2} = \frac{729}{27} = 27 \text{ units.}$$

Alternatively, if the firm uses less capital and more labor, such as $L_2 = 3$ units, to produce the 9 units of output, then

$$K_2 = \frac{9^3}{27(3)^2} = \frac{729}{27(9)} = 3 \text{ units.}$$

Our analysis has been conducted for only one level of output, $\overline{Q}_1$, and as a result, it pertains to only one isoquant. If we specify Q at levels other than $\overline{Q}_1$, such as $\overline{Q}_2$, $\overline{Q}_3$, $\overline{Q}_4$, and so forth, then it is possible to develop an entire map containing a different isoquant for each level of output. We can compute the *MRTS* for each (L,K) combination on any particular isoquant. Recall that the *MRTS* is equal to the negative of the slope of an isoquant, $-dK/dL$, or the ratio of the marginal products, MP_L/MP_K. Thus, for the original isoquant, where $\overline{Q}_1 = 9$ units of output,

$$K = \frac{\overline{Q}_1^3}{27L^2} = \frac{1}{27}\overline{Q}_1^3 L^{-2}$$

and

$$\frac{dK}{dL} = -\frac{2}{27}\overline{Q}_1^3 L^{-3} = -\frac{2}{27}\frac{\overline{Q}_1^3}{L^3},$$

or

$$MRTS = -\frac{dK}{dL} = \frac{2}{27}\frac{\overline{Q}_1^3}{L^3}.$$

Evaluating this term for $\overline{Q}_1 = 9$ units and $L_1 = 1$ unit yields

$$MRTS = -\frac{dK}{dL} = \frac{2}{27}\frac{(9)^3}{(1)^3} = \frac{2}{27}\cdot\frac{729}{1} = 54.$$

This result indicates that at the input combination $L_1 = 1$ unit and $K_1 = 27$ units, the firm is able to substitute 1 unit of labor for 54 units of capital and still produce 9 units of output. Alternatively, the firm can substitute 54 units of capital for 1 unit of labor, while still producing 9 units of output. We can also compute this value for the $MRTS$ by using the more common method that involves determining the ratio of the marginal products. Thus, for this example

$$MRTS = \frac{MP_L}{MP_K} = \frac{2K^{1/3}L^{-1/3}}{K^{-2/3}L^{2/3}} = \frac{2K}{L}.$$

where at the input combination $K = 27$ units and $L = 1$ unit

$$MRTS = \frac{2K}{L} = \frac{2(27)}{1} = 54$$

Note that this value is the same as the one we computed earlier for the negative of the slope of the isoquant.

9.5   CHARACTERISTICS OF ISOQUANTS

Before we use isoquants in any further analysis of production theory, it is necessary to note several of their characteristics. You may recognize that these characteristics closely parallel those related to indifference curves, which we presented in Section 3.5 of Chapter 3. First, the isoquant map is everywhere dense, indicating that all capital–labor combinations lie on some isoquant that is plotted in capital–labor space. This characteristic follows from our implicit assumption of smooth and continuous production functions from which we derive isoquants. Thus, when we focus on two alternative input combinations, one combination either clearly produces more output than the other, or they can be used to produce the same level of output. In the first case, the input combinations lie on two distinctly different isoquants, and in the second case, they lie on the same isoquant.

The second characteristic associated with isoquants is that they cannot intersect. Similar to the case involving indifference curves, a situation of intersecting isoquants violates one of two implicit assumptions: transitivity, or that an input combination containing greater amounts of inputs produces a greater level of output than a combination with lower levels of inputs.

The third characteristic related to isoquants is that, in general, they possess negative slopes, as we have demonstrated in Figure 9.3. This characteristic reflects some degree of substitutability between the inputs used in a production process. In other words, if a firm chooses to use less capital, it must use more labor in order to produce the same level of output, and the converse is true as well. Furthermore, the slope of an isoquant equals $-MP_L/MP_K$, and this slope remains negative throughout the relevant range of any isoquant where both MP_L and MP_K are positive. Recall from Chapter 8, that the range of input use for which both marginal products are nonnegative corresponds to the Stage II area of production, the stage in which a rational firm operates.[2] A hypothetical exception to negatively sloped isoquants occurs if one of the inputs becomes detrimental, meaning that its marginal product becomes negative. In this case, the isoquants acquire positive slopes. For example, if $MP_L < 0$, then $dK/dL = -(-MP_L/MP_K) > 0$. However, we have already reasoned that a firm will not rationally operate in this range; as a result, this exception is of little relevance to any useful economic analysis.

There are other exceptions to the characteristic of negatively sloped isoquants, with one being particularly noteworthy. This is a situation in which isoquants assume right-angle shapes, arising from the condition of fixed proportions we discussed earlier in this chapter. In this case, the underlying production function is of the fixed coefficient form

$$Q = \text{minimum}\left(\frac{K}{a}, \frac{L}{b}\right),$$

and the production process is restricted, in the extreme case, to only one input ratio by which output can be efficiently produced. As a result, additional amounts of either input beyond what is necessary to maintain this ratio become extraneous or useless.

We can best demonstrate this situation with a real-world example. Assume a firm is in the business of producing logs, and it produces them using saws (capital) and labor. The production process is restricted, however, because each saw requires two people to operate it. Specifically, each saw has two handles, and one person is not strong enough to operate the saw alone. Thus, the proportion by which the inputs, capital (saws) and labor (laborers), must be combined to produce the logs is one to two, respectively. The production function in this case is

$$Q = \text{minimum}\left(\frac{K}{1}, \frac{L}{2}\right),$$

which is the same type of production function we presented earlier in a generalized manner. Finally, assume that the relevant time period is one hour and that two laborers working with one saw can produce one log during that hour. If a second, third, or any number of additional saws is added to the production process, the output is still only one log, provided the firm continues to use just two laborers. Thus, these combinations of inputs lie on the same isoquant. Similarly, the inclusion of a third, fourth, or any number of additional laborers, using one saw, still results in the production of just one log. We have depicted the isoquant map representing this production process in Figure 9.5, where the isoquant just described is represented as $\overline{Q}_1 = 1$ log.

---

[2]Note that, technically, the Stage II area of production also includes the amounts of an input use for which $MP_K = 0$ and $MP_L = 0$.

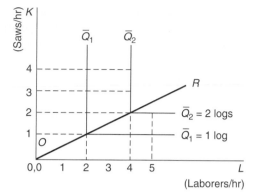

FIGURE 9.5 Isoquants for Fixed Coefficient Production Function where Inputs Are Perfect Complements

Note that the ray OR passes through the corners of each isoquant. These corners represent combinations of K and L that operate, according to the described production processes, to produce whole units of output. The slope of this ray, $K/L = 1/2$, reflects the proportion in which the inputs must be used in order to produce the output. Referring once again to Figure 9.5, we can see that if the firm produces two units of output, it must use at least two units of capital and four units of labor. In this case, additional units of capital beyond the necessary two, combined with four units of labor, still produce only two units of output. Alternatively, additional units of labor in excess of the fourth unit, combined with two units of capital, still produce only two units of output. Although we can apply these right-angle isoquants to some production situations, it is important that you note that they remain a rather rare exception to the more general characteristic of negatively sloped isoquants.

The fourth, and final, characteristic associated with isoquants is that generally they are strictly convex toward the origin, as we have shown in Figures 9.3 and 9.4. This characteristic reflects the fact that, as a firm moves down to the right along an isoquant, using less capital and more labor, the slope of the isoquant, dK/dL, becomes less negative, or smaller, in absolute value terms. This type of movement along an isoquant corresponds to a diminishing $MRTS$, since the $MRTS$ represents the negative of the slope of an isoquant. Given that the $MRTS = MP_L/MP_K$, a diminishing $MRTS$ reflects the fact that this ratio of marginal products declines as more units of labor are substituted for capital in a firm's production process. It is tempting for us to say that this result follows from the law of diminishing marginal productivity. However, in a broad sense, diminishing marginal productivity of the inputs is neither necessary nor sufficient for a diminishing $MRTS$ to occur. Instead, this result only requires that the ratio of marginal products decline as labor is substituted for capital or for the ratio to increase if capital is substituted for labor.

For the specific production function underlying the majority of the analysis in this chapter, however, we can provide a more detailed rationale regarding the characteristic of strict convexity. Recall that we made two key assumptions regarding this production function. The first is the law of diminishing marginal productivity, which states that the marginal product of an input diminishes as more of that input is used, while holding other inputs constant. Our second assumption is that changing one input alters the marginal product of the other. Therefore, as a firm moves down an isoquant using less capital and more labor, the marginal product of labor diminishes, partly because of the law of diminishing marginal productivity and partly because the additional labor has less capital with which to work. Simultaneously, the marginal product of capital increases as capital is reduced, partly because the law of diminishing marginal productivity is reversed, thereby causing the marginal product of capital to rise. In addition, lower levels of capital are now combined with increasing amounts of labor, further enhancing its marginal productivity. Since the marginal rate of technical substitution, *MRTS*, is equal to the negative of the slope of an isoquant, we have also expressed it as the ratio of marginal products, or

$$MRTS = \frac{MP_L}{MP_K}.$$

Therefore, by observing this formula, you can see that a falling MP_L accompanied with a rising MP_K clearly causes the *MRTS* to diminish.

We can demonstrate this result by returning to the specific isoquant, which we derived earlier from the production function

$$Q = 3K^{1/3}L^{2/3}.$$

In that example, Q was specified at $\overline{Q}_1 = 9$ units and the input combination $K_1 = 27$ units and $L_1 = 1$ unit was selected for analysis, at which the *MRTS* = 54. We also chose an alternative input combination on this same isoquant and demonstrated the substitutability between this combination of inputs. This second input combination was $K_2 = 3$ units and $L_2 = 3$ units, and since $K_2 < K_1$ and $L_2 > L_1$, it lies further down the isoquant than the original. At this second combination

$$MRTS = \frac{MP_L}{MP_K} = \frac{2K}{L} = \frac{2(3)}{3} = 2,$$

which is considerably smaller than the previous value for the *MRTS*, which was 54. Thus, by moving down the isoquant, substituting labor for capital, the *MRTS* has clearly diminished.

There are some exceptions to the property of strict convexity of isoquants. One, which we have already discussed, pertains to the right-angle isoquants derived from fixed coefficient production functions. Another interesting exception relates to isoquants representing inputs that are perfect substitutes in a production process. If two inputs are perfect substitutes, they can be used interchangeably, and the use of one input does not affect the marginal productivity of the other. Similarly, using more of one input relative to the other does not cause its own marginal product to decline. The implication of this situation is that the marginal products do not change as a firm moves along such an isoquant. As a result, the *MRTS* remains constant since it is equal to the ratio of the two constant marginal products. Because the *MRTS* represents the negative of the slope of an isoquant, the specific isoquants in this case are linear rather

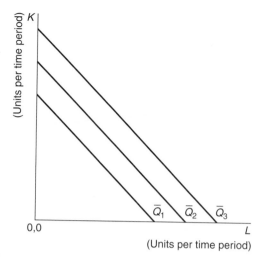

FIGURE 9.6 Isoquants for Inputs That Are Perfect Substitutes

than convex, as we have shown in Figure 9.6.[3] Although the characteristics of isoquants we have discussed in this section may seem rather esoteric to you at this time, they reflect many key economic concepts and provide a foundation for the extremely important optimization analysis that we will develop in the next chapter.

9.6   SUMMARY

The primary focus of this chapter has been on the technical, or engineering, aspects of firm behavior in the long run. In this vein, we developed the concept of an isoquant along with its associated marginal rate of technical substitution. In addition, we outlined the various characteristics typically associated with isoquants. A summary of the topics we covered in this chapter is as follows.

- Production processes for which a given level of output can be produced from an infinite number of input ratios exhibit the condition of variable proportions. Alternatively, production processes for which there exist a limited number of input ratios for producing a given level of output reflect the condition of fixed proportions.
- The set of input combinations capable of producing a particular level of output is known as an isoquant.
- The negative of the slope of an isoquant measures the marginal rate of technical substitution, indicating the rate at which a firm can substitute one input for the other while producing the same level of output.
- Isoquants typically possess the characteristics of an everywhere dense mapping, strict convexity, nonintersection, and negative slopes.

[3]Technically speaking, these isoquants are still convex but not strictly convex, which is the more common result. Strict convexity over an interval for a curve, such as an isoquant, implies that a line drawn between any two points on this interval lies above the curve.

KEY TERMS

- condition of fixed proportions, page 224
- condition of variable proportions, page 223
- isoquant, page 226
- marginal rate of technical substitution, page 229
- ridge lines for an isoquant mapping, page 225, 226

EXERCISES

9.1 Develop a logical proof demonstrating that isoquants cannot intersect.

9.2 The South China Sea Pearl Company produces pearl necklaces according to the fixed coefficient production function,

$$Q = \text{minimum}\left(\frac{K}{80}, \frac{L}{1}\right),$$

where K represents the number of pearls necessary to produce a single 16-inch necklace and L represents the number of laborers. Plot the isoquants associated with $Q = 1$ necklace and $Q = 2$ necklaces. What are the most efficient combinations of capital and labor that can be used to produce 1 necklace and 2 necklaces, respectively?

9.3 A Swiss watch manufacturer's production function is

$$Q = K^3 L.$$

a. Determine the firm's marginal product of labor function.
b. Determine if the marginal product of labor function exhibits diminishing marginal returns.
c. Determine the firm's marginal product of capital function.
d. Determine if the marginal product of capital function exhibits diminishing marginal returns.
e. Determine the function for the marginal rate of technical substitution.

9.4 Refer to the production function in Exercise 9.3.

a. Determine the function for this firm's isoquant when $Q = 2$ watches.
b. Plot the firm's isoquant when $Q = 2$ watches.
c. Compute the value of the marginal rate of substitution for three points lying on the $Q = 2$ watches isoquant. Does the marginal rate of technical substitution diminish as labor increases and capital decreases along this isoquant?

9.5 A catfish farmer's production function is

$$Q = KL.$$

a. Determine the farmer's marginal product of labor function.
b. Determine if the marginal product of labor function exhibits diminishing marginal returns.
c. Determine the farmer's marginal product of capital function.

d. Determine if the marginal product of capital function exhibits diminishing marginal returns.

e. Derive the function for the marginal rate of technical substitution.

9.6 Refer to the production function in Exercise 9.5.

a. Determine the function for the catfish farmer's isoquant when $Q = 400$ units of catfish.

b. Plot the farmer's isoquant when $Q = 400$ units of catfish.

c. Compute the value of the marginal rate of technical substitution at three points lying on the $Q = 400$ units of catfish isoquant. Does the marginal rate of technical substitution diminish?

9.7 A firm's production function is

$$Q = 32K + 16L.$$

a. Intuitively explain the relationship between the inputs, capital and labor, in this firm's production process.

b. Plot the isoquant for $Q = 480$ in input space.

c. Determine the marginal rate of technical substitution for three points that lie on the $Q = 480$ isoquant. Does the marginal rate of technical substitution diminish?

9.8 What factors will influence the length of time necessary for a firm to make long-run adjustments in its production?

CHAPTER 10

Long-Run Optimization for the Firm

10.1 INTRODUCTION

We have now laid the groundwork for analyzing a firm's production process from the perspective of both the short- and long-run time periods. In doing so, we developed the economic concepts of the production function, marginal product of labor, marginal product of capital, and marginal rate of technical substitution. However, up to this point, our discussion has not mentioned the cost a firm incurs in the production of goods and services. Typically, a firm must pay for the inputs it employs. Therefore, in order to be consistent with its goal of profit maximization, it is logical for a firm to produce its output at the least possible cost. Specifically, in the long run, where all inputs are variable, a firm achieves this goal of profit maximization by treating the amounts of inputs it employs as decision variables and adjusting their levels until they are used in the most cost-efficient manner. Thus, for a firm to be cost efficient, it not only will use efficient production techniques, but must also take into account the prices of the inputs it uses in its production process. Consider, say, a bean farmer, who can use many alternative combinations of farm machinery and laborers to plant and harvest his crop. Logically, this farmer takes into consideration the prices he pays for capital and labor when determining the amounts of these inputs he will use to minimize the cost of producing his beans.

In this chapter we will bring together production concepts from Chapters 8 and 9 with the idea of a firm's costs of production. Specifically, we will formulate a process known as constrained cost minimization, which we will use to determine a firm's cost-efficient input combinations associated with producing different levels of output.

10.2 ISOCOST EQUATIONS

In the long run, for most production functions, a firm has the ability to choose among an infinite number of input combinations when deciding to produce a particular level of output. In the two-input case, we assume that these inputs consist of capital and labor. In the previous chapter, we focused on a firm's use of inputs in production from purely an engineering perspective. However, from an economic point of view, a firm's choice of inputs is restricted in several ways. Specifically, assuming scarcity, the firm must pay for the resources it employs. Furthermore, if we assume that the prices of capital and labor are determined in perfectly competitive input markets by the interaction of all buyers and sellers of these resources, the firm exercises no control over these input prices. Therefore, firms must take the price of labor, P_L, and the price of capital, P_K, as given by the respective input markets.

Although the firm exercises no control over input prices, it does have some control over the amount of each input it purchases. If we assume predetermined input prices and a specific budget, or cost, $\overline{C}_1$, that the firm allocates for purchasing these inputs, then this budget equals the sum of the firm's expenditures on each input. This function, known as an **isocost equation**, represents *the set of all input combinations that a firm is able to purchase for a particular level of expenditure on inputs and a given set of input prices.* We can express the isocost equation for a firm purchasing capital, K, and labor, L, with total expenditures on these inputs equaling $\overline{C}_1$ dollars, as

$$\overline{P}_{K,1}K + \overline{P}_{L,1}L = \overline{C}_1, \tag{10.1}$$

where $\overline{P}_{K,1}$ and $\overline{P}_{L,1}$ represent the predetermined unit prices of capital and labor, respectively. Note that the isocost equation is a linear function containing the firm's decision variables, K and L.

Like the isoquant curve, we can plot the isocost equation in input space with labor, L, and capital, K, measured on the horizontal and vertical axes, respectively. Using simple algebra, we can isolate the variable K in equation (10.1) in order to determine the slope and vertical intercept of the isocost equation as

$$\overline{P}_{K,1}K + \overline{P}_{L,1}L = \overline{C}_1$$

$$\frac{\overline{P}_{K,1}K}{\overline{P}_{K,1}} = \frac{\overline{C}_1}{\overline{P}_{K,1}} - \frac{\overline{P}_{L,1}L}{\overline{P}_{K,1}}$$

$$K = \frac{\overline{C}_1}{\overline{P}_{K,1}} - \frac{\overline{P}_{L,1}L}{\overline{P}_{K,1}}. \tag{10.2}$$

Equation (10.2) is simply an algebraic transformation of the original isocost equation (10.1) into the general

$$Y = b + mx$$

format for a linear equation where b denotes the Y-intercept of the function and m represents the slope. Inspecting equation (10.2) reveals that the vertical, or K, intercept of the isocost equation is equal to $\overline{C}_1/\overline{P}_{K,1}$, or the value of the firm's total expenditures, $\overline{C}_1$, divided by the unit price of capital, $\overline{P}_{K,1}$. The value of the vertical intercept measures the maximum number of units of capital the firm can purchase if it allocates all of its budget to capital. Using equation (10.2), we compute this value by setting L equal to zero and solving for K. Similarly, we can determine the value of the intercept of the isocost equation with the labor axis by setting K equal to zero and solving for L in equation (10.1). The value of this intercept, $\overline{C}_1/\overline{P}_{L,1}$, represents the maximum number of units of labor that the firm can purchase if it spends all of its budget only on labor.

We determine the slope of the isocost equation, dK/dL, by taking the derivative of K with respect to L as

$$K = \frac{\overline{C}_1}{\overline{P}_{K,1}} - \frac{\overline{P}_{L,1}}{\overline{P}_{K,1}} L$$

$$\frac{dK}{dL} = 0 - \frac{\overline{P}_{L,1}}{\overline{P}_{K,1}} = \frac{-\overline{P}_{L,1}}{\overline{P}_{K,1}}$$

Thus, the slope of the isocost equation is simply the negative of the ratio of the unit price of labor to the unit price of capital, $-\overline{P}_{L,1}/\overline{P}_{K,1}$. We can interpret this slope of the isocost equation as measuring the rate, determined in the input markets, at which a firm can substitute one input for the other when purchasing capital and labor.

We have plotted an isocost equation in input space in Figure 10.1. All of the points that lie on a particular isocost line represent alternative combinations of labor and capital that the firm is able to purchase while spending all of its budget, $\overline{C}_1$, on these inputs. For example, if a firm has $12,000 to spend on either capital or labor, and if the unit price of capital is $100 per hour while the unit price of labor is $10 per hour, then the firm could choose to purchase only capital, in which case it could obtain a maximum of

$$\frac{\overline{C}_1}{\overline{P}_{K,1}} = \frac{\$12,000}{\$100} = 120 \text{ units of capital.}$$

Alternatively, the firm could choose to devote all of its budget to labor, in which case it could hire a maximum of

$$\frac{\overline{C}_1}{\overline{P}_{L,1}} = \frac{\$12,000}{\$10} = 1200 \text{ units of labor.}$$

The firm could also choose to hire any one of an infinite number of combinations of capital and labor that exhaust its budget, or cost, $\overline{C}_1$. For example, it could purchase 60

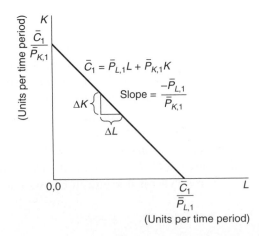

FIGURE 10.1 Isocost Equation

units of capital and 600 units of labor, since the sum of its expenditures on this input combination exactly equals its budget of $12,000. It should also be clear that in order for the firm to purchase more units of one input, it must decrease its purchases of the other in order to stay within its budget.

What happens if the firm allocates a larger budget to resource acquisition, say $\overline{C}_2$, where $\overline{C}_2 > \overline{C}_1$, assuming input prices remain constant? In such a case, the firm can buy more inputs than before. Graphically, we have depicted this situation in Figure 10.2 as a rightward parallel shift of the isocost equation. Note that its slope, $-\overline{P}_{L,1}/\overline{P}_{K,1}$, does not change since we have assumed that input prices are constant. However, the intercepts of the isocost equation with both the labor and capital axes, $\overline{C}_2/\overline{P}_{L,1}$ and $\overline{C}_2/\overline{P}_{K,1}$, respectively, increase since the new value of the firm's total expenditures on inputs, $\overline{C}_2$, is now larger than the initial value, $\overline{C}_1$. In Figure 10.2, the concept of an isocost mapping is illustrated, where we have plotted isocost equations $\overline{C}_1$ and $\overline{C}_2$ along with a third isocost equation pertaining to an even higher level of expenditure, or cost, $\overline{C}_3$. We can observe in this figure that isocost equations plotted further away from the origin pertain to higher total expenditures on capital and labor. As a result, the firm can purchase greater combinations of these inputs the further its isocost equation lies to the northeast.

A change in one of the input prices also has an impact on the isocost equation. Although it is true that a perfectly competitive firm has no control over input prices, these prices are likely to fluctuate since conditions in input markets can change. As an example, in the mid-1970s the world price of oil quadrupled over a very short period of time. This caused the price of energy, an input used to produce many goods and services, to rise dramatically relative to other input prices. A change in the price of one input relative to the price of another alters the slope of the isocost equation, since its slope is measured as the negative of the input price ratio, $-\overline{P}_{L,1}/\overline{P}_{K,1}$. Note that in addition to

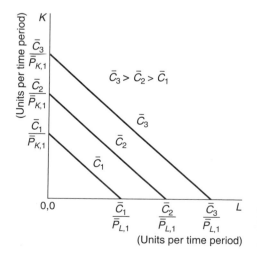

FIGURE 10.2 Isocost Mapping for Different Levels of Cost

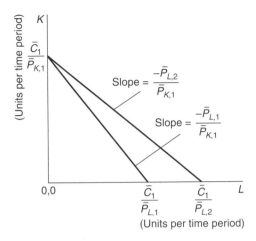

FIGURE 10.3 Effect of a Decrease in the Price of Labor on an Isocost Equation

the slope changing, one of the intercepts of the isocost equation is also affected. For example, if the price of labor decreases to $\overline{P}_{L,2}$, then the isocost line becomes flatter since the value of its slope, $-\overline{P}_{L,2}/\overline{P}_{K,1}$, has decreased, in absolute value terms. In addition, the value of the labor intercept increases to $\overline{C}_1/\overline{P}_{L,2}$, indicating that the firm can purchase more units of labor if it spends all of its budget on this input. The value of the capital intercept remains unaltered in this case, since neither the value of the firm's total expenditures on inputs, $\overline{C}_1$, nor the price of capital, $\overline{P}_{K,1}$, has changed. We have depicted this situation in Figure 10.3.

In the next section, we will bring together the notion of the isoquant, discussed in Section 9.3 of the previous chapter, with the isocost equation so as to determine the particular combination of capital and labor that minimizes a firm's expenditure, or cost, associated with producing a predetermined level of output.

10.3 CONSTRAINED COST MINIMIZATION

We typically assume that firms behave rationally to the extent that they make business decisions that optimize some predetermined objective, while at the same time taking into consideration any constraints they may face. Our focus in this chapter is on production in the long run, where it is logical for us to assume that in order for a firm to remain consistent with the broader goal of profit maximization, it will seek to produce its output by utilizing its inputs in their most efficient combinations. The most common method by which this goal can be achieved is known as constrained cost minimization.

Specifically, using this procedure, a rational firm seeks to employ a unique combination of capital and labor that is capable of producing a predetermined level of output, $\overline{Q}_1$, at the least possible cost. In this analysis we assume that the firm takes as given the prices of the two inputs it employs, $\overline{P}_{K,1}$ and $\overline{P}_{L,1}$, since these prices are determined in competitive input markets. Thus, the decision variables for the firm are the quantities of capital, K, and labor, L, that it purchases and uses in its production process.

The notions underlying the constrained cost minimization problem are depicted graphically in Figure 10.4, where we have plotted a single isoquant representing a predetermined level of output, $\overline{Q}_1$. In the constrained cost minimization problem, the isoquant acts as the constraint faced by the firm, since it represents the predetermined level of output the firm wants to produce. The objective function, which is to be minimized, is represented by an isocost equation. In Figure 10.4, we have plotted three different isocost equations, represented as C_1, C_2^*, and C_3, where $C_3 > C_2^* > C_1$. In addition, we have assumed that the firm has the ability to substitute labor for capital, or vice versa, in its production process, as we demonstrated in the discussion of negatively sloped isoquants in Section 9.5 of Chapter 9.

In general, any isocost equation that lies entirely below the isoquant constraint represents a level of cost that the firm cannot attain since the expenditures corresponding to any input combination lying on this isocost equation are not sufficient to purchase enough inputs to produce the predetermined level of output, $\overline{Q}_1$. We have depicted such a situation in Figure 10.4 with isocost equation C_1, where we can observe that this isocost equation and the isoquant constraint possess no common (L,K) combinations.

Referring once again to Figure 10.4, it is clear that the firm could produce $\overline{Q}_1$ using input combinations (L_1,K_1) or (L_2,K_2), since they both lie on the $\overline{Q}_1$ isoquant. However, each of these input combinations results in a level of cost, C_3, that is not the minimum level of cost the firm is capable of incurring when producing $\overline{Q}_1$. If we focus first on input combination (L_1,K_1), we can observe in Figure 10.4 that if the firm moves down the isoquant constraint by reducing its use of capital from K_1 to K^*, while simultaneously increasing its use of labor from L_1 to L^*, it can produce $\overline{Q}_1$ at the lower cost, C_2^*. Similarly, with respect to input combination (L_2,K_2), if the firm moves up its isoquant constraint by reducing its use of labor from L_2 to L^* units and

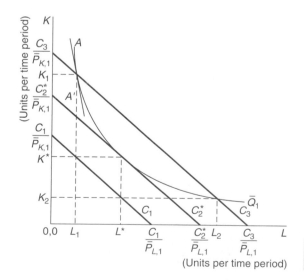

FIGURE 10.4 Constrained Cost Minimization Problem

increasing its use of capital from K_2 to K^* units, the firm can once again decrease its cost from C_3 to C_2^*.

The unique combination of capital and labor that minimizes the firm's cost subject to its predetermined level of output, $\overline{Q}_1$, is represented as (L^*,K^*) in Figure 10.4, and the corresponding minimum level of cost the firm incurs is C_2^*. Note that at this combination of labor and capital, known as the optimal combination, the isoquant $\overline{Q}_1$ is tangent to the isocost equation C_2^*. This tangency condition implies that the slope of the isoquant must be equal to the slope of the isocost equation, or

$$\overbrace{\text{slope of isoquant}} = \overbrace{\text{slope of isocost constraint}}$$

$$-MRTS = -\frac{MP_L}{MP_K} = \qquad -\frac{\overline{P}_{L,1}}{\overline{P}_{K,1}} \qquad\qquad \textbf{(10.3)}$$

or after multiplying all sides of equation (10.3) by -1

$$MRTS = \frac{MP_L}{MP_K} = \frac{\overline{P}_{L,1}}{\overline{P}_{K,1}}. \qquad\qquad \textbf{(10.4)}$$

Equation (10.4) is known as the necessary condition for a constrained cost minimum, and it must be satisfied for the firm to minimize its cost given some predetermined level of output.

From an economic perspective, this tangency condition embodies a wealth of information. Recall from Section 9.4 of Chapter 9 that the slope of the isoquant measures the rate at which the firm can substitute one input for the other while still producing the same level of output. Earlier in this chapter, we demonstrated that the slope of the isocost equation measures the rate in input markets at which purchases of capital and labor can be substituted for one another on the basis of their relative prices. Thus, in a general sense, the constrained cost minimization problem is solved by a firm adjusting its use of capital and labor to the point where the rate at which it can substitute one input for the other in its production process is just equal to the rate at which it can substitute one input for the other in its purchasing process.

Any input combination for which the necessary condition does not hold will not yield a constrained cost minimum solution. Recall that in Figure 10.4 the input combination (L_1,K_1) could be used to produce output level $\overline{Q}_1$. However, this input combination is not optimal because, by reducing K and increasing L, the firm can decrease its cost, ultimately to C_2^*. An alternative way for us to demonstrate that combination (L_1,K_1) is not optimal is by constructing a line, AA', drawn tangent to the isoquant at this input combination. Observe that this tangent to the isoquant has a considerably steeper slope than the isocost equation C_3. Since the slope of the isoquant is $-MRTS = -MP_L/MP_K$, and the slope of the isocost equation is $-P_L/P_K$, then at input combination (L_1,K_1)

$$-MRTS = -\frac{MP_L}{MP_K} < -\frac{P_L}{P_K},$$

or after multiplying by –1 to eliminate the minus signs

$$MRTS = \frac{MP_L}{MP_K} > \frac{P_L}{P_K}.$$

The necessary condition for an optimum does not hold true in this situation, and we can demonstrate that the firm can reduce its costs by adjusting its inputs while still producing Q_1. In Chapter 9 we demonstrated that, generally, if a firm decreases the amount of K and increases the amount of L it uses in its production process, MP_L declines and MP_K increases. In the above situation, the firm will engage in this substitution process because it results in successively lower costs for producing $\overline{Q}_1$ units of output, until eventually

$$MRTS = \frac{P_L}{P_K}.$$

This result occurs only at the optimal combination of inputs, (L^*, K^*), or the combination that produces the level of output, $\overline{Q}_1$, at the minimum cost, C_2^*. Using a similar analysis, you can verify that the necessary condition for an optimum does not hold at the input combination (L_2, K_2).

There is an alternative way for us to view this necessary condition that may be familiar from your principles of microeconomics course. By simultaneously dividing both sides of equation (10.4) by P_L and multiplying both sides by MP_K we can establish the relationship

$$\frac{MP_L}{\overline{P}_{L,1}} = \frac{MP_K}{\overline{P}_{K,1}}. \tag{10.5}$$

Equation (10.5) embodies the same essential information as equation (10.4); however, we can interpret it somewhat differently. Specifically, the equality $MP_L/P_L = MP_K/P_K$, indicates that the marginal product of labor per last dollar spent on labor is equal to the marginal product of capital per last dollar spent on capital. For example, if $MP_L/P_L = 5$ units of output for the last dollar spent on labor, while $MP_K/P_K = 2$ units of output for the last dollar spent on capital, then the firm can benefit by using more labor and less capital. By spending one dollar less on capital, the firm sacrifices 2 units of output. However, by transferring this dollar to expenditures on labor, it gains 5 additional units of output, thereby experiencing a net gain in its output of 3 units. Also, note that hiring more labor and less capital generally causes the marginal product of labor to decline and the marginal product of capital to rise. Thus, as this substitution takes place, an equality between MP_L/P_L and MP_K/P_K is ultimately achieved, after which there remains no incentive for any further adjustments.

10.3.1   Constrained Cost Minimization: Lagrangian Multiplier Method

We can now approach constrained cost minimization from a mathematical perspective. Specifically, we will apply the Lagrangian multiplier method, introduced in Chapter 2, to the constrained cost minimization problem for a firm. This mathematical procedure yields the optimal input combination, (L^*, K^*), the minimized value of total cost, C^*, and the optimal value of the Lagrangian multiplier, λ^*. We express the constrained cost minimization problem as

$$\text{Minimize} \quad C = \overline{P}_{K,1}K + \overline{P}_{L,1}L$$
$$\text{subject to} \quad \overline{Q}_1 = f(K,L)$$

where the isocost equation

$$C = \overline{P}_{K,1}K + \overline{P}_{L,1}L,$$

represents the objective function that is to be minimized and the production function

$$\overline{Q}_1 = f(K,L)$$

acts as the constraint. After we determine the solution values for labor and capital, respectively, L^* and K^*, we can compute the minimized value of C. The solution process is comprised of the following three steps:

Step 1   Set up the Lagrangian function.

$$\mathcal{L} = \mathcal{L}(K,L,\lambda) = C + \lambda[\overline{Q}_1 - f(K,L)]$$
$$\text{or, since } C = \overline{P}_{K,1}K + \overline{P}_{L,1}L$$
$$\mathcal{L} = \mathcal{L}(K,L,\lambda) = \overline{P}_{K,1}K + \overline{P}_{L,1}L + \lambda[\overline{Q}_1 - f(K,L)].$$

The Lagrangian function embodies the objective function, which in this case is the firm's isocost equation, the Lagrangian multiplier, λ, and the constraint, which in this problem consists of the predetermined level of output, $\overline{Q}_1$, minus the firm's production function. Note that we enter the constraint into the Lagrangian function so that it equals zero; therefore, its inclusion does not alter the value of the objective variable, C. Thus, minimizing $\mathcal{L}$ is equivalent to minimizing C, while still incorporating all of the information contained in the production constraint.

Step 2   Determine the first-order conditions by partially differentiating the Lagrangian function, $\mathcal{L}$, with respect to K, L, and λ, and setting the results equal to zero as

$$\frac{\partial \mathcal{L}}{\partial K} = \overline{P}_{K,1} - \lambda\frac{\partial f(K,L)}{\partial K} = 0 \tag{10.6}$$

$$\frac{\partial \mathcal{L}}{\partial L} = \overline{P}_{L,1} - \lambda\frac{\partial f(K,L)}{\partial L} = 0 \tag{10.7}$$

$$\frac{\partial \mathcal{L}}{\partial \lambda} = \overline{Q}_1 - f(K,L) = 0. \tag{10.8}$$

Step 3   Solve the first-order conditions simultaneously to determine the unique values of K, L, and λ that minimize the firm's expenditures on inputs while still attaining its predetermined level of output, $\overline{Q}_1$. There are several methods we can use to obtain these values. One of the simplest is for us to add the term $\lambda\,\partial f(K,L)/\partial K$ to both sides of equation (10.6) and the term $\lambda\,\partial f(K,L)/\partial L$ to both sides of equation (10.7), then divide the altered version of equation (10.7) by the altered version of equation (10.6) as

$$\frac{\overline{P}_{L,1}}{\overline{P}_{K,1}} = \frac{\lambda\dfrac{\partial f(K,L)}{\partial L}}{\lambda\dfrac{\partial f(K,L)}{\partial K}}. \tag{10.9}$$

Employing the reflexive property, as well as recognizing that $Q = f(K,L)$, we may restate equation (10.9) as

$$\frac{\dfrac{\partial Q}{\partial L}}{\dfrac{\partial Q}{\partial K}} = \frac{\lambda\overline{P}_{L,1}}{\lambda\overline{P}_{K,1}}. \tag{10.10}$$

After canceling the λ terms, and since $\partial Q/\partial L$ and $\partial Q/\partial K$ represent the marginal product of labor and the marginal product of capital, respectively, we can rewrite equation (10.10) as the familiar necessary condition for a constrained cost minimum, or

$$MRTS = \frac{MP_L}{MP_K} = \frac{\overline{P}_{L,1}}{\overline{P}_{K,1}}.$$

The following numerical example demonstrates the process by which we can apply the Lagrangian multiplier method to determine the optimal values of K, L, and λ associated with a constrained cost minimization problem.

Numerical Example: Constrained Cost Minimization Problem

$$\text{Minimize } C = \overline{P}_{K,1}K + \overline{P}_{L,1}L$$
$$\text{subject to } \overline{Q}_1 = 10K^{.5}L^{.5}$$

where the predetermined input prices are $\overline{P}_{K,1} = \$40$, $\overline{P}_{L,1} = \$10$, and the predetermined level of output, $\overline{Q}_1$, is 80 units.

Step 1   Set up the Lagrangian function.

$$\mathcal{L} = \mathcal{L}(K,L,\lambda) = \overline{P}_{K,1}K + \overline{P}_{L,1}L + \lambda(\overline{Q}_1 - 10K^{.5}L^{.5}).$$

Step 2   Determine the first-order conditions.

$$\frac{\partial \mathcal{L}}{\partial K} = \overline{P}_{K,1} - 5\lambda K^{-.5}L^{.5} = 0 \tag{10.11}$$

$$\frac{\partial \mathcal{L}}{\partial L} = \overline{P}_{L,1} - 5\lambda K^{.5}L^{-.5} = 0 \tag{10.12}$$

$$\frac{\partial \mathcal{L}}{\partial \lambda} = \overline{Q}_1 - 10K^{.5}L^{.5} = 0 \tag{10.13}$$

Step 3   Solve the first-order conditions simultaneously for the unique values of K, L, and λ that minimize the firm's total expenditures on inputs, C.

Thus, we rewrite equations (10.11) and (10.12), respectively, as

$$5\lambda K^{-.5}L^{.5} = \overline{P}_{K,1} \tag{10.11'}$$

and

$$5\lambda K^{.5}L^{-.5} = \overline{P}_{L,1}. \tag{10.12'}$$

We can divide equation (10.12′) by equation (10.11′) to determine the necessary condition for a constrained cost minimum as

$$\frac{5\lambda K^{.5}L^{-.5}}{5\lambda K^{-.5}L^{.5}} = \frac{\overline{P}_{L,1}}{\overline{P}_{K,1}},$$

or

$$\frac{K}{L} = \frac{\overline{P}_{L,1}}{\overline{P}_{K,1}}. \tag{10.14}$$

We can identify the term K/L as the *MRTS* since it represents MP_L/MP_K. After rearranging the terms of the necessary condition, we solve for K as

$$K = \frac{\overline{P}_{L,1}L}{\overline{P}_{K,1}}. \tag{10.15}$$

Substituting the expression for K from equation (10.15) into the constraint, represented by equation (10.13), and solving for L yields

$$\overline{Q}_1 - 10\left(\frac{\overline{P}_{L,1}}{\overline{P}_{K,1}}L\right)^{.5}L^{.5} = 0$$

$$\overline{Q}_1 - 10\frac{(\overline{P}_{L,1})^{.5}}{(\overline{P}_{K,1})^{.5}}L^{.5}L^{.5} = 0$$

$$\overline{Q}_1 - 10\frac{(\overline{P}_{L,1})^{.5}}{(\overline{P}_{K,1})^{.5}}L = 0$$

$$\overline{Q}_1 = 10\frac{(\overline{P}_{L,1})^{.5}L}{(\overline{P}_{K,1})^{.5}}$$

$$L^* = \frac{\overline{Q}_1(\overline{P}_{K,1})^{.5}}{10(\overline{P}_{L,1})^{.5}}. \tag{10.16}$$

By substituting the predetermined values $\overline{Q}_1 = 80$ units, $\overline{P}_{K,1} = \$40$, and $\overline{P}_{L,1} = \$10$ into equation (10.16), we determine the optimal value of L as

$$L^* = \frac{80(40)^{.5}}{10(10)^{.5}} = 16 \text{ units of labor.}$$

Substituting $L^* = 16$ along with the predetermined values of $\overline{P}_{L,1}$ and $\overline{P}_{K,1}$ into equation (10.15) yields the optimal value of K^* as

$$K^* = \frac{10(16)}{40} = 4 \text{ units of capital.}$$

We compute the minimum total cost incurred by the firm by substituting the optimal values of $L^* = 16$ units of labor and $K^* = 8$ units of capital, along with the predetermined values of the input prices into the objective function, yielding,

$$C^* = (\$40)(4) + (\$10)(16) = \$320.$$

Finally, using equation (10.11), we determine the value of λ^* as

$$(40) - 5\lambda(4)^{-.5}(16)^{.5} = 0$$
$$(40) - 5\lambda(.5)(4) = 0$$
$$40 = 10\lambda$$
$$\lambda^* = 4.$$

Recall from Chapter 2 that, in general, we can interpret the value of λ^* as the effect on the value of the objective function as the constraint changes by one unit. In this constrained cost minimization problem, the value of λ^* represents the dollar amount by which a firm's cost of production, C, changes if the predetermined level of production, $\overline{Q}_1$, changes by one unit. Recall from your principles of microeconomics course that marginal cost represents the change in a firm's total cost of production due to a one-unit change in its level of output. Therefore, in this problem we may also interpret λ^* as measuring the firm's long-run marginal cost, a topic that we will discuss in detail in Chapter 11. In this numerical example $\lambda^* = 4$, indicating that if the predetermined level of output decreases by one unit, from 80 to 79 units, the firm's minimum total expenditure on capital and labor decreases by \$4 from \$320 to \$316. Alternatively, if the predetermined level of output increases by one unit, from 80 to 81 units, the firm's minimum total expenditure increases by \$4 from \$320 to \$324.

10.4   EXPANSION PATHS

We have shown an optimal input combination to be one that is used to produce some predetermined level of output, $\overline{Q}_1$, at the least cost, C. In the previous section, only one solution of such input combinations was determined since we specified Q at a unique value. However, it is possible to repeat the firm's constrained cost minimization process numerous times for different values of the specified variable, Q. Note that we are holding input prices constant throughout the analysis at some specified values such as $\overline{P}_{K,1}$ and $\overline{P}_{L,1}$. By solving the optimization problem many times, we can generate an entire set of input combinations, $(L_1, K_1), (L_2, K_2), (L_3, K_3), \ldots$, that enable the firm to produce the predetermined levels of output, $\overline{Q}_1, \overline{Q}_2, \overline{Q}_3, \ldots$, at the least levels of cost, or expenditures, $C_1, C_2, C_3, \ldots$, respectively. These input combinations are shown in Figure 10.5.

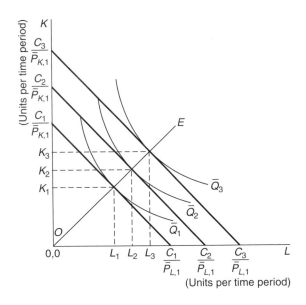

FIGURE 10.5 Expansion Path

Examining the graph in this figure, we can construct a ray, OE, starting at the origin, that passes through each of these optimal input combinations. Thus, the ray OE contains only points for which the necessary condition for a constrained cost minimum is satisfied. Since this necessary condition is

$$MRTS = \frac{P_L}{P_K},$$

and the input prices, P_L and P_K, are held constant, the $MRTS$ must be the same for every input combination on the ray OE. In a general sense, this ray consists of a set of optimal input combinations that a firm uses as it expands its output. As a result, we refer to a curve such as OE as an **expansion path**, or *a set of input combinations corresponding to constrained cost minimization solutions for different predetermined levels of output, while holding input prices constant.* We can also interpret this curve as representing a set of optimal input combinations for which the $MRTS$ remains constant.

The variables in the equation for an expansion path, such as the one represented in Figure 10.5 by the ray OE, are the inputs K and L. Therefore, it can be represented as either

$$K = K(L)$$

or

$$L = L(K),$$

since we can solve the expansion path equation for either input. Using the form

$$K = K(L),$$

this expansion path simply indicates that for any value of labor, L, we can determine the amount of capital, K, that must be combined with that value of labor to make the

Evidence of Increasing Substitution of Capital for Labor by U.S. Firms

Increasingly, American producers are pursuing productivity gains by investing more heavily in their operations. This investment has largely been in capital related to information technology, including computer hardware and software, as well as new plant and other types of equipment, such as robotics. Between 1992 and 1995, investment by businesses in computer technology rose an astounding 184.5% in constant dollars, while real spending on capital investments of all other types increased by 43.8% over the same time period.[1] Part of this expansion in capital investment can be explained by the fact that the associated cost has continued to fall due to innovations and productivity gains in the computer industry, while the relative cost of labor has risen.

These vast increases in capital investment have not been concentrated in just a few industries but have been widespread, thereby creating even more broadly encompassing productivity increases throughout the economy. For example, in 1995 Corning increased its capital investment in its fiber optics division by 30% to more than $500 million. First National Bank of Chicago invested $200 million per year in the mid-1990s on computer software and hardware. U.S. telecommunications provider MCI increased its capital spending in 1994 by approximately 70% to $2.9 billion on new transmission technology and increases in its routing system.

Evidence is also available that the vast increases in capital spending have led to decreases in the number of laborers firms need to employ. Such substitution of capital for labor is reported for Fannie Mae, a U.S. company that buys mortgages from lenders and then packages them into securities for commercial investors. In the first half of the 1990s, Fannie Mae more than doubled its investment in information technology. By utilizing scanners to image loan documents, thus enabling clerks to quickly verify data online, Fannie Mae was able to reduce the number of paper handlers by 67%, from 90 to 30. Furthermore, after installing optical character recognition equipment, Fannie Mae automated many of its document verification tasks. Similarly, steelmakers have also invested heavily in their operations. Over the past two decades, $50 billion have been spent on new plant and equipment in the U.S. steel industry. During the same period over 300,000 workers, or nearly three-quarters of its labor force, have been laid off permanently.[2] Such adjustments in input usage are consistent with the concept of moving up to the left along an isoquant, as the firm uses a more capital-intensive input combination to generate the same level of output. As these firms expand their production of output, they do so following a new expansion path that reflects the more intensive use of capital as opposed to labor.

---

[1] Joseph Spiers, "The Most Important Economic Event of the Decade," *Fortune*, April 3, 1995, pp. 33–40.

[2] "In America's Fiery Furnace," *The Economist*, September 19, 1998, pp. 73–75.

input combination optimal. As an example, recall the necessary condition for a constrained cost minimum that we generated by solving the numerical example in Section 10.3.1 as

$$\frac{K}{L} = \frac{\overline{P}_{L,1}}{\overline{P}_{K,1}} = \frac{10}{40} = \frac{1}{4}.$$

We can demonstrate the expansion path by merely rearranging this necessary condition as either

$$K = \frac{1}{4}L$$

or

$$L = 4K.$$

Examining the version

$$K = \frac{1}{4}L,$$

observe that for any value of L, we can solve for the value of K that makes the combination of inputs optimal. For example, we demonstrated earlier that if Q is specified as 80 units, the solution value for L is 16 units of labor. Thus, the corresponding optimal value of K is

$$K = \frac{1}{4}(16) = 4 \text{ units.}$$

More broadly, if we do not specify a value for Q, then an entire set of optimal (L,K) combinations are represented by this equation.[3] A major application of the expansion path will be evident in the next chapter where we will develop long-run cost functions. However, before making the transition from production theory to cost theory, we need to examine an additional concept related to production functions and expansion paths.

10.5 DEGREES OF HOMOGENEITY AND RETURNS TO SCALE

An expansion path is the path along which a firm, in the long run, optimally combines its inputs to expand its output. An interesting question arises at this point. As a firm moves up its expansion path, thus increasing its use of inputs, by what factor does its production of output expand? For example, if a firm chooses to double its inputs, K and L, along an expansion path, will output precisely double, or will it increase by some other factor? A comparison of two alternative situations should provide us with some insight into answering this question.

[3]Note that not all expansion paths are linear, such as that illustrated in the above example. However, this characteristic is common to those production functions described as being homogeneous, a topic we will discuss in Section 10.5.

Assume a firm has the production function

$$Q = K^{1/2}L^{1/2},$$

where it pays input prices of $\overline{P}_{K,1} = \$1$ and $\overline{P}_{L,1} = \$1$. Now, also assume that the firm predetermines its level of output as $\overline{Q}_1 = 1$ unit. We can solve this problem using the constrained cost minimization process, where you can verify that the optimal values for the inputs are $K_1 = 1$ unit and $L_1 = 1$ unit, and that the minimum level of cost incurred using this input combination is

$$C_1 = (\$1)(1) + (\$1)(1) = \$2.$$

Finally, you can also verify that the associated expansion path in this case is

$$K = L.$$

Now, suppose the firm decides to increase its predetermined level of output to 2 units. We can solve this problem again using this new set of circumstances to generate an optimal input combination of $K_2 = 2$ units and $L_2 = 2$ units, where the new minimum level of cost incurred is

$$C_2 = (\$1)(2) + (\$1)(2) = \$4.$$

This example clearly demonstrates that by doubling its input use, the firm exactly doubles its production of output. We have illustrated these results in Figure 10.6, where the ray OR represents the firm's expansion path.

More generally, observe that an equivalent change in the firm's inputs generates a proportional change in its output. Note that this result also holds true for a decrease in output. If the firm initially uses $K = 2$ units of capital and $L = 2$ units of labor to produce 2 units of output, and it reduces its inputs by one-half to $K = 1$ unit and $L = 1$ unit, then output falls by a factor of one-half, to $Q = 1$ unit. The economic implication

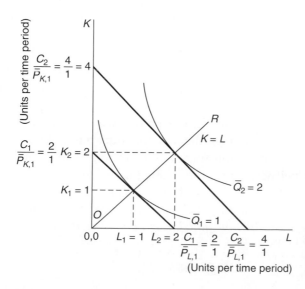

FIGURE 10.6 Isoquants, Isocosts, and Expansion Path for Constant Returns to Scale

of these results is that, as the firm either expands or reduces its production of output, it experiences neither an increase nor a decrease, respectively, in its production efficiency. This result simply indicates that there are no advantages or disadvantages associated with a firm becoming larger or smaller.

Does this result hold true universally? The answer to this question is no, and we can demonstrate this conclusion by analyzing a different underlying production function. Assume a firm has the production function

$$Q = K^{3/4}L^{3/4},$$

and pays the same input prices as in the previous example, $\overline{P}_{K,1} = \$1$ and $\overline{P}_{L,1} = \$1$. Once again, assume the firm sets its predetermined level of output at 1 unit. You can use the constrained cost minimization process to verify that the optimal values for the inputs are $K_1 = 1$ unit and $L_1 = 1$ unit. The minimum cost incurred by using this input combination is

$$C_1 = (\$1)(1) + (\$1)(1) = \$2,$$

and the expansion path is

$$K = L.$$

We have selected this problem to generate a set of initial results that are identical to those in the previous example. Now suppose the firm increases its predetermined level of output to 2.82 units. By solving the optimization problem once more, we generate a new optimal input combination of $K_2 = 2$ units and $L_2 = 2$ units. The new minimum level of cost incurred is

$$C_2 = (\$1)(2) + (\$1)(2) = \$4.$$

In this case a firm, by doubling its inputs, more than doubles its output, specifically increasing its output by a factor of 2.82. More generally stated, by increasing both of its inputs equivalently, the firm increases its output by a disproportionately greater amount. We have illustrated this result in Figure 10.7, where the expansion path is represented by the ray OS. The economic implication of this result is that the firm experiences an increase in production efficiency as it expands its output. Conversely, it will experience a decrease in production efficiency should it reduce its output.

The different results we have obtained from the two examples presented in this section follow from the different production functions underlying each analysis. Thus, we can categorize production functions according to their implications regarding production efficiency, where these categories reflect a concept known as the **degree of homogeneity** pertaining to these functions. This degree of homogeneity indicates the extent to which output changes subsequent to a change in a firm's input use. Specifically, *a production function is defined as homogeneous to the degree n if*

$$\delta^n Q = f(\delta K, \delta L),$$

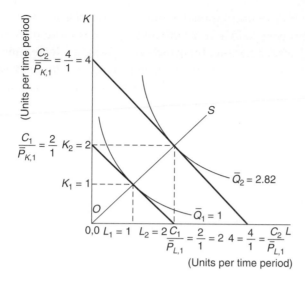

FIGURE 10.7 Isoquants, Isocosts, and Expansion Path for Increasing Returns to Scale

where the Greek letter delta, δ, represents some constant scaling factor. In the following discussion we will arbitrarily set the scaling factor, δ, at the value 2, and thus we can represent the above expression as

$$2^n Q = f(2K, 2L).$$

There are three categories regarding the degree of homogeneity, or the value of n. The first category pertains to $n = 1$ and therefore, in this case

$$2^1 Q = 2Q = f(2K, 2L).$$

We define this type of production function as homogeneous to the first degree, or linearly homogeneous. These functions indicate that if a firm simultaneously changes all of its inputs by some factor, δ, then its output is altered by the same factor, δ. Thus, if $\delta = 2$, doubling a firm's inputs results in doubling the firm's output. Production functions that are homogeneous to the first degree exhibit **constant returns to scale**, indicating that *a firm neither gains nor loses production efficiency as it proportionally expands or reduces its inputs, and thus its output proportionately increases or decreases, respectively.* Our earlier example relating to the production function

$$Q = K^{1/2} L^{1/2}$$

falls into this category.

The second category of degrees of homogeneity is for those production functions for which $n > 1$. For example, suppose $n = 2$, indicating that the production function is homogeneous to the second degree, then

$$\delta^n Q = \delta^2 Q = f(\delta K, \delta L),$$

or when $\delta = 2$

$$2^2 Q = 4Q = f(2K, 2L).$$

In such a situation, doubling a firm's inputs increases its output by a factor of 4. More generally, any equivalent change in a firm's inputs results in a more than proportional change in its output. These situations for which $n > 1$ exhibit **increasing returns to scale**, indicating that *a firm experiences increases in production efficiency as it proportionally increases its inputs and hence, it more than proportionally increases its output.* Conversely, in this case the firm experiences a decrease in production efficiency if it reduces its production of output by proportionately reducing its use of inputs. Our example, described earlier in this section, using the production function

$$Q = K^{3/4}L^{3/4},$$

falls into this category.

The third category relating to degrees of homogeneity is for those production functions for which $n < 1$, such as $n = 1/2$. Thus

$$\delta^n Q = \delta^{1/2}Q = f(\delta K, \delta L),$$

or when $\delta = 2$,

$$2^{1/2}Q = 1.41Q = f(2K, 2L).$$

In this scenario, doubling a firm's inputs increases its output by a factor of $2^{1/2} = 1.41$. More generally, any equivalent change in a firm's inputs results in a less than proportional change in the firm's output. These situations for which $n < 1$ exhibit **decreasing returns to scale** and indicate that *a firm experiences decreases in its production efficiency as it expands its output.*

We can easily compute the degree of homogeneity for any specific homogeneous production function. Referring back to the production function

$$Q = K^{1/2}L^{1/2},$$
$$\delta^n Q = (\delta K)^{1/2}(\delta L)^{1/2} = \delta^{1/2}K^{1/2}\delta^{1/2}L^{1/2},$$

or since $Q = K^{1/2}L^{1/2}$

$$\delta^n Q = \delta^1 K^{1/2}L^{1/2} = \delta^1 Q.$$

Thus, for this production function $n = 1$, and therefore it exhibits constant returns to scale. This characteristic holds true for any equivalent change in a firm's inputs, but it is more relevant when a firm is using its inputs optimally. In our earlier example related to this production function, we computed the optimal input combination as $K_1 = 1$ unit and $L_1 = 1$ unit when the predetermined level of output, Q, was 1 unit. When we doubled Q to 2 units, the optimal input combination also doubled to $K_2 = 2$ units and $L_2 = 2$ units. Now, we can obtain this same result by applying the degree of homogeneity associated with the production function. Since $n = 1$ in this case, changing the inputs by a factor of $\delta = 2$ also changes the production of output by a factor of 2 from some initial level, Q_1, to an altered level, Q_2, or

$$Q_2 = 2^1 Q_1 = 2(1) = 2 \text{ units.}$$

In the second example we discussed earlier, the production function was

$$Q = K^{3/4}L^{3/4}.$$

Therefore

$$\delta^n Q = (\delta K)^{3/4}(\delta L)^{3/4} = \delta^{3/4}K^{3/4}\delta^{3/4}L^{3/4},$$

or

$$\delta^n Q = \delta^{3/2}K^{3/4}L^{3/4} = \delta^{3/2}Q.$$

In this case, $n = 3/2 = 1.5$ and the production function exhibits increasing returns to scale. Thus, if both inputs are increased by a factor of $\delta = 2$, then output increases by a factor of

$$2^{3/2} = 2.82.$$

As a result

$$Q_2 = 2.82Q_1 = 2.82(1) = 2.82 \text{ units,}$$

the same result we generated earlier.

The concepts of constant, increasing, and decreasing returns to scale are somewhat difficult to grasp if you do not possess an engineering background. However, there is one basic example with which you should be familiar. Assume a firm is in the business of delivering oil to its customers by use of a pipeline. The area where the oil flows through the pipe is represented by the formula for the area of a circle. Thus

$$A = \pi r^2,$$

REAL-WORLD APPLICATION 10.2

Economies of Scale and Product Pricing

Recently, a major manufacturer of contact lens drops was placed under scrutiny for its pricing practice.[4] Bausch & Lomb was asked to justify the pricing of its eye drops that cost more than 24 times that of its own saline solution, despite the fact that the two products "share the same chemical formulation" and are thus virtually identical. In 1995 a 12-ounce bottle of Bausch & Lomb's Sensitive Eyes Saline Solution cost $2.79 or $0.23 per ounce, while a 1-ounce bottle of its Sensitive Eye Drops cost $5.65. Bausch & Lomb justified the higher price of its eye drops due to higher production costs involved in filling the much smaller bottles required by the U.S. Food and Drug Administration for all eye drops sold in the United States. Although there may likely be several reasons for this price differential, this explanation is, at least in part, consistent with the theory we presented earlier regarding scale economies. Recall, that an increase in the size of a cylindrical receptacle, such as a vat, or in this case a bottle, causes its holding capacity to expand fourfold. As a result, the per ounce packaging cost for 12-ounce bottles of saline solution is much less than that for 1-ounce bottles of eye drops. Thus, when using the smaller bottles, Bausch & Lomb is unable to capture the scale economies it enjoys with its saline solution when producing eye drops and chooses to pass these higher costs on to its consumers.

[4]Mark Maremont, "Eyeway Robbery: Contact Lens Wearers Pay Through the Nose for Drops," *Business Week*, February 27, 1995, p. 48.

where A is the area of the flow of output, π is the familiar constant equal to approximately 3.14, and r represents the radius of the pipe. In a sense, this is a simplified version of a production function where the radius represents a single input used in the production process. The degree of homogeneity is therefore

$$\delta^n A = \pi(\delta r)^2 = \pi \delta^2 r^2,$$

or

$$\delta^n A = \delta^2 \pi r^2 = \delta^2 A.$$

Thus, $n = 2$, and the production function exhibits increasing returns to scale. If the firm doubles its input, which in this case is the radius of the pipe, r, then its output, A, increases by a factor of 2^2 or 4. The point of this example is that the increase in production efficiency is mathematically intrinsic to the underlying production process. In the next two chapters, we will apply these concepts associated with production theory to analyze a firm's costs of production in both the long and short run.

10.6 SUMMARY

In this chapter, we developed and discussed a rational firm's long-run production decisions. Specifically, we showed how a profit-maximizing firm makes its production decisions by applying constrained optimization techniques. In addition, we discussed the concepts of returns to scale and a firm's expansion path. The key topics covered in this chapter are as follows.

- An isocost equation represents a set of input combinations that a firm is able to purchase for a given level of expenditures and a given set of input prices.
- The slope of an isocost equation measures the negative of the ratio of the price of a unit of labor to the price of a unit of capital. We interpret this slope as the rate at which a firm is able to substitute one input for the other in its purchasing process.
- We can solve a firm's constrained cost minimization problem by using the Lagrangian multiplier method to determine the levels of inputs that minimize its expenditures, or cost, subject to attaining a predetermined level of output.
- The necessary condition for a constrained cost minimum is that, at the optimal input combination, the marginal rate of technical substitution must be equal to the ratio of the input prices.
- An expansion path is a set of optimal input combinations that pertain to constrained cost minimization solutions for different levels of output.
- Production functions that are homogeneous to a degree greater than one, equal to one, or less than one, exhibit increasing, constant, or decreasing returns to scale, respectively.

KEY TERMS

- constant returns to scale, page 255
- decreasing returns to scale, page 256
- degree of homogeneity, page 254
- expansion path, page 250
- increasing returns to scale, page 256
- isocost equation, page 239

EXERCISES

10.1 State the necessary condition for a firm's constrained cost minimum and provide a verbal explanation for both sides of this equation. Illustrate this necessary condition graphically.

10.2 Assume the price of labor is $5.00 per hour while the price of capital is $25.00 per hour. Write the isocost equation when a firm's total expenditures on capital and labor are $2500.00. Determine the slope and intercepts of this isocost equation. Plot this isocost equation in input space.

10.3 Using the same input prices given in Exercise 10.2, now assume the firm's expenditures on inputs are $5000. Once again, determine the slope and intercept values for the associated isocost equation. Compare these values to those you computed in Exercise 10.2. Also plot the two isocost equations together in the same graph.

10.4 Primo Fungi, a mushroom firm, desires to produce 125 crates of Portobello mushrooms in the least costly manner. The firm's production function is

$$Q = K^2 + L^2,$$

where Q is the firm's level of output, K represents the amount of the capital input, and L is the amount of the labor input. The firm pays input prices of $4 and $2 per unit for its capital and labor, respectively.

  a. Determine the optimal combination of capital and labor that Primo Fungi should employ.

  b. What is the associated minimum cost incurred by the firm?

  c. How much additional cost will the firm incur if it increases its level of output to 126 crates?

10.5 A microbrewer desires to produce 120 cases of beer while incurring the least possible cost. The microbrewer's production function is

$$Q = 8K^{.5}L^{.5},$$

and it must pay input prices of $3 and $27 per unit, for labor and capital, respectively.

  a. What is the optimal combination of capital and labor the microbrewer should employ?

  b. Determine the minimum cost incurred by the microbrewer in producing 120 cases of beer.

10.6 Using the information in Exercise 10.5, derive the equation for the micro-brewer's expansion path. If the microbrewer uses 36 units of labor, how much capital must he also use in order to make the input combination optimal?

10.7 Assume a firm's production function is

$$Q = K^2 + KL + L^2,$$

where Q is the firm's level of output, and K and L represent the capital and labor inputs, respectively. Determine the degree of homogeneity associated with this production function. What type of returns to scale are exhibited in this case?

10.8 Assume a firm's production function is

$$Q = 4K^{1/4}L^{3/4}.$$

Suppose this firm is the subject of an antitrust suit, where the Justice Department is seeking to break it into several smaller firms. The firm counters by claiming that such an action would sacrifice efficiency. More specifically, it claims that it must be large to be efficient. Based on this production function, is this claim justified?

CHAPTER 11

Costs of Production in the Long Run

11.1 INTRODUCTION

Provided a firm must pay for the inputs it employs, it will incur costs associated with producing its output. In Chapter 10 we developed the concept of an isocost equation that expresses a firm's costs in terms of the amounts of inputs it employs, where we used this equation extensively in the analysis of production theory. Rather than expressing a firm's production costs in terms of the amounts of inputs it employs, economists often find it useful to define these costs in terms of the level of output the firm produces. We define such a relationship as a cost function, and our rationale for expressing a firm's costs in this manner stems from the way in which we usually define its profit function. A firm's profit, as we have noted, is the difference between its revenue and production costs, where revenue is the value of the output it sells. As a result, it is convenient to express a firm's costs as a function of output as well because, by doing so, we can express a firm's profit in terms of just one decision variable.

The basis for cost theory lies in the production theory we developed in the previous three chapters. Furthermore, just as we analyzed a firm's production process for both short- and long-run time periods, we can analyze the associated cost functions in the same manner. In this chapter, our focus is on a firm's production costs in the long run, where we will first conduct a transition from production theory to cost theory. The remainder of this chapter will be devoted to expressing a firm's long-run costs in various forms. Specifically, we will derive average and marginal cost functions, from long-run total cost functions, and provide a discussion of their various characteristics and interrelationships.

11.2 DEFINITIONS OF COST FUNCTIONS

In general, we can express a firm's production costs in terms of different types of economic variables, where the variables chosen as determinants of cost depend on how we focus our analysis. As we demonstrated in Chapter 10, for a specified set of input prices, a firm's costs can be expressed in terms of the amounts of the inputs, usually capital and labor, that it uses in its production process. We define this relationship as an isocost equation. It represents an integral component of the firm's constrained optimization process, which in turn is consistent with its broader goal of profit maximization. Specifically, if we treat the level of output produced as predetermined at some level, then the isocost equation represents the objective function to be minimized.

Thus, by applying a constrained cost minimization procedure, we can determine the optimal levels of the inputs, capital and labor, corresponding to a constrained cost minimum for a firm. These results pertain to the long run, a time period during which all of a firm's inputs are treated as variable. In the next chapter, we will demonstrate how to determine a firm's costs in the short run, a time period during which at least one of the firm's inputs remains fixed at some level. In the short run, a firm still seeks to produce output in the least costly manner in order to be consistent with its goal of profit maximization. However, isn't it logical to expect that the solution values for inputs and costs in the short run will typically be different from those we obtain in the long run, due to imposing the additional constraining factor of a fixed input?

Rather than defining a firm's costs in terms of the inputs it employs in its production process, we can derive a function that expresses its costs in terms of its production of output. This relationship, known as a **cost function**, *expresses a firm's costs in terms of the output it produces, ceteris paribus.* In terms of general notation, we express a cost function as

$$C = C(Q),$$

where C denotes a firm's cost, in dollars, and Q represents the units of output produced by the firm. Of course, there are other determinants of a firm's cost, in addition to the level of output it produces, such as the input prices it must pay and the state of technology affecting its production process. However, at the present time we will hold these factors constant and for the sake of clarity will not explicitly include them in the cost function above.

Before developing cost functions, it is necessary for us to distinguish two basic types of cost. First, **fixed cost** is *a firm's cost associated with the fixed input(s) it uses in its production process.* This type of cost is only applicable to the short run during which some inputs are treated as fixed. Since fixed inputs, by definition, cannot be altered as the level of output is changed, a firm's fixed cost clearly does not vary with its production of output.

The other type of cost is **variable cost**, or *a firm's cost associated with the variable input(s) it uses in its production process.* In the long run, we treat all inputs as variable, and as a result, all long-run costs are variable. By contrast, in the short run some inputs are treated as variable while others remain fixed, and thus short-run total costs represent the summation of fixed and variable costs.

11.2.1 Explicit and Implicit Costs

Before we develop various long-run cost functions in detail, it is in our interest to discuss the concept of a firm's costs from a more philosophical perspective. Specifically, within the context of economic analysis, the general concept of cost includes two distinct components: explicit cost and implicit cost. The term **explicit cost** represents *that component of a firm's cost associated with the nonowner-supplied inputs used in its production process*, while **implicit cost** is *that component of a firm's cost associated with those inputs supplied by the owners to their firm.* We measure implicit cost in terms of what the owner-supplied inputs could earn if employed in their next best alternative. Therefore, this type of cost is also known as the owners' opportunity cost.

Our rationale for including this implicit, or opportunity, cost as part of a firm's overall cost is related to the way economists define a firm's profit. Profit is the difference between the value of a firm's sales, or revenue, and its cost, where the economic definition of cost represents the summation of a firm's explicit and implicit costs. This definition of profit represents a concept known as economic profit, which we can contrast with that of accounting profit. You may recall from your principles of microeconomics course that accountants define profit as a firm's revenue less its explicit cost. As a result, we can interpret economic profit as equal to accounting profit less implicit cost.

The reason underlying these different definitions of profit stems from the different motives associated with the two professions. Generally, accountants tend to be concerned with measuring a firm's actual earnings and reporting these results to investors and tax authorities. Economists, on the other hand, are ultimately more concerned with the allocation of resources to and from various industries. More specifically, an economy that is allocatively efficient is one in which resources flow to their most highly valued uses, and the signal that motivates this flow of resources is economic profit. The reason for this interpretation is that, since economic profit is the difference between a firm's revenue and both its explicit and implicit costs, this definition of profit represents a gain or loss to the owners, compared to what they could earn elsewhere.

For example, if a firm's economic profit is positive, it represents a return above and beyond what its owners could earn if they used their same resources in the next best alternative. In this situation, the owners are motivated to remain in their current activity. In fact, if resources are free to flow to where they are most highly valued, we will expect that other firms will enter this market in the long run and engage in the same activity. Conversely, if a firm's economic profit is negative, then the owners of the firm are motivated to engage in some other activity since they could earn more by producing something else. We should emphasize that even if the accounting profit for a firm is positive, the owners still have an incentive to engage in some other type of economic activity, if they are earning negative economic profit. Finally, if a firm's economic profit is zero, there exists no incentive for the owners to abandon their current activity, nor is there any incentive for other producers to enter this market. In this case, the owners of the firm are earning the same amount they could earn if they engaged in their next best alternative.

We can illustrate these abstract concepts of economic cost and profit with a simple example. Suppose an economics professor, currently earning $50,000 per year, decides to leave the education profession and start up his own business—a restaurant. Thus, resources, specifically labor in this case, flow out of one industry, education, and into another, food service. Assume that after one year, this individual earns a revenue of $100,000 from operating the restaurant, while incurring $60,000 of explicit costs associated with purchasing supplies, hiring laborers, and renting the building and equipment necessary to conduct the business. In this case, the accounting profit equals the

$100,000 in revenue less the $60,000 explicit cost, or $40,000. However, to compute the economic profit, we must subtract the implicit cost, or the $50,000 the individual could have earned in the education profession, from the $40,000 accounting profit. Thus, the economic profit in this example is $40,000 – $50,000 = –$10,000, representing a loss to the individual. The significance of this result is that this negative economic profit, or loss, provides a motive for the individual to exit the restaurant business and return to the education profession. More generally, economic losses create an incentive for resources to flow out of one industry and into another. Note that we are ignoring noneconomic motives such as, in this example, the individual's desire to escape from committees or administrators, or simply the desire to possess his own business. However, it should be evident that economic profit plays an extremely important role regarding the efficient allocation of resources across industries in an economy. In order to analyze this role of economic profit effectively, we must compute it in a manner that takes into account both explicit and implicit costs.

11.3 LONG-RUN TOTAL COST

Since a firm is able to vary all of its inputs in the long run, it will rationally employ only optimal combinations of inputs when producing output during such a time period. Specifically, recall from Chapter 10 that optimal combinations of inputs are those corresponding to constrained cost minimization solutions. Thus, as a firm alters its level of output in the long run, it will adjust all of its inputs in order to remain consistent with this process of constrained cost minimization. This process is reflected by a firm's expansion path, or the set of input combinations pertaining to constrained cost minimization solutions for different levels of output. As a firm adjusts its inputs, moving along its expansion path, these constrained minimum levels of cost vary. Although we can express these minimum costs in terms of the optimal levels of inputs used in the production process, it is often more useful to express these costs in terms of the level of output produced. We described this relationship in Section 11.2 as representing a cost function. Specifically, a **long-run total cost function**, or curve, designated *LRTC*, is a function that expresses a firm's *minimum costs as a function of the level of output it produces, while holding input prices constant at some specified levels*. Notationally, we can express this function as

$$LRTC = C(Q),$$

where *LRTC* represents a firm's long-run total cost in dollars and Q denotes the firm's production of output in units. Note that the prices of the inputs employed to produce Q, as well as other underlying determinants of cost, are implicitly held constant.

We will first develop the long-run total cost function graphically, using the expansion path derived in Chapter 10 and illustrated once more in Figure 11.1. Earlier, we derived the isoquants representing the output levels Q_0, Q_1, and Q_2, from the production function containing two inputs

$$Q = f(K,L),$$

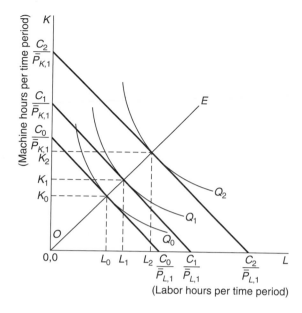

FIGURE 11.1 Derivation of Expansion Path

where we have treated both inputs, capital, K, and labor, L, as variable. The isocost equations illustrated in this figure pertain to three levels of total cost, C_0, C_1, C_2, where $C_2 > C_1 > C_0$. These levels of cost are expressed in the numerators of the K- and L-intercepts of the three isocost equations. The fixed input prices of capital and labor, denoted $\overline{P}_{K,1}$ and $\overline{P}_{L,1}$, respectively, are represented as the denominators of the K- and L-intercepts respectively. Finally the ray, OE, represents the firm's expansion path containing the set of (L,K) combinations, such as (L_0, K_0), (L_1, K_1), and, (L_2, K_2), corresponding to constrained cost minimization solutions. We can observe this result by the fact that this ray passes through the points of tangency between the isoquants and the isocost equations. Thus, it contains (L,K) combinations for which the marginal rate of technical substitution is equal to the ratio of the unit price of labor to the unit price of capital, or

$$MRTS = \frac{P_L}{P_K}.$$

Essentially, all of the information we need to derive a *LRTC* curve is contained in this figure. The cost values, C_0, C_1, and C_2, indicated in Figure 11.1 represent the minimum costs associated with producing the respective output levels Q_0, Q_1, and Q_2, since they pertain to the constrained cost minimization solutions for which the inputs, K and L, are used at their optimal levels. As a result, these cost values, C_0, C_1, and C_2, represent long-run total cost values designated, $LRTC_0$, $LRTC_1$, and $LRTC_2$, respectively. In Figure 11.2 we have plotted these *LRTC* values, along with their corresponding output levels Q_0, Q_1, and Q_2, on the vertical and horizontal axes, respectively. The resulting curve is the firm's long-run total cost function. We have assumed the particular cubic

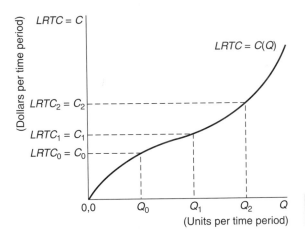

FIGURE 11.2 Long-Run Total Cost Function

shape of the curve shown in this figure for expository purposes because it demonstrates some frequently encountered economic characteristics. Specifically, this $LRTC$ curve indicates that as output increases from 0 to Q_1 units, the corresponding costs increase from 0 to C_1, but at a decreasing rate. This means that as Q increases, C increases, but by successively smaller increments. However, as output increases beyond Q_1, the level of output corresponding to the inflection point on the $LRTC$ curve, observe that costs increase at an increasing rate.

We will discuss the economic implications associated with the cubic shape of this $LRTC$ curve in subsequent sections of this chapter. However, at this point, it is important that we note several other characteristics associated not only with this particular $LRTC$ curve, but with all long-run total cost curves as well. First, the levels of a firm's long-run total cost always vary directly with output. In order to expand output, a firm must employ more units of its inputs, K and L, and with the input prices held constant, the associated cost of doing so must rise. Second, $LRTC$ curves always begin at the origin, indicating that if a firm produces zero output, its long-run total cost is equal to zero. This result reflects the fact that a firm possesses no fixed inputs, and hence no fixed costs, in the long run. At the origin, the firm is not employing any inputs since it is producing no output. Thus, at this point the firm is not only shut down but also has completely exited the market. Finally, we should reemphasize that every cost value, C, for the $LRTC$ curve represents the minimum cost at which any corresponding output level can be produced, barring changes in some underlying factors, such as a reduction in input prices, or an improvement in the state of technology.

We can also derive the $LRTC$ curve mathematically. This process, though rather laborious, is not difficult because it is just an extension of the constrained optimization problem we demonstrated in Chapter 10. The key components necessary for deriving the $LRTC$ curve are the production function

$$Q = f(K, L),$$

the isocost equation

$$C = \overline{P}_{K,1}K + \overline{P}_{L,1}L,$$

and the expansion path, represented as either

$$K = K(L)$$

or

$$L = L(K).$$

Recall from Chapter 10 that the expansion path is derived from the constrained optimization procedure and thus constitutes a representation of the necessary condition for a constrained cost minimum. We can describe the set of information outlined above as a system of three equations: the production function, the isocost equation, and the expansion path, containing four variables: the levels of the inputs, K and L, total cost, C, and output, Q. The process of mathematically deriving a $LRTC$ curve from this set of information consists of making a series of substitutions that ultimately reduce the system of three equations containing four variables, down to just one equation containing two variables. The resulting single equation is the $LRTC$ function containing the two variables, total cost, C, and output, Q.

We can best demonstrate this procedure with a specific numerical example. For the constrained cost minimization problem we solved in Chapter 10, the production function was

$$Q = 10K^{.5}L^{.5}, \tag{11.1}$$

and the isocost equation was

$$\overline{P}_{K,1}K + \overline{P}_{L,1}L = C, \tag{11.2}$$

where we specified the input prices as $\overline{P}_{K,1} = \$40$ and $\overline{P}_{L,1} = \$10$. We solved this problem to yield the expansion path as either

$$K = \frac{1}{4}L, \tag{11.3}$$

or

$$L = 4K. \tag{11.4}$$

Using the version of the expansion path represented by equation (11.3), we can substitute the term $1/4L$ for K in the production function, equation (11.1), yielding

$$Q = 10\left(\frac{1}{4}L\right)^{.5}L^{.5} = 10(0.25)^{.5}L^{.5}L^{.5} = 5L.$$

Next, solving for L in terms of Q yields the expression

$$L = \frac{Q}{5} = 0.2Q. \tag{11.5}$$

We have now expressed the optimal level of labor used by the firm in terms of its production of output. Similarly, we can substitute the term $4K$, from the version of the expansion path represented by equation (11.4), for L in equation (11.1), the production function, to obtain

$$Q = 10K^{.5}(4K)^{.5} = 10(4^{.5})K^{.5}K^{.5} = 20K.$$

Solving for K in terms of Q yields

$$K = \frac{1}{20}Q = 0.05Q. \tag{11.6}$$

Substituting the expressions for L and K from equations (11.5) and (11.6), respectively, into equation (11.2), the isocost equation, yields

$$C = \overline{P}_{K,1}(0.05Q) + \overline{P}_{L,1}(0.2Q).$$

Since $\overline{P}_{K,1} = \$40$ and $\overline{P}_{L,1} = \$10$, then

$$C = 40(0.05Q) + 10(0.2Q),$$

or

$$C = 2Q + 2Q = 4Q. \tag{11.7}$$

Finally, since the cost term, C, in this equation represents the minimum levels of cost associated with producing different levels of output, Q, we interpret equation (11.7) as a long-run total cost function, or

$$LRTC = C = 4Q. \tag{11.8}$$

Note that because of the particular production function used in this problem, this *LRTC* function is linear rather than cubic, as opposed to the more general *LRTC* function that we demonstrated graphically in Figure 11.2. However, this *LRTC* function

$$C = 4Q,$$

exhibits the other characteristics associated with long-run total cost functions described earlier. Specifically, it reflects a direct relationship between cost and output, it begins at the origin, thus exhibiting no fixed costs, and its C values represent the minimum costs associated with producing different levels of output.

11.4 LONG-RUN AVERAGE COST

In the process of analyzing a firm's long-run costs, particularly as they relate to the size of a firm, we frequently find it useful to express its costs on a per unit of output basis. This type of cost is **long-run average cost**, or *LRAC*, defined as *a firm's long-*

run total cost divided by the level of output produced. Notationally, we express this relationship as

$$LRAC = \frac{LRTC}{Q} = \frac{C(Q)}{Q},$$

and we can also represent it graphically by a *LRAC* curve, demonstrating long-run costs per unit of output as a function of the level of output produced. We have illustrated the graphical derivation of the *LRAC* curve from the *LRTC* curve in Figure 11.3. The cubic *LRTC* curve we discussed earlier is repeated in panel (A), while the corresponding

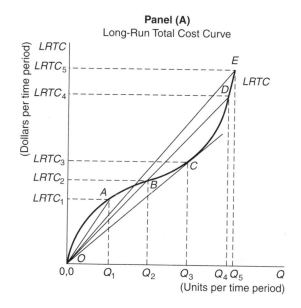

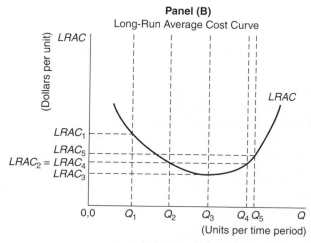

FIGURE 11.3 Derivation of Long-Run Average Cost Curve from Long-Run Total Cost Curve

LRAC curve is shown in panel (B). Since both *LRTC* and *LRAC* are functions of output, *Q*, the graphs of these two curves are linked by their common horizontal axes.

The graphical procedure we use to derive the *LRAC* curve from the *LRTC* curve consists of constructing rays from the origin to the *LRTC* curve and then determining the slopes of these rays, where these slopes represent the *LRAC* values corresponding to the different levels of *Q*. For example, observe in panel (A) that if a firm produces Q_1 units of output, the corresponding *LRTC* value is $LRTC_1$. The ray *OA* drawn from the origin to the *LRTC* curve at point *A*, corresponding to the $(Q_1, LRTC_1)$ combination, has the slope value

$$\frac{LRTC_1 - 0}{Q_1 - 0} = \frac{LRTC_1}{Q_1} = LRAC_1,$$

representing the value of the *LRAC* at this level of output. In panel (B), we have plotted this combination of long-run average cost, $LRAC_1$, and its corresponding Q_1 units of output, as one point on the *LRAC* curve. If the firm produces Q_2 units of output, the corresponding *LRTC* value is $LRTC_2$. We compute the value of *LRAC* associated with this level of output by determining the slope of the ray *OB*, drawn from the origin to point *B* on the *LRTC* curve, where this slope is

$$\frac{LRTC_2 - 0}{Q_2 - 0} = \frac{LRTC_2}{Q_2} = LRAC_2.$$

Observe that the ray *OB* is flatter than the preceding ray, *OA*, and thus it possesses a smaller slope value indicating that $LRAC_2 < LRAC_1$, as we have shown in panel (B) of Figure 11.3.

We can continue this process of determining the slopes of rays drawn from the origin to the *LRTC* curve until we derive the entire *LRAC* curve. Note that the rays *OA*, *OB*, and *OC*, constructed at output values of Q_1, Q_2, and Q_3, respectively, are successively flatter, indicating declining *LRAC* values up to Q_3 units of output, at which the ray *OC* is also tangent to the *LRTC* curve. As the production of output increases beyond Q_3, the rays *OD* and *OE*, constructed at Q_4 and Q_5 units, respectively, become successively steeper, indicating the successively higher *LRAC* values of $LRAC_4$ and $LRAC_5$ we have plotted in panel (B). In summary, the *LRAC* curve corresponding to a cubic *LRTC* curve possesses a quadratic, or U-shape, achieving a minimum value at the level of output for which a ray drawn from the origin to the *LRTC* curve is also tangent to this curve. In this example, this minimum value of *LRAC* occurs at Q_3 units of output. This particular U-shaped *LRAC* curve indicates that the firm achieves cost advantages from increasing its level of output up to Q_3 units and, by doing so, reduces its long-run per unit cost. Beyond Q_3, however, the firm becomes less cost efficient, and its per unit cost rises with further increases in *Q*.

We can also demonstrate the derivation of a *LRAC* curve mathematically, using nothing more than simple division. As an example, given the *LRTC* curve we derived earlier

$$LRTC = 4Q,$$

the corresponding $LRAC$ curve is

$$LRAC = \frac{LRTC}{Q} = \frac{4Q}{Q} = \$4/\text{unit}.$$

In this case, $LRAC$ is a constant value, indicating that the firm's long-run average cost neither decreases nor increases with increases in Q.

As another example, suppose a firm has a cubic long-run total cost curve, such as

$$LRTC = \frac{1}{3}Q^3 - 6Q^2 + 60Q.$$

In this case, the long-run average cost curve is

$$LRAC = \frac{LRTC}{Q} = \frac{\frac{1}{3}Q^3 - 6Q^2 + 60Q}{Q} = \frac{1}{3}Q^2 - 6Q + 60,$$

possessing the more common quadratic, or U-shape, we described earlier using graphical analysis. Given particular values of output, we can obtain the corresponding values of $LRAC$ by evaluating the $LRAC$ function at those Q values. For example, if $Q = 3$ units then

$$LRAC = \frac{1}{3}(3)^2 - 6(3) + 60 = \$45/\text{unit}.$$

By differentiating the $LRAC$ function with respect to Q and setting the term equal to zero, we can determine the value of Q at which the firm's long-run average cost achieves a minimum value. Thus

$$\frac{dLRAC}{dQ} = \frac{2}{3}Q - 6 = 0,$$

or

$$Q = \frac{3}{2}(6) = 9 \text{ units.}$$

You can verify this result by substituting increasing values of Q, up to $Q = 9$ units, into the above $LRAC$ function and determining the successively decreasing, corresponding values of $LRAC$. In addition, you can use a similar procedure to demonstrate that, for increasing values of Q beyond $Q = 9$ units, the corresponding values of $LRAC$ increase.

11.5   RELATIONSHIP BETWEEN RETURNS TO SCALE AND LONG-RUN AVERAGE COST

Earlier, in panel (B) of Figure 11.3, we showed that for a cubic $LRTC$ function, the long-run average cost curve is U-shaped, indicating that as the firm expands its output, initially its per unit costs of production fall, until it achieves a minimum, after which the long-run average cost rises as the firm continues to increase its output. Although there are several reasons for this U-shaped *LRAC* curve, the major rationale lies ultimately in the degree of homogeneity of the underlying production function.

In Chapter 10 we stated that the degree of homogeneity of a production function indicates the extent to which a firm's output changes as a result of a proportional change in all of its inputs. Specifically, a production function is homogeneous to the degree *n* if

$$\delta^n Q = f(\delta K, \delta L),$$

where the Greek letter delta, δ, represents some constant scaling factor by which all inputs are proportionately changed, and the degree of homogeneity of the production function is designated by the variable *n*. Recall, depending on whether the value of *n* is greater than, equal to, or less than one, the production function exhibits either increasing, constant, or decreasing returns to scale, respectively.

11.5.1 INCREASING RETURNS TO SCALE

In the case of increasing returns to scale, the degree of homogeneity of the production function, *n*, is greater than one, indicating that, if a firm alters its inputs by some factor, δ, its output changes by a disproportionably greater amount. For example, let us suppose $n = 2$, then

$$\delta^n Q = \delta^2 Q = f(\delta K, \delta L),$$

and if we assume the scaling factor, δ, is 2 then

$$2^2 Q = 4Q = f(2K, 2L).$$

Specifically, in this example, since the production function is homogeneous to the degree 2 and thus exhibits increasing returns to scale, a doubling of all inputs results in a more than proportionate increase in output. Indeed, in this example output quadruples when all inputs are scaled up by a factor of two. What causes this vast increase in output? In general, such a situation arises when a firm experiences increases in its production efficiency as it expands its scale of operation. This heightened production efficiency is due, in part, to the higher degree of specialization and division of labor in the workplace that arises as the entire production process grows larger. For example, assume a firm uses individualized workstations that enable capital and labor to work closely together on very specific tasks. This can result in the inputs becoming more proficient than if they were employed in a less structured manner. An additional explanation for increasing returns to scale lies in the production technology used by some firms. More specifically, in some situations, increases in production efficiency arise with increases in the size of the processing units. As an example, production processes that rely heavily on the use of large pipelines or vats are characterized by increasing returns to scale since a doubling of the radius of a pipe or vat results in a fourfold increase in the volume these apparatuses can accommodate. Oil, beer, and wine producers typically experience increasing returns to scale for this reason.

We can relate the effect of increasing returns to scale to long-run average cost in a direct and logical manner. Provided we assume that the prices of the inputs a firm uses are determined in perfectly competitive markets, then as the firm purchases additional amounts of these inputs, its total cost rises proportionately, since these input prices remain unchanged. Therefore, in this example where we assume that the scaling factor,

---

REAL-WORLD APPLICATION 11.1

The Difficulties in Achieving Economies of Scale in International Retailing

The world's largest retailer, Wal-Mart, is often cited as an example of a company that has successfully exploited the concept of economies of scale. By expanding the number of its large retail stores in the United States, it has been able to achieve significant cost savings via its increased production efficiency and its ability to negotiate lower prices from its various suppliers. However, Wal-Mart's domestic success has been difficult to replicate outside of the United States, as evidenced by the fact that its return on capital from its international operations is only 5.8%, well below its performance domestically.[1] Wal-Mart's difficulty in expanding internationally is not unique. For example, Carrefour, France's largest general merchandise retailer, earns operating margins domestically in excess of 6% of its sales, while simultaneously generating losses in Asia and Latin America. Carrefour opened only three stores in the United States, before it decided to abandon the U.S. market, when the retailer proved unable to capture the scale economies necessary to successfully compete with established U.S. retailers.

Several factors underlie the difficulties of general merchandise retailers in establishing scale economies in foreign markets. The foremost challenge faced by newcomers into a foreign market is the fact that their size and market share relative to the other established retailers tend to be small. As a result, foreign firms often have difficulty generating the revenue and profit necessary to justify creating a costly distribution network outside of their home countries, thereby further inhibiting growth and the attainment of scale economies. Foreign retailers also are often at a disadvantage when attempting to establish relationships with local suppliers, which are more likely to maintain stronger allegiances to the larger, established local retailers. In addition, cultural differences across countries in terms of product preferences and manner of service preclude general merchandise retailers from merely replicating their practices from one country to the next. Those few retailers that have had success internationally, such as the U.S.-based clothing retailer, the Gap, and the Swedish furniture retailer IKEA, have offered more narrowly focused product lines that have universal appeal, thereby facilitating the attainment of economies of scale across national borders. While general merchandise retailers face unique challenges in expanding outside of their home markets, perhaps the key to international retailing success is to aim toward marketing a specific product or service that possesses global appeal.

---

[1]"Shopping All Over the World," *The Economist*, June 19, 1999, pp. 59–61.

δ, is equal to two, a doubling of the amount of capital and labor employed by the firm causes the new value of long-run total cost, $LRTC_2$, to be twice the original value of long-run total cost, $LRTC_1$. However, the new level of output generated, Q_2, using twice as much capital and labor, is four times the original level of production, Q_1. Thus

$$LRAC_2 = \frac{LRTC_2}{Q_2} = \frac{2LRTC_1}{4Q_1} = \frac{1}{2} LRAC_1,$$

or $LRAC_2$ is one-half its original level. In general, the value of $LRAC$ decreases as the firm increases its output. Therefore, the slope of the long-run average cost curve, $dLRAC/dQ$, is negative when the firm experiences increasing returns to scale. In panel (A) of Figure 11.4, we have demonstrated the manner in which $LRAC$ declines from $LRAC_1$ to $LRAC_2$, as a firm experiencing increasing returns to scale expands its level of production from Q_1 to Q_2.

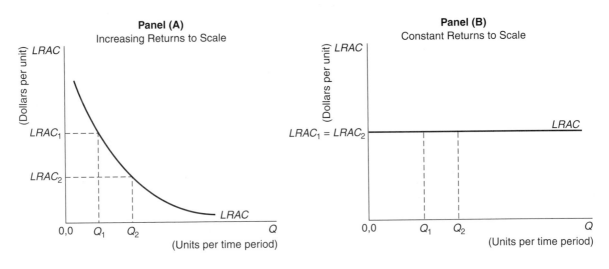

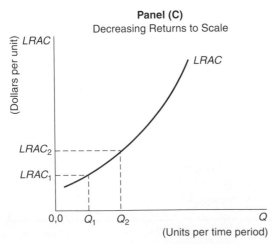

FIGURE 11.4 Long-Run Average Cost for Different Returns to Scale

A concept related to increasing returns to scale is that of economies of scale. Although the two phrases are often used interchangeably, we should note that there is an important distinction between them. The concept of increasing returns to scale refers to a situation for which a firm changes all of its inputs in a strictly proportionate manner, and as a result, its long-run average cost decreases. We consistently applied this concept to the preceding cost analysis. In contrast, the phrase, **economies of scale**, refers *to any production situation for which an increase in inputs, either in a proportionate or disproportionate manner, results in lower per unit costs of production.* Therefore, it is possible for us to categorize the concept of increasing returns to scale as a special case of economies of scale.

The phenomenon of economies of scale has some interesting implications in the real world. Consider a firm that consistently experiences economies of scale over a large range of its output due to having relatively high setup costs. The most cost-efficient outcome in such a situation may be for this firm to be the sole provider of the good. The reason for this result is that having multiple producers reduces each firm's market share, thus leading to higher average costs of production and ultimately higher prices for consumers. This scenario describes what is known as the natural monopoly argument, where competition from many firms in an industry characterized by economies of scale results in higher per unit costs of production than when the industry is monopolized. Electricity, water, and sewer service providers fall into such a category. Other real-world examples of industries characterized by economies of scale include automobile and aircraft manufacturing, brewing, and commercial airline service. As an exercise, it is left to you to suggest a rationale as to the source of economies of scale in each of these industries.

11.5.2 Constant Returns to Scale

Constant returns to scale arise when the degree of homogeneity, n, of the production function is equal to one. Specifically, if $n = 1$ then

$$\delta^n Q = \delta^1 Q = f(\delta K, \delta L),$$

indicating that, if the firm alters its inputs by some factor, δ, its output changes by a proportionate amount. For example, if we once again assume that the scaling factor, δ, equals 2, then

$$2^1 Q = f(2K, 2L).$$

Therefore, doubling the firm's inputs results in doubling its output. In this case of constant returns to scale, the firm neither gains nor loses productive efficiency as it proportionately increases its use of all inputs, since its output expands proportionately as well.

We can once again assess the effect of constant returns to scale on long-run average cost by examining the effect of a proportionate change in the use of all inputs on a firm's long-run total cost and its level of production. Earlier we demonstrated that, in the case of constant returns to scale, doubling all inputs results in a doubling of output. Thus the new level of output produced, Q_2, is twice the original level of production,

Q_1. In addition, the acquisition of twice as many inputs when the firm scales up its production process causes the firm's long-run total cost to double, relative to its original level, $LRTC_1$. Thus, after a firm doubles its scale of operation, the resulting new long-run average cost, $LRAC_2$, is

$$LRAC_2 = \frac{LRTC_2}{Q_2} = \frac{2LRTC_1}{2Q_1} = \frac{LRTC_1}{Q_1} = LRAC_1,$$

indicating no change in the value of the firm's long-run average cost. In addition, it should be clear that the slope of the firm's long-run average cost curve, $dLRAC/dQ$, equals zero when the firm experiences constant returns to scale, since the value of $LRAC$ remains unchanged when the firm scales up its production process. As a result, the long-run average cost curve is horizontal, as we have shown in panel (B) of Figure 11.4.

This $LRAC$ curve illustrated in panel (B) demonstrates constant returns to scale for the entire range of production. In some cases, however, constant returns to scale might not arise until a firm achieves a certain level of production. In this situation, the firm reaches a point on its long-run average cost curve known as its minimum efficient scale, where increasing returns to scale have been replaced by constant returns to scale, and at this point its $LRAC$ is minimized. We can observe in Figure 11.5 that the firm's minimum efficient scale of production, or where $LRAC$ first reaches its minimum value, occurs at Q' where the associated value of $LRAC$ is $LRAC'$. Prior to achieving this level of production, the firm experiences increasing returns to scale as it increases its output. After reaching Q', constant returns to scale continue to characterize the firm's production process, and $LRAC$ remains at its minimum value, as the firm increases its output to Q''.

Once a firm achieves its minimum efficient scale of production, its most logical course of action is to replicate its current production process by establishing multiple identical plants rather than expanding the size of a single plant. A real-world example may help us clarify this point. Restaurants for many fast-food chains are typically designed identically because after much engineering and cost analysis these chains have

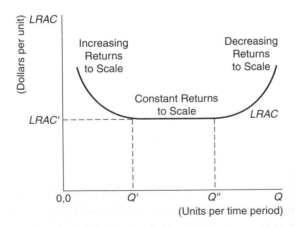

FIGURE 11.5 Long-Run Average Cost Function Demonstrating Increasing, Constant, and Decreasing Returns to Scale

determined the optimal, or per unit cost-minimizing, size of a restaurant. Given sufficient demand for its food, a fast-food chain then locates multiple, identical restaurants in a market rather than constructing one very large restaurant to accommodate its customers.

11.5.3   Decreasing Returns to Scale

The third possible type of returns to scale, decreasing returns, arises when the degree of homogeneity, n, of a production function is less than one, indicating that if a firm alters its inputs by some factor, δ, its output changes by a disproportionately lesser amount. For example, if $n = 1/2$, then

$$\delta^n Q = \delta^{1/2} Q = f(\delta K, \delta L),$$

and if we assume the scaling factor, δ, is 2, then

$$2^{1/2} Q = 1.41 Q = f(2K, 2L).$$

Specifically, in this example, because the production function is homogeneous of degree $\frac{1}{2}$ and thus exhibits decreasing returns to scale, doubling a firm's inputs results in a less than proportionate increase in its production of output. In general, a firm that exhibits decreasing returns to scale experiences a loss of production efficiency as it expands its scale of operation. We can relate the effect of decreasing returns to scale to long-run average cost, once again using the same analysis as in the earlier cases. When the scaling factor, δ, equals 2, using twice as much capital and labor results in output rising by a less than proportionate factor of 1.41, meaning the new level of output, Q_2, is equal to 1.41 times the original level of output, Q_1. In addition, the acquisition of twice as many inputs causes the firm's new long-run total cost, $LRTC_2$, to rise by a factor of two, relative to its original level, $LRTC_1$. Applying this information to the definition of long-run average cost yields

$$LRAC_2 = \frac{LRTC_2}{Q_2} = \frac{2LRTC_1}{1.41Q_1} = 1.41 LRAC_1.$$

Thus, the new value, $LRAC_2$, is 1.41 times its original level, $LRAC_1$. Since the value of $LRAC$ rises as the firm increases its output, the slope of the long-run average cost curve, $dLRAC/dQ$, is positive. We have demonstrated this result in panel (C) of Figure 11.4, where we can observe that as the firm increases its output from Q_1 to Q_2, the per unit cost of production rises from $LRAC_1$ to $LRAC_2$.

A concept very closely related to decreasing returns to scale is that of **diseconomies of scale**, defined as *any production situation for which an increase in the use of inputs, in either a proportionate or disproportionate manner, results in higher per unit costs of production.* As in the case of increasing returns to scale and the related concept of economies of scale, the distinction between decreasing returns to scale and diseconomies of scale lies in the manner in which the firm's inputs are adjusted. As mentioned earlier, in the case of decreasing returns to scale, all inputs are changed by the same proportion. However, in the less restrictive case of diseconomies of scale, the firm may increase its output by scaling up its inputs in either a proportionate or non-proportionate manner. Therefore, we can categorize decreasing returns to scale as a special case of diseconomies of scale.

The underlying rationale for the loss of production efficiency and the subsequent higher per unit costs, as a firm increases its scale of production, is often managerially based. In such cases, the scale of the production operation has grown too large to be effectively managed. Duplication of tasks or the undertaking of tasks that are counterproductive creates losses in production efficiency, resulting in an overall increase in per unit costs. Another factor often contributing to diseconomies of scale is that, as a firm expands production, it may experience disproportionate increases in its transportation costs. These cost increases can be associated with either acquiring additional amounts of inputs or delivering greater amounts of the final product to consumers, *ceteris paribus*. Overall, once a firm encounters decreasing returns to scale, then based solely on efficiency grounds, it is in its best interest to downsize. By doing so, the firm can establish better control over its resources, thereby enhancing its efficiency and lowering its per unit costs of production.

11.6   ECONOMIES OF SCOPE

The concepts of economies and diseconomies of scale pertain to a firm's production of a single output. However, sometimes a firm may enjoy cost advantages by engaging in the production of several related goods. Specifically, a firm experiences **economies of scope** if it *can achieve lower per unit costs of production by producing multiple outputs rather than by producing only one good or service.* Several possible rationales may underlie economies of scope. One explanation is a situation in which the production of one good also generates a marketable byproduct. Such an example is the slaughter of cattle for beef, since this also results in the production of hides that can be used to produce leather goods. Another example of economies of scope occurs when a firm is capable of using its inputs to produce different products. For example, an automobile manufacturer that can also use its capital and labor to produce trucks and sport utility vehicles will often engage in such diversity in its product line if it results in lower per unit costs of production. Finally, a firm may choose to become involved in the manufacture of intermediate goods, or those goods used in the production of its other goods, if there are cost advantages in doing so. For example, it is quite common for manufacturers of primary metals to also be involved in the mining of the ores that go into these metals. Although the phenomenon of economies of scope is quite prevalent in the real world, our cost analysis presented in this chapter is conducted under the assumption that firms engage in the production of just a single output. Therefore, for the sake of theoretical consistency, we will assume that the firms under analysis in this chapter do not experience economies of scope.

Economies of Scale and Scope for Firms in the Financial Services Industry

The commercial banking industry in the United States has been undergoing a considerable amount of consolidation since the mid-1980s. This consolidation has taken place in the form of mergers and takeovers, the majority of which have involved commercial banks such as Bank of America and Nations Bank, as well as First Chicago NBD and Bank One. In fact, there has been so much consolidation in recent years that the number of commercial banks in the United States has declined during the past 15 years from over 14,000 to approximately 9000. In addition to these types of mergers, however, there has also been a developing trend involving mergers of commercial banks and nonbank financial institutions, such as insurance companies and brokerage firms. The most notable of such mergers involved Citicorp Bank and Travelers Insurance.

From a legal perspective, the trend toward consolidation has been made possible by the government's deregulation of the financial services industry over the past 20 years. The economic rationale underlying mergers between commercial banks and nonbank financial institutions stems more from economies of scope than from economies of scale. These mergers have been made possible largely by the repeal of the Glass-Steagall Act in 1999. This act, passed in the 1930s, prohibited commercial banks from engaging in securities market activities, such as the underwriting of securities or the sale of mutual funds. With the repeal of the Glass-Steagall Act, many commercial banks are now acting to expand their scope of operations in order to compete in these additional markets. Recall that a firm experiences economies of scope if it can achieve lower per unit costs by producing multiple outputs as opposed to producing only one good or service. The likelihood of realizing such economies of scope is greatly enhanced if these multiple outputs are related to some degree. Commercial banks, for example, can use many of their existing inputs, including computers, software, and customer databases, to provide a wide variety of financial services in a number of related areas. Thus, commercial banks' acquisitions of other financial intermediaries, such as investment banks, brokerage firms, and insurance companies, enable them to produce and cross-sell what have historically been considered nonbank financial services (e.g., brokerage transactions and insurance policies) to their existing customers. In addition, they are now able to produce and sell their traditional banking services to customers of what previously were designated nonbank financial institutions.[2] In summary, these activities are the manifestation of economies of scope, leading to lower overall per unit costs for these financial institutions.

[2]Mark Zandi, "Why Are Banks Merging?" [Online]. http://www.dismal.com/thoughts/merger.stm.

11.7 LONG-RUN MARGINAL COST

We can derive yet another type of long-run cost and related cost function from the long-run total cost function. This cost is known as **long-run marginal cost**, or **LRMC**, defined as *the change in long-run total cost due to a change in the production of output.* In subsequent chapters, we will show how this type of cost plays a particularly important role in determining a firm's long-run profit. Notationally, we can represent the long-run marginal cost function as the derivative of the *LRTC* function, or

$$LRMC = \frac{dLRTC}{dQ} = \frac{dC(Q)}{dQ}.$$

The graphical derivation of this function is illustrated in Figure 11.6, where in panel (A) we have reproduced the cubic *LRTC* function used earlier, and in panel (B) we have plotted the associated *LRMC* function. Both functions are linked by their common horizontal axes measuring *Q*. As is the case with all marginal functions, we can interpret the *LRMC* function as representing the instantaneous slope of some corresponding total function. Specifically, the *LRMC* function represents the instantaneous slope values of the *LRTC* curve at different levels of output, *Q*. Therefore, we can compute the values of *LRMC* by constructing tangents to the *LRTC* curve at different levels of *Q* and determining the value of the slope of each of these tangents.

Referring to panel (A) of Figure 11.6, observe that if the firm produces Q_1 units of output, it incurs a long-run total cost of $LRTC_1$. The corresponding value of *LRMC* is represented by the slope of the line AA' drawn tangent to the *LRTC* curve at Q_1. We have plotted this value, designated $LRMC_1$, in panel (B) representing one point on the *LRMC* curve. If the firm produces Q_2 units of output, incurring a total cost of $LRTC_2$, we compute the corresponding value of *LRMC* as the slope of the line BB' drawn tangent to the *LRTC* curve at Q_2, designated as $LRMC_2$ in panel (B). Note that both tangents, AA' and BB', as well as all other tangents, possess positive slopes, thus indicating positive values for *LRMC*. Also note that the tangent BB' is flatter than the tangent AA', reflecting a lower slope, or *LRMC*, value at Q_2 than at Q_1. We have illustrated this result in panel (B), where you can observe that the *LRMC* values are decreasing up to Q_2 units of output.

The point $(Q_2, LRTC_2)$, shown in panel (A), corresponds to the inflection point on the *LRTC* curve. The lines we have drawn tangent to the *LRTC* curve at successively increasing values of output beyond Q_2, such as CC' at Q_3 and DD' at Q_4, become successively steeper, indicating higher slope, or *LRMC*, values. These values are represented as $LRMC_3$ and $LRMC_4$, respectively. Thus, we can observe in panel (B) that beyond Q_2, the *LRMC* curve rises with increases in *Q*. In summary, the *LRMC* curve we derived from a cubic *LRTC* curve assumes a quadratic, or U-shape, as did the *LRAC* curve derived earlier from a cubic *LRTC* curve. However, we must empha-

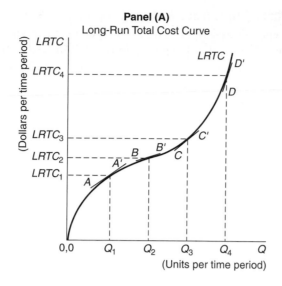

Panel (A)
Long-Run Total Cost Curve

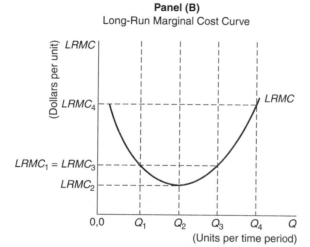

Panel (B)
Long-Run Marginal Cost Curve

FIGURE 11.6 Derivation of Long-Run Marginal Cost Curve from Long-Run Total Cost Curve

size that, although these curves possess similar general shapes in this case, they do not coincide because they are different curves.

Mathematically, we compute the *LRMC* function by taking the derivative of the *LRTC* function with respect to output. Returning to our earlier numerical example where

$$LRTC = 4Q,$$

we find that the long-run marginal cost function is then

$$LRMC = \frac{dLRTC}{dQ} = \$4.$$

In this case we have determined that *LRMC* is a constant value, indicating that for an infinitesimally small change in output, *LRTC* changes by \$4 regardless of the initial level of *Q*. We can also observe that for this example, $LRMC = LRAC = \$4$. However, this coincidence between long-run marginal and average costs does not hold true for most *LRTC* functions.

In the second numerical example we presented earlier, the long-run total cost function was cubic, specified as

$$LRTC = \frac{1}{3}Q^3 - 6Q^2 + 60Q.$$

In this case we compute the associated long-run marginal cost function as

$$LRMC = \frac{dLRTC}{dQ} = 1.0Q^2 - 12Q + 60.$$

This *LRMC* curve possesses the usual quadratic shape. You can determine particular values of *LRMC* corresponding to different levels of output very easily. For example, if a firm produces $Q = 10$ units of output, then

$$LRMC = (10)^2 - 12(10) + 60 = \$40.$$

11.8 RELATIONSHIPS AMONG LONG-RUN TOTAL COST, LONG-RUN MARGINAL COST, AND LONG-RUN AVERAGE COST

There are some *LRTC* functions for which the *LRMC* and *LRAC* functions are coincident, such as the linear *LRTC* we analyzed earlier demonstrating that $LRMC = LRAC$. However, for the more typical case of the cubic *LRTC* function, this result does not occur. Thus, it is of interest to examine the relationship between its associated *LRMC* and *LRAC* curves. These curves, which we constructed separately in earlier graphical analyses, are reproduced in panel (B) of Figure 11.7 and related to the cubic *LRTC* curve shown in panel (A) from which they are both derived.

The *LRAC* curve represents the slopes of rays drawn from the origin to (*Q*, *LRTC*) points on the *LRTC* curve, and the *LRMC* represents the slopes of the lines drawn tangent to the *LRTC* curve at these (*Q*, *LRTC*) points. Therefore, a ray drawn from the origin to the *LRTC* curve, which is also tangent to this curve, corresponds to an output value for which $LRMC = LRAC$. This particular level of output occurs at Q_3 units; thus, the *LRMC* and *LRAC* curves shown in panel (B) intersect at this level of *Q*. Furthermore, this level of output also corresponds to the minimum level of *LRAC*. We can observe that for levels of output less than Q_3, the lines drawn tangent to the *LRTC* curve, such as those at Q_1 and Q_2, possess smaller slope values than the slopes of the rays drawn from the origin to the curve at these points. As a result, for output levels less than Q_3, $LRMC < LRAC$, and we can also observe that for this range of *Q* values, *LRAC* decreases with increments to *Q*. For output levels greater than Q_3, the slope values of the lines drawn tangent to the *LRTC* curve, such as those at Q_4 and Q_5, are greater than the slope values pertain-

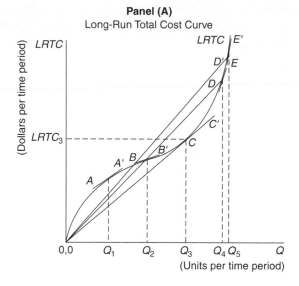

Panel (A)
Long-Run Total Cost Curve

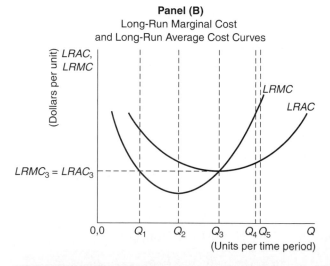

Panel (B)
Long-Run Marginal Cost
and Long-Run Average Cost Curves

FIGURE 11.7 Relationships among Long-Run Total Cost, Long-Run Marginal Cost, and Long-Run Average Cost

ing to the rays drawn from the origin to the $LRTC$ curve and thus $LRMC > LRAC$ at those values of Q. Also, observe that $LRAC$ increases as Q increases over this range.

We can also mathematically prove that $LRMC = LRAC$ when $LRAC$ achieves its minimum value by minimizing the $LRAC$ function with respect to Q. Since

$$LRAC = \frac{LRTC}{Q} = \frac{C(Q)}{Q} = C(Q)Q^{-1},$$

the first-order condition for a minimum is found by applying the product rule to the above formulation for $LRAC$. Thus, we obtain the derivative of $LRAC$ with respect to Q and set it equal to zero as

$$\frac{dLRAC}{dQ} = C(Q)\frac{dQ^{-1}}{dQ} + Q^{-1}\frac{dC(Q)}{dQ} = 0$$

$$= -C(Q)Q^{-2} + Q^{-1}\frac{dC(Q)}{dQ} = 0.$$

Multiplying the above equation by Q yields

$$-C(Q)Q^{-1} + \frac{dC(Q)}{dQ} = 0,$$

or

$$\frac{dC(Q)}{dQ} = \frac{C(Q)}{Q}.$$

We can recognize the terms $dC(Q)/dQ$ and $C(Q)/Q$ as the $LRMC$ and $LRAC$ functions respectively, and thus $LRMC = LRAC$ when $LRAC$ is minimized.[3]

Previously, we observed that $LRMC < LRAC$ as $LRAC$ declines with increases in Q. This fact can be explained intuitively. Since marginal costs represent the incremental total costs associated with increasing Q, we expect that if $LRMC < LRAC$, such increments will cause the average cost, $LRAC$, to decrease. Conversely, if $LRMC > LRAC$, then the increments to total cost exceed the average cost and any increases in Q cause the average cost to rise.

A numerical application of this result should provide you with some additional insight regarding the fact that $LRMC = LRAC$ when $LRAC$ achieves a minimum value. Recall the specific cubic $LRTC$ function we used throughout this chapter

$$LRTC = \frac{1}{3}Q^3 - 6Q^2 + 60Q,$$

for which we computed the associated $LRAC$ function as

$$LRAC = \frac{LRTC}{Q} = \frac{1}{3}Q^2 - 6Q + 60.$$

We determined the level of output at which $LRAC$ achieves a minimum value by taking the derivative of $LRAC$ with respect to Q, setting this derivative equal to zero, and solving for Q as

$$\frac{dLRAC}{dQ} = \frac{2}{3}Q - 6 = 0$$

or

$$Q = 9 \text{ units.}$$

---

[3]We have assumed in this proof that the second-order condition for a minimum, $d^2LRAC/dQ^2 > 0$, is fulfilled.

Thus, the minimized value of *LRAC* is

$$LRAC = \frac{1}{3}(9)^2 - 6(9) + 60 = \$33/\text{unit}.$$

The *LRMC* function derived from the *LRTC* function was

$$LRMC = \frac{dLRTC}{dQ} = Q^2 - 12Q + 60.$$

Since *LRMC* = *LRAC* when *LRAC* is at its minimum value, we can also determine the corresponding level of *Q* at which this result occurs by equating *LRMC* and *LRAC* as

$$Q^2 - 12Q + 60 = \frac{1}{3}Q^2 - 6Q + 60$$

$$\frac{2}{3}Q^2 - 6Q = 0$$

$$Q\left(\frac{2}{3}Q - 6\right) = 0,$$

or

$$Q = \frac{3}{2}(6) = 9 \text{ units.}$$

The value of long-run marginal cost at this level of output is

$$LRMC - 9^2 - 12(9) \mid 60 = \$33,$$

where these results for output and cost are the same as those we obtained by minimizing the *LRAC* function.

11.9   SUMMARY

Our focus in this chapter has been on defining a firm's costs from a conceptual perspective and, in particular, on analyzing the various costs incurred by a firm in the process of producing a good or service in the long run. We demonstrated how various types of long-run costs can be represented by total, average, and marginal cost functions. In addition, we also discussed the interrelationships among these various cost functions. The key topics covered in this chapter are as follows.

- In the long run, since all of a firm's inputs are variable, the firm incurs only variable costs.
- A firm's explicit costs refer to those costs that are associated with nonowner supplied inputs used in its production process, while implicit costs are those costs associated with inputs supplied by the owners to their firm.
- A long-run total cost function expresses a firm's minimum cost of production in terms of its level of output, assuming input prices and the state of technology are held constant.
- We compute long-run average cost by dividing a firm's long-run total cost by the level of output it produces.

- The slope of a firm's long-run average cost curve varies, depending on the type of returns to scale it experiences.
- A firm experiences economies of scope if it achieves lower per unit production costs by producing multiple outputs than by producing only one good or service.
- A firm's long-run marginal cost function measures the change in its long-run total cost arising from a change in its level of production.
- The long-run average cost and long-run marginal cost curves intersect at an output level that corresponds to the minimum value of long-run average cost.

KEY TERMS

- cost function, page 262
- diseconomies of scale, page 277
- economies of scale, page 275
- economies of scope, page 278
- explicit cost, page 262

- fixed cost, page 262
- implicit cost, page 262
- long-run average cost, page 268
- long-run marginal cost, page 280

- long-run total cost function, page 264
- production externality, page 288
- social cost, page 288
- variable cost, page 262

EXERCISES

11.1 Assume an individual is employed as a school teacher and earns a salary of $40,000/year. He also possesses $200,000 in wealth that he has invested in a money market account earning a return of 5%/year. Suppose this individual decides to quit teaching school and uses the $200,000 to purchase a store in which he works full time. After one year, the store generates a total revenue of $80,000 and $35,000 in explicit costs. Based solely on economic considerations, should this individual continue to own and operate the store or return to the teaching profession?

11.2 Sketch a cubic total function that starts at the origin. From an economic perspective, what does this lack of an intercept indicate? Does this curve depict a short-run or a long-run total cost function? What does the cubic shape reflect about the nature of a firm's costs?

11.3 A firm's production function is

$$Q = K^{1/3}L^{1/3},$$

where Q = units of output produced per year
   K = units of capital used per year
   L = units of labor used per year.

a. Determine the degree of homogeneity associated with this firm's production function.

b. As this firm changes the amount of output it produces, does it experience increasing, constant, or decreasing returns to scale?

c. What does this particular production function imply about the firm's long-run average cost curve?

11.4 For each of the following long-run total cost functions,

    i. $LRTC = C(Q) = 250Q$

    ii. $LRTC = C(Q) = 10Q^2 + 5Q$

    iii. $LRTC = C(Q) = 100Q - Q^2$

a. Compute and graph the long-run average cost function.

b. State what type of returns to scale the firm is experiencing and provide an explanation for your response.

c. Provide a real-world example of a firm whose $LRAC$ behaves in a manner similar to each of these situations.

11.5 Given the following long-run total cost function

$$LRTC = C(Q) = 200Q - 24Q^2 + Q^3,$$

a. Compute and graph the firm's long-run average cost function.

b. Over what range of output levels does the firm experience increasing returns to scale?

c. Over what range of output levels does the firm experience decreasing returns to scale?

11.6 A firm's long-run total cost function is

$$LRTC = C(Q) = Q^3 - 16Q^2 + 1800Q.$$

a. Determine the firm's long-run average cost function.

b. Determine the level of output at which long-run average cost is minimized.

c. Determine the minimum value of long-run average cost.

d. Compute the value of long-run marginal cost when $LRAC$ is minimized.

11.7 Two of the largest U.S. producers of soda pop have recently begun producing and selling bottled water. What economic justification can you provide for this business decision?

11.8 Based solely on efficiency grounds, will a rational entrepreneur produce that level of output at which his U-shaped long-run marginal cost is minimized? Supplement your answer with graphical analysis using typical U-shaped long-run average cost and long-run marginal cost curves.

Appendix

11.A PRIVATE COSTS VS. SOCIAL COSTS

In this chapter, we have defined a firm's costs of production as a function of the level of output it produces. Implicit in this definition is the assumption that the production of output by one firm has no impact on other firms' production and costs. However, this assumption may not always hold true. Consider a situation where a cloth dyeing firm, firm A, is located upstream from a fish hatchery, firm B. Also assume that firm A freely disposes of significant amounts of hot wastewater, generated in its production process, into the stream. The increased water temperature of the stream adversely alters the natural environment and results in a decrease in the fish population, thereby affecting the production of output by the hatchery, firm B.

From an economic perspective, we can say that firm A generates a negative production externality that adversely affects the production efforts, and therefore costs, of another firm, in this case firm B. More generally, this situation represents a type of **production externality**, defined as *either a negative or beneficial side effect associated with the production of a good or service by one firm that affects at least one other firm's production, and therefore generates uncompensated costs or benefits to the affected firm(s)*. As a result, these external costs or benefits are not accounted for in the prices of the goods produced by the firm generating the externality. We should note that, in addition to the previously mentioned example of a negative production externality, it is also possible for a firm to generate a positive production externality that benefits other firms' production. An example of such a case is that of a bee keeper whose bees help to pollinate the peach trees in a nearby orchard. In this case the production of honey generates a benefit for the fruit farmer.

Returning to a negative production externality scenario, such as the one involving firms A and

288

B, firm A has not been held accountable for the damage its production methods inflict on the environment. It freely releases its wastewater into the stream, subsequently affecting the production capabilities of firm B. In this scenario, the private production costs borne directly by firm A do not take into account the external costs associated with its production. Therefore, we need an alternative measure that accurately reflects the cost of producing goods that generate production externalities. Such a measure, known as **social cost**, is *a cost that includes a firm's private production costs plus any costs or minus any benefits generated by its production externality*. Mathematically, we can state this relationship as

Social Cost = Private Cost + External Cost,

or

Social Cost = Private Cost − External Benefits.

Since firm A, the cloth dyeing company, is generating an external cost, its private costs are less than its social costs. As a result, this firm offers its product at a price that is too low, since it is not truly covering all of the costs associated with producing its output. Ultimately, this situation leads to a misallocation of resources since the artificially low price associated with firm A's output causes this product to be both overconsumed and overproduced from a social perspective. In contrast, the output of the fish hatchery, the adversely affected firm, is underproduced due to the negative production externality associated with firm A's output. Specifically, as the fish hatchery tries to counteract the raised stream temperature by employing additional technology for which it must bear the cost, it is forced to charge a higher price for its output. This higher price subsequently causes the quantity demanded of the fish hatchery's output to decrease.

CHAPTER 12

Costs of Production in the Short Run

12.1 INTRODUCTION

In the previous chapter we developed various types of long-run cost functions and demonstrated their associated relationships, where our analysis was based on the assumption that the firm was free to vary all of its inputs. As a result, all of these long-run costs represent the minimum costs associated with producing any given level of output. However, a firm must also make production decisions in the short run, a time period during which at least one of the firm's inputs remains fixed. Thus, in the short run, a firm incurs both fixed and variable costs associated with its use of fixed and variable inputs, respectively. Our focus in this chapter is on analyzing these short-run costs. As with our analysis of long-run costs, once we complete the transition from production theory to cost theory, attention will be devoted to expressing a firm's short-run costs in various forms. Specifically, we will derive short-run average and marginal cost functions from short-run total cost functions, and discuss their interrelationships. We will also demonstrate that short- and long-run costs are not concepts developed independently of one another. After all, doesn't it make sense that every long-run solution must correspond to some particular short-run solution? The answer is yes, and accordingly, we will analyze the relationships between these two broad categories of cost.

12.2 SHORT-RUN TOTAL COST

Since a firm's variable cost is that cost associated with its variable input, we can also express this cost as a function of the firm's production of output. However, we cannot express its fixed cost in the same manner, because in the short run, the only way a firm can adjust its production is by changing its variable input(s). As a result, in the short run, a firm is generally not able to employ optimal combinations of its inputs, and thus its associated short-run costs generally do not represent constrained cost minimums. The exception to this result is a situation for which the firm chooses to produce a level of output requiring a level of the variable input(s) that, when combined with the fixed input(s), just happens to correspond to an optimal or cost-minimizing input combination. However, since this situation pertains to only one level of output, a firm in the short run is forced to use suboptimal input combinations if it chooses to produce any other level of output. We represent these short-run costs by a **short-run total cost function** designated *SRTC*, defined as *a function that expresses a firm's costs in terms of its*

289

production of output, holding constant the level of at least one input, as well as the prices of all inputs.

As we stated earlier, a firm's short-run total cost consists of the summation of its fixed and variable cost, or

$$SRTC = FC + VC,$$

where FC and VC represent the firm's fixed and variable costs, respectively. We should emphasize that any particular $SRTC$ function pertains to a particular level(s) for the fixed input(s).

We can derive the $SRTC$ functions by returning once again to the production function containing two inputs

$$Q = f(K,L),$$

and the isocost equation

$$C = \overline{P}_{K,1}K + \overline{P}_{L,1}L,$$

for which the prices of capital and labor have been specified at $\overline{P}_{K,1}$ and $\overline{P}_{L,1}$, respectively. In the short run, we typically treat the capital input, K, often considered as representing a firm's plant size, as the fixed input, while treating labor, L, as the variable input. Thus, we designate the short-run production function, also known as the total product of labor curve, as

$$TP_L = Q = f(\overline{K}_1,L).$$

Since the amount of capital is fixed at $\overline{K}_1$ units, we can solve this short-run production function for the amount of labor, L, that must be used to produce various levels of output, Q, as

$$L = L(Q,\overline{K}_1).$$

Substituting this expression for L, along with the fixed amount of capital, $\overline{K}_1$, into the firm's isocost equation

$$C = \overline{P}_{K,1}K + \overline{P}_{L,1}L,$$

yields

$$SRTC^{\overline{K}_1} = C^{\overline{K}_1} = \overline{P}_{K,1}\overline{K}_1 + \overline{P}_{L,1}L(Q,\overline{K}_1).$$

Conceptually, this equation represents the firm's short-run total cost function when $K = \overline{K}_1$ units of capital. The term $\overline{P}_{K,1}\,\overline{K}_1$ is the firm's fixed cost, $\overline{FC}_1$, and $\overline{P}_{L,1}\,L(Q,\overline{K}_1)$ represents the firm's variable cost, VC. Since variable cost is a function of the amount of output produced, given a fixed value for the price of the variable labor input, $\overline{P}_{L,1}$, and the amount of the fixed capital input, $\overline{K}_1$, we can express VC more concisely as

$$VC = VC(Q,\overline{P}_{L,1},\overline{K}_1),$$

and thus represent the $SRTC^{\overline{K}_1}$ function in the form

$$SRTC^{\overline{K}_1} = C^{\overline{K}_1} = \overline{P}_{K,1}\overline{K}_1 + VC(Q,\overline{P}_{L,1},\overline{K}_1).$$

If the firm's capital is fixed at a different level, say $\overline{K}_2$, then we can derive a new short-run total cost function as

$$SRTC^{\overline{K}_2} = C^{\overline{K}_2} = \overline{P}_{K,1}\overline{K}_2 + VC(Q,\overline{P}_{L,1},\overline{K}_2).$$

More generally, we can derive an entire set of short-run total cost functions, one for each fixed level of capital, expressed as

$$SRTC^{\overline{K}_1} = C^{\overline{K}_1} = \overline{P}_{K,1}\overline{K}_1 + VC(Q,\overline{P}_{L,1},\overline{K}_1)$$
$$SRTC^{\overline{K}_2} = C^{\overline{K}_2} = \overline{P}_{K,1}\overline{K}_2 + VC(Q,\overline{P}_{L,1},\overline{K}_2)$$
$$SRTC^{\overline{K}_3} = C^{\overline{K}_3} = \overline{P}_{K,1}\overline{K}_3 + VC(Q,\overline{P}_{L,1},\overline{K}_3)$$
$$\vdots \qquad \vdots \qquad \vdots \qquad \vdots \qquad ,$$

where the broad function representing the basis for this family of short-run total cost curves is

$$SRTC = C = \overline{P}_{K,1}K + VC(Q,\overline{P}_{L,1},K).$$

Note that if $\overline{K}_3 > \overline{K}_2 > \overline{K}_1$, then $\overline{FC}_3 > \overline{FC}_2 > \overline{FC}_1$, meaning, with constant input prices, that greater amounts of the fixed input, capital, correspond to greater levels of fixed costs. The variable cost component, VC, is also affected by the level at which capital, K, is fixed, a result that may not be readily apparent. However, recall that for most production processes, having more capital with which to work makes the variable input, labor, more productive. Therefore, doesn't it make sense that this increase in labor productivity will reduce its associated variable cost, *ceteris paribus*?

   We can further demonstrate the derivation of short-run total cost functions with a specific numerical example. Recall from Chapter 10, the production function

$$Q = 10K^{1/2}L^{1/2},$$

and the isocost equation

$$C = \overline{P}_{K,1}K + \overline{P}_{L,1}L,$$

for which $\overline{P}_{K,1} = \$40$ and $\overline{P}_{L,1} = \$10$. We can solve the production function for the amount of labor employed, L, as

$$L^{1/2} = \frac{Q}{10K^{1/2}} = 0.1QK^{-1/2},$$

or

$$L = 0.01Q^2K^{-1}.$$

Thus, the amount of labor used by the firm depends on its production of output, Q, and on the level of capital, K, it employs where, in the short run, this amount of K is fixed at some level. Substituting the above representation for L into the isocost equation yields

$$SRTC = C = \overline{P}_{K,1}K + \overline{P}_{L,1}(0.01Q^2K^{-1}),$$

and if $\overline{P}_{K,1} = \$40$ and $\overline{P}_{L,1} = \$10$ then

$$SRTC = C = 40K + 10(0.01\ Q^2K^{-1})$$
$$= 40K + 0.1Q^2K^{-1}. \tag{12.1}$$

Equation (12.1) represents the basis for a set of *SRTC* functions, where we can derive each specific *SRTC* function by fixing capital, K, at some specific value.

As an example, assume the firm's level of capital is fixed at $\overline{K}_1 = 4$ units. In this case, we derive the corresponding *SRTC* function by substituting this amount of capital into equation (12.1), yielding

$$SRTC^{\overline{K}_1} = C^{\overline{K}_1} = 40(4) + 0.1Q^2(4)^{-1}$$
$$= 160 + 0.025Q^2.$$

This equation represents the short-run total cost function for the firm, provided capital is fixed at $\overline{K}_1 = 4$ units, and we can relate it to the *LRTC* function derived in Chapter 11 using the same production function and input prices. Recall that this function was

$$LRTC = 4Q.$$

If the firm produces $Q = 80$ units of output, then

$$LRTC = 4(80) = \$320,$$

and

$$SRTC^{\overline{K}_1} = 160 + 0.025(80)^2 = \$320.$$

Thus, when the firm produces 80 units of output, $SRTC^{\overline{K}_1} = LRTC$. However, this equality between *SRTC* and *LRTC* occurs only when $Q = 80$ units, because to produce this level of output, the firm must combine *16* units of labor with the fixed *4* units of capital. As a result, this input mix corresponds to both a short-run and a long-run optimal input combination. In other words, for any short-run situation there exists one combination of inputs that turns out to be optimal. Thus, the associated short-run total cost for the level of output produced at this combination represents a constrained cost minimum and is therefore equal to the long-run total cost. You can verify the particular outcome in this case by reviewing the results of the constrained optimization problem for this example that we determined in Chapter 10.

If the firm produces some level of output other than $Q = 80$ units, the short- and long-run total costs will differ with $SRTC^{\overline{K}_1} > LRTC$ because the short-run costs will no longer correspond to a constrained cost minimization solution. For example, suppose the firm produces $Q = 100$ units of output while still holding K constant at $\overline{K}_1 = 4$ units of capital, then

$$SRTC^{\overline{K}_1} = 160 + 0.025(100)^2 = \$410$$

and

$$LRTC = 4Q = 4(100) = \$400.$$

Alternatively, assume the firm produces $Q = 60$ units of output, then

$$SRTC^{\overline{K}_1} = 160 + 0.025(60)^2 = \$250$$

and

$$LRTC = 4(60) = \$240.$$

As these computations indicate, $SRTC^{\overline{K}_1} > LRTC$, for values of Q other than $Q = 80$ units.

Note that we derived the above short-run total cost function for the amount of capital fixed at $\overline{K}_1 = 4$ units. If we fix the capital input at a different level, say $\overline{K}_2 = 5$ units, while holding input prices constant, then we must derive a new $SRTC$ function as

$$SRTC^{\overline{K}_2} = C^{\overline{K}_2} = \overline{P}_{K,1}\overline{K}_2 + \overline{P}_{L,1}L(Q,\overline{K}_2).$$

For our specific example, after substituting $\overline{P}_{K,1} = \$40$, $\overline{P}_{L,1} = \$10$, and $\overline{K}_2 = 5$ units, into equation (12.1), then

$$SRTC^{\overline{K}_2}= C^{\overline{K}_2} = 40(5) + 0.1Q^2(5)^{-1}$$
$$= 200 + 0.02Q^2.$$

Note that this increase in the amount of the fixed K alters both the fixed and variable cost components of the $SRTC$ function. We can show that the level of output for which $SRTC^{\overline{K}_2} = LRTC$ occurs at $Q = 100$ units since

$$SRTC^{\overline{K}_2} = 200 + 0.02(100)^2 = \$400$$

and

$$LRTC = 4(100) = \$400.$$

At this higher level of capital, $K_2 = 5$ units, $SRTC^{\overline{K}_2} = LRTC$ at a greater level of output, $Q = 100$ units, than when $\overline{K}_1 = 4$ and $SRTC^{\overline{K}_1} = LRTC$ at $Q = 80$ units. This is logical, because if capital is fixed at a higher level, such as $\overline{K}_2 = 5$ units $> \overline{K}_1 = 4$ units, then the firm must produce a greater level of output in order to use a level of labor pertaining to an optimal input combination. If the firm varies its production of output away from $Q = 100$ units, then $SRTC^{\overline{K}_2} > LRTC$, since the $SRTC$ levels no longer represent constrained cost minimums. You can verify this fact by substituting values for Q, other than $Q = 100$ units, into the $SRTC^{\overline{K}_2}$ and $LRTC$ functions and comparing the results.

As stated earlier, we can generate an entire set of $SRTC$ curves, one for each fixed level of capital, where for each $SRTC$ curve there is one level of output at which $SRTC = LRTC$. In addition, as we fix the level of capital at higher values, this equality occurs at respectively greater values of Q for each corresponding $SRTC$ curve. In fact, every point on the $LRTC$ curve corresponds to one point on some particular $SRTC$ curve. We can reaffirm this relationship between long-run and short-run total costs by deriving the $LRTC$ function directly from the set of $SRTC$ functions. Employing the specific example we used earlier, for which the production function was

$$Q = 10K^{1/2}L^{1/2}$$

and input prices were $\overline{P}_{K,1} = \$40$ and $\overline{P}_{L,1} = \$10$, recall that we derived equation (12.1) representing the basis for the set of $SRTC$ functions as

$$SRTC = C = 40K + 0.1Q^2K^{-1}.$$

We can determine the value of the fixed input, K, that minimizes $SRTC$ for any given level of Q by taking the partial derivative of $SRTC$ with respect to K and setting it equal to zero as

$$\frac{\partial SRTC}{\partial K} = 40 - 0.1Q^2K^{-2} = 0.$$

We solve this equation for K as

$$\frac{0.1Q^2}{K^2} = 40$$

$$K^2 = \frac{0.1Q^2}{40} = 0.0025Q^2,$$

or

$$K = 0.05Q.$$

Substituting this expression for K into equation (12.1) yields

$$SRTC = C = 40(0.05Q) + 0.1Q^2(0.05Q)^{-1}$$
$$= 2Q + 2Q = 4Q.$$

This equation represents the minimum values of $SRTC$ at which any given level of Q can be produced because the firm has chosen the optimal level of K, or plant size, in each case. Conceptually, this relationship also represents the long-run total cost, $LRTC$, and we can recognize the expression

$$C = 4Q$$

as the $LRTC$ function derived for this example in Chapter 11.

In Figure 12.1, we have illustrated the relationships between the two $SRTC$ functions, $SRTC^{\overline{K}_1}$ and $SRTC^{\overline{K}_2}$, and the $LRTC$ function, all of which have been derived from the production function

$$Q = 10K^{1/2}L^{1/2}.$$

Note that this particular $LRTC$ function is linear and, as with all $LRTC$ functions, begins at the origin, indicating that there are no fixed costs in the long run. The $SRTC^{\overline{K}_1}$ and $SRTC^{\overline{K}_2}$ curves, derived in this example, are quadratic functions possessing positive cost intercepts reflecting the corresponding fixed costs

$$\overline{P}_{K,1}\,\overline{K}_1 = \$40(4) = \$160$$

and

$$\overline{P}_{K,1}\,\overline{K}_2 = \$40(5) = \$200,$$

respectively. In addition, the $SRTC^{\overline{K}_1}$ curve, derived for $\overline{K}_1 = 4$ units, is tangent to the $LRTC$ curve at $Q_1 = 80$ units, indicating that $SRTC^{\overline{K}_1} = LRTC = \$320$ at this point due to the use of an optimal input combination. For any levels of output other than $Q_1 = 80$ units, with $\overline{K}_1 = 4$ units, $SRTC^{\overline{K}_1} > LRTC$ because the firm is now using suboptimal

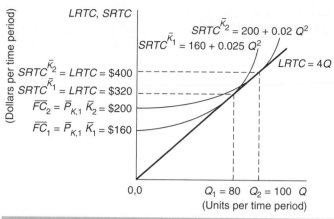

FIGURE 12.1 Relationships among Short-Run Total Cost Curves and Long-Run Total Cost Curve for $LRTC = 4Q$

input combinations in the short run. The $SRTC^{\overline{K}_2}$ curve derived for $\overline{K}_2 = 5$ units of capital, is tangent to the $LRTC$ curve at $Q_2 = 100$ units, indicating that $SRTC^{\overline{K}_2} = LRTC = \$400$, thus reflecting the use of another optimal input combination. In this case, for any levels of output other than $Q_2 = 100$ units, $SRTC^{\overline{K}_2} > LRTC$, again due to the use of suboptimal input combinations in the short run.

In Figure 12.1, we only illustrated two $SRTC$ curves. However, we can derive a different $SRTC$ curve for each level of the fixed input, K, generating an entire set of $SRTC$ curves as shown in Figure 12.2. Observe that each $SRTC$ curve is tangent to the $LRTC$ curve at only one output level, where the higher the K values, the greater is the Q value at which each $SRTC$ curve is tangent to the $LRTC$ curve. Our graphical depiction of the $SRTC$ curves and the $LRTC$ curve in Figure 12.2 illustrates the mathematical

FIGURE 12.2 Relationships among Quadratic Short-Run Total Cost Curves and Linear Long-Run Total Cost Curve

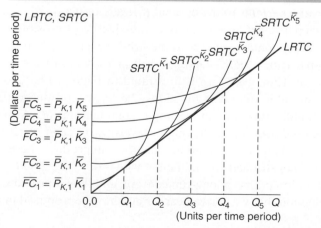

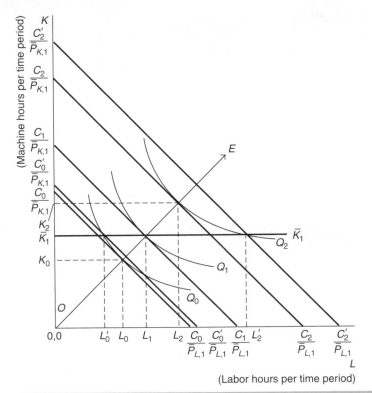

FIGURE 12.3 Derivation of Short-Run and Long-Run Total Cost Curves

relationship between these short- and long-run cost curves that we discussed earlier. Economists often describe the $LRTC$ curve as an envelope curve because it envelops an entire set of $SRTC$ curves. In fact, every point on the $LRTC$ curve represents a point on some $SRTC$ curve for which the input combination is optimal. In other words, the $LRTC$ curve pertains to the optimal K levels, or plant sizes, that enable the firm to produce each particular level of output at the least cost possible.

We can also apply graphical analysis to the firm's constrained optimization problem to derive any particular $SRTC$ curve, as well as to demonstrate its relationship with the $LRTC$ curve. This procedure is illustrated in Figures 12.3 and 12.4 for the more general case of cubic total cost functions. We have reproduced the expansion path in Figure 12.3, indicating the optimal input combinations (L_0, K_0), (L_1, K_1), and (L_2, K_2) that can be used to produce the output levels Q_0, Q_1, and Q_2, respectively. By employing these optimal input combinations, the firm can produce these output levels, Q_0, Q_1, and Q_2, at the constrained cost minimum values of C_0, C_1, and C_2, respectively. Recall that the expansion path is a long-run concept, and thus it provides the basis for the cubic $LRTC$ function that we derived earlier and have reproduced in Figure 12.4.

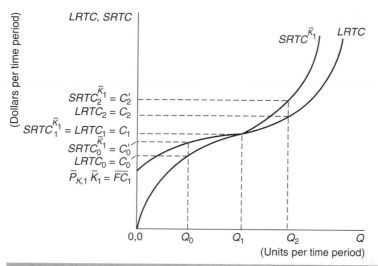

FIGURE 12.4 Relationship between Long-Run Total Cost and Short-Run Total Cost

Now assume a particular short-run situation for which capital is fixed at $\overline{K}_1$ units. If the firm chooses to produce $\overline{Q}_1$ units of output, it uses input combination $(L_1, \overline{K}_1)$ in both the short and long run. It incurs a total cost of C_1, which we represent in the numerator of the intercepts for the isocost equation

$$C_1 = \overline{P}_{K,1}K + \overline{P}_{L,1}L,$$

shown in Figure 12.3. At Q_1, $C_1 = SRTC^{\overline{K}_1} = LRTC_1$, as we can observe in Figure 12.4 by the fact that the two curves are tangent at this level of output. However, if the firm varies its output away from Q_1, the input combinations employed are different for the short- and long-run situations. Thus, the short- and long-run total costs are different as well.

For example, assume that the firm chooses to produce Q_2 amount of output, where $Q_2 > Q_1$. In the long run, it will use input combination (L_2, K_2) and incur a cost of C_2. However, in the short run the firm is not free to vary its capital, and as a result, it can only increase Q by using additional amounts of labor. Therefore, the firm produces Q_2 in the short run using input combination $(L'_2, \overline{K}_1)$, where $L'_2 > L_2$, and $K_1 < K_2$. The short-run cost associated with this input combination is C'_2, represented by the isocost equation passing through the intersection of the line representing $\overline{K}_1$ amount of capital and the isoquant representing Q_2 units of output. This short-run total cost, C'_2, exceeds the long-run total cost, C_2, associated with producing Q_2 units of output because the short-run input combination is no longer optimal. We can observe this result in Figure 12.3 by the fact that the isoquant representing Q_2 is not tangent to the isocost equation for C'_2. Instead, the two curves intersect at $(L'_2, \overline{K}_1)$, with the slope of the isoquant being greater (less negative) than the slope of the isocost equation.

Thus, at this input combination $MRTS < \overline{P}_{L,1}/\overline{P}_{K,1}$, violating the necessary condition for a constrained cost minimum we discussed in Chapter 10.

This result occurs in the short run because the firm cannot change its capital; therefore, it must produce Q_2 units of output using a suboptimally small amount of K and a suboptimally large amount of L, or $\overline{K}_1 < K_2$ and $L'_2 > L_2$. We have also demonstrated the resulting difference in costs in Figure 12.4 where we can observe that at Q_2, $C'_2 > C_2$, or $SRTC_2^{\overline{K}_2} > LRTC_2$. If the firm chooses to produce a level of output, say Q_0 where $Q_0 < Q_1$, we will once again observe that its short-run costs exceed its long-run costs. The firm produces Q_0 in the long run using an optimal input combination, $(L_0,K_0,)$, incurring costs of C_0. However, in the short run, with $K = \overline{K}_1$ units, the firm produces Q_0, using suboptimal input combination $(L'_0,\overline{K}_1)$, where $\overline{K}_1 > K_0$ and $L'_0 < L_0$. In this situation $MRTS > \overline{P}_{L,1}/\overline{P}_{K,1}$ because the firm is using too much capital and too little labor as compared to the optimal input combination (L_0,K_0). As a result, it incurs short-run costs of C'_0 that are greater than the associated long-run cost of C_0 at this level of output. We have demonstrated this outcome in Figure 12.3 by the higher isocost curve associated with C'_0, and also in Figure 12.4, where we can observe that $SRTC_0^{\overline{K}_1} > LRTC_0$. In summary, for $K = \overline{K}_1$ units of capital, $SRTC^{\overline{K}_1} > LRTC$ at all levels of output other than Q_1.

We have derived the particular $SRTC$ curve demonstrated in Figure 12.4 for the fixed level of capital, $\overline{K}_1$ units. If capital is held constant at a higher level, say $\overline{K}_2$ units, then we can derive another $SRTC$ curve exhibiting a higher vertical intercept value and a point of tangency with the $LRTC$ curve at a greater level of output. These results follow from the fact that higher K values yield higher fixed costs, $\overline{P}_{K,1}K$, and necessitate greater levels of output for which the input combination is optimal. As demonstrated earlier, we can derive an entire set of $SRTC$ curves, one for each value of K, with each $SRTC$ curve being tangent to the $LRTC$ curve at only one level of out-

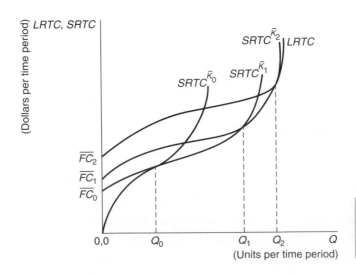

FIGURE 12.5 Relationships among Cubic Short-Run Total Cost Curves and Cubic Long-Run Total Cost Curve

put. This relationship between the set of *SRTC* curves and the *LRTC* curve is illustrated once again in Figure 12.5. In this case, we have assumed that the *SRTC* and *LRTC* curves possess the more common cubic shape.

Now, let's focus on any one *SRTC* curve in particular, say $SRTC^{\overline{K}_1}$. Recall that a firm's short-run total cost is equal to the summation of its fixed and variable cost components as

$$SRTC = FC + VC$$

or, if $K = \overline{K}_1$

$$SRTC^{\overline{K}_1} = \overline{P}_{K,1}\overline{K}_1 + VC(Q, \overline{P}_{L,1}, \overline{K}_1).$$

In Figure 12.6, we have represented the single cubic $SRTC^{\overline{K}_1}$, curve along with its fixed and variable component cost curves. As noted earlier, the *SRTC* curve possesses a positive vertical intercept equal to the firm's fixed cost, *FC*. The fixed cost in this case is $\overline{P}_{K,1}\,\overline{K}_1$, or the cost associated with the firm's fixed input, $\overline{K}_1$. Since *FC* does not vary with the firm's production of output, we represent it as a horizontal curve beginning at the vertical intercept, indicating that even if the firm shuts down production completely, it still incurs costs in the short run equal to the amount of its fixed cost. Variable costs, however, change as the firm alters its production of output. Should the firm shut down production, it logically uses no variable inputs and thus it incurs no variable costs. As a result, the firm's variable cost curve begins at the origin and always possesses a positive slope, indicating that this cost varies directly with the production of output. The fact that the *VC* curve in this example assumes a cubic shape follows from our assumption that the *SRTC* curve is cubic. Logically, any change in *SRTC* with respect to a change in output must reflect a similar change in the variable cost, since the fixed cost component of *SRTC* is constant. Thus, *SRTC* and *VC* curves are parallel to each other, separated vertically at any level of output by the value of the fixed cost.

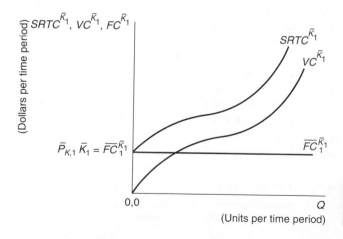

FIGURE 12.6 Short-Run Total Cost, Variable Cost, and Fixed Cost Curves

12.3 SHORT-RUN AVERAGE COSTS

As was the case for long-run costs, we frequently find it useful to express a firm's short-run costs in average, or per unit of output, terms. In general, the computation of average costs is a simple process that involves dividing the total costs by the level of output produced. Therefore, since

$$SRTC = FC + VC,$$

dividing each term by Q yields

$$\frac{SRTC}{Q} = \frac{FC}{Q} + \frac{VC}{Q}.$$

The term $SRTC/Q$ represents the **average total cost**, or **ATC**, defined as *a firm's short-run total cost per unit of output produced*. The term FC/Q represents the **average fixed cost**, or **AFC**, defined as *a firm's fixed cost per unit of output produced*. Finally, the term VC/Q is the **average variable cost**, or **AVC**, defined as *a firm's variable cost per unit of output produced*. Clearly, average total cost is equal to the summation of average fixed and average variable costs, or

$$ATC = AFC + AVC.$$

We can represent these average costs with curves that we derive graphically by determining the slopes of rays drawn from the origin to the respective total cost curve. In Figure 12.7 we have illustrated the derivation of the AFC curve, where the FC and AFC curves possess common horizontal axes representing Q. The FC curve described earlier is shown in panel (A), where it is represented by a horizontal line starting at the vertical intercept, indicating that fixed costs do not vary with the production of output. We have drawn the rays, OA, OB, and OC, from the origin to the $\overline{FC}_1$ curve at Q_1, Q_2, and Q_3 levels of output, respectively, where in general, the slope of each ray is equal to

$$\frac{\overline{FC}_1 - 0}{Q - 0} = AFC.$$

For example, at Q_1 the slope of the ray OA is

$$\frac{\overline{FC}_1 - 0}{Q_1 - 0} = \frac{\overline{FC}_1}{Q_1} = AFC_1,$$

where we have plotted this value in panel (B) as a point on the AFC curve. We can repeat this process at Q_2, Q_3, and so forth, until the entire AFC curve is constructed. Observe that the slopes of the rays OA, OB, and OC, drawn at Q_1, Q_2, and Q_3, respectively, become successively flatter, indicating successively declining slope, or AFC, values. More generally, the AFC curve forever declines with increasing values of Q, assuming the hyperbolic shape indicated by its formula, $AFC = \overline{FC}_1/Q$. Thus, although fixed cost is a constant value, average fixed cost is a decreasing function of output.

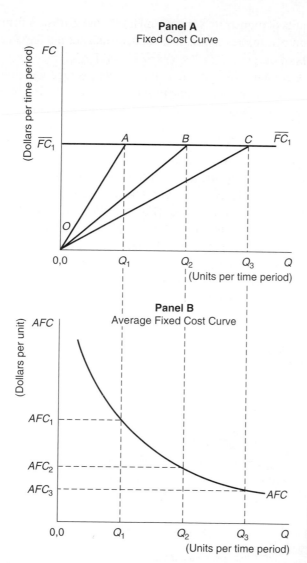

FIGURE 12.7 Derivation of Average Fixed Cost Curve from Fixed Cost Curve

As an example, assume a firm incurs $1000 in fixed costs, then for $Q_1 = 1$ unit of output

$$AFC_1 = \frac{\$1000}{1} = \$1000/\text{unit},$$

for $Q_2 = 2$ units

$$AFC_2 = \frac{\$1000}{2} = \$500/\text{unit},$$

for $Q_3 = 3$ units

$$AFC_3 = \frac{\$1000}{3} = \$333.33/\text{unit},$$

and so forth. These results demonstrate what we mean by the phrase, a firm is "spreading its fixed costs": it simply implies that a firm reduces its average fixed costs by producing greater amounts of output.

In Figure 12.8, we have illustrated the derivation of an average variable cost curve. We determine the values of AVC by computing the slopes of the rays drawn from the origin to the VC curve as shown in panel (A), where by definition these slopes are equal to

$$\frac{VC - 0}{Q - 0} = \frac{VC}{Q} = AVC.$$

Note that the rays OA, OB, and OC drawn from the origin to the VC curve at output levels Q_1, Q_2, and Q_3, respectively, become successively flatter indicating successively declining slope, or AVC values, as Q increases. Thus, the AVC curve we have plotted in panel (B) exhibits these declining values up to Q_3 units of output. Note that at Q_3 units the ray OC in panel (A) is also tangent to the VC curve. For increasing values of Q beyond Q_3, the rays from the origin to the VC curve, such as OD and OE, drawn at Q_4 and Q_5, respectively, become successively steeper, thus possessing successively higher slope, or AVC, values. In panel (B), observe that the AVC curve is increasing with increases in

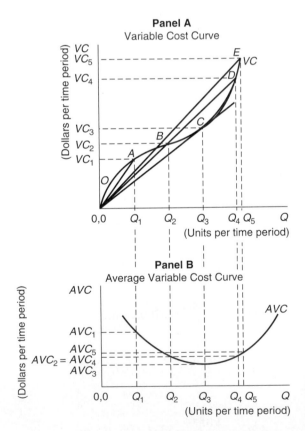

FIGURE 12.8 Derivation of Average Variable Cost Curve from Variable Cost Curve

Q beyond Q_3. In summary, provided the VC curve is cubic, the corresponding AVC curve is quadratic, or U-shaped, indicating that AVC declines for a range of increasing Q values, achieves a minimum, and rises thereafter with further increases in Q.

We can derive the average total cost curve directly from the $SRTC$ curve, or alternatively, by summing the component AFC and AVC curves that we have already established. The direct approach is illustrated in Figure 12.9, where we construct the ATC curve by once again determining the slopes of rays drawn from the origin to the corresponding total cost curve, which in this case is the $SRTC$ curve. In general, we compute the slopes of these rays as

$$\frac{SRTC - 0}{Q - 0} = ATC,$$

where you can observe in panel (A) that the rays OA, OB, OC, and OD drawn from the origin to the $SRTC$ curve at Q_1, Q_2, Q_3, and Q_4, respectively, become successively flatter, indicating the declining values for ATC that are demonstrated in panel (B). Note that at Q_4, the ray OD is also tangent to the $SRTC$ curve and that rays drawn to the $SRTC$ at successively increasing values of Q beyond Q_4, such as OE drawn at Q_5, become

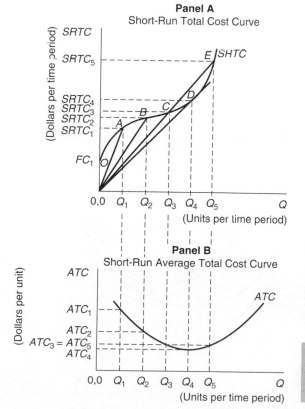

Panel A
Short-Run Total Cost Curve

Panel B
Short-Run Average Total Cost Curve

FIGURE 12.9 Derivation of Average Total Cost Curve from Short-Run Total Cost Curve

successively steeper, indicating increasing values of ATC. The ATC curve we have constructed in panel (B) is quadratic, or U-shaped, as was the AVC curve. However, since

$$ATC = AFC + AVC,$$

the ATC curve lies above the AVC curve for each value of Q. Also note that the ATC curve achieves a minimum value at a greater level of output, Q_4 than does the AVC curve that reaches a minimum value at Q_3.

We can reinforce this result by graphically deriving the ATC curve as the summation of the AFC and AVC curves as illustrated in Figure 12.10. In this figure we demonstrate the process of obtaining the ATC curve as a vertical summation of the two component curves, AFC and AVC. We achieve this result by determining the values of AFC and AVC at each level of Q and summing them to determine the corresponding value of ATC. Thus, at Q_3

$$ATC_3 = AFC_3 + AVC_3,$$

at Q_4

$$ATC_4 = AFC_4 + AVC_4,$$

and so forth. For increasing levels of output up to Q_3, observe that both AFC and AVC decline, and thus ATC declines as well. However, for levels of output greater than Q_3, when Q increases AFC declines while AVC rises. As a result, the net impact on ATC depends on which component changes by the greater amount. For example, as Q increases from Q_3 to Q_4, AFC declines by an amount greater than the increases in AVC and therefore, ATC decreases. As Q increases beyond Q_4, AVC rises more than AFC declines, and as a result ATC increases. In summary, the ATC curve achieves a minimum at a higher

FIGURE 12.10 Relationships among Average Total Cost, Average Variable Cost, and Average Fixed Cost Curves

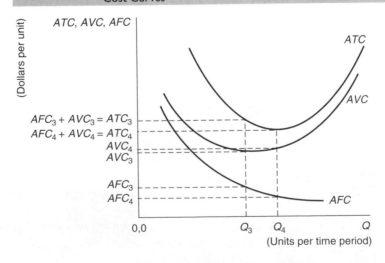

level of Q than does the AVC curve because the forever declining AFC more than off-sets the rising AVC for some range of Q. Specifically, this result occurs between Q_3 and Q_4 levels of output for the case we have illustrated in Figure 12.10.

12.4   SHORT-RUN MARGINAL COST

There is one more type of short-run cost that we can derive from the $SRTC$ function. It is known as **short-run marginal cost**, or **SRMC**, defined as *the change in a firm's short-run total cost due to a change in its production of output*. We can express this cost by a curve representing the derivative of the $SRTC$ function with respect to output, or

$$SRMC = \frac{dSRTC}{dQ} = \frac{d(FC + VC)}{dQ}.$$

Since, in the short run, we treat capital as fixed at some level, say $\overline{K}_1$, then

$$SRTC^{\overline{K}_1} = \overline{P}_{K,1}\overline{K}_1 + VC(Q, \overline{P}_{L,1}, \overline{K}_1),$$

and

$$SRMC^{\overline{K}_1} = \frac{dSRTC^{\overline{K}_1}}{dQ} = \frac{d\overline{P}_{K,1}\overline{K}_1}{dQ} + \frac{dVC(Q, \overline{P}_{L,1}, \overline{K}_1)}{dQ} = \frac{dVC(Q, \overline{P}_{L,1}, \overline{K}_1)}{dQ}.$$

Thus, $SRMC$ is the derivative, or slope, of either the $SRTC$ or the VC curve with respect to Q. This result is quite logical since the two curves are parallel to each other, possessing identical slopes at each value of Q.

We have illustrated the derivation of a $SRMC$ curve in Figure 12.11, where we compute the values for $SRMC$ as the slopes of the lines drawn tangent to either the $SRTC$ or the VC curve at various values of Q. Observe in panel (A) that the lines drawn tangent to the $SRTC$ curve, such as AA' and BB', and to the VC curve, such as AA'' and BB'', are respectively parallel to each other. We have drawn these lines tangent to both curves at Q_1 and Q_2, respectively, where the slopes of the tangents represent the $SRMC$ values at these levels of output. Since the tangents BB' and BB'', both drawn at Q_2, are flatter than the tangents AA' and AA'', drawn at Q_1, we can conclude that $SRMC_2 < SRMC_1$, as demonstrated by the declining portion of the $SRMC$ curve plotted in panel (B). Also, observe that Q_2 corresponds to the inflection points on the $SRTC$ and VC curves shown in panel (A), and as a result, the $SRMC$ curve achieves its minimum value at this level of output. For levels of output greater than Q_2, such as Q_3, Q_4, and Q_5, the lines drawn tangent to either the $SRTC$ or the VC curve become successively steeper, indicating that the corresponding values for $SRMC$ become successively greater. We have illustrated this result in panel (B) by the positively sloped portion of the $SRMC$ curve corresponding to values of Q that are greater than Q_2. In summary, a $SRMC$ curve derived from either a cubic $SRTC$ curve or its cubic VC component assumes a quadratic, or U-shape.

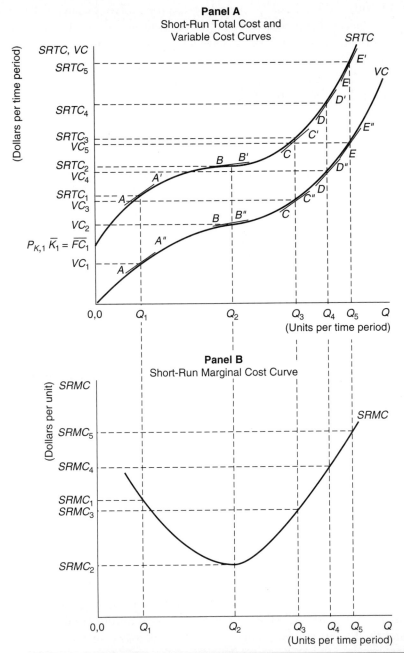

FIGURE 12.11 Derivation of Short-Run Marginal Cost Curve from Short-Run Total Cost or from Variable Cost Curve

12.5 RELATIONSHIPS AMONG SHORT-RUN AVERAGE AND MARGINAL COSTS

We can establish a relationship between the *SRMC* curve and both the *AVC* and *ATC* curves. Recall that we derive the *AVC* and *ATC* curves by determining the slopes of rays drawn from the origin to the *VC* and *SRTC* curves, respectively, at various levels of *Q*. This process was demonstrated in Figures 12.8 and 12.9, where we showed that the *AVC* and *ATC* curves achieve minimum values at output levels Q_3 and Q_4, respectively. At these output levels, the rays drawn from the origin to the respective *VC* and *SRTC* curves are also tangent to those curves. Also recall, as demonstrated in Figure 12.11, that we derive the *SRMC* curve by determining the slopes of lines drawn tangent to either the *VC* or *SRTC* curves at various levels of *Q*. Wherever a ray drawn from the origin to either the *VC* or the *SRTC* curve is also tangent to the respective curve, then its slope represents the value of both the average and marginal functions at that corresponding level of output. Thus, at Q_3 units of output, *SRMC* = *AVC*, and at Q_4 units, *SRMC* = *ATC*. Also, note that these equalities occur at the levels of output corresponding to the minimum values, AVC_3 and ATC_4, of the respective average cost curves.

We can also mathematically prove that short-run marginal costs are equal to average variable and average total costs at their respective minimum values. To do so, we take the derivative of each of these average cost functions with respect to output, set the result equal to zero, and solve for the respective values of *Q* that minimize *AVC* and *ATC*. Since we define *AVC* as

$$AVC = \frac{VC}{Q}$$

and *VC* as

$$VC = VC(Q,\overline{P}_{L,1},\overline{K}_1),$$

then

$$AVC = VC(Q,\overline{P}_{L,1},\overline{K}_1)Q^{-1}.$$

Taking the derivative of this function with respect to *Q* and setting the result equal to zero yields

$$\frac{dAVC}{dQ} = VC(Q,\overline{P}_{L,1},\overline{K}_1)\frac{dQ^{-1}}{dQ} + Q^{-1}\frac{dVC(Q,\overline{P}_{L,1},\overline{K}_1)}{dQ} = 0$$

$$= -VC(Q,\overline{P}_{L,1},\overline{K}_1)Q^{-2} + Q^{-1}\frac{dVC(Q,\overline{P}_{L,1},\overline{K}_1)}{dQ} = 0.$$

Multiplying both sides of this equation by *Q* results in

$$-VC(Q,\overline{P}_{L,1},\overline{K}_1)Q^{-1} + \frac{dVC(Q,\overline{P}_{L,1},\overline{K}_1)}{dQ} = 0$$

or

$$\frac{dVC(Q,\overline{P}_{L,1},\overline{K}_1)}{dQ} = \frac{VC(Q,\overline{P}_{L,1},\overline{K}_1)}{Q}.$$

We can recognize the terms on the left- and right-hand sides of this equality as the *SRMC* and *AVC* functions, respectively.[1] As an exercise, it is left to you to apply a similar procedure to demonstrate that *SRMC* = *ATC*, after minimizing the *ATC* function with respect to *Q*.

We have illustrated the relationships among the *SRMC*, *AVC*, and *ATC* curves in Figure 12.12. Observe that the *SRMC* curve intersects the *AVC* and *ATC* curves at their minimum values corresponding to Q_3 and Q_4, respectively. Also note that *SRMC* < *AVC*, as *AVC* decreases with increases in *Q*. Similarly, *SRMC* < *ATC*, as *ATC* declines with increases in *Q*. The rationale for these results is the same as the one discussed in Chapter 11. Recall that whenever the increments to *VC* and *SRTC* are less than their corresponding average costs, the average costs must decrease with increases in *Q*. Conversely, we have also demonstrated in Figure 12.12 that whenever *SRMC* exceeds either *AVC* or *ATC*, then that corresponding average cost rises with increases in *Q*.

We can demonstrate the derivation of *AFC*, *AVC*, *ATC*, and *SRMC* curves, along with their associated relationships, with a specific example. Assume that, for a particular fixed level of capital, a firm's *SRTC* curve is

$$SRTC = 8 + 3Q - 1.5Q^2 + 0.25Q^3.$$

Thus, the firm's fixed costs, *FC*, or those costs that do not vary with output, *Q*, are

$$FC = \$8$$

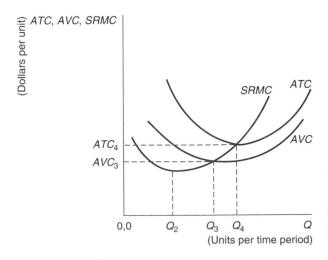

FIGURE 12.12 Relationships among Average Total Cost, Average Variable Cost, and Short-Run Marginal Cost Curves

---

[1]We are assuming that the second-order condition for a minimum is fulfilled, specifically, $d^2AVC/dQ^2 > 0$.

and the variable costs, or those costs that vary with output, are represented by the function

$$VC = 3Q - 1.5Q^2 + 0.25Q^3.$$

We derive the firm's average fixed and average variable cost curves as

$$AFC = \frac{FC}{Q} = \frac{8}{Q} = 8Q^{-1}$$

and

$$AVC = \frac{VC}{Q} = \frac{3Q - 1.5Q^2 + 0.25Q^3}{Q} = 3 - 1.5Q + 0.25Q^2.$$

To compute the average total cost curve, we sum these two component curves as

$$ATC = AFC + AVC$$

or

$$ATC = 8Q^{-1} + 3 - 1.5Q + 0.25Q^2.$$

Finally, the associated short-run marginal cost curve is

$$SRMC = \frac{dSRTC}{dQ} = \frac{dVC}{dQ} = 3 - 3Q + 0.75Q^2.$$

We can compute the level of output at which the *AVC* curve achieves its minimum value by taking the derivative of *AVC* with respect to Q, setting this derivative equal to zero, and solving for Q as

$$\frac{dAVC}{dQ} = -1.5 + 0.50Q = 0$$

or

$$Q = \frac{1.5}{0.50} = 3 \text{ units.}$$

Furthermore, at this level of Q

$$AVC = 3 - 1.5(3) + 0.25(3)^2 = \$0.75/\text{unit.}$$

Alternatively, since *SRMC* = *AVC* when *AVC* reaches its minimum value, we can compute these same results by equating the *SRMC* and *AVC* curves and solving for Q as

$$3 - 3Q + 0.75Q^2 = 3 - 1.5Q + 0.25Q^2$$
$$0.50Q^2 = 1.5Q$$
$$0.50Q = 1.5$$
$$Q = \frac{1.5}{0.50} = 3 \text{ units.}$$

The value of *SRMC* is therefore

$$SRMC = 3 - 3(3) + 0.75(3)^2 = \$0.75,$$

which is the same value that we computed for *AVC* at $Q = 3$ units of output.

We can also demonstrate that *SRMC* = *ATC* at the level of output where the *ATC* curve achieves its minimum value as

$$\frac{dATC}{dQ} = -8Q^{-2} - 1.5 + 0.50Q = 0,$$

or after multiplying both sides by Q^2

$$-8 - 1.5Q^2 + 0.50Q^3 = 0$$
$$0.50Q^3 - 1.5Q^2 = 8$$
$$0.50Q^2(Q - 3) = 8$$
$$Q^2(Q - 3) = 16,$$

and therefore

$$Q = 4 \text{ units.}$$

At this level of output, *ATC* achieves its minimum value of

$$ATC = 8(4)^{-1} + 3 - 1.5(4) + 0.25(4)^2 = \$3/\text{unit.}$$

We can derive these same results by applying the condition that *SRMC* = *ATC* when *ATC* achieves its minimum value, thus

$$3 - 3Q + 0.75Q^2 = 8Q^{-1} + 3 - 1.5Q + 0.25Q^2$$
$$0.50Q^2 - 1.5Q = \frac{8}{Q}$$
$$0.50Q^3 - 1.5Q^2 = 8$$
$$0.50Q^2(Q - 3) = 8$$
$$Q^2(Q - 3) = 16$$
$$Q = 4 \text{ units.}$$

The value of *SRMC* at $Q = 4$ units is

$$SRMC = 3 - 3(4) + 0.75(4)^2 = \$3,$$

the same value as *ATC* at this level of output. Note that the *ATC* curve reaches its minimum value at a greater level of output, 4 units, than does the *AVC* curve that achieves a minimum value at 3 units of output.

In Table 12.1, we have shown the values and relationships associated with various short-run costs for the *SRTC* function

$$SRTC = 8 + 3Q - 1.5Q^2 + 0.25Q^3,$$

corresponding to several levels of output. We can identify many characteristics associated with the different types of costs using the data presented in this table. For example, observe that the value of *AFC* continuously declines with increases in output.

TABLE 12.1 Various Short-Run Costs Generated from the Short-Run Total Cost Function, $SRTC = 8 + 3Q - 1.5Q^2 + 0.25Q^3$

Q	SRTC	FC	VC	AFC	AVC	ATC	SRMC
0	$8.00	$8.00	$ 0	$—	$—	$—	$—
1	9.75	8.00	1.75	8.00	1.75	9.75	1.75
2	10.00	8.00	2.00	4.00	1.00	5.00	0.25
3	10.25	8.00	2.25	2.67	0.75	3.42	0.25
4	12.00	8.00	4.00	2.00	1.00	3.00	1.75
5	16.75	8.00	8.75	1.60	1.75	3.35	4.75
6	26.00	8.00	18.00	1.60	3.00	4.33	9.25
7	41.25	8.00	33.25	1.14	4.75	5.89	15.25

Also observe that the *AVC* and *ATC* values decline with increases in output until they achieve their minimum values at $Q = 3$ units and $Q = 4$ units, respectively, and increase thereafter with further increases in output. It is important that we make a clarification regarding the *SRMC* values shown in this table. Note that the values of *SRMC* are not identical to those we computed earlier using calculus. For example, at $Q = 3$ units, $SRMC = \$0.25$ in the table, where earlier it was shown that $SRMC = AVC = \$0.75$/unit at this level of output. This discrepancy occurs because in the table we computed *SRMC* for finite, one-unit changes in output, or $SRMC = \Delta SRTC/\Delta Q = \Delta VC/\Delta Q$, whereas using calculus we computed these values for infinitesimally small changes in output, or

$$SRMC = \frac{dSRTC}{dQ} = \frac{dVC}{dQ}.$$

12.6 RELATIONSHIPS AMONG SHORT-RUN PRODUCT CURVES AND SHORT-RUN COST CURVES

We can further explain the conceptual rationale underlying the shapes of many short-run cost curves by directly linking the *SRMC* and *AVC* curves to the MP_L and AP_L curves discussed in Chapter 8. For the production function containing two inputs, capital and labor, we treat one of these inputs, usually capital, as fixed in the short run. As a result, we will focus our short-run production analysis on the marginal and average product functions for labor, MP_L and AP_L, respectively. In Chapter 8 we demonstrated in Figure 8.10, that, for the particular production function underlying our analysis, increases in labor use cause the value of the MP_L to increase up to L_2 units, at which MP_L achieves a maximum and then diminishes thereafter. We also demonstrated in this figure that for increases in labor use, the value of the AP_L increases up to L_3 units of labor, at which AP_L reaches a maximum and then declines thereafter. We base our rationale for these increases and decreases in MP_L and AP_L on the amount of the variable input, labor, that is used relative to the fixed input, capital. If a firm is using a small amount of labor relative to its fixed capital, then employing additional amounts of labor causes the MP_L to rise. Conversely, if the firm uses a large amount of labor relative to its fixed capital, then additional units of labor cause the MP_L to diminish. We also explained in Chapter 8 that for increases in labor use, if $MP_L > AP_L$, then AP_L increases, while if $MP_L < AP_L$, then AP_L decreases.

Since short-run cost theory is based on short-run production theory, we can apply our rationale for explaining the behavior of the MP_L and AP_L curves to short-run cost behavior as well. Specifically, we can relate the MP_L and AP_L functions to the $SRMC$ and AVC functions. Although we can link these two cost functions in terms of output, it is also possible for us to express them in terms of the variable input, L. This result follows because in the short run, the only way a firm can vary its production of output is by altering the amount of the variable input, L, it uses.

We can derive a formula demonstrating the relationship between $SRMC$ and MP_L as follows. Recall that

$$SRMC = \frac{dSRTC}{dQ} = \frac{dVC}{dQ},$$

and we can define variable cost, VC, as the product of the variable input price and the amount of the variable input employed as

$$VC = \overline{P}_{L,1}L.$$

Therefore,

$$SRMC = \frac{dVC}{dQ} = \frac{d\overline{P}_{L,1}L}{dQ} = \overline{P}_{L,1}\frac{dL}{dQ}.$$

Since $MP_L = dQ/dL$, once K is held constant, the term dL/dQ is the reciprocal of the MP_L, and therefore, we can express $SRMC$ as

$$SRMC = \overline{P}_{L,1}\left(\frac{1}{MP_L}\right) = \frac{\overline{P}_{L,1}}{MP_L}. \tag{12.2}$$

Equation (12.2) demonstrates that a firm's $SRMC$ is simply the monetized reciprocal of the marginal product of labor, and thus the $SRMC$ and MP_L are inversely related.

We have illustrated this relationship in panels (A) and (B) of Figure 12.13, where both the MP_L and $SRMC$ are plotted as functions of the amount of labor employed.

In a sense, the two curves are mirror images of each other, indicating that, as a firm employs additional amounts of labor up to L_2 units, then as MP_L increases, $SRMC$ correspondingly decreases. This result is intuitively logical, since the reason MP_L increases is that the firm is using successively more efficient input combinations. As a result, we expect the associated marginal costs to decline. Also observe that as MP_L achieves a maximum at L_2 units of labor, $SRMC$ reaches its minimum value at L_2. Finally, as MP_L diminishes with increases in labor use beyond L_2, $SRMC$ rises.

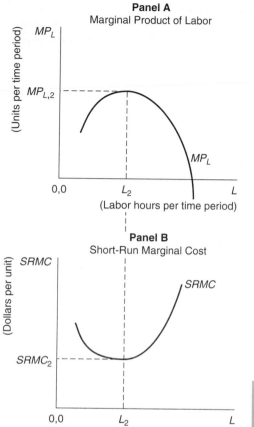

FIGURE 12.13 Relationship between Marginal Product of Labor and Short-Run Marginal Cost

We can also derive a formula demonstrating the relationship between AVC and AP_L. Recall that

$$AVC = \frac{VC}{Q},$$

and because $VC = \overline{P}_{L,1}L$, then

$$AVC = \frac{\overline{P}_{L,1}L}{Q} = \overline{P}_{L,1}\left(\frac{L}{Q}\right).$$

Since $AP_L = Q/L$, we can recognize the term L/Q as the reciprocal of AP_L, and therefore

$$AVC = \overline{P}_{L,1}\frac{1}{AP_L} = \frac{\overline{P}_{L,1}}{AP_L}. \tag{12.3}$$

Thus, we can describe the AVC as the monetized reciprocal of the AP_L, and clearly equation (12.3) indicates an inverse relationship between them. We have illustrated this relationship in Figure 12.14, where the AP_L and AVC curves are plotted as functions of L in panels (A) and (B), respectively. Observe that the AVC and AP_L curves effectively mirror each other, reflecting the fact that as AP_L rises with increases in labor use up to L_3 units, AVC declines. As AP_L achieves a maximum value at L_3 units of labor, AVC reaches its minimum value. Finally, as additional amounts of labor are employed beyond L_3 units, AP_L decreases, and AVC correspondingly increases.

We can also demonstrate these relationships between $SRMC$ and MP_L, and between AVC and AP_L with a mathematical example. Recall the production function

$$Q = 10K^{1/2}L^{1/2},$$

and assume a short-run situation for which capital is fixed at $\overline{K}_1 = 4$ units and the price of labor is $\overline{P}_{L,1} = \$10$. The total product of labor curve is

$$TP_L = Q = f(\overline{K}_1, L) = 10(4)^{1/2}L^{1/2} = 20L^{1/2},$$

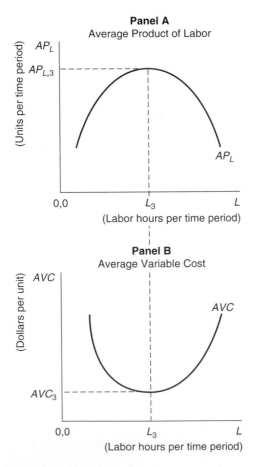

Panel A
Average Product of Labor

Panel B
Average Variable Cost

FIGURE 12.14 Relationship between Average Product of Labor and Average Variable Cost

and thus the marginal product of labor function is

$$MP_L = \frac{dTP_L}{dL} = \frac{dQ}{dL} = 10L^{-1/2} = \frac{10}{L^{1/2}}.$$

Using equation (12.2), we can represent the short-run marginal cost function as

$$SRMC = \overline{P}_{L,1}\left(\frac{1}{MP_L}\right) = \overline{P}_{L,1}\frac{1}{\dfrac{10}{L^{1/2}}} = \frac{\overline{P}_{L,1}L^{1/2}}{10}$$

and if $\overline{P}_{L,1} = \$10$, then

$$SRMC = \frac{10L^{1/2}}{10} = L^{1/2}.$$

If the amount of labor employed is initially $L_1 = 1$ unit, and is subsequently increased to $L_2 = 4$ units, then the respective values of the marginal product of labor are

$$MP_{L,1} = \frac{10}{1^{1/2}} = 10 \text{ units of output}$$

and

$$MP_{L,2} = \frac{10}{4^{1/2}} = 5 \text{ units of output.}$$

Note that for the type of production function we have used in this problem, the MP_L always diminishes with increases in the amount of labor used. Accordingly, in this case, short-run marginal costs always increase with increases in labor use, once again reflecting the inverse relationship between $SRMC$ and MP_L. Thus, for our selected labor values of $L_1 = 1$ unit and $L_2 = 4$ units

$$SRMC_1 = L^{1/2} = 1^{1/2} = \$1$$

and

$$SRMC_2 = 4^{1/2} = \$2.$$

We can compute the average product of labor function from the TP_L curve associated with $\overline{K}_1 = 4$ units as

$$AP_L = \frac{TP_L}{L} = \frac{20L^{1/2}}{L} = 20L^{-1/2} = \frac{20}{L^{1/2}}.$$

We derive the AVC curve in this case by substituting this representation for AP_L into equation (12.3) as

$$AVC = \overline{P}_{L,1}\frac{1}{AP_L} = \overline{P}_{L,1}\frac{1}{\dfrac{20}{L^{1/2}}} = \frac{\overline{P}_{L,1}L^{1/2}}{20},$$

and since $\overline{P}_{L,1} = \$10$,

$$AVC = \frac{10L^{1/2}}{20} = \frac{L^{1/2}}{2}.$$

By substituting increasing values for L into these AP_L and AVC functions, you can verify that successive values of AP_L decrease while successive values of AVC increase.

12.7 RELATIONSHIPS AMONG LONG-RUN AND SHORT-RUN AVERAGE AND MARGINAL COSTS

In Section 12.2, we described the long-run total cost curve as an envelope curve. This concept indicates that each $(Q,LRTC)$ point on the $LRTC$ curve corresponds to one $(Q,SRTC)$ point on a particular $SRTC$ curve from a set of $SRTC$ curves. For both the long- and short-run cases, the conversion from total to average cost consists of dividing the corresponding total cost by the level of output. Therefore

$$LRAC = \frac{LRTC}{Q}$$

and

$$ATC = \frac{SRTC}{Q},$$

indicating that the process of deriving these average costs is simply a matter of recalibrating the long- and short-run costs into per unit of output terms. Furthermore, this process does not alter the conceptual relationship between long- and short-run costs. Therefore, just as the $LRTC$ curve is the envelope of the set of $SRTC$ curves, the $LRAC$ is the envelope of the corresponding set of ATC curves, where each ATC curve is derived for one fixed level of capital, K.

We have illustrated the relationship between a $LRAC$ curve and its associated set of ATC curves, along with their respective $LRMC$ and $SRMC$ curves, in Figure 12.15. In this figure, we have presented only three ATC curves, one for each fixed level of capital, K, where $\overline{K}_2 > \overline{K}_1 > \overline{K}_0$. However, there are an infinite number of values at which we can fix the level of capital, and thus there exist an infinite number of associated ATC curves. Observe in Figure 12.15 that each ATC curve is tangent to the $LRAC$ curve at a particular level of output, where this level of output is different for each ATC curve. Each of these points of tangency pertains to levels of output that are produced by employing an optimal input combination in each short-run situation, reflected by a respective ATC curve. In fact, every point on the $LRAC$ curve, each of which reflect the use of an optimal input combination, pertains to a point on some particular ATC curve, each of which is derived for a particular level of the fixed input, capital.

For example, if we fix capital at $\overline{K}_0$ units, then we can represent the corresponding average total cost by the curve $ATC^{\overline{K}_0}$. If the firm chooses to produce Q_0 units of output, $ATC_0^{\overline{K}_0} = LRAC_0$, since at this level of output the amount of labor employed,

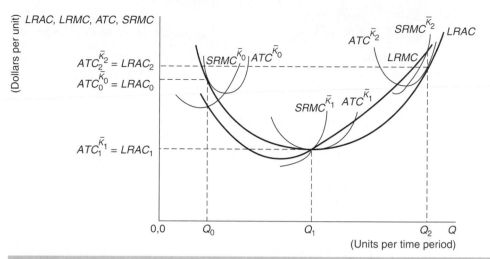

FIGURE 12.15 Relationships among Long-Run and Short-Run Average and Marginal Cost Curves

combined with the fixed level of capital, $\overline{K}_0$, represents an optimal input combination. For any level of output other than Q_0, $ATC^{\overline{K}_0} > LRAC$ because, in the short run, the input combination used to produce Q is no longer optimal. If we fix capital at a different level, say $\overline{K}_1$ units, where $\overline{K}_1 > \overline{K}_0$, we represent the corresponding average total cost by the curve $ATC^{\overline{K}_1}$. In this case, the optimal input combination occurs at Q_1 units of output, and accordingly $ATC_1^{\overline{K}_1} = LRAC_1$ at this point. For a level of output other than Q_1, $ATC^{\overline{K}_1} > LRAC$. If we set capital at $\overline{K}_2$ units, the optimal input combination occurs at Q_2 units, and $ATC_2^{\overline{K}_2} = LRAC_2$ at this level of output. Logically, the higher the value of K, the greater is the level of Q at which $ATC = LRAC$. This is because the greater the K value, or plant size, the greater is the amount of labor needed to make the input combination optimal.

Figure 12.15 illustrates some additional characteristics and relationships. Note that the $LRAC$ is U-shaped, reflecting increasing returns to scale as the production of output increases to Q_1 units, and decreasing returns to scale as output increases beyond Q_1 units. Thus, the minimum value for $LRAC$ occurs at Q_1 units, where the firm is using $\overline{K}_1$ units of capital and $ATC_1^{\overline{K}_1} = LRAC_1$, reflecting the most cost-efficient plant size, $\overline{K}_1$, in the long run. Why is this so? The answer is that the firm is using the optimal input combination to produce a level of output that enables it to realize all cost advantages associated with increasing returns to scale. Yet at this level of Q the firm is not producing so much output that it experiences the cost disadvantages associated with decreasing returns to scale.

In Figure 12.15 we have also included the long- and short-run marginal cost curves. As we described earlier, the $LRMC$ curve intersects the $LRAC$ at its minimum value, and each $SRMC$ curve intersects its respective ATC curve at its minimum value. Also note that each $SRMC$ curve intersects the $LRMC$ curve at output values corresponding to the points of tangency between each respective ATC curve and the $LRAC$

Economies of Scale and Negative Externalities in Swine Production

The face of agriculture in the United States has changed significantly over the past 50 years. Through improved technology and higher capital requirements, the trend in agricultural production for several decades has been toward both increased specialization and size of operation. The number of farms in the United States decreased from approximately 5.6 million in 1950 to 2.2 million by 1998, while the size of a typical farm increased.[2]

This trend has been most apparent in the swine industry, where since 1970, with only a slight decline in the total number of hogs raised, the number of small hog farms has declined by nearly 70%. In one of the largest swine-producing states, North Carolina, over 80% of all hogs are raised on large-scale farms, each with more than 2000 animals. In Iowa, some 4000 small hog farmers exited the business in 1994 alone. These small swine producers have been replaced by the introduction of large-scale mega producers raising as many as 320,000 piglets per year.[3]

The foremost reason underlying this trend is the large economies of scale associated with the industry. Swine production can take place within several different types of systems or facilities, ranging from pasture facilities where hogs have little shelter, to systems in which hogs are totally confined, or enclosed in buildings. These total confinement systems are very capital-intensive. As we have noted, one of the major reasons underlying economies of scale is that as a firm's scale of operation expands, it is often accompanied by qualitative improvements in the capital employed in the production process. This, in turn, leads to lower long-run costs per unit of output produced. In the case of swine production, larger producers who undertake the greater capital requirements involved with the total confinement system are able to realize the advantages this system provides due largely to having greater control over the hogs' environment. A confinement system enables the producer to take greater advantage of efficiency in animal health and feeding, and improved animal genetics, as well as increased mechanization. As a result, large-scale hog producers are able to achieve production and cost advantages that smaller producers cannot.

There is an additional issue surrounding large-scale swine production. Raising a very large number of pigs in a relatively small area creates a problem regarding the inevitable byproduct, namely manure. For smaller operations, the manure is simply spread on surrounding fields and serves as a valuable fertilizer. However, in the case of larger scale operations, often too much manure is created for the surrounding croplands to absorb, thus leading to the possible pollution of local streams and water tables from the runoff generated. In addition, the concentration of so much manure creates an offensive odor to which many area residents are subjected. In the jargon of economics, this manure disposal problem is an example of a negative externality. Unless the producer properly disposes of the manure, the social cost of swine production will exceed the private cost, resulting in an overproduction of the good. As a result, some states have passed laws requiring large livestock facilities to develop state-approved plans for disposing of their manure. Ultimately, the cost of disposing of this manure, once fully borne by the producer, may counteract some of the economies of scale advantages mentioned earlier and reduce the optimal size of swine production operations.

---

[2]"True Grit," *The Economist*, August 28, 1999, pp. 21–22.
[3]"Stink, Inc. Pig-farming," *The Economist*, September 2, 1995, pp. 23–24.

curve. Thus, for each fixed value of K, the corresponding $SRMC$ is equal to $LRMC$ at output levels for which the input combinations are optimal for each respective short-run situation, as well as for the long run.

These results can be explained by returning to Figure 12.5, where we can observe that each $SRTC$ curve is tangent to the $LRTC$ curve at the same output levels for which each corresponding ATC curve is tangent to the $LRAC$ curve in Figure 12.15. Recall that the slope values of the $LRTC$ and $SRTC$ curves at each level of output are represented by the corresponding values of $LRMC$ and $SRMC$, respectively. As a result, wherever a particular $SRTC$ curve is tangent to the $LRTC$ curve, the slopes of each of these curves are equal and the corresponding $SRMC$ is equal to the $LRMC$. In Figure 12.5, observe that $SRTC^{\overline{K}_0}$ is tangent to $LRTC$ at Q_0, $SRTC^{\overline{K}_1}$ is tangent to $LRTC$ at Q_1, and $SRTC^{\overline{K}_2}$ is tangent to $LRTC$ at Q_2. As a result, as we have demonstrated in Figure 12.15,

$$SRMC^{\overline{K}_0} = LRMC, \quad SRMC^{\overline{K}_1} = LRMC, \quad \text{and} \quad SRMC^{\overline{K}_2} = LRMC$$

at these same values of output, Q_0, Q_1, and Q_2, respectively. Furthermore, these are the same levels of output at which $ATC^{\overline{K}_0} = LRAC$, $ATC^{\overline{K}_1} = LRAC$, and $ATC^{\overline{K}_2} = LRAC$, respectively. The development and discussion of these relationships among the various types of cost functions may seem very meticulous at this point. However, it is necessary that we establish a good understanding of cost theory before broader models of firm behavior can be developed. In the next five chapters we will employ the various cost functions discussed in this chapter, along with the demand and revenue functions we established earlier, to develop distinct models of firm behavior.

12.8   SUMMARY

Our focus in this chapter has been on the various costs incurred by a firm when producing a good or service in the short run, a time period during which at least one of the firm's inputs remains fixed. We have devoted particular attention to analyzing the relationships among the different types of short-run costs, as well as their relationships to long-run costs. The key topics covered in this chapter are as follows.

- A short-run total cost function expresses a firm's costs as a function of its level of output, while holding at least one input and all input prices constant.
- A firm's short-run total cost equals the summation of its fixed and variable costs.
- There exists an entire set of short-run total cost curves, one for each fixed level of capital, where for each short-run total cost curve there is one level of output at which short-run total cost equals long-run total cost.
- Dividing each of the components in a firm's short-run total cost function by the level of output it produces enables us to derive short-run average costs, where the firm's average total cost is equal to the summation of its average fixed cost and average variable cost.

- A firm's short-run marginal cost function measures the change in either a firm's short-run total cost or variable cost, resulting from a change in its level of production.
- If a firm's short-run total cost function is cubic, then its associated average total, average variable, and marginal cost curves are quadratic, or U-shaped. In addition, the short-run marginal cost curve intersects the average total and average variable cost curves at their respective minimum values.
- We can express the short-run marginal cost as the monetized reciprocal of the marginal product of the variable input. Similarly, we can express the average variable cost as the monetized reciprocal of the average product of the variable input.
- The long-run average cost curve is the envelope of the corresponding set of average total cost curves, where we derive each *ATC* curve for a fixed level of capital. In addition, the *SRMC* curves intersect the *LRMC* curve at output levels for which the respective *ATC* curves are tangent to the *LRAC* curve.

KEY TERMS

- average fixed cost, page 300
- average total cost, page 300
- average variable cost, page 300
- short-run marginal cost, page 305
- short-run total cost function, page 289

EXERCISES

12.1 A firm's short-run total cost function is generally specified as

$$SRTC = \text{SRTC}(Q),$$

and its short-run marginal cost function is generalized as

$$SRMC = SRMC(Q) = \frac{dSRTC}{dQ},$$

where $SRTC$ = short-run total cost in dollars per year
Q = output produced in units per year
$SRMC$ = short-run marginal cost in dollars per year.

Assume that the above functions possess the following properties:
i. When $Q = 0$; $SRTC = 50$, $SRMC > 0$, and $dSRMC/dQ < 0$.
ii. When $0 < Q < 25$; $SRTC > 50$, $SRMC > 0$, and $dSRMC/dQ < 0$.
iii. When $Q = 25$; $SRTC > 50$, $SRMC > 0$, and $dSRMC/dQ = 0$.
iv. When $Q > 25$; $SRTC > 50$, $SRMC > 0$, and $dSRMC/dQ > 0$.

a. Using the preceding information, accurately sketch the firm's total, marginal, and fixed cost functions, each in a separate graph, one beneath the other.

b. For the total cost, identify the ranges of Q over which the function is convex, concave, and also identify any inflection points.

c. At what level of output is $SRMC$ minimized? State a rationale for your response.

12.2 Refer to the following table of total costs for a firm producing chocolate truffles.

Q	TC
0	$ 25
1	45
2	53
3	55
4	57
4.5	59.875
5	65
6	85
7	123

a. Do the data in this table represent long-run or short-run total costs? Explain your response.

b. Using the data in the table, append additional columns to the table and compute FC, VC, ATC, AFC and AVC for the chocolate truffle producer.

12.3 Refer to the data, as well as your answers, for Exercise 12.2.

a. Plot TC and FC in the same graph.

b. Beneath the graph of TC and FC, plot ATC and AVC together in a graph.

12.4 The total cost function for a firm producing titanium golf clubs is given as

$$SRTC(Q) = 8Q^2 + 100.$$

a. Determine the firm's variable cost function, $VC = VC(Q)$.

b. Determine the firm's fixed cost function, FC.

c. Determine the firm's average total cost function, $ATC = ATC(Q)$.

d. Determine the firm's average variable cost function, $AVC = AVC(Q)$.

e. Determine the firm's average fixed cost function, $AFC = AFC(Q)$.

f. Determine the firm's short run marginal cost function, $SRMC = MC(Q)$.

12.5 Using the total cost function from Exercise 12.4 and the various cost functions you computed in parts a–f of that problem, complete the following cost table for the titanium golf club producer.

Quantity of Titanium Golf Clubs Produced	SRTC	VC	FC	AFC	AVC	ATC	SRMC
0	$	$	$	$	$	$	$
5							
10							
20							
35							
50							
75							
100							

12.6 A firm's production function is given as

$$Q = f(K,L) = 10K^{1/2}L^{1/2},$$

and its isocost equation is

$$C = \overline{P}_{K,1}K + \overline{P}_{L,1}L.$$

a. Using this production function, express the amount of labor employed by the firm as a function of the level of output it produces and the amount of capital it employs.

b. Using your result from part a, along with the isocost equation, determine the firm's short-run total cost function, assuming the price of capital, $\overline{P}_{K,1}$, is \$40, the price of labor, $\overline{P}_{L,1}$, is \$10, and the level of capital is held constant at 8 units.

c. Using your result from part b, along with the fact that the firm's long-run total cost function is $LRTC = 4Q$, determine the level of output, Q, at which the firm's short-run total cost is equal to its long-run total cost. Also determine the optimal amount of labor that must be combined with the 8 units of capital to produce this level of output.

d. Using your result from part c, determine the values of short- and long-run total costs.

12.7 A hotdog vendor's short-run total cost function is

$$SRTC = 2Q^3 + 128.$$

a. Determine the hotdog vendor's short-run marginal cost function.

b. Determine the hotdog vendor's average total cost function.

c. Determine the number of hotdogs the vendor must produce in the short run in order to minimize his per unit cost of production.

d. What is the minimum value of average total cost?

12.8 An Italian sausage maker's production function is

$$Q = f(K,L) = 8K^{1/4}L^{3/4},$$

where the price of capital is \$4, the price of labor is \$24, and the amount of capital is fixed at 32 units. Determine the sausage maker's short-run marginal and average variable costs, provided he uses 2 units of labor.

CHAPTER 13

Perfect Competition in the Short Run

13.1 INTRODUCTION

Throughout the past five chapters we have analyzed firm behavior from the perspective of production efficiency. Our analysis resulted in the development of firms' cost functions for both the short- and long-run time periods. An implicit assumption underlying this analysis is the broader goal of profit maximization, which requires that a rational firm produces any given level of output in the most cost-efficient manner. A question that we did not address in those chapters, however, is, just how does a firm determine the profit-maximizing level of output it desires to produce? Also, how do we determine other important variables such as the price that a firm receives for its product and the profit it earns?

We will demonstrate in this, as well as the following five chapters, that the determination of important firm performance variables such as output, price, cost, and profit is largely affected by the market structure within which a firm operates. The term *market structure* generally refers to the number and size distribution of buyers and sellers operating in a market. Additional characteristics related to this concept are the degree of differentiation among goods produced by the firms in a particular market and the ease by which firms may enter or exit this market. Market structures can range from that of perfect competition, with its many buyers and sellers of a homogeneous good, to that of monopoly, consisting of a single seller of a good that is differentiated from those sold by all other firms.

Our purpose in this chapter is to analyze firm behavior in the short run within the context of a perfectly competitive market structure. We will initially focus on defining the particular characteristics that uniquely define a market structure of this type and on examining the immediate implications regarding typical firm behavior. Afterward, we will direct our attention to developing models of firm behavior in the short run, subject to perfectly competitive market conditions. These models will include an analysis of the behavior of a typical firm and of the perfectly competitive market as a whole. We will use these models to demonstrate various results for output, price, cost, and profit, as well as other economic variables.

13.2 CHARACTERISTICS OF A PERFECTLY COMPETITIVE MARKET STRUCTURE

In previous chapters, we limited our discussion of firm behavior to examining their choice of input combinations and the subsequent effects on the firms' costs. More broadly, individual producers operate within the context of a **market**, defined as *an*

323

aggregation of actual or potential buyers and sellers of a good or service who, through their interactions, determine the equilibrium price and quantity of that good or service being bought and sold. Defining the market for a particular good or service is considerably more difficult than you might expect. The critical issue is that the relevant market for a product must be defined in a manner that includes those goods or services perceived by consumers as constituting close substitutes for each other. Therefore, defining a market depends on such factors as the nature and attributes of the goods and services we include in the product definition, and often on the geographical location of the buyers in relation to the sellers.

Our task of product definition is a matter of degree. Depending on the analysis undertaken, we define some products rather narrowly, including only those goods with very similar attributes. Alternatively, we define some products more broadly, encompassing a collection of goods for which the attributes may be somewhat varied. For example, consider the market for corn. For the moment, ignoring geographical location, this product definition includes the output of corn produced by all farmers, since, once graded or classified, each farmer's corn is virtually identical. Excluded from this definition are other grains such as rice, wheat, and rye, although they can represent fairly good substitutes for corn in certain situations. This product definition is relatively narrow, and as a result, the market demand for this commodity is rather small and relatively elastic, compared to a more broadly defined product, owing to the existence of several close substitutes. Alternatively, suppose we define the relevant product market more broadly as grain. In this case, our product definition includes the output of corn, rice, and wheat, as well as other grains. As a result, the market demand is greater and less elastic than the demand for corn because there are few substitutes for grain in general.

Geographical location also plays a role in defining the relevant market for a good or service since the buyers and sellers of a particular product cannot be isolated from each other if transactions are to take place. Relevant geographical markets can be regional, national, or international, and are often delineated on the basis of governmental restrictions or the costs of information and transportation associated with obtaining the product. A good example of local geographical markets resulting from governmental restrictions has been in the area of commercial banking. Historically, thousands of commercial banks have operated in the United States. Yet, until recently, federal restrictions preventing interstate bank branching, and some state restrictions preventing the branching of banks within states, have created many small local markets due to the inaccessibility of many banks' services to some potential customers.

Another reason for the existence of local geographic markets is the high cost of transportation associated with delivering some products to consumers. For example, the markets for ready-mix cement remain local because the cost of transporting cement is very high relative to the cost of producing it. Recently, however, many geographic markets have become increasingly large owing to the reduction of government restrictions, such as bank branching constraints, tariffs, and import quotas. Furthermore, geographic market areas have also been enlarged through improvements in transportation, new technologies, and the creation of cyberspace that has greatly facilitated the exchange of information between buyers and sellers via personal computers. However, our overall point is that the definition of a relevant market for a good or service is a critical prerequisite in the process of defining market structures and in the subsequent analysis of firm behavior.

In microeconomic analysis, it is convention to define the **market structure** within which a firm operates according to the following set of structural criteria:

1. The number and size distribution of buyers and sellers operating in the market.
2. The degree of product differentiation within the market for the good.
3. The ease with which firms can enter and exit the market.
4. The amount of market-related information available to typical consumers and producers.

Since these characteristics play important roles in defining the specific type of market structure within which a firm operates, they ultimately have several implications regarding firm behavior.

Using this set of structural criteria, we can specify those characteristics that define a market structure known as perfect competition. Specifically, a **perfectly competitive market** possesses the following characteristics:

1. A large number of insignificantly small buyers and sellers, such that each firm produces an imperceptibly small share of total output in the market, and similarly, each buyer constitutes an extraordinarily small portion of total market demand.
2. The good or service produced is nondifferentiated, or homogeneous, and therefore, one firm's output is indistinguishable from another's.
3. Entry and exit of firms into or from the market is very easy, reflecting no barriers to entry such as government licenses, patent restrictions, scale economies, or high setup costs.
4. All buyers and sellers in the market have equal access to complete information regarding prices, technology, qualities of goods, and other market-related data.

There is an immediate implication associated with these characteristics defining a perfectly competitive market. Since there are so many sellers and buyers, with each respectively producing and consuming an imperceptibly small amount of the marketwide output of a homogeneous good, no one seller or buyer has the ability to exert any direct control over the price of the product. Rather, the price of a good or service sold in a perfectly competitive market is determined through the interaction of many small consumers and producers comprising the market. Traditionally, we can cite a number of agricultural markets in the United States as real-world examples of perfect competition. Many agricultural commodities are typically regarded as homogeneous, and therefore, one farmer's output is viewed as indistinguishable from that of another (see Real World Application 14.1). Furthermore, since there are a large number of relatively small producers of each of these homogeneous products, no individual farmer is capable of exerting any direct control over the price he receives for his output, and thus he must act as a price taker.

13.2.1 Price Determination in a Perfectly Competitive Market

Formally, we can describe the process by which the price of a good is determined in a perfectly competitive market in terms of the interaction of the market own-price demand and market supply curves for the good at a point in time. In Chapter 6, we developed the economic concept of the market demand function for some good X, denoted X_M. As noted, we can define this function, representing the aggregation of all of the individual consumers' demand functions, as

$$X_M = X_M(P_X, P_Y, P_W, \ldots, P_Z, I_M, T_M, N).$$

In this function, P_X represents the own price of the good; P_Y, P_W, $\ldots$, P_Z, are the prices of alternative goods, Y, W, $\ldots$, Z, respectively, that constitute either gross substitutes or gross complements relative to good X; I_M denotes the aggregate money income of consumers in the market; T_M represents some measure of consumers' tastes; and N denotes the number of consumers demanding good X. By specifying particular values for each determinant of market demand, other than the own price of good X, P_X, we derive the market own-price demand curve, D^M, for this good as

$$X_M = X_M(P_X, \overline{P}_{Y,1}, \overline{P}_{W,1}, \ldots, \overline{P}_{Z,1}, \overline{I}_{M,1}, \overline{T}_{M,1}, \overline{N}_1).$$

For the sake of clarity, let's recode X_M as Q^D, and P_X as simply P. Therefore, we can express this own-price market demand curve as

$$Q^D = Q^D(P, \overline{P}_{Y,1}, \overline{P}_{W,1}, \ldots, \overline{P}_{Z,1}, \overline{I}_{M,1}, \overline{T}_{M,1}, \overline{N}_1).$$

In general, an inverse relationship exists between the quantity demanded of a good, Q^D, and its own price, P. This result follows from our discussion in Chapters 5 and 6, where we demonstrated that, for normal goods, the income and substitution effects reinforce each other to produce a total effect that always indicates an inverse relationship between the quantity demanded of a good and its own price. Furthermore, even if a good is inferior, statistical results have historically demonstrated that, with the rare exception of a Giffen good, the inverse substitution effect exceeds the direct income effect, thus producing an inverse total effect for this case as well. Finally, we should note that, although market own-price demand curves represent the summation of individual own-price demand curves, this summation process virtually never changes the directionality of the relationship between the quantity demanded of a good and its own price.[1]

---

[1] One possible exception to this conclusion would be in the case of an extremely large snob effect. This snob effect was discussed in Chapter 6, where we showed that it tends to run counter to the change in the quantity demanded of a good resulting from a change in its own price. However, in general, we would not expect this effect to be so large that it more than offsets the effect of a change in own price on the quantity demanded of a good.

The market supply function for a good, such as X, expresses the quantity supplied by all firms in the market in terms of several important determinants. We can represent such a supply function as

$$Q^S = Q^S(P, P_L, \overline{K}_1, TEC, N_F).$$

Once again, P denotes the price of the good; P_L represents the price of labor; $\overline{K}_1$ denotes the level at which the capital input is fixed, thereby distinguishing the above equation as a short-run market supply function; TEC denotes the state of technology; and N_F represents the number of firms operating in the industry. Although this list of determinants is by no means comprehensive, it includes most of the important factors that affect the quantity supplied of a good. By fixing the values of all the determinants of market supply for a good, with the exception of its own price, P, we can derive a **short-run market supply curve**, or *a curve that expresses the quantity supplied of a good by all firms in a market, explicitly in terms of its price, holding all other determinants constant*. In terms of the notation used above, we can represent the short-run market supply curve as

$$Q^S = Q^S(P, \overline{P}_{L,1}, \overline{K}_1, \overline{TEC}_1, \overline{N}_{F,1}).$$

Generally, the relationship between the quantity supplied of a good, Q^S, and its own price, P, is direct, indicating a curve with a positive slope. Later in this chapter, we will demonstrate that this characteristic shows that firms can generally increase their profit by expanding their production of output in response to an increase in the price of the good.

This direct relationship between the quantity supplied of a good and its own price has an alternative explanation. Since the level of the capital input is fixed, the supply function described here constitutes a short-run supply function. Thus, for firms to expand their production of output, they must do so by employing additional units of their variable input, labor, along with their fixed input, capital. As a result, these firms experience diminishing marginal productivity associated with the labor input, and accordingly, their short-run marginal costs increase. Furthermore, in some instances due to scarcity of labor, its price rises as the demand for this input increases. Therefore, to induce firms to produce more output, they must be offered a higher price for the good so as to cover these higher production costs.

We can rearrange both the market own-price demand and supply curves into their inverse forms as

$$P = P^D(Q^D, \overline{P}_{Y,1}, \overline{P}_{W,1}, \ldots, \overline{P}_{Z,1}, \overline{I}_{M,1}, \overline{T}_{M,1}, \overline{N}_1)$$

and

$$P = P^S(Q^S, \overline{P}_{L,1}, \overline{K}_1, \overline{TEC}_1, \overline{N}_{F,1}),$$

respectively, where both of these functions are illustrated in Figure 13.1, representing the market for a good. The interaction of these market supply and demand curves determines the market equilibrium price that is subsequently taken as predetermined by the individual perfectly competitive firms. An **equilibrium price** is *a stable price, or a*

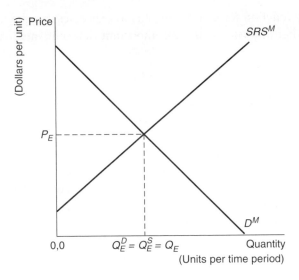

FIGURE 13.1 Equilibrium in a Perfectly Competitive Market

price that can be maintained in the absence of changes in the underlying determinants of the market own-price supply and demand curves. Given the set of underlying determinants, represented as the factors we hold constant in the own-price supply and demand curves, the forces that drive a market price to its equilibrium level are excess supplies, or surpluses, and excess demands, or shortages, of a good. Therefore, we characterize the absence of such forces as an **equilibrium condition**, defined as *a condition for which the quantity supplied of a good is equal to its quantity demanded.* Since the price corresponding to this condition is stable, in that there are no forces operating to change it, this price represents the equilibrium price. Graphically, a market equilibrium occurs where the market supply and own-price demand curves, SRS^M and D^M, respectively, intersect, as we have illustrated in Figure 13.1. At this point of intersection, the quantity demanded, Q_E^D, is equal to the quantity supplied, Q_E^S, or

$$Q_E^D = Q_E^S = Q_E.$$

The corresponding price, P_E, is the equilibrium price since it corresponds to neither an excess demand nor an excess supply in the market.

We can describe the process by which this equilibrium result is achieved as follows. If the price exceeds the equilibrium price, P_E, then $Q^D < Q^S$ and a surplus of the good exists, such as that depicted in panel (A) of Figure 13.2. At the price $P_1 > P_E$, the quantity demanded, Q_1^D, is less than the quantity supplied, Q_1^S, and there is a surplus, or excess supply, equal to $(Q_1^S - Q_1^D)$. As a result, this price, or any other price in excess of the equilibrium price, is not stable, for there exists pressure for firms to lower the price of the good in order to clear the market of excess stocks. As the price decreases, firms reduce the amount of the good they supply to the market, and, simultaneously consumers purchase more units of the good. This process continues until the price falls to P_E at which $Q_E^D = Q_E^S$. However, if the price of the good is lower than the equilibrium price of P_E, then $Q^D > Q^S$ and there exists a shortage, or excess demand, of the

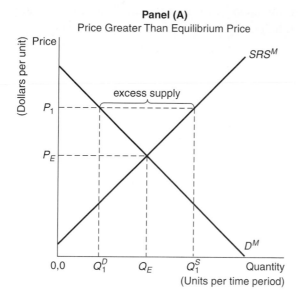

Panel (A)
Price Greater Than Equilibrium Price

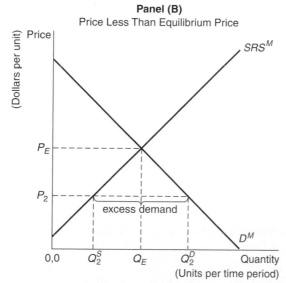

Panel (B)
Price Less Than Equilibrium Price

FIGURE 13.2 Disequilibrium in a Perfectly Competitive Market

good. We have illustrated this situation in panel (B) of Figure 13.2 for a price such as P_2, which is lower than the equilibrium price, P_E. At P_2, the quantity demanded, Q_2^D, exceeds the quantity supplied, Q_2^S. As a result, there is a shortage, or excess demand, equal to $(Q_2^D - Q_2^S)$. Therefore, P_2 is not a stable price since the price of the good will rise as consumers bid up the amount that they are willing to pay to acquire the relatively scarce good. Simultaneously, firms respond to this rising price by producing more units of the good. This process continues until the price rises to P_E at which $Q_E^D = Q_E^S$.

We can also analyze the concept of market equilibrium mathematically. Assume that the market supply and demand curves for a good, respectively, are

$$Q^S = -150 + 6P$$

and

$$Q^D = 180 - 4P.$$

REAL-WORLD APPLICATION 13.1

Economically Rational Vending Machines

We demonstrated earlier that in a perfectly competitive market the equilibrium price of a good is determined by the interaction of its associated market supply and demand curves. Specifically, an equilibrium price clears the market for a product during a particular time period by equating the quantity demanded to the quantity supplied of that product. If the time period is particularly short in duration, it is reasonable for us to treat the quantity supplied in that time period as a constant, and thus the inverse supply curve assumes a vertical shape. However, the own-price demand curve still possesses a negative slope, reflecting the inverse relationship between the quantity demanded of the good and its own price. Also recall that the own price demand curve for a good contains several determinants of quantity demanded, all of which are held constant, with the exception of the own price. Therefore, a change in any of these fixed determinants, such as consumers' income, the prices of other goods, or consumers' tastes, causes the own-price demand curve to shift, ultimately affecting the equilibrium price of the good.

For some products it may be possible to break down the taste determinant into more specific, measurable components that comprise this factor. This type of decomposition has been proposed by the Coca-Cola Company, the world's largest maker of soft drinks.

One of the most important components of consumers' tastes for soft drinks is the prevailing temperature at a particular point in time, where there exists a direct relationship between the demand for soft drinks and the temperature. Following this line of reasoning, Coca-Cola is working on a vending machine that automatically raises the price of soda pop as the temperature increases.

Analytically, we can think of an increase in temperature causing the own-price demand curve for the soda pop to shift to the right, creating an excess demand at the prevailing price and thus placing upward pressure on the price of the good. In the case of a temperature-sensing vending machine, the machine is simply reacting to changes in this factor affecting demand for the product and automatically changing the price to clear the market. Coca-Cola chairman, Doug Ivester, has been quoted as saying that "the machine was designed to reconcile supply and demand by raising the price when demand is increased." He has also been quoted as saying "Coca-Cola is a product whose utility varies from moment to moment."[2] At this point, the machine has been tested in Japan and is currently being evaluated for use in other markets.

[2]CNN America, Inc., *Coke Price Rises with Heat* [Online]. Available: http://www.cnnfn.com/1999/10/27/Companies/Coke.

Note that we have held all of the determinants of market supply and demand constant, at specified levels, with the exception of the own price of the good. As a result, these fixed values for the factors affecting market demand, $\overline{P}_{Y,1}, \overline{P}_{W,1}, \dots,$ $\overline{P}_{Z,1}, \overline{I}_{M,1}, \overline{T}_{M,1}$, and $\overline{N}_1$, are collectively embodied in the intercept of the market own-price demand equation. Similarly, those fixed values of the factors affecting market supply, $\overline{P}_{L,1}, \overline{K}_1, \overline{TEC}_1, \overline{N}_{F,1}$, are collectively embodied in the intercept of the market supply equation. We determine the equilibrium price by setting $Q^S = Q^D$ and solving for P as

$$-150 + 6P = 180 - 4P$$
$$10P = 330$$
$$P = \$33.$$

We can determine the equilibrium quantity by substituting this equilibrium price of $33 into either the market supply or market own-price demand curve, since at this price $Q^S = Q^D$. Using the market supply curve, we find that the equilibrium quantity is

$$Q^S = -150 + 6(33)$$
$$= -150 + 198 = 48 \text{ units,}$$

which is also equal to Q^D.

13.2.2   Relationships Between a Perfectly Competitive Firm and Its Associated Perfectly Competitive Market

We refer to a perfectly competitive firm as a price taker because each firm sells such an imperceptibly small portion of total market output that no one producer can exert any influence on the market price by altering its level of production. If a perfectly competitive firm attempts to sell its output at a price that exceeds the market-determined price, it loses its completely informed customer base to the many other producers who offer an identical product at the lower market determined price. From a theoretical perspective, a perfectly competitive firm is able to sell any quantity of its output, as long as it sells the good at the market price. As a result, a perfectly competitive firm's own-price demand curve is perfectly elastic, and hence horizontal, at the market-determined equilibrium price. We have illustrated this situation in panel (B) of Figure 13.3 where we have shown the equilibrium price of a good, P_1, as corresponding to the point where the market own-price demand curve, D^M, and the short-run market supply curve, SRS^M, intersect. The own-price demand curve for a typical perfectly competitive firm's output is represented in panel (A) of this figure as the horizontal curve D that intercepts the vertical axis at the value of the equilibrium market price, P_1.

We can also show that the own-price demand curve for a typical perfectly competitive firm's output also represents its marginal and average revenue functions. Recall from Chapter 7 that a firm's total revenue, representing the value of its sales, is

$$TR = PQ,$$

REAL-WORLD APPLICATION 13.2

E-Tailing: Is it the Dawn of the Perfectly Competitive Market in Retailing?

The fast-paced evolution of the Internet has brought a plethora of information to producers and consumers alike regarding numerous products and their prices. Moreover, access to this information is relatively cheap in terms of acquisition time and fees. As a result, some economists have touted the growth in electronic commerce, which totaled $3 billion in 1998 and was expected to triple to $9 billion in 1999, as the "new age of perfectly competitive markets."[3] If this is the case, then economic theory regarding perfectly competitive markets suggests that the prices charged by sellers of homogeneous products should be identical. This follows because buyers would possess perfect information with respect to products and their prices, and any firms that try to sell an identical good at a price higher than the lowest price prevailing in the marketplace will see their sales dwindle to zero as rational consumers purchase the product from other, lower-priced vendors.

In an effort to discern how competitive the up-and-coming world of e-tailing is relative to the conventional retail sales market, three recent studies have examined the price dispersion for identical goods sold in conventional retail stores with those sold over the Internet. Two of these studies were carried out by researchers at the Massachusetts Institute of Technology's Sloan School of Man-

agement and the University of Maryland, and the third was performed by a researcher at the University of Pennsylvania's Wharton School of Business. At first glance, the results of these studies are rather surprising. In comparing the price dispersion for books, CDs, and computer software, researchers found it to be no smaller for online purchases than for conventional retail sales. In comparing the prices of identical goods offered by online retailers only, the studies indicated that prices for books and CDs differed by as much as 50% and averaged 33% for books and 25% for CDs, while prices of identical airline tickets differed on average by 18%.

The researchers explain such price dispersion largely in terms of consumer trust. Given the existence of web-based programs, such as pricescan.com and mySimon.com, which search the Internet for the best prices on goods, consumers, especially those who are risk averse, still tend to be willing to pay higher prices in order to do business with a better known e-tailer. This issue is particularly important in light of the fact that with Internet retail purchases, consumers must pay up front and therefore cannot be sure as to whether or when their purchases will be delivered. We should emphasize, however, that online shopping is a relatively new phenomenon. Therefore, the potential still exists for these markets to evolve into the perfectly competitive prototype, especially as technology improves and consumers become even more price savvy.

---

[3]"Frictions in Cyberspace," *The Economist*, November 20, 1999, p. 94.

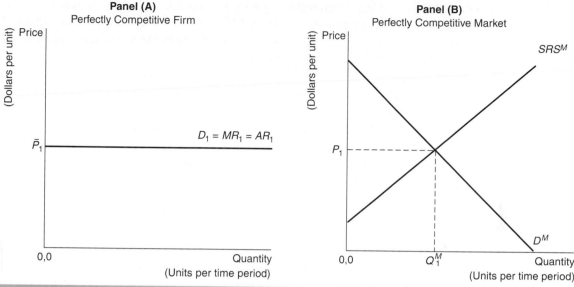

FIGURE 13.3 Perfectly Competitive Firm and Market

and since a perfectly competitive firm takes the price of its output as predetermined in the market at some value, such as $\overline{P}_1$, then

$$TR = \overline{P}_1 Q.$$

Also recall that marginal revenue is the change in a firm's total revenue due to a change in the amount of output it sells. Thus, we determine a firm's marginal revenue function by taking the derivative of the total revenue function with respect to Q as

$$MR = \frac{dTR(Q)}{dQ} = \frac{d\overline{P}_1 Q}{dQ} = \overline{P}_1 \frac{dQ}{dQ} = \overline{P}_1.$$

Another related measure is **average revenue**, which is simply the *value of a firm's sales, or total revenue, per unit of output it sells.* Therefore,

$$AR = \frac{TR}{Q} = \frac{\overline{P}_1 Q}{Q} = \overline{P}_1.$$

In summary, the perfectly elastic own-price demand curve for a perfectly competitive firm also represents its marginal revenue function as well as its average revenue function, all of which are equal to the market-determined price of the good.

13.3   GOAL OF A RATIONAL FIRM

Since a perfectly competitive firm acts as a price taker, it is placed in the position of reacting to whatever price is determined in the market. We have already reasoned that each firm can theoretically sell as much output as it desires at the prevailing market price. Therefore, the limitation regarding how much output a firm ultimately sells is established by its costs of production. Recall from Chapter 11 that we can express a firm's costs as a function of the level of output it produces. As a result, it is the level of output that a perfectly competitive firm treats as its decision variable.

We can model perfectly competitive firm behavior as an optimization problem for which the objective variable has been the subject of some debate. Specifically, what is the goal of a rational firm? Some economists contend that a firm may possess multiple goals that vary with different circumstances. Included in this list are such goals as maximization of revenue or market share, maximization of managerial salaries and benefits, or achievement of more altruistic goals such as community development or a more equal distribution of wealth. Although an interesting subject, we will leave the discussion of such multiple goals and how firms achieve them to business management texts. In this book, we assume that the goal of a rational firm is to maximize its profit. This goal is very straightforward and provides the basis for constructing models that have historically proven to be quite accurate in explaining and predicting firm behavior and resource allocation. Furthermore, this goal is particularly suitable as applied to perfectly competitive firms, since the underlying characteristic of free entry and exit forces these firms to behave in their most cost-efficient manner if they are to survive in a particular market.

In summary, we assume that the goal of a perfectly competitive firm is to determine the level of its decision variable, output, that corresponds to the maximum level of its objective variable, profit, and we can apply this decision-making process to both the short- and long-run time periods. Recall that the difference between these two time periods is that in the short run the firm possesses at least one fixed input, whereas in the long run all of its inputs are treated as variable. As a result, the firm possesses both fixed and variable costs in the short run, while in the long run all of its costs are variable. In this chapter, we will focus on analyzing short-run profit-maximizing behavior of a perfectly competitive firm.

13.4 SHORT-RUN PROFIT MAXIMIZATION

We define a firm's short-run profit as the difference between the value of its sales, or total revenue, and its short-run total cost. Note that, as we discussed in Chapter 12, these costs include the opportunity cost of the owners' inputs that are supplied to their firm. Therefore, this definition of profit represents an economic profit, or a return to the owners that is different from what they could earn if their resources were employed in their next best alternative. Mathematically, we express a firm's short-run profit function, $SR\pi$, as

$$SR\pi = TR - SRTC, \tag{13.1}$$

where TR is the firm's total revenue and $SRTC$ represents the firm's short-run total cost as discussed in Chapter 12. More specifically, we express total revenue, TR, as

$$TR = \overline{P}_1 Q, \tag{13.2}$$

where we specify the product price, P, at some level, $\overline{P}_1$, since it is determined in the marketplace and treated as a predetermined variable by the individual firm. Thus, for a specified price, the firm's total revenue is an increasing linear function of the amount of output it sells. Recall from Chapter 12 that we can also express a firm's short-run total cost in terms of its level of output, or

$$SRTC = \overline{FC}_1 + VC(Q,\overline{K}_1,\overline{P}_{L,1}). \tag{13.3}$$

Since fixed cost is the product of the firm's fixed capital input, $\overline{K}_1$, and the predetermined price of this input $\overline{P}_{K,1}$, we can express equation (13.3) as

$$SRTC = \overline{P}_{K,1}\overline{K}_1 + VC(Q,\overline{K}_1,\overline{P}_{L,1}).$$

Note that we are also holding the price of labor constant at $\overline{P}_{L,1}$. Substituting equations (13.2) and (13.3) into equation (13.1) yields the short-run profit function

$$SR\pi = \overline{P}_1 Q - \overline{FC}_1 - VC(Q,\overline{K}_1,\overline{P}_{L,1}). \tag{13.4}$$

We can determine the level of the decision variable, Q, that corresponds to the maximum value of the objective variable, $SR\pi$, by differentiating $SR\pi$ with respect to Q and setting the result equal to zero as

$$\frac{dSR\pi}{dQ} = \frac{d\overline{P}_1 Q}{dQ} - \frac{d\overline{FC}_1}{dQ} - \frac{dVC(Q,\overline{K}_1,\overline{P}_{L,1})}{dQ} = 0,$$

or, since $d\overline{FC}_1/dQ = 0$, and $d\overline{P}_1 Q/dQ = \overline{P}_1$, then

$$\frac{dSR\pi}{dQ} = \overline{P}_1 - \frac{dVC(Q,\overline{K}_1,\overline{P}_{L,1})}{dQ} = 0.$$

Finally, we can rearrange the above expression as

$$\overline{P}_1 = \frac{dVC(Q,\overline{K}_1,\overline{P}_{L,1})}{dQ}. \tag{13.5}$$

Recall from Section 13.2.2 that marginal revenue is

$$MR = \frac{dTR}{dQ} = \frac{d\overline{P}_1 Q}{dQ} = \overline{P}_1,$$

and from Chapter 12 that

$$SRMC = \frac{dVC(Q,\overline{K}_1,\overline{P}_{L,1})}{dQ}.$$

Therefore, we can interpret equation (13.5) as

$$MR_1 \equiv \overline{P}_1 = SRMC, \tag{13.6}$$

where we are applying the symbol $\equiv$ to indicate that MR and P can be used interchangeably in this equation. Conceptually, we can interpret equation (13.6) as indicating that a perfectly competitive firm maximizes its short-run profit by producing and selling a level of output at which the predetermined price is equal to its short-run marginal cost.[4] The rationale for this interpretation is quite straightforward. Since price is also the same as marginal revenue for a perfectly competitive firm, equation (13.6) indicates that a profit-maximizing firm produces output up to the point where the extra revenue from selling the last unit of output is just equal to the extra cost associated with producing that last unit. Recall that price, or marginal revenue, represents the rate of change of total revenue with respect to output, and marginal cost is the rate of change in total cost with respect to output. If this equality between price and marginal cost does not hold true, we can reason that the firm could adjust its level of output, and by doing so, increase its profit. For example, suppose a firm produces a level of output at which $P > SRMC$. Recall that $SR\pi = TR - SRTC$ and that both TR and $SRTC$ are increasing functions of output. Therefore, if the firm increases its production and sale of output when $P > SRMC$, TR will increase more than $SRTC$, and the difference between them, $SR\pi$, will rise. Conversely, if the firm produces some level of output at which $P < SRMC$, then by decreasing its production and sale of output, the firm can decrease $SRTC$ more than it decreases TR and again $SR\pi$ will rise. Logically, the only level of Q at which there is no possibility of making an adjustment to Q, and subsequently increasing profit, is that level at which $P = SRMC$.

We have illustrated the short-run profit maximization solution for a perfectly competitive firm in Figure 13.4, where this solution is shown from three different perspectives in panels (A), (B), and (C). Note that all three panels are linked by their common Q-axes. In panel (A), we have explicitly illustrated TR and $SRTC$ functions, or the components of the $SR\pi$ function. Specifically, since $SR\pi = TR - SRTC$, short-run profit at each level of output, Q, is indicated by the vertical distance between these two component functions. Note that for the situation we are illustrating, $SR\pi$ can assume a positive, negative, or zero value, depending on the level of Q chosen by the firm. Clearly, the behavior of the $SR\pi$ function depends on the behavior of the TR and $SRTC$ functions as the firm alters the value of Q. The TR function begins at the origin, because the firm receives no revenue if it sells no output, or

$$TR = \overline{P}_1(0) = 0.$$

Furthermore, TR is an increasing linear function of Q since its slope

$$\frac{dTR}{dQ} = MR \equiv \overline{P}_1,$$

is a positive constant value. The $SRTC$ function in this example is the familiar cubic cost function discussed in Chapter 12 and represented generally in equation (13.3). Recall that the intercept of this function is equal to the fixed cost, $\overline{FC}_1$, since the firm incurs this cost even if it produces no output.

---

[4]Technically, in order to ensure that the solution for Q corresponds to a maximum value for $SR\pi$, it is necessary that the second-order condition for a maximum be fulfilled, as $d^2SRTC/dQ^2 > 0$ or, since $SRMC = dSRTC/dQ$, then $dSRMC/dQ > 0$.

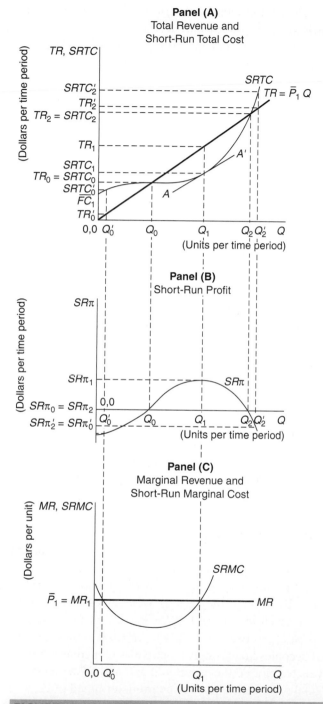

FIGURE 13.4 Relationships among Total Revenue, Total Cost, Profit, Marginal Cost, and Marginal Revenue for Perfectly Competitive Firm in the Short Run

As stated earlier, we compute the values of $SR\pi$ as the vertical distance between TR and $SRTC$ at each value of Q. For example, referring once again to panels (A) and (B) of Figure 13.4, if the firm produces and sells Q_0 units of output

$$SR\pi_0 = TR_0 - SRTC_0 = 0,$$

since at Q_0, $TR_0 = SRTC_0$. If the firm produces an amount of output less than Q_0, $SR\pi$ < 0. For example, if the firm produces Q_0' units, where $Q_0' < Q_0$

$$SR\pi_0' = TR_0' - SRTC_0' < 0,$$

since $TR_0' < SRTC_0'$. If the firm produces Q_2 units

$$SR\pi_2 = TR_2 - SRTC_2 = 0$$

since $TR_2 = SRTC_2$. For any level of output greater than Q_2, $SR\pi < 0$. For example, if the firm produces Q_2' units, where $Q_2' > Q_2$

$$SR\pi_2' = TR_2' - SRTC_2' < 0,$$

because $TR_2' < SRTC_2'$. Finally, observe that $SR\pi > 0$ for levels of output between Q_0 and Q_2 units, exclusively, since $TR > SRTC$ for output levels within this range. However, the goal of the firm is not just to earn a positive profit, if possible, but to earn a maximum profit, which in this example occurs at Q_1 units of output. At this value of Q

$$SR\pi_1 = TR_1 - SRTC_1,$$

and we can observe in panel (A) of Figure 13.4 that it is at this level of Q that TR exceeds $SRTC$ by the greatest amount.

We can demonstrate that this graphical solution for the profit-maximizing level of output, Q_1 units, is consistent with the profit maximization condition, $MR \equiv \overline{P}_1 = SRMC$, we established earlier. To prove this consistency, we construct a tangent to the $SRTC$ curve at Q_1 units of output, and we compare its slope to that of the TR function. Observe that this line, AA', drawn tangent to the $SRTC$ function at Q_1 units of output, is parallel to the TR function, indicating that the slopes of the TR and $SRTC$ functions are equal at this level of output. In general, since the slope of the TR function is $dTR/dQ = MR \equiv P$, and the slope of the $SRTC$ function is $dSRTC/dQ = SRMC$, then $MR \equiv P = SRMC$ at the level of Q corresponding to a profit maximum.

These results, demonstrated in panel (A), are also shown in panels (B) and (C) of Figure 13.4. In panel (B) we have plotted the $SR\pi$ function in terms of output, and therefore, we can directly observe the various $SR\pi$ values corresponding to different levels of Q. For output levels less than Q_0, $SR\pi < 0$, where $SR\pi$ rises with increases in Q until it equals zero at Q_0. Between Q_0 and Q_2, $SR\pi > 0$, achieving a maximum at Q_1. At Q_2, $SR\pi = 0$ and becomes increasingly negative as Q increases beyond Q_2.

In panel (C) we have plotted the associated MR and $SRMC$ curves as functions of output. Since marginal revenue is equal to the predetermined price, we represent it as a horizontal curve established at $\overline{P}_1$. We have derived the short-run marginal cost curve from the cubic short-run total cost curve shown in panel (A), and thus it is the familiar quadratic, or U-shaped, curve discussed in Chapter 12. Observe that the

$SRMC$ curve in this example intersects the $P \equiv MR$ curve at two values of output, the profit-maximizing level, Q_1, and also at the level Q_0'. However, Q_0' does not represent a profit-maximizing level of output because $SR\pi < 0$ at this value. Rather, the fact that $P \equiv MR = SRMC$ at this point indicates a maximized local loss, as shown by the $SR\pi$ function in panel (B), where you can observe that

$$SR\pi_0' = TR_0' - SRTC_0' < 0.$$

Given that the goal of a firm is to maximize its profit, we can rule out this solution.

We can demonstrate the process of determining a perfectly competitive firm's profit-maximizing level of output with a mathematical example. Assume a firm's short-run total costs are represented by the curve

$$SRTC = \frac{1}{3}Q^3 - 5Q^2 + 40Q + 10,$$

and the market price is predetermined as $P = \$24$. The firm determines its profit-maximizing level of output by deriving its short-run marginal cost function and setting it equal to the market price. Thus

$$SRMC = \frac{dSRTC}{dQ} = Q^2 - 10Q + 40 = P,$$

and since $P = \$24$,

$$Q^2 - 10Q + 40 = 24$$
$$Q^2 - 10Q + 16 = 0,$$

or

$$(Q - 2)(Q - 8) = 0,$$

yielding the roots $Q = 2$ and $Q = 8$ units. We determine the profit-maximizing value of Q by substituting each of the values for Q into the firm's profit function and comparing the results. Recall that

$$SR\pi = TR - SRTC$$

then if $Q = 2$ units

$$SR\pi = PQ - \left(\frac{1}{3}Q^3 - 5Q^2 + 40Q + 10\right)$$

$$= 24(2) - \frac{1}{3}(2)^3 + 5(2)^2 - 40(2) - 10$$

$$= 48 - \frac{8}{3} + 20 - 80 - 10 = \$-24.66.$$

Alternatively, if $Q = 8$ units then

$$SR\pi = 24(8) - \frac{1}{3}(8)^3 + 5(8)^2 - 40(8) - 10$$

$$= 192 - 170.67 + 320 - 320 - 10 = \$11.33,$$

demonstrating that the profit-maximizing level of output for this firm is $Q = 8$ units.

We often find it useful to express a firm's revenue, costs, and profit on a per unit of output basis. Thus, we can demonstrate the determination of a perfectly competitive firm's short-run profit-maximizing level of output and its corresponding amount of short-run profit, using average functions. We convert a firm's short-run total profit function

$$SR\pi = TR - SRTC,$$

into an average profit function by dividing both sides of the equation by the amount of output produced as

$$\frac{SR\pi}{Q} = \frac{TR}{Q} - \frac{SRTC}{Q}.$$

The term on the left-hand side of this equation, $SR\pi/Q$, represents a firm's short-run average profit, $SR\ AVE\pi$. Recognize, the term TR/Q is the firm's average revenue function, AR, defined earlier, and the term $SRTC/Q$ is the firm's ATC function we derived in Chapter 12. Thus, we can write the short-run average profit function more concisely as

$$SR\ AVE\pi = AR - ATC.$$

Furthermore, recall that

$$AR = \frac{TR}{Q} = \frac{\bar{P}_1 Q}{Q} = \bar{P}_1,$$

for a perfectly competitive firm, and since $P = MR$, then $AR = MR$ as well.

We have illustrated the two component functions of $SR\ AVE\pi$, AR and ATC, in Figure 13.5, where the short-run average profit is represented as the vertical distance between these two functions, $AR - ATC$, at each level of Q.

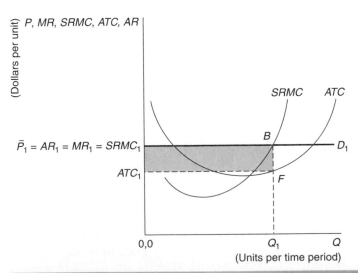

FIGURE 13.5 Short-Run Profit Earned by a Perfectly Competitive Firm

Also illustrated in this figure are the MR and $SRMC$ functions. The MR is identical to AR and P, and therefore, these terms correspond to the perfectly competitive firm's own-price demand curve discussed in Section 13.2.2. Note that the $SRMC$ function intersects the ATC function at a value of Q corresponding to a minimum value of ATC. This figure is actually just an extension of panel (C) in Figure 13.4, where now we have included an ATC function. The profit-maximizing level of output is once again Q_1, at which $\overline{P}_1 \equiv MR_1 = SRMC_1$. The short-run average profit at this level of output is

$$SR\,AVE\pi_1 = AR_1 - ATC_1$$

or

$$SR\,AVE\pi_1 = \overline{P}_1 - ATC_1,$$

represented by the vertical line BF. We compute the total profit as the product of the $SR\,AVE\pi$ and the profit-maximizing level of output, or $(SR\,AVE\pi_1)(Q_1)$, which is represented by the area of the shaded rectangle $\overline{P}_1\,B\,F\,ATC_1$. The amount of this total profit is the same as the value $SR\pi_1$, which we demonstrated in Figure 13.4.

Applying the earlier mathematical example where $P = \$24$, and the profit-maximizing level of output is $Q = 8$ units, we can compute the short-run average profit using the formula

$$SR\,AVE\pi = AR - ATC.$$

Since $AR = P$ and $ATC = SRTC/Q$, then

$$SR\,AVE\pi = 24 - \left(\frac{1}{3}Q^3 - 5Q^2 + 40Q + 10\right)\bigg/Q$$

$$= 24 - \frac{1}{3}Q^2 + 5Q - 40 - 10/Q$$

$$= 24 - \frac{1}{3}(8)^2 + 5(8) - 40 - \frac{10}{8} = \$1.42/\text{unit}.$$

Note that in both our graphical and mathematical examples, the maximized profit is positive. However, this is by no means always true. In the short run a firm's profit may be positive, negative, or zero, depending on the circumstances, specifically the market and cost conditions affecting the firm.

13.5   THE SHORT-RUN SUPPLY CURVE FOR A PERFECTLY COMPETITIVE FIRM

In the preceding section, we mathematically determined a firm's profit-maximizing level of output and profit for an assumed set of market supply and demand conditions and a specified set of cost curves. In the short run, a firm's cost curves cannot be altered since the level of capital, K, a firm employs is fixed, as are the other determinants of its cost, such as input prices and the state of technology. However, short-run market supply and demand conditions that determine the price to which the individual perfectly competitive firm must react are indeed likely to change. As a result, a firm's profit-maximizing level of output and associated short-run profit will change as well.

We can establish a boundary separating the price and output levels for which a firm chooses to operate from those for which the firm decides to shut down its operation and produce nothing. This is accomplished by examining how an individual firm responds to different prices resulting from changes in the market supply and demand conditions. Note that in the short run, if the firm chooses to shut down its production entirely, it still incurs its fixed cost because it possesses a fixed input. Since the firm is not earning any revenue in this situation, the firm's fixed cost equals its short-run profit, which is negative. We should emphasize that in the short run, a firm does not have the option of selling its capital input and reducing its total cost to zero because, by definition, this action constitutes a long-run adjustment. In fact, no firms, including both those outside of and within an industry, can change their level of capital in this situation. Thus, it follows that the concept of the short run, as we apply it to an entire industry, refers to a time period during which no entry or exit can occur.

In panel (B) of Figure 13.6, we have illustrated several different market prices, where each price results from the interaction of the short-run market supply curve, SRS^M, with each of five different respective market own-price demand curves. Assume that initially the market own-price demand curve is represented by D_1^M, and thus the equilibrium market price is established at P_1 for which $Q_1^{D,M} = Q_1^{S,M} = Q_1^M$. In panel (A), we have shown the revenue and cost functions for a typical perfectly competitive firm along with its associated average variable cost curve, AVC. If the market price is P_1, the firm determines its profit-maximizing level of output as Q_1, at which $MR_1 \equiv \overline{P}_1 = SRMC_1$, and its corresponding short-run average profit is

$$SR\,AVE\pi_1 = AR_1 - ATC_1,$$

or since $\overline{P}_1 = AR_1$,

$$SR\,AVE\pi_1 = \overline{P}_1 - ATC_1.$$

The firm's short-run total profit is the product of this short-run average profit and output, or

$$SR\pi_1 = (AR_1 - ATC_1)Q_1.$$

Since $AR_1 > ATC_1$, the short-run profit in this case is clearly positive. Returning to panel (B), suppose underlying market demand conditions change, for example, due to successive decreases in consumer tastes for the product or, assuming the good is normal, decreases in consumer money income. This would result in the market own-price demand curve shifting leftward from D_1^M to D_2^M, D_3^M, D_4^M and D_5^M, driving the market price down from P_1 to P_2, P_3, P_4, and finally to P_5, respectively.

We can observe the reaction of a typical firm to these different market prices in panel (A). If the market price falls from P_1 to P_2, the firm maximizes its short-run profit by reducing its production of output from Q_1 to Q_2 at which $MR_2 \equiv \overline{P}_2 = SRMC_2$. At this solution,

$$SR\,AVE\pi_2 = AR_2 - ATC_2 = \$0,$$

since $\overline{P}_2 = AR_2 = ATC_2$. The firm's short-run total profit is also equal to zero because

$$SR\pi = (SR\,AVE\pi)Q = (0)Q = \$0.$$

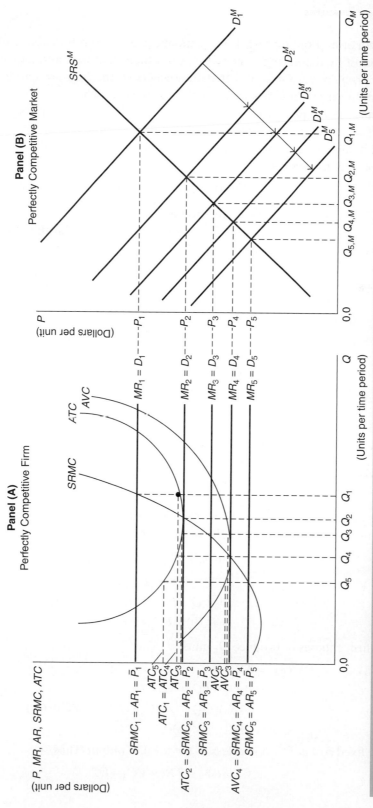

FIGURE 13.6 Reaction of Profit Maximizing Perfectly Competitive Firm to Decreases in Market Demand

This short-run profit represents an economic profit, or a return above what the owners could earn by employing their resources in their next best alternative. Thus, an economic profit of zero indicates that the owners of the firm are earning exactly what they could earn if these resources were employed elsewhere.

If the market price falls to P_3, the firm responds by decreasing its profit-maximizing level of output to Q_3, at which $MR_3 \equiv \overline{P}_3 = SRMC_3$. Although Q_3 represents the optimal output in this situation, observe in panel (A) of Figure 13.6 that the firm is experiencing negative profit. Specifically,

$$SR \, AVE\pi_3 = AR_3 - ATC_3 < 0,$$

since $AR_3 < ATC_3$ at Q_3. Since the firm is experiencing a negative short-run profit, or loss, it is confronted with the decision of producing Q_3 or shutting down its operation and producing nothing. However, in the short run, even if the firm produces nothing and thus earns zero revenue, it must still pay the cost associated with its fixed input, or its fixed cost, $\overline{FC}_1$. Thus, the decision whether to operate and produce Q_3 or shut down and produce nothing, is a matter of comparing the losses associated with each option and choosing the one yielding the smaller loss. Since this graphical analysis consists of average, rather than total, cost and revenue functions, the choice described above can be made by comparing $\overline{P}_3 = AR_3$ to the firm's average variable cost at Q_3 units, AVC_3. At $\overline{P}_3$, $AR_3 > AVC_3$, indicating that, on a per unit basis, the firm is earning a level of revenue that exceeds the cost associated with its variable input. The difference, $AR_3 - AVC_3$ or $\overline{P}_3 - AVC_3$, can then be applied to paying some of the firm's average fixed cost, represented by

$$AFC_3 = ATC_3 - AVC_3,$$

since $ATC = AFC + AFC$. Again, the average loss incurred by producing Q_3 units is

$$AR_3 - ATC_3 < 0,$$

where we can reason that the firm's total loss is less than its fixed cost. In total terms, if the firm shuts down production, its short-run profit is

$$SR\pi_0 = TR_0 - \overline{FC}_1 - VC_0$$

or

$$SR\pi_0 = \overline{P}_3 Q - \overline{FC}_1 - VC(Q, \overline{K}_1, \overline{P}_{L,1})$$
$$= \overline{P}_3(0) - \overline{FC}_1 - 0 = -\overline{FC}_1.$$

If the firm chooses to produce Q_3 units

$$SR\pi_3 = TR_3 - \overline{FC}_1 - VC_3$$
$$= \overline{P}_3 Q_3 - \overline{FC}_1 - VC_3$$
$$= (AR_3)(Q_3) - (AFC_3)(Q_3) - (AVC_3)(Q_3)$$
$$= (AR_3 - AVC_3)(Q_3) - \overline{FC}_1,$$

where fixed cost is $\overline{FC}_1$ regardless of the level of output. Thus

$$SR\pi_3 = TR_3 - VC_3 - \overline{FC}_1,$$

and since $AR_3 > AVC_3$, then $TR_3 - VC_3 > 0$. As a result, $SR\pi_3 > -\overline{FC}_1$, representing a smaller loss than that associated with producing zero output. In summary, at P_3 the firm will operate and produce Q_3 units despite the fact that its short-run profit is negative, since this choice minimizes its short-run loss.

Now suppose the market price decreases to P_4. At this price the firm could choose to produce Q_4 units at which $MR_4 \equiv P_4 = SRMC_4$, and at this level of output the firm will incur an average loss of

$$SR\ AVE\pi_4 = AR_4 - ATC_4 < 0.$$

Furthermore, note that the $\overline{P}_4 \equiv MR_4 = AR_4 = D_4$ curve is tangent to the AVC curve. As a result, $AR_4 = AVC_4$, indicating that the firm is just covering its variable cost by producing Q_4 units. Therefore, its short-run average profit, or loss, is

$$\begin{aligned} SR\ AVE\pi_4 &= AR_4 - ATC_4 \\ &= AR_4 - AFC_4 - AVC_4 = -AFC_4, \end{aligned}$$

since

$$AR_4 = AVC_4.$$

The firm's short-run total profit, or loss, in this situation is equal to the negative of its fixed cost, or

$$-\overline{FC}_1 = -(AFC_4)(Q_4).$$

This is the same loss the firm incurs if it shuts down and produces nothing, so it is clear that the firm gains nothing by producing Q_4 units. Thus, P_4 represents the price at which the firm shuts down its production.

We can reinforce this result by examining a situation for which the market price falls below P_4. For example, at P_5 in Figure 13.6, if the firm attempts to produce output, it would theoretically do so by producing Q_5 units at which $MR_5 \equiv P_5 = SRMC_5$. However, at this level of output the firm will experience a substantial loss, represented in average terms in panel (A) of Figure 13.6 as

$$SR\ AVE\pi_5 = AR_5 - ATC_5 < 0.$$

More importantly, from a decision-making perspective, $\overline{P}_5 = AR_5 < AVC_5$, indicating that by producing Q_5 units, the firm will not even cover all of its variable cost, let alone its fixed cost. Clearly, its loss includes not only this fixed cost but part of its variable cost as well. The loss attributed to the difference between its average revenue and its average variable cost, $AR_5 - AVC_5 < 0$, represents that additional contribution to the firm's average loss caused by operating and producing Q_5 units of output rather than shutting down its operation and producing nothing. In total terms, the firm's loss associated with producing Q_5 units is

$$\begin{aligned} SR\pi_5 &= (AR_5 - ATC_5)Q_5 \\ &= AR_5Q_5 - AFC_5Q_5 - AVC_5Q_5 \\ &= (AR_5 - AVC_5)Q_5 - \overline{FC}_1 < 0. \end{aligned}$$

This amount represents a greater loss than that associated with producing zero output, $\overline{FC}_1$, since $AR_5 < AVC_5$. Therefore, a profit-maximizing firm will choose to shut down and produce nothing at a market price of P_5 or, more generally, for any price less than P_4.

Our preceding discussion described how a perfectly competitive firm, in the short run, determines its set of profit-maximizing levels of output for a set of predetermined market prices. Conceptually, this analysis provides the basis for deriving a perfectly competitive firm's short-run supply curve, which in turn, underlies the market short-run supply curve defined in Section 13.2.1. Recall that a short-run supply curve expresses the total amount of a good supplied in terms of the market price of that good, with at least one input and the prices of all inputs fixed at specified levels. At this point, we can apply this definition to an individual firm. In Figure 13.6, we have shown that for the market prices P_1, P_2, P_3, P_4, and P_5, the firm produces Q_1, Q_2, Q_3, Q_4, and zero units of output, respectively. We determined these output levels, corresponding to prices P_1, P_2, P_3, and P_4, respectively, where $MR \equiv P = SRMC$, provided $P = AR \geq AVC$. For any price below P_4, such as P_5, we have determined that the firm will shut down rather than produce the output levels corresponding to the $MR \equiv P = SRMC$ condition because at those levels $P = AR < AVC$. Applying these results to the definition of a supply curve, we conclude that the short-run supply curve for a perfectly competitive firm is that portion of its $SRMC$ curve for which $P \geq AVC$, and that portion of the vertical axis where $Q = 0$, when $P < AVC$.

A mathematical example should provide us with some additional insight into the derivation of a short-run supply curve. Assume that a firm has the short-run total cost function

$$SRTC = \frac{1}{3}Q^3 - 5Q^2 + 42Q + 81,$$

and therefore

$$SRMC = \frac{dSRTC}{dQ} = Q^2 - 10Q + 42.$$

We can determine the firm's profit-maximizing levels of output for various market prices by applying the $MR \equiv P = SRMC$ rule. For example, if $P = \$42$

$$42 = Q^2 - 10Q + 42$$
$$Q^2 - 10Q = 0$$
$$Q(Q - 10) = 0,$$

yielding roots of $Q = 0$ and $Q = 10$ units. We can verify that the profit-maximizing level of output is $Q = 10$ units by substituting these two values of Q into the $SR\pi$ function and comparing the results. Thus, for $Q = 10$ units, the firm's short-run profit is

$$SR\pi = TR - SRTC$$
$$= PQ - \left(\frac{1}{3}Q^3 - 5Q^2 + 42Q + 81\right)$$
$$= 42(10) - \frac{1}{3}(10)^3 + 5(10)^2 - 42(10) - 81$$
$$= \$85.67.$$

If $P = \$33$, the firm's new level of production can once again be determined by equating P to $SRMC$ as

$$33 = Q^2 - 10Q + 42$$
$$Q^2 - 10Q + 9 = 0$$
$$(Q - 1)(Q - 9) = 0,$$

yielding roots of $Q = 1$ and $Q = 9$. Now, we can verify that the profit-maximizing level of output is $Q = 9$ units. Therefore, when $Q = 9$ units, the firm's short-run profit is

$$SR\pi = 33(9) - \frac{1}{3}(9)^3 + 5(9)^2 - 42(9) - 81$$

$$= \$0.$$

If $P = \$23.25$, then

$$\$23.25 = Q^2 - 10Q + 42$$
$$Q^2 - 10Q + 18.75 = 0$$
$$(Q - 2.5)(Q - 7.5) = 0,$$

yielding roots of $Q = 2.5$ units and $Q = 7.5$ units. We can determine that $Q = 7.5$ units represents the profit-maximizing level of output, yielding

$$SR\pi = (23.25)(7.5) - \frac{1}{3}(7.5)^3 + 5(7.5)^2 - 42(7.5) - 81$$

$$= \$ -81.00.$$

Thus, if $P = \$23.25$ and the firm produces 7.5 units, its short-run profit is $\$ -81.00$, which is the same amount as its fixed cost, the loss it incurs if it produces no output. For any price less than $\$23.25$, the firm will opt to shut down and produce nothing since it cannot cover its variable cost. Therefore, $P = \$23.25$ and $Q = 7.5$ units represents the point at which the firm will shut down its production. The firm's short-run supply curve, denoted SRS, is its $SRMC$ curve, or

$$SRS = SRMC = Q^2 - 10Q + 42,$$

provided $P \geq AVC$. Furthermore, since the firm determines its profit-maximizing level of output where $P = SRMC$, then we can represent its SRS curve in inverse form as

$$P = Q^2 - 10Q + 42.$$

This firm will shut down at $P = \$23.25$, where we have computed its profit-maximizing level of output as $Q = 7.5$ units because

$$AVC = \frac{VC}{Q} = \left(\frac{1}{3}Q^3 - 5Q^2 + 42Q\right)/Q$$

$$= \frac{1}{3}Q^2 - 5Q + 42$$

$$= \frac{1}{3}(7.5)^2 - 5(7.5) + 42 = \$23.25/\text{unit}.$$

Thus, at the price $P = \$23.25$, the firm is just covering its variable cost, indicating that

$$SR\pi = -FC = \$ -81.00,$$

the same loss it incurs if it shuts down and produces nothing.

13.6   SHORT-RUN MARKET SUPPLY CURVE

The short-run supply curve we have just derived pertains to only one of many firms comprising a perfectly competitive market. We can repeat the above process for each of these firms, thereby generating an entire set of short-run perfectly competitive firm supply curves. In each case, the supply curve is represented by the firm's *SRMC* curve, provided $P \geq AVC$, and that portion of the *P*-axis for which $P < AVC$. We can represent this set of N_F numbers of individual firm supply curves as

$$Q^{S,1} = Q^{S,1}(P, \overline{K}_1^1, \overline{P}_{L,1}, \overline{TEC}_1)$$
$$Q^{S,2} = Q^{S,2}(P, \overline{K}_1^2, \overline{P}_{L,1}, \overline{TEC}_1)$$
$$\vdots \qquad \vdots \qquad \vdots$$
$$Q^{S,N_F} = Q^{S,N_F}(P, \overline{K}_1^{N_F}, \overline{P}_{L,1}, \overline{TEC}_1),$$

where Q^S represents the amount of output supplied by each firm, P is the price of the output, $\overline{K}_1$ is the level of the fixed input, capital, $\overline{P}_{L,1}$ is the fixed input price of labor, and $\overline{TEC}_1$ is the fixed state of technology. Although these short-run firm supply curves are similar, they are generally somewhat different from each other because the underlying individual firm cost conditions are likely to vary.

These individual firm supply curves provide the basis for constructing the short-run market supply curve we introduced in Section 13.2.1. Recall that this market supply curve is represented as

$$Q^{S,M} = Q^S(P, \overline{K}_1, \overline{P}_{L,1}, \overline{TEC}_1, \overline{N}_{F,1}).$$

The terms in this function are essentially the same as those defined for the individual firm supply curves, with the exception that $Q^{S,M}$ represents the quantity of output supplied by the entire market and N_F represents the number of firms comprising the market. Our inclusion of this last determinant, N_F, in the market supply curve implies that such a curve consists of an aggregation of the individual firm supply curves. Logically, the greater the number of firms supplying the product, *ceteris paribus*, the greater is the quantity supplied in the market at each price. Thus, the process of deriving a short-run market supply curve is simply one of horizontally summing the individual firm supply curves, as we have illustrated in Figure 13.7. Panel (A) contains the *SRS* curve for firm 1. The *SRS* curve for firm 2 is shown in panel (B), and the *SRS* curve for the N_F^{th} firm in the market is illustrated in panel (C). We have plotted the quantity supplied by each individual firm on the horizontal axis in each of the first three panels and the market price on each vertical axis. Technically, these *SRS* curves are inverse supply functions represented as

$$P = P^S(Q^S, \overline{K}_1, \overline{P}_{L,1}, \overline{TEC}_1).$$

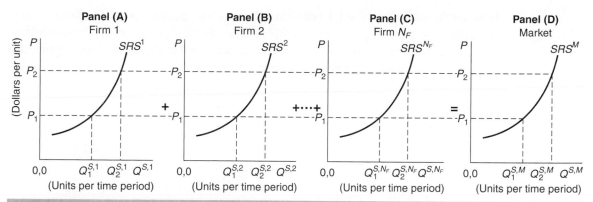

FIGURE 13.7 Derivation of Short-Run Market Supply Curve for a Perfectly Competitive Market When Variable Input Price Remains Constant

The product price is the same for all firms because they all react to the same market price. Therefore, we can link all of the panels in Figure 13.7 because of their common vertical axes. Panel (D) contains the short-run market supply curve, where the market quantity supplied, $Q^{S,M}$, is plotted on the horizontal axis.

We can determine the market quantity supplied at each price by selecting a price, determining the quantity of output supplied by each firm at that price, and then summing these quantities. Referring to Figure 13.7, if the market price is P_1, firm 1 produces $Q_1^{S,1}$, firm 2 produces $Q_1^{S,2}$, and so forth, up through firm N_F that produces Q_1^{S,N_F}. Thus, the market quantity supplied at P_1 is

$$Q_1^{S,M} = Q_1^{S,1} + Q_1^{S,2} + \ldots + Q_1^{S,N_F}.$$

If the market price is P_2, then the individual firms $1, 2, \ldots, N_F$, produce $Q_2^{S,1}, Q_2^{S,2}, \ldots, Q_2^{S,N_F}$, respectively, and the market quantity supplied is

$$Q_2^{S,M} = Q_2^{S,1} + Q_2^{S,2} + \ldots + Q_2^{S,N_F}.$$

By repeating this procedure at various market prices, we can construct the market supply curve, SRS^M, as shown in panel (D).

We can also demonstrate this horizontal summation process with a mathematical example. Suppose the market consists of two firms, for which the supply curve for firm 1 is of the linear form

$$Q^{S,1} = b_{0,1} + b_{1,1}P,$$

where $b_{0,1} \le 0$, $b_{1,1} > 0$, and $P \ge -b_{0,1}/b_{1,1}$,

and the supply curve for firm 2 is

$$Q^{S,2} = b_{0,2} + b_{1,2}P,$$

where $b_{0,2} \le 0$, $b_{1,2} > 0$, and $P \ge -b_{0,2}/b_{1,2}$.

The terms $b_{0,1}$ and $b_{0,2}$ represent the Q^S intercept coefficients for the supply curves pertaining to firms 1 and 2, respectively, and the terms $b_{1,1}$ and $b_{1,2}$, denote the respective slope coefficients. You should note that these intercept and slope coefficients most likely differ across these two firms' supply curves. Since supply curves are conventionally plotted in inverse form, we can rearrange the terms in these two supply functions to obtain the corresponding inverse supply functions as

$$P = \frac{-b_{0,1}}{b_{1,1}} + \frac{1}{b_{1,1}} Q^{S,1},$$

and

$$P = \frac{-b_{0,2}}{b_{1,2}} + \frac{1}{b_{1,2}} Q^{S,2}.$$

The conditions regarding the intercept and slope coefficients

$$b_{0,1} \le 0, \quad b_{0,2} \le 0, \quad b_{1,1} > 0, \quad b_{1,2} > 0, \quad P \ge \frac{-b_{0,1}}{b_{1,1}}, \quad \text{and} \quad P \ge \frac{-b_{0,2}}{b_{1,2}},$$

are necessary to ensure that the range for each firm's supply curve pertains to nonnegative values for price and quantity supplied. For example, regarding firm 1, if $P = -b_{0,1}/b_{1,1}$, the quantity supplied by that firm, $Q^{S,1}$, equals zero, where for prices greater than $-b_{0,1}/b_{1,1}$, the firm supplies positive amounts of the product, or $Q^{S,1} > 0$. Similarly, for firm 2, if $P = -b_{0,2}/b_{1,2}$, $Q^{S,2} = 0$, and thus $Q^{S,2} > 0$ provided $P > -b_{0,2}/b_{1,2}$. Recall, since $b_{0,1}$ and $b_{0,2}$ are restricted to be negative, the terms $-b_{0,1}/b_{1,1}$ and $-b_{0,2}/b_{1,2}$ both have positive values. Since $P \ge -b_{0,1}/b_{1,1}$ for firm 1 and $P \ge -b_{0,2}/b_{1,2}$ for firm 2, then if $-b_{0,1}/b_{1,1} < -b_{0,2}/b_{1,2}$, firm 1 begins supplying output at a lower price than does firm 2. Only when $P > -b_{0,2}/b_{1,2}$ will we observe both firms supplying output to the market. Thus, the technique for obtaining the market supply curve is a summation process, subject to the restrictions on P for each firm.

Perhaps an easier way for us to illustrate this process is with a specific example. Assume the individual firm supply curves for firms 1 and 2, respectively, are

$$Q^{S,1} = -9 + 3P, \quad \text{for} \quad P \ge -\left(\frac{-9}{3}\right), \quad \text{or} \quad P \ge 3,$$

and

$$Q^{S,2} = -5 + P, \quad \text{for} \quad P \ge -\left(\frac{-5}{1}\right), \quad \text{or} \quad P \ge 5.$$

If $P < 3 < 5$, neither firm supplies any output. If $3 < P < 5$, firm 1 supplies some output, while firm 2 does not. As a result, for $3 < P < 5$, the market supply curve is simply the same as the supply curve for firm 1, or

$$Q^{S,M} = Q^{S,1} = -9 + 3P.$$

For example, if $P = \$4$

$$Q^{S,M} = -9 + 3(4) = 3 \text{ units.}$$

If $P \geq 5 > 3$, both firms will supply output, and the market supply curve consists of the summation of the individual supply curves for both firms

$$Q^{S,M} = Q^{S,1} + Q^{S,2},$$

or

$$Q^{S,M} = (-9 + 3P) + (-5 + P)$$
$$Q^{S,M} = -14 + 4P.$$

Thus, for example, if $P = \$6$

$$Q^{S,M} = -14 + 4(6) = 10 \text{ units},$$

where firm 1 supplies

$$Q^{S,1} = -9 + 3(6) = 9 \text{ units},$$

and firm 2 supplies

$$Q^{S,2} = -5 + (6) = 1 \text{ unit}.$$

Summarizing, we define the market supply curve in segments, where each segment depends on the coefficients pertaining to each individual firm's supply curve, and therefore, on the minimum price at which each firm finds it profitable to supply output.

There is yet another qualification for deriving a short-run market supply curve. Each firm's short-run supply curve consists of its $SRMC$ curve provided $P \geq AVC$, where $SRMC = dSRTC/dQ$. Recall that each $SRTC$ curve contains the price of the variable labor input, P_L, as a determinant that is held constant at some level. Since $SRMC$ is the derivative of $SRTC$ with respect to Q, it also depends on the level of P_L. In the short run, the only way a firm can change the level of output it produces is by changing the amount of the variable labor input it employs. As a result, this process may cause a change in the associated input price, P_L. We will present a detailed discussion of the rationale underlying this possibility in Chapter 20. At this point, however, we can explain this potential outcome in terms of the abundance of the variable input, labor. Generally, this abundance depends on such factors as geographic mobility and the level of skill associated with this input. If the firms comprising the market are able to use labor that is relatively abundant because it is, say, unskilled, then they can employ additional units without paying a higher price for this input. However, if the firms must use skilled labor that is relatively scarce, then they are forced to pay a higher input price in order to attract additional units of this type of labor. This criterion regarding the effect of changes in the quantity of output supplied by firms on the price of the variable labor input, P_L, impacts the derivation of market supply curves.

Assuming that the horizontal summation process illustrated in Figure 13.7 is based on the assumption of P_L remaining constant, then we expect that as the output price rises, the individual firms are able to increase the quantity of output supplied more substantially than if P_L varies directly with the quantity of output. We can best demonstrate this point with the graphical analysis shown in Figure 13.8. The individual

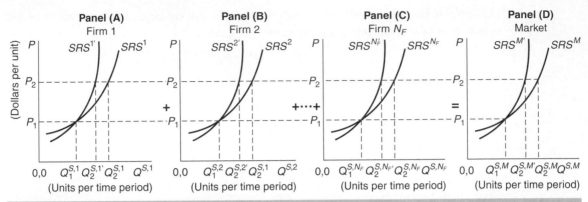

FIGURE 13.8 Comparison of Short-Run Market Supply Curve Derivation Process for Cases of Constant and Increasing Variable Input Price

firm supply curves $SRS^1, SRS^2, \ldots, SRS^{N_F}$, are the same short-run supply curves illustrated in Figure 13.7, where we established these curves on the assumption that P_L does not vary with the quantity of output supplied by each firm. As a result, the market supply curve in this case is the relatively flatter curve, SRS^M, indicating that as the product price increases from P_1 to P_2, $Q^{S,M}$ correspondingly increases by the substantial amount $Q_2^{S,M} - Q_1^{S,M}$. By contrast, if we assume that P_L varies directly with the quantity of output supplied by the firms in the market, then we represent the firm supply curves as $SRS^{1'}, SRS^{2'}, \ldots, SRS^{N'_F}$, where each of these curves can be observed to be steeper than $SRS^1, SRS^2, \ldots, SRS^{N_F}$, respectively. Therefore, in this situation, if the output price increases from P_1 to P_2, each firm increases its supply of output to only $Q^{S,1'}, Q^{S,2'}, \ldots, Q^{S,N'_F}$, respectively, where $Q^{S,1'} < Q^{S,1}, Q^{S,2'} < Q^{S,2}, \ldots, Q^{S,N'_F} < Q^{S,N_F}$. Each firm increases its quantity supplied by a smaller amount than in the preceding case because as P rises and each firm's Q^S increases, so does P_L. As a result, each firm's $SRMC$ rises by a greater amount than when P_L remains constant, causing its profit-maximizing level of output to increase by a comparatively smaller amount. Thus, when the price rises to P_2, the market quantity supplied, $Q^{S,M'}$, also increases by a smaller amount than in the preceding case, or

$$Q_2^{S,M'} = Q_2^{S,1'} + Q_2^{S,2'} + \ldots + Q_2^{S,N'_F} < Q_2^{S,M} = Q_2^{S,1} + Q_2^{S,2} + \ldots + Q_2^{S,N_F}.$$

In summary, if the variable input price, P_L, varies directly with the quantity of output supplied, the market supply curve will be steeper, indicating a weaker response in the quantity of output supplied to a change in the product price than for the case in which P_L remains constant.

13.6.1 Short-Run Supply Curves and Comparative Statics

After constructing a model, we can solve it to obtain solution values for the variables under analysis. We can also use a model to examine the impact on these solution values caused by a change in some underlying determinant. This latter analysis is known as comparative statics, and we can apply it to the supply and demand model constructed in the preceding sections of this chapter. As an example, recall the short-run total cost curve for a firm

$$SRTC = 160 + 0.025Q^2$$

that we derived in Chapter 12. This curve is based on the production function

$$Q = 10K^{1/2}L^{1/2},$$

where Q is the level of output and the terms K and L represent the amounts of capital and labor inputs, respectively, used by the firm in its production process. The prices of the capital and labor inputs are $P_K = \$40$ and $P_L = \$10$, and the amount of capital employed is fixed at $K = 4$ units. We will assume that this firm operates in a perfectly competitive market consisting of 100 identical firms. In addition, let's assume that the market own-price demand curve for the good is

$$Q^{D,M} = 10,000 - 500P,$$

where $Q^{D,M}$ is the market quantity demanded of the good and P is the price of the good. We can use this information to derive the short-run supply curve for both this typical firm and the entire market. In addition, we can determine the equilibrium price, the equilibrium quantities demanded and supplied of the good, and the typical firm's short-run total profit.

A firm's short-run supply curve is the same as its short-run marginal cost curve, provided it is greater than or equal to its average variable cost. Therefore, since

$$SRTC = 160 + 0.025Q^2,$$

then

$$SRMC = \frac{dSRTC}{dQ} = 0.05Q,$$

and since

$$AVC = \frac{0.025Q^2}{Q} = 0.025Q,$$

then $SRMC \geq AVC$ for any nonnegative value of Q. Recall that a perfectly competitive firm determines its profit-maximizing level of output in the short run where $P = SRMC$. Therefore, we can represent this firm's short-run supply curve as

$$P = 0.05Q,$$

or

$$Q^{S,F} = \frac{1}{0.05}P = 20P.$$

The short-run market supply curve, $Q^{S,M}$, is the summation of the individual firms' short-run supply curves. Since we are assuming that the market is comprised of 100 identical firms, then

$$Q^{S,M} = 100Q^{S,F} = 100(20P) = 2000P.$$

We can simultaneously solve the market supply and own-price demand curves, along with the equilibrium condition, to determine the equilibrium values of P, $Q^{D,M}$ and $Q^{S,M}$. Since the equilibrium condition is

$$Q^{D,M} = Q^{S,M},$$

then

$$10,000 - 500P = 2000P$$
$$P^* = \$4,$$

and

$$Q^{D,M^*} = Q^{S,M^*} = 2000(4) = 8000 \text{ units.}$$

The typical firm maximizes its short-run profit by producing a level of output, Q^{F^*}, where $P = SRMC$. Thus

$$4 = 0.05Q$$

or

$$Q^{F^*} = \frac{4}{0.05} = 80 \text{ units.}$$

The firm's short-run profit is computed as

$$SR\pi = TR - STRC = PQ - SRTC$$
$$= 4(80) - [160 + 0.025(80)^2]$$
$$= \$0.$$

We can demonstrate the process of comparative statics by assuming that the price of labor increases to $P_L = \$40$, where this increase affects all firms comprising the market. As an additional exercise, you can verify that if $P_L = \$40$, the firm's short-run total cost curve is

$$SRTC = 160 + 0.10Q^2.$$

In this case, the firm's short-run marginal cost curve is

$$SRMC = \frac{dSRTC}{dQ} = 0.20Q,$$

and its inverse short-run supply curve is

$$P = 0.20Q.$$

Thus the firm's short-run supply curve, $Q^{S,F}$ is

$$Q^{S,F} = \frac{1}{0.20} P = 5P.$$

Since this increase in P_L affects all firms in the industry, we compute the new short-run market supply curve, $Q^{S,M}$, as

$$Q^{S,M} = 100 \ Q^{S,F} = 100(5P) = 500P.$$

The equilibrium price and quantity are determined as

$$10,000 - 500P = 500P.$$

where

$$P* = \$10,$$

and

$$Q^{D,M} = Q^{S,M} = 500(10) = 5000 \text{ units.}$$

Each perfectly competitive firm determines its profit-maximizing level of output according to the rule $P = SRMC$; thus

$$10 = 0.20Q,$$

and

$$Q^{F*} = \frac{10}{0.20} = 50 \text{ units.}$$

At these levels of price and output, we compute the typical firm's short-run total profit as

$$SR\pi = TR - SRTC = PQ - SRTC$$
$$10(50) - [160 + 0.10(50)^2]$$
$$= 500 - 160 - 250 = \$90.$$

13.6.2   Short-Run Elasticity of Supply

We can describe the degree of responsiveness between the quantity of output supplied in the short run and the own price of a good in terms of the **short-run elasticity of supply**, where this concept is *the ratio of the percentage change in the quantity supplied of a good, in the short run, to the percentage change in its own price*. Procedurally, this concept is analogous to the own-price elasticity of demand we discussed in Chapter 7. We express the formula for elasticity of supply, denoted $E_{Q^S,P}$, as

$$E_{Q^S,P} = \frac{\%\Delta Q^S}{\%\Delta P} = \frac{\dfrac{\Delta Q^S}{Q^S}}{\dfrac{\Delta P}{P}} = \frac{\Delta Q^S}{\Delta P}\frac{P}{Q^S} = \frac{\partial Q^S}{\partial P}\frac{P}{Q^S},$$

where Q^S and P represent the short-run market quantity supplied of a good and the price of that good, respectively. Since short-run market supply curves generally possess nonnegative slope values, or $\partial Q^S / \partial P \geq 0$, the computed values for $E_{Q^S,P}$ are generally greater than or equal to zero. In addition, the greater the percentage response in quantity supplied, $\%\Delta Q^S$, resulting from a percentage change in price, $\%\Delta P$, the greater is the value of $E_{Q^S,P}$.

Several underlying factors influence the responsiveness of the quantity supplied of a good to changes in its price, thus affecting the computed value of $E_{Q^S,P}$. Most of these factors, such as the process by which the good is produced and the prevailing state of technology, are reflected by the change in each firm's *SRMC* due to a change in its production of output. This relationship between *SRMC* and Q^S also reflects the extent of diminishing marginal productivity associated with each firm's variable input. As we discussed in Chapter 9, the greater the marginal product of an input diminishes with increases in the production of output, the greater is the rise in marginal cost, and thus the steeper, or less elastic, is the *SRS* curve for each firm and for the market as a whole. The other major factor underlying the elasticity of a market supply curve is the degree to which input prices vary with the production of output. We demonstrated previously that if the price of the variable input varies directly with the production of output, the market supply curve is steeper, or less elastic, than if that input price remains constant. Logically, the greater the amount by which an input price varies directly with the production of output, the steeper, or less elastic, is the market supply curve because in this situation it becomes increasingly expensive for firms to expand their production of output.

The actual computation of elasticity of supply is very simple, and we can best demonstrate this procedure with a numerical example. Recall the short-run market supply curve we derived earlier:

$$Q^{S,M} = -14 + 4P.$$

For some value of price, say $P = \$6$

$$Q^{S,M} = -14 + 4(6) = 10 \text{ units,}$$

and therefore we compute the elasticity of supply as

$$E_{Q^S,P} = \frac{\partial Q^S}{\partial P}\frac{P}{Q^S} = 4\left(\frac{6}{10}\right) = \frac{24}{10} = 2.4.$$

How can we interpret this value? This result indicates that at this point on the market supply curve, a 1% change in price results in a 2.4% change in quantity supplied, in the same direction. In the next chapter, we will shift our focus from analyzing perfectly competitive firm and market behavior in the short run to the long-run time period.

13.7 SUMMARY

This is the first of seven chapters in which we examine various types of market structures within which firms operate. In this chapter, we defined a perfectly competitive market structure and cited its unique characteristics. We also developed and analyzed the behavior of firms operating within this market structure for the short-run time period. The main topics covered in this chapter are as follows.

- A market for a good or service is an aggregation of actual or potential buyers and sellers who by their interactions determine the equilibrium price and quantity of that good or service.
- A perfectly competitive market is defined by the following structural characteristics: (1) a large number of insignificantly small buyers and sellers, (2) a

homogeneous good or service, (3) easy entry and exit of firms into or from the market, and (4) all buyers and sellers' equal access to perfect information relevant to the market.

- A perfectly competitive firm acts as a price taker in the market because each firm produces an imperceptibly small portion of total market amount sold.
- A perfectly competitive firm's own-price demand curve is perfectly elastic, and therefore horizontal, at the market-determined equilibrium price. The firm's own-price demand curve also represents its marginal and average revenue functions.
- The goal of a perfectly competitive firm is to maximize its profit. It achieves this goal by producing the level of output at which $MR \equiv P = SRMC$.
- The short-run supply curve for a perfectly competitive firm is its $SRMC$ curve for $P \geq AVC$, and the portion of the vertical axis, or where $Q = 0$, for $P < AVC$.
- If the price of a variable input varies directly with the quantity of output supplied, then the market supply curve is steeper than for the case in which the price of the variable input remains constant.
- We compute the short-run elasticity of supply as the ratio of the percentage change in quantity supplied of a good to the percentage change in the price of that good.

KEY TERMS

- average revenue, page 333
- equilibrium condition, page 328
- equilibrium price, page 327
- market, page 323
- market structure, page 325
- perfectly competitive market, page 325
- short-run elasticity of supply, page 355
- short-run market supply curve, page 327

EXERCISES

13.1 Discuss the fundamental characteristics of a perfectly competitive market structure.

13.2 How common are perfectly competitive markets in the real world? Provide a real-world example of such a market structure. Of what significance is the study of the perfectly competitive market model?

13.3 What are some of the difficulties in defining the market for a good or service?

13.4 The market for good X is assumed to be perfectly competitive, with market supply and own-price demand curves given as

$$Q^{S,M} = -25{,}000 + 3000P$$
$$Q^{D,M} = 135{,}000 - 5000P.$$

Determine the equilibrium price and quantity exchanged in the market for good X.

13.5 Refer to the market supply and own-price demand curves in Exercise 13.4.

 a. Plot the market supply and own-price demand curves in their inverse forms and indicate market equilibrium.

 b. If the price of good X is regulated to be \$25, determine the value of excess supply or excess demand in the market, and discuss the process by which equilibrium will be restored in the market.

13.6 The short-run total cost function for a perfectly competitive producer of good X is

$$SRTC(Q) = 2 + 28Q - 3Q^2 + \frac{1}{3}Q^3.$$

Using this information, as well as your response to Exercise 13.4, determine a typical firm's profit-maximizing level of output of good X and the amount of profit (or loss) earned. Also calculate the number of firms operating in this industry.

13.7 Define each of the following profit measures for a firm.

 a. short-run profit, $SR\pi$

 b. short-run marginal profit, $SRM\pi$

 c. short-run average profit, $SR\,AVE\pi$

13.8 Assuming the market price received by a perfectly competitive firm for its output is \$40 and the firm's short-run total cost function is

$$SRTC(Q) = \frac{1}{3}Q^3 - 4Q^2 + 56Q + 2,$$

 a. Formulate the $SR\pi$ function, and determine the firm's profit-maximizing level of output and amount of profit earned.

 b. Formulate the firm's $SRM\pi$ function and determine the value of $SRM\pi$ when the firm is producing at its profit-maximizing level of output.

 c. Formulate the firm's $SR\,AVE\pi$ function and determine the value of $SR\,AVE\pi$ when the firm is producing at its profit-maximizing level of output.

CHAPTER 14

Perfect Competition in the Long Run

14.1 INTRODUCTION

In the preceding chapter, we analyzed firm behavior within the context of a perfectly competitive market for the short-run time period. Specifically, we demonstrated how a typical perfectly competitive firm and the market within which it operates interact to determine short-run equilibrium values of such variables as price and output for both the market and a typical firm. During the short run, a firm is confined to a fixed amount of capital, or plant size, and thus it must make its decisions regarding the amount of output it produces subject to the limitations imposed by this constraining factor.

In the long run, however, firm behavior is not constrained in this manner because each firm is able to adjust its output by varying all of its inputs, including the amount of capital it uses. In addition, perfectly competitive firms are free to enter and exit markets. Therefore, in the long run, established firms are not only free to adjust their level of capital if they remain in the market, but are also able to sell their capital and exit the market entirely. In addition, new firms are free to enter the market if they choose to do so, where the motive for this event, as well as those mentioned above, is the goal of profit maximization.

As an example, consider a farmer who is currently using all of his inputs to produce corn. Assume that due to changing conditions in the soybean market, the farmer discovers that he can increase his profit by $20,000 by switching to soybean production. Thus, in the long run, we expect that the higher profit this farmer could earn by producing soybeans provides an incentive for him to exit the corn market and move his resources into the production of soybeans, *ceteris paribus*. In this chapter, we will examine the impact of such entry and exit on the long-run performance of a typical perfectly competitive firm and its associated market. In addition, we will evaluate the performance outcomes of this market structure from a broad social perspective.

14.2 LONG-RUN EQUILIBRIUM IN A PERFECTLY COMPETITIVE MARKET

We stated earlier that the entry and exit of firms to and from markets is motivated by the goal of profit maximization. The existence of positive economic profits earned by incumbent firms provides an incentive for new firms to enter a market. This result follows because a positive economic profit indicates a return to the owners that is greater than their opportunity costs. Conversely, negative economic profits, or losses, incurred

359

by some firms provide an incentive for those firms to exit a market since their owners are earning less than their opportunity costs. Thus, the existence of either positive or negative profits represents unstable situations in perfectly competitive markets that cannot be sustained in the long run.

We can demonstrate this instability of nonzero profits by first recalling that a short-run market supply curve represents the summation of individual firm supply curves, and, therefore, it depends on the number of firms comprising the market. Thus, in the case of entry, the short-run market supply curve shifts to the right, subsequently driving down the market price of the good. We discussed in Chapter 13 that, in the short run, a typical firm responds to decreases in the market price by decreasing its profit-maximizing level of output according to the $MR \equiv P = SRMC$ rule. Thus, as the price falls, the equilibrium value of the firm's $SRMC$ must decline by an equal amount. This decrease in output also causes the firm's average total costs to fall, but by amounts less than the decreases in price. Since price is the same as average revenue, and short-run average profit, $SR\ AVE\pi$, is represented as

$$SR\ AVE\pi = AR - ATC,$$

then $SR\ AVE\pi$ falls as the firm decreases its production of output.

In the long run, however, the firm will make an additional adjustment in an attempt to protect its profit from a declining market price. Specifically, this entails altering its level of capital. In the event of a price decline, the firm will decrease its plant size to a level that enables it to produce the associated level of output in the most cost-efficient manner. The firm will then be using an optimal input combination, producing a level of output where $ATC = LRAC$. However, if the market price and the corresponding profit-maximizing level of output continue to decline, then, for the general case of a quadratic LRAC curve, a firm will only decrease its plant size so far, indicating that its $LRAC$ can only be decreased to a certain point. Specifically, this occurs at the particular level of output at which the firm adjusts its plant size until $ATC = LRAC$, corresponding to the minimum point on its $LRAC$ curve. At this point, the firm produces a level of output at which it realizes all economies of scale advantages, yet experiences none of the disadvantages associated with diseconomies of scale.

It is also true that at this level of production

$$P = AR = LRAC = ATC,$$

and therefore the firm's profit is zero. Recall that even when a firm earns zero economic profit, it is still covering its opportunity cost,—that is, it is doing as well in this industry as it could elsewhere. As a result, there is no longer an incentive for new firms to enter the market, and the downward pressure on market price ceases. If the price falls below $LRAC$, firms experience negative profits, or losses, and some will choose to exit the market. The exit of firms from the market drives up the market price until $P = LRAC$, at which point each firm's profit once again equals zero. In summary, when long-run equilibrium in a perfectly competitive market is achieved, each firm's long-run profit is zero, all firms produce their output using an optimal input combination, and each firm produces a level of output at which its long-run average cost is at the minimum value.

We represent a firm's long-run profit function, $LR\pi$, as the difference between its total revenue, TR, and its long-run total cost, $LRTC$, where

$$LRTC = C(Q, \overline{P}_{K,1}, \overline{P}_{L,1}).$$

Thus

$$LR\pi = TR - LRTC$$
$$= TR - C(Q, \overline{P}_{K,1}, \overline{P}_{L,1}),$$

and since

$$TR = \overline{P}_1 Q,$$
$$LR\pi = \overline{P}_1 Q - C(Q, \overline{P}_{K,1}, \overline{P}_{L,1}).$$

We can determine the firm's profit-maximizing level of output by differentiating $LR\pi$ with respect to Q and setting the result equal to zero as

$$\frac{dLR\pi}{dQ} = \frac{d\overline{P}_1 Q}{dQ} - \frac{dC(Q, \overline{P}_{K,1}, \overline{P}_{L,1})}{dQ} = 0,$$

or

$$P_1 = \frac{dC(Q, \overline{P}_{K,1}, \overline{P}_{L,1})}{dQ}.$$

Previously, we demonstrated that for a perfectly competitive firm, $P \equiv MR$, while the term $dC(Q, \overline{P}_{K,1}, \overline{P}_{L,1})/dQ$ can be recognized as the firm's long-run marginal cost, $LRMC$, discussed in Chapter 11. Therefore, the necessary condition for a long-run profit maximum is

$$MR \equiv P = LRMC.$$

We can use this condition to determine a firm's long-run profit-maximizing level of output. Furthermore, because of the condition of free entry and exit, it follows that this level of output corresponds to zero long-run profit for each firm.

The process by which a long-run equilibrium is established for a perfectly competitive firm is illustrated in Figure 14.1. We initially assume that the market price is established at P_2, where the market own-price demand curve, D^M, and supply curve, SRS_2^M, intersect. This price corresponds to the equilibrium condition, that the quantity supplied equals quantity demanded, or $Q_2^{S,M} = Q_2^{D,M}$, as we have shown in panel (B). The behavior of a typical firm is illustrated in panel (A), where we can observe that the firm determines its profit-maximizing level of output to be Q_2, at which

$$MR_2 \equiv \overline{P}_2 = LRMC_2.$$

Firm behavior in the long run involves adjusting the level of K so as to produce its profit-maximizing level of output in the most cost-efficient manner. Therefore, when

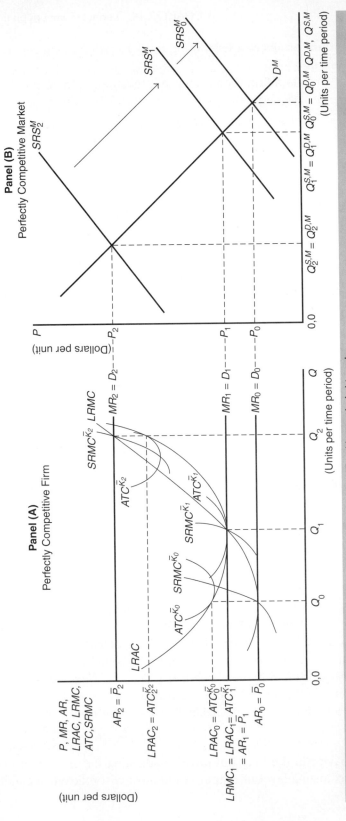

FIGURE 14.1 Process By Which Long-Run Perfectly Competitive Equilibrium Is Achieved

the market price is $\overline{P}_2$, the firm adjusts its level of capital to $\overline{K}_2$ units, generating the short-run cost curves $ATC^{\overline{K}_2}$ and $SRMC^{\overline{K}_2}$. It can then produce the associated level of output, Q_2, using an optimal input combination. Once the optimal level of K is established, the firm determines its profit-maximizing level of output, from a short-run perspective, by employing the rule

$$MR_2 \equiv \overline{P}_2 = SRMC_2^{\overline{K}_2}.$$

In this case, the level of output is Q_2, or the same amount we determined using the long-run profit maximization condition

$$MR_2 \equiv \overline{P}_2 = LRMC_2.$$

These results are identical because the long- and short-run situations are not determined independently of one another. Tying the two conditions together, we find that Q_2 is established where

$$MR_2 \equiv \overline{P}_2 = LRMC_2 = SRMC_2^{\overline{K}_2}.$$

However, this solution is not a stable one because at Q_2

$$LR\,AVE\pi_2 = SR\,AVE\pi_2 = AR_2 - LRAC_2 = AR_2 - ATC_2^{\overline{K}_2} > \$0/\text{unit}.$$

In other words, this situation yields a positive long-run profit that ultimately cannot be maintained because this profit entices new firms to enter the market since they can earn more profit in this industry than elsewhere. We have represented this new firm entry in panel (B) of Figure 14.1 by the rightward shift of the short-run market supply curve from SRS_2^M to SRS_1^M. As a result, the market price is driven down to P_1, and the firm determines its profit-maximizing level of output to be Q_1 at which

$$MR_1 \equiv \overline{P}_1 = LRMC_1 = SRMC_1^{\overline{K}_1}.$$

Note that since $Q_1 < Q_2$, the firm reduces its level of capital from $\overline{K}_2$ to $\overline{K}_1$ in order to use a lower optimal input combination, where this decrease in capital use is reflected by the short-run cost curves, $ATC^{\overline{K}_1}$ and $SRMC^{\overline{K}_1}$. We can observe in panel (A) that at Q_1 the firm's average profit is

$$LR\,AVE\pi_1 = SR\,AVE\pi_1 = AR_1 - LRAC_1 = AR_1 - ATC_1^{\overline{K}_1} = \$0/\text{unit}.$$

Since the level of profit is zero, there no longer exists any incentive for new firms to enter the market, so the market price remains stable at P_1. Therefore, we designate the production of Q_1 units of output by the typical firm, using a plant size of $\overline{K}_1$, as a **long-run perfectly competitive equilibrium**, or *a situation for which a typical firm produces a level of output corresponding to its minimum long-run average cost and zero profit.* This is a stable equilibrium since there are no forces operating to change it. Specifically, since all firms are earning zero profit, there is no incentive for entry or exit, and the firms are not able to make any further input adjustments to lower their costs.

To complete our analysis of this important result, let's assume that so many firms enter the market that the short-run market supply curve shifts to SRS_0^M, driving the market price down to P_0. In this case, the typical perfectly competitive firm maximizes its profit by producing Q_0 at which

$$MR_0 \equiv \overline{P}_0 = LRMC_0 = SRMC_0^{\overline{K}_0}.$$

Note that the firm is using a smaller plant size $\overline{K}_0$, where $\overline{K}_0 < \overline{K}_1$, so as to produce Q_0 in the most cost-efficient manner. However, at this level of output the firm's average profit is

$$LR\,AVE\pi_0 = SR\,AVE\pi_0 = AR_0 - LRAC_0 = AR_0 - ATC_0^{\overline{K}_0} < \$0/unit.$$

This negative profit indicates that the firm is not covering all of its opportunity costs and, therefore, can earn a greater profit if it invests its resources in some other industry. As a result, this situation is not stable in the long run since some firms will exit the market, causing the market supply curve to shift back to SRS_1^M where the market price rises to P_1. The remaining firms will react by increasing their plant sizes to $\overline{K}_1$ units and producing the long-run equilibrium level of output, Q_1 units. We have reproduced the long-run equilibrium result for a perfectly competitive firm in Figure 14.2, where the typical firm produces Q_1 units at which

$$MR_1 \equiv \overline{P}_1 = LRMC_1 = SRMC_1^{\overline{K}_1} = LRAC_1 = ATC_1^{\overline{K}_1}.$$

We can also demonstrate the long-run equilibrium outcome for a perfectly competitive firm with a mathematical example. Assume that the firm's constrained optimization process yields the total cost function

$$C = \frac{1}{3}Q^3 - 5Q^2 + 60Q - KQ + 0.25K^2, \tag{14.1}$$

from which we can generate a family of $SRTC$ curves, one for each possible fixed value of capital, K. We determine the optimal level of capital for producing different

FIGURE 14.2 Long-Run Equilibrium for a Perfectly Competitive Firm

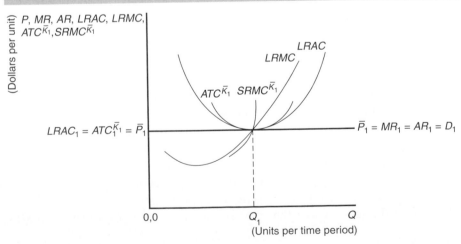

levels of output by partially differentiating this cost function with respect to K and setting the result equal to zero as

$$\frac{\partial C}{\partial K} = -Q + 0.5K = 0,$$

and therefore

$$K = 2Q. \tag{14.2}$$

Substituting this result into equation (14.1) yields the firm's $LRTC$ function as

$$LRTC = \frac{1}{3}Q^3 - 5Q^2 + 60Q - 2Q(Q) + 0.25(2Q)^2$$

$$= \frac{1}{3}Q^3 - 5Q^2 + 60Q - 2Q^2 + Q^2$$

$$= \frac{1}{3}Q^3 - 6Q^2 + 60Q. \tag{14.3}$$

This function indicates the minimum cost at which each level of output can be produced, because in the long run the firm employs optimal levels of both inputs, labor and capital. Now let's assume the market price is $P = \$40$. The firm maximizes its long-run profit by producing a level of output at which $P = LRMC$. Therefore, since

$$LRMC = \frac{dLRTC}{dQ} = Q^2 - 12Q + 60,$$

then equating $LRMC$ to $P = \$40$ yields

$$Q^2 - 12Q + 60 = P = \$40,$$

or

$$Q^2 - 12Q + 20 = 0$$
$$(Q - 2)(Q - 10) = 0,$$

resulting in the roots $Q = 2$ and $Q = 10$ units. You can verify that the profit-maximizing level of output is $Q = 10$ units, corresponding to a maximum, although unstable, long-run profit that we compute as

$$LR\pi = PQ - LRTC$$

$$= 40(10) - \left(\frac{1}{3}Q^3 - 6Q^2 + 60Q\right)$$

$$= 400 - \frac{1}{3}(10)^3 + 6(10)^2 - 60(10) = \$66.67.$$

This long-run response to a market price includes the firm producing its profit-maximizing level of output by using the optimal plant size, K. Thus, in order to produce $Q = 10$ units in the most cost-efficient manner, the firm will adjust its level of capital according to equation (14.2) to be

$$K_2 = 2Q = 2(10) = 20 \text{ units.}$$

We can obtain the short-run total cost curve pertaining to this level of capital by substituting $K = 20$ units into equation (14.1), yielding

$$C = SRTC^{\overline{K}_2} = \frac{1}{3}Q^3 - 5Q^2 + 60Q - 20Q + 0.25(20)^2$$

$$= \frac{1}{3}Q^3 - 5Q^2 + 40Q + 100.$$

Now, we can compute the same profit-maximizing level of output as determined above by employing the rule $MR \equiv P = SRMC$. Thus

$$C = SRMC^{\overline{K}_2} = \frac{dSRTC^{\overline{K}_2}}{dQ} = Q^2 - 10Q + 40,$$

and since $P_2 = \$40$, then by setting short-run marginal cost equal to the market price, we determine the value of Q as

$$Q^2 - 10Q + 40 = \$40$$
$$Q^2 - 10Q = 0$$
$$Q(Q - 10) = 0,$$

yielding the roots $Q = 0$ and $Q = 10$ units. By substituting these values for Q into the short-run profit function, you can verify that the profit-maximizing value of output is $Q = 10$ units. We compute the maximized short-run profit as

$$SR\pi_2 = TR - SRTC$$
$$= P_2Q - \left(\frac{1}{3}Q^3 - 5Q^2 + 40Q + 100\right)$$
$$= 40(10) - \frac{1}{3}(10)^3 + 5(10)^2 - 40(10) - 100 = \$66.67.$$

Note that these values for Q and $SR\pi$ are the same as those we computed earlier employing the condition $P = LRMC$.

These results are not stable, however, inasmuch as this positive profit will, in the long run, entice the entry of new firms into the market, subsequently driving down the market price. The firm reacts to this lower market price by reducing its profit-maximizing level of output and by reducing the level of capital, as well as the amount of labor, it employs. For example, assume that the market price is ultimately driven down to $\overline{P}_1 = \$33$. The firm now determines its profit-maximizing level of output as

$$\overline{P}_1 = LRMC$$
$$33 = Q^2 - 12Q + 60$$
$$Q^2 - 12Q + 27 = 0$$
$$(Q - 3)(Q - 9) = 0.$$

Although this equation yields the roots $Q = 3$ and $Q = 9$ units, you can verify that $Q = 9$ units represents the profit-maximizing level of output. At this level of output the firm's long-run profit is

$$LR\pi = TR - LRTC$$

$$= \overline{P}_1 Q - \left(\frac{1}{3}Q^3 - 6Q^2 + 60Q\right)$$

$$= 33(9) - \frac{1}{3}(9)^3 + 6(9)^2 - 60(9) = \$0.$$

Consequently, these values for P, Q, and $LR\pi$ correspond to a long-run equilibrium since there exists no incentive for firms to either enter or exit the market.

   We can obtain the same results using the relevant short-run analysis. In order to produce $Q = 9$ units of output efficiently, the firm adjusts its level of capital according to equation (14.2) as

$$K_1 = 2Q = 2(9) = 18 \text{ units.}$$

Once again using equation (14.1), we find that this level of capital yields the short-run total cost curve

$$C = SRTC^{\overline{K}_1} = \frac{1}{3}Q^3 - 5Q^2 + 60Q - 18Q + 0.25(18)^2$$

$$= \frac{1}{3}Q^3 - 5Q^2 + 42Q + 81.$$

Now, after determining the optimal value of capital, we can compute the firm's short-run profit-maximizing level of output, where this value will be the same as that we determined earlier for the long run. The short-run marginal cost function is

$$SRMC^{\overline{K}_1} = \frac{dSRTC^{\overline{K}_1}}{dQ} = Q^2 - 10Q + 42,$$

and applying the condition, $MR \equiv P = SRMC$, we determine the profit-maximizing level of output when $\overline{P}_1 = \$33$ as

$$Q^2 - 10Q + 42 = \$33$$
$$Q^2 - 10Q + 9 = 0$$
$$(Q - 1)(Q - 9) = 0.$$

You can verify that the short-run profit-maximizing level of output is the same value, $Q = 9$ units, that we obtained earlier for the long-run analysis. The corresponding short-run profit is

$$SR\pi_1 = \overline{P}_1 Q - \left(\frac{1}{3}Q^3 - 5Q^2 + 42Q + 81\right),$$

and since $\overline{P}_1 = \$33$ and $Q = 9$

$$SR\pi_1 = 33(9) - \frac{1}{3}(9)^3 + 5(9)^2 - 42(9) - 81 = \$0.$$

This short-run profit of zero corresponds to producing $Q = 9$ units in the least costly manner and thus yields the same amount as the long-run profit when $\overline{P}_1 = \$33$.

In long-run equilibrium, the typical firm produces its profit-maximizing level of output at the minimum value of long-run average cost, reflecting the fact that it realizes all economies of scale, while experiencing no diseconomies. We can determine the minimum $LRAC$ value by differentiating $LRAC$ with respect to Q and setting the term equal to zero. We expressed the $LRTC$ function in equation (14.3) as

$$LRTC = \frac{1}{3}Q^3 - 6Q^2 + 60Q.$$

Thus

$$LRAC = \frac{LRTC}{Q} = \left(\frac{1}{3}Q^3 - 6Q^2 + 60Q\right)/Q$$

$$= \frac{1}{3}Q^2 - 6Q + 60.$$

Taking the derivative of $LRAC$ with respect to Q and setting this result equal to zero yields

$$\frac{dLRAC}{dQ} = \frac{2}{3}Q - 6 = 0,$$

which we can solve for Q as

$$Q = 6\left(\frac{3}{2}\right) = 9 \text{ units.}$$

This is the value of Q corresponding to the minimum point on the $LRAC$ curve, which you can also recognize as the level of output we determined earlier corresponding to a long-run competitive equilibrium for the firm. The minimum value of $LRAC$ associated with this value of Q is

$$LRAC = \frac{1}{3}(9)^2 - 6(9) + 60 = \$33/\text{unit,}$$

or the same as the market-determined value of P or AR, reflecting the fact that long-run profit for the firm is equal to zero when $Q = 9$ units.

14.3 LONG-RUN INDUSTRY SUPPLY

Now that we have demonstrated long-run equilibrium for a perfectly competitive firm and corresponding market, we will direct our attention to developing the associated long-run market supply curve. A **long-run market, or industry, supply curve** comprises *the set of quantity–price combinations that constitute long–run equilibria in a perfectly competitive market.* Specifically, it is a curve that expresses the market quantity supplied of a good in terms of its price, where all firms in the market produce a level of output at which they have adjusted their plant sizes to a level that enables them to operate at minimum long-run average cost. In addition, due to the condition of free entry and exit, the typical firm incurs a profit equal to zero.

In the previous section, we developed long-run equilibrium on the implicit assumption that entry or exit, along with the subsequent changes in both the market quantity of output supplied and the associated demand for inputs, has no effect on the input prices of labor and capital. Thus, since these input prices are determinants in firms' cost functions, it follows that the cost structures for these firms remain unaffected. However, for some industries this will not be the case, as our assumption of constant input prices does not apply. In the next section, we will demonstrate that the slope of the long-run industry, or market, supply curve is determined by whether input prices are affected by the market supply of output. Two possible scenarios will be analyzed in detail, the first of which is known as a constant cost industry and the second as an increasing cost industry.

14.3.1   Constant Cost Industry

A **constant cost industry** is *an industry for which the input prices do not vary with changes in the demand for the inputs.* Why don't these input prices change in this case? This result occurs because the capital and labor inputs used by firms in a constant cost industry are assumed to be unspecialized and plentiful in supply. As a result, greater or lesser amounts of these inputs can be hired without affecting their prices. As an example, consider a firm that uses unskilled labor to provide dog-walking services. As the demand for labor in this market changes, there will be no change in input prices, assuming unskilled labor is plentiful.

To derive a long-run industry supply curve, we must first choose a situation in which a perfectly competitive market, along with any typical firm operating in the market, is in long-run competitive equilibrium. In panel (B) of Figure 14.3, we have illustrated such a long-run equilibrium at the quantity–price combination (Q_1^M, P_1), where the market supply curve, SRS_1^M, and market own-price demand curve, D_1^M, intersect. At this market clearing price, P_1, the market quantity demanded is equal to the market quantity supplied, or $Q_1^{D,M} = Q_1^{S,M} = Q_1^M$.

The perfectly competitive firm reacts to this market price, where the price is equal to its own-price demand, D_1, marginal revenue, MR_1, and average revenue, AR_1, curves, as we have illustrated in panel (A). The firm determines its profit-maximizing level of output, as Q_1, by applying the condition

$$LRMC_1 = SRMC_1^{\overline{K}_1} = MR_1 = \overline{P}_1.$$

At this level of output $AR_1 = ATC_1^{\overline{K}_1} = LRAC_1$, indicating that this typical firm is earning zero profit in both the long and short run. As a result, there is no incentive for firms to either enter or exit the market, indicating that P_1 is a long-run equilibrium price. Also note that at Q_1 the firm produces at the minimum value of its long-run average cost curve, $LRAC_1$, as well as at the minimum value of its average total cost curve, $ATC_1^{\overline{K}_1}$, where its level of capital is fixed at $\overline{K}_1$ units. Thus, it is producing its output in the most cost-efficient manner.

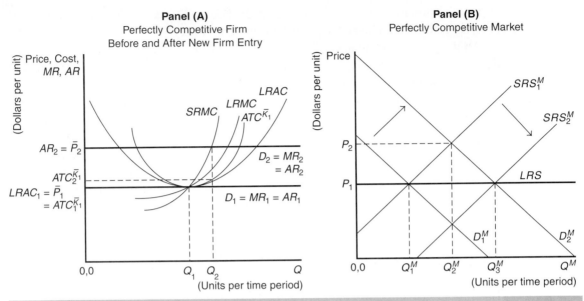

FIGURE 14.3 Derivation of Long-Run Industry Supply Curve for Constant Cost Industry

Now assume there is a change in some underlying factor that alters this equilibrium situation. Let's suppose the market demand for the good increases, perhaps because of changes in consumer incomes or tastes. We have illustrated this increase in market own-price demand in panel (B) by the rightward shift of D_1^M to D_2^M, which subsequently increases the price and market quantities supplied and demanded until a new short-run equilibrium is established at (Q_2^M, P_2), where SRS_1^M and D_2^M intersect.

For the perfectly competitive firm, this increase in market price from P_1 to P_2 causes an upward shift in its own-price demand curve from D_1 to D_2, as we have shown in panel (A). In the short run, this firm maximizes its profit by increasing its level of output to Q_2 units, where $P_2 = SRMC_2$. At this new level of production, the firm earns a positive short-run average profit of $(AR_2 - ATC_2^{\bar{K}_1})$. However, this positive profit provides an incentive for new firms to enter the industry, and thus the market equilibrium established at (Q_2^M, P_2) pertains only to the short run.

In the long run, a positive profit attracts new firms into the industry, causing the short-run market supply curve to shift to the right, subsequently increasing market supply and decreasing the price, *ceteris paribus*. For a constant cost industry, the firm's cost structures are not affected, since the supply of inputs used in this industry are so plentiful that the associated increase in demand for these inputs does not drive up their prices. However, the falling product price ultimately reduces the positive short-run profits for the incumbent firms to zero, thus eliminating any incentive for the additional entry of new firms. This result occurs once the short-run market supply curve shifts to SRS_2^M, as we have shown in panel (B) of Figure 14.3, where the market price has decreased to its original level, P_1. The typical firm maximizes its short-run profit by equating this price to its short-run marginal cost, and it reduces its output from Q_2 back to its original level, Q_1, at which its profit is, once again, equal to zero.

The new market equilibrium occurs at (Q_3^M, P_1), and since there no longer exists any incentive for either firm entry or exit, this quantity–price combination pertains to both short- and long-run equilibrium. Note that each firm produces its original level of output, Q_1; yet because more firms are now operating in the market, total industry output has increased to Q_3^M. We can now construct the long-run industry supply curve by sketching a line through the two long-run competitive equilibria, (Q_1^M, P_1) and (Q_3^M, P_1), shown as the curve LRS in panel (B). Note that in the case of a constant cost industry, this long-run industry supply curve is horizontal, indicating that, for this type of industry, marketwide output of the good can increase without the necessity of a long-run increase in its price.

14.3.2   The Effects of an Excise Tax on Short- and Long-Run Competitive Equilibrium

Now that we have examined the behavior of a typical perfectly competitive firm operating in a constant cost industry in both the short and long run, we can analyze a real-world situation. Specifically, using comparative static analysis, we will analyze the short- and long-run impacts of an excise tax on some good as it affects both consumers and producers. In this analysis, we assume that a typical perfectly competitive firm produces its output experiencing constant returns to scale, operates within a constant cost industry, and is initially in long-run equilibrium. Now suppose the government imposes a per unit tax, such as an excise tax, on the output produced and sold by all firms comprising the market.

We have illustrated the initial long-run equilibrium in Figure 14.4, where the typical perfectly competitive firm is depicted in panel (A) and the perfectly competitive market is shown in panel (B). Since the firm experiences constant returns to scale, its long-run average cost curve, $LRAC$, and long-run marginal cost curve, $LRMC$, are both horizontal, where $LRAC = LRMC$ for all levels of Q. Also, because the market is a constant cost industry, the long-run market supply curve, LRS, is also horizontal. Initially, the equilibrium price is determined where the market demand curve, D^M, the short-run market supply curve, SRS_1^M, and the long-run market supply curve, LRS, intersect. Therefore, the initial equilibrium price is P_1, and the equilibrium quantity demanded and supplied in the market is Q_1^M. The typical firm maximizes its profit by producing Q_1^F units of output at which its $SRMC = LRMC = \overline{P}_1$. Since $P = AR$, the firm's average profit at this level of output is

$$\overline{P}_1 - ATC_1 = \overline{P}_1 - LRAC_1 = 0,$$

corresponding to a long-run perfectly competitive equilibrium.

In the short run, after a per unit tax, t, is imposed on the good, the $SRMC$ and ATC curves shift up by the amount of the tax, and thus we represent them by the

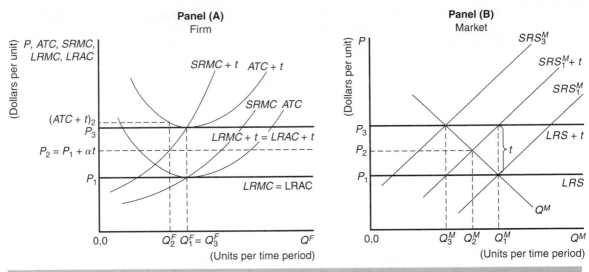

FIGURE 14.4 Incidence of a Per Unit Tax in the Short and Long Run

curves $SRMC + t$ and $ATC + t$, respectively, in panel (A) of Figure 14.4. This result applies to all firms comprising the market. Since the short-run market supply curve is the summation of individual firms' short-run marginal cost curves, the short-run market supply curve also shifts up by the amount of the tax, where we represent this new supply curve as $SRS_1^M + t$ in panel (B). The new after-tax price increases to

$$P_2 = P_1 + \propto t,$$

where $0 \leq \propto \leq 1$ is the fraction of the per unit tax passed on to the consumers. The equilibrium market quantity demanded and supplied decreases to Q_2^M units owing to the increase in the after-tax price. Thus, in the short run, consumers pay

$$P_2 - P_1 = \propto t$$

amount of the tax per unit, and the typical firm pays the remainder,

$$P_3 - P_2 = (1 - \propto)t.$$

The typical firm maximizes its short-run profit according to the condition

$$P_2 = SRMC + t,$$

where it produces Q_2^F units of the good, experiencing a per unit loss equal to

$$[P_2 - (ATC + t)_2].$$

This short-run loss induces some firms to exit the market in the long run, causing the short-run market supply curve to shift further to the left, represented by SRS_3^M. As a result, the market equilibrium price increases to P_3, while the equilibrium quantity demanded and supplied decreases to Q_3^M. For the remaining firms, the tax causes the long-run marginal and average cost curves to shift up to $LRMC + t$ and $LRAC + t$, respectively. Thus, the typical firm increases its output back to its original level, or $Q_3^F = Q_1^F$, at which

$$P_3 = SRMC + t = LRMC + t.$$

At this point, the typical firm is once again in long-run equilibrium and earns an average profit of

$$P_3 - (ATC + t) = P_3 - (LRAC + t) = \$0.$$

Thus, in long-run equilibrium the consumer pays, on a per unit basis, the amount

$$t = P_3 - P_1,$$

or the entire burden of the tax.

14.3.3   Increasing Cost Industry

An **increasing cost industry** is *an industry for which input prices vary directly with changes in the demand for the inputs.* Specifically, the inputs used in this type of industry must be specialized and therefore relatively scarce. In this case, increases in the production of the good, leading to increases in the demand for these inputs, causes the input prices to rise, ultimately creating a higher set of cost curves for the firms. Many industries fall into this category, since many production processes use at least one resource that is specialized and thus scarce. For example, due to the aging baby boom generation, demand for physicians who are cardiac specialists has increased. Accordingly, to attract more physicians into this medical specialty and compensate them for the necessary additional training, the wages paid to cardiologists must rise, thus increasing the costs of the hospitals that employ them.

We have illustrated the derivation of a long-run industry supply curve for an increasing cost industry in Figure 14.5. In panel (C) we have illustrated a long-run perfectly competitive equilibrium in the market at quantity–price combination (Q_1^M, P_1). The firm reacts to this price, P_1, and determines its profit-maximizing level of output as Q_1, according to the condition $\overline{P}_1 = SRMC_1^{\overline{K}_1} = LRMC_1$, as we have shown in panel (A). At this level of output, the firm earns zero profit in both the short and long run since $AR_1 = ATC_1^{\overline{K}_1} = LRAC_1$. As a result, no new firms have an economic incentive to enter the market, nor do any incumbent firms have an incentive to exit.

Now suppose there is an increase in market demand from D_1^M to D_2^M, as we have illustrated in panel (C), resulting in a new market equilibrium at (Q_2^M, P_2). For the firm, this increase in market price from P_1 to P_2 causes the own-price demand curve for its output to increase from D_1 to D_2, as shown in panel (A). The firm maximizes its profit by increasing its output until $\overline{P}_2 \equiv MR_2 = SRMC_2$, where it produces Q_2 units of output. At this level of production, the firm earns a positive short-run profit equal to $AR_2 - ATC_2^{\overline{K}_1}$.

Once again, these positive profits received by incumbent firms provide an incentive for new firms to enter the industry, thus distinguishing (Q_2^M, P_2) as only a short-run market equilibrium. The entry of new firms into an increasing cost industry not only causes the short-run market supply curve to shift to the right, but also increases the

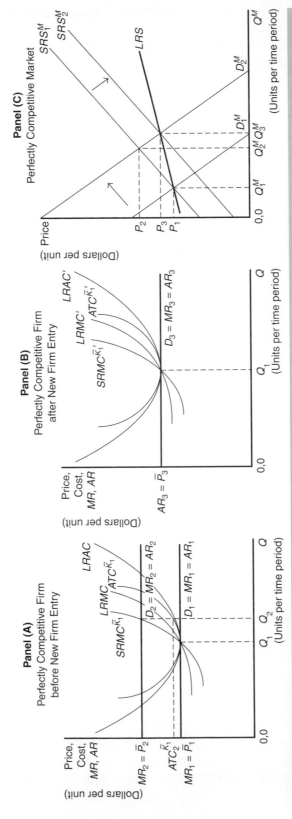

FIGURE 14.5 Derivation of Long-Run Industry Supply Curve for Increasing Cost Industry

cost structures of all firms operating in the industry. This latter result is due to the increase in the demand for scarce inputs that subsequently increases the prices of these resources. Note that this increase in demand for inputs also reflects the fact that incumbent firms are now using more of the variable input, labor, to expand their production of output in the short run.[1] In panel (B), we have illustrated the subsequent upward shift in the firm's cost structure. Specifically, by comparing the cost curves illustrated in panels (A) and (B) of Figure 14.5, observe that $LRAC' > LRAC$, $LRMC' > LRMC$, $ATC^{\overline{K}_1}{}' > ATC^{\overline{K}_1}$, and $SRMC^{\overline{K}_1}{}' > SRMC^{\overline{K}_1}$, for all values of output. Note that the primed cost curves reflect the higher input prices.

As new firms continue to enter the industry, thus shifting the short-run market supply curve to the right, the market price decreases, *ceteris paribus*. Entry continues until the short-run market supply curve reaches SRS_2^M, corresponding to price–output combination (Q_3^M, P_3), at which the firm determines its new profit-maximizing level of output where

$$\overline{P}_3 \equiv MR_3 = SRMC^{\overline{K}_1}{}' = LRMC'.$$

The particular level of output at which this condition holds true is somewhat ambiguous from a theoretical perspective. Essentially, it depends on the relative amounts by which the input prices change and on the degree of substitutability between the inputs used in the underlying production process. For the sake of simplicity, we have assumed that the $LRAC$ curve shifts directly upward so that the output level corresponding to its minimum value remains unchanged. Thus, all of the other cost curves also shift upward, and the firm continues to use the original amount of capital, $\overline{K}_1$ units. As a result, at P_3 the firm produces its original level of output, Q_1 units, as we have shown in panel (B), where both long- and short-run profits are equal to zero since at this level of output, $AR_3 = ATC^{\overline{K}_1}{}' = LRAC'_1$. In the long run, the firm's profits have been eliminated because of both the decreased product price and its increased costs. Since profits are equal to zero, there no longer exists any incentive for firm entry, and thus the output–price combination (Q_3^M, P_3) corresponds to a long-run competitive equilibrium. At Q_1 the firm produces at the minimum value of its new long-run average cost curve, $LRAC'$, as well as at the minimum value of its new short-run average total cost curve, $ATC^{\overline{K}_1}{}'$.

We can now construct the long-run industry supply curve by sketching the positively sloped line labeled LRS through the two long-run competitive equilibria, (Q_1^M, P_1) and (Q_3^M, P_3), in panel (C). Thus, in the case of an increasing cost industry, any increase in market output in the long run must be accompanied by a long-run increase in the price of the good. This result reflects the fact that firms comprising this type of industry must receive a higher price in order to pay the higher input prices associated with producing more units of the good.

---

[1]Technically, in the short run, the increase in the price of labor causes the set of short-run cost curves to shift up, dampening the incumbent firms' expansion of output. However, we have chosen not to illustrate these additional short-run effects, for the sake of graphical clarity.

There exists a third possibility in which a long-run industry supply curve possesses a negative slope. This situation can arise if the entry of new firms into the industry leads to an increase in the supply of inputs used to produce the good, thus decreasing the associated input prices. These lower input prices then reduce the cost structures of the firms operating in the industry. The very existence of this scenario, defined as a decreasing cost industry, is debatable and considered extremely rare. Therefore, we will reserve any further discussion of this topic for more advanced texts in microeconomic theory.

14.3.4 Long-Run Elasticity of Supply

In Chapter 13 we developed a measure for evaluating the degree of responsiveness between the quantity of output supplied in the short run and its own price, known as the short-run elasticity of supply. Similarly, we can also evaluate this type of responsiveness in the long run. The **long-run elasticity of supply** measures *the ratio of the percentage change in the market quantity supplied of a good in the long run to a percentage change in its own price*. We express the formula for the long-run elasticity of supply, denoted $E_{Q_L^S, P}$, as

$$E_{Q_L^S, P} = \frac{\%\Delta Q_L^S}{\%\Delta P} = \frac{\dfrac{\Delta Q_L^S}{Q_L^S}}{\dfrac{\Delta P}{P}} = \frac{\Delta Q_L^S}{\Delta P} \frac{P}{Q_L^S} = \frac{\partial Q_L^S}{\partial P} \frac{P}{Q_L^S},$$

where Q_L^S and P represent the long-run market quantity supplied of a good and its own price, respectively. Thus, the term $\partial Q_L^S/\partial P$ measures the slope of the long-run industry supply curve. Since all firms' inputs are variable in the long run, they have a greater capability of reacting to changes in the market price of their good compared to how they can respond in the short run. Thus, for any specific quantity of output selected, the value for elasticity of supply is generally greater in the long run than it is in the short run.

Another important factor we must take into consideration when evaluating long-run elasticity of supply is the effect that entry has on input prices. If this entry has no impact on input prices, as is the case with a constant cost industry, then the slope of the long-run industry supply curve, $\partial Q_L^S/\partial P$, is equal to positive infinity, as is the value of $E_{Q_L^S, P}$. These conclusions are consistent with the long-run industry supply curve that we illustrated for a constant cost industry in panel (B) of Figure 14.3. In this figure we plotted the *LRS* curve in its inverse form, and thus $\partial P/\partial Q_L^S = 0$. In the case of an increasing cost industry, the entry of new firms drives up input prices, thereby causing an increase in the firms' cost structures. As a result, the long-run industry supply curve we have illustrated in panel (C) of Figure 14.5 is positively sloped, or $\partial Q_L^S/\partial P > 0$, and therefore, the value of $E_{Q_L^S, P} = (\partial Q_L^S/\partial P)(P/Q_L^S)$ is also positive. Finally, in the rare case of a decreasing cost industry, the entry of new firms results in an increase in the supply of inputs. The prices of these inputs subsequently decrease, and accordingly, the cost structures of the firms decrease as well. In this situation, the long-run industry supply curve possesses a negative slope, where the associated value of the long-run elasticity of supply is also negative.

14.4   EVALUATION OF PERFECTLY COMPETITIVE MARKET PERFORMANCE

We can summarize and evaluate many of the outcomes associated with firm behavior within a perfectly competitive market from a broad social perspective. To conduct this evaluation, however, we must first establish some criteria by which these outcomes can be judged. These criteria are ultimately based on each society's underlying values and goals, and thus our definition and interpretation of these criteria involve some degree of subjectivity. There does seem to be a general consensus among economists that the following criteria reflect the values and goals that are common to most societies. These criteria are production efficiency, allocative efficiency, and dynamic efficiency. An additional, and more subjective, goal considered by some economists is that of fairness. Although we can establish a more complete perspective on the performance outcomes associated with a perfectly competitive market after analyzing other market structures, it is still possible at this point for us to make a preliminary evaluation.

The highly subjective goal of fairness essentially involves equal opportunity and a reasonably equitable distribution of income and wealth. Many economists consider the perfectly competitive outcome to be fair because it embodies the characteristic of free entry and exit, as well as zero long-run profits for all firms. Free entry and exit reflect equal opportunity in that individual entrepreneurs are free, at least in theory, to enter any market they choose. However, free entry does not guarantee success, since the failure of inefficient firms is an inevitable outcome associated with the efficiency of a perfectly competitive market.

Although the absence of long-run profit does not necessarily reflect an equal distribution of income or wealth in a society, it is logically more consistent with this result than a sustainable long-run profit. We consider positive short-run profits as desirable phenomena since they provide incentives for the flow of resources to their most highly valued uses. In addition, short-run profit is not considered an unfair return to a firm's owners since it represents a reward for assuming risk, introducing new products into a market, and implementing more efficient production processes. A long-run profit, however, is the result of some barrier to entry that enables the owners to sustain returns beyond their opportunity costs. In this situation, the product price cannot be driven down by the process of new firm entry, and thus it ultimately represents a transfer of income from consumers to the owners of firms. However, as we demonstrated earlier, a stable long-run profit cannot prevail in a perfectly competitive market due to the condition of free entry. It would perhaps be an overstatement for us to characterize the perfectly competitive outcome as being unambiguously fair, since the term "fair" is rather subjective. Yet, we can say that a perfectly competitive market does embody fewer characteristics associated with a less equitable distribution of income than other types of market structures. This generalization should become clearer after we analyze the performance results associated with other market structures in subsequent chapters.

The first formal criterion we use for judging market performance is **production efficiency**, defined as *producing any given level of output in the least costly manner and* *producing a level of output that corresponds to a firm's minimum long-run average cost.* When firms behave in a manner consistent with this criterion, they produce a level of output that corresponds to their optimal plant size. By doing so, they can take advantage of all economies of scale without experiencing the disadvantages associated with diseconomies of scale. Specifically, this level of production occurs at the minimum point on each firm's *LRAC* curve that we demonstrated in earlier analysis to be the level of each firm's output corresponding to a long-run competitive equilibrium.

Production efficiency also involves producing any given level of output at the least cost possible. There are two assumptions associated with this point, which until now we have not stated explicitly. First, we assume that a firm's management has the desire to purchase and employ its inputs efficiently. Second, we also assume that the firm obtains the maximum use from the inputs it employs. If these two assumptions hold true, then we can state that a condition of **X-efficiency** is achieved. This term, coined by Harvey J. Leibenstein, is a *condition for which a firm's management is able to minimize the cost associated with producing each level of output.* The lack of X-efficiency, known as X-inefficiency, is often characterized as the tolerance for a sheer waste of resources, such as overstaffing or the continued use of obsolete equipment. The presence of X-inefficiency is often prevalent in those firms for which there exists a significant separation between ownership and management. In these cases, it is often tempting for a firm's managers to be more concerned with maximizing their own benefits than the firm's profit. In terms of our earlier mathematical and graphical analyses, we would represent the introduction of any X-inefficiencies as creating an upward shift in the firm's cost curves, thus reflecting the higher costs associated with producing various levels of output. The important point we need to establish here is that, because of the pressures of firm entry and the associated elimination of long-run profit, a perfectly competitive firm is unable to tolerate these X-inefficiencies if they are to remain in the market. As a result, society benefits since the subsequent cost savings are reflected in lower product prices.

The second criterion we use for evaluating market outcomes is **allocative efficiency**, or *the flow of resources to their most highly valued uses.* In an economy that is allocatively efficient, resources flow into industries producing those goods and services most highly valued by consumers. This result enables consumers to ultimately choose amounts of those goods and services proportionate with their tastes and preferences. Perfectly competitive markets are allocatively efficient because the firms determine their profit-maximizing levels of output according to the $MR \equiv P = MC$ rule. Our rationale as to why this process leads to allocative efficiency is simply a matter of interpreting what these price and marginal cost terms represent. At the profit-maximizing level of output produced and sold, we can interpret the corresponding price as representing the value consumers place on the extra, or last, unit of output purchased, since they are willing to pay this amount. We can interpret marginal cost at this level of output as the cost associated with producing the extra, or last, unit of output. This is the extra cost incurred by the firm producing the good, but in a larger sense, it also represents the extra cost to society as a whole. Thus, if output is produced and sold up to the

REAL-WORLD APPLICATION 14.1

U.S. Agriculture: Moving Even Closer toward Perfect Competition

U.S. agriculture has traditionally been cited as one of the closest real-world examples of a perfectly competitive market structure. Recent data on wheat farming in the United States substantiates this claim. In 1995, aggregate output of this homogeneous commodity reached 2.2 billion bushels. Thus, with an average productivity of 36 bushels of wheat per acre, a 2000-acre farm produced 72,000 bushels per year, or just 3/1000 of 1% of total market output. Further evidence of the perfectly competitive nature of U.S. agriculture is provided below in the table containing 1997 selected U.S. agricultural data.

Sweeping revisions in federal farm policy under the 1996 Federal Agricultural Improvement and Reform Act (FAIR), better known to farmers as the Freedom to Farm Act, have created an even more competitive environment for American farmers.[2] One of the major provisions under FAIR is the phasing out of billions of dollars in farm subsidies, enacted during the Franklin Roosevelt

[2]"The Farmbelt Breaks Free," *The Economist*, July 12, 1997, pp. 21–22.

administration, in exchange for the lifting of production restrictions that previously limited what farmers could plant on their land. Specifically, the act reduced the amount of federal paperwork burdening farmers and freed them from seemingly arbitrary acreage restrictions and crop-rotation mandates. Farmers are now free to develop production plans in direct response to market changes. For example, in 1996 when agricultural commodity prices hit historic highs, due to unprecedented increases in expected export demand for grains from Canada, Mexico, and China, farmers in the United States responded by planting some of their largest crops since the 1980s. However, the new freedom to respond to higher market prices under FAIR also applies in cases of falling commodity prices. No longer are farmers protected from market declines by government price supports. As a result, U.S. farmers are increasingly relying on futures and options trading at the Chicago Board of Trade, along with revenue insurance policies, to manage the risks associated with the more competitive commodity markets in which they now operate.

1997 Selected U.S. Agricultural Data

Crop	Total Output (millions of bushels)	Number of Farms	Average Farm Size (acres)	Average Output (bushels/acre)
Corn	8579	430,711	162	123
Wheat	2204	243,568	242	37
Soybeans	2504	354,692	186	38

Source: 1997 Census of Agriculture, Volume 1: Geographic Area Series, Table 1: County Summary Highlights, 1997.

point where the value of the extra unit of output, meaning its price, is equal to the additional cost associated with producing the extra unit of output, or its marginal cost, then the allocatively efficient amount of the good is being produced. If this is not the case, say the firms produce and sell some amount of output at which $P > MC$, then society would value the last unit of output more than the cost of producing it, and we can reason that the good is underproduced, reflecting a misallocation of resources.

The final criterion regarding our evaluation of market performance is **dynamic efficiency**, or *technological progress*, a term that describes the development and adoption of new technology over time. There are essentially two points of view concerning perfectly competitive market performance as it relates to dynamic efficiency. The first is that perfectly competitive firms are dynamically efficient since this is the only way they can generate short-run profit. Recall that the entry of new firms drives down the price of a good, thus eliminating profit in the long run. As a result, the only way a competitive firm can continue to earn a short-run profit is by developing better production processes, introducing new cost-saving techniques, or improving its product. Logically, to accomplish these results, the firm must engage in research and development leading to new innovations. Furthermore, all firms must ultimately engage in the same research and development activity, or they will ultimately suffer a loss and be forced to exit the market.

The alternative viewpoint is that perfectly competitive markets are not successful in promoting dynamic efficiency owing to the lack of sustainable profit from which the necessary research and development can be financed. In addition, perfectly competitive firms are generally unable to obtain patent protection for the results of their research and development, thus lowering the incentive for them to engage in such activity. Both viewpoints are valid from a theoretical perspective, and thus the question of whether perfectly competitive markets are conducive to dynamic efficiency is one that must be resolved statistically.

Having now examined the behavior of perfectly competitive firms operating in both the short and long run, we will next direct our attention to analyzing firm behavior within the context of other market structures. Specifically, the most imperfectly competitive market structure, that of monopoly, will be our focus in Chapters 15 and 16, while Chapters 17, 18, and 19 will be devoted to other types of market structures, in particular, those of oligopoly and monopolistic competition. The performance outcomes pertaining to a perfectly competitive market structure will prove useful in serving as a benchmark against which we can compare the outcomes associated with these other market structures.

14.5   SUMMARY

Our focus in this chapter has been on the behavior of perfectly competitive firms and markets in the long run. We also evaluated the performance outcomes associated with this market structure from a social perspective. The primary topics covered in this chapter are as follows.

- In the long run, a perfectly competitive firm produces its profit-maximizing level of output using an optimal, or constrained cost minimizing, combination of inputs.
- In the long run, the existence of profit serves as the incentive for firms to enter or exit a market.
- A long-run perfectly competitive equilibrium is achieved in an industry when all firms produce a level of output that corresponds to minimum long-run average cost and zero economic profit.
- A long-run industry supply curve comprises the set of quantity–price combinations that constitute long-run equlibria in a perfectly competitive market.
- In the case of a constant cost industry, the long-run industry supply curve is horizontal.
- The long-run industry supply curve associated with an increasing cost industry exhibits a positive slope.
- Long-run elasticity of supply measures the ratio of the percentage change in the market quantity supplied of a good in the long run to a percentage change in its own-price.
- The outcomes associated with a perfectly competitive market structure are generally considered to fulfill the following criteria: production efficiency, allocative efficiency, and dynamic efficiency.

KEY TERMS

- allocative efficiency, page 378
- constant cost industry, page 369
- dynamic efficiency, page 380
- increasing cost industry, page 373

- long-run elasticity of supply, page 376
- long-run market, or industry, supply curve, page 368

- long-run perfectly competitive equilibrium, page 363
- production efficiency, page 377
- X-efficiency, page 378

EXERCISES

14.1 a. Plot a perfectly competitive firm's long-run average cost, marginal cost, and marginal revenue curves when it is in long-run equilibrium.

b. In your graph from part a, indicate the long-run equilibrium level of output for the firm. What force drives the firm to this level of output?

c. Why is the perfectly competitive firm's long-run equilibrium level of output described as efficient? Use your graph from part a to supplement your response.

14.2 A perfectly competitive wheat farmer's short-run total cost function is given as

$$SRTC(Q) = Q^3 - Q^2 + 12Q + 10.$$

How high must the market price of wheat be for the farmer to produce and sell his crop? How much wheat will he supply to the market at this price?

14.3 Graphically derive the long-run industry supply curve for each of the following types of industries:
a. constant cost industry
b. increasing cost industry
Provide an explanation of your graphical derivation and a real-world example for each case.

14.4 A perfectly competitive firm has the long-run total cost function

$$LRTC = 0.25Q^3 - 1.5Q^2 + 3Q.$$

a. Derive the firm's long-run average and long-run marginal cost functions.
b. If the firm is in long-run equilibrium, what level of output will it produce?
c. In long-run equilibrium, what price does this firm receive for its product?

14.5 A perfectly competitive firm's long-run total cost function is

$$LRTC = \frac{1}{3}Q^3 - 18Q^2 + 120Q.$$

a. Derive the firm's long-run average and long-run marginal cost functions.
b. What level of output will this firm produce when it is earning zero profit in the long run?
c. If there are 1000 firms in this competitive industry, determine the total industry output when it is at a long-run competitive equilibrium.

14.6 Suppose for some reason that a firm produces output where $P < MC$. Is this situation allocatively efficient? Since consumers are receiving the good at a price that is less than the cost of producing it, at the margin, is this outcome desirable from a social perspective? Explain your response.

14.7 Samantha operates a firm in a perfectly competitive industry.
a. How likely is Samantha to invest in research and development of new production methods for her product? Explain your response.
b. How likely is Samantha to adopt a new, more efficient production technology? Explain your response.

14.8 From a social perspective, what is the significance of a long-run competitive equilibrium? Support your response with an appropriate graph.

CHAPTER 15

Monopoly

15.1   INTRODUCTION

In the preceding two chapters, we demonstrated that the market structure within which a firm operates significantly affects that firm's behavior. Specifically, we analyzed the behavior of a firm operating in a perfectly competitive market structure for both short- and long-run time periods. In this chapter, we will examine the behavior of a firm operating in a very different type of market structure, one that, in a sense, represents the extreme opposite from that of perfect competition. This market structure, known as monopoly, is a market consisting of only one seller of a good, where by definition there are no close substitutes for this good. For this type of market structure to arise and be sustained, entry into the relevant market by other firms must be prevented through some type of barrier. Since one firm controls 100% of the marketwide sales, the performance results for monopoly, regarding its output, price, cost, and profit, generally differ from those for perfect competition. In this chapter, we will demonstrate that the lack of competitive pressure results in performance outcomes for a monopolist that are generally undesirable from a consumer's perspective and, more broadly, from a social perspective. It makes intuitive sense that if consumers have no options other than a single firm's product, then that firm will possess considerable leverage over the amount of output it sells, as well as the price it charges. Our initial focus in this chapter is on some of the important barriers to entry that may constitute causes of monopoly. Afterward, we will analyze the behavior of a monopolistic firm for both short- and long-run time periods.

15.2   DEFINITION OF MONOPOLY

A **monopoly** is *a market structure consisting of a single seller of a good*. We can elaborate on this definition by referring back to the basic criteria defining a market structure presented in Chapter 13. The first criterion is the number and size distribution of buyers and sellers operating in the market for a good. In the case of monopoly, the number of sellers is very small, specifically consisting of only one seller. Thus, the size distribution is such that this single firm controls 100% of the marketwide sales of the good. With regard to the purchasing side of the market, we will assume that the good in question has many buyers. The situation in which a market structure contains only a single buyer, defined as monopsony, will be analyzed in Chapter 22.

The second criterion for defining a market structure is the degree of product differentiation within the market for the good. A monopolist's product must be substantially differentiated from all other firms' products, to the point where it has no good substitutes. If viable substitutes exist, then, by definition, the market cannot be a pure monopoly, since there would exist more than one seller in the market for the product.

The third criterion is the ease with which firms can enter or exit a market. In the case of monopoly, entry into the market must be very difficult. Otherwise, once the firm earns a profit, entry will occur and the monopoly ceases to exist. Thus, the existence and continuance of a monopoly are contingent on some type of barrier to entry that prevents all but one firm from operating in the market.

The last criterion defining a market structure is the amount of market-related information available to consumers and producers. In this case, the consumers' lack of information is not a necessary prerequisite for establishment of a monopoly. However, imperfect information regarding such variables as product prices and the attributes of the goods produced by various firms can play a contributing role in creating and sustaining a monopoly. For example, if consumers are unaware of the existence of good substitutes for a particular firm's product, then that firm may be able to enjoy a monopoly position based on this lack of information.

The key implication associated with these characteristics is that a monopolist will not act as a price taker, as does a perfectly competitive firm, but instead possesses some influence over the market price of its product. This result follows from the fact that a monopolist controls 100% of the sales in a market, and thus its own-price demand curve and the market own-price demand curve for the product are the same. In addition, since market own-price demand curves typically exhibit an inverse relationship between the quantity demanded of a good and its own price, a monopolist is able to influence the price of the good by adjusting the amount of output it sells. More specifically, by restricting output, a monopolist can increase the scarcity of the good and drive up its price.

Notationally, we can express a typical market own-price demand curve for a good, which also represents the monopolist's own-price demand curve, as

$$Q^D = Q^D(P, \overline{P}_{Y,1}, \overline{P}_{W,1}, \ldots, \overline{P}_{Z,1}, \overline{I}_{M,1}, \overline{N}_1),$$

where the terms in this function are the same as those we defined in Chapters 6 and 13. In particular, Q^D is the quantity demanded of the good; P represents its price; $\overline{P}_{Y,1}$, $\overline{P}_{W,1}, \ldots, \overline{P}_{Z,1}$, are the prices of related goods $Y, W, \ldots Z$; and $\overline{I}_{M,1}$ and $\overline{N}_1$ represent money income and the number of consumers of the good, respectively. We have fixed all determinants of Q^D at specified levels, with the exception of its own price, P. Note that if any of the related goods, $Y, W, \ldots, Z$, represent substitutes for the good in question, they must be very poor substitutes. This result follows from the characteristic that there are no close substitutes for a monopolist's product. For most of our subsequent analysis, we will express the monopolist's own-price demand curve in its inverse form as

$$P = P^D(Q, \overline{P}_{Y,1}, \overline{P}_{W,1}, \ldots, \overline{P}_{Z,1}, \overline{I}_{M,1}, \overline{N}_1),$$

and for the sake of brevity, we can simply express it as

$$P = P^D(Q).$$

However, you should understand that the other determinants in the inverse demand curve, $\overline{P}_{Y,1}, \overline{P}_{W,1}, \ldots, \overline{P}_{Z,1}, \overline{I}_{M,1}, \overline{N}_1$, still influence P but have been omitted from the equation simply for the sake of clarity.

15.2.1 Natural Limitations on Monopoly Power

Before discussing several origins of monopoly power and constructing the monopoly model, we should note that a monopolist's ability to influence the price of its product is not without some natural limitations. This qualification will become readily apparent once we develop the associated model of firm behavior, but at this point it may be useful to dispense with some misconceptions. Since a monopolist controls 100% of the market, and thus can directly influence the market price of its product by changing its level of production, it is tempting to believe that it can charge any price it desires. This belief, however, is simply not true for a rational firm, since it will logically seek a profit-maximizing price for its product. At this point, we can reason that because price and quantity demanded are inversely related, or alternatively stated, since the monopolist's own-price demand curve is negatively sloped, then as the firm raises the price of its product, the quantity demanded declines. As a consequence, the firm desires to restrict output and raise the price of its product, only to a point.

The underlying reasons for this result are that although no good substitutes exist for a monopolist's product, in reality, there are virtually always some imperfect substitutes for any product. For example, if some consumers determine that the price of some leisure good, say powerboats, has risen to a level above what they are willing to pay, these consumers may switch to other unrelated leisure products constituting indirect substitutes for powerboats, such as snow skiing or mountain climbing equipment. Moreover, the consumer always has the alternative of simply doing without a good if its price is considered to be prohibitively high. These arguments are not being made to suggest that the monopoly outcomes regarding such performance variables as price and output are desirable from a consumer's perspective. Rather, we are pointing out the natural limitations on a monopolist's power to restrict output and raise price.

15.3 BARRIERS TO ENTRY AND THE ORIGINS OF MONOPOLY AND MONOPOLY POWER

In reality, there are very few examples of pure monopoly—a market structure consisting of only a single seller of a differentiated product. However, there are many examples of markets containing only a few sellers of a product, often behaving in concert with each other, or markets in which one firm has only some degree of product differentiation. As a result, the monopoly model serves as a useful approximation of firm behavior in many of these situations. We describe firms operating under these circumstances as possessing some amount of **monopoly power**, or *the ability to influence the price of a product*. The degree of control over price is dependent on the characteristics underlying the particular market structure, such as the amount of product differentiation or the effectiveness of the barriers to entry. In the remainder of this section, we will provide a more detailed discussion of several of the origins of pure monopoly. However, we may also consider these origins more broadly as representing causes of monopoly power.

In general, monopoly arises due to the existence of some type of **barrier to entry**, or *a factor that restricts the number of firms operating in a particular market*. We can group these barriers into essentially three categories: those inherent to the structure of the industry, those resulting from firm conduct, and those arising from government intervention. The first two categories are often viewed as intertwined because industry structure affects firm conduct and vice versa. As a result, these two categories comprise what we term the structure–conduct–performance school of thought. The third category of entry barriers, those resulting from government intervention, is the main focus of the free market-oriented Chicago school of thought, which contends that government-erected barriers to entry are the main source of monopoly power.

Among those entry barriers inherent to the structure of an industry, the major underlying cause of monopoly is economies of scale over the entire feasible range of marketwide output. In such a case, a firm's long-run average cost continues to decline as it expands its production of output to meet the entire market demand for the product. As a result, a single firm can produce the good at a cheaper per unit cost than could a group of smaller firms. Formally, we define this situation as a natural monopoly in that the market can accommodate only one cost-efficient firm. Another possible cause of monopoly that is related to structure arises when the capital requirements necessary for entering some industries are very high, thus making it too costly for many firms to enter. Interpreting high capital requirements as a barrier to entry, however, is rather debatable. Understandably, some smaller firms might be affected, but at the same time, there exist larger firms with access to capital markets that should be able to enter the industry as easily as the initial firm. Thus, we expect that the barrier to entry aspect of these high capital requirements exists only to the extent that they contribute to the large economies of scale barrier we discussed earlier.

The second category of barriers to entry consists of those created by the behavior of a firm operating in the industry. One such type of barrier is the exclusive control by one firm of some essential input necessary to produce the good. This type of behavior prevents other firms from producing the same good, creating a market structure known as an input control monopoly. The classic example of this type of monopoly occurred in the production of aluminum prior to World War II. At that time, the Aluminum Company of America (ALCOA) was the sole producer of aluminum, owing to its control of bauxite ore, the essential raw material from which aluminum metal is produced.

Yet other types of firm behavior may, arguably, create barriers to entry. For example, a firm might establish excess production capacity by building suboptimally high levels of plant and equipment, thereby enabling it to expand production quickly when it is deemed desirable. By maintaining excess capacity, an incumbent firm may be able to block entry through its ability to quickly increase production and engage in price warfare, ultimately creating an unprofitable situation for prospective entrants. An example of this type of behavior is evident in the U.S. titanium metal industry, where the present authors have conducted a study revealing that incumbent firms, acting in concert, have significantly reduced the probability of entry by maintaining levels of excess capacity.[1] However, there is an alternative view regarding the intentional use of excess capacity as a barrier to entry. This view contends that a profit-maximizing firm will decrease, rather than increase, production if entry occurs, in order to maintain a profit-maximizing price level. If this is the case, it makes no sense for firms to intentionally maintain excess capacity, for it would not constitute a credible barrier to entry.

Two final types of firm behavior that may be considered as barriers to entry are advertising and limit pricing. Through advertising, a firm may be able to substantially differentiate its product, thereby creating a degree of consumer loyalty that is very difficult for new entrants to overcome. In addition, advertising expenditures can also increase a firm's capital requirements, contributing to high economies of scale, both of which are potential barriers we discussed previously. In general, for advertising to constitute a successful barrier to entry, it must create a situation for which the costs of a new entrant are higher than those for an incumbent firm.

The final type of firm behavior representing a potential barrier to entry is limit pricing, which involves an incumbent firm charging a seemingly suboptimally low price so as not to create a profitable situation for a new entrant. Note that we consider a limit price as suboptimal only in the absence of entry. However, this price may actually constitute an optimal price in a broader sense in that it maximizes the firm's profit in the long run by deterring entry. However, one of the criticisms of limit pricing is that it runs contrary to the excess capacity argument presented earlier, where an incumbent firm will not lower its price until entry actually occurs.

The third broad category of entry barriers pertains to those created by government intervention. This category manifests the Chicago school of economic thought, which is essentially based on the idea that monopoly and monopoly power cannot persist over time unless some type of government-enforced barrier to entry is in place. There are indeed numerous examples of such government-erected barriers. One set of examples is the vast array of government licenses limiting the number of firms that may operate in many industries. One of the most often cited examples of such a licensing policy occurs in New York City where a taxi medallion must be obtained to operate a cab. A very limited number of these medallions have been issued by the Taxi and Limousine Commission controlling this industry in New York City, where the average price of a medallion sold in 1997 was a staggering $243,000.[2] Another example of government licensing restrictions is the limitation imposed on the number of liquor licenses issued to bars and restaurants in some states. In Pennsylvania, for example, a fixed number of these licenses have been issued and allocated according to population—one for every 3000 people in a municipality. Because of the fixed number of such licenses, any new bar or

---

[1] Stephen Mathis and Janet Koscianski, "Excess Capacity as a Barrier to Entry in the U.S. Titanium Industry," *International Journal of Industrial Organization*, 15 (1996): 263–281.

[2] New York City Taxi and Limousine Commission, *Price of Medallions Since 1970* [Online]. Available: http://www.ci.nyc.ny.us/html/tlc/value.html.

restaurant must purchase a license from an existing establishment, often paying hundreds of thousands of dollars per license (see Real-World Application 16.1).

The list of examples of government licensing restrictions is quite long. Commercial banks must be chartered by either federal or state governments. Many professions, such as those in medicine, law, and accounting, require licenses. Even barbers and beauticians must be licensed before they can practice their trade. Of course, the

---

REAL-WORLD APPLICATION 15.1

Barriers to Entry at European Airports

At several major European airports, the national carrier controls the majority of the takeoff and landing slots. For example, in 1995 approximately 70% of the takeoff and landing slots at Rome's Fiumicino Airport were controlled by Alitalia.[3] In Frankfurt, 60% were held by Lufthansa, while 55% of Copenhagen's airport slots were controlled by S.A.S. Such market dominance by national carriers in Europe is of no surprise given that takeoff and landing slots were originally allocated, free of charge, to these carriers by their respective national governments. In addition, the incumbents' market strength is further intensified by "grandfather rights" that guarantee an airline's rights to a slot for the following season as long as it uses it in the present. In fact, an airline can only be forced to relinquish a slot if it fails to use it. In light of the recent wave of alliances between many European national carriers and other major airlines located elsewhere throughout the world, the degree of competition at European airports is in even greater jeopardy.

Obviously, the barrier to entry created by these national governments, via their system for allocating takeoff and landing rights, has stifled airline competition in many European cities. What is not clear is whether merely opening the existing market to allow for the buying and selling of airport slots would make the situation more competitive. Specifically, potential new entrants would undoubtedly find the high start-up costs, which are associated with acquiring a sufficient number of slots to be a viable player in a market, to act as a barrier to entry. For example, ownership of the takeoff and landing slots at London's Heathrow Airport had an estimated value of $2.5 billion in 1997. Furthermore, incumbent national airlines may also purchase additional slots, thereby strengthening their monopoly control over certain air routes.

Perhaps a more competitive outcome could be achieved by completely overhauling the takeoff and landing slot allocation system throughout Europe. By placing all slots up for grabs to the highest bidder, the various national carriers would be forced to compete with other interested airlines for takeoff and landing rights in Europe. In addition, by abolishing the previously mentioned grandfather rights currently enjoyed by the national carriers, airport slots would continuously be bought and sold. This would allow the market to redistribute them over time on the basis of their worth to air carriers. Such competition should ultimately lead to a more efficient allocation of takeoff and landing slots, lower airfares for consumers, and ultimately air travel routes that more accurately reflect the flying public's needs.

[3]"Let the Market Take-off," *The Economist*, January 18, 1997, p. 74.

expressed rationale for these various licenses is not that they create barriers to entry and subsequently confer the privileges of monopoly power to various firms. Rather, those granting and receiving such licenses usually state that they are merely attempting to ensure safety and high-quality products and services for consumers. However, the market restriction aspect of these licenses is generally quite real, and it is often difficult to separate the extent to which these licenses actually provide quality control from the extent to which they simply create market restrictions.

Another type of government-erected barrier to entry is that of patent protection. A patent gives the inventor of a particular product or production process the exclusive right to that product or process for a period of 20 years. The rationale for patents is that they encourage invention and innovation, thus promoting dynamic efficiency by enabling a firm to exclusively reap the rewards associated with investing in research and development of new products or production processes. However, at the same time, a patent also creates a barrier to entry, conferring monopoly power to the firms receiving such protection.

The list of entry barriers created by government intervention is too long to be thoroughly detailed in this text, so we will mention only a few more. Local governments often apply zoning laws to prevent new firms from locating in certain areas, usually under the presumption of preventing parking problems or maintaining orderly community development. Local government authorities frequently issue governmental franchises, allowing one firm to provide a particular service to a municipality. These franchises are often sold to firms that provide utilities such as natural gas, electricity, and cable television. Finally, on a national level, the federal government has from time to time imposed tariffs and import quotas on many different types of goods and services, thus protecting domestic firms from international competition. In summary, the category of government-erected barriers to entry is quite encompassing. It is indeed amazing how many markets that have the potential for competition are instead characterized by the prevalence of monopoly power due to such regulation.

15.4 MONOPOLY BEHAVIOR IN THE SHORT RUN

As we stated earlier, the critical implication of a monopoly is that the single firm in the market can influence the price of its product by adjusting the amount of output it chooses to produce and sell. Another characteristic, related to this implication, is that the firm's marginal revenue is a function of its production of output, and, unlike a perfectly competitive firm, its marginal revenue is not equal to the price of the good. Deriving a monopolist's marginal revenue function is exactly the same as deriving the marginal revenue function for a market own-price demand curve. This follows from the fact that the monopolist's own-price demand curve and the market own-price demand curve are the same. Since we have already presented this derivation in an earlier chapter, we will repeat it rather briefly here. You are encouraged to return to Section 7.3.2 of Chapter 7 to review the lengthier discussion of marginal revenue and its relationship with the own-price demand curve.

A monopolist's total revenue, TR, is the value of the sales associated with its product, Q, or

$$TR = PQ.$$

This is essentially the same definition of total revenue as that for a perfectly competitive firm but with one major difference. Unlike a perfectly competitive firm, for which the price of its output is predetermined, the monopolist's price is a function of the level of output it sells, represented by the inverse own-price demand curve

$$P = P^D(Q).$$

We compute the monopolist's marginal revenue function, expressing the change in revenue due to a change in the amount of output sold, as the derivative of TR with respect to Q. Since P is now a variable, we must employ the product rule when taking the derivative of TR as

$$MR = \frac{dTR}{dQ} = P\frac{dQ}{dQ} + Q\frac{dP}{dQ},$$

or

$$MR = P + Q\frac{dP}{dQ}.$$

We can observe in this formula that marginal revenue is not equal to price. More specifically, since own-price demand curves possess negative slopes, meaning that $dP/dQ < 0$, we can reason that $MR < P$. The rationale for this result is that, since price is inversely related to output, the monopolist must decrease its price in order to sell additional units of its good. Moreover, we are assuming in this analysis that the firm does not price discriminate, meaning that it charges the same price for all units sold, once the optimal price is determined. This assumption implies that in order to increase sales of its product a monopolist must lower the price it charges, not only for the extra unit it sells, but also for all other units that were previously sold at a higher price.

We will briefly repeat a specific example of this result that was demonstrated previously in Section 7.3.2 of Chapter 7 and illustrated in Figure 7.1. The inverse own-price demand curve in that example is

$$P_X = 10 - X,$$

from which we can derive the TR and MR functions. Recoding X to be Q and P_X as simply P, we can rewrite this inverse demand curve as

$$P = 10 - Q, \tag{15.1}$$

and thus the total revenue function is

$$TR = PQ = (10 - Q)Q = 10Q - Q^2, \tag{15.2}$$

yielding the marginal revenue function

$$MR = \frac{dTR}{dQ} = 10 - 2Q \tag{15.3}$$

By substituting any value of Q other than zero into equation (15.1), the inverse demand curve, and equation (15.3), the MR function, and then comparing results, you can verify that $MR < P$. We have illustrated the relationships among equations (15.1–15.3) in Figure 15.1, by plotting the TR function in panel (A) and the inverse own-price demand curve, as well as the MR function, in panel (B). In addition, we have also shown the ranges of own-price elasticity of demand in this figure. Recall from Chapter 7 that the elastic range lies above the midpoint on the inverse own-price demand curve. The point of unitary elasticity corresponds to the midpoint, and the inelastic range lies below the midpoint. Furthermore, the elastic range corresponds to positive values for marginal revenue, the point of unitary elasticity occurs at a level of

FIGURE 15.1 Relationships among Own-Price Demand, Total Revenue, and Marginal Revenue Curves

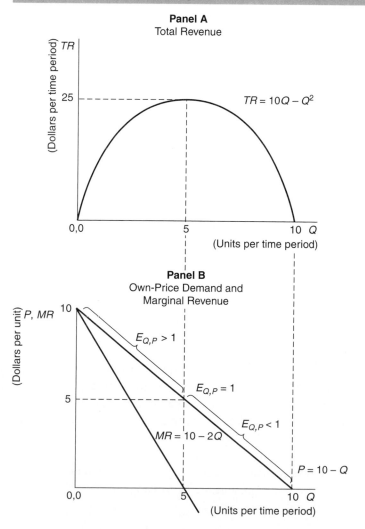

Panel A
Total Revenue

$TR = 10Q - Q^2$

Panel B
Own-Price Demand and
Marginal Revenue

$E_{Q,P} > 1$

$E_{Q,P} = 1$

$E_{Q,P} < 1$

$MR = 10 - 2Q$

$P = 10 - Q$

output for which marginal revenue is equal to zero, and the inelastic range corresponds to negative values for marginal revenue.

In Figure 15.1, we have demonstrated two important characteristics pertaining to a monopolist. First, observe in panel (B) that the *MR* function, with the exception of its vertical intercept, lies below the inverse own-price demand curve, reflecting the concept that *MR < P*. Second, the inelastic portion of this inverse own-price demand curve corresponds to negative values for *MR*. Thus, it also corresponds to that portion of the *TR* function that declines with decreases in *P* and increases in *Q*. As a result, it is irrational for a firm to decrease the price of its product to any level below the midpoint of its inverse own-price demand curve, in this case occurring at *P* = $5, because by doing so *TR* declines. For these reasons, a monopolist never operates on the inelastic portion of its inverse own-price demand curve.

The result that *MR < P* has several important ramifications regarding a monopolist's performance that will become evident once we analyze the monopoly model of firm behavior. However, before we construct this model, it is first necessary to establish the monopolist's goal. As we did in the case of a perfectly competitive firm, we will assume that the monopolist's goal is profit maximization. We mentioned in Chapter 13 that this goal involves some degree of controversy, which in the case of monopoly becomes somewhat more pronounced. For example, if the monopolist engages in limit pricing or in maintaining excess capacity, it is not maximizing its profit per se in the short run. However, as we discussed earlier, the viability of these types of conduct is also controversial. Furthermore, models based on profit maximization have historically performed quite well in explaining firm behavior. As a result, we will maintain the assumption of profit maximization for both short- and long-run models of monopoly behavior.

Recall, a firm's short-run profit, $SR\pi$, is simply the difference between its total revenue, *TR*, and its short-run total cost, *SRTC*, or

$$SR\pi = TR - SRTC.$$

In this case, the short-run total cost curve for a monopolist is exactly the same as that for a perfectly competitive firm, or

$$SRTC = \overline{FC}_1 + VC$$
$$= \overline{P}_{K,1}\overline{K}_1 + VC(Q,\overline{P}_{L,1},\overline{K}_1),$$

where $\overline{FC}_1 = \overline{P}_{K,1}\overline{K}_1$ represents the firm's fixed cost, and $VC = VC(Q,\overline{P}_{L,1},\overline{K}_1)$ is the firm's variable cost. This *SRTC* function is no different from the function we used in the perfectly competitive model because we are assuming that the firm, while behaving as a monopolist in its market for output, acts as a perfect competitor, or price taker, in its input markets. Thus, the difference between a monopolist's $SR\pi$ function and that for a perfectly competitive firm lies in the fact that, for the monopolist, $P = P^D(Q)$, and as a consequence, it faces a different *TR* function than does a perfectly competitive firm. Thus, we represent the short-run profit function for a monopolist as

$$SR\pi = PQ - \overline{P}_{K,1}\overline{K}_1 - VC(Q,\overline{P}_{L,1},\overline{K}_1),$$

for which the firm determines its profit-maximizing levels of Q and P. Since $P = P^D(Q)$, we can determine these values by totally differentiating $SR\pi$ with respect to Q and setting the result equal to zero as

$$\frac{dSR\pi}{dQ} = \frac{dPQ}{dQ} - \frac{d\overline{P}_{K,1}\overline{K}_1}{dQ} - \frac{dVC(Q,\overline{P}_{L,1},\overline{K}_1)}{dQ} = 0$$

$$= P + Q\frac{dP}{dQ} - \frac{dVC(Q,\overline{P}_{L,1},\overline{K}_1)}{dQ} = 0,$$

or

$$P + Q\frac{dP}{dQ} = \frac{dVC(Q,\overline{P}_{L,1},\overline{K}_1)}{dQ}.$$

The terms $P + Q\, dP/dQ$ and $dVC(Q,\overline{P}_{L,1},\overline{K}_1)/dQ$ are the firm's marginal revenue, MR, and short-run marginal cost, $SRMC$, respectively. Thus, the monopolist determines its profit-maximizing level of Q by producing and selling output to the point where

$$MR = SRMC. \tag{15.4}$$

We describe this result as the necessary condition for a short-run profit maximum, and we can easily explain it intuitively. For example, if a firm produces some level of output at which $MR > SRMC$, then by increasing its production and sale of output, the firm's total revenue rises more than its short-run total cost and accordingly, its short-run profit rises as well. If the firm produces some level of output at which $MR < SRMC$, then by decreasing its production and sale of output, the firm can reduce its short-run total cost by an amount greater than its reduction in total revenue, and again its short-run profit increases. Thus, the only level of Q at which the firm cannot make an adjustment that will increase its profit is the level at which $MR = SRMC$. We determine the price corresponding to this profit-maximizing level of output by substituting this value of Q into the inverse demand curve

$$P = P^D(Q),$$

and solving for P. Also note that this value of P is greater than the value of marginal revenue at this profit-maximizing level of Q.

We have illustrated the short-run profit maximization model for a monopoly in Figure 15.2, where the $SR\pi$ function is plotted as a function of output in panel (B); the two component functions comprising the profit function, TR and $SRTC$, are shown in panel (A); and the corresponding marginal functions, MR and $SRMC$, are demonstrated in panel (C). Referring to panels (A) and (B), observe that if the firm produces Q_0 units of output, $TR_0 = SRTC_0$ and thus $SR\pi_0 = 0$. Should the firm produce any level of output less than Q_0 units, then $TR < SRTC$, and therefore $SR\pi < 0$. If the firm produces Q_2 units of output, $TR_2 = STRC_2$ and $SR\pi_2 = 0$. For any level of output greater than Q_2, $TR < SRTC$ and again $SR\pi < 0$. Thus, we can conclude in this example that $SR\pi > 0$ between output levels Q_0 and Q_2, exclusively. The firm's goal is to produce a

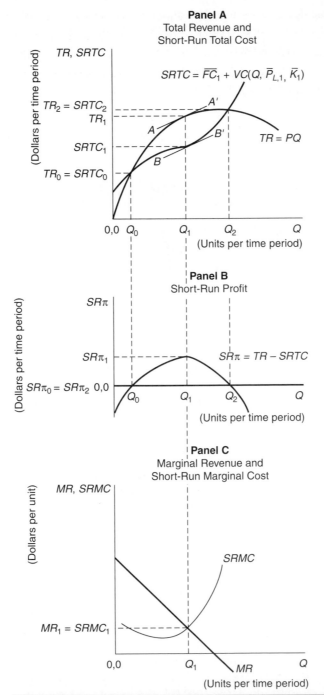

Panel A
Total Revenue and
Short-Run Total Cost

$SRTC = \overline{FC}_1 + VC(Q, \overline{P}_{L,1}, \overline{K}_1)$

$TR = PQ$

(Units per time period)

Panel B
Short-Run Profit

$SR\pi = TR - SRTC$

(Units per time period)

Panel C
Marginal Revenue and
Short-Run Marginal Cost

$SRMC$

MR

(Units per time period)

FIGURE 15.2 Relationships among Total Revenue, Total Cost, Profit, Marginal Cost, and Marginal Revenue for a Monopolist in the Short Run

level of Q corresponding to a maximum value for its $SR\pi$. We can observe that this result occurs in panel (A) at Q_1 units, where $TR > SRTC$ by the greatest amount, or specifically, where $SR\pi_1 = TR_1 - SRTC_1$. We can reinforce this conclusion by referring to panel (B) and observing that $SR\pi$ reaches its maximum value at Q_1 units of output.

We can also demonstrate that the necessary condition for a short-run profit maximum, established in equation (15.4), holds true at this level of output, by drawing the lines AA' and BB' tangent to the TR and $SRTC$ curves, respectively, at Q_1 units of output. As we demonstrated in panel (A), these two tangent lines are parallel to each other, indicating identical slope values, dTR/dQ and $dSRTC/dQ$, for the TR and $SRTC$ curves, respectively. Since these slope values represent the respective values for MR and $SRMC$, then $MR = SRMC$ at output level Q_1, corresponding to the maximum value for $SR\pi$. The result is also demonstrated in panel (C), where we can observe that $MR_1 = SRMC_1$ at Q_1 units of output.[4]

It is often convenient to present the profit maximization model in terms of average rather than total functions. We accomplish this by simply dividing the firm's short-run profit function by Q, enabling us to express all terms in this function on a per unit of output basis. Therefore, since

$$SR\pi = TR - SRTC,$$

then

$$\frac{SR\pi}{Q} = \frac{TR}{Q} - \frac{SRTC}{Q},$$

or

$$SR\,AVE\pi = AR - ATC.$$

The firm's short-run average profit is the difference between its average revenue, AR, and its average total cost, ATC. These are the same terms we defined in previous chapters, the only difference being that in the case of a monopolist

$$AR = \frac{TR}{Q} = \frac{PQ}{Q} = P,$$

where $P = P^D(Q)$. Specifically, price, or average revenue, varies inversely with the firm's sale of output rather than being taken as a predetermined constant. We have illustrated the short-run profit maximization result using marginal and average curves in Figure 15.3, where the shapes of these cost curves were explained previously in Chapter 11. The firm determines its short-run profit-maximizing level of output as Q_1 units, where $MR = SRMC$. We compute the corresponding price, and hence average revenue, by substituting Q_1 units of output into the inverse own-price demand curve, as

$$AR_1 = P_1 = P^D(Q_1).$$

---

[4]It is possible that $MR = SRMC$ at some lower value of Q as well. However, the second-order condition for a profit maximum is that $dSRMC/dQ > 0$, indicating that $SRMC$ must be rising with increases in Q. Therefore, the solution for a profit maximum occurs at Q_1 units in this analysis.

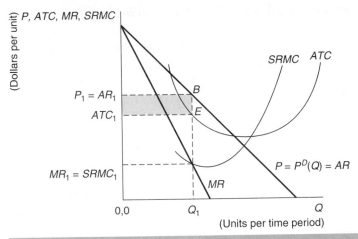

FIGURE 15.3 Short-Run Profit for a Monopolist

We determine the corresponding value of average total cost as ATC_1 by substituting Q_1 units into the ATC function. Thus, the maximized value of short-run average profit is

$$SR\,AVE\pi_1 = AR_1 - ATC_1,$$

represented in Figure 15.3 as BE, the vertical distance between the inverse own-price demand, or AR, curve, $P = P^D(Q)$, and the ATC curve at Q_1 units of output. The corresponding maximum short-run total profit is the product of the short-run average profit and the profit-maximizing level of output, Q_1, or

$$SR\pi_1 = (SR\,AVE\pi_1)Q_1,$$

represented in Figure 15.3 as the area of the rectangle $P_1B\,E\,ATC_1$.

In our example, the monopolist is earning a positive short-run profit. Is this always true? The answer is no. Depending on the circumstances, it is possible for a monopolist's short-run profit to be less than or equal to zero. At first glance, this possibility may seem somewhat strange to you because the monopolist has some influence over the price, or average revenue, of the product it sells. However, a positive short-run profit is ultimately dependent on the demand and cost conditions under which the firm must operate. For example, a firm may possess a monopoly in the market for mechanical slide rules, but in the age of personal computers and pocket calculators, it is unlikely that this firm could earn a positive profit.

By solving a specific mathematical example, we can provide some additional insight into the monopolist's process of short-run profit maximization. Assume a monopolist has the inverse demand curve

$$P = 52 - 1.5Q \tag{15.5}$$

and the cost function

$$C = \frac{1}{3}Q^3 - 5Q^2 + 60Q - KQ + 0.25K^2, \tag{15.6}$$

from which we can generate a family of $SRTC$ curves, one for each fixed level of capital, K. The firm's total revenue function is

$$TR = PQ = (52 - 1.5Q)Q$$
$$= 52Q - 1.5Q^2.$$

Thus, we derive the associated marginal revenue function as

$$MR = \frac{dTR}{dQ} = 52 - 3Q.$$

Assume the firm's level of capital, or plant size, is fixed at $\overline{K}_2 = 26$ units. By substituting this value for K into equation (15.6), we can derive the firm's particular short-run total cost curve as

$$SRTC^{\overline{K}_2} = \frac{1}{3}Q^3 - 5Q^2 + 60Q - 26Q + 0.25(26)^2$$

$$= \frac{1}{3}Q^3 - 5Q^2 + 34Q + 169.$$

The associated short-run marginal cost function is therefore

$$SRMC^{\overline{K}_2} = \frac{dSRTC^{\overline{K}_2}}{dQ} = Q^2 - 10Q + 34.$$

The firm determines its short-run profit-maximizing level of output by equating its marginal revenue to its short-run marginal cost. Thus, we solve for Q as

$$MR = SRMC^{\overline{K}_2}$$
$$52 - 3Q = Q^2 - 10Q + 34$$
$$Q^2 - 7Q - 18 = 0$$
$$(Q + 2)(Q - 9) = 0,$$

yielding the positive root $Q = 9$ units. The price of the firm's product is determined by substituting $Q = 9$ units into its inverse own-price demand curve, yielding

$$P = 52 - 1.5(9) = \$38.50.$$

Previously, we stated that this price is greater than the value of MR at the profit-maximizing level of output, as we can verify by computing this value of MR as

$$MR = 52 - 3Q = 52 - 3(9) = \$25.$$

Finally, we compute the monopolist's short-run total profit by substituting these values for output and price into its short-run total profit function, yielding

$$SR\pi_1 = TR - SRTC^{\overline{K}_2} = PQ - \left[\frac{1}{3}Q^3 - 5Q^2 + 34Q + 169\right]$$

$$= (38.50)(9) - \frac{1}{3}(9)^3 + 5(9)^2 - 34(9) - 169 = \$33.50,$$

where the short-run average profit is

$$SR\,AVE\pi_1 = \frac{SR\pi_1}{Q_1} = \frac{\$33.50}{9} = \$3.72/\text{unit}.$$

We can contrast monopoly performance to that of perfect competition by referring to the numerical problem we presented in Section 13.6.1 of Chapter 13. In that problem we assumed the market for a good to be perfectly competitive. The short-run total cost curve for a typical firm was

$$SRTC = 160 + 0.025Q^2,$$

where we derived this cost curve with the capital input fixed at $K = 4$ units. The market own-price demand curve for the good was

$$Q^{D,M} = 10{,}000 - 500P.$$

In this problem we demonstrated that the equilibrium price is $P^* = \$4$, the market quantity demanded and supplied is $Q^{M*} = 8000$ units, and the typical firm produces $Q^{F*} = 80$ units. Finally, at this level of output the firm's short-run profit is equal to zero. Now assume that a single firm gains control of the entire market for this good, thus becoming a monopolist. Assuming that all other conditions remain the same, we can compute the level of output produced and sold by this monopolist in the short run, the price it charges, and the level of short-run profit it receives.

Since a monopolist controls all of the market for a good, its own-price demand curve and that for the entire market are the same. Thus, the monopolist's demand curve is

$$Q^D = 10{,}000 - 500P,$$

that we can express in inverse form as

$$P = 20 - 0.002Q.$$

Using this information, we compute the firm's total revenue function, TR, to be

$$TR = PQ = (20 - 0.002Q)Q = 20Q - 0.002Q^2,$$

and its associated marginal revenue function, MR, as

$$MR = \frac{dTR}{dQ} = 20 - 0.004Q.$$

Since

$$SRTC = 160 + 0.025Q^2,$$

we derive the short-run marginal cost curve as

$$SRMC = \frac{dSRTC}{dQ} = 0.05Q$$

A monopolist maximizes its short-run profit by producing a level of output where $MR = SRMC$. Thus, we compute its profit-maximizing level of output to be

$$20 - 0.004Q = 0.05Q$$
$$Q^* = 370 \text{ units.}$$

We obtain the price the monopolist charges by substituting $Q^* = 370$ into the inverse own-price demand curve, yielding

$$P^* = 20 - 0.002(370) = \$19.26.$$

Finally, we compute the firm's short-run profit as

$$SR\pi = TR - SRTC$$
$$= 19.26(370) - [160 + 0.025(370)^2]$$
$$= \$3543.70.$$

Comparing these results for a monopolist to those we computed earlier for a perfectly competitive market, we can observe that the monopolist significantly restricts the amount of output it sells to a level far below that for perfect competition. Accordingly, the monopolist charges a significantly higher price. Note that for this problem the output restriction by the monopolist is very extreme. This is due, in part, to the fact that this is a short-run problem, where we have confined the firm to a very small level of capital, specifically $K = 4$ units.

In all of our examples in this section, the monopolist's short-run profits are determined to be positive. However, note that in the short run a monopolist's profit can also be less than or equal to zero, depending on the firm's demand and cost conditions. In this sense, the monopoly outcome in the short run seems rather similar to that for a perfectly competitive firm. However, this is not entirely true, since the monopolist's ability to restrict output and raise price enables it to generate a higher level of short-run profit than can a perfectly competitive firm, *ceteris paribus*. We will expand on this fact in the next chapter, where we provide a more detailed comparison between the monopoly outcome and that associated with perfect competition.

15.5 MONOPOLY BEHAVIOR IN THE LONG RUN

We will now focus on analyzing monopoly behavior in the long run, where we can immediately establish a striking dissimilarity between the monopoly results and those for a perfectly competitive firm. This difference is that a monopolist can earn a positive long-run profit, a result we demonstrated in Chapter 14 to be impossible for a perfectly competitive firm. The reason for this difference lies in the fact that a monopolist's profit is protected by entry barriers, unlike a perfectly competitive firm that enjoys no such protection.

A positive profit for a perfectly competitive firm entices the entry of new firms into the market, driving down the market price of its product. As a result, in the long run, after all adjustments have been completed, including the entry and exit of firms to and from the market, the typical perfectly competitive firm's profit is equal to zero. For the monopolist, however, this process is preempted by entry barriers, making it feasible for the firm to generate and sustain a positive profit in the long run. Furthermore, like a perfectly competitive firm in the long run, a monopolist adjusts its inputs, including its level of capital, or plant size, so as to produce its output in the most cost-efficient manner. Thus, the goal of a monopolist in the long run is to produce a level of output corresponding to a maximum value for its long-run profit. Achieving this goal also entails that the monopolist produce its profit-maximizing level of output using an optimal amount of capital as well as labor.

We can determine the necessary condition for a long-run profit maximum as follows. The monopolist's long-run profit is the difference between its total revenue, TR, and its long-run total cost, $LRTC$, or

$$LR\pi = TR - LRTC,$$

where

$$LRTC = C(Q, \overline{P}_{L,1}, \overline{P}_{K,1}).$$

The terms $\overline{P}_{L,1}$ and $\overline{P}_{K,1}$ represent the predetermined prices of the inputs labor and capital, respectively. Also note the absence of any fixed input, such as K, in the $LRTC$ function. Since

$$TR = PQ$$

and

$$P = P^D(Q),$$

then after making the appropriate substitutions, we can express the $LR\pi$ function as

$$LR\pi = PQ - C(Q, \overline{P}_{L,1}, \overline{P}_{K,1}).$$

We determine the profit-maximizing level of output by differentiating $LR\pi$ with respect to output, setting the result equal to zero, and solving for Q as

$$\frac{dLR\pi}{dQ} = \frac{dPQ}{dQ} - \frac{dC(Q, \overline{P}_{L,1}, \overline{P}_{K,1})}{dQ} = 0,$$

$$= P + Q\frac{dP}{dQ} - \frac{dC(Q, \overline{P}_{L,1}, \overline{P}_{K,1})}{dQ} = 0,$$

or

$$P + Q\frac{dP}{dQ} = \frac{dC(Q, \overline{P}_{L,1}, \overline{P}_{K,1})}{dQ}.$$

The terms on the left- and right-hand sides of this equation can be recognized as marginal revenue, MR, and long-run marginal cost, $LRMC$, respectively. Thus, the monopolist maximizes its long-run profit by producing output to the point where

$$MR = LRMC,$$

or where the extra revenue from selling an additional unit of output is equal to the extra cost of producing it. Also, recall that for reasons we discussed earlier, $P > MR = LRMC$ at this level of Q.

We have illustrated the monopolist's long-run profit maximization results in Figure 15.4. At first glance, this figure appears to be very similar to Figure 15.2, in which we illustrated the monopolist's short-run profit determination. However, the panels in Figure 15.4 contain long-run cost functions and hence demonstrate an analysis of long-run profit. Specifically, panel (B) shows the long-run profit function, $LR\pi$, panel (A) contains the component functions of $LR\pi$, TR and $LRTC$, and panel (C) demonstrates the associated marginal functions, MR and $LRMC$. Since we have expressed all functions in terms of output, the panels are linked by their common horizontal axes. Since total revenue is measured as $TR = PQ$, from either a short- or long-run perspective, the TR function shown in panel (A) is identical to that used in our earlier short-run profit analysis. However, this panel contains a $LRTC$ function rather than a $SRTC$ function, which we can identify as such because it begins at the origin, reflecting no fixed cost. The vertical distance between the TR and $LRTC$ functions is equal to $LR\pi$ at each value of Q, as illustrated in panel (B). The goal of a monopolist is to produce the level of output that corresponds to a long-run profit maximum, where we observe this level occurring at Q_1 units. At this value of Q, $TR > LRTC$ by the greatest amount, and thus the $LR\pi$ function achieves its maximum value as

$$LR\pi_1 = TR_1 - LRTC_1.$$

We can demonstrate the necessary condition for a long-run profit maximum, $MR = LRMC$, by drawing the lines AA' and BB', tangent to the TR and $LRTC$ functions, respectively, and observing that their slopes are equal. As a result, we can conclude that at Q_1 units, $MR_1 = LRMC_1$, corresponding to the maximum value for $LR\pi$. We can also observe this necessary condition for an $LR\pi$ maximum in panel (C) where $MR_1 = LRMC_1$ at Q_1 units. This example illustrates a case for which $LR\pi > 0$. However, it is possible to have a situation in which $LR\pi = 0$, even for a monopolist. In this case the TR and $LRTC$ curves would be tangent to each other, still reflecting the necessary condition for a profit maximum, $MR = LRMC$, but a long-run profit of zero since $TR = LRTC$. Note that a negative long-run profit is nonsensical in that a monopolist, after making all possible adjustments, would not be covering its opportunity costs. In this case, the monopolist will leave the industry and seek a positive profit elsewhere.

We can also use average functions to analyze the long-run profit maximization process for a monopolist, where we convert the total profit function into an average one by simply dividing it by Q as

$$\frac{LR\pi}{Q} = \frac{TR}{Q} - \frac{LRTC}{Q},$$

or

$$LR\,AVE\pi = AR - LRAC.$$

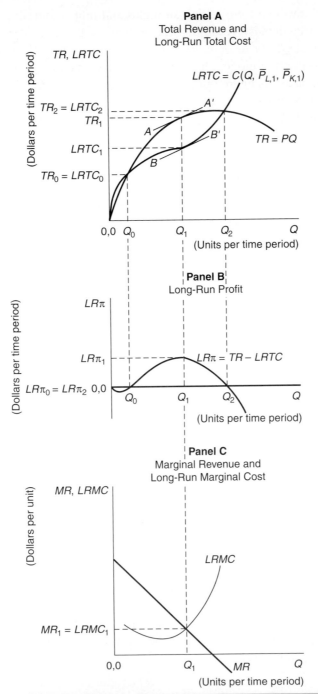

FIGURE 15.4 Relationships among Total Revenue, Total Cost, Profit, Marginal Cost, and Marginal Revenue for a Monopolist in Long Run

In Figure 15.5, we have illustrated these component functions of *LR AVEπ*, *AR*, and *LRAC* along with the associated marginal functions, *MR* and *LRMC*. Recall that the *AR* function is the inverse own-price demand curve, $P = P^D(Q)$. We determine the firm's long-run profit-maximizing level of output to be Q_1 units, at which $MR_1 = LRMC_1$. We compute its corresponding price, or *AR*, by substituting Q_1 units into the inverse own-price demand curve, yielding

$$P_1 = P^D(Q_1) = AR_1.$$

Thus, the maximum long-run average profit is equal to *EF*, the vertical distance between the inverse own-price demand curve and the *LRAC* function at Q_1, or

$$LR\,AVE\pi_1 = AR_1 - LRAC_1.$$

The total long-run profit is the product of $LR\,AVE\pi_1$ and Q_1, or

$$LR\pi_1 = (LR\,AVE\pi_1)(Q_1),$$

and is represented in Figure 15.5 as the area of the rectangle $P_1\,E\,F\,LRAC_1$. It is important for us to reemphasize that a long-run profit is possible for a monopolist because of the presence of barriers to entry. Moreover, this profit can be sustainable, subject to changes in underlying demand and cost conditions.

We can provide some additional insight into the long-run profit maximization solution by recalling that the short- and long-run cost functions are not independent of one another. In Chapter 12, we established the fact that long-run total and average cost curves represent envelope curves, where each output–cost combination on a long-run cost curve corresponds to a different single combination pertaining to each curve in a set of short-run cost curves. Furthermore, since in the long run, the firm is able to vary all of its inputs, each of these output–cost combinations pertains to a constrained cost minimization solution. As a result, a monopolist's long-run profit maximization

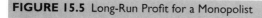

FIGURE 15.5 Long-Run Profit for a Monopolist

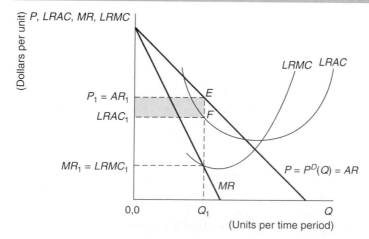

solution consists of determining the optimal (profit-maximizing) levels of output and price, and in addition, determining the amount of capital, or plant size, at which it can produce this level of output in the least costly manner. Thus, the optimal level of capital at which the firm produces this long-run profit-maximizing level of output is also represented by the corresponding set of short-run cost curves for that particular amount of capital. This being the case, the long-run profit maximization solution is the same as the corresponding short-run profit maximization solution.

In Figure 15.6 we have illustrated the relationship between long-run average and short-run or average total cost curves, for a long-run profit maximization solution. In this figure, we have repeated the long-run solution shown in Figure 15.5, while including a short-run marginal cost curve, $SRMC^{\overline{K}_1}$, and an average total cost curve, $ATC^{\overline{K}_1}$, pertaining to the use of the optimal amount of capital, $\overline{K}_1$, for producing Q_1 units of output. We can determine this profit-maximizing level of output, Q_1, from either the necessary condition for a long-run profit maximum

$$MR = LRMC,$$

or the necessary condition for a short-run profit maximum, on the condition the firm uses $\overline{K}_1$ units of capital

$$MR = SRMC^{\overline{K}_1}.$$

The corresponding price is $P_1 = AR_1$, and the maximum average profit is

$$LR\,AVE\pi_1 = SR\,AVE\pi_1^{\overline{K}_1} = AR_1 - LRAC_1 = AR_1 - ATC_1^{\overline{K}_1}.$$

We can reinforce the concept of long-run profit maximization and the process of selecting the optimal level of capital for producing the profit-maximizing level of output by returning to the mathematical example presented in Section 15.4. In that example, the monopolist's inverse own-price demand curve was represented by equation (15.5) as

$$P = 52 - 1.5Q,$$

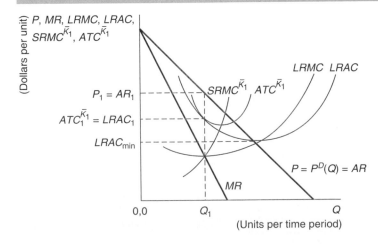

FIGURE 15.6 Relationship between Long-Run and Short-Run Monopoly Profit

while the basis for the firm's family of short-run total cost curves was represented by equation (15.6) as

$$C = \frac{1}{3}Q^3 - 5Q^2 + 60Q - KQ + 0.25K^2.$$

Furthermore, we assumed that the firm, in the short run, used a fixed amount of the capital input, $\overline{K}_2 = 26$ units. Thus, we computed the firm's short-run total cost function as

$$SRTC^{\overline{K}_2} = \frac{1}{3}Q^3 - 5Q^2 + 34Q + 169.$$

We determined the short-run profit-maximizing level of output by equating MR to $SRMC$, yielding a value of $Q = 9$ units. The corresponding values for price and short-run profit were computed as $P = \$38.50$, and $SR\pi_2 = \$33.50$, respectively. Given its underlying cost conditions and the market own-price demand curve, the firm is doing the best it can, provided it has no choice but to use $\overline{K}_2 = 26$ units of capital. However, for this short-run solution, there is no reason to believe that this amount of capital is necessarily optimal, or constrained cost minimizing. Specifically, for this example, we can demonstrate that the firm is not using an optimal level of capital, given the particular own-price demand curve. The reason for this result is that the firm does not have sufficient time to make appropriate adjustments to its plant size.

In the long run, however, the firm is free to vary all of its inputs, including the amount of capital it employs, and it produces its long-run profit-maximizing level of output using an optimal input combination. We can demonstrate this result by first minimizing the firm's cost with respect to the amount of capital employed. Thus, using equation (15.6), or

$$C = \frac{1}{3}Q^3 - 5Q^2 + 60Q - KQ + 0.25K^2,$$

we take the partial derivative of C with respect to K and set the result equal to zero, yielding

$$\frac{\partial C}{\partial K} = -Q + 0.5K = 0,$$

and we solve for K as

$$K = 2Q. \tag{15.7}$$

This equation expresses the optimal levels of capital, K, that the firm uses to produce different amounts of output. By substituting this expression for K from equation (15.7) into equation (15.6), we derive the firm's long-run total cost function as

$$C = LRTC = \frac{1}{3}Q^3 - 5Q^2 + 60Q - 2Q(Q) + 0.25(2Q)^2,$$

or

$$LRTC = \frac{1}{3}Q^3 - 6Q^2 + 60Q.$$

This function represents the minimum total cost associated with producing each level of output. We can determine the profit-maximizing level of Q according to the $MR = LRMC$ condition by first computing $LRMC$ as

$$LRMC = \frac{dLRTC}{dQ} = Q^2 - 12Q + 60.$$

Earlier, we derived the total revenue function to be

$$TR = PQ = (52 - 1.5Q)Q = 52Q - 1.5Q^2,$$

and the corresponding marginal revenue function as

$$MR = \frac{dTR}{dQ} = 52 - 3Q.$$

Thus, equating MR to $LRMC$,

$$52 - 3Q = Q^2 - 12Q + 60$$
$$Q^2 - 9Q + 8 = 0$$
$$(Q - 1)(Q - 8) = 0,$$

we obtain the roots of $Q = 1$ unit and $Q = 8$ units. You can verify that the profit-maximizing level of output in this example is $Q = 8$ units. The corresponding price is

$$P = 52 - 1.5(8) = \$40,$$

and the long-run profit is

$$LR\pi = TR - LRTC$$
$$= 40(8) - \frac{1}{3}(8)^3 + 6(8)^2 - 60(8) = \$53.33.$$

This long-run solution for the monopolist's output price and capital differs from the earlier short-run solution for which $\overline{K}_2 = 26$ units of capital. We expect long-run profit to exceed short-run profit because, in the long run, the firm produces its output using an optimal input combination, whereas in the short run this is generally not the case.

We can further clarify this process of long-run profit maximization by determining, for the example above, the particular short-run situation within which the firm operates, after adjusting its amount of capital to the optimal level. To produce $Q = 8$ units of output in the least costly manner, the firm alters the amount of capital it employs according to equation (15.7), yielding

$$\overline{K}_1 = 2(8) = 16 \text{ units.}$$

We then compute the relevant short-run total cost function as

$$SRTC^{\overline{K}_1} = C = \frac{1}{3}Q^3 - 5Q^2 + 60Q - 16Q + 0.25(16)^2$$

$$= \frac{1}{3}Q^3 - 5Q^2 + 44Q + 64,$$

where the short-run marginal cost function is

$$SRMC^{\overline{K}_1} = \frac{dSRTC^{\overline{K}_1}}{dQ} = Q^2 - 10Q + 44.$$

After determining the optimal level of capital, we can obtain the solution values for Q, P, and π by applying the necessary condition for short-run profit maximization as

$$MR = SRMC^{\overline{K}_1}$$
$$52 - 3Q = Q^2 - 10Q + 44$$
$$Q^2 - 7Q - 8 = 0$$
$$(Q + 1)(Q - 8) = 0,$$

yielding a positive root of $Q = 8$ units. Once again we find the corresponding value for price by substituting $Q = 8$ into the inverse own-price demand curve

$$P = 52 - 1.5Q.$$

Thus

$$P = 52 - 1.5(8) = \$40,$$

and therefore the value for short-run profit is

$$SR\pi^{\overline{K}_1} = TR - SRTC^{\overline{K}_1}$$
$$= 40(8) - \frac{1}{3}(8)^3 + 5(8)^2 - 44(8) - 64 = \$53.33.$$

These values for output, price, and profit are the same as those we obtained earlier using the long-run cost functions. Having now examined the basic monopoly model in both the short- and long-run time periods, we will direct our focus in the following chapter to some additional topics uniquely related to monopoly behavior.

15.6   SUMMARY

In this chapter, we first discussed some of the primary origins of monopoly and monopoly power. Afterward, we devoted our attention to determining outcomes for such performance variables as output, price, and profit for a monopolistic market structure during both short- and long-run time periods. A summary of the various topics we covered in this chapter is as follows.

- Monopoly is a market structure consisting of a single seller of a good where, by definition, this good is substantially differentiated from the products of all other firms.
- A monopolist, unlike a perfectly competitive firm, possesses some influence over the price of the good it sells.
- A monopolistic market structure is generally the result of barriers to entry that prevent other firms from entering the industry.

- Marginal revenue is less than market price for a monopolist.
- A profit-maximizing monopolist determines its output where $MC = MR$ for the last unit it produces.
- Due to the lack of entry, a monopolist may be able to sustain a positive economic profit in the long run.

KEY TERMS

- barrier to entry, page 386
- monopoly, page 383
- monopoly power, page 385

EXERCISES

15.1 Discuss the characteristics that define a monopolistic market structure.

15.2 Discuss five different types of barriers to entry and explain how each can result in a monopoly. Provide a real-world example of each type of entry barrier.

15.3 Compare the own-price demand curve faced by a monopolist to that for a perfectly competitive firm. Also compare the marginal revenue curve the monopolist faces to that associated with a perfectly competitive firm, and explain why they are different.

15.4 Why does a profit-maximizing monopolist never elect to produce a level of output that falls within the inelastic portion of its own-price demand curve? To support your written response, draw a vertical sequence of three graphs depicting (a) the market own-price demand curve and the marginal revenue curve, (b) the total revenue curve, and, (c) the marginal cost and marginal revenue curves.

15.5 Assume that a monopolist faces the inverse own-price demand curve

$$P = P^D(Q) = 10 - 0.10Q,$$

and the total cost curve

$$TC(Q) = 2Q + 0.025Q^2.$$

a. Determine the monopolist's profit-maximizing levels of output and price, as well as the amount of profit earned.

b. Do your results from part a correspond to a long- or short-run outcome for the monopolist, or both? Explain your response.

15.6 Suppose the own-price demand curve faced by a monopolist is

$$Q^D = 25 - P,$$

and its short-run total cost curve is

$$SRTC(Q) = \frac{1}{12}Q^3 - 2.50Q^2 + 30Q + 100.$$

a. Determine the inverse market own-price demand curve facing the monopolist.

b. Determine the monopolist's total revenue curve.

c. Determine the monopolist's short-run marginal cost curve.

15.7 Referring to the information in Exercise 15.6, compute the profit-maximizing level of output produced by the monopolist, the price it changes, and the amount of profit it earns in the short run.

15.8 Since a monopolist has some discretion over the price of its product, how is it possible for this firm ever to experience a short- run loss? Specifically, why can't the firm simply charge a price that always exceeds its costs?

CHAPTER 16

Additional Topics Related to Monopoly

16.1 INTRODUCTION

In this chapter we will extend our analysis of monopoly, paying particular attention to the performance outcomes associated with this market structure. Using the same set of performance criteria we applied in Chapter 14 to the perfectly competitive market, we will similarly evaluate monopoly performance and compare the associated output, price, profit, and cost outcomes to those for perfect competition. In addition, we will expand this comparison by developing and applying concepts known as consumer and producer surplus that represent the benefits received by consumers and firms, respectively, from participating in a marketwide process.

Another concept we will explore is price discrimination by the seller of a good, a topic unique to firms possessing some degree of monopoly power, or price-setting ability. Undoubtedly, you are familiar with stores that offer discounted prices to specific groups of people. For example, a firm may engage in price discrimination by offering senior citizens' discounts, reflecting the fact that senior citizens have relatively more elastic demand than other customers. We will show that by pricing its good differently, in accordance with the own-price elasticity of demand of its various categories of consumers, a firm can increase its total revenue and profit. Finally, many monopolists produce their output using more than one plant, and thus we will extend the basic monopoly model to analyze a multiplant monopolist.

16.2 EVALUATION OF MARKET PERFORMANCE UNDER MONOPOLY

In Chapter 14 we evaluated several performance variables associated with perfectly competitive markets from a social perspective. We can conduct a similar analysis regarding monopoly market performance. Although much of this analysis involves an implicit comparison between the outcomes associated with monopoly and those for perfect competition, we will defer our direct comparison of these results to Section 16.3.1.

As discussed in Chapter 14, the formal criteria we use for evaluating market performance are production efficiency, allocative efficiency, and dynamic efficiency. In addition, we also considered the less formal criterion of fairness, taking into consideration the concepts of equal opportunity and a reasonably equitable distribution of income and wealth. Keeping in mind that the idea of fairness involves some degree of subjectivity, we generally believe that the monopoly outcome does not fulfill the criterion of fairness for essentially two reasons. First, monopoly is characterized by the existence of barriers to entry that enable one firm to operate in an industry, thus preventing other firms from entering the market. The result of such barriers, which may exist for many reasons, can hardly be characterized as reflecting equal opportunity. A second reason centers around the monopolist's potential for generating long-run profit. This result reflects the fact that a monopolist may be able to sustain a return that is greater than his opportunity cost, and because of the presence of entry barriers, there exists no natural market pressure to eliminate this long-run profit. Furthermore, since this profit is due to the monopolist's ability to restrict the production of output and increase price, most of this profit is derived at the consumer's expense.

The first formal criterion we use for evaluating market performance is production efficiency, which involves producing output in the most cost-efficient manner possible. Production efficiency entails two major aspects. First, a firm must produce a level of output using an optimal plant size that enables it to produce this output at minimum long-run average cost. By doing so, a firm can realize all the advantages associated with economies of scale, yet experience none of the disadvantages connected with diseconomies of scale. A monopolist can produce a level of output corresponding to the minimum point on its $LRAC$ curve, but there is no guarantee of this result. Once again, as a result of entry barriers, the natural pressures that would force the monopolist to be cost efficient in this manner are absent. Essentially, the monopolist can generally increase its profit by restricting output and raising price, even though it may experience the associated disadvantage of higher per unit costs of production. The resulting outcome, though rational from the monopolist's perspective, is cost inefficient from a social perspective. We demonstrated this result in Figure 15.6, where the monopolist maximizes its long-run profit by producing Q_1 units of output at a corresponding long-run average cost of $LRAC_1$, a level that is clearly above the minimum value, $LRAC_{min}$.

Another concern regarding production efficiency is the possibility of X-inefficiency. As described in Chapter 14, X-inefficiency involves a tolerance for wasting resources. Although irrational from an omniscient perspective, this phenomenon becomes a likely possibility for a monopolist. As we discussed earlier, a monopolist can earn a long-run profit that is shielded from the pressures of entry; as a result, this firm is in a position to squander some of its resources. This is not to say that it will necessarily do so, but the monopolist is not forced to be cost efficient in order to merely survive, as is the case for a perfectly competitive firm. Thus, the temptation for managers to behave in a slack manner or to maximize their own salaries and benefits rather than the firm's profit can become rather strong, particularly if there exists a significant separation between ownership and management of the firm.

The second criterion for evaluating market performance is allocative efficiency, or the flow of resources to their most highly valued uses. Simply stated, the monopoly outcome is not allocatively efficient because the firm underproduces its product. This conclusion follows from the fact that a monopolist determines its profit-maximizing level of output according to the $MR = MC$ rule, and since the price it charges exceeds

---

REAL-WORLD APPLICATION 16.1

Barriers to Entry in Small-Town America and
Their Impact on Market Performance

The following excerpts from an editorial appeared in a weekly newspaper published in Shippensburg, Pennsylvania.[1] It succinctly details many of the negative impacts of a government-imposed barrier to entry on local economic development.

[E]conomic development takes in everything from big industry to the availability of gas stations, grocery and convenience stores and restaurants. The last—restaurants—has steadily become more of a factor. People want all kinds, from fast food to fine cuisine. We are an *eat-out* society.

Appetites for restaurants have increased although ways of gauging fine restaurants haven't. And to most people, fine food is accompanied by wine, a cocktail, or, perhaps, an imported or microbrewery beer.

But the liquor laws of Pennsylvania make it easier to have a lineup of fast-food outlets than places for fine food. That's because the state of Pennsylvania long has had a law that so stringently limits liquor licenses that it can become prohibitive for an aspiring restaurateur to acquire one. The law restricts regular liquor licenses for bars and restaurants to one for every 3,000 people in a municipality. No new ones have been issued for decades, making transfers from one business to another costly

ventures. [We] have heard of liquor licenses selling for more than $100,000 in Cumberland County [PA]. There is a loophole in the law that allows granting unlimited special licenses for establishments within 15 miles of "resort" communities. And this has been abused as it is loosely defined in many instances. As proof, 344 municipalities in this state now have resort status. . . . We have heard of restaurant operations that waited a long time to come into Cumberland County because of liquor license limitations.

So it's not a system that demands fair distribution; it's one where the sly fox gets the goods. But it is a system that can inhibit "local economic development" because good restaurants can help to make a community more vital. And the more the merrier because having a number of good restaurants means people will keep coming back to your town for more. We have heard of restaurant operations that waited a long time to come into Cumberland County because of liquor license limitations and some have not located here because they can't get a liquor license.

Now along comes a bill that would dump the "resort" gimmick and allow new licenses if food accounts for 70 percent of the restaurant's sales. So far, so good. We'll vote for that. It would provide more variety for would-be diners and would be . . . fairer to those who want to open a business.

But, most importantly, it's a matter of letting free enterprise work fairly—instead of through dishonest ploys.

[1]"Change in Liquor Laws Could Help Economy," *Shippensburg Sentinel*, Shippensburg, PA, August 5, 1998, p. A4.

its marginal revenue, this price also exceeds its marginal cost. We can interpret the price of a good as representing the value consumers place on the extra, or last, unit of the good sold, while marginal cost represents the extra cost associated with the last unit of the good produced. Since a monopolist maximizes its profit by producing a level of output at which $P > MC$, then at this level of production, consumers value the last unit more than it costs the firm to produce it. This conflict between the best interest of consumers and the best interest of the firm will not be resolved, for a rational monopolist will continue to restrict its production of output in order to charge the higher price. This being the case, we can conclude that monopoly behavior causes a good to be underproduced, thus misallocating resources.

The final criterion for evaluating market performance is dynamic efficiency, or the development and adoption of technological progress. With regard to this criterion, the monopoly outcome is rather ambiguous. Essentially, there are two conflicting viewpoints, which ultimately can only be resolved statistically. One viewpoint is that monopoly is conducive to a high level of dynamic efficiency, primarily because it can generate a long-run profit from which it can support the research and development necessary to sustain technological progress. In addition, because of entry barriers, it is logical to believe that a monopolist is virtually assured that it can exclusively reap any rewards associated with this type of investment. An alternative viewpoint is that, although a monopolist is in a good position to engage in research and development, it may not actually undertake such investment owing to a lack of competitive pressure. After all, if a monopolist is already generating a secure long-run profit, where is the incentive to take on the cost and risk associated with many research and development projects?

In summary, our evaluation of monopoly market performance, within the context of fairness, production efficiency, allocative efficiency, and dynamic efficiency, leads us to the conclusion that the overall outcome is not particularly desirable from a social perspective. We will reinforce this conclusion in the following section by directly comparing various outcomes associated with monopoly with those for perfect competition.

16.3 CONSUMER SURPLUS AND PRODUCER SURPLUS

Before proceeding with our direct comparison of the monopoly and perfectly competitive market outcomes, we will introduce two related economic concepts, consumer surplus and producer surplus. **Consumer surplus** is *the difference between the value consumers place on each unit of a good and the price they actually pay for that unit, summed over all units purchased.* Since the prices associated with the market own-price demand curve for a good represent the different values consumers place on each unit of that good, consumer surplus is the amount by which the social value of each unit of the good exceeds its price, summed over all units sold. Essentially, it is the advantage received by consumers from participating in a marketwide process. Once a market price is established for a good, all units are purchased at that price regardless of the fact that, for an own-price demand curve possessing a negative slope, all but the last unit purchased are valued more highly than this market price. Thus, the total consumer surplus is represented as the area under the inverse own-price demand curve, less the area under the market price, both measured from zero units to the equilibrium quantity of output purchased.[2] This result is contingent on the absence of price discrimination, a process by which sellers identify the value consumers place on different units of a good and then correspondingly charge different prices for these units. We will reserve our discussion of price discrimination and its implications for the next section.

A concept similar to consumer surplus is **producer surplus**, or *the difference between the price a producer receives from selling each unit of a good and the marginal cost associated with producing each respective unit, summed over all units sold*. We can readily apply the concept of producer surplus to ideas previously developed. For example, in the short run, a perfectly competitive firm's profit is equal to its producer surplus less its fixed cost. This result follows because the summation of the prices of all units sold is equal to the firm's total revenue, $TR = PQ$, and the summation of its short-run marginal costs are equal to its variable cost, VC. More importantly, since the short-run market supply curve for a perfectly competitive industry consists of the summation of the individual firms' $SRMC$, or SRS curves, it is possible to demonstrate producer surplus for the entire market.

We have illustrated producer surplus, along with the previously discussed concept of consumer surplus, in Figure 16.1 for a perfectly competitive market in the short run. This figure contains a market own-price demand curve, D^M, represented in inverse form as

$$P = b_0' - b_1' Q^D,$$

and a short-run market supply curve, SRS^M, also expressed in inverse form as

$$P = \alpha_0 + \alpha_1 Q^S.$$

Thus, the vertical, or price, intercepts for the inverse own-price demand and supply curves are b_0' and α_0, respectively. Observe, that the equilibrium price is established at P_E where $Q_E^D = Q_E^S = Q_E$. For the last unit of output produced and sold, Q_E, consumer surplus is equal to zero since P_E is the value consumers place on this last unit. In addi-

---

[2]Technically, total consumer surplus is the area under an inverse compensated demand curve less the area under the market price of the good, measured from zero to the equilibrium quantity of output purchased. The distinction between these two types of curves is that a compensated own-price demand curve does not include income effects associated with changes in the price of a good, whereas ordinary own-price demand curves include these effects. In practice, it is the ordinary own-price demand curve that is commonly observed and empirically estimated using real-world data. As a result, it is often convention to ignore the income effects and measure consumer surplus using the ordinary own-price demand curve as we have described.

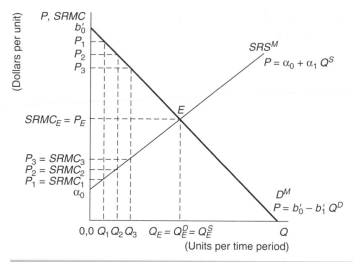

FIGURE 16.1 Consumer Surplus and Producer Surplus for a Perfectly Competitive Market

tion, the producer surplus associated with this last unit is also equal to zero since $P = SRMC$ at this unit. However, for all units produced and sold prior to the Q_E unit, there exist successively declining amounts of both consumer and producer surplus associated with increases in Q.

For example, at $Q_1 = 1$ unit of output, a consumer may value this unit at a price of P_1, and accordingly receives $(P_1 - P_E)$ amount of consumer surplus from purchasing this unit, provided he pays the market price, P_E. The producer surplus associated with this $Q_1 = 1$ unit of output equals $(P_E - SRMC_1)$, since this unit is produced at a marginal cost of $SRMC_1$. For the second unit, $Q_2 = 2$, the consumer surplus equals $(P_2 - P_E)$, and the producer surplus is $(P_E - SRMC_2)$. Thus, we can compute the entire amount of consumer surplus, CS, by summing the consumer surplus pertaining to each unit of output up to the last unit purchased as

$$CS = (P_1 - P_E) + (P_2 - P_E) + \ldots + (P_E - P_E).$$

Technically, the consumer surplus associated with the Q_E unit is zero, since $P_E - P_E = 0$. However, for some applications we will interpret the increments in Q as infinitesimally small, and thus we include this Q_E unit in the computation of CS. The total amount of consumer surplus is illustrated in Figure 16.1 as the area of the triangle $P_E b_0' E$, which we can compute by recalling the formula for the area of a right triangle, $1/2$ (base) (height). In this example, the area for consumer surplus is

$$CS = \frac{1}{2}(Q_E - 0)(b_0' - P_E). \tag{16.1}$$

We can also determine the entire producer surplus, PS, by summing the producer surplus associated with each unit of output sold up through the Q_E unit, or

$$PS = (P_E - SRMC_1) + (P_E - SRMC_2) + \ldots + (P_E - SRMC_E).$$

In Figure 16.1, this total amount of producer surplus is represented by the area of the triangle $P_E E \propto_0$, computed as

$$PS = \frac{1}{2}(Q_E - 0)(P_E - \propto_0). \qquad \textbf{(16.2)}$$

We can further demonstrate the computation of consumer and producer surplus with a mathematical example. Assume a perfectly competitive market in which the market own-price demand and short-run market supply curves are

$$Q^D = 40 - 0.2P$$

and

$$Q^S = -5 + 0.25P,$$

respectively. The equilibrium level of output, Q_E, occurs where $Q^D = Q^S$; therefore, we determine the equilibrium level of price as

$$40 - 0.2P = -5 + 0.25P$$
$$0.45P = 45$$
$$P_E = \$100.$$

We compute the equilibrium amount of output by substituting this value for price into either the market own-price demand or the short-run market supply curve. Selecting the market own-price demand curve yields

$$Q^D = 40 - 0.2(100) = 40 - 20 = 20 \text{ units,}$$

and thus, in equilibrium

$$Q^D = Q^S = Q_E = 20 \text{ units.}$$

Rearranging the market own-price demand and short-run market supply curves into their inverse forms allows us to express them as

$$P = 200 - 5Q^D$$

and

$$P = 20 + 4Q^S,$$

respectively, yielding price intercept values of $b_0' = 200$ and $\propto_0 = 20$. Finally, we compute the values for consumer surplus, CS, and producer surplus, PS, by substituting the appropriate values into equations (16.1) and (16.2), respectively. Thus, for this example

$$CS = \frac{1}{2}(Q_E - 0)(b_0' - P_E)$$

$$= \frac{1}{2}(20 - 0)(200 - 100) = \$1000$$

and

$$PS = \frac{1}{2}(Q_E - 0)(P_E - \infty_0)$$
$$= \frac{1}{2}(20 - 0)(100 - 20) = \$800.$$

16.3.1 Comparison of Monopoly and Perfectly Competitive Market Outcomes in Terms of Consumer Surplus

The concepts of consumer and producer surplus are very useful in comparing the outcomes associated with monopoly and perfect competition as we have illustrated in Figure 16.2. In this figure, we have reproduced the perfectly competitive market equilibrium outcome shown in Figure 16.1, again using the inverse market own-price demand and supply curves,

$$P = b_0' - b_1' Q^D,$$

and

$$P = \infty_0 + \infty_1 Q^S,$$

respectively. The equilibrium price is P_C, where $Q_C^D = Q_C^S = Q_C$, and we represent the consumer surplus, CS_C, and producer surplus, PS_C, by the areas of the triangles $P_C b_0' E$ and $P_C E \infty_0$, respectively. Also included in Figure 16.2 is the outcome for the same market under the condition of monopoly. As a result, we can also interpret the market own-price demand curve, D^M, as the monopolist's own-price demand curve from which we derive the associated marginal revenue curve, MR. In addition, on the basis

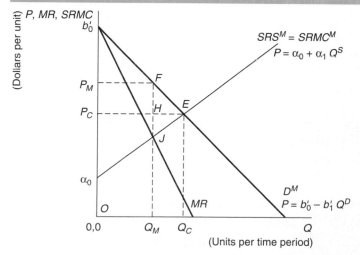

FIGURE 16.2 Comparison of Consumer and Producer Surpluses under Perfect Competition and Monopoly

of some simplifying assumptions, such as no X-inefficiency, we can consider the market supply curve, SRS^M, as the monopolist's short-run marginal cost curve, $SRMC^M$. The monopolist determines its profit-maximizing level of output as Q_M, where $MR = SRMC^M$, and its corresponding price as P_M. The monopolist's ability to restrict its production of output and raise its price results in both a lower level of output and a higher price, compared to that for perfect competition. These results are illustrated in Figure 16.2, where $Q_M < Q_C$, and $P_M > P_C$.

We can also compare the amounts of consumer and producer surplus corresponding to the perfect competition and monopoly outcomes. The consumer surplus associated with perfect competition, the area of the triangle $P_C b_0' E$, is reduced by the area of the quadrilateral $P_C P_M F E$ once the market is monopolized, leaving a consumer surplus under monopoly equal to the area of the smaller triangle $P_M b_0' F$. This loss of consumer surplus has two components. One component is the area of the rectangle $P_C P_M F H$ that, rather than comprising part of consumer surplus, is now part of the monopolist's total revenue represented by the area of the rectangle $OP_M F Q_M$. As a result, this component of lost consumer surplus ultimately becomes part of the monopolist's profit. The other component of lost consumer surplus is the area of the triangle HFE. This loss is due to the output restriction from Q_C to Q_M, and it is a complete loss because it is not received by either the consumers or the monopolist. The monopoly outcome also results in a lower amount of producer surplus as compared to that under perfect competition. For monopoly, the producer surplus is equal to the area of the quadrilateral $P_M F J \infty_0$, which is part of the monopolist's total revenue. However, compared to perfect competition, the monopolist loses the producer surplus represented by the area of the triangle HEJ due to restricting output from Q_C to Q_M.

The summation of the areas of the triangle HFE—the consumer surplus lost and received by no one—and the triangle HEJ—the producer surplus lost and received by no one—is equal to the area of the triangle JFE. This triangle, JFE, represents the **deadweight loss** attributable to monopoly, or *the complete loss of consumer and producer surplus due to monopoly output restriction*. This deadweight loss does not involve a transfer of surplus from one party to another, such as from consumers to a firm. Instead, it represents a measure of true loss to society due to the misallocation of resources caused by monopoly behavior.

Our comparison of monopoly and perfectly competitive market outcomes, for such performance variables as output, price, profit, consumer surplus, and deadweight loss, can also be demonstrated with a mathematical example. Assume the inverse own-price market demand curve for a good is

$$P = 200 - 5Q^D,$$

which in the case of monopoly also represents the firm's own-price demand curve. Also assume that the long-run total cost curve for the industry is

$$LRTC = 20Q,$$

and as a result, we compute the firm's corresponding long-run marginal and average costs as

$$LRMC = \frac{dLRTC}{dQ} = \frac{d20Q}{dQ} = \$20$$

and

$$LRAC = \frac{LRTC}{Q} = \frac{20Q}{Q} = \$20,$$

respectively. Thus, in this example both long-run marginal and average costs are equal to the same constant value, or

$$LRMC = LRAC = \$20.$$

Furthermore, we also assume these values to be identical regardless of whether the market is treated as perfectly competitive or monopolistic. If the market is perfectly competitive, we interpret this value as representing the market supply curve. To determine the perfectly competitive level of output, we equate price to marginal cost as

$$P = LRMC$$
$$200 - 5Q^D = 20$$
$$Q_C = \frac{180}{5} = 36 \text{ units,}$$

and the perfectly competitive price is simply

$$P_C = MC = \$20.$$

As expected, the perfectly competitive level of long-run average profit is equal to zero, or

$$LR\,AVE\pi = AR - LRAC$$
$$= 20 - 20 = \$0,$$

since $P = AR$.

Of course, the long-run total profit equals zero as well, since

$$LR\pi = (LR\,AVE\pi)(Q) = (0)Q_C = \$0.$$

These results are illustrated in Figure 16.3, where we can observe that the corresponding consumer surplus, CS_C, is the area of the triangle $P_C b_0' E$, or

$$CS_C = \frac{1}{2}(36 - 0)(200 - 20) = \$3240.$$

In this example, there exists no producer surplus since $P - MC = 0$ at each level of output.

If we treat this market as a monopoly, the values of the performance variables differ from those we just computed for the perfectly competitive outcome. A monopolist determines its profit-maximizing level of output by equating marginal revenue to marginal cost, where we obtain the *MR* function by taking the derivative of the monopolist's *TR* function as

$$TR = PQ$$
$$= (200 - 5Q)Q = 200Q - 5Q^2$$
$$MR = \frac{dTR}{dQ} = 200 - 10Q.$$

Thus, equating *MR* to *LRMC*, the monopolist's profit-maximizing level of output, Q_M, is

$$200 - 10Q = 20$$
$$Q_M = \frac{180}{10} = 18 \text{ units},$$

and we compute the corresponding price, P_M, from the inverse own-price demand curve as

$$P_M = 200 - 5(18) = \$110.$$

This outcome reflects the monopolist's ability to restrict output and raise price, as $Q_M < Q_C$ and $P_M > P_C$. These results are illustrated in Figure 16.3, which shows that the amount of consumer surplus corresponding to the monopoly outcome is substantially lower than that for perfect competition. The consumer surplus pertaining to the monopoly outcome is represented by the area of the triangle $P_M b_0' F$, or

$$CS_M = \frac{1}{2}(18 - 0)(200 - 110) = \$810,$$

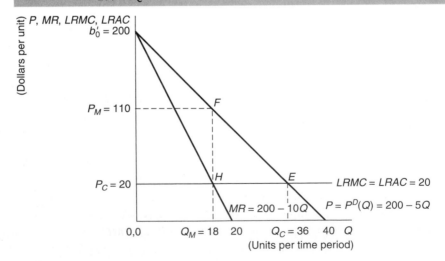

FIGURE 16.3 Comparison of Monopoly and Perfect Competition Outcomes When $P = P^D(Q) = 200 - 5Q$

an amount considerably smaller than the $3240 we computed for the market, assuming perfect competition. The monopolist's profit is

$$LR\pi_M = TR - LRTC$$
$$= PQ - 20Q$$
$$= 110(18) - 20(18) = \$1620,$$

a value substantially larger than the long-run perfectly competitive profit of zero. In Figure 16.3, we have represented this monopoly profit as the area of the rectangle $P_C P_M FH$. This figure also shows that this profit is generated at the expense of some of the consumer surplus corresponding to the perfectly competitive outcome, CS_C. In addition, CS_C is reduced by the area of the triangle HFE, representing the deadweighted loss, DWL, attributed to monopoly, which we compute as

$$DWL = \frac{1}{2}(36 - 18)(110 - 20) = \$810.$$

16.4   PRICE DISCRIMINATION

We briefly referred to price discrimination in Chapter 7, as well as earlier in this chapter. However, our discussion of this topic was deferred until we could develop the concept of consumer surplus. Specifically, **price discrimination** is *the charging of different price to marginal cost ratios for different units of a good that are of the same grade and quality, once an equilibrium price is established*. We must clarify two important points at the outset. First, any price differentials across the units of a good sold that are cost justified do not constitute price discrimination. For example, differences in the geographic location of a firm's customers affect its transportation costs, resulting in different delivered prices. However, this result does not constitute price discrimination. Second, price discrimination is a phenomenon found only in those markets characterized by some degree of monopoly power. Clearly, for a firm to price discriminate, it must have some discretion over the price it charges.

16.4.1   First-Degree Price Discrimination

We typically describe price discrimination in terms of three categories, separated by the degree to which firms are able to identify the values consumers place on different amounts of a good. The first category, first-degree price discrimination, is the practice of charging a different price for each unit of a good sold that is equal to the maximum value consumers place on each of these units. By doing so, a firm is able to extract all of the consumer surplus and incorporate this amount into its revenue and profit. We can demonstrate this result by returning to the monopoly outcome derived both mathematically and graphically in the preceding example. In that example, we assumed that the monopolist does not price discriminate, and thus it determines its profit-maximizing level of output to be $Q_M = 18$ units, at which $MR = LRMC$. It charges a uniform price of $P_M = \$110$ for each of these 18 units sold, and it receives a profit equal to $LR\pi_M = \$1620$.

Now, if the monopolist engages in first-degree price discrimination, it charges the maximum prices consumers are willing to pay for each unit of the good. Not only does this behavior result in a set of different prices for the units sold, but it also changes how the monopolist determines its profit-maximizing level of output.

In the absence of price discrimination, we compute the monopolist's marginal revenue as

$$MR = P + Q\frac{dP}{dQ},$$

and since $dP/dQ < 0$, then $MR < P$. This means that the monopolist must decrease its price in order to sell each additional unit of output, and if no price discrimination is involved, the price is decreased for units that could have been sold at higher prices. With first-degree price discrimination, a monopolist does not decrease the price for these more highly valued units, but only for the extra, or marginal, unit. As a result, in the marginal revenue equation above

$$Q\frac{dP}{dQ} = 0,$$

and therefore $MR = P$. In this case, marginal revenue, or the additional revenue associated with selling one more unit of output, is equal to the price of the additional unit sold multiplied by that one extra unit. Thus, marginal revenue is simply equal to the price of the good. However, the price charged by a monopolist is not a predetermined constant value; rather,

$$P = P^D(Q),$$

reflecting the fact that P varies inversely with Q. Since, for a price-discriminating monopolist, $MR = P$, we can express the profit-maximizing condition, $MR = MC$, as $P = MC$, which we then use to determine a monopolist's profit-maximizing level of output.

With regard to the numerical example we used earlier in this section, a price-discriminating monopolist determines Q_M according to the rule

$$P = LRMC,$$

and therefore

$$200 - 5Q = 20,$$

or

$$Q_M = 36 \text{ units}.$$

This amount is the same output value we computed earlier for the perfectly competitive market. Thus, from a social perspective, the ability to price discriminate provides an incentive for a monopolist to expand output—in this case, to the allocatively efficient level. However, the firm can significantly increase its revenue and profit at the expense of consumers by charging a different price for each unit of the good that is equal to the maximum price consumers are willing to pay for each of these units. In this example, the monopolist charges 36 different prices for each of the 36 units sold. For the first unit, the firm charges

$$P_1 = 200 - 5(1) = \$195,$$

for the second unit,

$$P_2 = 200 - 5(2) = \$190,$$

and so forth until, for the 36th and last unit sold

$$P_{36} = 200 - 5(36) = \$20 = LRMC.$$

If we assume that the increments in Q are infinitesimally small, the total increase in the monopolist's profit due to this type of price discrimination equals the summation of the consumer surplus for a nondiscriminating monopolist, CS_M, and the deadweight loss, DWL. Therefore, the total profit for a price-discriminating monopolist, $LR\pi_{M'}$, is equal to the sum of CS_M and DWL, plus the profit received by a nondiscriminating monopolist, $LR\pi_M$, or

$$LR\pi_{M'} = CS_M + DWL + LR\pi_M$$
$$= \$810 + \$810 + \$1620 = \$3240.$$

Note that $LR\pi_{M'}$ is also equal to the entire consumer surplus for the perfectly competitive outcome, corresponding to $Q = 36$ units, or

$$LR\pi_{M'} = CS_C = \frac{1}{2}(36 - 0)(200 - 20) = \$3240.$$

Thus, a monopolist engaging in first-degree price discrimination increases its level of profit beyond the amount it receives in the absence of such discrimination. From a realistic perspective, however, first-degree price discrimination is a highly unlikely phenomenon, because it requires a degree of product valuation and customer identification on the part of the monopolist that is virtually impossible.

16.4.2   Second-Degree Price Discrimination

Second-degree price discrimination is a more viable possibility because it requires less information on the part of the firm. Essentially, this behavior represents a modification of first-degree price discrimination, where in this case, the firm is not able to determine the values consumers place on each unit of the good. Rather, it is able to break down the demand for its product by grouping multiple units of the good and assigning them to different blocks for which it can determine consumer value. It then charges different prices for these different blocks of the good. In this case, the firm cannot extract the entire amount of consumer surplus due to its inability to perfectly identify consumers' valuations of each unit of the good purchased. However, it can extract some consumer surplus and subsequently increase its revenue and profit.

We illustrate second-degree price discrimination in Figure 16.4, where the monopolist is shown to produce Q'_M units of output corresponding to $P = LRMC$. In this example, the firm groups the units of the good it sells into three blocks—$(Q_1 - 0)$ units,

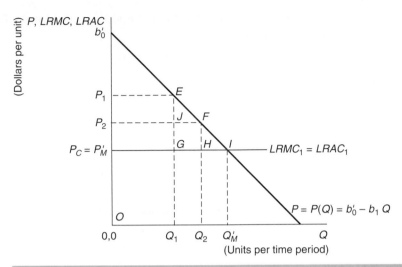

FIGURE 16.4 Second-Degree Price Discrimination

$(Q_2 - Q_1)$ units, and $(Q'_M - Q_2)$ units—and determines the value consumers place on each block. The firm charges prices of P_1, P_2, and P'_M for the blocks $(Q_1 - 0)$, $(Q_2 - Q_1)$, and $(Q'_M - Q_2)$ units, respectively, where $P_1 > P_2 > P'_M$. Thus, its revenue is the summation of the products of the number of units comprising each block and the corresponding price of that block, or

$$TR = P_1(Q_1 - 0) + P_2(Q_2 - Q_1) + P'_M(Q'_M - Q_2),$$

where these products, $P_1(Q_1 - 0)$, $P_2(Q_2 - Q_1)$, and $P'_M(Q'_M - Q_2)$, are represented in Figure 16.4 as the areas of the rectangles, $0P_1EQ_1$, Q_1JFQ_2, and $Q_2HIQ'_M$, respectively. We express the firm's total revenue, when it engages in second-degree price discrimination, as the summation of these rectangles, or

$$TR = 0P_1EQ_1 + Q_1JFQ_2 + Q_2HIQ'_M.$$

Since the firm's long-run total cost, $LRTC$, is equal to its long-run average cost, $LRAC$, multiplied by the total units of output it produces, then

$$LRTC_1 = LRAC_1(Q'_M),$$

represented in Figure 16.4 by the area of the rectangle $OP'_MIQ'_M$. The corresponding profit, $LR\pi$, is therefore

$$LR\pi_1 = TR - LRTC_1$$
$$= P_1(Q_1 - 0) + P_2(Q_2 - Q_1) + P'_M(Q'_M - Q_2) - LRTC_1,$$

or in terms of areas

$$LR\pi_1 = OP_1EQ_1 + Q_1JFQ_2 + Q_2HIQ'_M - OP'_MIQ'_M$$
$$= P'_MP_1EG + GJFH.$$

With second-degree price discrimination, the monopolist is not able to extract all of the consumer surplus and incorporate it into its profit. Specifically, consumers still receive the consumer surplus represented by the areas of the triangles, $P_1 b_0' E$, JEF, and HFI, due to the monopolist's inability to identify differing consumer values associated with every unit of the good within each block.

16.4.3   Third-Degree Price Discrimination

The final and most realistic category of price discrimination is third-degree discrimination. A firm can implement this practice if it can identify and separate two or more distinct types of consumers purchasing its good into submarkets and then price the output sold in each submarket differently. Formally, we characterize the various types of customers as possessing different own-price demand curves, yielding distinct own-price elasticities for comparable amounts of the good. These different own-price demand curves and corresponding elasticities reflect different customer tastes and alternative perceptions regarding the closeness of possible substitutes for the product. Later in this section, using a numerical example, we will demonstrate that the firm charges the highest price in the submarket characterized by the least elastic own-price demand curve.

One of the best real-world examples of third-degree price discrimination is found in the structure of different prices, or rates, charged for long-distance phone calls. Telephone companies charge different rates for calls depending on the day of the week and on the time of day the call is made. Typically, weekend rates are lower than week day rates, and evening rates are lower than daytime rates. By engaging in this practice, the telephone companies are effectively separating the demand for their service into different submarket demands based on the type of customers using their service. They then charge different prices in these submarkets based on the different own-price elasticities of demand.

Specifically, customers making calls on weekdays and during the daytime tend to be businesspeople who perceive their phone calls as virtual necessities. As a result, their corresponding own-price demand curve is relatively inelastic. Alternatively, customers using the telephone on weekends or during evening hours tend to be people making calls for social purposes that they generally do not perceive as essential. Consequently, the own-price demand curve for this second submarket is characterized as being relatively elastic. The end result is that the telephone companies charge a higher price in the relatively inelastic submarket, comprised of those customers making weekday and daytime calls, and charge a lower price in the relatively elastic submarket consisting of those customers making weekend and evening calls.

The total market own-price demand curve for the firm's product represents the horizontal summation of these different submarket demand curves. Assuming two such submarket own-price demand curves, where one curve is less elastic than the other at comparable levels of output, we have illustrated this horizontal summation process in Figure 16.5. The own-price demand curves pertaining to submarkets one and two are illustrated in panels (A) and (B), respectively, and we have constructed the total market own-price demand curve in panel (C) by employing the horizontal

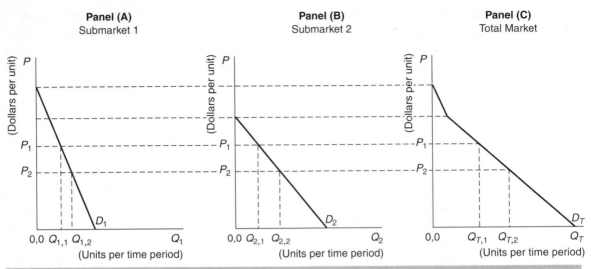

FIGURE 16.5 Construction of a Firm's Total Market Demand Curve from Two Submarket Demand Curves Reflecting Different Own-Price Elasticities

summation process discussed in Chapter 6. Specifically, at price P_1, consumers in submarket one demand $Q_{1,1}$ units, where, the first subscript refers to the submarket and the second subscript refers to price level, P_1. In the second submarket, consumers demand $Q_{2,1}$ units at P_1, and thus the total market quantity demanded at this price is

$$Q_{T,1} = Q_{1,1} + Q_{2,1} \text{ units.}$$

At the price P_2, the quantity demanded in submarket one is $Q_{1,2}$ units and in submarket two it is $Q_{2,2}$ units. Thus, the corresponding total quantity demanded in the market at this price is

$$Q_{T,2} = Q_{1,2} + Q_{2,2} \text{ units.}$$

By repeating this procedure for different price levels, we can construct the total market own-price demand curve, D_T. We have repeated these three own-price demand curves in panels (A), (B), and (C) of Figure 16.6. Also included in this figure are the marginal revenue curves, MR_1, MR_2, and MR_T, corresponding to each submarket own-price demand curve, D_1 and D_2, as well as the total market own-price demand curve, D_T, respectively. In addition, we have illustrated the firm's marginal cost curve, assuming that marginal cost is the same regardless of the market in which the firm sells its output. As a result, the MC curve is extended across both submarkets as well as the total market.

The firm determines its overall profit-maximizing level of output by equating MR_T to MC, as we have illustrated in panel (C). Thus, it produces Q_T^* units of output in total, where by construction

$$Q_T^* = Q_1^* + Q_2^*.$$

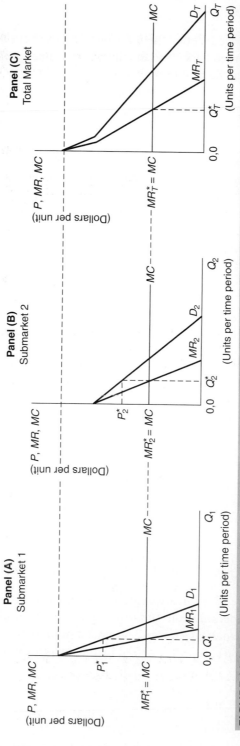

FIGURE 16.6 Third-Degree Price Discrimination

This result reflects the fact that the firm determines the profit-maximizing amounts of its output sold in each submarket by equating the marginal revenue in each submarket to its marginal cost. Thus, the firm determines Q_1^* where $MR_1^* = MC$, and Q_2^* where $MR_2^* = MC$, and since MC is the same in both submarkets, as well as the total market, then

$$MR_1^* = MR_2^* = MC = MR_T^*.$$

It is logical that $MR_1^* = MR_2^*$ at the profit-maximizing levels of output, for if this equality is not true, the firm can increase its profit by reallocating sales from one submarket to the other. For example, if the firm is selling output levels in its submarkets where $MR_1 > MC$, and $MR_2 < MC$, and therefore $MR_1 > MR_2$, then it can increase its profit by selling more units of the good in submarket one and fewer units in submarket two. Once the firm determines its profit-maximizing levels of output in each submarket, it then computes the corresponding prices by substituting these output values into the respective inverse own-price demand curves. We illustrate this process in Figure 16.6, where the firm charges P_1^* in submarket one and P_2^* in submarket two. Observe that $P_1^* > P_2^*$, indicating that the firm charges the higher price in the market characterized by the relatively less elastic own-price demand curve.

We can confirm these results using the formula derived in Chapter 7, which relates marginal revenue to own-price elasticity of demand, $E_{Q,P}$. This formula is

$$MR = P\left(1 - \frac{1}{E_{Q,P}}\right),$$

and since, at the profit-maximizing levels of output for the two submarkets, $MR_1^* = MR_2^*$, then

$$P_1^*\left(1 - \frac{1}{E_{Q_1,P}}\right) = P_2^*\left(1 - \frac{1}{E_{Q_2,P}}\right), \tag{16.3}$$

where $E_{Q_1,P}$ and $E_{Q_2,P}$ represent the own-price elasticities of demand for submarkets one and two, respectively. In this example, since we are assuming $E_{Q_1,P} < E_{Q_2,P}$, it follows that

$$\left(1 - \frac{1}{E_{Q_1,P}}\right) < \left(1 - \frac{1}{E_{Q_2,P}}\right),$$

and thus to ensure the equality expressed in equation (16.3), P_1^* must exceed P_2^*.

We can also demonstrate the results pertaining to third-degree price discrimination with a mathematical example. Assume a monopolist separates its consumers into two distinct submarkets characterized by the own-price demand curves

$$Q_1^D = 30 - 0.25P_1,$$

for submarket one and

$$Q_2^D = 50 - 0.5P_2,$$

for submarket two. The corresponding inverse own-price demand curves are

$$P_1 = 120 - 4Q_1^D$$

and

$$P_2 = 100 - 2Q_2^D.$$

We can verify that for any specific quantity of output selected, the value of the own-price elasticity of demand in submarket one is less elastic than that for submarket two. For example, at $Q_1 = Q_2 = 5$ units, $P_1 = \$100$ and $P_2 = \$90$, and using the formula

$$E_{Q,P} = \left| \frac{\partial Q}{\partial P} \frac{P}{Q} \right|,$$

we determine the value of the own-price elasticity of demand in submarket one as

$$E_{Q_1,P} = \left| (-0.25)\left(\frac{100}{5}\right) \right| = 5,$$

and for submarket two as

$$E_{Q_2,P} = \left| (-0.5)\left(\frac{90}{5}\right) \right| = 9.$$

Assume that the cost of producing the good is identical regardless of the submarket in which the good is sold and that this cost is represented by the total cost function

$$TC = 40Q_T,$$

where $Q_T = Q_1 + Q_2$. Thus, the firm's marginal and average cost functions are identical, computed respectively, as

$$MC = \frac{dTC}{dQ_T} = \$40/\text{unit}$$

and

$$AC = \frac{TC}{Q_T} = \frac{40Q_T}{Q_T} = \$40/\text{unit}.$$

A price-discriminating firm determines its profit-maximizing level of output sold in each submarket by equating the corresponding marginal revenue in each submarket to its marginal cost. Thus, for submarket one

$$TR_1 = P_1Q_1 = (120 - 4Q_1)Q_1$$
$$= 120Q_1 - 4Q_1^2,$$

and therefore

$$MR_1 = \frac{dTR_1}{dQ} = 120 - 8Q_1.$$

By equating MR_1 to MC, we determine the profit-maximizing level of output sold in submarket one as

$$120 - 8Q_1 = 40$$
$$Q_1^* = 10 \text{ units.}$$

For submarket two

$$TR_2 = P_2Q_2 = (100 - 2Q_2)Q_2$$
$$= 100Q_2 - 2Q_2^2$$

and therefore

$$MR_2 = \frac{dTR_2}{dQ_2} = 100 - 4Q_2.$$

By equating MR_2 to MC, we determine the profit-maximizing level of output sold in submarket two as

$$100 - 4Q_2 = 40$$
$$Q_2^* = 15 \text{ units.}$$

We compute the corresponding prices charged in each submarket by substituting each profit-maximizing level of output into its respective inverse own-price demand curve. Thus, for submarket one

$$P_1^* = 120 - 4(10) = \$80,$$

and for submarket two

$$P_2^* = 100 - 2(15) = \$70.$$

The result that $P_1^* > P_2^*$ follows from our earlier discussion that a price-discriminating firm charges the higher price in the submarket characterized by the less elastic own-price demand curve.

Finally, we calculate the firm's total profit, π_T, associated with its price-discriminating behavior, as the difference between the summation of the total revenues earned in each submarket and its overall cost of producing the good, expressed as

$$\pi_T = TR_1 + TR_2 - TC,$$

or more specifically

$$\pi_T = P_1Q_1 + P_2Q_2 - 40Q_T.$$

Substituting the appropriate values for the prices and quantities into this equation and recalling that

$$Q_T = Q_1 + Q_2,$$

yields the firm's total profit as

$$\pi_T^* = \$80(10) + \$70(15) - 40(10 + 15) = \$850.$$

We can place these results regarding price, output, and profit for a price-discriminating firm in better perspective by analyzing the same firm's behavior on the assumption that it does not price discriminate. In this case, we derive the total own-price demand curve for the firm, Q_T^D, by summing the submarket own-price demand curves, yielding

$$Q_T^D = Q_1^D + Q_2^D,$$

or

$$Q_T^D = (30 - 0.25P) + (50 - 0.5P),$$
$$Q_T^D = 80 - 0.75P.$$

The corresponding inverse own-price demand curve is therefore

$$P = \frac{80}{0.75} - \frac{1}{0.75} Q_T^D = 106.67 - 1.33Q_T^D,$$

where we should note that the value of the P-intercept, 106.67, is only theoretical since for $P > 100$, the total own-price demand is represented exclusively by the own-price demand curve for submarket one. As a result, the total own-price demand curve possesses two segments, one for $P > 100$ and one for $P \leq 100$. However, we will demonstrate that for this problem the segment pertaining to $P \leq \$100$ is the only relevant portion for determining the profit-maximizing level of output, given the particular cost function we have assumed for this problem. The firm's total revenue function for this segment is

$$TR_T = PQ_T = (106.67 - 1.33Q_T)Q_T = 106.67Q_T - 1.33Q_T^2$$

and therefore, we compute its marginal revenue function as

$$MR_T = \frac{dTR}{dQ_T} = 106.67 - 2.66Q_T.$$

We determine the profit-maximizing level of total output, Q_T, by equating MR_T to MC as

$$106.67 - 2.66Q_T = 40,$$

and therefore

$$Q_T^* = 25 \text{ units},$$

or the same level of total output we computed earlier for the price-discriminating case, where

$$Q_T^* = Q_1^* + Q_2^* = 10 + 15 = 25 \text{ units}.$$

However, if the firm chooses not to price discriminate, it charges the uniform price P_T^*, computed as

$$P_T^* = 106.67 - 1.33(25) = \$73.42.$$

Thus, in this case we determine the firm's profit to be

$$\pi_T^* = 73.42(25) - 40(25) = \$835.50,$$

a lesser amount than the $850 it receives by engaging in price discrimination.

Price-Discriminating Vending Machines

First-degree price discrimination involves a seller charging a price for each unit of a good sold that is equal to the maximum value consumers place on each unit of that good. By doing so, a seller can enhance her revenue and profit by extracting all of the consumer surplus associated with sales of a product. In practice, this type of price discrimination is very difficult to implement since, in order to be successful, the seller has to ascertain consumers' tastes to such a fine degree that is considered to be virtually impossible. However, given recent advances in technology and consumer profiling, the ability of sellers to fine tune their perceptions of consumers' tastes may eventually become a reality, making first-degree price discrimination an economically viable possibility.

We can offer an example of such a situation, albeit hypothetical at the present time, by returning to the temperature-sensitive vending machine proposed by the Coca-Cola Company, which we described in Real-World Application 13.1. Recall that this machine can automatically adjust the price of soft drinks based on the outdoor temperature. Now suppose that such a machine is eventually modified to also take into account other determinants of demand, such as time of day or affluence of customers. Although this analysis consists of a bit of science fiction at this point, it is not too much of a stretch to imagine that such a machine could determine the highest price that a particular consumer is willing to pay for a unit of the good, at any point in time, under specific circumstances. Should this occur, and the machine adjusts the price accordingly, then the result would be an example of first-degree price discrimination. Although written tongue in cheek, the following article by Jeff Brown of *The Philadelphia Inquirer*

paints an interesting picture of what the future may hold.

Computer chips may soon enable vending machines to constantly adjust prices according to any number of factors that cause momentary fluctuations in supply and demand, not just weather.

So, some busy fall evening in the not-too-distant future, you sidle up to a well-lit Coke machine in South Philly. The box has no buttons, does not display any prices. A spotlight shines on your face as sensors zoom in on your vital signs. A head-high video screen flickers on. The machine sees you're in jeans, not a suit, so it scans its library of personalities, skipping the erudite Englishman and the slinky French model. It displays the good natured face of Sylvester Stallone.

"Yo!" the Coke machine calls. "What can I do ya for?" Sly smiles, thinking of his royalty, perhaps.

"A Coke Classic, please."

"No problem. Four bucks."

"Whoa! They're 50 cents at the supermarket."

The machine pauses while its accent analyzer determines you aren't from the neighborhood.

"You see a supermarket around here?" it says. "Four dollars."

You decide to bluff. "Look, the machine around the corner gave me Pepsi for half that."

"When?"

"A couple of hours ago."

"Yea, it's rush hour now. You won't get a two-dollar soda anywhere." The head on the screen shakes from side to side sympathetically. Then the red and white machine goes silent, letting you sweat.

This is going to be tougher than you'd thought. You pull out your Palm Pilot X, link to the Internet, and go to sodamachines.com.

"There are 14 soda machines within four blocks," you report, holding up the Palm Pilot for the machine to see. "You're telling me I can't beat four dollars?"

The Coke machine tallies the 90 seconds it has expended on this negotiation. Its motion sensor detects two customers moving around impatiently behind you. Its atomic clock reports that rush hour is winding down.

"Okay, three dollars," it offers, peeved.

"No way." You stuff your wallet into your pants and step back.

The Coke machine focuses an infrared scanner on your lips, calibrating your thirst. It counts its inventory and finds a surplus of Diet Coke. Its hard drive whirs for a second.

"I'll give you a Coke lite for $2.50," it offers resentfully.

"Terrible aftertaste," you say.

"With a bag of nuts."

"Nah."

"Look, pal, if you're not buyin' move along."

Traffic is getting lighter. The two people behind you give up and leave.

"All right," the box grumbles.

You deposit two dollars, get your can, and turn to go.

"How about those peanuts?" the machine asks hopefully. "Fifty cents."

"I'm allergic," you answer.

The machine pauses a nanosecond while electrons zip around its circuits. It's a week day. Rush hour. Statistics suggest you work nearby. You'll be back. The machine activates it customer relations software.

"Have a nice evening, bud," it calls as you turn away, the face smiling widely."[3]

---

[3]Jeff Brown, "Have a Coke, and Big Brother Is Sure to Smile," *The Philadelphia Inquirer*, October 31, 1999, pp. E1, E5.

16.5 MULTIPLANT MONOPOLY

There are many subtopics related to monopoly behavior, the majority of which we will reserve for Industrial Organization texts. However, because of its real-world prevalence, there is one additional topic that we will explore here. In all of the monopoly models discussed previously, we assumed that the firm produces its output using only one plant. Realistically, however, many monopolistic firms produce their output using several plants, where each plant may be subject to different cost conditions. This characteristic follows from the fact that these plants are usually located in different geographical regions characterized by different infrastructures, such as roads and utilities. They also face different labor markets that may vary with respect to both the amount and skill level of labor available to the firm. Other possible reasons for varying cost conditions include differences in the quality of the capital input(s) used in the various plants and differences in the skill levels of the various plant managers. Generally, through a combination of these factors, a monopolist's production of output across various plants is subject to different cost conditions that we can represent with different cost functions. As a result, the multiplant monopolist must not only determine its profit-maximizing level of total output and price, but also simultaneously determine the least costly manner to produce the output using more than one plant.

At first thought, it would seem that the monopolist would produce all of its output in the plant characterized by the lowest set of cost functions. This is generally not the case, however, since the marginal cost pertaining to a single plant ultimately rises as output produced in that plant increases. We may recall that, in the short run, marginal costs rise as the production of output increases due to diminishing marginal productivity of the variable input, while in the long run, these costs rise primarily due to diseconomies of scale. Our point of emphasis is that a profit-maximizing multiplant firm produces each additional unit of output in the plant yielding the lowest marginal cost *value*. Focusing on the short run, logically, the firm produces its first unit of output in the plant characterized by the lowest marginal cost curve. Depending on the particular marginal cost curves for each of the firm's plants, this will most likely be true for the first few units of output produced. However, as the firm continues to expand its level of production, the marginal costs of producing output in this plant will rise in the short run, due to diminishing marginal productivity of the variable input. This reflects a situation in which the firm is using too much of its variable input, labor, relative to its fixed input, the plant size. Therefore, it becomes cost efficient for the firm to begin using another plant, even though it may be characterized by a set of relatively higher cost curves. This result follows because the value of the marginal cost in this second plant is lower than in the first, since the firm is producing fewer units of output in the second plant.

We have illustrated this situation in Figure 16.7 for a multiplant monopolist using two plants. The marginal cost curves for plants one and two are shown in panels (A) and (B), respectively, where plant two is subject to the higher MC curve. We can verify this by selecting any value of MC common to both plants and observing that a greater level of output is produced in the first plant than in the second. For example, observe at $MC_{1,1} = MC_{2,1}$ that $Q_{1,1}$ and $Q_{2,1}$ units of output are produced in plants one and two, respectively, where $Q_{1,1} > Q_{2,1}$. Note that the first subscript refers to the plant and the second subscript to the particular values of output produced.

We obtain the overall marginal cost curve for the monopolist, MC_T, shown in panel (C), by horizontally summing the MC curves for each plant. As we described earlier, at $MC_{1,1} = MC_{2,1}$, plants one and two produce $Q_{1,1}$ and $Q_{2,1}$, respectively, and the monopolist's total production of output is therefore

$$Q_{T,1} = Q_{1,1} + Q_{2,1}.$$

FIGURE 16.7 Multiplant Monopoly with Different Marginal Cost Curves

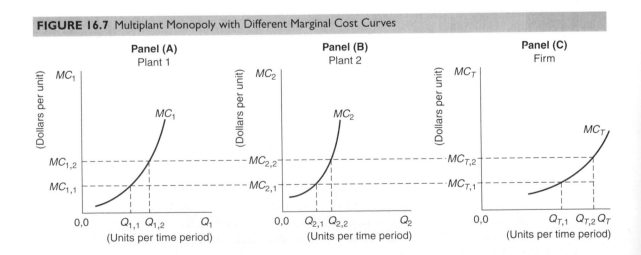

At $MC_{1,2} = MC_{2,2}$, plant one produces $Q_{1,2}$, plant two produces $Q_{2,2}$, and thus

$$Q_{T,2} = Q_{1,2} + Q_{2,2}.$$

By continuing this process, we can construct the monopolist's MC_T curve.

The MC curves illustrated in Figure 16.7 are reproduced in Figure 16.8, where in panel (C) we have also included the monopolist's own-price demand curve and associated marginal revenue curve. The monopolist's profit-maximizing level of output, $Q_{T,1}^*$, and price, P^*, are determined in the same manner as we demonstrated in earlier analyses. Specifically, the firm determines $Q_{T,1}^*$ by equating MR to MC_T and then computes P^* by substituting this value of $Q_{T,1}^*$ into its own-price inverse demand curve. However, a multiplant monopolist faces the additional problem of how to allocate its production of output between its two plants. The firm solves this problem by equating the marginal cost values in each plant to its marginal revenue. Thus, Q_1^* and Q_2^* are determined using the rule

$$MC_1 = MC_2 = MR = MC_T.$$

If this equality does not hold true, say $MC_1 > MC_2$, at some levels of output for the two plants, then the firm could increase its profit by reallocating the last unit of output produced from plant one to plant two, since it can produce that unit at a lower cost by making such an adjustment. The firm continues this reallocation, causing the value of MC_1 to fall and the value of MC_2 to rise, until $MC_1 = MC_2$, corresponding to the output value Q_1^* for plant one and Q_2^* for plant two, where $Q_1^* + Q_2^* = Q_T^*$. At these output levels, the firm can no longer increase its profit by reallocating its production of output from one plant to the other. We have illustrated this outcome in Figure 16.8 by essentially reversing the horizontal summation process described earlier.

We can also demonstrate the multiplant monopoly outcome with a mathematical example. Assume a monopolist has the inverse own-price demand curve

$$P = 300 - \frac{1}{2}Q_T,$$

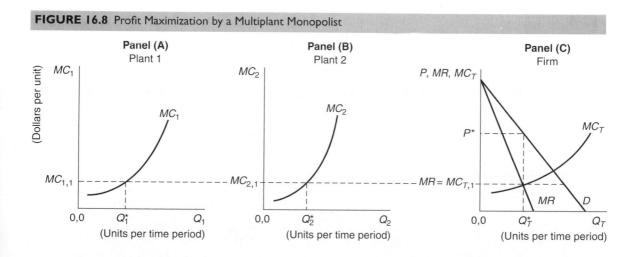

FIGURE 16.8 Profit Maximization by a Multiplant Monopolist

where Q_T is the total amount of output produced and sold by the firm. We also assume that the monopolist uses two plants, where Q_1 and Q_2 represent the output levels produced in plants one and two, respectively. Since the monopolist's total production of output, Q_T, is the summation of the output produced in each plant, or

$$Q_T = Q_1 + Q_2, \tag{16.4}$$

we can express the inverse own-price demand curve as

$$P = 300 - \frac{1}{2}(Q_1 + Q_2). \tag{16.5}$$

Now assume the short-run total cost curves pertaining to plants one and two are, respectively,

$$SRTC_1 = 500 + 20Q_1 \tag{16.6}$$

and

$$SRTC_2 = 1000 + \frac{1}{4}Q_2^2. \tag{16.7}$$

The firm's total revenue function is

$$TR = PQ_T = \left(300 - \frac{1}{2}Q_T\right)Q_T$$
$$= 300Q_T - \frac{1}{2}Q_T^2,$$

and we derive its marginal revenue function as

$$MR = \frac{dTR}{dQ_T} = 300 - Q_T,$$

or since

$$Q_T = Q_1 + Q_2,$$

then

$$MR = 300 - (Q_1 + Q_2)$$
$$= 300 - Q_1 - Q_2.$$

The short-run marginal cost functions, $SRMC_1$ and $SRMC_2$ for plants one and two are, respectively,

$$SRMC_1 = \frac{dSRTC_1}{dQ_1} = \frac{d(500 + 20Q_1)}{dQ_1} = 20$$

and

$$SRMC_2 = \frac{dSRTC_2}{dQ_2} = \frac{d\left(1000 + \frac{1}{4}Q_2^2\right)}{dQ_2} = \frac{1}{2}Q_2.$$

We determine the profit-maximizing levels of output produced in each plant by equating the firm's marginal revenue to the marginal cost in each plant, or

$$MR = SRMC_1$$
$$300 - Q_1 - Q_2 = 20 \qquad \textbf{(16.8)}$$

and

$$MR = SRMC_2$$
$$300 - Q_1 - Q_2 = \frac{1}{2}Q_2. \qquad \textbf{(16.9)}$$

By solving equations (16.8) and (16.9) simultaneously, we determine the profit-maximizing values for Q_1 and Q_2. Solving equation (16.9) for Q_2 yields

$$Q_2 = 200 - \frac{2}{3}Q_1, \qquad \textbf{(16.10)}$$

and substituting this expression for Q_2 into equation (16.8) yields the solution value for Q_1 as

$$300 - Q_1 - \left(200 - \frac{2}{3}Q_1\right) = 20$$

$$300 - Q_1 - 200 + \frac{2}{3}Q_1 = 20$$

$$\frac{1}{3}Q_1 - 80$$

$$Q_1^* = 240 \text{ units.}$$

Substituting this value for Q_1 into equation (16.10) provides the solution value for Q_2 as

$$Q_2^* \; 200 - \frac{2}{3}(240) = 40 \text{ units,}$$

where the total output, Q_T^*, produced by the monopolist is

$$Q_T^* = Q_1^* + Q_2^* = 240 + 40 = 280 \text{ units.}$$

Specifically, the monopolist produces its first 40 units of output in plant two since for $Q \le 40$ units, $SRMC_2 \le SRMC_1$, and produces the next 240 units in plant one, since for $Q > 40$, $SRMC_2 > SRMC_1$. We compute the price charged by the firm as

$$P^* = 300 - \frac{1}{2}(Q_T^*) = 300 - \frac{1}{2}(Q_1^* + Q_2^*)$$

$$= 300 - \frac{1}{2}(240 + 40) = \$160,$$

and the monopolist's corresponding profit as

$$SR\pi^* = P^*Q_T^* - SRTC_1^* - SRTC_2^*$$
$$= 160(280) - 500 - 20(240) - 1000 - \frac{1}{4}(40)^2$$
$$= \$38,100.$$

A more concise approach to solving the multiplant monopoly problem is to construct the firm's profit function and then maximize its profit by partially differentiating this function with respect to Q_1 and Q_2. After setting these partial derivatives equal to zero, we can solve the resulting system of two equations simultaneously to obtain the profit-maximizing values of Q_1 and Q_2. The monopolist's short-run profit function is represented by the difference between its total revenue and the summation of its short-run total cost functions for each plant, or

$$SR\pi = TR - (SRTC_1 + SRTC_2)$$
$$= PQ_T - (SRTC_1 + SRTC_2). \qquad \textbf{(16.11)}$$

After substituting the expressions for Q_T, P, $SRTC_1$, and $SRTC_2$ from equations (16.4), (16.5), (16.6), and (16.7), respectively, into equation (16.11), we can express the $SR\pi$ function as

$$SR\pi = \left[300 - \frac{1}{2}(Q_1 + Q_2) \right](Q_1 + Q_2) - \left(500 + 20Q_1 + 1000 + \frac{1}{4}Q_2^2 \right)$$
$$= 300(Q_1 + Q_2) - \frac{1}{2}(Q_1 + Q_2)^2 - 500 - 20Q_1 - 1000 - \frac{1}{4}Q_2^2$$
$$= 300Q_1 + 300Q_2 - \frac{1}{2}Q_1^2 - 1.0Q_1Q_2 - \frac{1}{2}Q_2^2 - 1500 - 20Q_1 - \frac{1}{4}Q_2^2.$$

Partially differentiating $SR\pi$ with respect to Q_1 and Q_2, and setting the results equal to zero, yields

$$\frac{\partial SR\pi}{\partial Q_1} = 300 - Q_1 - Q_2 - 20 = 0 \qquad \textbf{(16.12)}$$

and

$$\frac{\partial SR\pi}{\partial Q_2} = 300 - Q_1 - Q_2 - \frac{1}{2}Q_2 = 0. \qquad \textbf{(16.13)}$$

Solving equation (16.13) for Q_2 in terms of Q_1 yields

$$Q_2 = 200 - \frac{2}{3}Q_1. \qquad \textbf{(16.14)}$$

By substituting the expression for Q_2 from equation (16.14) into equation (16.12), we determine the profit-maximizing value for Q_1 as

$$300 - Q_1 - \left(200 - \frac{2}{3}Q_1 \right) - 20 = 0$$

$$80 - \frac{1}{3}Q_1 = 0$$

$$Q_1^* = 240 \text{ units.}$$

Then, substituting this value for Q_1 into equation (16.14) yields the solution value for Q_2 as

$$Q_2^* = 200 - \frac{2}{3}(240) = 40 \text{ units.}$$

Note that these values for Q_1^* and Q_2^* are the same as we computed earlier, where you can verify that the values for P^* and $SR\pi^*$ are identical as well.

Although real-world examples of pure monopoly are relatively rare, many economists believe the monopoly model provides a useful approximation of firm behavior in many industries. There are other industries, however, characterized by some degree of monopoly power, for which the model of pure monopoly is not considered to provide a sufficient explanation of firm behavior. These industries are categorized into two additional types of market structures, specifically, oligopoly and monopolistic competition. These market structures will be our focus in the next three chapters.

16.6   SUMMARY

Our primary purpose in this chapter has been to examine several topics related to a monopolistic market structure. First, we compared the outcomes generated by a monopoly to those associated with a perfect competition. We also analyzed some additional topics related to monopoly, specifically, price discrimination and multiplant monopoly. A summary of the various topics covered in this chapter is as follows.

- Consumer surplus is measured as the difference between the value consumers place on each unit of a good and the price they actually pay for that unit, summed over all units sold.
- Producer surplus is measured as the difference between the price a producer receives from selling each unit of a good and the marginal cost associated with producing each respective unit, summed over all units sold.
- The monopoly outcome leads to a transfer of part of the consumer surplus generated under perfect competition to the monopolist's profit. In addition, under monopoly there is also a loss of both consumer and producer surplus that is received by no one, known as deadweight loss.
- Firms possessing some degree of monopoly power may engage in price discrimination that involves charging different price to marginal cost ratios for different units of a good that are of the same grade and quality, once an equilibrium price has been established.
- There are three categories of price discrimination separated on the basis of the degree to which firms are able to discern the values consumers place on different amounts of a good sold.
- A multiplant monopoly arises when the firm allocates its production of output over more than one plant, so as to take advantage of differing cost conditions.

KEY TERMS

- consumer surplus, page 413
- deadweight loss, page 418
- price discrimination, page 421
- producer surplus, page 414

EXERCISES

16.1 Compare the monopoly outcome to that in a perfectly competitive market for the following performance factors.
   a. price charged for the good
   b. level of output produced
   c. efficient use of resources
   d. consumer surplus
   e. producer surplus
   f. deadweight loss

16.2 Distinguish between first-, second-, and third-degree price discrimination. Also, draw a graph depicting each type of price discrimination.

16.3 Assume the market own-price demand curve faced by a monopolist is

$$Q^D = 500 - 10P,$$

and its short-run total cost function is

$$SRTC(Q) = 25 + 2Q.$$

   a. Derive the inverse market own-price demand curve for the monopolist, $P = P^D(Q)$.
   b. Using the result obtained in part a, derive the monopolist's total revenue curve, $TR = TR(Q)$.
   c. Compute the firm's short-run marginal cost curve, $SRMC$.
   d. Using the results obtained in parts b and c, determine the monopolist's short-run profit-maximizing level of output.
   e. Determine the price charged by the monopolist and the amount of profit earned.

16.4 Using your results from Exercise 16.3, in a single graph plot the inverse own-price demand curve, the marginal revenue curve, and the short-run marginal cost curve faced by the monopolist. Indicate the level of output produced and the price charged by the profit-maximizing monopolist, as well as the area depicting consumer surplus.

16.5 Assume a monopolist is able to separate the own-price demand for its product into two separate markets. Therefore, the own-price demand curves for markets one and two are, respectively, represented as

$$Q_1^D = 1000 - 4P$$

and

$$Q_2^D = 1200 - 4P.$$

The short-run total cost curve for the firm is

$$SRTC = 100 + 0.25Q^2.$$

   a. Compute the quantity of the good that the monopolist sells in each market, assuming it is maximizing its profit.
   b. What type of behavior can you attribute to this monopolist?

16.6 Refer to Exercise 16.5. Compute the own-price elasticity of demand for each market at the optimal price–quantity combination. What do these elasticity values indicate? How are they consistent with the results computed in Exercise 16.4?

16.7 Assume a monopolist produces its output using two different plants, where the production processes in the two plants are characterized by two different cost curves, reflecting the fact that one plant is more efficient than the other. In general, why doesn't the monopolist simply always produce all of its output in the plant possessing the lower cost curve? Illustrate your response with graphs.

16.8 Assume you are a business consultant for a monopolist selling pork rinds. The monopolist tells you that his customers in the South are very loyal to his product, while his customers in the North are not. Develop a marketing plan for this monopolist based on economic theory.

CHAPTER 17

Oligopoly

17.1 INTRODUCTION

In previous chapters, we examined firm behavior both within a perfectly competitive market structure and within a monopolized market, demonstrating significantly different performance outcomes regarding such economic variables as output, price, cost, and profit. The models we use to analyze these market structures are very deterministic in that they are based on very clear assumptions and therefore provide us with most precise results. However, some of the assumptions on which we base these models tend to be quite restrictive; as a result, many economists believe these models to be less than exact in approximating many real-world situations.

For example, the perfect competition model is based on the key assumption that all firms comprising the market produce and sell homogeneous goods that constitute perfect substitutes for each other. In reality in few, if any, markets are the firms' products truly homogeneous. The products sold by most firms in a market nearly always differ to some degree, where, for example, even the proximity of the firms to their customers affects the substitutability of these products. Regarding the applicability of the monopoly model, only in the rare market does a single firm account for 100 percent of the sales. This is mainly because there are very few real situations for which a firm's product is totally differentiated from all other firms' products. Do the above arguments suggest that the models of perfect competition and monopoly are not useful? The answer is no, since generally, they serve as good benchmarks to which we can compare many real-world market situations. However, for the many market situations that do not conform to the rather strict assumptions underlying perfect competition or monopoly, we can construct new models that are less pure in nature but tailored to fit many real-world circumstances.

Our purpose in this chapter is to analyze several of these models pertaining to a market structure known as oligopoly. This is a market structure consisting of a few sellers of a good, and it lies between the polar extremes of perfect competition and monopoly. Furthermore, the goods sold may be either homogeneous or differentiated to some degree. Since only a few firms comprise a market in the case of oligopoly, the central characteristic of this market structure is interdependent behavior on the part of the firms; that is, each firm takes into account the actions of its rivals in determining its own behavior. This interdependence can be manifested in different forms; therefore, we must discuss several different models of oligopoly. The first model we will present is the cartel model, which involves explicit agreements by firms to jointly determine values of such strategic variables as output and price. Afterward, since interdependent firm behavior is frequently manifested through some type of tacit collusion, we will develop several models to analyze these situations. In these models, the firms do not adhere to any explicit agreements, but instead consider the decisions of their rivals when determining their own strategic behavior. Many market structures are oligopolistic, including those of automobile manufacturers, personal computer makers, and textbook publishers.

17.2 GENERAL CHARACTERISTICS OF OLIGOPOLY

An **oligopoly** is *a market structure generally consisting of a few sellers of a good, where each seller accounts for a significant portion of marketwide sales of the good.* As with the market structures discussed in previous chapters, we can describe oligopoly more specifically by applying the basic criteria for defining a market structure presented in Section 13.2 of Chapter 13. The first criterion is the number and size distribution of buyers and sellers operating in the market. As we stated earlier, oligopoly contains a few sellers of a good; however, an exact specification of the term *few* is rather ambiguous. To distinguish this market structure from that of monopoly, there must be more than one seller. However, the upper limit for the number of significant sellers comprising the market is considerably more difficult to establish, since this number may vary across markets for different types of goods. Essentially, this upper limit must be small enough that each firm produces a significant portion of the marketwide sales of the good and is therefore able to exert a discernible impact on the market price by altering its level of production. As a result, the business decisions made by one firm do not go unnoticed by the other sellers of the good.

For example, in the United States currently just two firms produce primary titanium metal, and only eleven produce primary copper. The cigarette industry, consisting of only eight firms, is also an oligopoly. Even the breakfast cereals industry, containing 42 producers, is considered to be an oligopoly because the eight largest firms collectively produce 98 percent of that industry's total output.[1] In each of these cases, we expect that, owing to the small number of firms comprising the market, each firm is aware of its rivals' behavior.

The second criterion for defining a market structure is the degree of product differentiation across the goods sold by different firms in the market. In the case of oligopoly, we may characterize the sellers' goods as either homogeneous or somewhat differentiated from each other. With regard to the latter, however, we should note that no seller's good can be completely differentiated from all others' or the market structure for that firm reverts to monopoly.

The third criterion is the ease with which firms can enter or exit the market. In this regard, oligopoly is very similar to monopoly in that, for essentially the same reasons, entry into the market is very difficult. Specifically, oligopoly is sustained owing to the presence of some barrier to entry. As we discussed previously, these entry barriers may

---

[1]U.S. Department of Commerce, Bureau of the Census, 1992 Census of Manufacturers, *Concentration Ratios in Manufacturing*, Subject Series MC 92-S-2, 1997.

arise due to the structure of the industry, as with large-scale economies or high capital requirements. Alternatively, they may be due to the conduct of incumbent firms operating within the industry, such as the exclusive control over some essential input, the establishment of excess capacity, or the use of a limit pricing strategy. Finally, entry barriers may arise as a result of government intervention in the form of licensing, zoning, patent, or import restrictions, to name a few. For a more detailed discussion of these various barriers to entry, you are encouraged to return to Section 15.3 of Chapter 15.

The final criterion for describing a market structure is the amount of market-related information available to consumers and producers. Although not a prerequisite for oligopoly, incomplete information on the part of consumers regarding prices and the substitutability of different firms' products can help create and sustain an oligopoly. This possibility becomes more pronounced if the firms engage in a substantial amount of persuasive advertising. This tactic, often prevalent in oligopoly, is designed to create a perception of product differentiation in the minds of consumers. From the sellers' perspective, oligopoly is characterized by a substantial degree of information acquired by firms regarding the behavior of other producers in the market. This characteristic largely follows because the market consists of such a small number of firms. Thus, it is relatively easy and inexpensive for them to acquire information about each others' behavior regarding the values of such strategic variables as price, output, and costs. Later in this chapter we will demonstrate that this easy access to information on the part of the firms facilitates some type of collusive behavior, subsequently leading to various degrees of monopoly power, or price-setting ability. Thus, perfect information on the part of the firms ironically generates performance results that we generally consider to be detrimental for consumers.

17.3 MODELS OF OLIGOPOLY

In the previous four chapters, we demonstrated that the behavior of a firm is greatly influenced by the market structure within which it operates. In the case of a perfectly competitive market, there are many firms, each selling an imperceptibly small amount of the marketwide output of a homogeneous good. As a result, the competition among these many firms is completely impersonal, where each firm determines the level of output it sells by reacting to a market-determined price. In a monopolistic market structure there is only one seller of a differentiated good; therefore, the firm has the ability to influence the price it receives for its product by adjusting the amount of output it sells. In the case of monopoly there exists no competition, impersonal or otherwise, because the market consists of only one firm. An oligopoly consists of a few significant sellers of either a homogeneous or somewhat differentiated product. In one sense, oligopolistic firm behavior is similar to that of a monopoly since, generally, each firm sells a large enough share of the marketwide output to perceptibly influence the price of the good. However, there is a difference in that, unlike monopoly, an oligopoly is comprised of more than one firm that can exert this influence. For this reason, oligopolistic firm behavior also differs from that of perfectly competitive firms, where each firm is a price taker. In addition, unlike a perfectly competitive market, the competition among firms comprising an oligopoly is quite personal, since each firm's profit is affected by the price and output behavior of other firms in the market. As a result, an oligopolistic firm takes into account the behavior of its rivals when determining its own profit-maximizing levels of price and output. Furthermore, if the oligopoly is characterized by some degree of product differentiation, this interdependence will most likely affect other types of strategic behavior such as the amount and type of advertising a firm chooses to undertake. Technically, in economic jargon, we do not consider the impact of one firm's behavior on another as competition per se but rather as a type of rivalry.

In a broad sense, we can separate interdependent firm behavior into two categories: overt collusion and covert collusion. Overt collusion includes such activities as price fixing or market sharing. This type of behavior generally involves an explicit agreement on the part of the firms to jointly determine the values of such variables as price and output in a manner that maximizes the overall profit of the firms engaged in the agreement. By doing so, this group of firms can restrict the overall production of output and subsequently increase the price of their good. A group of firms behaving in this manner is formally known as a cartel.

The second type of collusion is covert, or tacit, in that it does not involve any explicit agreements on the part of the firms. Instead, it reflects the fact that oligopolistic firms, because they are so few in number, rationally take into account the actions of their rivals when determining the optimal values of their own strategic variables. However, even such a subtle type of collusion on the part of firms can lead to less than desirable results for consumers and society as a whole. Because numerous behavioral options are available to oligopolistic firms when taking into account the actions of their rivals, we will examine several models of covert collusion. For a more exhaustive analysis of these models, we refer you to textbooks in Industrial Organization, the field of economics devoted to the study of market structures.

17.3.1   Cartel Model

As discussed earlier, a **cartel** is *a group of firms that, through some type of explicit agreement, collude to jointly determine the values of strategic variables such as price and output.* A cartel involves overt collusion by a group of firms, with the goal of maximizing the groups' overall profit. Technically, cartels are illegal in the United States because the courts have repeatedly found their behavior to be in violation of the Sherman Act. This act constitutes the major U.S. antitrust law specifying agreements in restraint of trade and attempts to monopolize an industry as illegal activities. However, cartels are allowed in many European and Asian countries, and though illegal here, they still exist from time to time in various U.S. industries too. As a result, the cartel model warrants close examination, for the worldwide impact of this type of oligopoly is quite significant.

Excess Capacity as a Barrier to Entry in the U.S. Titanium Metal Industry

Excess capacity exists when the firms in an industry possess more production capacity than they need to satisfy the demand for their good. Sometimes this excess capacity occurs as a result of unanticipated fluctuations in demand. Other times firms intentionally build more production capacity than they ordinarily expect to use so as to have the ability to prevent new firms from entering an industry. They can achieve this result by using their excess capacity to quickly increase their output when it becomes apparent that a new firm is going to attempt to enter the industry. By increasing their output, these incumbent firms can drive down the price of the good until it becomes unprofitable for new firms to enter the market. Such preemption of entry obviously restricts the number of firms in the industry, enabling the incumbent firms to earn higher profits than would be the case if entry occurred.

The U.S. titanium metal industry exhibits many of the classic characteristics associated with oligopoly, specifically a small number of relatively large firms selling homogeneous products, a common price for their products, and significant barriers to entry. Historically, the number of firms operating in this industry has ranged from two to six. Because of the cyclical nature of the civilian aerospace industry and the unpredictability of government orders for military aircraft, the demand for titanium metal has been characterized by extreme fluctuations. These phenomena indicate that excess capacity, which ranged from 12 percent of production capacity in 1988 to nearly 60 percent in 1983, is, in part, inherent to the titanium industry. It is often difficult to prove when firms are using excess capacity as a barrier, especially in those industries characterized by a widely fluctuating demand for their product.

The authors of this text conducted a study demonstrating a statistically significant, inverse relationship between expected levels of capacity expansion and the probability of firm entry into the U.S. titanium metal industry.[2] In that study, we disentangled the components of excess capacity, capacity, and production, and estimated the predicted values for these variables separately from the effects of underlying cycles in titanium demand and production, making it possible to draw some inferences regarding any incumbent firms' actions to preempt entry. Our results indicate that increases in the projected three-year average levels of production capacity for incumbent firms, while controlling for changes in demand, adversely affect the entry of new firms into the titanium industry. Although we can draw no conclusions from this study regarding the intent of the titanium firms to deviate from profit-maximizing behavior to prevent new firms from entering the industry, our results do indicate that excess capacity does act as an effective barrier to entry in this industry.

---

[2]Stephen Mathis and Janet Koscianski, "Excess Capacity as a Barrier to Entry in the U.S. Titanium Industry," *International Journal of Industrial Organization*, 15 (1996): 263–281.

Two of the most well-known examples of cartels are the Organization of Petroleum Exporting Countries (OPEC) and the Central Selling Organization (CSO). OPEC, which includes many of the world's largest exporters of petroleum, such as Saudi Arabia, Iran, Kuwait, Venezuela, and Nigeria, was established in 1960. However, it was not until the 1970s that OPEC was able to effectively restrict the production of crude oil and dramatically increase the price of this essential commodity. From 1973 to 1974, OPEC increased the price of crude oil from $2.59 per barrel to $11.05 per barrel, and by 1981 the price increased to $36.00 per barrel. However, since the early 1980s, the effectiveness of OPEC has decreased significantly for a number of reasons. Specifically, increases in the world demand for oil have been curtailed significantly by such consumer responses as the use of more fuel-efficient automobiles, the increased use of home insulation, and changes in residential living patterns. Furthermore, cartels tend to be somewhat unstable inasmuch as individual members have an incentive to cheat on the production agreements by expanding their own output. This has been the more recent experience of OPEC: the cartel has had difficulty maintaining the overall production restrictions necessary to maintain a high price for oil.

Historically, an even more effective cartel is the Central Selling Organization, known more popularly by the name of its controlling company, DeBeers, the world's largest diamond producer. This cartel has been extremely successful in restricting the number of diamonds marketed throughout the world, controlling approximately 85 percent of this product. As a result, the high price of diamonds, at least in part, reflects the successful cartel arrangement enforced by DeBeers.

The cartel model we will analyze in this chapter is based on the simplifying assumption that 100 percent of the sales of a good are incorporated into the cartel. By making this assumption, we can then treat the cartel as a multiplant monopoly, where the member firms are analogous to the plants operated by a monopolist. We developed the multiplant monopoly model in Section 16.5 of Chapter 16. Recall that, in general, the goal of a firm is to determine the level of output that maximizes its profit, and to be consistent with this goal, a multiplant monopolist must also determine the various portions of its total output that it produces in each of its plants. We demonstrated that a multiplant firm determines the profit-maximizing level of output for these plants by equating the marginal cost of producing output in each plant to its overall marginal revenue. Thus, for $1, 2, \ldots, N$ plants, we express this condition as

$$MC_1 = MC_2 = \ldots = MC_N = MR.$$

We can apply this same condition to a cartel, where we interpret the cartel as representing the monopolist and the different firms comprising the cartel as the plants. Thus, the goal of the cartel is to maximize the overall profit of the group of firms.

We provided a specific example of a multiplant monopoly in Section 16.5 of Chapter 16, assuming the monopolist uses two plants. We can now reinterpret this example as representing a two-firm oligopoly, or duopoly, behaving as a cartel. Also, note that we are implicitly assuming that the two firms' products are homogeneous. The own-price demand curve for the monopolist, now interpreted as a cartel, is

$$P = 300 - \frac{1}{2}(Q_T),$$

where Q_T represents the overall output of the cartel, equal to the summation of the output levels Q_1 and Q_2 produced by firms one and two, respectively. Thus, since

$$Q_T = Q_1 + Q_2,$$

we can express the own-price demand curve as

$$P = 300 - \frac{1}{2}(Q_1 + Q_2).$$

Finally, the short-run total cost curves for the two plants are

$$SRTC_1 = 500 + 20Q_1,$$

and

$$SRTC_2 = 1000 + \frac{1}{4}Q_2^2,$$

where now these cost curves, $SRTC_1$ and $SRTC_2$, pertain to firms one and two, respectively. The profit function we will maximize is the difference between the total revenue for the cartel and the summation of the short-run total costs associated with each firm, or

$$SR\pi = TR - (SRTC_1 + SRTC_2),$$
$$= PQ_T - SRTC_1 - SRTC_2,$$
$$= P(Q_1 + Q_2) - SRTC_1 - SRTC_2.$$

Since we solved this model in Chapter 16, only a summary of the results will be presented here. We determined the optimal values for output, price, and profit as, respectively, $Q_1^* = 240$ units, $Q_2^* = 40$ units, $Q_T^* = 280$ units, $P^* = \$160$, and $SR\pi^* = \$38,100$.

There is an important difference when interpreting these results for a cartel solution as opposed to that for a multiplant monopoly. If we interpret the results to represent the profit-maximizing solution for a multiplant monopolist, then they represent stable values in that the two plants are clearly part of a single firm. The optimal outcome, which requires the vast majority of the overall output, 240 units, to be produced in the lower cost plant, while the higher cost plant produces only 40 units, is quite logical. There is no need to compute the profit associated with each plant per se, because they are simply parts of the same firm. However, when we interpret this model as representing a cartel, then we must remember that, although the firms are behaving jointly, they are indeed truly separate firms. The potential problem here is that the firm receiving the smaller production allocation subsequently receives a smaller share of the cartel's overall profit. Thus, the cartel arrangement, though good for the two firms

as a whole, may not provide a satisfactory outcome for one of the individual participants unless some type of profit-sharing arrangement is established. In this example,
the profit attributed to firm one is

$$
\begin{aligned}
SR\pi_1^* &= TR_1 - SRTC_1 \\
&= P^*Q_1^* - (500 + 20Q_1^*) \\
&= 160(240) - 500 - 20(240) = \$33,100,
\end{aligned}
$$

and for firm two

$$
\begin{aligned}
SR\pi_2^* &= TR_2 - SRTC_2 \\
&= P^*Q_2^* - \left(1000 + \frac{1}{4}Q_2^{*2}\right) \\
&= 160(40) - 1000 - \frac{1}{4}(40)^2 = \$5000.
\end{aligned}
$$

Clearly, the share of the total profit earned by firm two is substantially lower than that
earned by firm one. This disparity between the two firms' profits is an example of why
economists often consider cartels to be inherently unstable arrangements. Often individual firms in a cartel have an incentive to cheat on the agreement and attempt to expand their output and profit unilaterally. However, if this occurs, the effectiveness of
the cartel to restrict output and maximize overall profit is substantially diminished.

17.3.2   Cournot Model

The cartel model requires the firms to adhere to an explicit collusive agreement. In all
other models of oligopoly, the firms involved do not formulate such agreements. However, in these models they tacitly collude, meaning that each firm takes into account
the behavior of the other firms when determining the profit-maximizing values of its
own output and price.

The first of these other models, the Cournot model, is named after nineteenth-
century French economist Augustin Cournot. In this model each firm determines its
own profit-maximizing level of output, on the assumption that the other firms in the
oligopoly sell some fixed amount of the good. Thus, although each firm reacts to
changes in the output sold by the other firms, it does not expect the other firms to respond to changes in its own output. However, in reality, if each firm behaves in this
manner, they will all react to changes in each other's output levels. Note that the term
react is used within a static, or point in time, context. Specifically, each firm in the
Cournot model takes into account the level of output sold by its rivals when determining its own profit-maximizing level of output. In no way should the term *react* be interpreted as implying that the Cournot model is dynamic, or applicable across time, for it
is not. The Cournot model is simply based on the additional, and somewhat unrealistic,
assumption that as the firms observe each other's behavior, each firm does not alter its
original assumption of expecting all other firms to leave their output levels unchanged.

In order to simplify the model, let's assume that the oligopoly consists of only two
firms and that their products are homogeneous. Accordingly, the market output, Q_T, is

simply the summation of the output levels Q_1 and Q_2 sold by firms one and two, respectively, or

$$Q_T = Q_1 + Q_2.$$

The market own-price demand curve, expressed in inverse form, is therefore

$$P = f(Q_T) = f(Q_1 + Q_2),$$

indicating that the price of the good is dependent on the levels of output sold by both firms. The short-run total cost functions for firms one and two are

$$SRTC_1 = \overline{FC}_1 + VC_1(Q_1, \overline{P}_{L,1}, \overline{K}_{1,1})$$

and

$$SRTC_2 = \overline{FC}_2 + VC_2(Q_2, \overline{P}_{L,1}, \overline{K}_{2,1}).$$

The terms $\overline{FC}_1$ and $\overline{FC}_2$ represent the firms' respective fixed costs, and the variable costs for firms one and two are, respectively, VC_1 and VC_2. These variable costs are functions of each firm's respective level of output, the price of the variable labor input, $\overline{P}_{L,1}$, and each firm's respective level of capital, $\overline{K}_{1,1}$ and $\overline{K}_{2,1}$.

The short-run profit function for firm one is the difference between its total revenue and its short-run total cost function, or

$$
\begin{aligned}
SR\pi_1 &= TR_1 - SRTC_1 \\
&= PQ_1 - [\overline{FC}_1 + VC_1(Q_1, \overline{P}_{L,1}, \overline{K}_{1,1})],
\end{aligned}
$$

and since

$$P = f(Q_1 + Q_2),$$

then

$$SR\pi_1 = f(Q_1 + Q_2)Q_1 - \overline{FC}_1 - VC_1(Q_1, \overline{P}_{L,1}, \overline{K}_{1,1}). \tag{17.1}$$

Observe that the interdependence between the firms' behavior is reflected by the fact that the inverse own-price demand curve contains the output sold by both firms as determinants of the price of the good. We determine the profit-maximizing level of output sold by firm one by first taking the derivative of its short-run profit function with respect to the level of output it sells and setting the result equal to zero. Thus, applying the product rule

$$\frac{dSR\pi_1}{dQ_1} = f(Q_1 + Q_2)\frac{dQ_1}{dQ_1} + Q_1\frac{df(Q_1 + Q_2)}{dQ_1} - \frac{d\overline{FC}_1}{dQ_1} - \frac{dVC_1(Q_1, \overline{P}_{L,1}, \overline{K}_{1,1})}{dQ_1} = 0,$$

or

$$= f(Q_1 + Q_2) + Q_1\left[\frac{\partial f(Q_1 + Q_2)}{\partial Q_1}\frac{dQ_1}{dQ_1} + \frac{\partial f(Q_1 + Q_2)}{\partial Q_2}\frac{dQ_2}{dQ_1}\right] -$$

$$\frac{dVC(Q_1, \overline{P}_{L,1}, \overline{K}_{1,1})}{dQ_1} = 0. \tag{17.2}$$

The term dQ_2/dQ_1, which appears in equation (17.2), denotes an important concept known as a **conjectural variation**, or *how one firm thinks another will react to its own adjustments in some strategic variable*. In this case, dQ_2/dQ_1 represents how firm one thinks firm two will change its output in response to firm one changing its level of output. Recall that a critical characteristic associated with the Cournot model is that each firm determines its profit-maximizing level of output on the assumption that the other firms sell a fixed amount of the good. An alternative, and more formal, way to express this characteristic is to assume that the conjectural variations for each firm are equal to zero. As a result, once we set firm one's conjectural variation regarding firm two's behavior, dQ_2/dQ_1, equal to zero, equation (17.2) reduces to the form

$$\frac{dSR\pi_1}{dQ_1} = f(Q_1 + Q_2) + Q_1 \frac{\partial f(Q_1 + Q_2)}{\partial Q_1} - \frac{dVC_1(Q_1, \overline{P}_{L,1}, \overline{K}_{1,1})}{dQ_1} = 0.$$

After adding $dVC_1(Q_1, \overline{P}_{L,1}, \overline{K}_{1,1})/dQ_1$ to both sides of the above equation and substituting Q_T for $Q_1 + Q_2$, the equation becomes

$$f(Q_T) + Q_1 \frac{\partial f(Q_T)}{\partial Q_1} = \frac{dVC_1(Q_1, \overline{P}_{L,1}, \overline{K}_{1,1})}{dQ_1}.$$

Finally, since $P = f(Q_T)$, we can express this equation as

$$P + Q_1 \frac{\partial P}{\partial Q_1} = \frac{dVC_1(Q_1, \overline{P}_{L,1}, \overline{K}_{1,1})}{dQ_1}, \tag{17.3}$$

where we can recognize the terms on the left and right sides of this equation as the marginal revenue, MR_1, and the short-run marginal cost, $SRMC_1$, respectively, for firm one. Thus, firm one determines its profit-maximizing level of output by the familiar rule

$$MR_1 = SRMC_1,$$

or by producing and selling output to the point where the additional revenue is just equal to the additional cost from doing so. The difference between this outcome and that associated with monopoly is that because $P = f(Q_1 + Q_2)$, the marginal revenue term, $P + Q_1 \, \partial P/\partial Q_1$, reflects the output levels sold by more than just one firm. In fact, it contains the output levels sold by all firms in the oligopoly.

We can rearrange a firm's profit maximization condition into a form known as a **reaction function**, or *a function that expresses one firm's profit-maximizing level of output in terms of the output sold by another*. In this case, we can express the reaction function for firm one as

$$Q_1 = \delta_1(Q_2),$$

indicating the profit-maximizing levels of output sold by firm one, Q_1, corresponding to each value of output sold by firm two, Q_2.

In the Cournot model, all firms behave in the same manner, specifically determining their profit-maximizing levels of output on the assumption that the other firms' levels of output sold remain fixed. Thus, in our two-firm model, we can develop a reaction function for firm two using a procedure similar to that we demonstrated for firm one, yielding

$$Q_2 = \delta_2(Q_1).$$

This reaction function expresses the profit-maximizing levels of output sold by firm two, corresponding to different levels of output sold by firm one. Thus, we have now derived two reaction functions, one for each firm in the duopoly. Ironically, we have developed these reaction functions on the assumption that neither firm believes the other will react, when in fact both firms do react to changes in the other's output. In general, for both reaction functions, we expect an inverse relationship between the quantities produced and sold by the two firms, Q_1 and Q_2. This expectation follows from the fact that the price of the good is inversely related to both outputs, and thus if one firm increases the level of output it sells, the other firm will be inclined to decrease its level of output to maintain this price.

Since the reaction functions for the two firms contain the same variables, Q_1 and Q_2, we can solve these functions simultaneously to determine the particular profit-maximizing levels of output for both firms. These values represent stable, or equilibrium, values for the firms' outputs since, once both firms are maximizing their profits simultaneously, there is no incentive for either firm to change the level of output it sells.

We can provide some additional insight into the process by applying the Cournot assumptions to the specific numerical example we used earlier for the cartel model. By using the same own-price demand and cost curves, we can compare the solutions generated by the two models. Recall, in this example, that the market consists of a duopoly, where the two firms sell homogeneous products. The market own-price demand curve, represented in inverse form, expresses the price of the good in terms of the outputs sold by both firms and is of the form

$$P = 300 - \frac{1}{2}(Q_1 + Q_2). \tag{17.4}$$

The short-run total cost curves for firms one and two are

$$SRTC_1 = 500 + 20Q_1 \tag{17.5}$$

and

$$SRTC_2 = 1000 + \frac{1}{4}Q_2^2, \tag{17.6}$$

respectively. In the Cournot model, the two firms will not overtly collude, and therefore, they do not act as one firm maximizing an overall profit. Instead, each firm maximizes its own profit function on the assumption that the other firm leaves its output unchanged, or, alternatively stated, the conjectural variations are equal to zero. Thus, the short-run profit function for firm one is

$$SR\pi_1 = TR_1 - SRTC_1$$
$$= PQ_1 - SRTC_1$$
$$= \left[300 - \frac{1}{2}(Q_1 + Q_2)\right]Q_1 - (500 + 20Q_1)$$
$$= 300Q_1 - \frac{1}{2}Q_1^2 - \frac{1}{2}Q_1Q_2 - 500 - 20Q_1$$
$$= 280Q_1 - \frac{1}{2}Q_1^2 - \frac{1}{2}Q_1Q_2 - 500.$$

The simplest mathematical technique for determining the profit-maximizing level of output for firm one is to take the partial derivative of $SR\pi_1$ with respect to Q_1 and set the result equal to zero. By employing a partial derivative, we are treating all other independent variables as constant, thus eliminating the conjectural variation. In this case the only other independent variable is Q_2, and therefore

$$\frac{\partial SR\pi_1}{\partial Q_1} = 280 - 1.0Q_1 - \frac{1}{2}Q_2 = 0,$$

or

$$Q_1 = 280 - \frac{1}{2}Q_2. \tag{17.7}$$

Equation (17.7) expresses the profit-maximizing levels of Q_1 corresponding to any given level of Q_2, or more concisely, it represents the reaction function for firm one.

Firm two behaves in a similar manner where its short-run profit function is

$$SR\pi_2 = TR_2 - SRTC_2$$
$$= PQ_2 - SRTC_2$$
$$= \left[300 - \frac{1}{2}(Q_1 + Q_2)\right]Q_2 - \left(1000 + \frac{1}{4}Q_2^2\right)$$
$$= 300Q_2 - \frac{1}{2}Q_1Q_2 - \frac{1}{2}Q_2^2 - 1000 - \frac{1}{4}Q_2^2$$
$$= 300Q_2 - \frac{1}{2}Q_1Q_2 - \frac{3}{4}Q_2^2 - 1000.$$

Maximizing the short-run profit for firm two with respect to its own level of output, Q_2, on the assumption that Q_1 remains constant, yields

$$\frac{\partial SR\pi_2}{\partial Q_2} = 300 - \frac{1}{2}Q_1 - \frac{3}{2}Q_2 = 0,$$

or

$$Q_2 = 200 - \frac{1}{3}Q_1, \tag{17.8}$$

that represents the reaction function for firm two. Therefore, although neither firm believes the other will react, each firm does react to changes in the output of the other, and equilibrium is achieved when both firms maximize their profits simultaneously. Thus, substituting the expression for Q_2 in equation (17.8), the reaction function for firm two, into equation (17.7), the reaction function for firm one, yields the unique profit-maximizing level of output for firm one as

$$Q_1^* = 280 - \frac{1}{2}\left(200 - \frac{1}{3}Q_1\right) = 216 \text{ units.}$$

Substituting this value for Q_1 into equation (17.8) yields the unique profit-maximizing level of output for firm two as

$$Q_2^* = 200 - \frac{1}{3}(216) = 128 \text{ units.}$$

We obtain the price of the good by substituting these values for Q_1 and Q_2 into the market inverse own-price demand curve yielding

$$P^* = 300 - \frac{1}{2}(216 + 128) = \$128.$$

We compute each firm's short-run profit by substituting this value for price along with the corresponding level of output sold by each firm into its respective profit function. Thus, for firm one

$$SR\pi_1^* = 128(216) - 500 - 20(216) = \$22,828,$$

and for firm two

$$SR\pi_2^* = 128(128) - 1000 - 0.25(128)^2 = \$11,288.$$

It is interesting to contrast these results for the Cournot model with those we obtained earlier for the cartel model. In the Cournot case, the total output sold by both firms is

$$Q_T = Q_1 + Q_2 = 216 + 128 = 344 \text{ units,}$$

a greater amount than the $Q_T = 280$ units sold in the cartel case. Accordingly, the price of the good is less in the Cournot model, where $P = \$128$, than the price corresponding to the cartel where $P = \$160$. Finally, the total profit for the Cournot case is

$$SR\pi_T = SR\pi_1 + SR\pi_2 = \$22,828 + \$11,288 = \$34,116,$$

a lesser amount than the profit generated by the cartel, where $SR\pi = \$38,100$. In summary, from the consumer's perspective, the type of covert rivalry characterized in the Cournot model yields better performance results than those generated by the overt collusion associated with the cartel model.

We can also demonstrate the Cournot duopoly model with a graphical analysis. Figure 17.1 contains two panels so that we can analyze different types of firm behav-

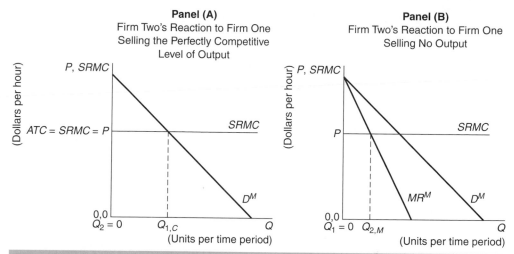

FIGURE 17.1 Profit-Maximizing Behavior Underlying Firms' Reaction Functions for a Cournot Duopoly

ior. Both panels contain identical short-run marginal cost, *SRMC*, and market own-price demand curves, D^M, where panel (B) also includes the associated marginal revenue curve, MR^M. To simplify the analysis, we are assuming that the two firms have identical cost functions. In addition, we will also assume that the short-run total cost curve common to both firms is linear. As a result, we can interpret the horizontal cost curve included in each panel as representing both the short-run marginal and average total cost curve for either firm. Using this information, we can derive the reaction functions for the two firms. Referring to panel (A), if firm one chooses to produce all of the output in the market, then it does so by producing $Q_{1,C}$ units according to the $P = SRMC$ condition for profit maximization. At this level of output, its profit would be equal to zero since $SRMC = ATC$, and thus

$$SR\ AVE\pi = AR - ATC = P - ATC = \$0.$$

Also, we can interpret this level of output, $Q_{1,C}$ as representing the perfectly competitive quantity of output since it is determined by the condition $P = SRMC$. At this level of output for firm one, there is nothing left in the market for firm two to sell, and hence, $Q_2 = 0$ in this situation. We have plotted this combination where $Q_1 = Q_{1,C}$ and $Q_2 = 0$, in Figure 17.2 as the Q_1 intercept of the reaction function for firm two.

Returning to Figure 17.1, as illustrated in panel (B), if firm one chooses to sell no output, then firm two will act as a monopolist and sell $Q_{2,M}$ units of output according to the profit-maximizing condition $MR = SRMC$. This combination, $Q_1 = 0$ and $Q_2 = Q_{2,M}$, is shown in Figure 17.2 as the Q_2 intercept for firm two's reaction function. Of course, an infinite number of (Q_1, Q_2) combinations lie between these intercepts, where each of these combinations represents the profit-maximizing level

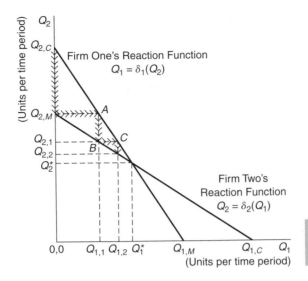

FIGURE 17.2 Reaction Functions for Firm One and Firm Two

of output for firm two, corresponding to each level of output sold by firm one. Conceptually, this curve, designated

$$Q_2 = \delta_2(Q_1),$$

is the reaction function for firm two. As an exercise, you can conduct a similar analysis to obtain the reaction function for firm one, or

$$Q_1 = \delta_1(Q_2).$$

From this perspective, if firm two sells a perfectly competitive level of output, $Q_{2,C}$, where $P = SRMC$, then firm one sells no output. This combination, $Q_1 = 0$ and $Q_2 = Q_{2,C}$, is shown in Figure 17.2 as the Q_2 intercept of the reaction function for firm one. Finally, if firm two chooses to sell no output, then firm one acts as a monopolist and sells $Q_{1,M}$ level of output where $MR = SRMC$. We have plotted this combination, $Q_1 = Q_{1,M}$ and $Q_2 = 0$, in Figure 17.2 as the Q_1 intercept for firm one's reaction function.

Each firm adjusts its profit-maximizing level of output along its reaction function until an equilibrium is established. This occurs when both firms maximize their profits simultaneously as demonstrated in Figure 17.2. We can describe the process by which this equilibrium is achieved. At the Q_2 intercept of the reaction function for firm one, firm one sells no output. As a result, the output sold by firm two, $Q_{2,C}$, is not a stable solution since firm two can now act as a monopolist and increase its profit by restricting its output to $Q_{2,M}$. However, once it does so, firm one will react to this reduction in output by firm two by increasing the amount of output it sells from zero to $Q_{1,1}$, corresponding to point A on its reaction function. Firm two responds by decreasing its level of output further to $Q_{2,1}$, corresponding to point B on its reaction function. Firm one then reacts by increasing its level of output to $Q_{1,2}$ corresponding to point C, causing firm two to respond by decreasing its output to $Q_{2,2}$. This process continues until firms one and two sell Q_1^* and Q_2^* levels of output, respectively, at which both firms' profits are maximized simultaneously. In Figure 17.2 these solution values for Q_1 and Q_2 correspond to the point of intersection of the two reaction functions, and at these levels of output there is no incentive for any further adjustments by either firm. Note that the analysis we have just described is actually static since the situations we have presented refer to possibilities that exist at a particular point in time, as opposed to those occurring over time. As an exercise, it is left to you to determine the path of adjustment to an equilibrium if the process starts at the Q_1 intercept, $Q_{1,C}$.

17.3.3   Stackelberg Model

The critical assumption underlying the Cournot model—that the oligopolists' conjectural variations are equal to zero—has led many economists to challenge the applicability of this model to real-world situations. What is particularly bothersome is that each firm continues to believe that its rivals will not react to changes in the level of output it sells, despite historical evidence to the contrary. The first attempt at expanding the model of covert collusion to allow for different types of firm behavior was conducted by the German economist, Heinrich von Stackelberg in the 1930s. In the construction of his model of oligopoly behavior, Stackelberg allowed for the possibility that some or all of the firms comprising an oligopoly may form conjectural variations that are not necessarily equal to zero. As a result, Stackelberg expanded the model of covert collusion to allow for differing assumptions about these conjectural variations. In a sense, the Cournot model we described earlier is now reduced to a special subcase of the broader Stackelberg model, where in the Cournot case both firms behave as followers, reacting to changes in the other's output.

There are also other possibilities. Focusing on the duopoly model, it is possible that one firm may anticipate the other's reaction, thus incorporating a nonzero conjectural variation into its profit function. By doing so, this firm becomes a leader while the other firm, provided it maintains a conjectural variation equal to zero, remains a follower. Note that these roles could be reversed where the second firm might choose to be the leader and the first firm remains the follower. Finally, it is also possible that both firms may anticipate the other's reaction, causing both firms to act as leaders. However, in subsequent analysis we will show that if both firms choose to operate as leaders, it is impossible to determine a true equilibrium, since both firms cannot simultaneously maximize their profits. This is a situation known as a Stackelberg disequilibrium.

We will first demonstrate the general case of one firm acting as a leader by returning to equation (17.1), the profit function for firm one. If this firm decides to act as a leader, it will anticipate the reaction function for firm two, $Q_2 = \delta_2(Q_1)$, and incorporate it into its own profit function. Accordingly, equation (17.1), becomes

$$SR\pi_1 = f[Q_1 + \delta_2(Q_1)]Q_1 - \overline{FC}_1 - VC_1(Q_1, \overline{P}_{L,1}, \overline{K}_{1,1}),$$

and we can maximize $SR\pi_1$ with respect to the output sold by firm one. Alternatively, since we have already established the derivative, $dSR\pi_1/dQ_1$ in equation (17.2), the same modification can be accomplished by substituting $Q_2 = \delta_2(Q_1)$ for Q_2 in this equation. In addition, we can compute the conjectural variation for firm one, dQ_2/dQ_1, from the reaction function for firm two as

$$\frac{dQ_2}{dQ_1} = \frac{d\delta_2(Q_1)}{dQ_1},$$

and substitute this expression into equation (17.2) yielding

$$\frac{dSR\pi_1}{dQ_1} = f[Q_1 + \delta_2(Q_1)] + Q_1 \left\{ \frac{\partial f[Q_1 + \delta_2(Q_1)]}{\partial Q_1} + \frac{\partial f[Q_1 + \delta_2(Q_1)]}{\partial Q_2} \frac{d\delta_2(Q_1)}{dQ_1} \right\}$$
$$- \frac{dVC_1(Q_1, \overline{P}_{L,1}, \overline{K}_{1,1})}{dQ_1} = 0.$$

We can now solve this equation for Q_1^*, the profit-maximizing level of output for firm one. Note that we can conduct a similar profit-maximizing process for firm two if it decides to act as a leader.

Given the difficulty in comprehending these notational equations, we believe that the Stackelberg leader–follower cases can be demonstrated more clearly with a specific numerical example. Once again, assume a duopoly with homogeneous products. The market inverse own-price demand curve and the two firms' short-run total cost functions are given in equations (17.4), (17.5), and (17.6), respectively. The short-run profit function for firm one is

$$\begin{aligned} SR\pi_1 &= TR_1 - SRTC_1 \\ &= PQ_1 - (500 + 20Q_1) \\ &= \left[300 - \frac{1}{2}(Q_1 + Q_2) \right] Q_1 - 500 - 20Q_1 \\ &= 300Q_1 - \frac{1}{2}Q_1^2 - \frac{1}{2}Q_1Q_2 - 500 - 20Q_1. \end{aligned}$$

The reaction function for firm two, which we presented earlier for the Cournot model, is represented by equation (17.8) as

$$Q_2 = 200 - \frac{1}{3}Q_1.$$

If firm one behaves as a leader and firm two behaves as a follower, then substituting the reaction function for firm two into the profit function for firm one yields

$$\begin{aligned} SR\pi_1 &= 300Q_1 - \frac{1}{2}Q_1^2 - \frac{1}{2}Q_1\left(200 - \frac{1}{3}Q_1\right) - 500 - 20Q_1 \\ &= 300Q_1 - \frac{1}{2}Q_1^2 - 100Q_1 + \frac{1}{6}Q_1^2 - 500 - 20Q_1. \end{aligned}$$

We determine the profit-maximizing level of output for firm one by taking the derivative of $SR\pi_1$ with respect to Q_1, setting the result equal to zero, and solving as

$$\frac{dSR\pi_1}{dQ_1} = 300 - Q_1 - 100 + \frac{1}{3}Q_1 - 20 = 0$$

$$= 180 - \frac{2}{3}Q_1 = 0,$$

or

$$Q_1^* = 270 \text{ units.}$$

If firm two behaves as a follower, we determine its profit-maximizing level of output by substituting $Q_1^* = 270$ units into its reaction function and solving to obtain

$$Q_2^* = 200 - \frac{1}{3}(270) = 110 \text{ units.}$$

Substituting these amounts for Q_1 and Q_2 into the market inverse own-price demand curve yields the price of the good as

$$P^* = 300 - \frac{1}{2}(270 + 110) = \$110.$$

Finally, we compute the profits for firms one and two as

$$SR\pi_1 = TR_1 - SRTC_1$$
$$= PQ_1 - 500 - 20Q_1$$
$$= 110(270) - 500 - 20(270) = \$23,800$$

and

$$SR\pi_2 = TR_2 - SRTC_2$$
$$= PQ_2 - 1000 - \frac{1}{4}Q_2^2$$
$$= 110(110) - 1000 - \frac{1}{4}(110)^2 = \$8075.$$

Thus, the total profit for the duopoly is

$$SR\pi_T = SR\pi_1 + SR\pi_2 = \$23,800 + \$8075 = \$31,875.$$

We can also solve this model on the assumption that firm two chooses to act as a leader and firm one as a follower. In this case, the short-run profit function for firm two is

$$SR\pi_2 = TR_2 - SRTC_2$$
$$= PQ_2 - 1000 - \frac{1}{4}Q_2^2$$
$$= \left[300 - \frac{1}{2}(Q_1 + Q_2)\right]Q_2 - 1000 - \frac{1}{4}Q_2^2$$
$$= 300Q_2 - \frac{1}{2}Q_1Q_2 - \frac{1}{2}Q_2^2 - 1000 - \frac{1}{4}Q_2^2.$$

In this situation, firm two anticipates the reaction function for firm one, represented in equation (17.7) as

$$Q_1 = 280 - \frac{1}{2}Q_2,$$

which we determined earlier for the Cournot model. Substituting this expression for Q_1 into the short-run profit function for firm two yields

$$SR\pi_2 = 300Q_2 - \frac{1}{2}\left(280 - \frac{1}{2}Q_2\right)Q_2 - \frac{1}{2}Q_2^2 - 1000 - \frac{1}{4}Q_2^2$$

$$= 300Q_2 - 140Q_2 + \frac{1}{4}Q_2^2 - \frac{1}{2}Q_2^2 - 1000 - \frac{1}{4}Q_2^2$$

$$= 160Q_2 - \frac{1}{2}Q_2^2 - 1000,$$

and therefore

$$\frac{dSR\pi_2}{dQ_2} = 160 - Q_2 = 0$$

$$Q_2^* = 160 \text{ units.}$$

Assuming that firm one acts as a follower, we determine its profit-maximizing level of output by substituting $Q_2 = 160$ units into its reaction function and solving as

$$Q_1^* = 280 - \frac{1}{2}(160) = 200 \text{ units,}$$

and therefore we obtain the price of the good as

$$P^* = 300 - \frac{1}{2}(200 + 160) = \$120.$$

The short-run profits for the two firms are correspondingly,

$$SR\pi_1 = 120(200) - 500 - 20(200) = \$19,500,$$

and

$$SR\pi_2 = 120(160) - 1000 - \frac{1}{4}(160)^2 = \$11,800,$$

yielding a total profit for the oligopoly equal to

$$SR\pi_T = SR\pi_1 + SR\pi_2 = \$19,500 + \$11,800 = \$31,300.$$

Finally, if both firms decide to behave as leaders, assuming the other follows its own reaction function, a Stackelberg disequilibrium is encountered. This result follows because neither firm behaves as the other expects. Thus, neither firm is able to achieve its intended result of maximizing its profit subject to the assumption that the other firm behaves as a follower.

17.3.4 Dominant Firm Model

Another type of oligopoly market structure consists of one large firm accounting for a significantly large portion of the marketwide output, and a large number of small firms with each selling an insignificantly small portion. Although we consider this structure as an oligopoly, it is somewhat different from the oligopoly models we developed earlier. In this situation, we assume the single large firm can sell a large enough percentage of total market sales so as to influence the price of the good. However, we consider each of the small firms as having an imperceptible effect on market sales and price. As a result, each of these firms behaves as a price taker, and the price that these small firms take as predetermined is influenced by the single large firm. Therefore, we can analyze this type of market structure using a price leadership model, known as the dominant firm model, because the single dominant firm acts as the price leader. There is yet another important aspect associated with this model. We are assuming that the dominant firm, because it can influence the price of the good, could increase its output and decrease the price to the point of driving the small firms out of the market. However, it chooses not to do so for various reasons, perhaps out of fear of an antitrust suit or the potential entry of a strong rival into the market. Thus, the goal of the dominant firm is to determine a level of output that maximizes its profit, subject to the condition that it does not wish to drive the small firms out of the market.

We will first demonstrate this model graphically as illustrated in Figures 17.3 and 17.4. Figure 17.3 contains the market own-price demand curve, D^M, and the short-run supply curve for the group of small firms, SRS^S. As noted earlier, a short-run supply curve represents the summation of the individual firms' short-run marginal cost curves, and thus in this case we represent it as $\sum_{i=1}^{N} SRMC_i^S$, for $i = 1, 2, \ldots, N$ small

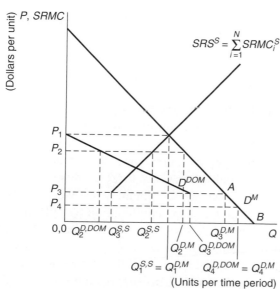

FIGURE 17.3 Derivation of Own-Price Demand Curve for a Dominant Firm

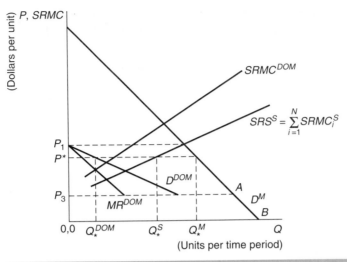

FIGURE 17.4 Profit Maximization Results for Dominant Firm Model

firms. Our first step in analyzing the dominant firm model is to derive the own-price demand curve for the dominant firm. We can observe in Figure 17.3 at the price level P_1, the quantity of output supplied by the small firms is $Q_1^{S,S}$ where $P_1 = \sum_{i=1}^{N} SRMC_i^S$. This amount, $Q_1^{S,S}$ is also equal to the quantity of the good demanded, $Q_1^{D,M}$. Note that the second superscript on $Q_1^{S,S}$ refers to the fact that this term represents the summation of the quantities of output supplied by all of the small firms. Since at P_1, $Q_1^{S,S} = Q_1^{D,M}$, then all of the market demand for the good is sold by the small firms. The dominant firm sells no output at this price, and as a result, P_1 represents the vertical intercept of the dominant firm's inverse own-price demand curve.

At the lower price, P_2, the small firms supply the amount $Q_2^{S,S}$, determined where $P_2 = \sum_{i=1}^{N} SRMC_i^S$. However, at P_2 the market quantity demanded is $Q_2^{D,M}$. Therefore, the small firms do not satisfy all of the market demand at P_2, leaving the amount $Q_2^{D,M} - Q_2^{S,S}$ to be supplied by the dominant firm. We can recalibrate this amount of output, designated as $Q_2^{D,DOM}$, to begin at the origin. This combination $(Q_2^{D,DOM}, P_2)$ represents another point on the dominant firm's own-price demand curve.

At the price level P_3, the small firms will sell $Q_3^{S,S}$, leaving the remainder of the market demand, $Q_3^{D,M} - Q_3^{S,S}$, for the dominant firm. We can set this amount, $Q_3^{D,M} - Q_3^{S,S}$, equal to $Q_3^{D,DOM}$ and thus the combination $(Q^{D,DOM}, P_3)$ represents yet another point on the dominant firm's own-price demand curve. Note that P_3 represents the price at which the small firms begin supplying output, reflecting the fact that any price below P_3 does not cover the small firms' average variable costs. Thus, for any price below P_3, say P_4, the small firms supply no output, and the entire market demand is available to the dominant firm. Therefore, for any price less than P_3, the dominant firm's own-price demand curve is represented by the corresponding portion of the market own-price demand curve and is illustrated in Figure 17.3 by the segment AB.

Once we have derived the dominant firm's own-price demand curve, analyzing the dominant firm oligopoly model is quite straightforward. Our analysis is illustrated in Figure 17.4, which contains all of the information shown in Figure 17.3, including the dominant firm's own-price demand curve. In addition, this figure also includes the marginal revenue function, MR^{DOM}, associated with the dominant firm's own-price demand curve, as well as its short-run marginal cost curve, $SRMC^{DOM}$. The dominant firm determines its profit-maximizing level of output by the familiar rule, $MR^{DOM} = SRMC^{DOM}$, and sells Q_*^{DOM} units of output yielding the price of the good as P^*. At this price, the small firms behaving as price takers, determine their output according to the $P = \sum_{i=1}^{N} SRMC_i^S$ rule and collectively sell Q_*^S units of output. By construction $Q_*^{DOM} + Q_*^S = Q_*^M$, and thus all of the market demand at this price is satisfied. In summary, the dominant firm has achieved its goal of determining a profit-maximizing level of output and price, subject to allowing the small firms to remain and operate in the market.

We can also demonstrate the dominant firm oligopoly model with a specific mathematical example. Assume a market own-price demand curve of the form

$$Q^{D,M} = 200 - P, \tag{17.9}$$

which we can also express in inverse form as

$$P = 200 - Q^{D,M}.$$

Since the products sold by all of the firms are homogeneous, the market own-price demand is equal to the summation of the quantities sold by the dominant and the small firms, or

$$Q^{D,M} = Q^{D,DOM} + Q^{D,S}.$$

Assume the short-run marginal cost functions for the dominant and small firms are

$$SRMC^{DOM} = 20 + 0.2Q^{DOM} \tag{17.10}$$

and

$$SRMC^S = 20 + 4Q^S, \tag{17.11}$$

respectively. Our first step in solving this model is to derive the own-price demand curve for the dominant firm. As we have seen, we accomplish this by determining the amounts of output supplied by the small firms at various prices and then computing the dominant firm's own-price demand curve as the difference between the market demand and the total amount supplied by the small firms.

The small firms collectively determine their profit-maximizing levels of output at various prices by equating price to short-run marginal cost, or

$$P = SRMC^S.$$

Since

$$SRMC^S = 20 + 4Q^S,$$

then

$$P = 20 + 4Q^S,$$

or

$$Q^{S,S} = -5 + 0.25P, \tag{17.12}$$

representing the short-run supply curve for the small firms. The quantity of output demanded for the dominant firm is the difference between the market demand and the quantity of output supplied by the small firms, or

$$Q^{D,DOM} = Q^{D,M} - Q^{S,S}.$$

After substituting the expressions for $Q^{D,M}$ and $Q^{S,S}$ from equations (17.9) and (17.12), respectively, into the above equation, we can express the own-price demand curve for the dominant firm as

$$\begin{aligned} Q^{D,DOM} &= (200 - P) - (-5 + 0.25P) \\ &= 205 - 1.25P, \end{aligned} \tag{17.13}$$

or in inverse form

$$P = 164 - 0.8Q^{D,DOM}. \tag{17.14}$$

The total revenue function for the dominant firm is

$$TR^{DOM} = PQ^{D,DOM},$$

where substituting the expression for P from equation (17.14) into the above equation yields

$$\begin{aligned} TR^{DOM} &= (164 - 0.8Q^{D,DOM})Q^{D,DOM} \\ &= 164Q^{D,DOM} - 0.8(Q^{D,DOM})^2. \end{aligned}$$

Therefore, the marginal revenue for the dominant firm is

$$MR^{DOM} = \frac{dTR^{DOM}}{dQ^{D,DOM}} = 164 - 1.6Q^{D,DOM}. \tag{17.15}$$

We compute the profit-maximizing level of output for the dominant firm according to the condition

$$MR^{DOM} = SRMC^{DOM}.$$

Substituting the expressions for MR^{DOM} and $SRMC^{DOM}$ from equations (17.15) and (17.10) into the above equation yields

$$164 - 1.6Q^{D,DOM} = 20 + 0.2Q^{D,DOM}$$

$$D_*^{D,DOM} = \frac{144}{1.8} = 80 \text{ units.}$$

We obtain the corresponding price by substituting this value for $Q^{D,DOM}$ into equation (17.14) as

$$P^* = 164 - 0.8(80) = \$100.$$

Finally, we compute the quantity of output supplied by the small firms by substituting this value for P into equation (17.12), yielding

$$Q^{S,S} = -5 + 0.25P = -5 + 0.25(100) = 20 \text{ units,}$$

and thus the total market quantity demanded of this good sold is

$$Q^{D,M}_* = Q^{D,DOM}_* + Q^{S,S}_* = 80 + 20 = 100 \text{ units.}$$

17.3.5 Sweezy Kinked Demand Curve Model

The final oligopoly model we will present is the Sweezy kinked demand curve model. Understand, however, that we have by no means exhausted the list of oligopoly models, for they are far too numerous to be comprehensively covered in this text. We have chosen to include the kinked demand curve model because it is rather popular and is often encountered in microeconomics texts, perhaps because of its simplicity. This model was developed in the 1930s by economist Paul Sweezy with the intent of rationalizing the price rigidities frequently observed to occur in oligopolistic markets. More specifically, the prices charged by oligopolistic firms often appear to remain stable for extended periods of time, after which they change abruptly and often significantly.

We have demonstrated the basis for the kinked demand curve model in Figure 17.5, where our focus is on one typical firm within an oligopoly. We are assuming in this case that there is a slight degree of product differentiation for this firm's good. In Figure 17.5, observe that this particular firm faces two potential own-price demand

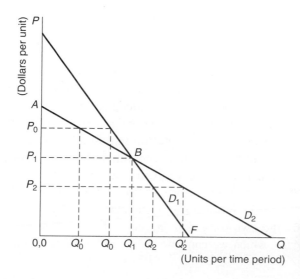

FIGURE 17.5 Two Potential Own-Price Demand Curves for an Oligopolistic Firm

curves for its product, the comparatively steeper, or less price elastic curve, D_1, and the comparatively flatter, or more price elastic, curve, D_2. We have assumed the profit-maximizing levels of output and price for this firm to be (Q_1, P_1), corresponding to the intersection point of the two potential own-price demand curves. Why does this firm face two potential own-price demand curves? The underlying reason is based on whether its rival firms respond to changes in the price this firm charges for its product. For example, if the firm decreases its price from P_1 to P_2, and the rival firms choose not to reduce their prices accordingly, then the quantity demanded of this firm's product increases from Q_1 to Q_2', as indicated by moving down the more elastic curve D_2. Part of this increase in the firm's sales is due to an increase in the overall market quantity demanded resulting from the decrease in its price. However, another part comes at the expense of the other firms' market shares because they have not lowered their prices in response. Alternatively, if the rival firms reduce their prices in response to this firm decreasing its price from P_1 to P_2, then the quantity demanded for this firm's product increases from Q_1 to only Q_2, as indicated by the less elastic curve D_1. This increase in sales, measured as $Q_2 - Q_1$, is due strictly to the firm's share of the overall market expansion resulting from the price decrease. We should emphasize that none of the increase in sales comes at the expense of its rivals' market shares. This latter amount is indicated in Figure 17.5 as $Q_2' - Q_2$, and would only be realized by this firm in the former situation, where the rival firms choose not to lower their prices.

If the firm increases its price from P_1 to P_0, and the rival firms choose not to raise their prices accordingly, then the quantity demanded of this firm's product decreases from Q_1 to Q_0', part of which, represented as $Q_1 - Q_0$, is due to an overall market contraction resulting from the higher price. The other part, $Q_0 - Q_0'$, is due to the loss in market share by this firm to its rivals because they do not raise their prices. Alternatively, if the rival firms choose to increase their prices in response to this firm's price increase, then the quantity of output demanded for the firm in question decreases from Q_1 to Q_0, owing only to its share of the overall market contraction resulting from the price increase.

At this point we need to apply two critical assumptions, imposed by Sweezy, regarding oligopolistic firm behavior. The first is that, if a firm decreases the price of its product, its rival firms will respond by lowering their prices to protect their market shares. As a result, observe in Figure 17.5 that for any price below the initial price, P_1, the own-price demand curve for the firm in question is segment BF pertaining to the less price elastic curve, D_1. The second assumption imposed by Sweezy is that if the firm increases its price, its rival firms do not respond, and thus, by not raising their prices, they can increase their market shares at the expense of the firm in question. Therefore, for any price above the initial price, P_1, the firm's own-price demand curve is segment AB pertaining to the more price elastic curve, D_2. In summary, based on the Sweezy assumptions, the own-price demand curve for the firm under analysis is the segmented curve ABF, which we can observe as possessing a kink at the initial price, P_1.

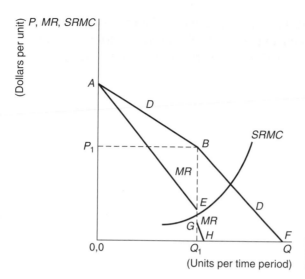

FIGURE 17.6 Sweezy Kinked Demand Curve Solution

We have repeated this "kinked" demand curve in Figure 17.6 while including the marginal revenue curves associated with each segment. Recall that for a linear own-price demand curve, the associated marginal revenue curve possesses the same vertical intercept, one-half the horizontal intercept, and twice the slope, in absolute value terms, as the own-price demand curve from which it is derived. Thus, for portion AB of the own-price demand curve, the associated marginal revenue curve is represented by the segment AE, whereas for portion BF the associated marginal revenue curve is the segment GH. The overall marginal revenue curve, including both segments, AE and GH, is discontinuous at the quantity–price combination (Q_1, P_1) corresponding to the kink in the own-price demand curve. The size of this gap, or discontinuity, in the marginal revenue curve, EG, depends on the difference in the own-price elasticities for the two segments of the own-price demand curve. Specifically, the greater the difference in these elasticities, the greater is the gap in the marginal revenue curve.

To complete the kinked demand curve model, we introduce a short-run marginal cost curve, $SRMC$, assuming that it passes through this gap in the marginal revenue curve. This being the case, then small upward or downward shifts in the $SRMC$ curve, caused by changes in underlying factors such as technology or input prices, will not disturb the quantity–price solution (Q_1, P_1), provided these shifts in the $SRMC$ curve remain within the gap in the MR curve. As noted earlier, the original intent of the kinked demand curve model is to provide a rationale for observed price rigidities in oligopolistic markets. According to this model, a firm will not alter its profit-maximizing levels of price and output unless its marginal cost curve shifts to the point where it intersects the MR curve outside its range of discontinuity. If the marginal cost curve does so, then the firm will change its price and quantity combination according to the $MR = SRMC$ condition for profit maximization.

We can also use this model to rationalize the phenomenon of a rigid price under different own-price demand conditions. For example, if the two segments of the own-price demand curve both shift either to the left or to the right, owing perhaps to changes in consumer tastes or incomes, while maintaining constant slopes, then the equilibrium quantity sold changes. However, the price does not change; rather, it remains constant at the new kink in the own-price demand curve. This result is contingent on assuming that the original marginal cost curve passes through the gap in the marginal revenue segments for the new kinked own-price demand curve.

In the final analysis, the kinked demand curve model, though rather interesting, is not particularly popular with many economists. The major criticism of this model is that it involves constructing a "model" around a predetermined solution. Recall that we simply assumed the solution values for the initial quantity–price combination that acts as the starting point of the model. Thus, we developed the critical kink in the own-price demand curve, as well as other aspects of the model, around this assumption. Good models, however, are supposed to work the other way around. Specifically, we design them to generate solutions, not just to rationalize them.

17.4 SUMMARY

Our focus in this chapter has been on the imperfectly competitive market structure of oligopoly. Although our list of oligopoly models is by no means complete, we have analyzed some of the most prominent models, including the cartel, Cournot, Stackelberg, Sweezy, and dominant firm models. In each of these models, we devoted particular attention to the type and degree of interdependence existing among the firms comprising the market. The main concepts covered in this chapter are as follows.

- An oligopoly is a market structure consisting of a few sellers of a good, where each seller accounts for a significant portion of marketwide sales.
- Since so few firms comprise an oligopoly, the behavior of these firms is interdependent, reflecting the fact that each firm can perceptibly influence market output and price, thereby affecting other firms' profits.
- A cartel is a group of firms that, through some type of explicit agreement, collude to jointly determine the levels of price and output of their product. From a theoretical perspective, we can model the behavior of firms comprising a cartel as a multiplant monopoly.
- In the Cournot model of oligopoly behavior, we assume that, while each firm reacts to changes in the output of other firms, it does not expect the other firms to respond to changes in its own output.
- A conjectural variation measures how one firm thinks another firm will react to its own adjustments to some strategic variable. In the case of the

Cournot model, we assume that the conjectural variations for each firm are equal to zero. In the Stackelberg model of oligopoly behavior, we assume that some or all of the firms in an oligopoly may employ conjectural variations that are not equal to zero.

- A reaction function expresses one firm's profit-maximizing level of output as a function of the output sold by another firm.
- The dominant firm model is a type of oligopoly containing one large firm, accounting for a significantly large portion of the sales in a market, and a large number of small firms, each of which sells an insignificantly small portion of the marketwide sales.
- In the Sweezy kinked demand curve model, we assume that an oligopolistic firm faces two potential own-price demand curves for its product, where each curve reflects a different own-price elasticity of demand, depending on whether the firm's rivals respond to a change in the price it charges. We use this model to rationalize price rigidities in oligopolistic market structures.

KEY TERMS

- cartel, page 445
- conjectural variation, page 451
- oligopoly, page 443
- reaction function, page 451

EXERCISES

17.1   A firm has two plants with the following marginal cost functions:

$$MC_1 = 30 + 2Q_1$$

and

$$MC_2 = 20 + 5Q_2,$$

where MC_1 is the marginal cost in the first plant, MC_2 is the marginal cost in the second plant, Q_1 is the output produced in the first plant, and Q_2 is the output produced in the second plant.

a. If the firm is minimizing its costs and if it is producing 5 units of output in the first plant, how many units of output will it produce in the second plant? Explain your response.

b. Generate a schedule showing the marginal cost of producing each successive unit in each plant up to 9 units in total. Identify which units are produced in each plant.

17.2 Assume an industry is characterized by a duopoly with the market own-price demand curve

$$P = 100 - 0.1(Q_1 + Q_2)$$

and with cost curves for the two firms represented as

$$C_1 = 400 + 20Q_1$$
$$C_2 = 800 + 0.25Q_2^2.$$

a. Assuming the two firms form a cartel, specify the profit function to be maximized.
b. Determine the values for Q_1 and Q_2 that maximize the cartel's profit.
c. Determine the price charged by the cartel.
d. What is the cartel's profit?

17.3 Using the information in Exercise 17.2, assume both firms behave as followers.
a. What type of model is this?
b. Set up the profit functions provided the two firms behave as followers.
c. Determine the reaction functions for each firm.
d. Solve for the profit-maximizing levels of output, Q_1^* and Q_2^*, for each firm.

17.4 What are conjectural variations? Do these terms play a role in the Cournot model? What is the major criticism associated with the Cournot model?

17.5 What is the major contribution to models of oligopoly attributed to Stackelberg? Now, refer to the information in Exercise 17.3.
a. If firm one is a leader and firm two is a follower, what is the conjectural variation pertaining to firm two?
b. Solve for the corresponding values of Q_1 and Q_2, given that firm two is a leader and firm one is a follower. Also, determine the price of the product.

17.6 What is the purpose of the Sweezy kinked demand curve model, or what is it intended to demonstrate? Illustrate this model graphically. What does the kink in this demand curve reflect? Is there a conceptual problem with this model, and if so what is it?

17.7 Assume a market structure consisting of one large firm that controlls a very large portion of market sales, and many small firms, with each of these small firms selling an insignificantly small portion. The inverse own-price demand curve for the market is

$$P = 595 - Q^{D,M},$$

where P represents the price of the good and $Q^{D,M}$ is the total market sales. Furthermore, the marginal cost curves for the large firm and group of small firms are represented as

$$MC^{DOM} = 10 + \frac{2}{3}Q^{DOM}$$

and

$$MC^S = 10 + 2Q^S,$$

respectively, where Q^{DOM} is the amount of the good sold by the large firm and Q^S is the amount sold by the group of small firms. Assume that the large firm desires to maximize its profit subject to allowing the group of small firms to remain in the market.

a. Derive the supply curve for the group of small firms.
b. Derive the own-price demand curve for the large firm.
c. Compute the level of output sold by the large firm.
d. What is the price of the good?
e. Compute the level of output sold by the group of small firms.
f. What is the total amount of the good sold?

17.8 Using the dominant firm model, graphically demonstrate how the dominant firm's own-price demand curve is constructed. Now, complete the dominant firm model, showing the profit-maximizing levels of output and price for both the dominant firm and the group of small firms.

Appendix

17A COMPARISON OF CARTEL, COURNOT, STACKELBERG, AND PERFECTLY COMPETITIVE OUTCOMES

Just as it was in our interest to compare the economic results generated by the perfectly competitive and monopolistic market models, it is also useful for us to make some comparisons of the results generated by the cartel, Cournot, Stackelberg, and perfect competition models. We will make these comparisons by assuming a simple market inverse own-price demand curve of the form

$$P = 10 - Q_T,$$

where Q_T represents the market output in all of the subsequent models demonstrated in this section. Furthermore, since the differences in behavior and outcomes are the result of how we treat the own-price demand curve, we will assume that all costs equal zero in order to simplify the analysis. We will first determine the perfectly competitive solution so as to establish a benchmark for subsequent comparisons. Recall that we compute the perfectly competitive equilibrium level of output, $Q_{T,C}$, where $P = MC$, and since all costs are assumed to be zero, $Q_{T,C}$ is

$$10 - Q_{T,C} = 0,$$

or

$$Q_{T,C}^* = 10 \text{ units.}$$

The perfectly competitive price is

$$P_C^* = MC = \$0,$$

and the profit, π_C, is the difference between total revenue, TR, and total cost, TC, or

$$\begin{aligned} \pi_C^* &= TR - TC \\ &= PQ_C - 0 \\ &= 0(100) - 0 = \$0. \end{aligned}$$

If we treat the market as a duopoly, where the firms agree to behave as a cartel, then the profit-maximizing level of output is the same as that for a monopoly, $Q_{T,M}$. Since

$$\begin{aligned} TR &= PQ_{T,M} \\ &= (10 - Q_{T,M})Q_{T,M} \\ &= 10Q_{T,M} - Q_{T,M}^2, \end{aligned}$$

then

$$MR = \frac{dTR}{dQ_T} = 10 - 2Q_{T,M},$$

where we determine $Q_{T,M}$ by the rule $MR = MC$, or

$$10 - 2Q_{T,M} = 0,$$

and therefore

$$Q_{T,M}^* = 5 \text{ units.}$$

Thus, the two firms behaving as a cartel restrict the total sales of output to one-half of that for the perfectly competitive solution. Since the firms' marginal costs are equal, the allocation of the amount of output to be produced by either firm is indeterminate, since there is no cost advantage attributed to either one. The price of the good in this case is

$$\begin{aligned} P_M^* &= 10 - Q_{T,M} \\ &= 10 - 5 = \$5, \end{aligned}$$

and the profit for the cartel is

$$\begin{aligned} \pi_M^* &= TR_M - 0 \\ &= 5(5) = \$25. \end{aligned}$$

If the two firms behave according to the Cournot assumptions, meaning they both act as followers, then

$$Q_T = Q_1 + Q_2,$$

and

$$P = 10 - Q_1 - Q_2,$$

where the profit function for firm one is

$$\pi_1 = TR_1 - 0$$
$$= PQ_1 = (10 - Q_1 - Q_2)Q_1$$
$$= 10Q_1 - Q_1^2 - Q_1Q_2.$$

We determine this firm's reaction function as

$$\frac{\partial \pi_1}{\partial Q_1} = 10 - 2Q_1 - Q_2 = 0,$$

or

$$Q_1 = 5 - \frac{1}{2}Q_2. \qquad \textbf{(17A.1)}$$

The profit function for firm two is

$$\pi_2 = TR_2 - 0$$
$$= PQ_2 = (10 - Q_1 - Q_2)Q_2$$
$$= 10Q_2 - Q_1Q_2 - Q_2^2,$$

and its reaction function is

$$\frac{\partial \pi_2}{\partial Q_2} = 10 - Q_1 - 2Q_2 = 0,$$

or

$$Q_2 = 5 - \frac{1}{2}Q_1. \qquad \textbf{(17A.2)}$$

We determine the equilibrium values for Q_1 and Q_2 by solving the two reaction functions simultaneously. Substituting the expression for Q_2 from equation (17A.2) into equation (17A.1) yields

$$Q_1 = 5 - \frac{1}{2}\left(5 - \frac{1}{2}Q_1\right)$$

$$= 5 - \frac{5}{2} + \frac{1}{4}Q_1$$

$$\frac{3}{4}Q_1 = \frac{5}{2}$$

$$Q_1^* = 3\frac{1}{3} \text{ units.}$$

Then, substituting this value for Q_1 into equation (17A.2) yields

$$Q_2^* = 5 - \frac{1}{2}\left(3\frac{1}{3}\right) = 3\frac{1}{3} \text{ units.}$$

In this example, both firms sell the same level of output because their costs are equal. The total market output in this case is

$$Q_T = Q_1 + Q_2 = 3\frac{1}{3} + 3\frac{1}{3} = 6\frac{2}{3} \text{ units,}$$

which is less than the perfectly competitive level of output, $Q_{T,C} = 10$ units, but more than the total output for the cartel, or monopoly solution, $Q_{T,M} = 5$ units. The price of the product for the Cournot solution is

$$P^* = 10 - 3\frac{1}{3} - 3\frac{1}{3} = \$3.33,$$

which is greater than the perfectly competitive price of zero but less than the cartel price of \$5. The profits for firms one and two are

$$\pi_1^* = TR_1 - 0$$
$$= (3.33)(3.33) = \$11.09,$$

and

$$\pi_2^* = TR_2 - 0$$
$$= (3.33)(3.33) = \$11.09,$$

respectively, yielding a total profit for the duopoly of

$$\pi_T = \pi_1^* + \pi_2^* = \$11.09 + \$11.09 = \$22.18.$$

This overall profit is greater than the perfectly competitive profit of zero but less than the cartel profit of \$25.

If we represent this duopoly by the Stackelberg model, where firm one acts as a leader and firm two acts as a follower, then we substitute the reaction function for firm two into the profit function for firm one yielding

$$\pi_1 = (10 - Q_1 - Q_2)Q_1$$
$$= 10Q_1 - Q_1^2 - Q_1Q_2$$
$$= 10Q_1 - Q_1^2 - Q_1\left(5 - \frac{1}{2}Q_1\right)$$
$$= 10Q_1 - Q_1^2 - 5Q_1 + \frac{1}{2}Q_1^2$$
$$= 5Q_1 - \frac{1}{2}Q_1^2,$$

and therefore

$$\frac{\partial \pi_1}{\partial Q_1} = 5 - Q_1 = 0,$$

or

$$Q_1^* = 5 \text{ units.}$$

Since firm two is a follower, we determine its level of output by substituting $Q_1^* = 5$ units into its reaction function and solving it as

$$Q_2^* = 5 - \frac{1}{2}(5) = 2.5 \text{ units.}$$

The total output for the duopoly in this case is

$$Q_T = Q_1^* + Q_2^* = 5 + 2.5 = 7.5 \text{ units,}$$

and the price of the good is

$$P^* = 10 - 5 - 2.5 = \$2.50.$$

The profit for firm one is

$$\pi_1^* = \$2.50(5) = \$12.50$$

and for firm two

$$\pi_2^* = \$2.50(2.5) = \$6.25,$$

yielding a total profit for the duopoly as

$$\pi_T = 12.50 + 6.25 = \$18.75,$$

which is less than the total profit for the Cournot case.

Another Stackelberg possibility is for firm two to act as a leader and firm one to act as a follower. In this situation, the roles of the two firms are reversed, compared to the model we developed above. As an exercise, it will be left to you to verify that the solution values in this case are $Q_2^* = 5$ units, $Q_1^* = 2.5$ units, $Q_T = 7.5$ units, $P^* = \$2.50$, $\pi_2^* = \$12.50$, $\pi_1^* = \$6.25$, and $\pi_T = \$18.75$.

The final possibility for the Stackelberg model is when both firms act as leaders. This situation leads to a Stackelberg disequilibrium, since both firms cannot truly maximize their profits simultaneously. Comparing the results associated with the leader–follower model above to those for the Cournot, or follower–follower, model presented earlier, we can observe that the consumer benefits more in the leader–follower case. Specifically, market output is greater, price is lower, and the combined profit for the duopoly is lower for the leader–follower case compared to the follower–follower situation. In general, we conclude that the more aggressive the rivalry, as with the leader–follower situation, the better are the results for consumers. Applying this line of reasoning, the leader–leader model, though a disequilibrium case, can provide the best results for consumers, with the extreme outcome yielding the same results as those corresponding for perfect competition. In the Stackelberg example, we demonstrated that if either of the firms acts as a leader, assuming the other is a follower, it sells 5 units of output. Thus, the market output, provided both firms behave in this manner, is

$$Q_T = Q_1^* + Q_2^* = 5 + 5 = 10 \text{ units,}$$

or the same amount sold in a perfectly competitive market. The price is

$$P^* = 10 - Q_T = 10 - 10 = \$0,$$

and the profit for each firm is also equal to zero since

$$\pi = TR = PQ = 0(Q) = \$0$$

for both firms.

CHAPTER 18

Applications of Game Theory to Oligopolistic Firm Behavior

18.1   INTRODUCTION

In our analysis of oligopoly in the previous chapter, we demonstrated the interdependent behavior of firms operating in this market structure. Recall that firms in this type of industry act strategically by considering the actions of other firms when making their own business decisions. This was clearly the case in the Cournot, cartel, and dominant firm models we developed in Chapter 17. Furthermore, some oligopolistic firms also consider the reactions of other firms to changes in their own strategic variables, as we demonstrated with the Stackelberg and Sweezy models. In this chapter we will continue our analysis of oligopoly using an alternative method of modeling the strategic behavior of firms, known as game theory.

Developed in the 1940s by John Von Neuman and Oskar Morgenstern, game theory is a mathematically based methodology for analyzing rational decision making under conditions of interdependent choiccs. It is applicable to virtually any situation characterized by strategic decision making. For example, we can use game theory to analyze the choices made by players in games of chance, ethical or personal decisions made by individuals, and strategic decisions made by oligopolistic firms.

One of the most commonly discussed games is known as the Prisoners' Dilemma. In this game two individuals, we'll call them Steve and Jan, are arrested for a crime they have committed together. They are placed in separate rooms by police authorities for questioning and are not allowed to communicate with one another. Each prisoner has two strategies available: confessing to the crime, thereby implicating the other person, or denying involvement. If only one prisoner confesses, that person will serve six months in prison, while the other will receive the maximum sentence of 20 years. If both confess, each will serve 10-year terms; however, if neither confesses, each will serve one year, on a technicality.

So what should the prisoners do? Let's examine this problem from Jan's perspective first. If she assumes that Steve will confess, then the best strategy for Jan is also to confess. By doing so, Jan will receive a 10-year sentence, half the amount of time she would have to serve if she chooses not to confess when Steve confesses. If Jan thinks Steve will not confess, then once again, she can minimize her time in jail by confessing. In such a situation, Jan will serve six months and Steve will get a 20-year sentence.

Now let's analyze this problem from Steve's perspective. If he thinks Jan will confess, then Steve's best strategy is also to confess. By doing so, he will be sentenced to 10 years, half the time he would have to serve if he does not confess when

Jan confesses. If Steve believes that Jan will not confess, he can minimize his time in jail by confessing and receiving a six-month sentence, while Jan will have to serve 20 years. Interestingly, in this game if Jan acts to minimize the amount of time she serves in jail, given Steve's possible choices, and Steve also acts to minimize the time he spends in jail, given Jan's possible choices, then both will confess to the crime. This will result in 10-year sentences for both Steve and Jan. However, if both can trust one another to not confess, then they will only serve one-year terms.

At this point, you may be asking yourself, "What does the Prisoners' Dilemma game have to do with economics?" In this chapter we will formulate games similar to the Prisoners' Dilemma in order to analyze the interdependent decision-making processes of firms. Just as Steve and Jan in the Prisoners' Dilemma game formulate their choices on the basis of which strategy will result in the shortest jail time, given the strategy chosen by the other prisoner, oligopolistic firms also make decisions based on the choices made by the other firms in the oligopoly. For example, a firm operating in an oligopoly may have to decide whether to change the price of its good, or change its production of output, on the basis of how the choices made by the other firms in the oligopoly affect its profit. In addition to the Prisoners' Dilemma, we will also use other concepts from game theory, such as dominant strategies, maximin and minimax strategies, as well as repeated and sequential games, to analyze the strategic decision-making behavior of firms operating in oligopolistic market structures.

18.2 ELEMENTS OF GAME THEORY

We will begin our analysis of game theory by defining this concept along with some of the terms we frequently use in this type of analysis. **Game theory** is a *mathematically based framework for modeling optimal decision making under conditions of strategic interactions among players in a game*, where a **game** is *any situation in which two or more participants, or players, directly compete to make optimal strategic decisions*. We can construct a game to model and predict the optimal choices for rational decision makers in virtually any situation that involves participants that interact strategically. Each game consists of three fundamental elements: the players, the strategies, or choices available to each of the players, and the payoffs associated with each combination of strategies chosen by the players in the game. The **players**, or participants, in a game are defined as *rational decision makers with the goal of selecting the strategy that yields the best payoff to the player, given the strategies available to the other players in the game*. The players may represent individuals, national or political entities, or, as will typically be the case in this chapter, competing firms. Since we can best apply game theory to oligopolistic market structures, the number of players, or firms, in the games we analyze will typically be limited to an oligopoly with two firms, also known as a duopoly.

A second element of a game are the **strategies**, collectively defined as *the set of all alternative choices available to all of the players in a game*. We assume that each player possesses perfect information regarding the alternative strategies it faces, as well as all of the possible strategies available to the other players in the game. However, a player typically will not know with certainty the strategy its opponent will select. For example, depending on the type of game, the strategies may include whether to raise, hold, or fold in a game of poker, whether to advance troops or retreat in war, or whether a firm engages in a particular business decision. Our primary interest is to apply game theory to firms operating in an oligopolistic market structure. Some specific examples of strategies facing such firms include whether to increase or decrease their level of output, whether to enter an industry, or whether to introduce a new product into the market. Any one of these strategies chosen by an oligopolistic firm could potentially affect the optimal business strategies chosen by other firms operating in the oligopoly.

The third and final element of game theory is the **payoff** that *measures the return a player in a game receives from selecting a particular strategy, contingent on the strategies chosen by the other players in the game.* Payoffs can be measured in a variety of ways, including utils that reflect the level of utility the player receives, or more commonly, in monetary units such as dollars. We will typically measure payoffs in dollars in the examples we present in this chapter. Specifically, the payoffs received by oligopolistic firms depicted in a game will generally reflect the amount of profit each firm receives from selecting a particular strategy, given the specific strategies chosen by the other firms participating in the game. Having formally defined the concept of game theory, as well as the essential elements of a game, we can now focus our attention on specific types of games and demonstrate how they can be applied to firms operating in an oligopolistic market structure.

18.3   DOMINANT STRATEGIES

The Prisoners' Dilemma situation we introduced earlier demonstrates the strategic decision-making processes of two criminals with game theory. Our primary focus in this chapter, however, is applying game theory to the interdependent decision-making processes of oligopolistic firms. Just as we assumed there were two players in the Prisoners' Dilemma game, we make the assumption in models of firm behavior we develop that there are two firms engaging in strategic decision making. We also assume that each firm faces two options, or strategies, where the payoffs associated with each of the possible strategy combinations in the game are known with certainty.

We can use game theory to analyze the behavior of firms in a cartel. Assume that there are two producers of a good, firm A and firm B, that agree to act as a monopoly and produce the combined level of output that maximizes their joint profit. Each firm knows its specific production allocation of the cartel's profit-maximizing level of output. We also assume that each firm in the cartel has identical costs of production. In this game each firm faces two possible strategies: abide by its production agreement or cheat on it. You may note that this problem closely resembles the Prisoners' Dilemma game. However, rather than choosing between confessing or not confessing to a crime, the players, or firms, in this game must choose between cheating or not cheating on their production agreements.

The payoffs associated with this cartel's game appear in Table 18.1. The two strategies available to firm A are stated beside the rows of the payoff table, while the two strategies available to firm B appear as column headings. Note that we have divided each cell in this payoff table by a diagonal line. The number appearing in the lower triangle of each cell refers to the profit firm A receives when it selects the strategy stated next to that particular row, given that firm B engages in the strategy listed above the column. For example, firm A receives $20,000 in profit if it cheats on its production agreement, given that firm B abides by the production agreement. Similarly, the number appearing in the upper triangle of each cell of the payoff table indicates the profit received by firm B when it selects the strategy listed above the column, given that firm A engages in the strategy listed beside the corresponding row.

Let's analyze this problem from firm A's perspective first. If firm A thinks firm B will abide by its production agreement, then firm A can earn more profit by cheating. Specifically, if firm B abides by its production agreement, firm A receives $20,000 in profit if it cheats, which is $5000 more than if it elected not to cheat. If firm A thinks firm B will cheat on its production agreement, then the best strategy for firm A to pursue is also to cheat on the production agreement. By doing so, firm A will earn $10,000 in profit. However, if firm A chooses to abide by the agreement when firm B cheats, then firm A will receive only $5000 in profit.

We can also analyze this game from firm B's perspective. If firm B thinks firm A will abide by its production agreement, then firm B can earn $5000 more in profit by cheating than by abiding by the production agreement. In such a situation, firm B will earn $20,000 in profit if it cheats but only $15,000 if it did not cheat. If firm B thinks firm A will cheat on the production agreement, then once again firm B will maximize its profit by also cheating. By doing so, firm B will receive $10,000 in profit rather than the $5000 it will receive if it did not cheat on the agreement when firm A had. We can

TABLE 18.1   Cartel Production Game with Dominant Strategies

| | | *Firm B's Strategies* | |
		Abide by Its Production Agreement	**Cheat on Its Production Agreement**
Firm A's Strategies	**Abide by Its Production Agreement**	$15,000 / $15,000	$20,000 / $5000
	Cheat on Its Production Agreement	$5000 / $20,000	$10,000 / $10,000

observe in the cartel payoff matrix in Table 18.1 that if each firm chose to cheat on the production agreement, the combined profit earned by the cartel would be $20,000, since each firm would receive $10,000 in profit. However, this is not the maximum amount of profit the cartel could earn. If each firm abided by the production agreement, then the cartel could earn $30,000 in profit, since each firm would receive $15,000 if both did not cheat. This is precisely the outcome we would expect, given our analysis of cartel behavior in Chapter 17. Recall that the firms comprising a cartel must collectively act as a monopolist and set their combined output where $MC = MR$ in order to maximize the cartel's profit. If these firms cheat on the production agreement, the cartel's output will no longer correspond to its profit-maximizing level.

In this game, regardless of the strategy firm B chooses, firm A always maximizes its profit if it cheats on the production agreement. We refer to firm A's strategy to cheat on the production agreement as a **dominant strategy**, defined as *a strategy that consistently optimizes a player's payoff in a game, regardless of the strategies chosen by the other players in the game*. Similarly, regardless of the strategy firm A chooses, firm B consistently maximizes its profit by cheating on the production agreement. Therefore, firm B's strategy to cheat on its production agreement is also a dominant strategy for this firm.

Game theory is also useful in analyzing the pricing strategies of two firms in an oligopoly, or duopoly.[1] Assume that the two firms are contemplating lowering the price of the homogeneous good they both produce. Thus, each firm has two strategies: lower the price of its good or don't lower the price. We will also assume that each firm knows with certainty the payoff, measured as profit, associated with each of its pricing strategies, given the strategy chosen by the other firm. These strategies and their associated payoffs are summarized in Table 18.2.

TABLE 18.2   Duopoly Pricing Game with Dominant Strategies

		Firm B's Strategies	
		Lower Price	**Don't Lower Price**
Firm A's Strategies	**Lower Price**	$30 \\ $30	$20 \\ $40
	Don't Lower Price	$50 \\ $10	$15 \\ $18

---

[1]This game is based on the well-known Bertrand model in which firms compete by setting their prices. Specifically, firms attempt to increase their sales by undercutting their rivals' prices.

We will assume that the goal of each firm is to choose the pricing strategy that maximizes its profit, given the strategy chosen by the other firm. Do the firms in this game have dominant strategies? To answer this question, let's first examine this game from firm A's perspective. If firm A believes that firm B will lower its price, then firm A will maximize its profit by also lowering its price. By doing so firm A will earn $30, or $20 more than if it did not lower its price when firm B lowered its price. However, if firm A thinks firm B will not lower its price, then firm A could earn $40 by lowering its price. This is more than twice the amount of profit it will earn if it did not lower the price of its good, given that firm B also did not lower its price. Since lowering the price of its good is the best, or profit-maximizing, strategy for firm A regardless of the strategy chosen by firm B, we can designate it as firm A's dominant strategy.

Now let's analyze this problem from firm B's perspective. If firm B assumes that firm A will lower its price, then firm B will earn more profit by lowering its price than by not lowering it. Specifically, if both firms lower their prices, each will receive $30 in profit. However, if firm B elects not to lower its price when firm A does, then firm B's profit will only be $20. If firm B assumes that firm A won't lower its price, then firm B will again choose to lower its price since this strategy earns firm B more profit than not lowering its price. Specifically, firm B earns $50 if it lowers its price when firm A does not. This is $35 more profit than if firm B chooses to not lower its price, given that firm A also chooses not to lower its price. This analysis indicates a dominant strategy in this game for firm B. In particular, firm B's dominant strategy is to lower its price, since it maximizes its profit by following this strategy, regardless of the strategy chosen by firm A. In a game such as this one, where each player has a dominant strategy, we can establish a unique equilibrium. Specifically, the equilibrium of a game characterized by dominant strategies describes the unique combination of strategies undertaken by all the players in the game. In this firm-pricing game, an equilibrium exists when both firms select the strategy to reduce the price of their good. The payoff received by each firm, $30 for firm A and $30 for firm B, when each follows its dominant strategy, represents the equilibrium value of this game.

18.4 NASH EQUILIBRIUM

Not all games are characterized exclusively by dominant strategies that clearly yield a unique equilibrium or set of optimal strategies for the players. In fact, in the real world we are far more likely to encounter strategic game situations where the optimal strategy chosen by one player varies depending on the strategies undertaken by the other players in the game. Such a situation is known as a **Nash equilibrium**, defined as *an outcome in a game where each player selects the strategy that optimizes its payoff, given the strategies chosen by the other players*. A Nash equilibrium relies on two important assumptions. First, each player acts rationally by selecting its optimal strategy, contingent on the strategies it believes the other players will choose, and second, each player's conjectures regarding the strategies the other players choose are correct.

As an example of a Nash equilibrium, we should recall the Cournot duopoly model we developed and analyzed with a numerical example in the appendix to Chapter 17. Using static analysis, we demonstrated that each firm in a Cournot model determines its own optimal level of output simultaneously by taking the output level of the other firm in the oligopoly as fixed. As a result, once equilibrium is established, neither firm has the incentive to deviate from its chosen level of output, since each firm is maximizing its profit given the production decisions made by its rivals. Therefore, the equilibrium output associated with the Cournot model also constitutes a Nash equilibrium. The Prisoners' Dilemma game is also characterized by a Nash equilibrium. In that game, Steve's best strategy is not to confess, regardless of the strategy Jan chooses. Similarly, Jan's best strategy is not to confess regardless of the strategy Steve chooses. Earlier, we stated that both of the prisoners' optimal choices are dominant strategies. We can now also identify a game possessing dominant strategies, such as the Prisoners' Dilemma game, as a special case of a Nash equilibrium.

Not all games possess a Nash equilibrium. Thus, for such games there does not exist a set of strategies that represent the best strategy for each player, contingent on the strategies chosen by the other players. For example, consider the game depicted in Table 18.3 where two automobile manufacturers, firm T and firm H, are considering whether to add a sport utility vehicle (SUV) to their product lines. For the sake of simplicity, we will assume that the two firms incur no sunk costs when producing an SUV, thus making it easy for them to add this type of vehicle to their product lines. Upon analyzing the payoff data for this game in Table 18.3, it is clear to us that if firm T chooses to introduce an SUV, then firm H will maximize its profit by also adding an SUV to its product line. However, this combination of strategies will not constitute a Nash equilibrium, since if firm H elects to introduce an SUV, then firm T's optimal

TABLE 18.3 Duopoly Game Without a Nash Equilibrium

		Firm H's Strategies	
		S_1^H **Introduce Sport Utility Vehicle**	S_2^H **Don't Introduce Sport Utility Vehicle**
Firm T's Strategies	S_1^T **Introduce Sport Utility Vehicle**	$h_{11} =$ $2.5 million / $t_{11} =$ $2 million	$h_{12} =$ $1 million / $t_{12} =$ $3 million
	S_2^T **Don't Introduce Sport Utility Vehicle**	$h_{21} =$ $2 million / $t_{21} =$ $3 million	$h_{22} =$ $3 million / $t_{22} =$ $1 million

strategy will be to not introduce an SUV. Specifically, firm H's profit will be $3 million rather than $2 million if it also chooses to introduce an SUV when firm T follows the same business strategy. Similarly, if firm T chooses not to introduce an SUV, then firm H will earn a maximum profit of $3 million by also not introducing an SUV. Once again, this outcome does not constitute a Nash equilibrium since if firm H chooses not to add an SUV to its product line, then firm T will want to switch its strategy to introduce an SUV in order to maximize its profit of $3 million. We can see that the players in this game will end up in an infinite loop. They will continuously cycle around the set of possible strategies and never achieve a stable equilibrium combination of strategies. There is, however, a way to determine a stable equilibrium solution to this game using a technique known as mixed strategies. We will develop the concept of mixed strategies and apply it to this SUV game, in the appendix to this chapter, 18A: Mixed Strategies.

18.5 MAXIMIN AND MINIMAX STRATEGIES

Our previous analysis of a Nash equilibrium was based on the assumption that all players in a game act rationally. In the real world, however, one or more players in a game may act irrationally either intentionally or by mistake. This type of behavior can be detrimental to those players who choose their strategies on the false assumption that their rivals are also selecting strategies rationally. It is possible for us to develop strategy selection processes that minimize the risk a player faces if it is not certain that its rivals in a game are acting rationally. Specifically, a **maximin strategy** is *a strategy that maximizes the minimum gain that a player can earn in a game*. A maximin strategy is a cautious or risk-averse approach to a game. Specifically, a player following a maximin strategy selects the strategy that maximizes the minimum gain possible among all the choices available to the player.

We can demonstrate the conservative maximin approach using a game that involves two firms, firm A and firm B, which are the sole producers of a good. In this game each firm must decide on the manner in which it will advertise its product. The firms are faced with two alternative advertising strategies. Specifically, the firms must choose to follow either an aggressive advertising strategy or a limited advertising strategy. The payoffs received by the firms in this game are measured in terms of market share. Since firms A and B generate the total supply of this good in the market, then the market share collectively held by these two firms must be the constant sum of 100 percent. Therefore, this game also represents an example of a **constant sum game**, or *a game for which the sum of the payoffs to all players in the game is a constant value for all possible strategy combinations*. The firms in this game are in direct competition with one another, since any gain in market share by one firm represents a loss in market share by the other firm.

In Table 18.4 we have presented the payoffs corresponding to all of the possible strategy combinations for firm A and firm B. Specifically, we have listed the two strategies available to firm A, Aggressive Advertising, and Limited Advertising, beside the

TABLE 18.4 Constant Sum Game Using Maximin and Minimax Strategies

		Firm B's Strategies		Minimum of Firm A's Row Gains
		Aggressive Advertising	**Limited Advertising**	
Firm A's Strategies	**Aggressive Advertising**	55	95	55 (Maximum)
	Limited Advertising	5	10	5
Maximum of Firm B's Column Losses		55 (Minimum)	95	

rows of the table, while the two advertising strategies for firm B, Aggressive Advertising and Limited Advertising, serve as column headings. Each cell in the table, or payoff matrix, contains a single entry. In the case of constant sum games, we typically express the payoff matrix in terms of the gains received by the player whose strategies are listed next to the rows of the table, or alternatively as the losses incurred by the other player whose strategies are stated above the columns of the table. For example, referring once again to Table 18.4, if firm A chooses to follow an aggressive advertising strategy, it would claim 55 percent of the market, provided firm B simultaneously pursues an aggressive advertising strategy. Alternatively stated, firm B will lose 55 percent of the market to firm A if firm B chooses an aggressive advertising strategy when firm A chooses the same type of advertising strategy. If, however, firm A chooses to advertise its product in a limited manner while firm B chooses to advertise its product aggressively, then firm A will claim only 5 percent of the market, thereby leaving 100% − 5% = 95% of the market for firm B. It should now be very clear to you that in this constant sum game, the constant sum that is redistributed between the two players as they choose alternative strategies is 100, which reflects 100 percent of the market share for the product both firms are selling.

We begin our analysis by examining this game from firm A's perspective, where we assume that firm A follows a maximin strategy. If firm A chooses to pursue an aggressive advertising strategy and firm B also follows an aggressive advertising strategy, then firm A will capture 55 percent of the market share. However, if firm A selects an aggressive advertising policy, when firm B engages in only limited advertising of its product, then firm A will gain 95 percent of the market. Therefore, the minimum payoff firm A will receive if it follows an aggressive advertising strategy is a 55 percent market share. Alternatively, if firm A chooses to follow a limited advertising strategy when firm B advertises aggressively, then firm A will only capture 5 percent of the market. However, if both firms follow their limited advertising strategies, then firm A will capture only 10 percent of the market share while firm B receives 90 percent of the market. Thus, the minimum payoff firm A will receive if it follows a limited advertising strategy is a 5 percent market share.

We can now demonstrate how firm A determines its advertising policy using a maximum strategy. Since firm A does not know a priori the particular advertising strategy firm B will pursue, then firm A will choose the strategy that maximizes the minimum payoff it can possibly receive. In the column to the right of the payoff matrix in Table 18.4, we have indicated the minimum payoffs firm A will receive for each of its alternative advertising strategies. These payoffs include a 55 percent market share if firm A pursues an aggressive advertising strategy and a 5 percent market share if it advertises its product in a limited manner. Thus, the maximum of these minimum payoffs firm A can possibly receive if it follows a conservative maximin strategy is a 55 percent market share, given that both firm A and firm B adopt aggressive advertising campaigns.

Now let's determine the strategy firm B will follow. Recall that the payoff matrix in Table 18.4 reflects the losses in market share by firm B for each of the alternative strategy combinations chosen by the two firms. In this game, firm B will follow a **minimax strategy** defined as *a strategy that minimizes the maximum loss that a player can earn in a game*. Like the maximin strategy that firm A follows, the minimax strategy is a risk-averse approach to a game. Referring to the payoff matrix in Table 18.4, we can observe that if firm B selects an aggressive advertising strategy and firm A does the same, then firm B will relinquish 55 percent of the market to firm A. However, if firm B follows an aggressive advertising strategy while firm A advertises in a limited manner, then firm B will only lose 5 percent of the market to firm A. Therefore, the maximum loss in market share that firm B can possibly experience if it chooses to follow an aggressive advertising strategy is 55 percent. Alternatively, if firm B chooses to advertise its product in a limited manner, while firm A pursues an aggressive advertising strategy, then firm B will lose 95 percent of the market to firm A. Finally, if both firms follow limited advertising strategies, firm B will lose just 10 percent of the market to firm A.

Inasmuch as firm B has no way of knowing which strategy firm A will select, coupled with firm B's risk-averse nature, firm B will choose the strategy that minimizes the maximum losses it can possibly experience. In the row beneath the payoff matrix in Table 18.4, we have indicated the values of the maximum losses firm B will incur for each of its possible advertising strategies, given the advertising strategy chosen by firm A. Specifically, firm B will experience a 55 percent loss in market share if it follows an aggressive advertising strategy, or a 95 percent loss in market share if it engages in a limited advertising strategy. Thus, the minimum loss in market share that firm B can possibly experience if it follows a risk-averse strategy will be the 55 percent loss it will incur if both firms A and B follow aggressive advertising strategies.

In this particular game, the optimal risk-minimizing strategies for the two firms are identical. Specifically, firm A will choose to pursue an aggressive advertising strategy and as a result capture 55 percent of the market. Firm B's risk-minimizing strategy, also an aggressive advertising strategy, results in a 55 percent loss in market share to firm A, or alternatively stated, a 45 percent market share for firm B. This equilibrium situation is known as a **saddle point**, or *a solution to a game in which players follow maximin and minimax strategies and no player has an incentive to change its strategy, given the strategies chosen by each of the other players in the game.* This outcome also represents a stable, Nash equilibrium since the strategies chosen by the firms are optimal given the firms' risk-averse nature. It is important for us to note that not all games possess an equilibrium solution. In the following section we will investigate this type of game.

18.6 REPEATED AND SEQUENTIAL GAMES

Our analysis of game theory to this point has focused on single-stage games in which players choose their strategies on the basis of a single round of play. However, often many firms' decisions are repeatedly made in direct response to the choices made by their rivals in a previous decision period. We can model this type of firm behavior using a **repeated game**, or *a game that is played over and over again, where each player has complete knowledge of the strategies previously chosen by each of its rivals.* We can further categorize repeated games on the basis of how often they are repeated. Specifically, if a game is repeated a finite number of times, thus indicating that it has a fixed end, then it is known as a finitely repeated game. In such a game, we compute its payoff simply by summing the payoffs accruing to each player at each stage of the game. By contrast, if a game has no end, we refer to it as an infinitely repeated game, where we typically compute its payoff as the sum of the discounted expected payoffs associated with the infinite stages of the game. In the analysis that follows, we will assume, for the sake of clarity, that the repeated games have a definite endpoint.

We can once again model the behavior of two firms operating within a cartel. This time, however, we will do so using a finitely repeated game. Recall that in the case of a cartel, the firms act collusively to determine the profit-maximizing level of output for the cartel, and afterward they allocate this production among its members. However, individual cartel members typically have an incentive to cheat on their production quotas. Recall from our earlier analysis of a cartel using game theory that cheating on the production agreement in a single-stage game results in even higher profits for a single firm, assuming that the other cartel member abides by its output quota. However, by analyzing the firms' strategic choices from the perspective of a repeated game, we can show that cooperation among the firms comprising a cartel is a better strategy than cheating.

This result follows from the fact that in a repeated game, if one firm chooses to cheat on its agreed production quota, in subsequent stages of the game its rivals can retaliate by also cheating on their quotas and so reduce the amount of profit received by the firm that initially cheated in the cartel. Conversely, if this firm initially chooses to abide by its output quota rather than cheat, then this obedient behavior will be rewarded by the other firms which will also choose to abide by their production quotas in the subsequent rounds of the game. This behavior, known as **tit-for-tat**, is *a strategy in which players in a repeated game immediately reward their rivals for cooperative behavior or penalize them for noncooperative behavior in the subsequent round of the game.* We can more simply, and personally, express the tit-for-tat strategy as: if you don't cheat in this round of the game, then I won't cheat in the next round; however, if you cheat in this round, then I will cheat in the next round. The tit-for-tat strategy, though simplistic, is quite effective and is often employed by oligopolistic firms in the real world. This strategy was found to be more effective than many others examined in computer simulations of infinitely repeated games by Robert Axelrod.[2] However, in a finitely repeated game, the tit-for-tat strategy loses its effectiveness as the game approaches its final stages. At that time it becomes advantageous for players to cheat, since the negative impacts of cheating will be short lived.

We can easily demonstrate the concepts of a repeated game and the tit-for-tat strategy for the game depicted in Table 18.5. In this game we assume that two firms, firm one and firm two, have initially entered on a cooperative production agreement designed to maximize the combined profits of the two firms comprising the cartel. Once the production agreement is in place, however, each firm must choose on a monthly basis whether to abide by the agreement or cheat on its production quota. We also assume that the two firms make their decisions simultaneously and that neither firm possesses any prior information as to the strategy its rival will select that month. In this game, the payoffs are measured as profit. The payoffs corresponding to each of the possible strategy combinations appear in Table 18.5. Note that the payoffs given in the lower and upper triangles of each cell of the payoff matrix indicate the profits received by firm one and firm two, respectively. If we assume that both firms initially abide by their production quotas, each firm receives $50,000 in profit, thus yielding a maximum profit of $100,000 for the cartel.

TABLE 18.5 Repeated Game for a Cartel

	Firm Two's Strategies	
	Abide by Its Production Quota	**Cheat on Its Production Quota**
Abide by Its Production Quota	$50,000 \ $50,000	$70,000 \ $−5000
Cheat on Its Production Quota	$−5000 \ $70,000	$10,000 \ $10,000

Firm One's Strategies

[2]Robert Axelrod, *The Evolution of Cooperation* (New York: Basic Books, 1984).

If one firm cheats on its production quota, however, while the other firm abides by the original production agreement, the cheating firm will significantly increase its profit. In light of this information, assume that in the following month both firms once again simultaneously choose a strategy to follow for the next 30 days. Assume that firm one chooses to cheat on its production quota, while firm two abides by its original production agreement. As a result, firm one will increase its monthly profit from $50,000 to $70,000. However, firm two will incur a loss of $5000, thereby reducing the combined profit for the cartel from $100,000 to $70,000 + $–5000 = $65,000 for that month.

Upon learning of its rival's cheating on the production agreement, firm two will logically retaliate by also cheating on its production quota in its next round of the game. Specifically, this tit-for-tat strategy takes place during the third stage of the game, when both firms opt to cheat on their production quotas, thereby reducing the profit firm one receives to $10,000 and raising firm two's payoff from $–5000 to $10,000. The vast reduction in firm one's profit from $70,000 to $10,000 may be enough incentive to convince it to change its strategy from cheating to abiding by its original production quota. If we assume that firm two's tit-for-tat strategy succeeds in reestablishing cooperation between the two firms, at stage four of this repeated game both firms will return to abiding by their original production agreements. This will increase the cartel's profit to $100,000, since each firm will receive $50,000. Thus, if each firm perceives the tit-for-tat strategy as a credible threat, then the rational strategy for each firm is to abide by its original production quota. This strategy combination will remain effective until the firms approach the end of the repeated game. At that time, cheating will once again become a viable strategy, since the possibility of retaliation in subsequent rounds by either firm is very limited.

Another type of game that we can apply to oligopolistic firm behavior is a **sequential game**, defined as *a game in which the order of the players' participation is prespecified prior to the start of the game.* Thus, in a sequential game we dismiss the assumption of simultaneous selection of strategies by players, which we used in repeated games. Sequential games are highly applicable to oligopolistic behavior since these firms often select their business strategies in response to the strategies chosen by their rivals. We can analyze the Stackelberg duopoly model, which we previously developed in Section 17.3.3 and the appendix to Chapter 17, within the framework of a sequential game. Recall that in the Stackelberg model each firm must choose between acting as a leader in setting its level of output or as a follower by determining its level of production in response to the amount of output produced by its rival. Therefore, we must analyze four possible outcomes: both firms acting as followers; both acting as leaders; firm one acting as a follower and firm two acting as a leader; and firm one acting as a leader and firm two acting as a follower. The payoffs, or profit, associated with each of these four strategy combinations, and the level of output produced by each firm, appear in the payoff matrix in Table 18.6.

In our previous analysis of the Stackelberg model in Chapter 17, we did not prespecify the order of firm participation, since the firms simultaneously selected their

TABLE 18.6   Summary of Outcomes from Stackelberg Model Numerical Example

		Firm Two's Strategies	
		Act as Follower	**Act as Leader**
Act as Follower	$11.09 $Q_1 = 3.33$ units	$11.09 $Q_2 = 3.33$ units	$12.50 $Q_2 = 5$ units $6.25 $Q_1 = 2.50$ units
Act as Leader	$12.50 $Q_1 = 5$ units	$6.25 $Q_2 = 2.50$ units	$0 $Q_2 = 5$ units $0 $Q_1 = 5$ units

strategies. Therefore, if firm one chooses to be a leader and firm two also elects to pursue a leader strategy, both firms will earn zero profit. This result, though the best outcome for consumers since the level of output produced is greatest as compared with that generated in any of the other three strategy combinations, is the worst possible combined outcome from the firms' perspective. Each firm will earn more profit if either selectes a different strategy. Therefore, if subsequent moves are allowed, the leader-leader strategy combination will not constitute a stable equilibrium because each firm has a very strong incentive to deviate from its leader strategy in order to increase its profit.

We can also demonstrate that the leader–leader outcome does not constitute a Nash equilibrium either. Referring to the payoffs in Table 18.6, we can observe that if firm one knows that firm two is going to adopt a leader strategy, then firm one will receive a maximum profit of $6.25 by choosing a follower strategy. Similarly, if firm two knows that firm one will choose a leader strategy, then firm two will also maximize its profit at $6.25 by selecting a follower strategy. Therefore, if either firm knows that its rival is choosing a leader strategy, the other profit-maximizing firm will never subsequently also adopt a leader strategy.

The follower–follower strategy combination is also unstable, since each firm can increase its profit from $11.09 to as much as $12.50 by choosing a different strategy. Specifically, if firm one has advance knowledge that firm two will choose a follower strategy, then firm one will maximize its profit and receive $12.50 by selecting a leader strategy. Similarly, if firm two knows that firm one will choose a follower strategy, then firm two will also earn a maximum profit of $12.50 by selecting a leader strategy. Both the follower–leader and the leader–follower strategy combinations constitute Nash equilibrium situations, since neither firm can increase its profit by changing its strategy.

Using a sequential game, we can determine that if firm one moves first by selecting its leader strategy, then the optimal strategy for firm two in response to firm one's choice is to be a follower. Given the choice of leader by firm one, firm two will receive a higher payoff of $6.25 if it chooses to be a follower than if it chooses to be a leader and earn a payoff of $0. As a result, in this case, if firm one moves first and chooses to be a leader, and firm two subsequently elects to be a follower, then firm one will receive a profit of $12.50, while firm two will only receive $6.25 in profit. Moreover, this sequence of strategies represents a stable Nash equilibrium since once firm one chooses its leader strategy, firm two has chosen its best, or profit-maximizing, strategy of follower. Since this set of strategy choices also results in a profit maximum for firm one, neither firm possesses an incentive to change its strategy.

If we reverse the order of strategy selection in the game and firm two first chooses its strategy, that of leader, then the best possible strategy for firm one to subsequently select is that of follower. Referring once again to the payoffs listed in Table 18.6, we can confirm that, given the choice of leader by firm two, firm one will receive a higher profit, $6.25, by choosing to be a follower than by choosing to be a leader and earning a profit of $0. The combination of sequential strategies of leader for firm two and follower for firm one results in $12.50 in profit for firm two and $6.25 profit for firm one. Once again, this strategy combination constitutes a stable, Nash equilibrium since once firm two has chosen its leader strategy, firm one responds by choosing its own profit-maximizing strategy of follower. Since this set of strategy choices also results in a profit maximum for firm two, neither firm has any incentive to deviate from its chosen strategy.

The order of play by the two firms participating in this game dictates which firm earns the greater profit. Specifically, the higher profit is consistently earned by the player, or in this case the firm, that selects its strategy first. This phenomenon, known as the first mover's advantage, occurs in many sequential games, since only the player making the first move has the ability to freely select a strategy that optimizes its payoff, without facing the constraints imposed by the strategy choices previously made by its rivals. Therefore, although the player that moves first does take into consideration the possible reactions of its competitors when selecting its strategy, unlike the players who follow, it is not forced to pursue a particular strategy due to the choices made by others.

The phenomenon of a first mover's advantage is abundantly evident in oligopolistic markets. For example, when a firm establishes itself as a leader in an industry by being the first to introduce a new product or technology, new firms that attempt to enter the market at a later time with their versions of a similar product may find it difficult to compete with the incumbent firm for market share. This was the case in the computer operating systems software industry when Microsoft introduced its DOS software. Because of Microsoft's first mover's advantage, DOS became the business computing operating system standard, thus making it extremely difficult for other operating system manufacturers to enter this market. Similarly, in the online auction market eBay has a first mover's advantage. Newer entrants into the online auction industry find it very difficult to compete with eBay because, logically, online auction buyers want to go where the most sellers are, and sellers want to post their goods

Evidence of Sequential Strategies in the Potato Chip Industry

In the United States, the $5.2 billion potato chip industry is an oligopoly, dominated by a single producer. The nationally known snack food producer, Frito-Lay, with its familiar potato chip brands of Lay's and Ruffles, stands as the dominant firm in this industry, and in many areas of the United States it faces little competition from regional potato chip producers. For example, west of the Rocky Mountains, only two regional potato chip companies compete with Frito-Lay's potato chips. However, in Pennsylvania the market for potato chips is considerably different. Six regional potato chip manufacturers are located in the southeastern part of the state, aptly known as the Potato Chip Belt. Twenty other smaller firms produce potato chips for their local market areas, all contributing to Pennsylvania's status as the number-one producer of potato chips in the United States, followed by Texas, the home-base of Frito-Lay, and California.[3]

The ability of so many small potato chip firms to successfully compete with such a dominant player in the United States potato chip oligopoly is a testament to their ability to develop and employ effective strategies in response to the business decisions made by Frito-Lay. For example, when Frito-Lay offers coupons or temporary reductions in the prices of its chips, the smaller, regional potato chip producers respond to the market leader, Frito-Lay, by reducing the prices of their chips. In addition, these smaller firms have reacted in a similar manner to the introduction of new products by Frito-Lay, such as low-fat baked potato chips, by offering their own renditions of these new snack foods.

We can describe the behavior of the firms comprising the potato chip oligopoly as a sequential game. Recall that in a sequential game the order of the players' participation is known prior to the start of the game. In this case, it is clear that the dominant player in the game is Frito-Lay. It acts as the leader; therefore, we would logically expect it to be the first firm to set forth a new business strategy regarding, for example, the pricing of its chips in a particular regional market or the introduction of a new variety of chips. Afterward, the other, smaller firms in the industry must each select an optimal strategy on the basis of the strategy chosen by the dominant firm. As a result, Frito-Lay is capable of maintaining its dominant firm position partly through its first mover's advantage, which enables it to freely choose a strategy that maximizes its profit without facing any constraints imposed by the strategies chosen by any of its rivals. Furthermore, given the declining trend in the number of potato chip plants in the United States, dropping from 400 in 1960 to 119 in 1997 (see accompanying table), it is expected that the ever increasing degree of consolidation in this oligopoly will enable Frito-Lay to become an even more formidable player in the potato chip industry in the future.

Year	Number of Potato Chip Plants in U.S.
1960	400
1965	342
1970	278
1975	213
1980	175
1985	156
1989	155
1996	122
1997	119

[3]Bob Fernandez, "Pa. Tops in Chips? It's in the Bag," *The Philadelphia Inquirer*, June 6, 1999, p. D-1.

Source: U.S. Department of Agriculture.

where the most buyers are online. In addition, new firms attempting to enter a market may find it difficult to compete with well-established brands. For example, new entrants into the sports drink market find competing with the well-known brand Gatorade difficult.

Although we have covered numerous topics relating to game theory in this chapter, our analysis is by no means exhaustive. Indeed, entire texts are devoted to game theory and its various applications to economic analysis, as well as other fields of study. However, we must point out that despite the various economic applications of game theory to firm behavior, researchers have yet to develop a generalized theory of oligopoly based on game theory. This may be because game theory models require a substantial amount of specific information regarding strategies, payoffs, and probabilities, which may not be available to all firms in a market. It will be interesting to see if further research in the area of game theory yields a comprehensive theory capable of consistently predicting oligopolistic firm behavior.

REAL-WORLD APPLICATION 18.2

Game Theory Taken a Bit Too Far

In their seemingly unrelenting quest to demonstrate the applicability of economic theory in the real world, some economists will even risk public chiding, as this article, which appeared in the British news weekly *The Economist*,[4] clearly demonstrates.

Economists, like football [i.e., soccer] pundits, are renowned for stating the obvious. So economic analysis of soccer seems pointless. Yet a new study applies "game theory" to football, with interesting results.

True, many of its conclusions will come as no surprise. The authors, Frederic Palomino, Luca Rigotti and Aldo Rustichini of Tilburg University in the Netherlands, "can only confirm the widespread opinion that . . . the skills of the two teams are a key component . . . in explaining the game of soccer". They also find that "teams react rationally to . . . changes in the current score" by attacking more when

they are losing, for instance. But it also finds behaviour "which is difficult to characterise as rational". The best example is that teams perform better at home than they do away.

Chuckles aside, the importance of "irrationality" in football seems greater than even most fans would claim. Skill (as measured by a team's scoring average and defensive strength for the season) has less effect on the likelihood of a team scoring than emotion (playing at home). According to data from 2,885 matches in Italy, England and Spain, a bad team playing at home is more likely to score than a good one playing away.

For economists, the research suggests that emotion and strategy interact in more complicated ways than they usually assume. For football fans, it provides support for many of their prejudices. Italian teams, for instance, are more likely to settle for a one-nil win than Spanish ones. It may also help explain the success of Arsene Wenger, Arsenal's manager, who led his team to the English "double" of both cup and championship last season. He happens to be an economics graduate.

---

[4]"The Invisible Foot," *The Economist*, April 3, 1999, pp. 62–63.

18.7 SUMMARY

In this chapter, we presented the topic of game theory and applied it to various situations characterized by interdependent decision making by the players in games. Our primary focus was on using game theory to model the strategic decision-making processes of oligopolistic firms. The main concepts we discussed in this chapter are as follows.

- Game theory is a mathematically based framework for modeling optimal decision making under conditions of strategic interactions among players in a game, where the term *game* refers to any situation in which two or more participants, or players, directly compete to make optimal strategic decisions.
- A dominant strategy is one that consistently optimizes a player's payoff in a game, regardless of the strategies chosen by the other players in the game.
- A Nash equilibrium exists in a game when each player selects the strategy that optimizes its payoff, given the strategies chosen by the other players. However, not all games possess a Nash equilibrium.
- In a constant sum game, the sum of the payoffs to all players is a constant value.
- A repeated game is played over and over again, where each player has complete knowledge of the strategies previously chosen by its rivals.
- In a repeated game, players can employ a strategy known as tit-for-tat whereby they reward their rivals for cooperative behavior or penalize them for noncooperative behavior in the subsequent round of the game.
- In a sequential game, the order of the players' participation is prespecified prior to the start of the game.

KEY TERMS

- constant sum game, page 482
- dominant strategy, page 479
- expected value, page 496
- game, page 476
- game theory, page 476
- maximin strategy, page 482
- minimax strategy, page 484
- mixed strategies, page 495
- Nash equilibrium, page 480
- payoff, page 477
- players, page 476
- repeated game, page 485
- risk, page 496
- saddle point, page 485
- sequential game, page 487
- strategies, page 476
- tit-for-tat, page 486
- uncertainty, page 496

EXERCISES

18.1 Using the payoff data for the game depicted in the following table, determine if either player possesses a dominant strategy in this game. If so, determine the value of the payoff of the game to each player.

Player B's Strategies

	S_1^B	S_2^B
S_1^A	$100 \diagdown $100	$60 \diagdown $120
S_2^A	$150 \diagdown $30	$45 \diagdown $55

Player A's Strategies

18.2 Using the information provided in Section 18.1 regarding the Prisoners' Dilemma game, construct the payoff matrix and determine the optimal strategy for each prisoner.

18.3 Distinguish between a repeated game and a sequential game. Provide an appropriate real-world application of each type of game.

18.4 What is a Nash equilibrium? Does the Prisoners' Dilemma game in Section 18.1 possess a Nash equilibrium? If so, what is it? Does the price-cutting game in Table 18.2 possess a Nash equilibrium? If so, what is it?

18.5 Under what conditions would a player in a game use a tit-for-tat strategy? Provide a real-world example of such a situation.

18.6 Firm G and firm H are the sole producers of a special jet engine. If neither firm reduces the price of its jet engines, each will earn $36,000 in profit. If both firms reduce their prices, each will earn $10,000 in profit. If one firm reduces the price of its jet engines while the other firm does not, then the firm that reduces its price will earn $50,000 in profit while the other firm will earn $5000 in profit.
   a. Construct the payoff matrix for this game.
   b. Determine the pricing strategy that firm G will follow if it acts rationally.
   c. Determine the pricing strategy that firm H will follow if it acts rationally.
   d. Is the solution to this game a Nash equilibrium?

18.7 Firm D and firm Z have decided to operate collusively as a cartel. If both firms abide by the cartel's production agreement, each will earn $100,000 in profit. If both firms cheat on their production agreement, then each firm will earn $25,000 in profit. If one firm cheats on its production agreement while the other firm abides by the production agreement, the firm that cheats will earn $150,000 in profit while the firm that does not cheat will earn $12,5000 in losses.
   a. Construct the payoff matrix for this game.
   b. Assume the firms are playing a repeated game in which firm D moves first. Determine the strategy choices of each firm for the first four rounds of the game.
   c. Does this game possess a stable equilibrium solution?

†18.8 Solve the game depicted in the following table using mixed strategies. Specifically, determine the probabilities at which firm A and firm B will select each of their strategies, or P_1^A, P_2^A, P_1^B, and P_2^B. Also determine the associated expected value of each firm's payoffs.

Firm B's Strategies

		S_1^B		S_2^B	
S_1^A	$5000	$2500	$0	$0	
S_2^A	$0	$0	$2500	$5000	

Firm A's Strategies

Appendix

18A   MIXED STRATEGIES

The method of mixed strategies is built on the assumption that no player in a game without dominant strategies knows a priori the strategies its opponents will choose. Therefore, a rational player attempts to formulate a random strategy selection process that makes him indifferent to the strategies that his opponents choose. Formally, **mixed strategies** is *a process that requires a player to select each of his strategies a particular percentage of the time so that the player's payoffs are equal regardless of the strategies chosen by his rivals.* This process involves the assignment of a probability value, denoted P_i, where $0 \leq P_i \leq 1, i = 1, 2, 3, \ldots, N$, to each player's feasible strategies, S_i, where $i = 1, 2, 3, \ldots, N$, such that the sum of these probabilities is equal to one or, $\sum_{i=1}^{N} P_i = 1.0$. Note that the sum of the probabilities must equal 1.0, since S_i includes all possible strategies for a player.

For example, if a game has two players, A and B, each facing two strategies, 1 and 2, we can denote the strategies available to player A as S_i^A, where $i = 1, 2$, while S_j^B, where $j = 1, 2$, refers to the strategies faced by player B. Associated with each of the possible combinations of strategies for the two players is a payoff value. In general, we denote these payoff values as a_{ij}

and b_{ij} for players A and B, respectively, where once again, the subscript $i = 1, 2$ indicates the number of the strategy chosen by player A and the subscript $j = 1, 2$ refers to the number of the strategy chosen by player B.

When the players in a game use mixed strategies, each determines the probabilities associated with his strategies so that the expected value of the payoff to the player from any of his strategies is equal, regardless of the strategies chosen by the other players in the game. In addition, mixed strategies make it difficult for rivals to accurately predict a player's strategy, and thus reduces their ability to benefit from knowing in advance the strategy a player will follow.

To help you better understand the concept of mixed strategies, as well as the process by which a player determines the probabilities associated with his strategies, we will first present a generalized mixed strategies game followed by a numerical example. Consider the two-player game depicted in Table 18A.1. In this game, we assume that each player faces two possible strategies. Specifically, player A chooses between strategy 1 and strategy 2, denoted respectively as S_1^A and S_2^A, while player B selects either strategy 1 or strategy 2, denoted

TABLE 18A.1   Payoff Matrix for a Generalized Mixed Strategies Game

		Player B's Strategies	
		S_1^B	S_2^B
Player A's Strategies	S_1^A	b_{11} / a_{11}	b_{12} / a_{12}
	S_2^A	b_{21} / a_{21}	b_{22} / a_{22}

S_1^B and S_2^B, respectively. We denote the payoff values associated with each of the possible strategy combinations as a_{ij} and b_{ij} for players A and B, respectively. In this case, $i = 1, 2$ and $j = 1, 2$ since each player possesses two possible strategies. Therefore, the value of the payoff player A receives when he chooses strategy 1, given that player B also chooses strategy 1, is denoted as a_{11}, while the payoff player A receives if he selects strategy 2 while player B chooses strategy 1 is denoted as a_{21}. Similarly, from player B's perspective, the value of the payoff he receives, if he selects strategy 1 when player A also selects strategy 1, is denoted as b_{11} and the value of the payoff to player B when he selects strategy 2 while player A chooses strategy 1 is denoted as b_{12}. The other four entries appearing in the payoff matrix in Table 18A.1—a_{21}, a_{22}, b_{21}, and b_{22}—represent the payoff values associated with the remaining possible combinations of strategies facing the two players.

Earlier, we stated that the method of mixed strategies is based on the assumption that the players do not know which strategies their rivals will choose. Therefore, from any player's perspective, there initially exists **uncertainty**, defined as *a situation in which a decision maker does not possess perfect information or any probabilities associated with the occurrence of a specific outcome.* However, when a player uses mixed strategies, he assigns probabilities to each of his possible strategies so that the expected values of his payoffs are equal, regardless of the strategies chosen by his rivals. By doing so, the player is no longer functioning in a state of uncertainty. Rather, it is operating in a situation of **risk**, or *a situation that exists when perfect information is unavailable to a decision-maker; however, the probabilities associated with all outcomes are known.* Therefore, it is important for you to possess at least an elementary understanding of probability theory in order to comprehend the concept of risk and its relationship to mixed strategies.

Recall from statistics that the probability associated with an event is simply a measure of the likelihood of the occurrence of a particular outcome. In some instances, we objectively know the values of these probabilities, since they are based on long-term historical experience. For example, we would objectively know that the probability of rolling a three on a single die is 1/6, since the probability of any value coming to the surface is equal to one out of the six unique values represented on the die. However, sometimes we cannot determine the probability of an outcome from past experience. In such a case we must deduce a subjective probability, simply our best estimate of the probability of an event's occurrence, based on the limited information available. For example, when a consumer assigns a probability to liking a new product, based only on seeing it in an advertisement and his preferences for similar goods, he is indicating a subjective probability.

Once the probabilities associated with each of the possible outcomes are determined, we can estimate the expected value of any one of these outcomes. Specifically, given some variable, X, that has the ability to take on a number of values, such as $X_1, X_2, X_3, \ldots, X_n$, the **expected value** of the variable X *(also known as the mean value of X) equals the summation of the products of each value of X multiplied by its probability of occurrence.* We can mathematically express the expected (or mean) value of the variable X, denoted $E(X)$, as

$$E(X) = Pr_1X_1 + Pr_2X_2 + Pr_3X_3 + \ldots + Pr_nX_n$$
$$= \sum_{i=1}^{n} Pr_iX_i,$$

where $Pr_1, Pr_2, Pr_3, \ldots, Pr_n$, represent the probabilities associated with the variable X assuming the values of $X_1, X_2, X_3, \ldots, X_n$, respectively. For example, we can determine the expected value of a coin toss game using this formula. Let's assume that the payoff associated with a heads outcome, X_H, is \$10, while a tails outcome, X_T, pays \$5. When we toss a coin, the probability of a heads appearing is 0.50, the same as that of a tails, or $Pr_H = Pr_T = 0.50$. We can compute the expected value of the game as

$$E(X) = Pr_H X_H + Pr_T X_T$$
$$= (0.50)(\$10) + (0.50)(\$5) = \$7.50.$$

Therefore, if we play this game a large number of times, the payoff we will expect to receive is \$7.50.

When we develop the method of mixed strategies, we must use the concept of an expected value of a random variable. In our mixed strategies example, we assume that the two players, A and B, each possess two possible strategies. Therefore, we must compute the probabilities associated with each player selecting a particular strategy, specifically $P_1^A, P_2^A, P_1^B,$ and P_2^B, where the superscript refers to the player and the subscript indicates the strategy. In this case, we only need to compute these four probabilities since their values are determined so that the expected value of the payoff to a player from pursuing either of his strategies is equal, regardless of the strategies chosen by the other players in the game. Therefore, from player A's perspective, the probability of player A selecting strategy 1, given that player B chooses strategy 1, denoted P_{11}^A, where the first subscript refers to the strategy chosen by player A and the second subscript indicates the strategy chosen by player B, must be equal to the probability of player A selecting strategy 1 when player B pursues strategy 2, denoted P_{12}^A. As a result, we can drop the second subscript, which denotes the strategy chosen by player B, since

$$P_{11}^A = P_{12}^A = P_1^A.$$

Similarly, from player A's perspective, the probability of player A selecting strategy 2, given

that player B chooses strategy 1, denoted P_{21}^A, must be equal to the probability of player A choosing strategy 2, given that player B selects strategy 2, denoted P_{22}^A. Therefore,

$$P_{21}^A = P_{22}^A = P_2^A.$$

From player B's point of view, the probability of player B choosing strategy 1, given that player A chooses strategy 1, denoted P_{11}^B, must be equal to the probability of player B selecting strategy 1 given that player A chooses strategy 2, denoted P_{12}^B. As a result, the first subscript, which denotes the strategy chosen by player A, may be dropped since

$$P_{11}^B = P_{21}^B = P_1^B.$$

In addition, the probability of player B selecting strategy 2, given that player A chooses strategy 1, denoted P_{21}^B, must be equal to the probability of player B selecting strategy 2, given that player A chooses strategy 2, denoted P_{22}^B. Once again, we can drop the first subscript since

$$P_{12}^B = P_{22}^B = P_2^B.$$

We can now apply the concept of an expected value to the payoffs associated with the various combinations of strategies represented in Table 18A.1. Since the payoff associated with a particular combination of strategies is known with certainty, the expected value of a payoff to a player is equal to the probability that the player chooses that strategy multiplied by the payoff associated with the strategy combination. Specifically, we can mathematically express the expected value of the payoff received by player A, given that player B chooses strategy 1, as

$$E(a_{i1}) = P_1^A a_{11} + P_2^A a_{21},$$

or since $P_1^A + P_2^A = 1$,

$$E(a_{i1}) = P_1^A a_{11} + (1 - P_1^A)a_{21}, \qquad \textbf{(18A.1)}$$

where P_1^A denotes the probability of player A selecting strategy 1 and $P_2^A = (1 - P_1^A)$ denotes the probability of player A not selecting strategy 1, instead choosing strategy 2. The expected value of the payoff to player A, assuming that player B chooses strategy 2, may be stated mathematically as

$$E(a_{i2}) = P_1^A a_{12} + P_2^A a_{22}$$

or

$$E(a_{i2}) = P_1^A a_{12} + (1 - P_1^A)a_{22}. \qquad \textbf{(18A.2)}$$

Similarly, we can mathematically express the expected value of the payoff received by player B, given that player A selects strategy 1, as

$$E(b_{1j}) = P_1^B b_{11} + P_2^B b_{12},$$

or since $P_1^B + P_2^B = 1$,

$$E(b_{1j}) = P_1^B b_{11} + (1 - P_1^B)b_{12}, \qquad \textbf{(18A.3)}$$

where P_1^B denotes the probability of player B selecting strategy 1 and $P_2^B = (1 - P_1^B)$ represents the probability of player B not selecting strategy 1, instead choosing strategy 2. The expected value of the payoff to player B, assuming that player A chooses strategy 2, is expressed as

$$E(b_{2j}) = P_1^B b_{21} + P_2^B b_{22},$$

or

$$E(b_{2j}) = P_1^B b_{21} + (1 - P_1^B)b_{22}. \qquad \textbf{(18A.4)}$$

Recall that when players follow a mixed strategies approach in a game, each seeks to determine the values of the probabilities for selecting its own strategies that render him indifferent among his strategies. This is because the expected values of the payoffs resulting from selecting either strategy in accordance with these probabilities are equal. For example, if player A is indifferent to the strategy chosen by player B, then the expected values of the payoffs to player A must be equal, regardless of the strategy chosen by player B. Therefore, we can set equations (18A.1) and (18A.2) equal to

each other, and determine the optimal value of the probability of player A choosing strategy 1, P_1^A, as

$$E(a_{i1}) = E(a_{i2}),$$

where $i = 1, 2$, or

$$E(a_{11}) + E(a_{21}) = E(a_{12}) + E(a_{22})$$
$$P_1^A a_{11} + (1 - P_1^A)a_{21} = P_1^A a_{12} + (1 - P_1^A)a_{22}$$
$$P_1^A a_{11} + a_{21} - P_1^A a_{21} = P_1^A a_{12} + a_{22} - P_1^A a_{22}$$
$$P_1^A a_{11} - P_1^A a_{21} - P_1^A a_{12} + P_1^A a_{22} = a_{22} - a_{21}$$
$$P_1^A(a_{11} - a_{21} - a_{12} + a_{22}) = a_{22} - a_{21}$$
$$P_1^A = \frac{a_{22} - a_{21}}{a_{11} - a_{21} - a_{12} + a_{22}}. \qquad \textbf{(18A.5)}$$

We can also compute the optimal value of the probability of player A not choosing strategy 1, and instead selecting strategy 2, $P_2^A = (1 - P_1^A)$, as

$$P_2^A = 1 - P_1^A = 1 - \left(\frac{a_{22} - a_{21}}{a_{11} - a_{21} - a_{12} + a_{22}}\right). \textbf{(18A.6)}$$

Similarly, from player B's perspective, in order for this player to be indifferent to the strategy chosen by player A, the expected value of the payoff to player B must be equal, regardless of the strategy chosen by player A. Thus, we set equations (18A.3) and (18A.4) equal to each other, and compute the optimal value of the probability of player B selecting strategy 1, P_1^B, as

$$E(b_{1j}) = E(b_{2j}),$$

where $j = 1, 2$, or

$$E(b_{11}) + E(b_{12}) = E(b_{21}) + E(b_{22})$$
$$P_1^B b_{11} + (1 - P_1^B)b_{12} = P_1^B b_{21} + (1 - P_1^B)b_{22}$$
$$P_1^B b_{11} + b_{12} - P_1^B b_{12} = P_1^B b_{21} + b_{22} - P_1^B b_{22}$$
$$P_1^B b_{11} - P_1^B b_{12} - P_1^B b_{21} + P_1^B b_{22} = b_{22} - b_{12}$$
$$P_1^B(b_{11} - b_{12} - b_{21} + b_{22}) = b_{22} - b_{12}$$
$$P_1^B = \frac{b_{22} - b_{12}}{b_{11} - b_{12} - b_{21} + b_{22}}. \qquad \textbf{(18A.7)}$$

Accordingly, the optimal value of the probability of player B not selecting strategy 1, and instead choosing strategy 2, $P_2^B = (1 - P_1^B)$, is

$$P_2^B = (1 - P_1^B)$$
$$= 1 - \left(\frac{b_{22} - b_{12}}{b_{11} - b_{12} - b_{21} + b_{22}}\right). \quad \textbf{(18A.8)}$$

Recall that since we know the values of the payoffs to player A, a_{11}, a_{12}, a_{21}, and a_{22}, and to player B, b_{11}, b_{12}, b_{21}, and b_{22}, with certainty, we can easily determine the values of P_1^A, $P_2^A = (1 - P_1^A)$, P_1^B, and $P_2^B = (1 - P_1^B)$ by merely substituting the appropriate payoff values into equations (18A.5), (18A.6), (18A.7), and (18A.8), respectively.

We can further demonstrate the method of mixed strategies with a numerical example. Specifically, we will use the payoff data pertaining to the duopoly game we discussed in Section 18.4 and depicted in Table 18.3. Recall that this game centers around two automobile manufacturers, firm H and firm T, which are contemplating introducing sport utility vehicles to their product lines. Each firm faces two possible strategies: specifically, strategy 1, to introduce a sport utility vehicle to its product line, and strategy 2, not to introduce a sport utility vehicle. We have denoted these strategies in Table 18.3 as S_1^H and S_2^H for firm H, and S_1^T and S_2^T for firm T. The payoffs associated with the possible strategy combinations are denoted t_{ij} and h_{ij} for firm T and firm H, respectively, where $i = 1, 2$ refers to the number of the strategy chosen by firm T and $j = 1, 2$ refers to the number of the strategy chosen by firm H. Since each firm faces two possible strategies, we must determine the probabilities associated with each firm selecting either of its strategies. Thus, we must compute P_1^T, P_2^T, P_1^H, and P_2^H, where the superscript refers to the firm and the subscript refers to the number of the strategy chosen.

Applying the concept of an expected value to the payoffs associated with the various combinations of strategies represented in Table 18.3, we can mathematically express the expected value of the payoff firm T will receive, given that firm H chooses to introduce an SUV, or firm H's strategy 1, as

$$E(t_{i1}) = P_1^T t_{11} + (1 - P_1^T)t_{21}, \quad \textbf{(18A.9)}$$

where P_1^T denotes the probability of firm T selecting strategy 1 and $P_2^T = (1 - P_1^T)$ represents the probability of firm T not selecting strategy 1 but rather choosing strategy 2. We can also mathematically express the expected value of the payoff to firm T, assuming firm H chooses strategy 2, not to introduce an SUV, as

$$E(t_{i2}) = P_1^T t_{12} + (1 - P_1^T)t_{22}. \quad \textbf{(18A.10)}$$

Following the method of mixed strategies, firm T seeks to determine the optimal values of the probability associated with selecting each of its alternative strategies that will render it indifferent to the strategy chosen by firm H. In order to determine these probabilities, the expected payoffs to firm T must be equal, regardless of the strategy chosen by its rival, firm H. Therefore, setting equations (18A.9) and (18A.10) equal to one another, we can determine the optimal value of the probability of firm T selecting strategy 1, P_1^T, as follows:

$$E(t_{i1}) = E(t_{i2}), \text{ where } i = 1, 2$$

or

$$E(t_{11}) + E(t_{21}) = E(t_{12}) + E(t_{22})$$
$$P_1^T t_{11} + (1 - P_1^T)t_{21} = P_1^T t_{12} + (1 - P_1^T)t_{22}$$
$$P_1^T t_{11} + t_{21} - P_1^T t_{21} = P_1^T t_{12} + t_{22} - P_1^T t_{22}$$
$$P_1^T t_{11} - P_1^T t_{21} - P_1^T t_{12} + P_1^T t_{22} = t_{22} - t_{21}$$
$$P_1^T(t_{11} - t_{21} - t_{12} + t_{22}) = t_{22} - t_{21}$$
$$P_1^T = \frac{t_{22} - t_{21}}{t_{11} - t_{21} - t_{12} + t_{22}}. \quad \textbf{(18A.11)}$$

We can now compute the specific values of P_1^T and $P_2^T = (1 - P_1^T)$ by substituting the appropriate payoff values for firm T from Table 18.3 into equation (18A.11) as follows:

$$P_1^T = \frac{\$1 \text{ mil} - \$3 \text{ mil}}{\$2 \text{ mil} - \$3 \text{ mil} - \$3 \text{ mil} + \$1 \text{ mil}}$$

$$= \frac{-2}{-3} = 0.67,$$

and

$$P_2^T = (1 - P_1^T) = 1 - 0.67 = 0.33.$$

Therefore, firm T will select strategy 1—to introduce a sport utility vehicle—67 percent of the time and will choose strategy 2—not to introduce a sport utility vehicle—33 percent of the time. By randomly selecting its strategies on the basis of these probabilities, the expected value of the payoff to firm T, regardless of the strategy selected by firm H, is determined by substituting the values of P_1^T and P_2^T that we just computed into either equation (18A.9) or equation (18A.10), along with the appropriate values of firm T's payoffs from Table 18.3. Thus, using equation (18A.9)

$$E(t_{i1}) = P_1^T(t_{11}) + (1 - P_1^T)t_{21},$$

where $i = 1, 2$,

$$P_1^T (\$2 \text{ mil}) + (1 - P_1^T) (\$3 \text{ mil})$$
$$= 0.67 (\$2 \text{ mil}) + (1 - 0.67) (\$3 \text{ mil})$$
$$= \$2.33 \text{ million}.$$

Similarly, we can determine firm H's optimal probability values associated with selecting each of its alternative strategies, which render it indifferent to the strategy chosen by firm T. Once again, we apply the concept of an expected value to firm H's payoffs associated with the various combinations of strategies represented in Table 18.3. Thus, we can mathematically express the expected value of the payoff received by firm H, contingent on firm T selecting strategy 1, introducing an SUV, as

$$E(h_{1j}) = P_1^H h_{11} + (1 - P_1^H)h_{12}, \quad \textbf{(18A.12)}$$

where P_1^H denotes the probability of firm H selecting strategy 1 and $P_2^H = (1 - P_1^H)$ represents the probability of firm H not selecting strategy 1, instead choosing strategy 2. The expected value of the payoff to firm H, given that firm T chooses strategy 2, not to introduce an SUV, is expressed mathematically as

$$E(h_{2j}) = P_1^H h_{21} + (1 - P_1^H)h_{22}. \quad \textbf{(18A.13)}$$

Using the method of mixed strategies, firm H seeks to determine the optimal values of the probabilities associated with its strategies, which renders it indifferent to the strategy chosen by firm T. In order to determine these probabilities, the expected values of firm H's payoffs associated with choosing either strategy must be equal. Therefore, setting equations (18A.12) and (18A.13) equal to one another, we determine the optimal value of the probability of firm H selecting strategy 1, P_1^H, as

$$E(h_{1j}) = E(h_{2j}),$$

where $j = 1, 2$

or

$$E(h_{11}) + E(h_{12}) = E(h_{21}) + E(h_{22})$$
$$P_1^H h_{11} + (1 - P_1^H)h_{12} = P_1^H h_{21} + (1 - P_1^H)h_{22}$$
$$P_1^H h_{11} + h_{12} - P_1^H h_{12} = P_1^H h_{21} + h_{22} - P_1^H h_{22}$$
$$P_1^H h_{11} - P_1^H h_{12} - P_1^H h_{21} + P_1^H h_{22} = h_{22} - h_{12}$$
$$P_1^H(h_{11} - h_{12} - h_{21} + h_{22}) = h_{22} - h_{12}$$

$$P_1^H = \frac{h_{22} - h_{12}}{h_{11} - h_{12} - h_{21} + h_{22}}. \quad \textbf{(18A.14)}$$

We can compute the values of P_1^H and $P_2^H = (1 - P_1^H)$ by substituting the corresponding payoff values for firm H from Table 18.3 into equation (18A.14) as

$$P_1^H = \frac{\$3 \text{ mil} - \$1 \text{ mil}}{\$2.5 \text{ mil} - \$1 \text{ mil} - \$2 \text{ mil} + \$3 \text{ mil}}$$

$$= \frac{2}{2.5} = 0.80,$$

and

$$P_2^H = (1 - P_1^H) = 1 - 0.80 = 0.20.$$

Thus, by using the method of mixed strategies, firm H optimally chooses strategy 1—introducing a sport utility vehicle—80 percent of the time and selects its strategy 2—not to introduce a sport utility vehicle to its product line—20 percent of the time. We can determine the expected value of the payoff to firm H by substituting the values of P_1^H and P_2^H we just computed, along with the appropriate values of firm H's payoffs from Table 18.3, into either equation (18A.12) or (18A.13). Thus, using equation (18A.12),

$$E(h_{1j}) = P_1^H h_{11} + (1 - P_1^H)h_{12},$$

where $j = 1, 2$

$$
\begin{aligned}
P_1^H\ (\$2.5\ \text{mil}) &+ (1 - P_1^H)\ (\$1\ \text{mil}) \\
&= 0.80\ (\$2.5\ \text{mil}) + (1 - 0.80)\ (\$1\ \text{mil}) \\
&= \$2.2\ \text{mil}.
\end{aligned}
$$

Logically, either firm would be at a disadvantage if it revealed the optimal probabilities at which it selects its strategies to its rival. Therefore, each firm will rationally attempt to keep this information confidential.

CHAPTER 19

Monopolistic Competition

19.1 INTRODUCTION

In the preceding six chapters, we examined three market structures—perfect competition, monopoly, and oligopoly—and generally showed the performance results to vary across these different industries. There is yet one more market structure that we need to discuss: monopolistic competition. As you can probably infer from the name, it contains some elements of both perfect competition and monopoly. Specifically, monopolistic competition is characterized by a large number of firms but with each firm selling a slightly differentiated product. The fact that it has a large number of sellers, reflecting no barriers to entry, gives this market structure a similarity to perfect competition. However, the characteristic that the firms' products are slightly differentiated from one another gives it a similarity to monopoly in that these firms possess some degree of discretion over the prices of their products.

Many goods are produced in markets characterized as monopolistically competitive, including soaps, lotions, and deodorants, to name a few. The markets for these goods contain many sellers, but the firms' products are not quite the same, often further differentiated through advertising and packaging. Our focus in this chapter is on analyzing monopolistic competition, whose structure describes these types of markets, for both the short- and long-run time periods. In addition, we will discuss some of the unique outcomes associated with this type of industry.

19.2 CHARACTERISTICS OF MONOPOLISTIC COMPETITION

Formally, **monopolistic competition**, is *a market structure consisting of a large number of firms selling slightly differentiated products.* As was the case with our discussions of other market structures, we can describe monopolistic competition in terms of the basic criteria defining a market structure presented in Chapter 13. Once again our focus is on the sellers' side of the market. Recall that the first criterion for describing a market structure is the number and size distribution of sellers in a market. As we stated earlier, in monopolistic competition the number of sellers is quite large. However, there is some ambiguity regarding their size within the relevant market. This ambiguity is related to the next criterion for defining a market structure—the degree of product differentiation within the market for the good. In the case of monopolistic competition, the sellers' products are slightly differentiated from each other. Logically, these products cannot be homogeneous or they will constitute perfect substitutes for each other, and we would treat the market as perfectly competitive. Alternatively, the products cannot be significantly differentiated from each other or they will be very poor substitutes. In this situation, the overall market would break down into a number of different markets characterized by monopolies, one for each firm. Thus, by definition, the products sold by monopolistically competitive firms can only be slightly differentiated, representing imperfect substitutes for each other.

This ambiguity associated with defining the degree of product differentiation in monopolistic competition creates some difficulty in establishing the relevant market for the firms' products. Earlier we defined a market to include those goods consumers perceive as close substitutes for each other. In the case of monopolistic competition, this is clearly a matter of degree because the firms' products are interpreted as rather imperfect substitutes. As a result, economists have attempted to circumvent this difficulty of appropriate market definition by focusing on the concept of a product group rather than on a market per se. A **product group** is *a set of heterogeneous but closely related goods*. Thus, referring to the concept of size distribution we mentioned earlier, we see that each monopolistically competitive firm accounts for only an insignificantly small portion of the sales of the entire product group and yet controls 100 percent of the sales of its own uniquely defined product. Thus, each firm possesses a small degree of monopoly power or discretion over the price of its product.

As a real-world example of monopolistic competition, consider the vast number and variety of restaurants existing in any large metropolitan area in the United States. In addition, we can characterize the women's dress industry as monopolistically competitive, given that it is comprised of nearly 4000 firms, with the eight largest firms producing only 17 percent of total industry output.[1] Some additional examples of monopolistic competition are in product groups such as detergents, toothpastes, soft drinks, and retailing, where each firm's product is slightly differentiated, and therefore, some consumers are willing to pay small price premiums for particular products.

There are two additional criteria for defining a market structure, or more appropriately in this case, product group: (1) the ease by which firms can enter or exit the market and (2) the amount of market-related information available to consumers and producers. For a monopolistically competitive product group, entry and exit to and from the group is quite easy and without restriction, thus accounting for the large number of firms comprising the product group. With regard to the amount of market-related information, consumers' lack of such information may affect their perceptions regarding the degree of product differentiation, thus helping to create the underlying structure associated with monopolistic competition. Consumer perceptions regarding product differentiation can be affected by significant amounts of persuasive advertising, a characteristic quite prevalent for these types of firms.

The actual model of monopolistic competition was developed in the 1930s by economist Edward Chamberlin. We will demonstrate this model for a typical firm with the understanding that it is just one of many firms that make up a monopolistically competitive industry. Figure 19.1 illustrates the fundamental basis for this model. The

---

[1] U.S. Department of Commerce, Bureau of the Census, 1992 Census of Manufacturers, *Concentration Ratios in Manufacturing*, Subject Series MC 92–S–2, 1997.

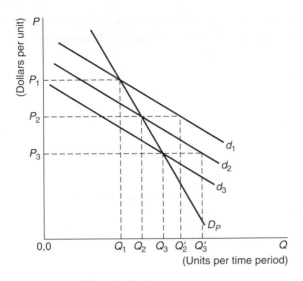

FIGURE 19.1 Proportional and Perceived Own-Price Demand Curves for a Monopolistically Competitive Firm

curve labeled D_P in this figure is known as the proportional own-price demand curve for a typical firm. A **proportional own-price demand curve** is *a set of quantity–price combinations representing the proportion of the total product group quantity demanded at each price attributed to one firm within the group.* For example, suppose the own-price demand curve for a product group is

$$Q^{D,G} = 1000 - 10P,$$

where $Q^{D,G}$ represents the quantity demanded and P is the price for all goods comprising the product group. If one firm accounts for 1/100th of the product group's sales, then we compute the proportional own-price demand curve for this firm as

$$Q^{D,P} = \frac{1}{100} Q^{D,G} = \frac{1}{100}(1000 - 10P) = 10 - 0.1P,$$

where $Q^{D,P}$ is the quantity demanded of this firm's product. The slope of the own-price demand curve for the product group is

$$\frac{dQ^{D,G}}{dP} = -10,$$

indicating that as the price changes by one unit, $Q^{D,G}$ changes by 10 units in the opposite direction. The slope of the proportional own-price demand curve for a typical firm is

$$\frac{dQ^{D,P}}{dP} = -0.1,$$

indicating that a one-unit change in price causes a one-tenth of a unit change in $Q^{D,P}$ in the opposite direction. Thus, a change in the price of all goods, P, causes the quantity demanded of a typical firm's product to change in the opposite direction by 0.1/10 = 1/100th of the quantity demanded for the entire product group. To conduct such a simple derivation and subsequent interpretation of a typical firm's proportional demand curve, it is necessary to assume that consumer preferences for all goods in the product group are uniformly distributed.

Referring back to Figure 19.1, the curves designated d_1, d_2, and d_3 represent what are known as perceived own-price demand curves for a typical firm, where, there exists an infinite number of such curves. Focusing on any one of the three that are illustrated, say d_1, we can observe that it is flatter, or more price elastic, than the proportional own-price demand curve, D_P. This characteristic reflects another one of Chamberlin's assumptions contending that since the product group contains a large number of sellers, each firm believes that changes in its own price go unnoticed by its rivals. Another way to explain this assumption is that each firm believes its product to be more differentiated than is actually the case. Thus, if the firm represented here decreases its price from P_1 to P_2, it believes that the other firms will not decrease the prices of their products in response. As a result, this firm believes the quantity demanded of its product will increase substantially from Q_1 to Q_2', as indicated by the relatively flatter, or more price elastic, own-price demand curve, d_1.

There is a discrepancy between perception and reality, however, in that the other firms do react to this price decrease and reduce their prices accordingly, resulting in a much smaller increase in the quantity demanded of this firm's product. Thus, the actual increase in quantity demanded is from Q_1 to Q_2 as indicated by the relatively steeper, or less price elastic, proportional own-price demand curve D_P. The typical firm remains unaware that its rivals will always match its price changes and that subsequently its sales are actually indicated by the proportional own-price demand curve, D_P. Instead, the firm believes that its own-price demand curve has simply shifted left from d_1 to d_2, due to any of a number of potential factors, such as decreases in the number of consumers or changes in consumers' tastes away from its product. Thus, at P_2, the firm perceives its own-price demand curve as d_2 and believes that if it decreases its price from P_2 to P_3, the quantity demanded of its product will increase to Q_3' because its rivals will not respond and decrease their prices accordingly. In reality, however, the rival firms will decrease their prices, and the quantity demanded of the firm's product increases only to Q_3, as indicated by the proportional own-price demand curve, D_P. At this point, the firm perceives its own-price demand curve as d_3 and so the process continues, or in the language of Chamberlin, the perceived own-price demand curve slides down the proportional own-price demand curve each time the firm decreases the price of its product.

19.3   SHORT-RUN EQUILIBRIUM FOR A MONOPOLISTICALLY COMPETITIVE FIRM

By using the above scenario, we can now demonstrate short-run equilibrium for a monopolistically competitive firm. Before doing so, we will make one last assumption. Since our analysis is conducted for a single firm, we must assume that all firms in the product group are subject to the same cost conditions so as to make the model representative of any one of the firms. However, the validity of this assumption is rather suspect because, by definition, the firms' products are somewhat differentiated. Thus, we would expect the costs of producing these goods to vary to some degree. Nevertheless, adhering to this assumption, we have illustrated a short-run equilibrium situation for a typical monopolistically competitive firm in Figure 19.2. This figure contains a proportional own-price demand curve, D_P, three perceived own-price demand curves, d_1, d_2, and d_3, as well as their respective marginal revenue curves, mr_1, mr_2, and mr_3. With the exception of the vertical intercept, each mr curve lies beneath its perceived own-price demand curve, reflecting the fact that $mr < P$ for own-price demand curves possessing negative slopes. Also illustrated in this figure are the short-run marginal cost curve, $SRMC^{\overline{K}_1}$, and the average total cost curve, $ATC^{\overline{K}_1}$, for this typical firm, where we have fixed the capital input at $\overline{K}_1$.

The firm seeks to determine its short-run profit-maximizing level of output according to the condition $mr = SRMC$, where both of these values are less than the price of the good for reasons discussed previously. To demonstrate the process by which a short run eqilibrium is achieved, assume the firm initially charges the price P_0 and correspondingly sells Q_0 units of output. The firm perceives its own-price demand curve to be d_1, and thus its associated marginal revenue curve is mr_1. This quantity–price combination (Q_0, P_0) does not constitute an equilibrium, since at Q_0 units of output, $mr_1 > SRMC^{\overline{K}_1}$. Thus, the firm will seek to increase its short-run profit by decreasing the price to P_1, at which the firm perceives that it can increase the level of output it sells to the profit-maximizing amount, Q'_1, at which $mr_1 = SRMC^{\overline{K}_1}$. However, at P_1 the firm will sell only Q_1 units of output as indicated by the proportional own-price demand curve D_P. The firm now believes its own-price demand curve to be d_2, and accordingly, its new perceived marginal revenue curve is mr_2, where at $Q_1, mr_2 > SRMC^{\overline{K}_1}$. Again, the firm will decrease its price

FIGURE 19.2 Short-Run Profit Maximization for a Monopolistically Competitive Firm

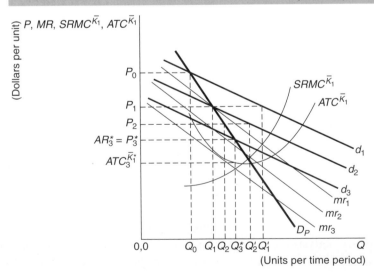

and increase output in order to achieve a profit maximum that it perceives to be at the price P_2, corresponding to output level Q_2', at which $mr_2 = SRMC^{\overline{K}_1}$. However, once again, perception differs from reality, and the firm sells only Q_2 units of output at price P_2. And so this process continues until an equilibrium is attained.

To achieve a short-run equilibrium, or stable result, two conditions must be met. First, the firm must ultimately determine levels of output and price that correspond to a maximum value for its short-run profit. Second, this profit-maximizing solution must occur at a point where perception and reality coincide, leaving no need for further adjustment. Specifically, the firm must determine profit-maximizing levels of output and price at which its perceived quantity demanded equals the proportional quantity demanded. In Figure 19.2, this short-run equilibrium occurs at Q_3^* units of output, corresponding to the price P_3^*. At this quantity–price combination, short-run profit is maximized because $mr_3 = SRMC^{\overline{K}_1}$. Simultaneously, perception and reality coincide for the firm, as we can observe by the fact that D_P and d_3 intersect at this combination. The corresponding maximum short-run average profit is represented as

$$SR\ AVE\ \pi_3^* = AR_3^* - ATC_3^{\overline{K}_1*} = P_3^* - ATC_3^{\overline{K}_1*},$$

and therefore, the short-run total profit is

$$SR\pi^* = (P_3^* - ATC_3^{\overline{K}_1*})Q_3^*,$$

which, in this example, is positive. As with any market structure, however, short-run profit for a monopolistically competitive firm can be positive, negative, or zero, depending on demand and cost conditions.

19.4 LONG-RUN EQUILIBRIUM FOR A MONOPOLISTICALLY COMPETITIVE FIRM

We will now demonstrate long-run equilibrium for a monopolistically competitive firm. Recall that in the long run firms can vary all inputs including their level of capital or plant size. As a result, firms will vary their inputs, labor and capital, so as to produce their output in the least costly manner, by using an optimal input combination. Furthermore, since the absence of barriers to entry is one of the major characteristics associated with monopolistic competition, firms are able to enter or exit the product group in the long run, where the incentives for such activity are the same as those for perfect competition. Specifically, positive short-run profits earned by incumbent firms provide an incentive for the entry of firms into the product group. Ultimately, this entry eliminates these profits as the entry of new firms decreases the market shares of the incumbent firms. Alternatively, negative short-run profits, or losses, received by incumbent firms provide an incentive for some of these firms to exit the product group. This exit ultimately eliminates the losses for the remaining firms as their market shares subsequently increase. Long-run equilibrium is established when there exists no incentive for entry or exit, or when the short-run, and long-run, profits earned by the incumbent firms are equal to zero. Thus, in this aspect, the long-run equilibrium solution for monopolistic competition resembles that for perfect competition.

We can further describe the process by which long-run equilibrium is achieved for a monopolistically competitive firm by returning to Figure 19.2, which illustrates a short-run equilibrium. In this case, the firm's short-run profit is positive, providing an incentive for new firms to enter the product group in the long run. As this entry occurs, the proportional own-price demand curve, along with its associated set of perceived own-price demand curves, shifts to the left, reflecting a decrease in the firm's share of the product group. After this shift, at the original profit-maximizing level of output, Q_3^*, the necessary condition for a profit maximum no longer holds true as $mr < SRMC$. Therefore, the firm will decrease its level of output as it seeks a new profit-maximizing level of Q. In addition, the firm attempts to protect its profit by reducing the level of capital as well as the amount of labor it uses in order to produce the lower level of output in the least costly manner. Entry into the product group, and these subsequent adjustments by incumbent firms, will continue until a long-run equilibrium is established. This situation occurs once the profits earned by incumbent firms equal zero; as a result, the incentive for entry is eliminated. Moreover, all firms now comprising the product group have adjusted all of their inputs so as to be producing their output at a constrained cost minimum.

The necessary condition for a long-run profit maximum is fulfilled by each firm producing output to the point where its marginal revenue, mr, is equal to its long-run marginal cost, $LRMC$, or

$$mr = LRMC.$$

In addition, this condition coincides with the necessary condition for a short-run profit maximum once the firm has determined its optimal level of capital, say $\overline{K}_0$, for producing the long-run profit-maximizing level of output. Thus

$$mr = LRMC = SRMC^{\overline{K}_0},$$

where the associated long- and short-run levels of profit are equal to zero.

Finally, in long-run equilibrium, as is the case for any short-run equilibrium for a monopolistically competitive firm, perception and reality must coincide. Specifically, the solution value for the profit-maximizing level of output must be common to both the proportional and the particular perceived own-price demand curve for the firm. We have illustrated such a long-run equilibrium situation for a monopolistically competitive firm in Figure 19.3. The profit-maximizing level of output for the firm, Q_0^*, is determined by the condition

$$mr_0' = LRMC_0 = SRMC_0^{\overline{K}_0},$$

where the corresponding price is P_0^*. At this quantity–price combination, observe that the proportional own-price demand curve, D_P', intersects the particular perceived own-price demand curve, d', and thus Q_0^* represents both the actual and perceived quantity demanded. Furthermore, we observe that the price P_0^*, which is also the firm's average revenue, AR_0^*, is equal to both the long-run average cost, $LRAC_0^*$, and the relevant average total cost, $ATC_0^{\overline{K}_0*}$. These equalities are reflected by the fact that

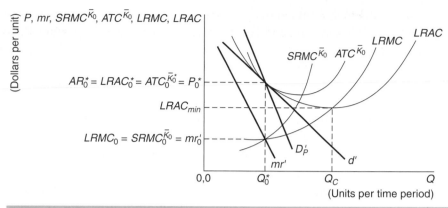

FIGURE 19.3 Long-Run Equilibrium for a Monopolistically Competitive Firm

the perceived own-price demand curve, d', is tangent to both of these cost curves. Accordingly, both long- and short-run average profits are equal to zero, or

$$LR\ AVE\pi_0 = AR_0^* - LRAC_0^* = SR\ AVE\pi_0 = AR_0^* - ATC_0^{\bar{K}_0*} = \$0.$$

We have demonstrated the process by which this long-run equilibrium is achieved by starting with a situation in which the incumbent firms' short-run profits are positive. As an exercise, you can analyze how long-run equilibrium is attained starting from a situation of short-run losses for the incumbent firms. In this case, the force driving these losses upward to zero is the exit by some firms from the product group.

19.5 EVALUATION OF MONOPOLISTIC COMPETITION OUTCOMES

As with other market structures, we can evaluate the outcomes associated with monopolistic competition from a social perspective. Embedded in our evaluation is an implicit comparison to the outcomes generated by perfect competition; thus you are encouraged to review those outcomes discussed in Section 14.4 of Chapter 14. We should also note that the outcomes for monopolistic competition are subject to some additional interpretations that are generally not associated with other market structures. Recall that the formal criteria we have used as the basis for evaluating market performance are production efficiency, allocative efficiency, and dynamic efficiency. In addition, we have also taken into account the rather subjective consideration of fairness when evaluating performance. With regard to fairness, monopolistic competition is characterized by no significant entry barriers, indicating that this market structure is consistent with the concept of equal opportunity. In addition, because of this characteristic, the firms receive no long-run economic profits, and therefore, their owners receive returns equivalent to only their opportunity costs.

In terms of production efficiency, owing to the slight degree of product differentiation, monopolistically competitive firms do not produce levels of output that are sufficiently high for them to realize all advantages associated with economies of scale. Referring back to Figure 19.3, observe that in long-run equilibrium, the typical firm incurs a long-run average cost of $LRAC_0^*$, associated with producing Q_0^* units of output rather than the Q_C units of output necessary to produce at the minimum point on its $LRAC$ curve, represented in this figure as $LRAC_{min}$. This combination $(Q_C, LRAC_{min})$ is the long-run equilibrium outcome for a perfectly competitive firm. We refer to the difference, $Q_C - Q_0^*$ as representing a firm's **excess capacity**, or *the difference between the perfectly competitive level of output and that for a monopolistically competitive firm, in long-run equilibrium*. Alternatively, a firm's excess capacity is the increase in output that is necessary to produce its output at minimum long-run average cost. Production efficiency also involves the concept of X-inefficiency, an event that is unlikely to be prevalent in monopolistic competition due to the lack of long-run profits. In other words, these firms are simply not in a position to squander resources if they are to survive.

Allocative efficiency involves producing a level of output at which price is equal to marginal cost. Again referring to Figure 19.3, observe that this is not the case for a monopolistically competitive firm as, at the profit-maximizing level of output, Q_0^*, $P_0^* > SRMC_0^{\overline{K}_0} = LRMC_0$. As a result, we can conclude that the firm restricts its production of output to a level less than the socially desirable amount, since at this output level consumers value the last unit of output sold more than the cost of producing it.

Our final criterion for evaluating market outcomes is dynamic efficiency, or the development and adoption of new technology. As with other market structures, it is difficult to evaluate monopolistic competition in terms of this criterion on a purely theoretical basis. Monopolistically competitive firms do not receive the long-run profits necessary to support the level of research and development needed to sustain a large amount of technological progress. However, monopolistic competition is characterized by some degree of product differentiation. As a result, these firms have an incentive to increase the amount of this differentiation to gain more discretion over the price they charge. Thus, as they attempt to accomplish this goal, the firms must engage in some degree of research and development. However, there is an alternative view contending that, since the degree of product differentiation across the product group is slight, much of the research and development is directed toward rather trivial endeavors such as elaborate packaging and persuasive advertising.

Earlier we stated that evaluating some of the outcomes associated with monopolistic competition is subject to some interpretation, where the most interesting is that provided by Edward Chamberlin. We can describe his interpretation of the monopolistically competitive outcome in terms of the excess capacity concept that reflects the loss of productive and allocative efficiency caused by the restrictions of output. Again referring back to Figure 19.3, we see that these characteristics are reflected by the fact that since the perceived own-price demand curve, d', possesses a negative slope, the long-run equilibrium solution of zero profit must occur on the downward-sloping portion of the $LRAC$ curve, thus yielding the excess capacity result. Conceptually, this negative slope for d' reflects the slight degree of product differentiation associated with a monopolistically competitive firm's output. By contrast, if all of the firms' products were homogeneous, the own-price demand curve for any typical firm would be horizontal. Combining this implication with the characteristic of free entry would yield the perfectly competitive outcome where the typical firm produces Q_C units of

---

The Perils of Launching a New Product in a Monopolistically Competitive Industry

In the broad realm of personal care products, one of the most fragmented product groups is that of hair shampoo. The market stands as a classic example of monopolistic competition, where numerous sellers use extensive advertising to convince the buying public that their ever so slightly differentiated product is superior to those of its many competitors. As an example, in 1993 the top-selling shampoo, Pert Plus, captured a mere 10 percent of the market, followed by Pantene, and Head and Shoulders, each with approximately 9 percent (see accompanying table).[2] Yet, despite the small market shares attributed to each firm's product characterizing this industry, the venerable hair care brand, Breck, tried to reestablish its position in the shampoo market by reviving its classic brand in 1993. Not surprisingly, Breck invested heavily in a new advertising campaign designed to promote a premium product having healthful properties. In addition, the shampoo was repackaged in peach-colored bottles and given a new fruity scent. Despite its costly efforts to revamp and promote its vitamin-enriched shampoo, Breck was only able to capture a meager 1.1 percent of the shampoo market, no doubt partly because of

a competitor's simultaneous introduction of yet another vitamin-enriched shampoo also packaged in peach-colored bottles.

Such paltry results are not uncommon in a market cluttered with numerous brands and customers possessing little brand loyalty. In 1991, the cost to introduce a new shampoo was estimated to range between $35 million and $40 million, with an astounding failure rate of 90 percent. Moreover, some market researchers claim that consumers have become at best, desensitized, and at worst, confused, by the excessive degree of product differentiation and advertising employed in the shampoo market. Such results obviously lend credence to the waste and inefficiency associated with a monopolistically competitive market structure.

Top-Selling Shampoo Brands, January 26 to April 18, 1993		
Ranking	*Shampoo*	*Percent of Market Share*
1	Pert Plus	10.4
2	Pantene	9.2
3	Head and Shoulders	8.7
4	Suave	6.5
5	Neutrogena	4.1
:	:	:
28	Breck	1.1

[2]Pauline Yoshihashi, "Reviving Breck: New Bottles, No 'Girls'," *Wall Street Journal*, June 1, 1993, p. B-1.

Source: Information Resources, Inc.

output, at minimum long-run average cost, and earns a long-run profit of zero. Since this is not the case with monopolistic competition, Chamberlin concluded that the excess capacity for a monopolistically competitive firm simply indicates the degree of product differentiation associated with its output. Thus, the output restriction and higher production costs attributed to monopolistically competitive firms reflect the cost to society of being able to choose from a variety of products, a cost that Chamberlin believed to be justified. The counterargument to Chamberlin's contention is that much of this variety is rather trivial and often results from the wasteful packaging and advertising strategies used by the firms to influence consumers' perceptions. The arguments on both sides of the issue become rather subjective, so we will let you draw your own conclusions.

19.6 SUMMARY

In this chapter, we focused on the market structure, or product group, known as monopolistic competition. After discussing its characteristics, we analyzed the formal model of monopolistic competition for both the short- and long-run time periods. Finally, we provided an evaluation of the outcomes associated with this model. The main topics covered in this chapter are as follows.

- A product group is a set of heterogeneous, but closely related, goods.
- Monopolistic competition is a product group consisting of a large number of firms selling slightly differentiated products.
- In a monopolistically competitive product group, each firm believes it possesses more price-setting discretion than actually exists.
- A proportional own-price demand curve indicates the proportion of the total product group sales demanded at each price, attributed to a single firm in the group.
- Short-run equilibrium occurs at an output level for which a firm's marginal revenue equals its marginal cost and, simultaneously, where its perceived own-price demand equals the proportional own-price demand for its product.
- Long-run equilibrium occurs at an output level for which a firm's marginal revenue equals its long- and short-run marginal costs, as well as where its perceived own-price demand equals the proportional own-price demand for its product.
- Due to the entry and exit of firms, a monopolistically competitive firm's long-run profits are equal to zero.
- Due to the restriction of output, long-run equilibrium for a monopolistically competitive firm is characterized by excess capacity. Specifically, the firm does not produce enough output to realize all economies of scale advantages.

KEY TERMS

- excess capacity, page 510
- monopolistic competition, page 502
- product group, page 503
- proportional own-price demand curve, page 504

EXERCISES

19.1 Name some real-world industries that you believe to be monopolistically competitive. Explain why you believe these industries can be described by this market structure.

19.2 What is a proportional own-price demand curve? Why is it less own-price elastic than any of the number of associated perceived own-price demand curves?

19.3 Graphically, illustrate a short-run equilibrium situation for a monopolistically competitive firm, assuming that its corresponding short-run profit is negative. What conditions must hold true for this equilibrium to occur?

19.4 Graphically, illustrate long-run equilibrium for a monopolistically competitive firm. What is the firm's profit in this situation and why is it this level? Finally, what other conditions must hold true in long-run equilibrium?

19.5 What is excess capacity? Why does it exist for the case of monopolistic competition? What are some of the advantages and disadvantages associated with it?

19.6 Sometimes we hear the phrase "a monopolistically competitive product group contains too many firms." What is meant by this phrase, and what are the associated implications?

CHAPTER 20

Demand for Labor

20.1   INTRODUCTION

In the preceding seven chapters, we discussed various models of firm behavior assuming the goal of the typical firm is profit maximization. Accordingly, we developed firm profit functions consisting of the difference between a firm's revenues and costs, treating the level of output produced and sold as the decision variable. To produce this output, a firm must use amounts of inputs in its production process, where we generally categorize these inputs as labor, representing human efforts, and capital, consisting of the created means of production such as plant and equipment.

In this chapter, we will formally demonstrate that, as a firm determines its profit-maximizing level of output, it simultaneously determines the optimal amounts of the inputs it uses to produce that level of output. In other words, these are not separate processes but are just different aspects of the profit maximization problem. Next, by allowing input prices to vary, we will develop input demand functions, with an emphasis on the demand for labor. This function has several important determinants, including the price of labor, the level of the capital input used, and the price of a firm's output. We frequently refer to input demand functions as derived demand functions because they ultimately depend on the market for the final product being sold. For example, the expansion of E-commerce in the 1990s greatly increased the demand for computer programmers and engineers. Conversely, the collapse of many of the "dot com" firms in the year 2000, had quite the opposite effect, shrinking the demand for this type of labor.

Initially, our focus in this chapter is on developing an individual firm's labor demand curve, both for the single variable input case and, later, for the more complex situation in which there are several variable inputs. Afterward, we will aggregate these individual firm labor demand curves to construct their industry counterparts. In the next chapter, we will develop labor supply curves that, when used with these labor demand curves, enable us to analyze how labor markets perform to determine the price of labor.

20.2   FIRM LABOR DEMAND CURVES WITH ONLY ONE VARIABLE INPUT

A firm maximizes its profit by producing and selling output to the point where the extra revenue is equal to the extra cost from doing so, or more formally, where marginal revenue is equal to marginal cost. To be consistent with the goal of profit maximization, the firm seeks to produce this level of output in the least costly manner, subject to its prevailing constraints. If this is not the case, the firm cannot be earning a maximum profit, in that it could adjust its input levels and increase its profit. The point we are emphasizing is that determining the profit-maximizing level of output and determining the profit-maximizing levels of inputs are related processes that lead to the same overall solution. As a result, we can express a firm's profit function in terms of either its level of output, as demonstrated in the preceding seven chapters, or alternatively, in terms of the inputs employed to produce this output. This latter approach requires that we express the two components of profit, revenue and cost, in terms of the inputs the firm uses, where, ultimately, a profit function defined in this manner provides the basis for deriving a firm's input demand curves.

Before proceeding with this analysis, it is necessary that we establish some underlying assumptions. Initially, we will assume that a firm uses only one variable input in its production process. Thus, for the familiar production function containing two inputs, capital, K, and labor, L, we will treat capital as fixed at some specified level, $\overline{K}_1$, and thus labor constitutes the only variable input. In addition, recall that a firm's profit-maximizing behavior depends on the market structure within which it operates. To simplify our analysis, we will initially assume that the firm operates in a perfectly competitive market for its output and therefore behaves as a price taker. In addition, we are assuming that the firm operates in a perfectly competitive market for the inputs it purchases and, as a result, behaves as a price taker in its input markets as well. This last assumption should be familiar to you, for we applied it throughout our analysis of optimal input combinations in Chapters 10 and 11.

Keeping the above assumptions in mind, we can now express a firm's revenue, cost, and profit functions in terms of the inputs it employs, and then use these functions to develop a firm's labor demand curve. Recall that a firm's total revenue is simply the product of the price of its output and the amount of output it sells, or

$$TR = \overline{P}_1 Q, \tag{20.1}$$

where the output price is specified at level $\overline{P}_1$, reflecting the fact that the firm is a price taker. Also recall that for a perfectly competitive firm, this price is equal to marginal revenue, MR.

The familiar short-run production function containing two inputs, capital and labor, is

$$Q = f(\overline{K}_1, L),$$

where we have fixed capital at the level $\overline{K}_1$. By substituting this expression for Q into equation (20.1), we can express the total revenue function, TR, in terms of the price of the product and the levels of the two inputs as

$$TR = \overline{P}_1 f(\overline{K}_1, L), \tag{20.2}$$

where L is the only independent variable not specified at some constant level.

We can use this expression for TR to determine a relationship between a firm's total revenue and the amount of the variable input it employs, known as the **value of**

the marginal product of an input, or VMP_{input}, defined as *the change in total revenue due to a change in the amount of an input used in a production process, holding the output price and all other inputs constant*. In this case, since labor is the variable input, we compute the value of the marginal product of labor, VMP_L, as the derivative of total revenue with respect to the amount of labor used as

$$VMP_L = \frac{dTR}{dL} = \frac{d\overline{P}_1 f(\overline{K}_1, L)}{dL} = \overline{P}_1 \frac{df(\overline{K}_1, L)}{dL},$$

or since $Q = f(\overline{K}_1, L)$, then

$$VMP_L = \overline{P}_1 \frac{dQ}{dL}.$$

We can recognize the term dQ/dL as the marginal product of labor, MP_L, or the change in the production of output resulting from a change in the amount of labor used, holding all other inputs constant. We represented this concept in Chapter 8 as the term, $\partial Q/\partial L$. However once we hold capital constant, there is no difference between the total or partial derivative of Q with respect to L, or $dQ/dL = \partial Q/\partial L$. Thus, we can finally express the value of the marginal product of labor function as

$$VMP_L = \overline{P}_1 MP_L,$$

where, ultimately, VMP_L is a function of the amount of the labor input used by the firm, since MP_L is a function of this variable.

We have illustrated the VMP_L function in Figure 20.1, where this curve assumes the general shape of the familiar MP_L curve, since it simply consists of MP_L multiplied by the constant price, $\overline{P}_1$. Note that for increases in labor use, VMP_L rises up to L_2 units, decreasing thereafter, reflecting the law of diminishing marginal productivity.

The other component of a firm's short-run profit function is its short-run total cost, $SRTC$, which we can express in terms of output, or alternatively, in terms of the inputs employed to produce that output. In Chapter 10 we represented a firm's costs in terms of the inputs it employs by the isocost equation as

$$C = \overline{P}_{K,1} K + \overline{P}_{L,1} L.$$

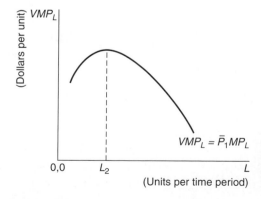

FIGURE 20.1 Value of the Marginal Product of Labor Curve

This equation indicates that a firm's total cost, C, is equal to the summation of its expenditures on the two inputs, capital and labor. We fixed the input prices of capital and labor at specified levels, $\overline{P}_{K,1}$ and $\overline{P}_{L,1}$, respectively, reflecting our earlier assumption that the firm is a price taker in its input markets. Once the capital input is fixed at level $\overline{K}_1$, we interpret this equation as a short-run total cost function, $SRTC$, or

$$SRTC = \overline{P}_{K,1}\overline{K}_1 + \overline{P}_{L,1}L, \qquad (20.3)$$

where the terms $\overline{P}_{K,1}\overline{K}_1$ and $\overline{P}_{L,1}L$ represent the firm's fixed and variable costs, respectively.

We can establish a relationship between $SRTC$ and the firm's variable input, known as the **marginal expense of an input**, or MEI_{input}, defined as *the change in total cost due to a change in the amount of an input employed, holding all other inputs constant*. In this case, since the variable input is labor, we compute the marginal expense of labor, MEI_L, by taking the derivative of $SRTC$ with respect to L as

$$MEI_L = \frac{dSRTC}{dL} = \frac{d\overline{P}_{K,1}\overline{K}_1}{dL} + \frac{d\overline{P}_{L,1}L}{dL} = \overline{P}_{L,1}.$$

This result that the MEI_L is equal to the constant price of labor reflects the fact that the firm is a price taker in its labor market.

We can apply the value of the marginal product and the marginal expense of an input concepts to demonstrate how a firm determines the amount of an input it should employ to maximize its profit. The short-run profit function for a firm is the difference between its total revenue and short-run total cost, or

$$SR\pi = TR - SRTC.$$

Substituting the expressions for TR and $SRTC$ from equations (20.2) and (20.3), respectively, into the above equation, enables us to define the profit function in terms of the inputs as

$$SR\pi = \overline{P}_1 f(\overline{K}_1, L) - (\overline{P}_{K,1}\overline{K}_1 + \overline{P}_{L,1}L) = \overline{P}_1 f(\overline{K}_1, L) - \overline{P}_{K,1}\overline{K}_1 - \overline{P}_{L,1}L.$$

We obtain the amount of labor corresponding to the maximum value of short-run profit by taking the derivative of $SR\pi$ with respect to L, setting the result equal to zero, and solving as

$$\frac{dSR\pi}{dL} = \frac{d\overline{P}_1 f(\overline{K}_1, L)}{dL} - \frac{d\overline{P}_{K,1}\overline{K}_1}{dL} - \frac{d\overline{P}_{L,1}L}{dL} = 0$$

$$= \overline{P}_1 \frac{df(\overline{K}_1, L)}{dL} - \overline{P}_{L,1} = 0,$$

or

$$\overline{P}_1 MP_L = \overline{P}_{L,1},$$

and therefore

$$VMP_L = MEI_L.$$

This equation indicates that a firm maximizes its profit by employing its variable input, labor, to the point where the extra revenue from using an extra unit of labor, VMP_L, is equal to the extra cost associated with hiring the extra unit of labor, MEI_L. Thus, the condition $VMP_L = MEI_L$, which in this case is equal to $\overline{P}_{L,1}$, represents an alternative version of the necessary condition for achieving a profit maximum.

In Figure 20.2, we have once again illustrated the VMP_L curve, as well as including several $MEI_L = P_L$ curves. Since VMP_L and P_L constitute dollar amounts, both are plotted on the vertical axis, while the amount of labor, L, is plotted on the horizontal axis. To simplify the graphical analysis, we are focusing on only the negatively sloped portion of the VMP_L curve. This portion reflects diminishing marginal productivity of the labor input and includes that range of labor use pertaining to a firm's Stage II area of production, or where MP_L and MP_K are both nonnegative.

Observe in Figure 20.2 that, if the market price of labor, generally considered to be the wage rate, is predetermined as $\overline{P}_{L,1}$, the firm maximizes its short-run profit by employing L_1 units of labor for which $VMP_{L,1} = MEI_{L,1} = \overline{P}_{L,1}$. The rationale for this result is very straightforward. For example, if the firm employs L_0 units of labor at $\overline{P}_{L,1}$, then $VMP_{L,0} > MEI_{L,1} = \overline{P}_{L,1}$. This inequality indicates that if the firm increases the amount of labor it uses, it can increase its total revenue more than its short-run total cost and therefore, increase its short-run profit. Alternatively, if the firm employs L_2 units of labor at $\overline{P}_{L,1}$, then $VMP_{L,2} < MEI_{L,1} = \overline{P}_{L,1}$, and the firm can increase its short-run profit by employing less labor, reducing its short-run cost more than its total revenue. Thus, at $\overline{P}_{L,1}$, the only level of labor for which there is no opportunity to increase short-run profit is L_1 units, where $VMP_{L,1} = MEI_{L,1} = \overline{P}_{L,1}$, and accordingly, at which short-run profit must achieve its maximum value.

If labor market conditions change such that the price of labor increases to $\overline{P}_{L,0}$, then the firm maximizes its short-run profit by reducing the amount of labor it employs to L_0 units, where $VMP_{L,0} = MEI_{L,0} = \overline{P}_{L,0}$. Alternatively, if the price of labor falls to $\overline{P}_{L,2}$, then the firm achieves a profit maximum by increasing the amount of labor it hires to L_2 units at which $VMP_{L,2} = MEI_{L,2} = \overline{P}_{L,2}$. For any predetermined market price of labor, we determine the profit-maximizing level of labor according to the $VMP_L = MEI_L = P_L$ condition.

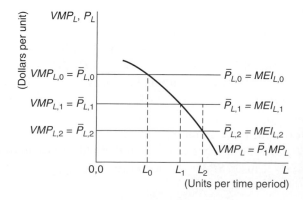

FIGURE 20.2 Profit-Maximizing Quantities of Labor for a Perfectly Competitive Firm with Only One Variable Input

We can provide some additional insight into the above discussion by demonstrating that a firm's determination of its profit-maximizing level of output and its profit-maximizing level of an input are parts of the same process. Recall that a perfectly competitive firm determines its short-run profit-maximizing level of output according to the rule $P = SRMC$. Also, in Chapter 12, we expressed a firm's short-run marginal cost as the monetized reciprocal of the marginal product of its variable input, which in this case is labor; thus

$$SRMC = \frac{P_L}{MP_L}.$$

Therefore, at the profit-maximizing level of output

$$P = SRMC = \frac{P_L}{MP_L},$$

or

$$P = \frac{P_L}{MP_L}.$$

Since the profit-maximizing level of labor is determined by the rule

$$VMP_L = PMP_L = P_L,$$

then dividing this equation by MP_L yields

$$\frac{PMP_L}{MP_L} = \frac{P_L}{MP_L},$$

or

$$P = \frac{P_L}{MP_L},$$

which is the same result we obtained above.

We have illustrated the $P = SRMC$ condition for determining a firm's profit-maximizing level of output in Figure 20.3. The curve $SRMC\ (\overline{P}_{L,1})$ represents the firm's short-run marginal cost when the price of labor is $\overline{P}_{L,1}$. Recall that a firm's short-run costs, including short-run marginal cost, contain the price of the variable input as one of the determinants. If the price of the output is $\overline{P}_1$, the firm determines its profit-maximizing level of output as Q_1 where $\overline{P}_1 = SRMC_1$. To produce Q_1 units of output, the firm uses L_1 units of labor at which $VMP_{L,1} = \overline{P}_1 MP_L = \overline{P}_{L,1}$, as we illustrated in Figure 20.2. Now, if the price of labor decreases to $\overline{P}_{L,2}$, the firm's $SRMC$ curve shifts down to $SRMC'(\overline{P}_{L,2})$ as shown in Figure 20.3, demonstrating that the firm can now produce any given level of Q at a lower short-run marginal cost than before, owing to the lower input price. Another way to view this result is by observing the formula, $SRMC = P_L/MP_L$, where we can reason that a decrease in the numerator of the right-hand term, P_L, causes $SRMC$ to decrease. At Q_1, $\overline{P}_1 > SRMC'_1$, and the

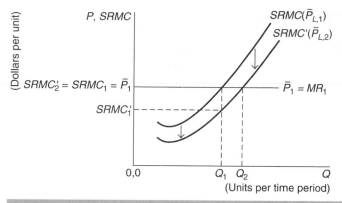

FIGURE 20.3 Profit-Maximizing Quantities of Output for Different Prices of Labor

firm can increase its short-run profit by increasing the level of output it produces to Q_2 units, at which $\overline{P}_1 = SRMC'_2$. Therefore, to produce this larger amount of Q, the firm must increase the amount of labor it uses, where we have shown this amount in Figure 20.2 as L_2 units at which $VMP_{L,2} = \overline{P}_{L,2}$.

Our major objective in this analysis is to derive the demand for labor curve. A demand curve, or more technically an own-price demand curve, is a function that expresses the quantity demanded of some good as a function of its own price, while holding all other determinants constant at some levels. In this case, the "good" we are analyzing is the quantity of labor employed by a firm, and the own price is the price of labor, P_L, generally considered to be the wage rate. As demonstrated in the preceding analysis, we determine the optimal, or profit-maximizing, quantity of labor by equating each price of labor with the value of its marginal product and then solving for the corresponding value of L. As a result, we can interpret the VMP_L curve as representing the firm's demand for labor curve, given our earlier assumptions that the firm uses only one variable input and that it acts as a price taker in both its output and input markets. We can express this demand for labor curve as

$$L^d = L^d(P_L, \overline{K}_1, \overline{P}_1),$$

where L^d represents the quantity of labor demanded by the firm. We have held constant at specified levels all determinants of L^d, with the exception of its own price, P_L. Observe, in Figures 20.1 and 20.2, that for reasons discussed earlier, the relationship between P_L and L^d is clearly inverse. Generally, we expect the relationship between L^d and the amount of capital, K, to be direct. This follows because an increase in K usually enhances the marginal productivity of labor, since labor receives a greater amount of plant and equipment with which to work. Finally, the demand for labor is also directly related to the price of the output, P, as an increase in this price clearly enhances the value of the extra amount of output produced, due to using an extra unit of labor, or the VMP_L.

We have demonstrated the firm's demand for one variable input curve while holding the level of capital held constant and treating labor as the variable input. This process can be conducted by holding the amount of labor constant and treating capital as the variable input, thus generating a firm's demand for capital curve. This process is analogous to our derivation of the firm's demand curve for labor, and thus it will be left to you as an exercise. However, we should mention that capital possesses some unique characteristics not attributed to labor; therefore, we will present a more extensive treatment of a firm's demand for capital in Chapter 22.

We can provide some additional insight into the derivation of a firm's demand for labor curve with a specific example. Assume a firm produces output in the short run according to the production function,

$$Q = 10\overline{K}_1^{1/2}L^{1/2},$$

where it receives a predetermined output price of $\overline{P}_1$, and must pay input prices $\overline{P}_{K,1}$, and $\overline{P}_{L,1}$ for its capital and labor inputs, respectively. The firm's short-run profit function is the difference between its total revenue and short-run total cost, or

$$SR\pi = TR - SRTC,$$

where

$$TR = \overline{P}_1 Q$$

and

$$SRTC = \overline{P}_{K,1}\overline{K}_1 + \overline{P}_{L,1}L.$$

Substituting these expressions for TR and $SRTC$ into the $SR\pi$ function yields

$$SR\pi = \overline{P}_1 Q - (\overline{P}_{K,1}\overline{K}_1 + \overline{P}_{L,1}L).$$

We can substitute the expression for Q from the production function into this equation, thus enabling us to define $SR\pi$ strictly in terms of inputs as

$$SR\pi = \overline{P}_1 10\overline{K}_1^{1/2}L^{1/2} - \overline{P}_{K,1}\overline{K}_1 - \overline{P}_{L,1}L.$$

We determine the profit-maximizing level of labor by first taking the derivative of $SR\pi$ with respect to L and setting the result equal to zero as

$$\frac{dSR\pi}{dL} = 5\overline{P}_1\overline{K}_1^{1/2}L^{-1/2} - \overline{P}_{L,1} = 0,$$

or

$$5\overline{P}_1\overline{K}_1^{1/2}L^{-1/2} = \overline{P}_{L,1}. \tag{20.4}$$

The terms on the left- and right-hand sides of this equation are the results of computing and dTR/dL and $dSRTC/dL$, respectively, and thus represent the expressions for VMP_L and the MEI_L, respectively. Therefore, equation (20.4) is the necessary condition for a profit maximum, from which we can compute the profit-maximizing levels of labor as

$$\frac{5\overline{P}_1\overline{K}_1^{1/2}}{\overline{P}_{L,1}} = \frac{1}{L^{-1/2}}$$

$$L^{1/2} = \frac{5\overline{P}_1\overline{K}_1^{1/2}}{\overline{P}_{L,1}}$$

$$L = \frac{25\overline{P}_1^2\overline{K}_1}{\overline{P}_{L,1}^2}.$$

We construct the firm's demand for labor curve by allowing the price of labor, P_L, to vary, while holding the output price, P, and the level of capital, K, fixed at specified levels, or

$$L = \frac{25\overline{P}_1^2\overline{K}_1}{P_L^2}. \tag{20.5}$$

If the values of P and K are known, say, for example, $\overline{P}_1 = \$1$ and $\overline{K}_1 = 4$ units, then we can write equation (20.5) more specifically as

$$L = \frac{25(1)^2\,4}{P_L^2} = \frac{100}{P_L^2}.$$

To reinforce the point that the two expressions of the necessary condition for a profit maximum, $P = SRMC$, and $VMP_L = MEI_L = P_L$, represent the same outcome, we can derive the firm's demand for labor curve using an alternative approach. To do so, we first solve the production function

$$Q = 10K_1^{1/2}L^{1/2}$$

for the labor input, as

$$L^{1/2} = \frac{Q}{10\overline{K}_1^{1/2}},$$

or

$$L = \frac{Q^2}{100\overline{K}_1}.$$

Substituting this expression for L into the $SRTC$ function

$$SRTC = \overline{P}_{K,1}\overline{K}_1 + \overline{P}_{L,1}L,$$

yields

$$SRTC = \overline{P}_{K,1}\overline{K}_1 + \overline{P}_{L,1}\left(\frac{Q^2}{100\overline{K}_1}\right).$$

Next we compute the firm's short-run marginal cost by taking the derivative of *SRTC* with respect to output as

$$SRMC = \frac{dSRTC}{dQ} = \frac{d\overline{P}_{K,1}\overline{K}_1}{dQ} + \frac{d\left(\dfrac{\overline{P}_{L,1}Q^2}{100\overline{K}_1}\right)}{dQ}$$

$$= \frac{2\overline{P}_{L,1}Q}{100\overline{K}_1} = \frac{\overline{P}_{L,1}Q}{50\overline{K}_1}. \tag{20.6}$$

Since the firm's profit-maximizing level of output is determined where $P = SRMC$ and $P = \overline{P}_1$, then we can express equation (20.6) as

$$\overline{P}_1 = \frac{\overline{P}_{L,1}Q}{50\overline{K}_1},$$

and after substituting the expression for Q from the production function, this expression becomes

$$\overline{P}_1 = \frac{\overline{P}_{L,1}10\overline{K}_1^{1/2} L^{1/2}}{50\overline{K}_1}.$$

We can now solve this equation for L as

$$L^{1/2} = \frac{5\overline{K}_1\overline{P}_1}{\overline{P}_{L,1}\overline{K}_1^{1/2}} = \frac{5\overline{P}_1\overline{K}_1^{1/2}}{\overline{P}_{L,1}}$$

$$L = \frac{25\overline{P}_1^2\overline{K}_1}{\overline{P}_{L,1}^2}.$$

After letting P_L vary, then

$$L = \frac{25\overline{P}_1^2\overline{K}_1}{P_L^2},$$

where this expression represents the firm's demand for labor curve we derived earlier.

20.3 FIRM INPUT DEMAND CURVES WITH MORE THAN ONE VARIABLE INPUT

In this section, we will extend our analysis to derive labor demand curves for a firm using more than one variable input. In order to make comparisons with our earlier analysis, we will maintain our assumptions that the firm acts as a perfect competitor in both its output and input markets. Furthermore, to continue focusing on the short run, we will include a third input in the production process, which we will hold constant at some level. We can now express the firm's production function as

$$Q = f(K, L, \overline{Z}_1),$$

where Q, K, and L are defined in the same manner as earlier, but in this case, we are treating both of these inputs as variable. The third input in the production function, Z, might represent an input such as land, which we are holding constant at level $\overline{Z}_1$.

Although our focus is on developing a firm's demand for labor curve, we will also derive its demand for capital curve, since both curves are related to the same process. Deriving a firm's demand for labor curve with two variable inputs is considerably more complex than the one variable input case. This additional complexity is based primarily on the fact that a change in the price of labor not only causes a change in the amount of labor demanded by a firm, but also affects its use of the other variable input, capital. As discussed in Chapter 8, for most production functions, a change in the use of one input typically has a direct effect on the marginal productivity of the others. For example, a decrease in the price of labor might increase the amount of capital, as well as labor, employed by a firm. In this case, the diminishing marginal product of labor, caused by additional use of this input, is partly offset, reflecting the fact that labor has more capital with which to work. In other words, additional capital makes the labor input more productive, ultimately increasing the firm's demand for labor.

The process of determining a firm's profit-maximizing levels of two variable inputs, and the associated firm input demand curves, is as follows. As stated earlier, the firm's short-run production function is

$$Q = f(K, L, \overline{Z}_1),$$

where the third input, Z, is fixed at level $\overline{Z}_1$. In this case, we represent the short-run total cost function for the firm as

$$SRTC = \overline{P}_{K,1}K + \overline{P}_{L,1}L + \overline{P}_{Z,1}\overline{Z}_1,$$

where $\overline{P}_{K,1}K + \overline{P}_{L,1}L$ represents the firm's variable cost and $\overline{P}_{Z,1}\overline{Z}_1$ is its fixed cost. The short-run profit function for the firm is

$$SR\pi = TR - SRTC,$$

or

$$SR\pi = \overline{P}_1 Q - (\overline{P}_{K,1}K + \overline{P}_{L,1}L + \overline{P}_{Z,1}\overline{Z}_1)$$
$$= \overline{P}_1 Q - \overline{P}_{K,1}K - \overline{P}_{L,1}L - \overline{P}_{Z,1}\overline{Z}_1,$$

where we treat the output price, $\overline{P}_1$, and the input prices $\overline{P}_{K,1}$, $\overline{P}_{L,1}$, and $\overline{P}_{Z,1}$ as predetermined. Substituting the expression for Q from the production function yields

$$SR\pi = \overline{P}_1 f(K, L, \overline{Z}_1) - \overline{P}_{K,1}K - \overline{P}_{L,1}L - \overline{P}_{Z,1}\overline{Z}_1.$$

We determine the firm's profit-maximizing levels of capital and labor by taking the partial derivative of $SR\pi$ with respect to each input and setting the results equal to zero as

$$\frac{\partial SR\pi}{\partial K} = \overline{P}_1 \frac{\partial f(K, L, \overline{Z}_1)}{\partial K} - \overline{P}_{K,1} = 0 \tag{20.7}$$

and

$$\frac{\partial SR\pi}{\partial L} = \overline{P}_1 \frac{\partial f(K,L,\overline{Z}_1)}{\partial L} - \overline{P}_{L,1} = 0. \tag{20.8}$$

Thus

$$\overline{P}_1 \frac{\partial f(K,L,\overline{Z}_1)}{\partial K} = \overline{P}_{K,1}$$

and

$$\overline{P}_1 \frac{\partial f(K,L,\overline{Z}_1)}{\partial L} = \overline{P}_{L,1}.$$

Since $Q = f(K,L,\overline{Z}_1)$, we can simplify these equations as

$$\overline{P}_1 \frac{\partial Q}{\partial K} = \overline{P}_{K,1}$$

and

$$\overline{P}_1 \frac{\partial Q}{\partial L} = \overline{P}_{L,1}.$$

Recognizing $\partial Q/\partial K$ and $\partial Q/\partial L$ as MP_K and MP_L, respectively, then

$$\overline{P}_1 MP_K = \overline{P}_{K,1} \tag{20.9}$$

and

$$\overline{P}_1 MP_L = \overline{P}_{L,1}. \tag{20.10}$$

Since we ultimately determine $\overline{P}_1 MP_K$ by computing $\partial TR/\partial K$, or the change in total revenue due to a change in the amount of capital used, it represents the value of the marginal product of capital function, VMP_K. Similarly, we determine $\overline{P}_1 MP_L$ by computing $\partial TR/\partial L$, or the change in total revenue due to a change in the amount of labor employed, and it thus represents the value of the marginal product of labor, VMP_L. The input prices, $\overline{P}_{K,1}$ and $\overline{P}_{L,1}$, result from taking the partials $\partial SRTC/\partial K$ and $\partial SRTC/\partial L$, respectively. Therefore, they represent the changes in a firm's short-run total cost due to respective changes in the amounts of capital and labor employed. Thus, $\overline{P}_{K,1}$ represents the marginal expense of the input capital, MEI_K, and $\overline{P}_{L,1}$ represents the marginal expense of the input labor, MEI_L. We can express equations (20.9) and (20.10) in the familiar form

$$VMP_K = \overline{P}_{K,1} = MEI_K \tag{20.11}$$

and

$$VMP_L = \overline{P}_{L,1} = MEI_L, \tag{20.12}$$

indicating that a firm maximizes its short-run profit by employing capital and labor to the point where the extra revenue is equal to the extra cost associated with using an additional unit of each respective input.

Formally, these equations represent the set of necessary conditions we define as the first-order conditions for a profit maximum. In this two variable input case, we obtain the profit-maximizing level of any one input, and therefore its subsequent input demand curve, by satisfying both first-order conditions simultaneously. This result occurs because the amount of either input used is related to the use of the other. Therefore, a change in the price of either of these inputs affects the firm's demand for both inputs. Solving these first-order conditions simultaneously yields the firm's input demand curves for labor and capital, represented as

$$K^d = K^d(P_K, \overline{P}_{L,1}, \overline{P}_1, \overline{Z}_1)$$

and

$$L^d = L^d(P_L, \overline{P}_{K,1}, \overline{P}_1, \overline{Z}_1),$$

respectively. Each input demand curve contains both input prices, P_L and P_K, as determinants, along with the price of the output, P, and the level of the fixed input, Z. In each case, we allow the own price of the input to vary, while holding all other determinants constant.

Focusing on the firm's demand for labor curve, we can make some inferences regarding the directionality of the relationships between each of the independent variables and L^d. First, the relationship between P_L and L^d is inverse, as in the single variable input case, although the rationale for this result is now based on substitution and output effects, which we will discuss later in this section. The relationship between P_K and L^d also depends on substitution and output effects, which in this case run counter to each other. As a result, it is impossible to determine a priori the direction of this relationship. However, the relationship between P and L^d is clearly direct, as an increase in the price of a firm's output enhances the value of the extra output produced from each extra unit of labor employed. Finally, the relationship between Z and L^d is generally direct, since for many production processes increasing the use of one input enhances the marginal productivity of the others.

We can provide some additional insight by using a specific example to derive a firm's input demand curves for the case of two variable inputs. Assume a firm has the production function

$$Q = K^{1/4} L^{1/4} \overline{Z}_1^{1/2},$$

where we hold the input Z, say land, constant at $\overline{Z}_1$ units, and thus capital, K, and labor, L, constitute the firm's variable inputs. Also assume that the price of the firm's output is predetermined as $\overline{P}_1$, and the input prices for capital, labor, and land are initially specified as $\overline{P}_{K,1}$, $\overline{P}_{L,1}$, and $\overline{P}_{Z,1}$, respectively. The firm's short-run profit function $SR\pi$ is

$$SR\pi = TR - SRTC$$

and therefore, after making the appropriate substitutions for TR and $SRTC$, then

$$SR\pi = \overline{P}_1 Q - (\overline{P}_{K,1}K + \overline{P}_{L,1}L + \overline{P}_{Z,1}\overline{Z}_1).$$

Substituting the expression for Q from the production function yields

$$SR\pi = \overline{P}_1 K^{1/4} L^{1/4} \overline{Z}_1^{1/2} - \overline{P}_{K,1} K - \overline{P}_{L,1} L - \overline{P}_{Z,1} \overline{Z}_1.$$

We compute the first-order conditions for a profit maximum as

$$\frac{\partial SR\pi}{\partial K} = \frac{1}{4} \overline{P}_1 K^{-3/4} L^{1/4} \overline{Z}_1^{1/2} - \overline{P}_{K,1} = 0 \qquad \textbf{(20.13)}$$

and

$$\frac{\partial SR\pi}{\partial L} = \frac{1}{4} \overline{P}_1 K^{1/4} L^{-3/4} \overline{Z}_1^{1/2} - \overline{P}_{L,1} = 0, \qquad \textbf{(20.14)}$$

where the first term in equation (20.13) is the VMP_K and the second term is the MEI_K. Similarly, the first term in equation (20.14) is the VMP_L, and the second term is the MEI_L. We can solve equations (20.13) and (20.14) simultaneously to determine the firm's input demand functions for labor and capital. This procedure can be accomplished in any of several ways, where one of the simplest is to first rearrange equations (20.13) and (20.14) and then divide equation (20.14) by equation (20.13), yielding

$$\frac{\frac{1}{4} \overline{P}_1 K^{1/4} L^{-3/4} \overline{Z}_1^{1/2}}{\frac{1}{4} \overline{P}_1 K^{-3/4} L^{1/4} \overline{Z}_1^{1/2}} = \frac{\overline{P}_{L,1}}{\overline{P}_{K,1}},$$

which reduces to the result

$$\frac{K}{L} = \frac{\overline{P}_{L,1}}{\overline{P}_{K,1}},$$

or

$$K = \frac{\overline{P}_{L,1}}{\overline{P}_{K,1}} L. \qquad \textbf{(20.15)}$$

Substituting this expression for K into equation (20.14) yields

$$\frac{1}{4} \overline{P}_1 \left(\frac{\overline{P}_{L,1}}{\overline{P}_{K,1}} L \right)^{1/4} L^{-3/4} \overline{Z}_1^{1/2} - \overline{P}_{L,1} = 0$$

$$\frac{1}{4} \overline{P}_1 \left(\frac{\overline{P}_{L,1}}{\overline{P}_{K,1}} \right)^{1/4} L^{-1/2} \overline{Z}_1^{1/2} = \overline{P}_{L,1}$$

$$\frac{\overline{P}_{L,1}}{L^{-1/2}} = \frac{1}{4} \overline{P}_1 \left(\frac{\overline{P}_{L,1}}{\overline{P}_{K,1}} \right)^{1/4} \overline{Z}_1^{1/2}$$

$$L^{1/2} = \frac{\overline{P}_1}{4 \overline{P}_{L,1}} \left(\frac{\overline{P}_{L,1}}{\overline{P}_{K,1}} \right)^{1/4} \overline{Z}_1^{1/2},$$

where we can finally solve for L by squaring both sides of this equation, yielding

$$L = \frac{\overline{P}_1^2 \overline{Z}_1}{16 \overline{P}_{L,1}^{3/2} \overline{P}_{K,1}^{1/2}}. \tag{20.16}$$

By allowing P_L to vary, while holding P, Z, and P_K constant, we can interpret this expression as the firm's demand for labor curve, or

$$L^d = \frac{\overline{P}_1^2 \overline{Z}_1}{16 P_L^{3/2} \overline{P}_{K,1}^{1/2}}. \tag{20.17}$$

Specifically, suppose $\overline{P}_1 = \$80$, $\overline{Z}_1 = 1$ unit, and $\overline{P}_{K,1} = \$1$; then in this case we compute the firm's demand for labor curve as

$$L^d = \frac{80^2(1)}{16 P_L^{3/2}(1)^{1/2}} = \frac{400}{P_L^{3/2}}.$$

This curve expresses the quantity of labor demanded by a firm explicitly as a function of its own price, *ceteris paribus*. For example, if $\overline{P}_{L,1} = \$4$, then the corresponding quantity of labor demanded by the firm is

$$L_1^d = \frac{400}{4^{3/2}} = 50 \text{ units},$$

and if P_L decreases to $\overline{P}_{L,2} = \$1$, then the quantity of labor demanded increases to the level

$$L_2^d = \frac{400}{(1)^{3/2}} = 400 \text{ units}.$$

We derive the firm's demand for capital curve in a similar manner. Substituting equation (20.16) into equation (20.15) yields

$$K = \frac{\overline{P}_{L,1}}{\overline{P}_{K,1}}\left(\frac{\overline{P}_1^2 \overline{Z}_1}{16 \overline{P}_{L,1}^{3/2} \overline{P}_{K,1}^{1/2}}\right) = \frac{\overline{P}_1^2 \overline{Z}_1}{16 \overline{P}_{L,1}^{1/2} \overline{P}_{K,1}^{3/2}},$$

and once P_K is allowed to vary, this expression becomes

$$K^d = \frac{\overline{P}_1^2 \overline{Z}_1}{16 \overline{P}_{L,1}^{1/2} P_K^{3/2}}, \tag{20.18}$$

or the firm's demand for capital curve. As an example, if $\overline{P}_1 = \$80$, $\overline{Z}_1 = 1$ unit and $\overline{P}_{L,1} = \$4$, the specific capital demand curve is

$$K^d = \frac{80^2(1)}{16(4)^{1/2} P_K^{3/2}} = \frac{200}{P_K^{3/2}},$$

and if $\overline{P}_{K,1} = \$1$, we compute the quantity of capital demanded by the firm as

$$K_1^d = \frac{200}{(1)^{3/2}} = 200 \text{ units}.$$

We can also use the preceding analysis to determine the firm's profit-maximizing level of output. Since the input values we calculate from input demand curves represent optimal, or profit-maximizing, levels of these inputs, then the corresponding levels of output also pertain to profit maximums. For this example, we can compute the specific output level by substituting the initial optimal values of the inputs K and L, along with the predetermined value of Z, into the production function, yielding

$$Q_1 = K_1^{1/4}L_1^{1/4}\overline{Z}_1^{1/2} = (200)^{1/4}(50)^{1/4}(1)^{1/2} = 10 \text{ units.}$$

More generally, by focusing on the input demand curves represented in equations (20.17) and (20.18), and allowing P, P_K, and P_L to vary, we can broaden these input demand curves to represent input demand functions, which can be substituted into the production function yielding

$$Q = \left(\frac{P^2\overline{Z}_1}{16P_L^{1/2}P_K^{3/2}}\right)^{1/4}\left(\frac{P^2\overline{Z}_1}{16P_L^{3/2}P_K^{1/2}}\right)^{1/4}\overline{Z}_1^{1/2}$$

$$= \left(\frac{P^{1/2}\overline{Z}_1^{1/4}}{2P_L^{1/8}P_K^{3/8}}\right)\left(\frac{P^{1/2}\overline{Z}_1^{1/4}}{2P_L^{3/8}P_K^{1/8}}\right)\overline{Z}_1^{1/2},$$

or

$$Q = \frac{P\overline{Z}_1}{4P_L^{1/2}P_K^{1/2}}. \tag{20.19}$$

This equation expresses the firm's profit-maximizing levels of output in terms of the output price, P, the prices of the two variable inputs, P_K and P_L, and the fixed input $\overline{Z}_1$. We can interpret equation (20.19) as the firm's short-run supply function for the case of two variable inputs. Then, once we fix the input prices, this function becomes the firm's short-run supply curve, expressing the levels of output supplied by the firm, Q^S, as a function of the price of the output, P, with all other determinants held constant at some specified levels, or

$$Q^S = Q^S(P,\overline{P}_{K,1},\overline{P}_{L,1},\overline{Z}_1).$$

20.3.1 Substitution and Output Effects

Earlier we stated that there is an inverse relationship between the price of labor and the quantity of labor demanded by a firm. However, our rationale for the directionality of this relationship in the two variable input case is somewhat more complex than in the single variable input case in that now a change in the price of labor affects both the amount of labor and capital used by the firm. Thus, as the price of an input changes, a firm alters the amount of that input it uses for two reasons. First, when the price of an input changes, holding the price of the other input constant, one input becomes more or less expensive relative to the other. Logically, the firm will substitute away from the increasingly expensive input and toward the one that becomes relatively less expensive. We refer to this result more formally as the familiar substitution effect, that in this context, is the effect of a change in the price of an input on the quantity demanded of that input, due strictly to the resulting change in relative input prices.

The second reason explaining why a firm alters its use of an input in response to a change in its price is that such a change affects the firm's *SRMC* curve, thus providing it with an incentive to adjust its output to maintain the $P = SRMC$ condition for a profit maximum. Thus, for a firm to alter the level of output it produces, it must change the level of inputs it uses. This result is known as the **output effect**, or *the effect of a change in the price of an input on the quantity demanded of that input, due strictly to the resulting change in the profit-maximizing level of output.* These substitution and output effects, when summed together, comprise the total effect of a change in an input price on the quantity demanded of that input. These effects that we apply to a firm are somewhat analogous to the substitution and income effects we developed in Chapter 5 as part of consumer theory. However, the analogy breaks down for the output effect because firms, unlike consumers, are not restricted to a particular level of expenditure, or cost, provided we assume they operate in perfect financial markets. Thus, given this assumption, firms are able to borrow all of the funds necessary to purchase the inputs they employ in their production processes.

In Figure 20.4, we have illustrated the substitution and output affects for the quantity of labor demanded by a firm, for the case of a decrease in the price of labor from $\overline{P}_{L,1}$ to $\overline{P}_{L,2}$. Initially, the firm operates at point D, producing Q_1 units of output at which the isoquant representing Q_1 is tangent to the isocost curve pertaining to the level of cost, $C_1 - \overline{P}_{K,1}K + \overline{P}_{L,1}L$. Thus, at point D the firm is operating at a constrained cost minimum by using L_1 units of labor and K_1 units of capital at which the necessary condition, $MRTS = \overline{P}_{L,1}/\overline{P}_{K,1}$, is satisfied. As noted in Chapter 10, this condition indicates that the firm has adjusted its inputs until the rate at which it is able to substitute one input for the other while producing the same level of output, or *MRTS*, is equal to the rate at which it is able to substitute one input for the other while incurring the same level of cost, or P_L/P_K. If the price of labor decreases from $\overline{P}_{L,1}$ to $\overline{P}_{L,2}$,

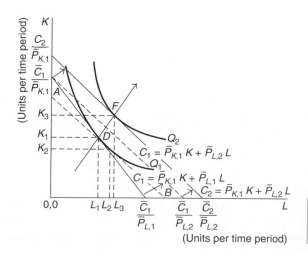

FIGURE 20.4 Substitution and Output Effects for a Decrease in the Price of Labor

ceteris paribus, the value of the L intercept for the isocost curve increases to $C_1/\overline{P}_{L,2}$, for this price decrease causes the isocost curve to rotate counterclockwise around the K intercept, $C_1/\overline{P}_{K,1}$, which remains constant.

This new isocost equation, $C_1 = \overline{P}_{K,1} K + \overline{P}_{L,2} L$, is unlikely to provide the final solution to the firm's optimization problem because ultimately the firm is seldom restricted to incurring a specific cost such as C_1. However, the slope of this new isocost equation, $-\overline{P}_{L,2}/\overline{P}_{K,1}$, is particularly relevant because it reflects the fact that labor has become increasingly less expensive relative to capital. Therefore, we can analyze the substitution effect associated with this decrease in the price of labor by constructing a compensated isocost constraint, represented in Figure 20.4 as the curve AB. We have drawn this curve parallel to the new isocost equation, $C_1 = \overline{P}_{K,1} K + \overline{P}_{L,2} L$, but tangent to the initial isoquant representing Q_1, in order to hold the production of output constant at that level. As a result, any change in the amount of labor or capital used by the firm is due strictly to the change in the relative input price ratio, P_L/P_K, since we have eliminated any output effect by holding Q constant. Observe in Figure 20.4 that the firm decreases the amount of capital it uses from K_1 to K_2 units and increases the amount of labor it employs from L_1 to L_2 units, reflecting the substitution effect of labor for capital due to the decrease in the relative price of labor. Thus, we can conclude that the substitution effect relating to the quantity demanded of an input and its own price is inverse.

To complete the analysis and therefore demonstrate the total effect of a decrease in P_L on L, it is necessary that we add the output effect to this substitution effect. We have already demonstrated in Section 20.2 that a decrease in the price of an input causes a firm's marginal cost curve to shift downward. This situation was illustrated in Figure 20.3, where a decrease in P_L causes the $SRMC$ curve to shift down, resulting in a situation for which $P_1 > SRMC_1'$ at the firm's original level of production, Q_1. As a result, the firm can increase its profit by expanding its production of output to Q_2 units, at which $P_1 = SRMC_2'$. To do so, in the two variable input case, the firm increases its use of both inputs by moving along the expansion path labeled DF in Figure 20.4. Accordingly, the firm produces its output using optimal input combinations and therefore produces its output in the least costly manner. Since the firm is not restricted to a particular level of cost, such as C_1, it produces the new profit-maximizing level of output, Q_2, at a constrained cost minimum of $C_2 = \overline{P}_{K,1} K + \overline{P}_{L,2} L$, where $C_2 > C_1$. In Figure 20.4, the firm now operates at point F, using K_3 units of capital and L_3 units of labor, at which the necessary condition for a constrained cost minimum, $MRTS = \overline{P}_{L,2}/\overline{P}_{K,1}$ is satisfied. This increase in labor use from L_2 to L_3 units constitutes the output effect, and when added to the substitution effect, $(L_2 - L_1)$, yields the total effect, $(L_3 - L_1)$. Assuming labor is not an inferior input, these substitution and income effects reinforce each other, creating an unambiguously inverse total effect. Alternatively stated, in this case, a decrease in the price of labor definitely results in an increase in the quantity of labor demanded by a firm. By plotting the associated combinations of L and P_L, we can construct the firm's labor demand curve for the two variable input case as illustrated in Figure 20.5. This labor demand curve contains the

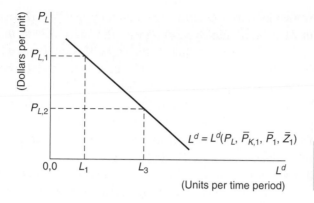

FIGURE 20.5 Firm Demand for Labor Curve with More Than One Variable Input

aforementioned combinations, $(L_1, P_{L,1})$ and $(L_3, P_{L,2})$, where $P_{L,2} < P_{L,1}$ and $L_3 > L_1$, demonstrating the net inverse relationship between L and P_L.

To emphasize that, generally, the firm's demand for labor curve in the two variable input case is not simply the VMP_L curve, we have provided an alternative derivation in Figure 20.6. If labor is the only variable input, with capital fixed at level $\overline{K}_1$, then the curve, $VMP_L(\overline{K}_1)$, constitutes the firm's demand for labor curve. Thus, if the price of labor decreases from $P_{L,1}$ to $P_{L,2}$, the firm's quantity of labor demanded increases from L_1 to L_2 units. However, in the two variable input case where capital is also allowed to vary, the decrease in P_L causes a change in the firm's use of capital. Specifically, the substitution effect associated with a decrease in P_L results in the firm using more labor and less capital. This decrease in capital, in most situations, causes the marginal product of labor to decrease, as labor now has less capital with which to work. This effect causes the VMP_L curve to shift left to $VMP(\overline{K}_0)$, as we have shown in Figure 20.6, where $\overline{K}_0 < \overline{K}_1$, dampening the increase in labor use to L_2' units.

The output effect, however, causes the firm to employ more units of both capital and labor, as the decrease in P_L shifts the firm's $SRMC$ curve downward. Ultimately, this effect provides an incentive for the firm to expand its output in order to maximize

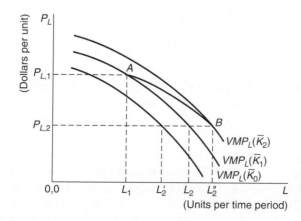

FIGURE 20.6 Alternative Derivation of Firm's Demand for Labor Curve with More Than One Variable Input

its profit, and thus the firm increases Q until once again, $P = SRMC$. The associated increase in the amount of capital employed enhances the marginal product of labor, which in turn causes the VMP_L curve to shift to the right. It is impossible for us to determine, *a priori*, whether the net shift in the VMP_L curve is to the left or to the right. However, the ultimate impact on the quantity of labor demanded, due to the decrease in P_L, is an increase beyond the initial L_1 units. The formal proof of this result is quite complex, and we will reserve it for higher level texts in microeconomics. However, we intuitively expect this result as both the substitution and output effects are inverse with respect to the relationship between P_L and L. Therefore, these effects reinforce each other, provided labor is not an inferior input. In Figure 20.6, we have assumed that the net shift in the VMP_L curve is to the right, represented by the curve $VMP(\overline{K}_2)$, where $\overline{K}_2 > \overline{K}_1$, and thus the net increase in the quantity of labor demanded is from L_1 to L_2'' units. As a result, we represent the firm's demand for labor curve by the curve labeled AB, which is constructed by connecting the points $(L_1, P_{L,1})$ and $(L_2'', P_{L,2})$.

20.3.2 Constant Output Demand for Input Curves

We can further demonstrate the decomposition of the total effect of a change in the price of labor on a firm's demand for labor into the substitution and income effects by returning to the specific example used earlier. In that example, the firm's short-run production function is

$$Q = K^{1/4} L^{1/4} \overline{Z}_1^{1/2},$$

and its short-run total cost function is

$$SRTC = \overline{P}_{K,1} K + \overline{P}_{L,1} L + \overline{P}_{Z,1} \overline{Z}_1,$$

where all terms have been defined previously. We derived the firm's demand for labor curve as

$$L^d = \frac{\overline{P}_1^2 \overline{Z}_1}{16 P_L^{3/2} \overline{P}_{K,1}^{1/2}},$$

or more specifically, for $\overline{P}_1 = \$80, \overline{Z}_1 = 1$ unit, and $\overline{P}_{K,1} = \$1$ as

$$L^d = \frac{400}{P_L^{3/2}}.$$

Using this curve, we demonstrated that if $\overline{P}_{L,1} = \$4$, then $L_1 = 50$ units, and if the price of labor decreases to $\overline{P}_{L,2} = \$1$, the quantity of labor demanded increases to $L_2 = 400$ units. This increase in L of $(400 - 50) = 350$ units constitutes the total effect on L due to the decrease in P_L.

We can mathematically separate this total effect into its two components, the substitution effect and the output effect. This procedure involves deriving a **constant output demand for an input curve**, or *a curve that expresses the quantity of an input de-*

manded as a function of its own price, holding output, and all other determinants of this input constant. Thus, any change in the quantity of labor demanded due to a change in its price, as reflected by a constant output demand for labor curve, is due strictly to the substitution effect. Our derivation of this curve results from the constrained cost minimization process developed in Chapter 10. Recall that this process consists of determining the levels of a firm's inputs that enable it to produce any given level of output at the least cost possible. In the present analysis, we will construct a Lagrangian function, containing the firm's short-run total cost function,

$$SRTC = \overline{P}_{K,1}K + \overline{P}_{L,1}L + \overline{P}_{Z,1}\overline{Z}_1,$$

as the objective function to be minimized, and the firm's production function, expressed such that it is equal to zero,

$$\overline{Q}_1 - K^{1/4}L^{1/4}\overline{Z}_1^{1/2},$$

as the constraint. Since our objective is constrained cost minimization, we are holding output, Q, constant at some predetermined level, such as $\overline{Q}_1$. We express the Lagrangian fnction, $\mathcal{L}$, for this problem as

$$\mathcal{L} = SRTC + \lambda(\overline{Q}_1 - K^{1/4}L^{1/4}\overline{Z}_1^{1/2}),$$

or

$$\mathcal{L} = \overline{P}_{K,1}K + \overline{P}_{L,1}L + \overline{P}_{Z,1}\overline{Z}_1 + \lambda\overline{Q}_1 - \lambda K^{1/4}L^{1/4}\overline{Z}_1^{1/2},$$

where λ is the Lagrangian multiplier discussed in Chapter 10. We determine the first-order conditions for a constrained cost minimum as

$$\frac{\partial\mathcal{L}}{\partial K} = \overline{P}_{K,1} - \frac{1}{4}\lambda K^{-3/4}L^{1/4}\overline{Z}_1^{1/2} = 0 \qquad \textbf{(20.20)}$$

$$\frac{\partial\mathcal{L}}{\partial L} = \overline{P}_{L,1} - \frac{1}{4}\lambda K^{1/4}L^{-3/4}\overline{Z}_1^{1/2} = 0 \qquad \textbf{(20.21)}$$

$$\frac{\partial\mathcal{L}}{\partial\lambda} = \overline{Q}_1 - K^{1/4}L^{1/4}\overline{Z}_1^{1/2} = 0. \qquad \textbf{(20.22)}$$

This system of first-order conditions consists of three equations containing three variables, K, L, and λ, which we solve simultaneously. Rearranging equations (20.20) and (20.21), and then dividing equation (20.21) by equation (20.20) yields

$$\frac{\overline{P}_{L,1}}{\overline{P}_{K,1}} = \frac{\frac{1}{4}\lambda K^{1/4}L^{-3/4}\overline{Z}_1^{1/2}}{\frac{1}{4}\lambda K^{-3/4}L^{1/4}\overline{Z}_1^{1/2}},$$

or

$$\frac{K}{L} = \frac{\overline{P}_{L,1}}{\overline{P}_{K,1}},$$

which you should recognize as the necessary condition for a constrained cost minimum, $MRTS = \overline{P}_{L,1}/\overline{P}_{K,1}$. Solving equation (20.23) for K as

$$K = \frac{\overline{P}_{L,1}}{\overline{P}_{K,1}} L, \qquad\qquad (20.23)$$

and substituting this result for K into equation (20.22) yields

$$\overline{Q}_1 - \left(\frac{\overline{P}_{L,1}}{\overline{P}_{K,1}} L\right)^{1/4} L^{1/4}\overline{Z}_1^{1/2} = 0,$$

or

$$\overline{Q}_1 - \left(\frac{\overline{P}_{L,1}}{\overline{P}_{K,1}}\right)^{1/4} L^{1/2}\overline{Z}_1^{1/2} = 0.$$

We can isolate the $L^{1/2}$ term as

$$L^{1/2} = \frac{\overline{Q}_1}{\left(\dfrac{\overline{P}_{L,1}}{\overline{P}_{K,1}}\right)^{1/4}\overline{Z}_1^{1/2}},$$

where, after squaring both sides of this equation and allowing P_L to vary, then

$$L^{d'} = \frac{\overline{Q}_1^2}{\left(\dfrac{P_L}{\overline{P}_{K,1}}\right)^{1/2}\overline{Z}_1} = \frac{\overline{P}_{K,1}^{1/2}\overline{Q}_1^2}{P_L^{1/2}\overline{Z}_1}. \qquad (20.24)$$

We interpret this equation as the constant output demand for labor curve because it expresses the firm's quantity of labor demanded in terms of its own price, P_L, with output, the price of capital, and the level of the input Z held constant. More specifically, equation (20.24) expresses the firm's optimal quantity of labor that it must use to produce Q_1 units of output at a constrained cost minimum. In order to minimize its costs of production, the firm must also use the corresponding optimal amount of the other variable input, capital. Thus, we determine the firm's constant output demand for capital curve by substituting the expression for $L^{d'}$ from equation (20.24) into equation (20.23), while holding the price of labor constant and allowing the price of capital to vary, yielding

$$K^{d'} = \frac{\overline{P}_{L,1}}{P_K}\left(\frac{P_K^{1/2}\overline{Q}_1^2}{\overline{P}_{L,1}^{1/2}\overline{Z}_1}\right) = \frac{\overline{P}_{L,1}^{1/2}\overline{Q}_1^2}{P_K^{1/2}\overline{Z}_1}. \qquad (20.25)$$

Keep in mind that our goal is to separate the substitution and output effects comprising a change in the quantity demanded of labor due to a change in its own price. Since any movement along a constant output demand for an input curve reflects the substitution effect and any movement along an ordinary demand for an input curve indicates the total effect, then the difference between the two represents the output effect. To measure these effects, we select a point common to each constant output demand for input curve and its respective ordinary input demand curve by focusing on the output value, Q, that corresponds to a profit maximum for the firm. In Section 20.3, for the particular values, $\overline{P}_1 = \$80, \overline{P}_{K,1} = \$1, \overline{P}_{L,1} = \$4$, and $\overline{Z}_1 = 1$ unit, we determined the optimal values for K and L to be $K_1 = 200$ units and $L_1 = 50$ units. Thus, the profit-maximizing level of output is

$$Q_1 = K_1^{1/4}L_1^{1/2}\overline{Z}_1^{1/2} = (200)^{1/4}(50)^{1/4}(1)^{1/2} = 10 \text{ units.}$$

We can determine the constant output amounts of labor, L', and capital, K', demanded by the firm at this level of output by substituting the predetermined values for P, P_K, P_L and Z, along with our computed value for Q, into equations (22.24) and (22.25), yielding

$$L_1^{d'} = \frac{\overline{P}_{K,1}^{1/2}\overline{Q}_1^2}{\overline{P}_{L,1}^{1/2}\overline{Z}_1} = \frac{1^{1/2}(10)^2}{(4)^{1/2}(1)} = 50 \text{ units,}$$

and

$$K_1^{d'} = \frac{\overline{P}_{L,1}^{1/2}\overline{Q}_1^2}{\overline{P}_{K,1}^{1/2}\overline{Z}_1} = \frac{4^{1/2}(10)^2}{1^{1/2}(1)} = 200 \text{ units,}$$

respectively. These values of labor and capital are the same as those we computed earlier from the ordinary input demand curves. Focusing on the labor input, we demonstrated earlier that if P_L decreases to $\overline{P}_{L,2} = \$1$, then the firm's total quantity of labor demanded increases to the amount

$$L_2^d = \frac{\overline{P}_1^2\overline{Z}_1}{16P_{L,2}^{3/2}\overline{P}_{K,1}^{1/2}} = \frac{80^2(1)}{16(1)^{3/2}(1)^{1/2}} = 400 \text{ units.}$$

We can also show that the corresponding amount of capital increases to the value

$$K_2^d = \frac{\overline{P}_1^2\overline{Z}_1}{16\overline{P}_{L,2}^{1/2}P_{K,1}^{3/2}} = \frac{80^2(1)}{16(1)^{1/2}(1)^{1/2}} = 400 \text{ units.}$$

Note that we have obtained these results on the assumption that the amount of output produced by the firm varies to its new profit-maximizing level, Q_2, computed as

$$Q_2 = K^{1/4}L^{1/4}\overline{Z}_1^{1/2} = (400)^{1/4}(400)^{1/4}(1)^{1/2} = 20 \text{ units.}$$

We obtain the corresponding substitution effect associated with a decrease in the price of labor from $\overline{P}_{L,1} = \$4$ to $\overline{P}_{L,2} = \$1$, by holding output constant at the initial level $\overline{Q}_1 = 10$ units. Therefore, by substituting $\overline{P}_{L,2} = \$1$, along with $\overline{P}_{K,1} = \$1$ and $\overline{Z}_1 = 1$ unit into equation (20.24), we now compute the constant output demand for labor as

$$L_2^{d'} = \frac{\overline{P}_{K,1}^{1/2}\overline{Q}_1^2}{\overline{P}_{L,2}^{1/2}\overline{Z}_1} = \frac{1^{1/2}(10)^2}{1^{1/2}(1)} = 100 \text{ units.}$$

We can also obtain the firm's constant output demand for capital by substituting the appropriate values for the determinants in equation (20.25), yielding

$$K_2^{d'} = \frac{\overline{P}_{L,1}^{1/2}\overline{Q}_1^2}{\overline{P}_{K,1}^{1/2}\overline{Z}_1} = \frac{1^{1/2}(10)^2}{1^{1/2}(1)} = 100 \text{ units.}$$

In summary, the decrease in the price of labor from $\overline{P}_{L,1} = \$4$ to $\overline{P}_{L,2} = \$1$, holding output constant at $\overline{Q}_1 = 10$ units, causes the firm to substitute

$$(L_2' - L_1') = (100 - 50) = 50 \text{ units of labor}$$

for

$$(K_2' - K_1') = |100 - 200| = 100 \text{ units of capital,}$$

REAL-WORLD APPLICATION 20.1

International Differences in Labor Productivity

Recently, two independent studies concerning labor productivity in Great Britain have concluded that British labor lags substantially behind labor in other western nations in terms of their output per labor hour (see accompanying table).[1] The results of these studies indicate that U.S. labor productivity, measured in output per labor hour, is more than 30 percent greater than that of Britain's, while German and French labor productivity, also measured in output per labor hour, is more than 20 percent ahead.

The primary reason cited for these international differences in labor productivity centered around Britain's lower levels of capital investment, which in turn adversely affected the productivity of its labor force. A possible explanation for the relatively lower levels of capital investment lies in risk-averse entrepreneurs who have been reluctant to make large long-term capital investments, particularly during the many boom-bust cycles that have characterized the British economy in recent years. Another factor cited in these studies placed partial blame for the low level of British labor productivity on a relatively poorly skilled workforce, inclusive of management. By comparison, American firms invested far more in on-the-job training of its labor force than did British employers, thus resulting in the substantially higher rates of labor productivity experienced in the United States.

We can analyze this real-world economic issue from a theoretical perspective. Assuming that the use of one input affects the productivity of another input, then we expect Britain's lower levels of investment in physical capital, as well as human capital (education and training), to cause both the marginal product of labor curve and the value of the marginal product of labor curve to lie to the left of those pertaining to other countries. It then follows that this lower amount of capital, and subsequent reduced marginal product of labor, result in comparatively less output per labor hour in Great Britain.

Labor Productivity in Selected Countries	
Country	*Output per Labor Hour*[2] *Britain = 100*
Britain	100
France	125
Germany	125
United States	137

Source: McKinsey Consultancy.

[1]McKinsey Consultancy, "Driving Productivity and Growth in the U.K. Economy," and Mary O'Mahony, "Britain's Relative Productivity Performance, 1950–1996: A Sectoral Analysis" (London: NIESR and Economic and Social Research Council, 1998) quoted in *The Economist,* "The British Disease Revisited," October 31, 1998, pp. 61–62.

[2]Average over the period 1994–1996.

in its production process. This result represents the inverse substitution effect, demonstrating that as P_L decreases, L_d increases. The remaining change in the quantity demanded of labor, due to the decrease in P_L, is

$$L_2 - L_2' = 400 - 100 = 300 \text{ units,}$$

representing the output effect. This effect reflects the fact that the firm ultimately increases its profit-maximizing level of output to $Q_2 = 20$ units, and to do so, it uses more units of both labor and capital. Note that the corresponding increase in capital due to the output effect is

$$K_2 - K_2' = 400 - 100 = 300 \text{ units.}$$

Finally, the total effect of the decrease in P_L on the quantity demanded of labor is the summation of these substitution and output effects, or

$$(L_2' - L_1') + (L_2 - L_2') = 50 + 300 = 350 \text{ units of labor.}$$

20.3.3 Elasticity of Substitution and Relative Input Shares

We demonstrated in Chapter 10 that when a firm uses two variable inputs such as capital, K, and labor, L, with constant input prices, P_K and P_L, respectively, the firm alters its level of output according to its expansion path, represented as

$$K = K(L).$$

Recall that a firm's expansion path is a set of input combinations pertaining to constrained cost minimization solutions for different levels of output, with input prices held constant. In other words, it is a set of input combinations for which the necessary condition for a constrained cost minimum is satisfied, or where the marginal rate of technical substitution, $MRTS$, between the two inputs is equal to the input price ratio, P_L/P_K. For many production functions, we represent an expansion path as a ray beginning at the origin when plotted in input, or $K - L$, space such as that illustrated in Figure 10.6. We compute the slope of such a ray, or expansion path, as the input ratio K/L. Along a particular expansion path this slope, representing the proportion by which a firm combines its inputs in an optimal manner in its production process, remains constant as a firm alters its production of output. However, if the price of an input changes, holding the price of the other input constant, then the necessary condition for a constrained cost minimum, $MRTS = P_L/P_K$, is altered and the firm moves to a new expansion path reflecting a different input, or K/L, ratio. We can formally prove this result by assuming a production function

$$Q = f(K,L),$$

that is homogeneous of degree one. Recall that for this type of production function, changing the inputs used in a firm's production process by some scale factor changes the level of output produced by the same factor. Therefore, defining the term $1/L$ as the scale factor, we can alter the production function as

$$\left(\frac{1}{L}\right)^{1} Q = f\left(\frac{K}{L}, \frac{L}{L}\right),$$

or

$$Q = Lf\left(\frac{K}{L}, 1\right) = Lf\left(\frac{K}{L}\right).$$

We can compute the marginal product functions from this expression for the two inputs K and L, MP_K and MP_L, respectively. Thus, for the marginal product of capital

$$MP_K = \frac{\partial Q}{\partial K} = \frac{\partial\left[Lf\left(\frac{K}{L}\right)\right]}{\partial K} = L\frac{\partial f\left(\frac{K}{L}\right)}{\partial K},$$

and after applying the chain rule

$$MP_K = L\frac{df\left(\frac{K}{L}\right)}{d\left(\frac{K}{L}\right)}\frac{\partial\left(\frac{K}{L}\right)}{\partial K},$$

or

$$MP_K = L\frac{df\left(\frac{K}{L}\right)}{d\left(\frac{K}{L}\right)}\frac{1}{L} = \frac{df\left(\frac{K}{L}\right)}{d\left(\frac{K}{L}\right)}.$$

For the marginal product of labor

$$MP_L = \frac{\partial Q}{\partial L} = \frac{\partial\left[Lf\left(\frac{K}{L}\right)\right]}{\partial L},$$

where after applying the product and chain rules

$$MP_L = f\left(\frac{K}{L}\right)\frac{\partial L}{\partial L} + L\frac{\partial f\left(\frac{K}{L}\right)}{\partial L}$$

$$= f\left(\frac{K}{L}\right) + L\frac{df\left(\frac{K}{L}\right)}{d\left(\frac{K}{L}\right)}\frac{\partial\left(\frac{K}{L}\right)}{\partial L}$$

$$= f\left(\frac{K}{L}\right) + L\,\frac{df\left(\frac{K}{L}\right)}{d\left(\frac{K}{L}\right)}\,(-KL^{-2})$$

$$= f\left(\frac{K}{L}\right) - \frac{K}{L}\,\frac{df\left(\frac{K}{L}\right)}{d\left(\frac{K}{L}\right)}.$$

In the above equations, we have expressed both marginal product functions strictly in terms of the input ratio (K/L). Thus, as a firm changes its inputs by some common scale factor in order to change its production of output, the marginal products remain unaltered. By definition, $MRTS = MP_L/MP_K$, and the necessary condition for a constrained cost minimum is

$$MRTS = \frac{MP_L}{MP_K} = \frac{P_L}{P_K}.$$

Therefore, if input prices remain constant, then so does the ratio of marginal products, or $MRTS$, and thus the input ratio, K/L, remains constant regardless of the level of output produced.

If the price of one of the inputs changes, however, holding the price of the other input constant, then not only does the input price ratio, P_L/P_K change, but so does the ratio of marginal products, MP_L/MP_K, or $MRTS$. Conceptually, this change in the $MRTS$ indicates that the firm is substituting the increasingly less expensive input for the other to reestablish the necessary condition for a constrained cost minimum. Therefore, the input ratio, K/L, changes due to this substitution, reflecting the new proportion by which the firm combines the inputs in its production process. The amount by which this K/L ratio changes in response to a change in the $MRTS$ or the input price ratio, reflects the ease with which one input can be substituted for the other in the firm's production process. We can measure this responsiveness with a unitless number known as the elasticity of substitution between the two inputs, capital and labor. Formally, this **elasticity of substitution**, denoted σ, is *the ratio of the percentage change in the capital–labor ratio to the percentage change in the marginal rate of technical substitution between two inputs, holding output constant*, or

$$\sigma = \frac{\%\Delta\left(\frac{K}{L}\right)}{\%\Delta MRTS}. \qquad\qquad (20.26)$$

This formula can be rearranged so that we can express it as

$$\sigma = \frac{\dfrac{\Delta\left(\dfrac{K}{L}\right)}{\dfrac{K}{L}}}{\dfrac{\Delta MRTS}{MRTS}} = \frac{\Delta\left(\dfrac{K}{L}\right)}{\dfrac{K}{L}}\frac{MRTS}{\Delta MRTS} = \frac{\Delta\left(\dfrac{K}{L}\right)}{\Delta MRTS}\frac{MRTS}{\dfrac{K}{L}}.$$

Alternatively, since for the optimal, or constrained cost-minimizing values of K and L, $MRTS = P_L/P_K$, then we can also express equation (20.26) in the form

$$\sigma = \frac{\%\Delta\left(\dfrac{K}{L}\right)}{\%\Delta\left(\dfrac{P_L}{P_K}\right)} = \frac{\dfrac{\Delta\left(\dfrac{K}{L}\right)}{\dfrac{K}{L}}}{\dfrac{\Delta\left(\dfrac{P_L}{P_K}\right)}{\dfrac{P_L}{P_K}}} = \frac{\Delta\left(\dfrac{K}{L}\right)}{\Delta\left(\dfrac{P_L}{P_K}\right)}\frac{\left(\dfrac{P_L}{P_K}\right)}{\left(\dfrac{K}{L}\right)}.$$

The elasticity of substitution, σ, is nonnegative as K/L and P_L/P_K vary directly, indicating that a firm substitutes toward the increasingly less expensive input when one of the input prices changes.

Our interpretation of the magnitude of any computed value for σ is straightforward. The higher the value of σ, the greater is the responsiveness between the input ratio, K/L, and the input price ratio, P_L/P_K, reflecting a greater degree of substitutability between the inputs, capital and labor. For example, if σ is relatively high, say greater than 1.0, then an increase in P_L resulting in an increase in the ratio P_L/P_K, causes a disproportionately greater response in K/L. This result occurs because the firm substitutes a large amount of the capital input for the increasingly expensive labor input, reflecting the ease with which K can be substituted for L in its production process. Conversely, if $\sigma < 1$, then an increase in P_L, and subsequently in P_L/P_K, results in a disproportionately low increase in K/L, reflecting the difficulty associated with substituting K for L. An example of this latter situation is in the business of harvesting some rather fragile fruits and vegetables. In this case, it is very difficult for a firm to substitute capital, or machines, for labor in this production process.

Elasticity of substitution values provides us with some important inferences regarding the value of the contribution made by one input to the total value of a firm's output compared to that provided by the other input. Specifically, assuming a firm operates as a perfect competitor in both its input and output markets, then we express the relative share of labor in terms of its contribution to the value of a firm's output as $P_L L/PQ$, where the term, $P_L L$, is the firm's total payment to the labor input and PQ is the value of the firm's output, or total revenue. Similarly, the relative share of capital in terms of its contribution to the value of a firm's output is $P_K K/PQ$. Therefore, the ratio of the relative share of labor to the relative share of capital is

$$\frac{\dfrac{P_L L}{PQ}}{\dfrac{P_K K}{PQ}} = \frac{P_L L}{P_K K}. \tag{20.27}$$

Often, we are interested in determining the impact of a change in the price of one of the inputs on this ratio of relative shares of inputs. For example, if the price of labor increases, holding the price of capital constant, we expect that the resulting increase in relative prices, P_L/P_K, causes the firm to substitute away from labor and toward capital, thus decreasing the input ratio expressed in equation (20.27) as L/K. The extent of any change in the share of labor relative to that of capital, or $P_L L/P_K K$, depends on the magnitude of the changes in the two ratios, P_L/P_K and L/K, comprising this term. This change in the input ratio, due to a change in the input price ratio, with both expressed on a percentage basis, constitutes the elasticity of substitution, σ. For this example, the magnitude of a decrease in L/K, or alternatively, an increase in K/L, reflecting the substitution of capital for labor caused by an increase in P_L, is indicated by the related value of σ. Thus, if $0 < \sigma < 1$, then the increase in P_L/P_K results in a disproportionately smaller increase in K/L, or a decrease in L/K, and the relative input share of labor to capital, $P_L L/P_K K$, rises. Conversely, if $\sigma > 1$, then an increase in P_L, and subsequently in P_L/P_K, results in a disproportionately larger increase in K/L or decrease in L/K, and the relative input share of labor to capital decreases.

20.4 LABOR DEMAND CURVE FOR AN INDUSTRY AND FOR THE LABOR MARKET

Earlier in this chapter, we developed input demand curves for a single firm. Focusing on the labor input, we find that the firm's demand for labor curve in the two-variable input case is

$$L^d = L^d(P_L, \overline{P}_{K,1}, \overline{P}_1, \overline{Z}_1).$$

Generally, we can develop a labor demand curve for each firm comprising the particular industry being analyzed, thus generating an entire set of such curves as

$$L^{d,1} = L^{d,1}(P_L, \overline{P}_{K,1}, \overline{P}_1, \overline{Z}_1^1)$$
$$L^{d,2} = L^{d,2}(P_L, \overline{P}_{K,1}, \overline{P}_1, \overline{Z}_1^2)$$
$$\vdots \quad \vdots \quad \vdots$$
$$L^{d,N} = L^{d,N}(P_L, \overline{P}_{K,1}, \overline{P}_1, \overline{Z}_1^N),$$

where the industry consists of $i = 1, 2, \ldots, N$ firms producing the good in question. All terms in the above set of equations are the same as those we have defined previously, but with the superscripts, $1, 2, \ldots, N$, added to the L and Z terms, denoting the particular firm to which the labor demand curve pertains.

Essentially, deriving the labor demand curve for this entire industry consists of selecting a price of labor, P_L, determining the quantity of labor demanded, L^d, by each firm at that price, and then summing these quantities to obtain the industrywide quantity demanded of labor. By repeating this procedure for several prices of labor, we can construct the associated industry demand curve. However, before demonstrating this procedure, we need to address one additional complication. Since individual firm demand for labor curves possess negative slopes, a decrease in the price of labor results in each firm increasing the amount of labor it employs. Part of this increase is due to the substitution effect as the firms substitute the increasingly less expensive labor for capital in their production processes. However, some of the increase in labor, as well as capital, occurs because the firms increase their profit-maximizing levels of output, reflecting the output effect. This increase in output on the part of all firms in the industry, caused by a decrease in P_L, is manifested by a rightward shift in the market supply of output curve, which in turn causes the price of the output to decline. Finally, since this output price is a determinant of each firm's demand for labor, each firm's demand for labor curve shifts left, thereby dampening the increase in the amount of labor demanded by each firm.

Intuitively, a decrease in the price of labor causes the *SRMC* curve for each firm to shift downward, resulting in a situation where $P > SRMC$. However, as the firms expand their profit-maximizing levels of output, the corresponding price declines as well, reducing the increase in Q necessary to fulfill the necessary condition for a profit maximum, $P = SRMC$. The ultimate result of this decrease in the price of the output is manifested in an industry demand for labor curve that is steeper, or less price elastic, than would occur if this output price remained constant.

This process is illustrated in Figure 20.7, where we have constructed an industry demand for labor curve. This figure contains four panels, where panels (A), (B), and (C) pertain to firms $1, 2, \ldots, N$ and panel (D) refers to the entire industry. For output price $\overline{P}_1$, the labor demand curves for firms $1, 2, \ldots N$ are labeled $L^{d,1}(\overline{P}_1)$, $L^{d,2}(\overline{P}_1)$, $\ldots, L^{d,N}(\overline{P}_1)$, respectively. Thus if the price of labor is $P_{L,1}$, then firms $1, 2, \ldots, N$ demand $L_1^{d,1}$, $L_1^{d,2}, \ldots, L_1^{d,N}$ units of labor, respectively, and the industry demand for labor is

$$L_1^{d,M} = L_1^{d,1} + L_1^{d,2} + \ldots + L_1^{d,N}.$$

If the price of labor decreases to $P_{L,2}$ then, provided the output price remains constant at $\overline{P}_1$, the respective firms increase their quantities of labor demanded to levels $L_2^{d,1}$, $L_2^{d,2}, \ldots, L_2^{d,N}$ units, and we compute the industry demand for labor as

$$L_2^{d,M} = L_2^{d,1} + L_2^{d,2} + \ldots + L_2^{d,N},$$

subsequently yielding the industry demand for labor curve, $L^{d,M}(\overline{P}_1)$. However, for reasons we mentioned earlier, this is not the case, as the decrease in P_L causes all of the firms to increase their production of output to maximize their profits according to

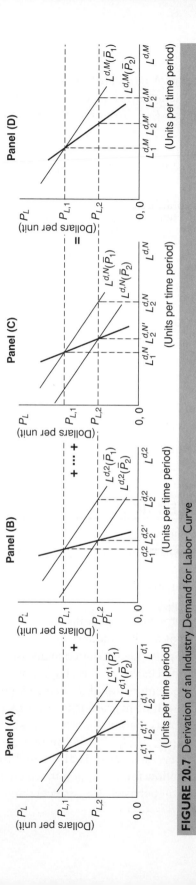

FIGURE 20.7 Derivation of an Industry Demand for Labor Curve

the $P = SRMC$ condition. As a result, the market price of the output decreases to level P_2. Thus, each firm's demand for labor curve shifts left represented by the curves, $L^{d,1}(\overline{P}_2)$, $L^{d,2}(\overline{P}_2), \ldots, L^{d,N}(\overline{P}_2)$, and the profit-maximizing levels of labor demanded by firms $1, 2, \ldots, N$ are $L_2^{d,1'}, L_2^{d,2'}, \ldots, L_2^{d,N'}$, respectively, where $L_2^{d,1'} < L_2^{d,1}$, $L_2^{d,2'} < L_2^{d,2}, \ldots, L_2^{d,N'} < L_2^{d,N}$. The industry demand for labor at $P_{L,2}$ is subsequently

$$L_2^{d,M'} = L_2^{d,1'} + L_2^{d,2'} + \ldots + L_2^{d,N'},$$

where $L_2^{d,M'} < L_2^{d,M}$. We have illustrated the corresponding industry demand for labor curve in panel (D) of Figure 20.7, as $L^{d,M}(\overline{P}_2)$. This curve is steeper, or less price elastic, than the curve $L^{d,M}(\overline{P}_1)$ that would exist if the output price remained constant at $\overline{P}_1$. Also note that the industry demand for labor curve always possesses a negative slope, indicating an inverse relationship between $L^{d,M}$ and P_L. This result follows because the leftward shifts in the firms' labor demand curves only dampen the increase in the amount of labor used by each firm. These shifts cannot completely offset the increased labor use because ultimately they are the result of firms using more labor to expand their output.

There is one last point we should recognize. The process we have described here pertains to the labor demand curve for a particular industry in that this curve is derived for a group of firms producing a homogeneous good. To derive the overall market labor demand curve requires yet another aggregation procedure that involves summing the particular industry demand for labor curves. Since this procedure can become increasingly complicated, we will reserve this topic for texts in Labor Economics.

20.5 MARGINAL REVENUE PRODUCT OF LABOR

In the preceding analysis, we assumed that the firms operated in perfectly competitive markets, thus behaving as price takers in their output markets. By adhering to this assumption, we were able to simplify the analysis somewhat and keep our focus on the input markets. However, many firms do not behave as perfect competitors in their output markets but instead possess some degree of monopoly power or influence over the price of their products. Since this situation occurs fairly often, it is in our interest to examine any impact that a firm's monopoly power in its output market has on its demand for inputs. To simplify the associated analysis, we will conduct it for the one variable input case, developed earlier in this chapter, where labor is treated as the variable input. For that case, we demonstrated that since a perfectly competitive firm behaves as a price taker in its output market, it maximizes profit by employing labor to the point where the value of its marginal product of labor, VMP_L, is equal to the marginal expense of its labor input, MEI_L. Furthermore, since we assumed the firm is a price taker in its input markets, this MEI_L is also equal to the price of labor. We will now modify this analysis to allow for a situation in which a firm operates as a monopolist in its output market but still behaves as a perfect competitor in its input markets.

As we demonstrated in Chapter 15, a monopolist has the incentive to restrict the output it sells to some amount below the perfectly competitive level, since by so doing it can increase the price of its good. Therefore, this firm correspondingly restricts the levels of the inputs, or in this case, the amount of the single variable input, labor, it employs. We can demonstrate this result by deriving the necessary condition by which a monopoly determines the profit-maximizing level of labor it uses. Recall the short-run production function

$$Q = f(\overline{K}_1, L),$$

that expresses output, Q, in terms of two inputs, capital and labor, where we fix capital at $\overline{K}_1$ units and thus treat labor as the only variable input. Also recall that the version of a firm's short-run total cost function, $SRTC$, that expresses its costs in terms of the inputs it employs is

$$SRTC = \overline{P}_{K,1}\overline{K}_1 + \overline{P}_{L,1}L,$$

where $\overline{P}_{K,1}$ and $\overline{P}_{L,1}$ are the market-determined prices of capital and labor, respectively. As always, the firm's short-run profit function is the difference between its total revenue and short-run total cost, or

$$SR\pi = TR - SRTC,$$

where after substituting the appropriate expressions for TR and $SRTC$ this profit function becomes

$$SR\pi = PQ - (\overline{P}_{K,1}\overline{K}_1 + \overline{P}_{L,1}L).$$

The critical difference between this analysis and that for a perfectly competitive firm is that the price of a monopolistic firm's output, P, is not predetermined, but instead is a function of the amount of output it sells, or $P = P(Q)$. Substituting this expression for P in the $SR\pi$ function yields

$$SR\pi = P(Q)Q - \overline{P}_{K,1}\overline{K}_1 - \overline{P}_{L,1}L,$$

and since $Q = f(\overline{K}_1, L)$, this function becomes

$$SR\pi = P[f(\overline{K}_1, L)]f(\overline{K}_1, L) - \overline{P}_{K,1}\overline{K}_1 - \overline{P}_{L,1}L.$$

We determine the firm's profit-maximizing level of labor use by first differentiating $SR\pi$ with respect to L and setting the result equal to zero. Thus, applying both the product and chain rules yields

$$\frac{dSR\pi}{dL} = P[f(\overline{K}_1, L)]\frac{df(\overline{K}_1, L)}{dL}$$
$$+ f(\overline{K}_1, L)\frac{dP[f(\overline{K}_1, L)]}{df(\overline{K}_1, L)}\frac{df(\overline{K}_1, L)}{dL}$$
$$- \frac{d\overline{P}_{K,1}\overline{K}_1}{dL} - \frac{d\overline{P}_{L,1}L}{dL} = 0,$$

or since $Q = f(\overline{K}_1, L)$ and $d\overline{P}_{K,1}\overline{K}_1/dL = 0$, then

$$\frac{dSR\pi}{dL} = P(Q)\frac{dQ}{dL} + Q\frac{dP(Q)}{dQ}\frac{dQ}{dL} - \overline{P}_{L,1} = 0,$$

or

$$\left[P(Q) + Q\frac{dP(Q)}{dQ}\right]\frac{dQ}{dL} = \overline{P}_{L,1}.$$

Finally, since $P = P(Q)$ this expression becomes

$$\left[P + Q\frac{dP}{dQ}\right]\frac{dQ}{dL} = \overline{P}_{L,1},$$

where we can recognize the term $(P + Q\ dP/dQ)$ as the firm's marginal revenue, MR, the term dQ/dL as the marginal product of labor, MP_L, and $\overline{P}_{L,1}$ as the marginal expense of labor, MEI_L. More concisely, this necessary condition for determining the profit-maximizing level of labor for a monopolist is

$$(MR)(MP_L) = MEI_L, \tag{20.28}$$

where the term on the left side of this equation is known as the marginal revenue product of labor. More generally, the **marginal revenue product of an input**, denoted MRP, is *the change in total revenue due to a change in the amount of that input used, holding all other inputs constant*. Note that this definition is extremely close to that for the value of the marginal product of an input, VMP, where the difference is that for MRP we do not have to take the output price as predetermined, as is the case with VMP. In a sense, we can interpret the VMP, for which price is predetermined, as a special subcase of the MRP, that allows the price of an output to vary with the amount of that output produced and sold by a firm, or for which $P = P(Q)$. Our interpretation of equation (20.28) is that a monopolist maximizes its short-run profit by using its labor input to the point where the associated extra revenue, MRP_L, is equal to the extra cost, MEI_L.

We have contrasted the MRP_L and VMP_L concepts in Figure 20.8 by illustrating a MRP_L curve, assuming the output market is a monopoly, and a market VMP_L curve, labeled VMP_L^M, for a group of firms based on the alternative assumption that this same output market is perfectly competitive. Observe that the MRP_L curve lies beneath the VMP_L^M curve, with the exception of the vertical intercept where $L = 0$ units, indicating that $MRP_L < VMP_L^M$ for any positive amount of labor employed. Since $MRP_L = (MR)(MP_L)$, and $VMP_L = \overline{P}_1 MP_L$, we expect this result since $MR < P$ at a monopolist's profit-maximizing level of output. Thus, for any price of labor, a monopolist employs a lower profit-maximizing amount of labor compared to that used in a perfectly competitive market, since $MRP_L = P_L$ at levels of labor less than the amount at which $VMP_L^M = P_L$. We have illustrated this result in Figure 20.8 where you can observe that at $\overline{P}_{L,1} = MEI_{L,1}$, the group of perfectly competitive firms employs $L_{1,C}$ units of labor at which $VMP_{L,1}^M = \overline{P}_{L,1}$, where a monopolist employs only $L_{1,M}$ units of

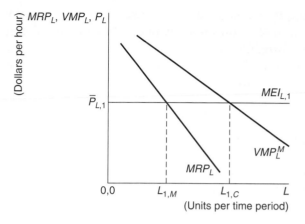

FIGURE 20.8 Comparison of the Optimal Amount of Labor Employed for a Monopolist and a Perfectly Competitive Market

labor for which $MRP_{L,1} = \overline{P}_{L,1}$. Intuitively, this result follows from the fact that a monopolist restricts the amount of output it produces below the perfectly competitive level in order to increase the price of its output. As it does so, it reduces the amount of labor it employs to an amount less than the perfectly competitive level.

20.6 SUMMARY

Our focus in this chapter has been on developing labor demand curves for both firms and industries. We have demonstrated that the nature of these demand curves depends on various underlying assumptions, such as the number of variable inputs and the type of output market under consideration. The key topics discussed in this chapter are briefly outlined as follows.

- The value of the marginal product of an input, or *VMP*, is the change in total revenue due to a change in the amount of that input used in a production process, holding the output price and other inputs constant.
- The marginal expense of an input, *MEI*, is the change in total cost due to a change in the amount of that input employed, holding other inputs constant.
- In the case where a firm treats only the labor input as variable in its production process, it maximizes its profit by employing that input to the point where $VMP_L = MEI_L$. As a result, the VMP_L curve represents the firm's demand for labor curve in this case.
- If a firm uses more than one variable input, say two inputs, capital and labor, it determines its profit-maximizing quantities of these inputs where the conditions $VMP_K = MEI_K$ and $VMP_L = MEI_L$ are satisfied simultaneously.
- If the price of an input changes, in the multiple variable input case, the effect on the quantity demanded of that input depends on the associated substitution and output effects.

- A constant demand for an input curve expresses the quantity demanded of an input as a function of its own price, with output and other determinants of that input held constant.
- The elasticity of substitution, σ, for two inputs is the ratio of the percentage change in the input ratio to the percentage change in the marginal rate of technical substitution between the two inputs.
- We can use the elasticity of substitution to determine the impact of a change in relative input prices on the ratio of the relative share of one input to the relative share of the other.
- The labor demand curve for a particular industry is the summation of all the demand for labor curves for the firms comprising that industry.
- The marginal revenue product of an input, MRP, is the change in total revenue due to a change in the amount of that input sued, holding other inputs constant. We apply this concept to firms that behave as monopolists in their output markets.

KEY TERMS

- constant output demand for an input curve, page 534
- elasticity of substitution, page 541
- marginal expense of an input, page 518
- marginal revenue product of an input, page 548
- output effect, page 531
- value of the marginal product of an input, page 517

EXERCISES

20.1 Suppose a firm produces its output according to the function

$$Q = 4\overline{K}_1^{1/4}L^{3/4}$$

where Q represents the firm's level of output and the terms K and L are the inputs, capital and labor, respectively. Also note that the capital input is fixed at $\overline{K}_1$ units. Finally, assume that the firm behaves as a perfect competitor in both its output and input markets. As a result, the prices of its output and inputs are $\overline{P}_1$, $\overline{P}_{K,1}$ and $\overline{P}_{L,1}$, respectively.

a. Determine the firm's value of the marginal product of labor curve.

b. What is the firm's marginal expense of the labor input curve in this case?

c. If $\overline{K}_1 = 4$ units, $\overline{P}_1 = \$2$, and $\overline{P}_{L,1} = \$3$, compute the profit-maximizing quantity of labor used by the firm.

20.2 Assume a firm has the production function

$$Q = K^{1/3}L^{1/3}Z^{1/3},$$

where Q is the firm's output and the terms K, L, and Z represent the firm's inputs capital, labor, and land, respectively. Furthermore, we fix land at some specified level, $\overline{Z}_1$. The firm behaves as a price taker in both its output and input markets, where P_1 is the price of the firm's output and $\overline{P}_{K,1}$, $\overline{P}_{L,1}$, and $\overline{P}_{Z,1}$ represent the input prices of capital, labor, and land, respectively.

a. Determine the firm's short-run profit function.

b. Derive the firm's demand for capital and demand for labor curves.

c. If $\overline{P}_1 = \$3$, $\overline{P}_{K,1} = \$2$, $\overline{P}_{L,1} = \$1$, and $\overline{Z}_1 = 4$ units, determine the firm's profit-maximizing levels of K and L.

d. What is the corresponding level of output?

20.3 Refer to the production function and information given in Exercise 20.2. Using the optimal level of output you determined in part d, derive the firm's constant output demand curves for capital and labor. What are the optimal values of K and L?

20.4 Again refer to the information given in Exercise 20.2. Assume the price of labor increases to $\overline{P}_{L,2} = \$2$. Now compute the optimal values of capital and labor corresponding to the constant output demand curves developed in Exercise 20.3. Also compute these optimal values for K and L using the results from Exercise 20.2. How do these results for the two exercises compare? Explain why they are different.

20.5 Compare two firms, both operating as perfect competitors in their input markets. However, one firm behaves as a perfect competitor in its output market, while the other is a monopolist. Which firm employs the greater amount of labor? What is the explanation for this result?

20.6 Assume a firm produces its output using two variable inputs, capital and labor. Graphically, illustrate both the substitution and output effects for an increase in the price of labor. Next, sum these two effects and illustrate the total effect of such a price increase on both labor and capital.

20.7 Suppose a firm has the production function

$$Q = K^{1/2}L^{1/2}.$$

The price of capital, K, is $P_K = \$1$ and the price of labor, L, is $P_L = \$4$. Assume the firm's profit-maximizing level of output is $\overline{Q}_1 = 100$ units.

a. Determine the firm's $MRTS$, as well as its optimal levels of K and L.

b. Determine the elasticity of substitution between the inputs. Explain what this result indicates.

20.8 Refer to the information in Exercise 20.7. Determine the ratio of the relative factor shares regarding capital and labor. Interpret your result.

CHAPTER 21

Supply of Labor

21.1 INTRODUCTION

In the previous chapter, we developed labor demand curves for both an individual firm and the corresponding industry within the context of several different scenarios. Our focus in this chapter is on deriving individual and market labor supply curves, and by so doing, we can complete our analysis of labor markets. In the preceding chapter, we assumed that all of the firms under analysis, including monopolistic firms, behave as perfect competitors in their input markets. By definition, each firm employs an imperceptibly small amount of each input relative to the entire market for that particular input. Therefore, each firm can employ as much of any input it desires without affecting its price. Accordingly, we can interpret the horizontal $P_L = MEI_L$ curve as the supply of labor curve to a particular firm.

More generally, a **labor supply curve**, is *a curve that expresses the quantity of labor supplied as a function of its own price, ceteris paribus.* Assuming labor is homogeneous, the quantity of labor supplied to the entire market for this input generally varies with its own price, P_L, as individual workers make rational choices regarding the amount of labor they are willing to supply. Essentially, these choices relate to how an individual decides to divide her time. Specifically, she may choose to spend some fraction of a given time period working and earning income. Simultaneously, she is also choosing to spend some amount of this time period not working, which we define as leisure time. Logically, this choice between income and leisure time is affected by a number of variables, where one of the most significant is the price of labor, more commonly known as the wage rate. Thus, for example, if the price of labor rises, will this individual choose to work more hours and earn more income, or alternatively, will she decide to work less and take more leisure time? The answer to this question varies across individuals possessing different preferences regarding income as opposed to leisure time. However, analyzing this choice process provides us with the basis for constructing individual labor supply curves. Once these curves are derived, we will then aggregate them to derive broader labor market supply curves. Ultimately, we can use these curves, along with the industry and market demand for labor curves developed in Chapter 20, to analyze how the price of labor is determined.

21.2. INDIVIDUAL SUPPLY OF LABOR CURVES

The motive as to why individuals choose to work or to supply labor is quite simple. It is to earn income that can be used to purchase the goods and services they consume in order to derive utility. Therefore, the decision-making process regarding the amount of labor individuals are willing to supply is the familiar one of rational consumer choice, which we analyzed in Chapter 4. In this case, we assume that individuals derive utility not from supplying labor, or work time itself, but instead from the goods and services they can purchase and consume from the income earned by supplying labor. It is convention in economic analysis to define time not spent working as constituting leisure time, a "good" from which individuals receive utility. As a result, we derive an individual's labor supply curve using an indirect approach that involves first deriving an individual's demand curve for leisure, a curve expressing the quantity of leisure time demanded in terms of the price of labor. Conceptually, this relationship follows from the fact that the price of labor represents the foregone income per hour from not working. Thus, we can interpret it as also representing the price of leisure time. Once an individual's demand for leisure curve is derived, we construct her supply of labor curve by simply subtracting the amount of leisure time consumed at each price of labor from some absolute amount of time representing the length of the period under focus.

21.2.1 Utility Function for Income and Leisure Time

We can generally describe the following analysis as an income–leisure model that is essentially an application of the consumer's constrained utility maximization problem. We will construct the model for a single individual, or consumer, possessing a utility function of the form

$$U = U(Le, y), \qquad (21.1)$$

where U represents the utility an individual derives from consuming amounts of the two "goods"—leisure time, Le, measured in hours, and real income, y, measured in constant, or inflation-adjusted dollars. It is because the income variable represents the non-leisure goods and services the individual is able to purchase and consume that we interpret it as the consumer's level of real income. By holding utility constant at a specified level, say $\overline{U}_1$, we can generate an indifference curve from this utility function representing the combinations of Le and y yielding this same level of utility, $\overline{U}_1$. More generally, by holding utility constant at different levels, $\overline{U}_1, \overline{U}_2, \overline{U}_3, \dots$, we can generate an entire set of indifference curves from this utility function, where $\overline{U}_3 > \overline{U}_2 > \overline{U}_1, \dots$. Three such indifference curves are illustrated in Figure 21.1 representing utility levels $\overline{U}_1, \overline{U}_2$, and $\overline{U}_3$.

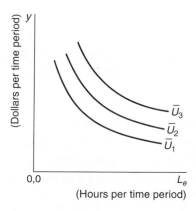

FIGURE 21.1 Consumer's Indifference Curves for Leisure Time and Income

The slope of any one of these indifference curves is represented as dy/dLe, which we compute from equation (21.1) by first totally differentiating U with respect to Le as

$$\frac{dU}{dLe} = \frac{\partial U(Le,y)}{\partial Le}\frac{dLe}{dLe} + \frac{\partial U(Le,y)}{\partial y}\frac{dy}{dLe}.$$

Since U is constant for any particular indifference curve, then $dU/dLe = 0$, and therefore

$$\frac{\partial U(Le,y)}{\partial Le} + \frac{\partial U(Le,y)}{\partial y}\frac{dy}{dLe} = 0.$$

Finally, substituting U for $U(Le,y)$ and solving for dy/dLe yields

$$\frac{dy}{dLe} = \frac{\dfrac{-\partial U(Le,y)}{\partial Le}}{\dfrac{\partial U(Le,y)}{\partial y}} = \frac{\dfrac{-\partial U}{\partial Le}}{\dfrac{\partial U}{\partial y}}, \tag{21.2}$$

where the term $\partial U/\partial Le$ is the change in utility due to a change in the consumption of leisure time, *ceteris paribus*, or the marginal utility of leisure time MU_{Le}. Similarly, the term $\partial U/\partial y$ is the change in utility due to a change in the consumption of income, or the marginal utility of income, MU_y. Thus, we can express equation (21.2), representing the slope of an indifference for this model, as

$$\frac{dy}{dLe} = \frac{-MU_{Le}}{MU_y},$$

conceptually indicating the negative of the rate at which the consumer can substitute leisure time for income, while receiving the same level of utility.

Recall from Chapter 3 that we define the ratio of the marginal utilities, or the negative of the slope of an indifference curve, as the marginal rate of substitution, *MRS*, between two goods, where in this case the two goods are leisure time and income. The particular value of the *MRS* at a point on any one indifference curve depends on the shape of the curve, which in turn depends on the nature of the underlying utility function from which it is derived. For example, some individuals possess a preference bias for leisure over income and thus require a substantial increase in income to sacrifice some leisure time. For other consumers the opposite may be true. We discussed the impact of these biases regarding the leisure-income tradeoff relationship in more detail in Section 3.4.2 of Chapter 3.

21.2.2 Budget Constraint for Income and Leisure Time

The purpose of our analysis is to demonstrate how a rational consumer determines the optimal levels of the goods, leisure time and income, comprising her utility function and ultimately to provide a basis for an individual's supply of labor curve. The goal of a rational consumer is to choose amounts of these goods that correspond to a maximum value for her level of utility. However, as we implied at the outset of this discussion, this choice is not made without the presence of some constraining factors. The number of these factors we include in a consumer's constrained utility maximization model depends on the level of complexity desired. However, some very important factors are common to virtually all of these models. The prices of the two goods, leisure time and income, play a role as they affect the amounts of these goods the consumer is able to purchase. Also, the total amount of time pertaining to the period we are analyzing must be included, since the solution to this type of optimization problem involves allocating portions of this time period to work and leisure. Furthermore, in more complex models, we include the amount of nonlabor income in the model, for this variable can also influence the leisure-income choice.

We can use these factors to develop an individual's budget constraint that limits the amounts of leisure time and income she is able to consume in a given time period. Initially, we will assume that nonlabor income is equal to zero, and thus all of the individual's income is earned by supplying labor, which is by definition not choosing leisure time. Thus, the amount of income, y, the individual earns equals the amount of labor supplied, L, multiplied by the market determined wage rate, or price of labor, $\overline{P}_{L,1}$, as

$$y = \overline{P}_{L,1}L. \tag{21.3}$$

Since the total amount of time for the period under analysis is some constant, $\overline{T}$, the individual's labor time, L, and leisure time, Le, must sum to this value as

$$Le + L = \overline{T}. \tag{21.4}$$

The period we are analyzing can represent any time period such as a day, month, or year, and can be measured in any units of time. For example, if T represents one day and our unit of measurement is hours, then $\overline{T} = 24$ hours. We can solve equation (21.4) for the amount of labor time, L, as

$$L = \overline{T} - Le,$$

and then substitute this express for L into equation (21.3) yielding

$$y = \overline{P}_{L,1}(\overline{T} - Le)$$

or

$$y = \overline{P}_{L,1}\overline{T} - \overline{P}_{L,1}Le. \tag{21.5}$$

This equation represents the consumer's budget constraint, or the set of combinations of leisure time and income the individual can select for given values of P_L and $\overline{T}$. This constraint is illustrated in Figure 21.2, where Le and y are plotted on the horizontal and vertical axes, respectively.

The vertical or y-intercept indicates the maximum amount of income the individual can earn in the given period $\overline{T}$. Since all income in this model is generated from supplying labor, this maximum level of income is the amount of income the individual

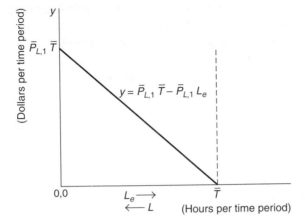

(Dollars per time period)

$y = \overline{P}_{L,1}\overline{T} - \overline{P}_{L,1}L_e$

$\overline{P}_{L,1}\overline{T}$

0,0

$L_e \longrightarrow$
$\longleftarrow L$

$\overline{T}$

(Hours per time period)

FIGURE 21.2 Budget Constraint for Leisure Time and Income

can earn provided she chooses zero leisure time and supplies labor for the entire time period, $\overline{T}$. As a result, we compute the y-intercept by substituting $Le = 0$ into the budget constraint, yielding

$$y = \overline{P}_{L,1}\overline{T} - \overline{P}_{L,1}(0) = \overline{P}_{L,1}\overline{T},$$

or the price of labor multiplied by the total units of time in the fixed period $\overline{T}$. The horizontal or Le intercept represents the maximum amount of leisure time the individual can choose, and we compute it by substituting $y = 0$ into the budget constraint, yielding

$$0 = \overline{P}_{L,1}\overline{T} - \overline{P}_{L,1}Le,$$

or

$$Le = \overline{T}.$$

This result indicates that the individual spends the entire time period consuming leisure time, thus supplying zero units of labor and earning zero income. Also, since the amount of labor time supplied is $L = \overline{T} - Le$, we can easily compute the value of L for any value of Le, where in Figure 21.2, labor time, L, is indicated on the horizontal axis, measured from right to left, beginning at $\overline{T}$ where $L = 0$. Finally, we compute the slope of this budget constraint as

$$\frac{dy}{dLe} = \frac{-\overline{P}_{L,1}}{1},$$

representing the rate at which the consumer is able to substitute one good for the other within this constraint. This term is the negative of the ratio of the price of leisure, $\overline{P}_{L,1}$, to the price of real income, where we can also interpret the price of labor as the price of leisure time. The price of real income is simply equal to 1.0 since it is measured in constant dollar amounts.

21.2.3   Constrained Utility Maximization for the Income-Leisure Model

Now that the individual consumer's utility function and budget constraint for the income-leisure model have been established, we can demonstrate how the consumer determines the solution values for Le and y corresponding to her constrained utility maximum. We solve this problem by constructing a Lagrangian function, $\mathcal{L}$, embodying the objective function

$$U = U(Le, y),$$

and the budget constraint, solved in the manner

$$y - \overline{P}_{L,1}\overline{T} + \overline{P}_{L,1}Le = 0.$$

Thus

$$\mathcal{L} = U + \lambda(y - \overline{P}_{L,1}\overline{T} + \overline{P}_{L,1}Le),$$

or

$$\mathcal{L} = U(Le, y) + \lambda y - \lambda \overline{P}_{L,1}\overline{T} + \lambda \overline{P}_{L,1}Le.$$

We determine the first-order conditions for a constrained utility maximum as

$$\frac{\partial \mathcal{L}}{\partial Le} = \frac{\partial U(Le, y)}{\partial Le} + \lambda \overline{P}_{L,1} = 0 \tag{21.6}$$

$$\frac{\partial \mathcal{L}}{\partial y} = \frac{\partial U(Le, y)}{\partial y} + \lambda(1) = 0 \tag{21.7}$$

$$\frac{\partial \mathcal{L}}{\partial \lambda} = y - \overline{P}_{L,1}\overline{T} + \overline{P}_{L,1}Le = 0. \tag{21.8}$$

Subtracting the term $\lambda \overline{P}_{L,1}$ from both sides of equation (21.6) and the term λ from both sides of equation (21.7), and then dividing the rearranged version of equation (21.6) by the rearranged version of equation (21.7), yields

$$\frac{\dfrac{\partial U(Le, y)}{\partial Le}}{\dfrac{\partial U(Le, y)}{\partial y}} = \frac{-\lambda \overline{P}_{L,1}}{-\lambda},$$

and since $U = U(Le, y)$, then

$$\frac{\dfrac{\partial U}{\partial Le}}{\dfrac{\partial U}{\partial y}} = \frac{\overline{P}_{L,1}}{1}.$$

We can recognize the terms $\partial U/\partial Le$ and $\partial U/\partial y$ as the marginal utility of leisure time, MU_{Le}, and the marginal utility of income, MU_y, respectively. Thus

$$\frac{MU_{Le}}{MU_y} = \frac{\overline{P}_{L,1}}{1},$$

where the term on the left-hand side of this equation, MU_{Le}/MU_y, is the marginal rate of substitution, MRS, between the two goods, leisure time, Le, and income, y. Thus, the necessary condition for a constrained utility maximum is

$$MRS = \frac{MU_{Le}}{MU_y} = \frac{\overline{P}_{L,1}}{1}.$$

This expression indicates that the consumer achieves a constrained utility maximum by adjusting the amounts of leisure time and income she consumes to the point where the rate at which she is willing to substitute one of these goods for the other while still receiving the same level of utility, or MRS, is equal to the rate at which she is able to substitute one of these goods for the other subject to the fixed amount of time $\overline{T}$, and the price of leisure time, P_L. Given specific values of P_L and $\overline{T}$, we can solve the set of first-order conditions simultaneously to determine the optimal values of Le, y, and if desired, λ and U. Furthermore, once the optimal value of Le is determined, we can obtain the corresponding value of labor time, L, from the equation $L = \overline{T} - Le$.

We have illustrated this constrained utility maximization solution in Figure 21.3, which includes the consumer's budget constraint and a set of three indifference curves, U_0, U_1, and U_2. Observe that the consumer achieves the highest level of utility subject to her budget constraint by consuming $L^*_{e_1}$ amount of leisure time and y^*_1 amount of income, indicated by the point where the indifference curve representing

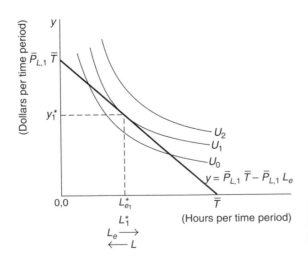

FIGURE 21.3 Constrained Utility Maximization Solution for Leisure Time and Income

utility level U_1 is tangent to the budget constraint. At this combination, $(L_{e_1}^*, y_1^*)$, the necessary condition for a constrained utility maximum is fulfilled, as the slope of the indifference curve, U_1, is equal to the slope of the budget constraint, or

$$-MRS = \frac{-MU_{Le}}{MU_y} = \frac{-\overline{P}_{L,1}}{1}.$$

After multiplying both sides of this equation by –1, we can recognize this expression as the necessary condition for a constrained utility maximum as

$$MRS = \frac{MU_{Le}}{MU_y} = \frac{\overline{P}_{L,1}}{1}.$$

Note that the corresponding value for the optimal amount of labor supplied by this consumer is

$$L_1^* = \overline{T} - L_{e_1}^*.$$

We have computed these results for a particular price of leisure time, $\overline{P}_{L,1}$. Logically, for a different value of P_L a new set of results for Le, y, U, and L can be generated. Thus, by allowing P_L to vary, we can use the constrained utility maximization results to establish a relationship between Le and P_L, representing the individual consumer's demand for leisure curve. This curve expresses the quantity of leisure demanded by a consumer as a function of its price, *ceteris paribus*, or

$$L_e^d = Le(P_L, \overline{T}),$$

where we have also included the length of the time period as a determinant of Le. Once the demand for leisure curve is derived, we can establish a relationship between the quantity of labor supplied, L, and its price, P_L, representing the individual consumer's labor supply curve. This curve expresses the quantity of labor supplied by an individual in terms of its price, *ceteris paribus*, or

$$L^s = L^s(P_L, \overline{T}).$$

This labor supply curve contains the same determinants as the demand for leisure curve. Because different outcomes are possible, we will defer our discussion regarding the directionality of the relationships between L^s and P_L, as well as that for L_e^d and P_L, until Section 21.2.4.

We can provide additional insight into this discussion by deriving an individual consumer's demand for leisure curve and subsequent supply of labor curve, using a specific mathematical example. Assume an individual receives utility, U, from consuming amounts of leisure time, Le, and income, y, according to the utility function

$$U = Le^{1/2} + y^{1/2},$$

and is subject to the budget constraint

$$y = \overline{P}_{L,1}\overline{T} - \overline{P}_{L,1}Le,$$

where P_L and $\overline{T}$ denote the same terms as defined earlier. We solve the consumer's constrained utility maximization problem by first constructing the Lagrangian function as

$$\mathcal{L} = U + \lambda(y - \overline{P}_{L,1}\overline{T} + \overline{P}_{L,1}Le)$$

or, since $U = Le^{1/2} + y^{1/2}$, then

$$\mathcal{L} = Le^{1/2} + y^{1/2} + \lambda y - \lambda \overline{P}_{L,1}\overline{T} + \lambda \overline{P}_{L,1}Le.$$

The first-order conditions are

$$\frac{\partial \mathcal{L}}{\partial Le} = \frac{1}{2}Le^{-1/2} + \lambda \overline{P}_{L,1} \quad = 0 \tag{21.9}$$

$$\frac{\partial \mathcal{L}}{\partial y} = \frac{1}{2}y^{-1/2} + \lambda = 0 \tag{21.10}$$

$$\frac{\partial \mathcal{L}}{\partial \lambda} = y - \overline{P}_{L,1}\overline{T} + \overline{P}_{L,1}Le = 0. \tag{21.11}$$

Rearranging equations (21.9) and (21.10) and dividing equation (21.9) by equation (21.10) yields the necessary condition for a constrained utility maximum as

$$\frac{\frac{1}{2}Le^{-1/2}}{\frac{1}{2}y^{-1/2}} = \frac{-\lambda \overline{P}_{L,1}}{-\lambda},$$

or

$$\frac{y^{1/2}}{Le^{1/2}} = \frac{\overline{P}_{L,1}}{1},$$

that we can solve for y in terms of Le as

$$y = \overline{P}_{L,1}^2 Le.$$

Substituting this expression for y into equation (21.11) yields

$$\overline{P}_{L,1}^2 Le - \overline{P}_{L,1}\overline{T} + \overline{P}_{L,1}Le = 0,$$

or

$$(\overline{P}_{L,1}^2 + \overline{P}_{L,1})Le - \overline{P}_{L,1}\overline{T} = 0,$$

that we solve for Le as

$$L_e^* = \frac{\overline{P}_{L,1}\overline{T}}{\overline{P}_{L,1}^2 + \overline{P}_{L,1}} = \frac{\overline{T}}{\overline{P}_{L,1} + 1}. \tag{21.12}$$

Thus, if $\overline{T} = 24$ hours, and say $\overline{P}_{L,1} = \$3/\text{hour}$, then we compute the optimal amount of leisure time the consumer chooses as

$$L_{e_1}^* = \frac{24}{3+1} = 6 \text{ hours.}$$

Since the amount of labor time supplied, L, is represented as $L = \overline{T} - Le$, then the optimal amount of labor time is

$$L_1^* = 24 - 6 = 18 \text{ hours,}$$

and the associated amount of income earned is

$$y_1^* = \overline{P}_{L,1}^2 Le = (3)^2(6) = \$54/\text{day,}$$

that we can alternatively obtain as

$$y_1^* = P_{L,1} L = 3(18) = \$54/\text{day.}$$

We can compute optimal values of Le, L, and y for various levels of P_L. For example, if P_L increases to $\overline{P}_{L,2} = \$5$, then

$$L_{e_2}^* = \frac{24}{5+1} = 4 \text{ hours}$$

$$L_2^* = 24 - 4 = 20 \text{ hours}$$

and

$$y^* = 5(20) = \$100.$$

More generally, we represent the consumer's demand for leisure curve by equation (21.12) once the price of leisure, P_L, is allowed to vary. As a result, this curve is

$$Le = \frac{\overline{T}}{P_L + 1},$$

where in this case, the directionality of the relationship between Le and P_L is inverse, as P_L appears only in the denominator of the right-hand side of this equation. The labor supply curve for this individual is

$$L = \overline{T} - Le = \overline{T} - \left(\frac{\overline{T}}{P_L + 1}\right) = \overline{T}\left(1 - \frac{1}{P_L + 1}\right),$$

or

$$L = \overline{T}\left(\frac{P_L + 1 - 1}{P_L + 1}\right) = \overline{T}\left(\frac{P_L}{P_L + 1}\right).$$

The relationship between L and P_L is direct because a change in P_L proportionally changes the numerator more than the denominator for the term on the right-hand side of this equation. In summary, for this specific example, an increase in P_L, which we can interpret as either the price of labor or the price of leisure time, results in the consumer demanding a smaller amount of leisure and supplying a greater amount of labor.

We can modify this specific income-leisure choice model to allow for the possibility that an individual may receive some nonlabor income in addition to her labor income. Realistically, many individuals receive some income in the form of interest, dividends, or capital gains, or from some other nonlabor source. We would expect the presence of this nonlabor income to have some impact on the individual's income-leisure choice process. For the sake of simplicity, let's assume that this nonlabor income is some type of lump sum, or constant amount, $\overline{N}$, for the time period $\overline{T}$. As a result, we modify the consumer's budget constraint as

$$y = \overline{P}_{L,1}L + \overline{N},$$

to account for the fact that the consumer's income is now equal to the summation of her labor income, $\overline{P}_{L,1}L$ and nonlabor income, $\overline{N}$. Since $L = \overline{T} - Le$, we can express this budget constraint as

$$y = \overline{P}_{L,1}(\overline{T} - Le) + \overline{N},$$

or

$$y = \overline{P}_{L,1}\overline{T} - \overline{P}_{L,1}Le + \overline{N}.$$

Assuming the same utility function as before

$$U = Le^{1/2} + y^{1/2},$$

the Lagrangian function for this constrained utility maximization problem is

$$\mathcal{L} = Le^{1/2} + y^{1/2} + \lambda(y - \overline{P}_{L,1}\overline{T} + \overline{P}_{L,1}Le - \overline{N}),$$

for which the first-order conditions are

$$\frac{\partial \mathcal{L}}{\partial Le} = \frac{1}{2}Le^{-1/2} + \lambda \overline{P}_{L,1} = 0 \qquad \textbf{(21.13)}$$

$$\frac{\partial \mathcal{L}}{\partial y} = \frac{1}{2}y^{-1/2} + \lambda = 0 \qquad \textbf{(21.14)}$$

$$\frac{\partial \mathcal{L}}{\partial \lambda} = y - \overline{P}_{L,1}\overline{T} + \overline{P}_{L,1}Le - \overline{N} = 0. \qquad \textbf{(21.15)}$$

These first-order conditions can be solved in the same manner as for the earlier problem. Rearranging equations (21.13) and (21.14) and dividing equation (21.13) by equation (21.14) yields

$$\frac{\frac{1}{2}Le^{-1/2}}{\frac{1}{2}y^{-1/2}} = \frac{-\lambda\overline{P}_{L,1}}{-\lambda}$$

$$\frac{y^{1/2}}{Le^{1/2}} = \overline{P}_{L,1},$$

or

$$y = \overline{P}_{L,1}^2 Le.$$

Substituting this result for y into equation (21.15) yields

$$\overline{P}_{L,1}^2 Le - \overline{P}_{L,1}\overline{T} + \overline{P}_{L,1}Le - \overline{N} = 0,$$

or

$$Le \, (\overline{P}^2_{L,1} + \overline{P}_{L,1}) = \overline{P}_{L,1}\overline{T} + \overline{N},$$

which we solve for Le as

$$L^*_e = \frac{\overline{P}_{L,1}\overline{T} + \overline{N}}{\overline{P}^2_{L,1} + \overline{P}_{L,1}} = \frac{\overline{P}_{L,1}\overline{T} + \overline{N}}{\overline{P}_{L,1}(\overline{P}_{L,1} + 1)}.$$

Once we allow the price of leisure, P_L, to vary, the above equation represents the consumer's demand for leisure curve, which in this case is

$$Le = \frac{P_L\overline{T} + \overline{N}}{P_L(P_L + 1)}.$$

The relationship between Le and P_L is inverse, for a change in P_L alters the denominator by a greater percentage amount than it does for the numerator in this expression. The corresponding supply of labor curve is

$$L = \overline{T} - Le = \overline{T} - \left[\frac{P_L\overline{T} + \overline{N}}{P_L(P_L + 1)}\right],$$

where the relationship between L and P_L must be direct since Le and P_L are inversely related.

Our inclusion of the nonlabor income term, $\overline{N}$, in the budget constraint affects the solution values for Le, L, and y. Using the same values for P_L and $\overline{T}$ as in the earlier example, $P_L = \$3$ and $\overline{T} = 24$ hours, assume that the amount of nonlabor income is $\overline{N} = \$12$ for this 24-hour period. As a result, the amount of leisure time the consumer now chooses is

$$L^{*'}_{e_1} = \frac{P_L\overline{T} + \overline{N}}{P_L(P_L + 1)} = \frac{3(24) + 12}{3(3 + 1)} = 7 \text{ hours,}$$

and the quantity of labor supplied is

$$L^{*'}_1 = \overline{T} - Le = 24 - 7 = 17 \text{ hours.}$$

The level of income is therefore

$$y^{*'}_1 = \overline{P}_{L,1}L + \overline{N} = 3(17) + 12 = \$63,$$

which is the consumer's total income for time period $\overline{T}$ including both labor and non-labor income, where the labor income, y^*_L, is

$$y^*_L = \overline{P}_{L,1}L = 3(17) = \$51.$$

We can compare the results computed for this example to those for the preceding case in which the consumer receives zero nonlabor income. In that case, the solution values for Le, L, and y are $L^*_{e_1} = 6$ hours, $L^*_1 = 18$ hours, and $y^*_1 = \$54$. In the latter case, for which we have included nonlabor income in the budget constraint, the consumer chooses more leisure time, 7 hours, supplies fewer units of labor, 17 hours, and earns less labor income, $51, as compared to the former case that does not include nonlabor income. The rationale for these different results lies in the fact that including nonlabor income in the consumer's budget constraint enables the individual to consume greater amounts of leisure time, as well as total income.

21.2.4   Substitution and Income Effects

In the preceding examples, we determined the relationships between Le and P_L, and subsequently between L and P_L, to be clearly inverse and direct, respectively. More generally, however, these relationships are ambiguous. Focusing on the consumer's demand for leisure, we find that this ambiguity is due to the conflicting directionality associated with the two component effects comprising the total effect of a change in the quantity demanded of leisure resulting from a change in its price. These two component effects are the familiar substitution and income effects stemming from a change in the price of a good. In our current context, the good is leisure time, where the substitution effect measures the impact of a change in the price of leisure on the quantity demanded of this good, due strictly to the resulting change in the relative price of leisure time to income. More specifically, it reflects the consumer's tendency to substitute away from the increasingly expensive good and toward the increasingly less expensive good. Thus, as always, the substitution effect produces an inverse relationship between the quantity demanded of a good and its own price. In this case, the income effect reflects the change in the quantity demanded of leisure time resulting from a change in its price, due strictly to the effect on income caused by the price change. Generally, we consider leisure time to be a normal good, indicating a positive relationship between Le and P_L as measured by the income effect. Specifically, a change in P_L directly affects the consumer's income, y, *ceteris paribus*, thereby directly affecting the amount of leisure time demanded, provided the good is normal.

Since the substitution and income effects resulting from a change in the price of leisure time run counter to each other, we cannot determine the directionality of the total effect of such a change on Le on the basis of pure theory. Instead, this directionality depends on the magnitudes of the opposing substitution and income effects, which ultimately must be determined statistically. We have illustrated two different outcomes for this total effect of a change in P_L on Le in panels (A) and (B) of Figure 21.4, where we are assuming P_L increases from $\overline{P}_{L,1}$ to $\overline{P}_{L,2}$. In both panels, for the initial price of labor, $\overline{P}_{L,1}$, we represent the consumer's budget constraint as

$$y = \overline{P}_{L,1}\overline{T} - \overline{P}_{L,1}Le,$$

possessing a y-intercept value of $\overline{P}_{L,1}\overline{T}$ and a slope value of $-\overline{P}_{L,1}$. As P_L increases to level $\overline{P}_{L,2}$, the budget constraint rotates clockwise, with the constant Le intercept, $\overline{T}$, as the pivot point. The new budget constraint is

$$y = \overline{P}_{L,2}\overline{T} - \overline{P}_{L,2}Le,$$

possessing a higher y-intercept value, $\overline{P}_{L,2}\overline{T}$, and a greater slope value, in absolute value terms, $\overline{P}_{L,2}$, than the initial budget constraint.

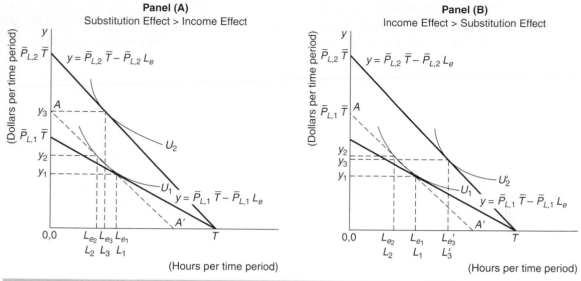

FIGURE 21.4 Substitution and Income Effects Associated with an Increase in the Price of Leisure Time

We can decompose the effect of this increase in the price of labor on the optimal amount of leisure time the consumer chooses into the associated substitution and income effects. An identical substitution effect is illustrated in panels (A) and (B) of Figure 21.4 using a compensated budget constraint, designated AA' in both panels. We have drawn this compensated constraint parallel to the new actual budget constraint to reflect the new set of relative prices, $P_{L,2}/1$, and tangent to the original indifference curve, U_1, to hold utility constant at U_1. By doing so, we have eliminated from the analysis any income effect, due to an increase in income resulting from the increase in P_L. Therefore, any impact on Le must be due strictly to the substitution effect or to the increase in the price of leisure relative to the price of income. This substitution effect is shown in both panels as $(Le_2 - Le_1) < 0$, representing the decrease in the amount of leisure time chosen by the consumer owing to the fact that it has become increasingly expensive relative to income. This decrease in leisure time from Le_1 to Le_2 corresponds to an increase in the amount of labor supplied by this consumer from L_1 to L_2, since $L = \overline{T} - Le$. Thus, the amount of income selected by this individual increases from y_1 to y_2, reflecting the increase in L. To obtain the total effect of this increase in P_L from $\overline{P}_{L,1}$ to $\overline{P}_{L,2}$ on Le and subsequently L, we must reintroduce the income effect into the analysis. Initially, as P_L increases, *ceteris paribus*, income increases, and, provided leisure time is a normal good, the consumer increases her consumption of leisure time as a result of this increase in income. However, as we stated earlier, the magnitude of the income effect relative to the substitution effect is a statistical question. Therefore, the directionality of the total effect is ambiguous from the perspective of pure theory, as the income and substitution effects run counter to each other.

We have illustrated two possible outcomes in panels (A) and (B) of Figure 21.4, where these outcomes differ only because of the difference in the magnitude of the income effect relative to the substitution effect. In panel (A), we have assumed that for an increase in P_L, the inverse substitution effect, $(Le_2 - Le_1)$, in absolute value terms, is greater than the direct income effect, $(Le_3 - Le_2)$. Thus, the total impact of the increase in P_L is a net decrease in the amount of leisure time consumed from Le_1 to Le_3, corresponding to utility level U_2, where $U_2 > U_1$. The amount of labor supplied ultimately increases to L_3 units, and the level of income increases to level y_3. In panel (B) of Figure 21.4, where once again the price of leisure increases from $\overline{P}_{L,1}$ to $\overline{P}_{L,2}$, we have assumed that the direct income effect, $Le_3' - Le_2$ exceeds the substitution effect, $Le_2 - Le_1$, in absolute value terms. Therefore, the total effect of the increase in P_L is a net increase in the amount of leisure time consumed from Le_1 to Le_3', corresponding to utility level U_2', where $U_2' > U_1$. Thus, in this case, the amount of labor supplied decreases to L_3' units.

The results generated in Figure 21.4 provide the basis for deriving both the consumer's demand for leisure curve and supply of labor curve, where essentially, we derive both of these curves simultaneously. We have plotted these curves, pertaining to the two different scenarios presented above, in Figures 21.5 and 21.6, where in both figures, panel (A) shows the consumer's demand for leisure curve and panel (B) demonstates the consumer's supply of labor curve. In Figure 21.5, both the demand for leisure and supply of labor curves are based on the assumption underlying the results in panel (A) of Figure 21.4, specifically, that the substitution effect, associated with the impact of a change in P_L on Le, exceeds the income effect.

Referring to panel (A) of Figure 21.4, for the price of leisure time, $P_{L,1}$, the amount of leisure time demanded is Le_1 and the quantity of labor supplied is L_1. We have plotted the corresponding combinations $(Le_1, P_{L,1})$ and $(L_1, P_{L,1})$ in panels (A)

FIGURE 21.5 Consumer's Demand for Leisure and Supply of Labor Curves where Substitution Effect Exceeds Income Effect

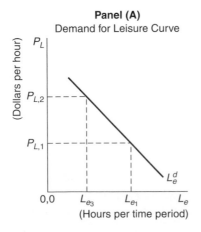
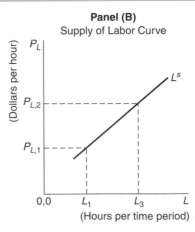

and (B), respectively, of Figure 21.5. As the price of leisure increases to $P_{L,2}$, the total effect of this price increase results in a decrease in the amount of leisure time chosen by the consumer from Le_1 to Le_3 units, and a corresponding increase in the quantity of labor supplied from L_1 to L_3 units. These combinations, $(Le_3, P_{L,2})$, and $(L_3, P_{L,2})$, are also plotted, respectively, in panels (A) and (B), of Figure 21.5. By connecting the combinations $(Le_1, P_{L,1})$ and $(Le_3, P_{L,2})$ in panel (A), we can construct the consumer's demand for leisure curve, L_e^d. This curve possesses a negative slope, indicating an inverse relationship between the quantity of leisure time demanded and its price, P_L. Similarly, we have constructed the consumer's supply of labor curve, L^S, in panel (B) by connecting the combinations $(L_1, P_{L,1})$ and $(L_3, P_{L,2})$. This curve possesses a positive slope, indicating a direct relationship between the quantity of labor supplied and the price of leisure time, which we can also interpret as the price of labor, P_L.

Panel (B) of Figure 21.4 represents a situation for which the income effect, associated with a change in P_L on Le and L, exceeds the substitution effect. We expect the consumer's demand for leisure and supply of labor curves derived for this case to possess different slopes from those derived above. As in our previous analysis, initially the price of leisure time is $P_{L,1}$ where the corresponding amount of leisure time demanded by the consumer is Le_1 units and the quantity of labor supplied is L_1 units. The corresponding combinations $(Le_1, P_{L,1})$ and $(L_1, P_{L,1})$, are plotted in panels (A) and (B), respectively, of Figure 21.6. As the price of leisure increases to $P_{L,2}$, the total effect on Le, in this case, is an increase in the amount of leisure time from Le_1 to Le_3' units and, correspondingly, a decrease in the quantity of labor supplied from L_1 to L_3' units. The associated combinations $(Le_3', P_{L,2})$ and $(L_3', P_{L,2})$ are plotted in panels (A) and (B), respectively, of Figure 21.6. We construct the consumer's demand for leisure curve, L_e^d, by connecting the combinations $(Le_1, P_{L,1})$ and $(Le_3', P_{L,2})$ in panel (A), where this curve possesses a positive slope indicating a direct relationship between L_e^d

FIGURE 21.6 Consumer's Demand for Leisure and Supply of Labor Curves where Income Effect Exceeds Substitution Effect

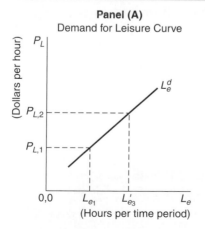
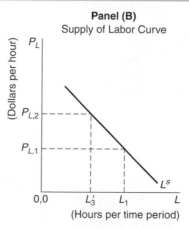

Panel (A)
Demand for Leisure Curve

Panel (B)
Supply of Labor Curve

and P_L. In panel (B), the consumer's supply of labor curve, L^S, is constructed by connecting the combinations $(L_1, P_{L,1})$ and $(L_3', P_{L,2})$, generating a curve possessing a negative slope, indicating an inverse relationship between the quantity of labor supplied and P_L.

Our determination as to which of the two preceding scenarios is appropriate depends on the magnitude of the substitution and income effects due to a change in P_L, that ultimately reflects the preferences of the particular consumer to which these demand for leisure and supply of labor curves pertain. A third case, often considered by economists, involves applying both of the two scenarios discussed above, where an individual's response to a change in the price of leisure, or labor, P_L, depends on the particular level of this price. Specifically, for many individuals, the substitution effect exceeds the income effect at relatively low prices of leisure. Thus, as P_L increases, the consumer chooses less leisure and supplies more labor as indicated by our analysis illustrated in panel (A) of Figure 21.4 and in both panels of Figure 21.5. However, as P_L continues to increase for these individuals, there is a level of P_L at which the income effect begins to dominate the substitution effect and continues to do so for further increases in P_L. As a result, for increases in P_L above this level, the consumer chooses more leisure and supplies less labor, similar to the results we demonstrated in panel (B) of Figure 21.4 and in both panels of Figure 21.6. The overall result is a labor supply curve possessing a "backward-bending" shape, as illustrated in Figure 21.7. When the price of labor is less than $P_{L,2}$, increases in P_L result in the individual increasing her quantity of labor supplied, but when the price of labor is greater than or equal to $P_{L,2}$, increases in P_L result in the individual decreasing her quantity of labor supplied.

Although this backward-bending portion of an individual's labor supply curve is a theoretical possibility, statistical estimates of labor supply curves indicate that most individuals do not earn a price of labor, or wage rate, that is sufficiently high for them to operate on the backward-bending portion of their labor supply curve. As a result, the majority of our analysis of labor markets focuses on the positively sloped portion of an individual's labor supply curve.

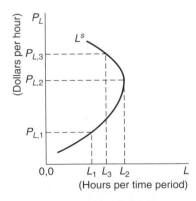

FIGURE 21.7 Backward-Bending Supply of Labor Curve

A More Realistic Definition of Leisure Time

In most income-leisure models of consumer behavior, including those developed in this chapter, we define leisure time simply as nonlabor time. The implicit assumption in these models is that labor time refers only to those services sold in the labor market outside the home. As a result, we consider domestic labor, including such tasks as meal preparation, cleaning, child care, and yardwork, conducted and consumed by an individual within the home, as constituting leisure time. From the perspective of someone other than an economist, this definition of leisure time must seem rather peculiar inasmuch as for many individuals these tasks are not perceived as generating utility or satisfaction. As evidence of this perception, there has been an increasing trend in recent years toward outsourcing many of these domestic tasks. For example, in the United States, consumer expenditures on restaurant meals in 1998 exceeded expenditures for home-prepared meals. Furthermore, regarding home-prepared food, the trend is toward pre-prepared or ready-to-eat meals, and firms such as Pea Pod and Net Grocer have enabled consumers to request delivery orders of groceries by fax, telephone, or the Internet.[1] These concepts of convenience and outsourcing have been taken further by firms such as Streamline, which is in the business of not only automatically replenishing grocery supplies, but also performing such tasks as returning dry cleaning and videos, posting letters for individuals, and delivering camera film to be developed.

Changing attitudes toward domestic labor and the related outsourcing of such tasks logically impacts our analysis of a consumer's income-leisure optimization problem. For example, this outsourcing should, to some extent, forestall the backward-bending portion of an individual's labor supply curve, as increases in the price of labor enable an individual to outsource more domestic tasks should she wish to do so. As a result, the decrease in "leisure time," associated with an increase in its price, comes at the expense of these domestic tasks that are no longer performed by the individual, rather than at the expense of more commonly defined free leisure time from which most individuals derive their utility. Given the increasing aversion of many consumers to domestic labor, we should develop a more realistic income-leisure time model of consumer choice that defines leisure as time spent not supplying labor to either the market or to the home, as well as factoring into account the price of outsourcing domestic work.

[1]"Homework," *The Economist*, September 26, 1998, pp. 68–69.

21.3 MARKET SUPPLY OF LABOR CURVE

Now that we have derived the supply of labor curve for an individual consumer, it is possible to construct a market supply of labor curve by horizontally summing these individual curves. We conduct this procedure by selecting particular values for P_L, determining the quantities of labor supplied by the different individuals at these prices of labor, and then summing these quantities to obtain the market quantity of labor supplied at each value of P_L. You should be familiar with the process of horizontal summation at this point, and therefore, we will leave it to you as an exercise. However, we should note some technical points regarding this process. First, there are some minimal values for P_L, below which some individuals supply zero units of labor. Therefore, you should conduct the horizontal summation process for ranges of P_L, yielding a market supply of labor curve that is segmented. Each segment, in part, depends on the number of individuals willing to supply units of labor over the corresponding ranges of P_L. Another complication is the fact that at certain values of P_L, the labor supply curve for some individuals may begin bending backward, generating a negative slope for their individual supply curves at high levels of P_L. This outcome causes a dampening of any increases in the overall market quantity of labor supplied, resulting from further increases in P_L.

Finally, we should note that the supply of labor curve pertaining to any one industry, where the output is homogeneous, is generally flatter, or more price elastic, than the market labor supply curve. This result follows because an increase in the price of labor in a particular industry generally results in an increase in the quantity of labor supplied to that industry, arising from not only some individuals choosing to consume less leisure time, but also from other individuals switching jobs from one particular industry to another.

21.4 MONOPSONY

We based our various analyses of the demand for labor in Chapter 20 on the assumption that the firms behave as perfect competitors in their input markets. The result of this assumption is that the equilibrium price of the labor input is determined by the interaction of the industry or market labor supply and demand curves. Thus, each firm takes the market price of labor as given and determines its profit-maximizing level of labor use according to the procedures described in that chapter. Since each firm is but one of many imperceptibly small firms operating in the market for its labor input, the firm's labor supply curve is subsequently represented by its horizontal MEI_L curve, where $MEI_{L,1} = \overline{P}_{L,1}$. This result indicates that the firm can employ as many units of labor as it desires without affecting the price of this input.

However, just as some output markets consist of a single seller possessing some discretion over the price it receives for its product, so there are also some input markets comprised of a single buyer possessing some discretion over the price that it pays for its inputs. This type of input market is known as a **monopsony**, or *a market structure in which a single firm acts as the sole purchaser of an input*. A monopsonist's discretion over the price it pays for an input follows from the fact that the particular industry or market supply curve for that input also represents the input supply curve to the monopsonistic firm, since this firm is the sole buyer of the input. The market supply of labor curve can be represented as

$$L^{s,M} = L^{s,M}(P_L, \overline{T}),$$

where $L^{s,M}$ represents the market quantity of labor supplied. In general, for relatively lower values of P_L, the relationship between $L^{s,M}$ and P_L is direct, or the market labor supply curve possesses a positive slope. We can express this curve in inverse form as

$$P_L = P_L(L^{s,M}, \overline{T}),$$

where in the case of monopsony, $L^{s,M}$, or simply L, is the amount of labor supplied to only one buyer. Therefore, as a monopsonist alters the level of labor, L, it employs, this firm can directly influence the price it pays for this input, P_L. Thus, a monopsonist has an incentive to restrict the amount of labor it hires in order to drive down the price of labor, where the restriction clearly affects the profit-maximizing level of labor the firm employs in its production process. As a result, the solution values regarding L and P_L for a monopsonist differ from those for a firm behaving as a perfect competitor in its input market. We can show that this difference is due to the impact that a monopsonist's discretion over its input price has on its marginal expense of an input (*MEI*) curve.

We will demonstrate this impact on the *MEI* curve for the single variable input case, where capital is fixed at $\overline{K}_1$ units, and therefore labor constitutes the only variable input. Recall that we can express the firm's short-run total cost curve, *SRTC*, as

$$SRTC = \overline{P}_{K,1}\overline{K}_1 + P_L L.$$

However, in the case of a monopsonist,

$$P_L = P_L(L, \overline{T}),$$

and thus

$$SRTC = \overline{P}_{K,1}\overline{K}_1 + P_L(L, \overline{T})L.$$

We derive the marginal expense of labor curve, MEI_L, by taking the derivative of *SRTC* with respect to L, yielding

$$MEI_L = \frac{dSRTC}{dL} = \frac{d\overline{P}_{K,1}\overline{K}_1}{dL} + \frac{dP_L(L, \overline{T})L}{dL}.$$

Recognizing that the term $d\overline{P}_{K,1}\overline{K}_1/dL = 0$, and applying the product rule to the term $dP_L(L, \overline{T})L/dL$, we can express this equation as

$$MEI_L = P_L(L, \overline{T})\frac{dL}{dL} + L\frac{dP_L(L, \overline{T})}{dL},$$

or since $P_L = P_L(L, \overline{T})$, as

$$MEI_L = P_L + L\frac{dP_L}{dL}. \tag{21.16}$$

This expression in equation (21.16) indicates that for a monopsonist $MEI_L > P_L$, or that the change in its cost due to a change in the amount of labor it employs exceeds the price it pays for its labor by the amount $L(dP_L/dL)$. The term, dP_L/dL, represents the slope of the inverse supply of labor curve, where $dP_L/dL > 0$, indicating that for this firm to attract additional units of labor, it must increase the price it pays for these units. At this point, it is necessary for us to introduce the important assumption that the firm does not discriminate in terms of the price of labor it pays its employees. As a result, as the monopsonist increases P_L to attract additional units of labor, it increases this price for all units of labor it employs, including those that could be hired at lower prices. Therefore, we can interpret the term, $L(dP_L/dL)$, as the extra cost to the firm associated with paying its "current" labor units the higher price necessary to hire one additional unit of labor. For example, if the initial price of labor is $P_{L,1}$ at which L_1 units of labor are employed by the firm, and $P_{L,2}$ is the higher price necessary to hire one additional unit of labor, then the marginal expense of the labor input associated with doing so is

$$MEI_L = P_{L,2}(L_2 - L_1) + L_1 \frac{P_{L,2} - P_{L,1}}{L_2 - L_1},$$

and since $L_2 - L_1 = 1$ unit of labor, then

$$MEI_L = P_{L,2} + L_1(P_{L,2} - P_{L,1}).$$

This example represents a discrete version of equation (21.16), where now we are measuring the change in the amount of labor in finite one-unit increments. The term $(P_{L,2} - P_{L,1})$ is the increase in the price of labor necessary to attract an additional unit of labor. Therefore, the term $L_1(P_{L,2} - P_{L,1})$ is that part of the MEI_L representing the increase in the wage bill that a nondiscriminating firm must pay for units of labor it previously employed at the price $P_{L,1}$.

To complete the model of monopsony, we will reintroduce the value of the marginal product of labor, VMP_L, curve that represents the firm's demand for labor curve in the one variable input case. Also, we are assuming that the firm being analyzed, though now a monopsonist in its labor market, remains a perfect competitor in its output market. Thus, the firm determines the profit-maximizing amount of labor it employs according to the familiar necessary condition

$$VMP_L = MEI_L,$$

reflecting the fact that it employs amounts of labor to the point at which the associated extra revenue, VMP_L, is equal to the extra cost, MEI_L. Note, however, that for a monopsonist, $MEI_L > P_L$. By substituting the expression for MEI_L from equation (21.16), we can express this necessary condition as

$$VMP_L = P_L + L\frac{dP_L}{dL},$$

reflecting the fact that since $MEI_L > P_L$, then at the profit-maximizing amount of labor employed, $VMP_L > P_L$ as well. Therefore, a monopsonist pays a price for the amount of labor it hires that is less than the extra revenue generated from employing the extra unit of labor. This result differs from the case in which a firm behaves as a perfect competitor in its input markets and thus determines its profit-maximizing level of labor according to the condition

$$VMP_L = MEI_L = P_L.$$

In this perfectly competitive case, the firm pays a price for its labor equal to the value of its marginal product. However, a monopsonist pays a lower price for labor than does the perfectly competitive firm. As a result, it also employs a lower quantity of labor. This result follows because the quantity of labor supplied to a monopsonist is a direct function of its price, P_L, as represented by the market supply of labor curve

$$L^{s,M} = L^{s,M}(P_L, \overline{T}).$$

We have illustrated these results in Figure 21.8 which includes the VMP_L, or demand for labor, curve for the one variable input case, the supply of labor curve in inverse form, $P_L = P_L(L, \overline{T})$, and the MEI_L curve, $MEI_{L,M} = P_L + L(dP_L/dL)$, for a monopsonist. The $MEI_{L,M}$ curve lies above the supply of labor curve, reflecting the fact that the $MEI_{L,M} > P_L$ for all positive values of L. Assuming this labor market is monopsonistic, we see that the firm employs L_M units of labor at which $VMP_L = MEI_{L,M}$, and pays the price $P_{L,M}$ for the units of labor it employs. Using Figure 21.8, we can compare these results to those for this same market, assuming it is perfectly competitive. In this latter case, the demand for labor curve, VMP_L, represents the horizontal summation of the perfectly competitive firms' demand for labor curves comprising this market. The amount of labor employed in this case is L_C, at which $L_C^d = L_C^s$, or $VMP_L = P_L$, and the corresponding price of labor is $P_{L,C}$. We can also observe in this figure that, as reasoned earlier, $L_M < L_C$ and $P_{L,M} < P_{L,C}$.

The occurrence of pure monopsony is relatively rare. However, we can mention a few examples of markets characterized by either monopsony or some degree of

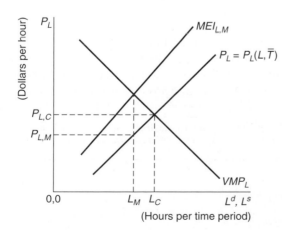

FIGURE 21.8 Comparison of Outcomes for Monopsony and a Perfectly Competitive Labor Market

---

The Draft System in Professional Sports

In this chapter we stated that prior to softening the reserve clause, owners of professional baseball teams were able to operate as monopsonists. This clause "reserved" to the owners of a professional sports team the right to unilaterally impose a new contract on a player if the team and this formerly contracted player could not agree to new terms. This reserve system has been significantly modified to varying degrees for all major professional sports: baseball, basketball, football, and ice hockey. However, some elements of the reserve system, and the subsequent monopsony power associated with it, still exist in these sports, primarily through the implementation of a draft system. A professional sports team that drafts a player possesses the rights to that player's services for one year. This draft system is largely the result of agreements between players' unions and team owners that free veteran players from the reserve system in exchange for imposing a draft system on rookie players.

As with many agreements pertaining to market restrictions, this draft system was supposedly instituted for reasons that have nothing to do with the resulting monopsony power. In this case, the rationale is that a draft system balances the competition across the teams comprising a professional sports league, in that the team with the worst win-loss record gets to select first. The team with the second worst record chooses second, and so forth. However, the alleged balancing effect of a draft is suspect because ultimately the draft applies to a very small number of top quality players, who are then bound to a team for only one year. More importantly, economic theory indicates that resources tend to flow to where they are most highly valued. In the case of professional sports, the resources (players) are usually most highly valued by teams located in cities characterized by large populations. It is no coincidence that, generally, these teams are able to acquire the most talented players; the weaker teams, often located in low-population cities, find it profitable to trade their rights to these high-quality players to the more successful teams.

If the draft system does not create a competitive balance across teams comprising a professional sports league, what does it accomplish? Essentially, it establishes a degree of monopsony power that enables the team owners to exploit the talents of first-year players, leading to a redistribution of income and wealth away from these rookie players toward team owners and to veteran players, who by their union agreements, are able to sell their services to the highest bidders. Furthermore, the draft system also results in a redistribution of income and wealth away from winning teams, located in high-population cities, to losing teams situated in low-population cities. Thus, although the draft does not balance competition, it does subsidize weaker opponents and, by so doing, maintains the stability of a professional sports league.[2]

---

[2]John J. Siegfried, "Sports Player Drafts and Reserve Systems," *Cato Journal*, 14, no. 3 (Winter 1995): 443–452.

monopsony power. One of the traditional cases of pure monopsony was that of major league baseball prior to the elimination of the reserve clause in 1976. Before that time, the reserve clause effectively bound a major league baseball player to a particular team owner. Thus, in order to sell their labor services, the players had no choice other than to play for a single owner, leading to salaries that in many cases were below the players' contributions to total revenue, or VMP_L, for the team. Once the reserve clause was overthrown by the courts in 1976, the salaries for many of the top baseball players skyrocketed by several multiples, leading to the multimillion dollar salaries received by many of today's baseball players.

Although examples of pure monopsony are relatively rare, we encounter cases for which some degree of monopsony power exists more frequently. These situations occur when individuals supplying units of labor believe their mobility to be restricted for some reason, perhaps related to personal or family matters. For the labor market, as with virtually any market, to allocate resources (units of labor) efficiently, these labor units need to flow to their most highly valued uses. If this is not the case, say for example, because some individuals believe themselves restricted to a particular geographic region, then these individuals must sell their labor to only a few firms, or in the most extreme case, to only one firm. As a result, this firm acquires some degree of monopsony power, or influence over the price, that it pays for its units of labor. More generally, if there are only a few firms purchasing units of labor in a particular market, we define this market structure as an oligopsony. In this case, the firms might be able to collude in some manner so as to decrease the price of the labor they hire, thus creating a market structure for inputs that is analogous to an oligopoly in a market for output.

21.5 SUMMARY

We have devoted this chapter to analyzing labor supply curves, where these curves, along with the labor demand curves developed in Chapter 20, provide the basis for analyzing labor markets. The key topics covered in this chapter are briefly outlined as follows.

- We determine the amount of an individual's labor supplied by solving her constrained utility maximization problem regarding the choice between income and leisure time.
- The slopes of a consumer's demand for leisure curve, and supply of labor curve, depend on the magnitudes of the substitution and income effects associated with a change in the price of leisure time.
- If the substitution effect exceeds the income effect, an individual's supply of labor curve possesses a positive slope. Conversely, if the income effect exceeds the substitution effect, then this supply of labor curve possesses a negative slope.
- A monopsony is a market structure consisting of a single buyer of an input. In this case, a firm employs an input, say labor, where $VMP_L = MEI_L$, but for

which the MEI_L exceeds the price of labor. As a result, a monopsonist employs less labor, and pays a lower price for this labor, than a group of firms behaving as perfect competitors in their input markets.

KEY TERMS

- labor supply curve, page 552
- monopsony, page 570

EXERCISES

21.1 Assume that an individual perceives leisure time as a normal good and that the substitution and income effects associated with a change in the price of leisure are equal, in absolute value terms. This being the case, what is the shape of the individual's supply of labor curve? Interpret this result intuitively.

21.2 Suppose an individual perceives leisure time as an inferior good. Graphically, show the substitution, income, and total effects for an increase in the price of leisure time. Next, illustrate the associated demand for leisure and supply of labor curves.

21.3 An individual has the utility function

$$U = 4Le^{1/2} + 2y^{1/2},$$

where U represents utility, Le is leisure time, in hours, and y is the individual's real income. Assuming the price of leisure time is $2/hour, construct this individual's budget constraint for a 24-hour period. Next, determine the optimal amounts of leisure time, labor time, and real income for this individual.

21.4 Referring to the information provided in Exercise 21.3, assume the individual receives $6/day in nonlabor income. Now, compute the individual's optimal levels of leisure time, labor time, and real income. In addition, compute the optimal amount of real income resulting strictly from providing labor. Intuitively, why are these results different from those for Exercise 21.3?

21.5 Once again, refer to the information given in Exercise 21.3. Derive the individual's demand for leisure and supply of labor curves. Note the slope for each of the curves. What do these slope values indicate about the individual's substitution and income effects associated with a change in the price of leisure time?

21.6 Assume an individual has the utility function

$$U = Le^{1/2}y^{1/2},$$

where U represents utility, Le is leisure time, in hours, and y is real income. For the time period $T = 24$ hours, determine the optimal values for Le, L (labor time), and y. *Note:* The price of leisure time is not given for this problem.

21.7 Refer to the information in Exercise 21.6. Derive and illustrate the individual's demand for leisure and supply of labor curves. What do these shapes reflect? How do they compare to the curves you derived in Exercise 21.5?

21.8 Graphically, demonstrate the monopsony model. Show the firm's optimal amount of labor hired and the wage rate it pays. On the same graph show the amount of labor hired and the wage rate if the labor market is made perfectly competitive, and contrast these results with those you obtained assuming the market is a monopsony. Finally, if the labor market is characterized by a monopsony, what happens to the optimal amount of labor hired if a union successfully increases the wage rate paid by the monopsonist?

CHAPTER 22

Capital Markets

22.1 INTRODUCTION

The focus of our analysis in the preceding two chapters was on the input market for labor. In this chapter, we will direct our attention to the market for the other major input included in most production functions, capital. As established in Chapter 8, the term *capital* refers to produced inputs such as plant and equipment, which in turn are used by firms to produce output. Analyzing capital markets is more complex than labor markets, primarily because capital possesses some degree of durability. Thus, regarding the demand for capital, if a firm chooses to purchase a unit of this input rather than rent it, the firm generally expects this capital to provide services for an extended period of time, usually several years. This durability introduces the dimension of time into our analysis, creating several complications. For example, over time a capital input tends to wear out or depreciate. In addition, its price may rise or fall, according to changing market conditions. The broader issue, however, is the mismatch regarding the time period in which capital is purchased by a firm and the several time periods during which its use contributes to the production of that firm's output and ultimately its profits. Specifically, a firm that purchases units of capital in the present time period generally receives the benefits of increased production and profit not only in the present time period, but also for several future time periods as well. Why is this a complicating factor? The answer, as we will demonstrate in the next section, is that income or profit received in future time periods is not valued as highly as present income or profit. As a result, this discrepancy between the immediate time period in which capital is purchased and the time periods during which it generates production and profit affects its purchase price and quantity demanded.

The supply of capital is ultimately created by those consumers who are willing to postpone some of their current consumption in order to increase their consumption in future time periods. We define this postponement of current consumption more commonly as that amount of a consumer's current income that is saved, and it provides the basis for financing the accumulation of capital by firms. However, consumers generally possess a bias favoring consumption in the present time period over that in the future. Consequently, individuals who save some of their current income expect to be rewarded for their postponement of current consumption. In turn, this reward affects the price and quantity supplied of capital. Implicit in our discussion of capital markets, regarding both firms and consumers, is the existence of a price that allocates resources across time periods to their most highly valued uses. This price is the interest rate, and we will show that it plays an extremely important role in the analysis of capital markets.

22.2   INTEREST RATES AND THE PROCESS OF DISCOUNTING

There are several related definitions and interpretations of an **interest rate**, the most direct being that it is *the ratio of the payment per annum generated by an asset to the value of that asset.* An individual or firm, which we often define as an economic agent, who owns an asset such as a bond is effectively a lender of funds. Thus, the per annum payment associated with the asset represents a form of income received by this owner. Note that, although firms are often treated as economic agents, they are ultimately owned by individuals. The economic agent who makes the payment is a borrower, and this payment represents a cost to this agent for obtaining use of the funds for some specified time period. This per annum payment is known as a flow variable, or one that we measure per unit of time, whereas the value of an asset represents a stock variable that we measure at a point in time. Thus, an interest rate relates a flow variable to a stock variable. For example, if the flow of payments from an asset is $100 per year and the value of the asset is $1000 at a particular point in time, then we compute the interest rate, r, as

$$r = \frac{\$100/\text{year}}{\$1000} = 10\%/\text{year}.$$

22.2.1   Real vs. Nominal Interest Rates

As we stated earlier, those individuals who save some of their income in the current time period ultimately become lenders of funds, and because of a general bias favoring consumption in the current time period, these savers expect a reward for postponing their current consumption. Specifically, these savers who ultimately become lenders, expect to receive at some time in the future, say one year, the original funds they have lent out, also known as the principal amount of the loan, plus a reward that is equal to the interest rate multiplied by this principal amount. Conversely, borrowers, many of whom are firms, expect to pay this same amount for obtaining the current use of these funds.

There is an important point we should note. The interest payment that lenders receive in the future time period is an amount representing the additional goods and services they expect to be able to purchase in the future as their reward for saving and lending. For example, if the interest rate is 10 percent, then they expect to be able to purchase 10 percent more goods and services in the future than they can purchase with the original principal amount in the present time period. They will not be able to do so, however, if the prices of goods and services increase in the future, unless these price increases are incorporated into the interest rate they charge to borrowers. Therefore, to demonstrate how the interest rate charged to borrowers is affected by the possibility of future price changes, we need to interpret an interest rate from two perspectives. The first is that of a **real interest rate**, or *a per annum percentage expressing a future payment in terms of the goods and services that can be purchased with this payment in the present time period.* The second perspective is that of a **nominal interest**

rate, or *a per annum percentage expressing a future payment in "current," dollar terms*. The term *current* refers to the year of the payment. It is this nominal interest rate that we actually observe, where it includes the real interest rate, along with some allowance for any expected change in the prices of goods and services over the period of a loan. We can formalize the relationship between real and nominal interest rates in terms of an expression known as the Fisher equation, named after economist Irving Fisher, renowned for his economic research related to interest rates.

To interpret the Fisher equation, it is necessary to view the concept of an interest rate from yet another perspective. Earlier, we defined an interest rate as the ratio of the payment per annum associated with an asset to the value of that asset, where this value often represents the principal amount of a loan. Thus, after a period of one year, the total value of this asset increases by the amount of the per annum payment. Defining r_N as the nominal interest rate and V_t as the initial dollar value of an asset, measured at the end of period, or year, t, then we find that the total value associated with this asset at the end of the next period, or year, V_{t+1}, equals the initial value, V_t, plus the interest payment, $r_N V_t$, or

$$V_{t+1} = V_t + r_N V_t. \tag{22.1}$$

Therefore, the change in the total value of the asset over the one-year period, $V_{t+1} - V_t$, is

$$V_{t+1} - V_t = r_N V_t,$$

where dividing both sides of this equation by V_t and applying the commutative property yields

$$r_N = \frac{V_{t+1} - V_t}{V_t}. \tag{22.2}$$

This expression indicates that the nominal interest rate represents a one-year percentage change in current, or noninflation-adjusted, dollar terms in the total value of an asset, or more concisely, it is the per annum growth rate in the value of an asset.

As we stated earlier, the prices of goods and services may change over time, or more relevantly, over the time period associated with a loan. We can demonstrate this change in the prices of goods and services by first computing weighted averages of these prices for the periods t and $t + 1$, represented by P_t and P_{t+1}, respectively. The change in these price averages over the one-year period between t and $t + 1$ is $P_{t+1} - P_t$, and dividing this term by the initial price average, P_t, yields the term

$$\frac{P_{t+1} - P_t}{P_t},$$

that represents the percentage change in the average price level over the one-year period between times t and $t + 1$. This term is also a growth rate, which we more commonly know as the rate of inflation, when $(P_{t+1} - P_t)/P_t > 0$, or alternatively, as the rate of deflation when $(P_{t+1} - P_t)/P_t < 0$. In the following analysis we will interpret this term as the rate of inflation, denoted $\dot{P}$, since historically inflation has been considerably more prevalent than deflation. At the time a loan is negotiated, the actual rate of inflation over the period of the loan, say one year, is unknown. As a result, it is the expected rate of inflation, designated $\dot{P}*$, that is incorporated into the nominal interest rate to compensate the lender for being repaid in depreciated dollars. Defining r_r as the real interest rate, we compute the total value of an asset, in nominal terms, after one year as

$$V_{t+1} = V_t + r_r V_t + \dot{P}* V_t + r_r \dot{P}* V_t, \tag{22.3}$$

where all terms have been defined previously. Thus, V_{t+1} equals the summation of the initial value of the asset, such as a loan, V_t, the real interest payment, $r_r V_t$, the increase in the value of the asset due to the expected rate of inflation, $\dot{P}* V_t$, and the real interest charge associated with this increase due to expected inflation, $r_r \dot{P}* V_t$. Subtracting V_t from both sides of equation (22.3) and factoring V_t from the remaining terms on the right-hand side yields

$$V_{t+1} - V_t = V_t(r_r + \dot{P}* + r_r \dot{P}*),$$

where dividing this equation by V_t yields

$$\frac{V_{t+1} - V_t}{V_t} = r_r + \dot{P}* + r_r \dot{P}*. \tag{22.4}$$

Since, from equation (22.2), $r_N = (V_{t+1} - V_t)/V_t$, we can express equation (22.4) as

$$r_N = r_r + \dot{P}* + r_r \dot{P}*.$$

Finally, since the term $r_r \dot{P}*$ is generally very small, we can simplify this expression as

$$r_N = r_r + \dot{P}*. \tag{22.5}$$

Formally, equation (22.5) is known as the Fisher equation, simply indicating that the nominal interest rate, r_N, equals the real interest rate, r_r, plus the expected rate of inflation, $\dot{P}*$. Our interpretation of this equation is straightforward, reflecting the fact that lenders add an expected inflation premium to the real interest rate to compute the nominal rate they actually charge borrowers. Lenders do this in order to protect themselves from being paid back in depreciated dollars resulting from inflation. Borrowers, on the other hand, are logically willing to pay this expected inflation premium to obtain use of the funds for the relevant time period because they also expect to pay back the loan in depreciated dollars. If the expected inflation rate equals zero, as we will assume for the sake of simplicity in much of the following analysis, then the nominal and real rates of interest will be equal, or

$$r = r_N = r_r.$$

Therefore, r represents the interest rate in either nominal or real terms. However, keep in mind that actual inflation, and consequently expected inflation, are frequently occurring real-world phenomena, and thus the nominal interest rate we observe must be adjusted accordingly to obtain the real interest rate.

22.2.2 Future and Present Values

Before analyzing capital markets, we need to address two additional concepts related to interest rates. The first is the **future value of an asset or payment**, denoted FV, defined as *the value of a present asset or payment in terms of what it is worth in some future time period*. This concept is implicit in equation (22.1), which expresses the value of an asset in the present time period t, or V_t, in terms of what it is worth in the period $t + 1$, or one year into the future. Thus, the term V_{t+1} represents the future value of the asset V_t. We can extend this concept to account for any number of years into the future. Letting $t = 0$ represent the present time period, we can express equation (22.1) as

$$FV_1 = V_1 = V_0 + rV_0 = (1 + r)V_0, \tag{22.6}$$

which measures the future value of asset V_0, after being lent for one year. If V_0 is lent for two years, then we compute the future value of V_0 after that amount of time, denoted FV_2, on the assumption that the new amount, V_1, is lent for the second year, yielding

$$FV_2 = V_2 = V_1 + rV_1 = (1 + r)V_1.$$

After substituting the expression for V_1 from equation (22.6) into this equation, this expression becomes

$$FV_2 = V_2 = (1 + r)(1 + r)V_0 = (1 + r)^2 V_0.$$

Similarly, we compute the future value of V_0 after three years as

$$FV_3 = V_3 = V_2 + rV_2 = (1 + r)V_2 = (1 + r)(1 + r)^2 V_0 = (1 + r)^3 V_0.$$

At this point, you should be able to discern a pattern such that for n periods into the future, we can generalize the formula for the future value of a present asset by the expression

$$FV_n = V_n = (1 + r)^n V_0. \tag{22.7}$$

For example, if $n = 3$ years, $r = 10\%$, and the value of a present asset, such as the principal amount of a loan, V_0, equals \$1000, then after three years the future value of this amount is

$$FV_3 = V_3 = (1 + 0.10)^3 (1000) = \$1331.$$

Note that for this computation, and for the generalized future value formula in equation (22.7), we are assuming the interest payment is computed, or compounded, only once each year.

The second concept related to interest rates which we need to address is the **present value of an asset** or payment, denoted PV, defined as *the value of a future asset or payment in terms of what it is worth in the present time period*. In the preceding analysis, the term V_0 represents the value of an asset in the present time period; therefore, we can interpret it as the present value, PV_0, of that asset in time period $t = 0$. We derive the formula for computing a present value by simply rearranging equation (22.7) to isolate the term V_0 as

$$PV_0 = V_0 = \frac{FV_n}{(1 + r)^n}. \tag{22.8}$$

Assuming the same values, $n = 3$ years and $r = 10\%$, as in the preceding example, and assuming the value of an asset three years in the future, FV_3, equals \$1331, we compute the present value of this asset as

$$PV_0 = \frac{\$1331}{(1 + 0.10)^3} = \$1000,$$

which is the same value for V_0 used in the earlier example.

More realistically, rather than receiving a single lump sum at one point several years into the future, firms or individuals often receive a stream of future payments, one for each time period, extending several years into the future. For example, an asset such as a bond or a unit of physical capital, such as a machine, may generate some amount of annual income or profit for a period of several years. We can derive a formula for computing the present value of this future annual income or profit stream by modifying equation (22.8). Assume that $FV_1, FV_2, \ldots, FV_n$, represent annual income generated by some asset for future years $i = 1, 2, \ldots, n$, respectively. We compute the present value of this future income stream as

$$PV_0 = \frac{FV_1}{(1 + r)^1} + \frac{FV_2}{(1 + r)^2} + \cdots + \frac{FV_n}{(1 + r)^n},$$

or more concisely

$$PV_0 = \sum_{i=1}^{n} \frac{FV_i}{(1 + r)^i}. \tag{22.9}$$

The formula in equation (22.9) embodies a process known as **discounting**, or *the determination of the present value of a stream of future payments generated by an asset*. For example, suppose some asset, such as a piece of capital equipment, generates an annual income or profit of \$1000/year for three years. If $r = 10\%$, the present value of this stream of future income is

$$PV_0 = \frac{1000}{(1 + 0.10)^1} + \frac{1000}{(1 + 0.10)^2} + \frac{1000}{(1 + 0.10)^3}$$
$$= 909.09 + 826.45 + 751.31 = \$2486.85.$$

Frequently, we are interested in determining not only the present value of a stream of future income associated with an asset, but also the present value of the asset itself, which is worth some amount in a future time period. For this case we modify the present value formula demonstrated in equation (22.9) as

$$PV_0 = \sum_{i=1}^{n} \frac{FV_i}{(1 + r)^i} + \frac{FV_A}{(1 + r)^n},$$

The Lump Sum vs. Annuity Options Associated with a Lotto Jackpot

A good application of discounting is encountered when determining which option a Lotto winner should select regarding how to receive her proceeds. Most state Lotto games offer the winner a choice between an annuity of 20 annual payments or a lump sum equal to the present value of the 20-year annuity.

The method of analyzing this choice involves comparing the after-tax proceeds from a lump sum to the present value of the alternative, an annual, after-tax, cash flow from an annuity. An example of such a comparison has been constructed by Allen B. Atkins and Edward A. Dyl.[1] In their example, it is assumed that a Lotto jackpot consists of $6 million, $300,000 of which is to be paid to the winner each year for a period of 20 years. In addition, they assume an interest rate, and hence a discount rate of 8 percent, along with average federal and state tax rates of 31.7 percent and 5 percent, respectively. For higher incomes, the federal tax is assumed to increase to $75,304.50 plus 39.6 percent of any amount over $250,000. We will show that the more lucrative alternative for the Lotto winner depends on his tax rates and the estimated interest rate.

To compare the after-tax value of the lump sum, it is first necessary that we determine the present value of the annuity, consisting of $300,000/year payments for a period of 20 years as

$$PV = \frac{300,000}{1 + .08} + \frac{300,000}{(1 + .08)^2}$$
$$+ \ldots + \frac{300,00}{(1 + .08)^{20}} = \$3,181,080.$$

---

[1]Allen B. Atkins and Edward A. Dyl, "The Lotto Jackpot: The Lump Sum Versus the Annuity," *Financial Practice and Education*, 5, no. 2, (Fall/Winter 1995): 107–111.

Next, we calculate the after-tax value of this $3,181,080 by subtracting [(75,304.50 + 0.396 (3,181,080 − 250,000)] dollars of federal taxes and [0.05 (3,181,080)] dollars of state taxes from this present value. Therefore, the present value of the $6 million lump sum payment is worth $1,786,014, after taxes.

Alternatively, the individual can choose the annuity option of receiving $300,000 per year for 20 years. Using the previously mentioned federal and state tax rates, we compute the annual after-tax cash flow from the annuity as

$$\$300,000 - [\$75,304.50 - 0.396(300,000 - 250,000) - 0.05(300,000)] = \$189,895/\text{year}.$$

To determine the present value of this flow of future income, it is necessary to discount these annual amounts by the after-tax interest rate. We determine this interest rate by computing the value of one minus the average federal tax rate, 31.7 percent, minus the average state tax rate, 5 percent, and then multiplying this amount by the interest rate, 8 percent, or

$$(1 - 0.317 - 0.05)(0.08) = 0.05064 = 5.064\%.$$

We then use this after-tax interest rate to determine the present value of the after-tax flows from the annuity as

$$PV = \frac{189,895}{(1 + 0.0564)} + \frac{189,895}{(1 + 0.0564)^2}$$
$$+ \ldots + \frac{189,895}{(1 + 0.0564)^{20}} = \$2,472,913.$$

Therefore, based on these computations, the better alternative for the Lotto winner is to select the annuity option.

where FV_i represents the income associated with an asset in each of $i = 1, 2, \ldots, n$ future time periods and FV_A is the future value of the asset itself in time period n. Suppose in the above example that the asset we are considering is a bond that matures after three years, at which time the owner receives the face, or par, value of the bond worth $10,000. We compute the present value of this bond, which includes the three $1000/year income payments, along with the face value of the bond, as

$$PV_0 = \frac{1000}{(1 + 0.10)} + \frac{1000}{(1 + 0.10)^2} + \frac{1000}{(1 + 0.10)^3} + \frac{10,000}{(1 + 0.10)^3} = \$10,000.$$

In this example PV_0 equals the face value of the bond, since by holding this bond to its maturity, the income payments are equal to the rate of interest multiplied by this face value, or

$$1000 = 10\%(10,000).$$

However, if the bond is sold after one year, and the interest rate has increased to 20 percent, then we compute the present value of the bond at this time, having two years left to maturity, as

$$PV_0 = \frac{1000}{(1 + 0.20)^1} + \frac{1000}{(1 + 0.20)^2} + \frac{10,000}{(1 + 0.20)^2} = \$8472.21.$$

In this case the present value of the bond, including annual income payments, is worth only $8472, because the interest rate has increased, although the annual income payments have remained constant. Logically, the present value of an asset indicates the price that is paid for an asset. This follows because the present value of an asset represents the current value associated with the future income generated by that asset, along with the current value associated with the value of the asset at some point in the future. It is also important for us to note that the present value, or price, of an asset varies inversely with the rate of interest, as demonstrated in the above example and, more generally, by equations (22.8) and (22.9).

22.3   SUPPLY OF CAPITAL

Ultimately, the supply of capital inputs, such as plant and equipment, in any particular time period depends on the level of saving in previous time periods because this saving provides the funds for purchasing capital. Specifically, it is the postponement of current consumption by some individuals that enables them to save some of their current income. These savings are then borrowed by firms for the purpose of purchasing capital that is used to produce output in subsequent time periods. In summary, the supply of capital in a given time period is the result of rational consumer choice in preceding time periods, regarding their desired levels of consumption in the current time period as opposed to consumption in future time periods. As a result, we can analyze the supply of capital by returning once again to the consumer's constrained utility maximization problem.

22.3.1 Intertemporal Utility Function

To simplify our analysis, we will assume an individual derives utility from consuming goods and services in only two time periods, say years, designated period one and period two. Therefore, we express this individual's utility function as

$$U = U(C_1, C_2),$$

where U represents the individual's level of utility and the terms C_1 and C_2 are the amounts of goods and services consumed by this individual in time periods one and two, respectively. By now you should be very familiar with the following analysis. By holding utility constant at some level, say $\overline{U}_1$, we can construct an indifference curve representing the various combinations of C_1 and C_2 corresponding to the same level of utility for the consumer. More generally, we can derive a set of such indifference curves, with each pertaining to a fixed level of utility. Three such indifference curves representing utility levels $\overline{U}_1, \overline{U}_2$, and $\overline{U}_3$, for which $\overline{U}_3 > \overline{U}_2 > \overline{U}_1$, are illustrated in Figure 22.1.

We compute the slope for any one of the indifference curves, dC_2/dC_1, by first totally differentiating U with respect to C_1 and setting the result equal to zero, since utility remains constant along any one indifference curve. Thus

$$\frac{dU}{dC_1} = \frac{\partial U(C_1,C_2)}{\partial C_1}\frac{dC_1}{dC_1} + \frac{\partial U(C_1,C_2)}{\partial C_2}\frac{dC_2}{dC_1} = 0,$$

and since $U = U(C_1,C_2)$, then

$$\frac{dU}{dC_1} = \frac{\partial U}{\partial C_1} + \frac{\partial U}{\partial C_2}\frac{dC_2}{dC_1} = 0,$$

where we can solve for the slope as

$$\frac{dC_2}{dC_1} = \frac{-\dfrac{\partial U}{\partial C_1}}{\dfrac{\partial U}{\partial C_2}}. \qquad (22.10)$$

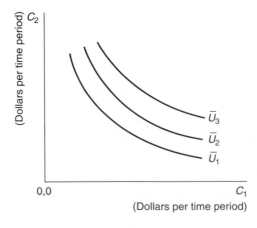

C_2
(Dollars per time period)

$\overline{U}_3$
$\overline{U}_2$
$\overline{U}_1$

0,0

C_1
(Dollars per time period)

FIGURE 22.1 Indifference Curves for an Individual's Consumption Levels of Goods and Services in Time Periods One and Two

The term $\partial U/\partial C_1$ measures the change in utility due to a change in the individual's consumption level of goods and services in period one, *ceteris paribus*, or the marginal utility of consumption in period one, MU_{C_1}. Similarly, the term $\partial U/\partial C_2$ measures the change in utility due to a change in the individual's consumption of goods and services in period two, *ceteris paribus*, or the marginal utility of consumption in period two, MU_{C_2}. Thus, we can express equation (22.10) as

$$\frac{dC_2}{dC_1} = \frac{-MU_{C_1}}{MU_{C_2}},$$

indicating that the slope of an indifference curve in this case is measured as the negative of the ratio of marginal utilities of consuming goods and services in the two time periods. We define this ratio of marginal utilities as the marginal rate of substitution, or *MRS*, between the two "goods" C_1 and C_2, where conceptually, it represents the rate at which the consumer is willing to substitute consumption in one period for consumption in the other, while receiving the same level of utility.

In general, the *MRS* is measured as the negative of the slope of an indifference curve, where in this particular application, we can refer to it as the marginal rate of time preference because it pertains to the substitution of consumption levels between two time periods. The value of the *MRS* at a point on an indifference curve depends on the particular (C_1, C_2) combination and on the shape of the indifference curve, where this shape reflects the individual's underlying utility function. For example, some consumers are more biased in favor of current consumption than others, and therefore generally require a larger increase in future consumption, C_2, for any decrease in current consumption, C_1, than those individuals who are less predisposed toward current consumption.

22.3.2   Intertemporal Budget Constraint

The goal of a rational consumer in this case is to choose consumption levels for the two time periods corresponding to a maximum value for his level of utility, where as usual, this process is subject to some constraining factors that ultimately limit the amounts of the two "goods," C_1 and C_2, the individual is able to consume. The number of such constraining factors we include in this model depends on the level of complexity desired. However, even in a simple model an individual's choice regarding amounts of C_1 and C_2 is constrained by the prices, $\overline{P}_1$ and $\overline{P}_2$, he must pay for the consumption levels of goods and services in the two time periods. Other basic constraining factors are the consumer's initial income levels, $\overline{I}_1$ and $\overline{I}_2$, for time periods one and two, respectively, and finally, the interest rate, r, that represents the price at which the individual can transfer income, and ultimately consumption, between the two time periods. We are assuming the levels of income for the two periods, $\overline{I}_1$ and $\overline{I}_2$, to be independent of interest income, and thus predetermined at specified levels. In the subsequent analysis, we will also assume that these initial levels of income remain constant. Therefore, a second subscript will not be added to the terms $\overline{I}_1$ and $\overline{I}_2$, as has been our convention throughout most of this text. This omission is simply for the purpose of maintaining clarity.

We can use the factors mentioned above to construct an intertemporal, or two-time-period, budget constraint for an individual consumer. In period one, an individual may choose to spend an amount on consumption, represented by the price level multiplied by the number of units of goods and services consumed in this period, $\overline{P}_1 C_1$, that is different from his income received during that period, $\overline{I}_1$. We define the difference between this income and the amount spent on consumption as that individual's level of saving, S, during period one, or

$$S = \overline{I}_1 - \overline{P}_1 C_1,$$

where this level of saving, should it exist, can be either positive or negative. If $S > 0$, then in period one, the individual ultimately becomes a lender, where alternatively if $S < 0$, he is a borrower. In this two-period model, the choice to postpone current consumption and save a positive amount, or to increase current consumption at the expense of future consumption and save a negative amount (dissave), is made in period one. This is because we are assuming there are no time periods left for this individual after period two. Economists often refer to this model as a life cycle model for which period one refers to the early time period in an individual's life and the second period as the later time period.

We represent the individual's total expenditure on goods and services in period two, $\overline{P}_2 C_2$, as

$$\overline{P}_2 C_2 = \overline{I}_2 + S + \overline{r}_1 S, \tag{22.11}$$

indicating that the amount spent on goods and services in period two equals the summation of the individual's income in period two, I_2, any amount saved during period one, S, and the interest payment associated with that level of saving $\overline{r}_1 S$. Both S and $\overline{r}_1 S$ can be either positive or negative, depending on whether the individual is a saver and lender, or whether the individual is a dissaver and borrower. We can rearrange equation (22.11) as

$$\overline{P}_2 C_2 = \overline{I}_2 + (1 + \overline{r}_1)S,$$

and since $S = \overline{I}_1 - \overline{P}_1 C_1$, then

$$\overline{P}_2 C_2 = \overline{I}_2 + (1 + \overline{r}_1)(\overline{I}_1 - \overline{P}_1 C_1),$$

or

$$\overline{P}_2 C_2 = \overline{I}_2 + (1 + \overline{r}_1)\overline{I}_1 - (1 + \overline{r}_1)\overline{P}_1 C_1.$$

Grouping the expenditure and income terms separately on the left and right-hand sides of this equation, respectively, yields

$$\overline{P}_2 C_2 + (1 + \overline{r}_1)\overline{P}_1 C_1 = \overline{I}_2 + (1 + \overline{r}_1)\overline{I}_1. \tag{22.12}$$

This equation represents the consumer's intertemporal budget constraint for years one and two, demonstrating the set of combinations of C_1 and C_2 the individual is able to consume for given values of income, $\overline{I}_1$ and $\overline{I}_2$, along with prices, $\overline{P}_1$ and $\overline{P}_2$, for a given value of the interest rate, $\overline{r}_1$.

The goal of our analysis is to demonstrate the effect of changes in the interest rate on the individual's consumption-saving decision and ultimately on the supply of capital. Therefore, in order to maintain this focus, we will simplify the analysis by making two assumptions. The first assumption is that the prices, $\bar{P}_1$ and $\bar{P}_2$, represent average price levels for all goods and services consumed in periods one and two, respectively. Therefore, we can simplify the intertemporal budget constraint by designating period one as the base time period for which $\bar{P}_1 = 1.0$. Second, we will assume that the price level remains unchanged over the two time periods, and thus $\bar{P}_1 = \bar{P}_2 = 1.0$. As a result, we can express the budget constraint represented by equation (22.12) as

$$C_2 + (1 + \bar{r}_1)C_1 = \bar{I}_2 + (1 + \bar{r}_1)\bar{I}_1, \qquad \textbf{(22.13)}$$

where this constraint is illustrated in Figure 22.2.

The vertical, or C_2, intercept of this constraint is the value of C_2 when $C_1 = 0$, or

$$C_2 = \bar{I}_2 + (1 + \bar{r}_1)\bar{I}_1,$$

representing the maximum amount of consumption possible in period two. This amount is equal to the individual's income in period two, $\bar{I}_2$, plus the term $(1 + \bar{r}_1)\bar{I}_1$, which we can recognize as the future value in period two associated with the individual's income received in period one, assuming the individual saves and lends all of his income received in that period. The horizontal, or C_1, intercept of this budget constraint is the value of C_1 when $C_2 = 0$, or

$$C_1 = \bar{I}_1 + \frac{\bar{I}_2}{1 + \bar{r}_1},$$

representing the maximum amount of consumption possible in period one. This amount consists of income received in period one, $\bar{I}_1$, plus the term, $\bar{I}_2/1 + \bar{r}_1$, that we can recognize as the present value in period one of the individual's income received in period two. In this case, in period one, the individual borrows an amount equal to the discounted value of his future income in order to increase his present consumption. The slope of this budget constraint, dC_2/dC_1, represents the rate at which consumption

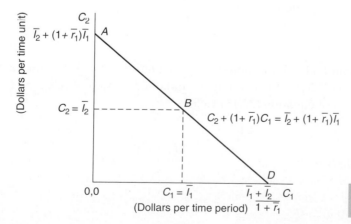

FIGURE 22.2 Intertemporal Budget Constraint

in one period can be substituted for consumption in the other, where we compute it by solving equation (22.13) for C_2 as

$$C_2 = \bar{I}_2 + (1 + \bar{r}_1)\bar{I}_1 - (1 + \bar{r}_1)C_1$$

and then taking the derivative of C_2 with respect to C_1 yielding

$$\frac{dC_2}{dC_1} = -(1 + \bar{r}_1).$$

For given values of I_1, I_2, and r, the intertemporal budget constraint represents the entire set of consumption-saving possibilities for a consumer. If an individual chooses to neither save nor borrow, then $S = 0$, $C_1 = \bar{I}_1$, and $C_2 = \bar{I}_2$, indicated in Figure 22.2 as point B on the intertemporal budget constraint. Thus, the range for which the individual is a net saver, or where $S > 0$, is represented by the upper segment, AB, of the budget constraint for which $C_1 < \bar{I}_1$ and $C_2 > \bar{I}_2$. Conversely, the range for which this individual is a net borrower, or where $S < 0$, is reflected by the lower segment of the budget constraint, BD, for which $C_1 > \bar{I}_1$ and $C_2 < \bar{I}_2$.

22.3.3 Intertemporal Constrained Utility Maximization

The goal of the consumer in this problem, is to determine the values of the consumption levels in the two time periods, C_1 and C_2, that correspond to a maximum value for his utility, subject to his intertemporal budget constraint. We can demonstrate this process by constructing a Lagrangian function containing the consumer's utility function as the objective function and the intertemporal budget equation, solved such that it is equal to zero, as the constraint, or

$$\mathcal{L} = U(C_1, C_2) + \lambda[\bar{I}_2 + (1 + \bar{r}_1)\bar{I}_1 - C_2 - (1 + \bar{r}_1)C_1].$$

The first-order conditions for a constrained utility maximum are

$$\frac{\partial \mathcal{L}}{\partial C_1} = \frac{\partial U(C_1, C_2)}{\partial C_1} - \lambda(1 + \bar{r}_1) = 0 \tag{22.14}$$

$$\frac{\partial \mathcal{L}}{\partial C_2} = \frac{\partial U(C_1, C_2)}{\partial C_2} - \lambda = 0 \tag{22.15}$$

$$\frac{\partial \mathcal{L}}{\partial \lambda} = \bar{I}_2 + (1 + \bar{r}_1)\bar{I}_1 - C_2 - (1 + \bar{r}_1)C_1 = 0. \tag{22.16}$$

Adding the term $\lambda(1 + \bar{r}_1)$ to both sides of equation (22.14), and the term λ to both sides of equation (22.15), and dividing the modified version of equation (22.14) by the modified version of equation (22.15) yields

$$\frac{\dfrac{\partial U(C_1, C_2)}{\partial C_1}}{\dfrac{\partial U(C_1, C_2)}{\partial C_2}} = \frac{\lambda(1 + \bar{r}_1)}{\lambda} = 1 + \bar{r}_1,$$

or since $U = U(C_1, C_2)$, then

$$\frac{\dfrac{\partial U}{\partial C_1}}{\dfrac{\partial U}{\partial C_2}} = 1 + \bar{r}_1. \tag{22.17}$$

We can recognize the terms on the left-hand side of this equation, $\partial U/\partial C_1$ and $\partial U/\partial C_2$, as the marginal utilities of C_1 and C_2, respectively. Therefore, this ratio of marginal utilities is the marginal rate of substitution, MRS, between the two goods, C_1 and C_2. As a result, we can express equation (22.17) as

$$MRS = \frac{MU_{C_1}}{MU_{C_2}} = 1 + \bar{r}_1,$$

where this equation represents the necessary condition for a constrained utility maximum.

Conceptually, this equation indicates that a consumer determines the optimal values for C_1 and C_2 where the MRS, or the rate at which he is willing to substitute consumption in one period for the other while receiving the same level of utility, is equal to $(1 + \bar{r}_1)$, or the rate at which he is able to substitute consumption in one period for the other, given a particular value of the interest rate. These values of C_1 and C_2 pertaining to constrained utility maximization solutions for two different individuals are illustrated in panels (A) and (B) of Figure 22.3.

The solution values for C_1 and C_2 shown in panel (A) are $C_{1,1}^*$ and $C_{2,1}^*$, respectively, where the second subscript refers to the particular values of C_1 and C_2. At this combination, $(C_{1,1}^*, C_{2,1}^*)$, the individual receives the highest level of utility attainable, represented by the indifference curve U_1^*, subject to the intertemporal budget constraint. We can observe this result by the fact that the indifference curve U_1^* is tangent to the intertemporal budget constraint. Thus, at $(C_{1,1}^*, C_{2,1}^*)$ the slope of the corresponding indifference curve equals the slope of the budget constraint, and the necessary condition for a constrained utility maximum, $MRS = 1 + r$, is satisfied. Observe, at this solution, $C_{1,1}^* < \bar{I}_1$ and $C_{2,1}^* > \bar{I}_2$. Therefore, in period one this individual saves the amount

$$S_1^* = \bar{I}_1 - C_{1,1}^* > 0,$$

which is used to increase his consumption in period two. In summary, the individual analyzed in panel (A) is predisposed toward future consumption, C_2, and we can describe him as a net saver.

Conversely, in panel (B) the solution for a constrained utility maximum occurs at combination $(C_{1,1}'^*, C_{2,1}'^*)$, corresponding to utility level $U_1'^*$ for which $C_{1,1}'^* > \bar{I}_1$ and $C_{2,1}'^* < \bar{I}_2$. Therefore, this individual dissaves, or borrows the amount

$$S_1'^* = \bar{I}_1 - C_{1,1}'^* < 0,$$

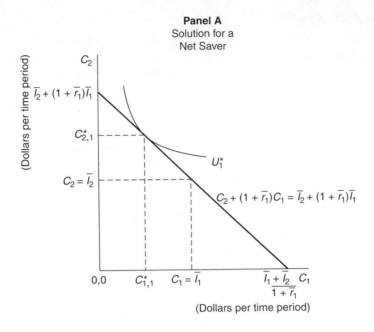

Panel A
Solution for a
Net Saver

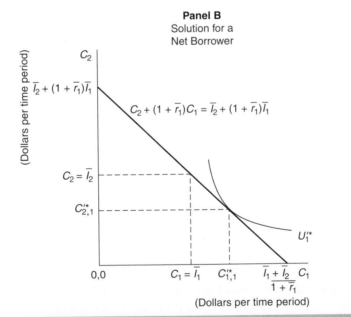

Panel B
Solution for a
Net Borrower

FIGURE 22.3 Constrained Utility Maximization Solutions for Two Different Types of Individuals

in period one so as to increase his consumption in that period. Accordingly, the analysis illustrated in panel (B) is for an individual who is predisposed toward present consumption, and we can describe him as a net borrower. Clearly, for a given rate of interest, whether an individual is a net saver or a net borrower depends on that individual's underlying utility function.

A change in the interest rate alters the intertemporal budget constraint, thereby ultimately affecting the solution values of C_1 and C_2 for both a net saver and a net borrower. We have illustrated such an alteration of the budget constraint in Figure 22.4 for an increase in the interest rate from $\bar{r}_1$ to $\bar{r}_2$. The initial budget constraint is

$$C_2 + (1 + \bar{r}_1)C_1 = \bar{I}_2 + (1 + \bar{r}_1)\bar{I}_1,$$

for which the C_1 and C_2 intercepts are $\bar{I}_2 + (1 + \bar{r}_1)\bar{I}_1$ and $\bar{I}_1 + \bar{I}_2/(1 + \bar{r}_1)$, respectively, and for which the slope is $-(1 + \bar{r}_1)$. An increase in the interest rate from $\bar{r}_1$ to $\bar{r}_2$ increases the C_2 intercept to the value $\bar{I}_2 + (1 + \bar{r}_2)\bar{I}_1$. This result follows because an increase in r increases the future value of income received in period one to the amount $(1 + \bar{r}_2)\bar{I}_1$, enabling the individual to potentially increase his consumption in period two. The C_1 intercept decreases to $\bar{I}_1 + \bar{I}_2/(1 + \bar{r}_2)$, due to the fact that the rise in r decreases the present value, in period one, of income received in period two, to the amount $\bar{I}_2/(1 + \bar{r}_2)$, thus reducing the maximum possible level of consumption in period one for this individual. Finally, the increase in r causes the slope of the budget constraint, $(1 + r)$, to become more negative, or greater in absolute value terms. Thus, we can observe in Figure 22.4 that this new constraint is steeper than it was initially. Conceptually, this increase in r increases the price at which levels of consumption can be substituted for each other across the two time periods.

FIGURE 22.4 Effect of an Increase in the Interest Rate on the Intertemporal Budget Constraint

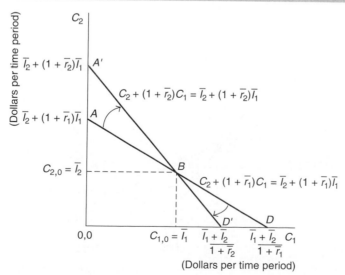

We have illustrated the impact of an increase in the interest rate on the intercepts and slope of the intertemporal budget constraint in Figure 22.4. Note that budget constraint rotates clockwise, with the combination $(C_{1,0}, C_{2,0})$ serving as the pivot point. At this combination the individual is neither a net saver nor a borrower, and therefore $C_{1,0} = \bar{I}_1$ and $C_{2,0} = \bar{I}_2$. If the individual neither saves and lends, nor borrows, a change in the interest rate has no impact on these consumption levels, $C_{1,0}$ and $C_{2,0}$. As a result, this combination $(C_{1,0}, C_{2,0})$ is common to both budget constraints. Finally, an increase in the interest rate increases the future value of current income and decreases the present value of future income, thus extending the upper portion of the budget constraint. This portion is represented in Figure 23.4 as $A'\,B$ as opposed to AB, and pertains to a net saver. Conversely, an increase in the interest rate reduces the lower portion from BD to BD', relating to a net borrower.

22.3.4 Substitution and Income Effects

The impact of an increase in the interest rate on an individual's constrained utility maximization solution is illustrated in Figures 22.5 and 22.6, where our focus is on the individual's consumption level in period one, C_1. The directionality of this impact of an increase in r on C_1 depends on whether the individual is a net borrower or a net saver, where the analysis illustrated in Figure 22.5 pertains to a net borrower. Initially,

FIGURE 22.5 Substitution and Income Effects Resulting from an Increase in the Interest Rate for a Net Borrower

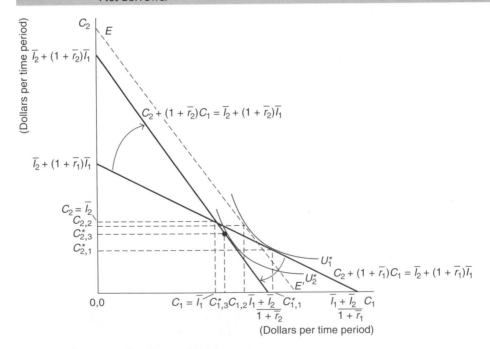

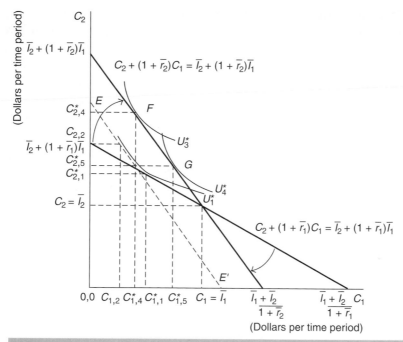

FIGURE 22.6 Substitution Effect and Two Different Income Effects Resulting from an Increase in the Interest Rate for a Net Saver

for $\bar{r}_1$, the individual maximizes his utility by choosing amounts of C_1 and C_2 as $C_{1,1}^*$ and $C_{2,1}^*$, respectively, at which the indifference curve representing utility level U_1^*, is tangent to the original budget constraint

$$C_2 + (1 + \bar{r}_1)C_1 = \bar{I}_2 + (1 + \bar{r}_1)\bar{I}_1.$$

An increase in the interest rate from $\bar{r}_1$ to $\bar{r}_2$, causes the budget constraint to rotate in the manner described earlier, and after the increase in r, we represent it as

$$C_2 + (1 + \bar{r}_2)C_1 = \bar{I}_2 + (1 + \bar{r}_2)\bar{I}_1.$$

The total effect of this increase in r on the optimal levels of C_1 and C_2 depends on the familiar substitution and income effects. In this case, we isolate the substitution effect by constructing a compensated budget constraint represented as the curve EE' shown in Figure 22.5. We have drawn this compensated constraint parallel to the new budget constraint to reflect the new relative price, $(1 + \bar{r}_2)$, indicating that the price of consumption in period one has increased relative to the price of consumption in period two. In addition, we have drawn this compensated constraint tangent to the original indifference curve to compensate the consumer for any change in income caused by the change in r. Thus, any resulting change in C_1 is due strictly to the change in relative prices. The substitution effect in this case is $(C_{1,2} - C_{1,1}^*) < 0$, reflecting a consumer's tendency to substitute away from the increasingly expensive good, C_1, and toward the other, C_2. Recall that the substitution effect always reflects an inverse relationship between the quantity demanded of a good—in this case C_1, and its price, $(1 + r)$.

To demonstrate the total effect of this increase in r on the amount of C_1 demanded, it is necessary that we reintroduce the associated income effect into the analysis. The increase in the interest rate reduces the present value of the individual's future income. Given that C_1 is a normal good, this decrease in the present value of income received in period two causes the individual to reduce his consumption of goods and services in period one, C_1. Thus, for a net borrower the income effect is also inverse regarding the relationship between r and C_1, and reinforces the inverse substitution effect. In Figure 22.5, the new solution for the optimal amount of C_1 chosen by the consumer occurs at $C_{1,3}^*$ at which the new budget constraint is tangent to the indifference curve representing U_2^*, where $U_2^* < U_1^*$. We have illustrated the income effect as $(C_{1,3}^* - C_{1,2}) < 0$. Therefore, the total effect, $(C_{1,3}^* - C_{1,1}^*)$, is the summation of the substitution and income effects, or

$$C_{1,3}^* - C_{1,1}^* = (C_{1,2} - C_{1,1}^*) + (C_{1,3}^* - C_{1,2}) < 0.$$

In summary, for the case of a net borrower, the total effect of an increase in the interest rate results in a decrease in the consumption of goods and services in period one. Furthermore, since saving, which is negative in this case, is defined as $S = \bar{I}_1 - C_1$, the decrease in C_1 increases the amount of saving, or more precisely, decreases the amount of dissaving for a net borrower in period one.

We have illustrated the substitution and income effects for an increase in the interest rate pertaining to a net saver in Figure 22.6. The substitution effect in this case is similar to that for a net borrower in that it once again reflects an inverse relationship between r and C_1. In Figure 22.6 this substitution effect is indicated by the reduction in C_1 from $C_{1,1}^*$ to $C_{1,2}$, where this new level of C_1, or $C_{1,2}$, occurs at the point for which we have drawn the compensated budget constraint, EE', tangent to the original indifference curve, representing utility level U_1. Thus, the inverse substitution effect is the amount $(C_{1,2} - C_{1,1}^*) < 0$. The directionality of the income effect, however, for a net saver is different from that for a net borrower. This difference follows because an increase in the interest rate increases the future value of an individual's income received in period one. In other words, a higher interest rate increases the value of period one savings in terms of what it is worth in period two. Given that C_1 is a normal good, the income effect reflects a direct relationship between C_1 and r for a net saver. Specifically, an increase in r that increases the future value of savings, and thus income for a net saver, results in an increase in that individual's consumption in period one. As a result, the substitution and income effects for a net saver run counter to each other. Therefore, the directionality of the total effect of an increase in r on C_1 depends on the magnitude of these conflicting effects, which we must determine statistically.

In Figure 22.6, we have presented two different scenarios regarding the magnitude of the income effect as compared to the substitution effect. The situation for which the direct income effect is less than the inverse substitution effect occurs at point F where the indifference curve representing U_3^*, is tangent to the new budget constraint

$$C_2 + (1 + \bar{r}_2)C_1 = \bar{I}_2 + (1 + \bar{r}_2)\bar{I}_1.$$

Accordingly, the income effect is $(C_{1,4}^* - C_{1,2}) > 0$, but it is less than the substitution effect, $(C_{1,2} - C_{1,1}^*) < 0$. In this case the total effect, which is the summation of these two component effects, is

$$(C_{1,2} - C_{1,1}^*) + (C_{1,4}^* - C_{1,2}) = (C_{1,4}^* - C_{1,1}^*) < 0.$$

Therefore, if the substitution effect exceeds the income effect for a net saver, then the total effect of a change in the interest rate on the consumption level in period one is inverse. Therefore, an increase in r results in a decrease in C_1 and an increase in saving, S.

Conversely, if the income effect is greater than the substitution effect for a net saver, then the total effect of a change in r on C_1, is direct, as we have illustrated in Figure 22.6 by the solution occurring at point G. At this solution, where the indifference curve representing U_4^* is tangent to the new budget constraint, the increase in r produces the direct income effect, $(C_{1,5}^* - C_{1,2}) > 0$, that exceeds the inverse substitution effect, $(C_{1,2} - C_{1,1}^*) < 0$. Therefore, the total effect in this case is

$$(C_{1,2} - C_{1,1}^*) + (C_{1,5}^* - C_{1,2}) = (C_{1,5}^* - C_{1,1}^*) > 0.$$

Thus, if the income effect exceeds the substitution effect for a net saver, the total effect of a change in r on C_1 is direct, and an increase in r yields an increase in C_1 and a subsequent decrease in saving.

22.3.5   Demand for Consumption Curves and Savings Curves

The optimal values for C_1 and S we have generated by solving the consumer's constrained utility maximization problem provide the basis for deriving the consumer's demand curve for consumption in period one, and ultimately for deriving the consumer's saving curve. Generally, the demand for C_1 curve is

$$C_1^d = C_1^d(r, \bar{I}_1, \bar{I}_2),$$

where the consumer's demand for period one consumption, C_1^d, is expressed as a function of the interest rate, r, and the levels of income in periods one and two, $\bar{I}_1$ and $\bar{I}_2$, respectively. These income levels are held constant at specified levels. We expect the relationship between C_1^d and each of the two income levels, $\bar{I}_1$ and $\bar{I}_2$, to be direct. However, the relationship between C_1^d and r depends on the underlying conditions discussed earlier, specifically, whether the individual is a net borrower or a net saver, and whether the substitution effect exceeds the income effect.

The individual's level of saving is the difference between her income and consumption in period one, or $S = \bar{I}_1 - C_1^d$. Therefore, we can express this level of saving for given values of income in periods one and two, $\bar{I}_1$ and $\bar{I}_2$, as

$$S = \bar{I}_1 - C_1^d(r, \bar{I}_1, \bar{I}_2),$$

or more concisely as

$$S = S(r, \bar{I}_1, \bar{I}_2). \tag{22.18}$$

This equation represents the individual's savings curve that expresses S in terms of the interest rate, r, and the fixed levels of income $\bar{I}_1$ and $\bar{I}_2$ for the two periods. The relationship between S and r depends on the aforementioned characteristics regarding the individual's behavior concerning consumption and saving.

In Figures 22.7, 22.8, and 22.9, we have illustrated three different sets of demand for C_1 curves, along with the corresponding savings curves. The curves in Figure 22.7 are derived from the constrained utility maximization process for a net borrower assuming that the interest rate increases from $\bar{r}_1$ to $\bar{r}_2$, as demonstrated in Figure 22.5. Initially, when the interest rate is r_1, the individual consumes $C_{1,1}$ amount of C_1, and after the interest rate increases to r_2, this individual decreases her consumption level of C_1 to $C_{1,3}^*$. These combinations, $(C_{1,1}^*, r_1)$ and $(C_{1,3}^*, r_2)$, are plotted in panel (A) of Figure 22.7, where C_1 and r are measured on the horizontal and vertical axes, respectively. By connecting these (C_1, r) combinations, we can construct the individual's demand curve for consumption in period one, C_1^d, demonstrating an inverse relationship

FIGURE 22.7 Net Borrower's Demand for Consumption and Supply of Saving in Period One

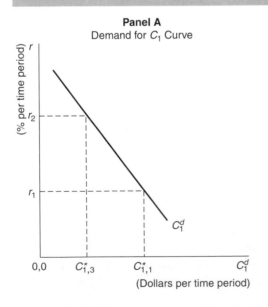

Panel A
Demand for C_1 Curve

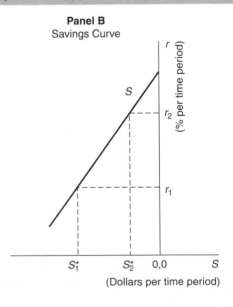

Panel B
Savings Curve

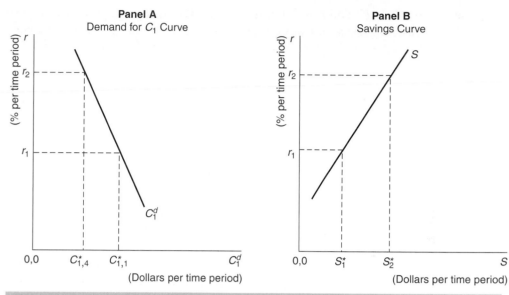

FIGURE 22.8 Net Saver's Demand for Consumption and Supply of Saving in Period One Where Substitution Effect Exceeds Income Effect

FIGURE 22.9 Net Saver's Demand for Consumption and Supply of Saving in Period One Where Income Effect Exceeds Substitution Effect

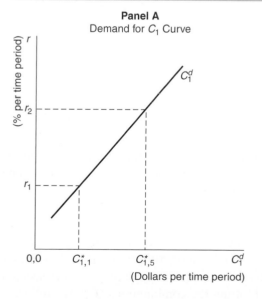

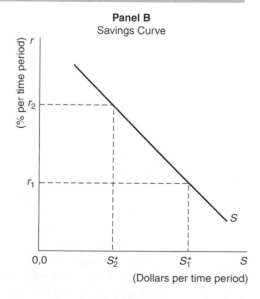

between C_1 and r for a net borrower. Once these values for C_1, corresponding to the different levels of r are obtained, we can compute the related values for savings, S, from the relationship

$$S = \bar{I}_1 - C_1.$$

Thus, for a fixed level of income, $\bar{I}_1$, the corresponding levels of saving are

$$S_1^* = \bar{I}_1 - C_{1,1}^*$$

and

$$S_2^* = \bar{I}_1 - C_{1,3}^*,$$

where $S_2^* > S_1^*$ because $C_{1,3}^* < C_{1,1}^*$.

The corresponding saving–interest rate combinations (S_1^*, r_1) and (S_2^*, r_2) are plotted in panel (B) of Figure 22.7, generating a savings curve expressing S in terms of the interest rate, r. The relationship between S and r is direct, indicating that an increase in r results in an increase in S. However, for this case involving a net borrower, note that saving is negative. Thus, the increase in saving is actually a reduction in dissaving by this individual.

In Figure 22.8 we have constructed the demand for period one consumption, C_1^d, and savings, S, curves for a net saver in panels (A) and (B), respectively, assuming the substitution effect exceeds the income effect for a change in r on C_1^d. The derivation of these curves is based on the results of the constrained utility maximization process illustrated in Figure 22.6, for which the increase in the interest rate from $\bar{r}_1$ to $\bar{r}_2$, yields a decrease in C_1 from $C_{1,1}^*$ to $C_{1,4}^*$. Plotting the combinations $(C_{1,1}^*, r_1)$ and $(C_{1,4}^*, r_2)$ in panel (A) of Figure 22.8 yields the consumer's demand curve for C_1. This reflects an inverse relationship between C_1^d and r, but a curve that is less elastic than that demonstrated for a net borrower. The corresponding levels of saving in this case are

$$S_1^* = \bar{I}_1 - C_{1,1}^*$$

and

$$S_2^* = \bar{I}_1 - C_{1,4}^*,$$

where

$$S_2^* > S_1^*.$$

Therefore, by plotting the combinations (S_1^*, r_1) and (S_2^*, r_2), we generate the savings curve illustrated in panel (B). This curve indicates a direct relationship between S and r, where for a net saver, these savings levels are positive.

Finally, in Figure 22.9 we have plotted the individual's demand for C_1 and savings curves for a net saver, assuming the income effect exceeds the substitution effect associated with the impact of a change in r on C_1^d. Referring to Figure 22.6 once again, we see that if the income effect exceeds the substitution effect, then an increase in the level of the interest rate from r_1 to r_2 results in the individual increasing her consumption of C_1 from $C_{1,1}^*$ to $C_{1,5}^*$. Plotting the combinations $(C_{1,1}^*, r_1)$ and $(C_{1,5}^*, r_2)$ in panel

(A) of Figure 22.9 yields the individual's demand for C_1 curve, which in this case possesses a positive slope indicating that an increase in r results in the individual increasing her consumption level of C_1. The corresponding levels of saving are

$$S_1^* = \bar{I}_1 - C_{1,1}^*$$

and

$$S_2^* = \bar{I}_1 - C_{1,5}^*,$$

where $S_2^* < S_1^*$. By plotting the combinations (S_1^*, r_1) and (S_2^*, r_2) in panel (B) of Figure 22.9, we construct the negatively sloped savings curve, indicating that an increase in r causes the individual to decrease her level of saving.

The different results yielded by the preceding situations demonstrate the complexity associated with analyzing the impact of changes in the interest rate on a particular individual's consumption–saving decision. Generally, for most individuals, a situation for which the savings curve possesses a negative slope is most likely to occur for relatively high interest rates. However, the savings curves we use in most economic models tend to reflect only the positively sloped range for such curves, over which relatively lower levels of interest rates are examined.

We can provide some additional insight into an individual's consumption–saving decision by combining some of the preceding analyses into one example, as illustrated in Figures 22.10 and 22.11. Assume the interest rate is initially $\bar{r}_1$, and thus the original intertemporal budget constraint is

$$C_2 + (1 + \bar{r}_1)C_1 = \bar{I}_2 + (1 + \bar{r}_1)\bar{I}_1,$$

as indicated in Figure 22.10. Also assume that the individual is initially a net borrower at this relatively low initial interest rate, $\bar{r}_1$, and therefore, she chooses $C_{1,1}^*$ level of consumption in period one and saves, or more precisely dissaves,

$$S_1^* = \bar{I}_1 - C_{1,1}^*,$$

where $S_1^* < 0$. Now suppose the interest rate increases to $\bar{r}_2$, causing the budget constraint to rotate clockwise around the $C_1 = \bar{I}_1$ and $C_2 = \bar{I}_2$ combination of consumption levels. The effect of this rotation is a reduction in that portion of the budget constraint for which $C_1 > \bar{I}_1$ and $C_2 < \bar{I}_2$, pertaining to net borrowers, or conversely, this rotation increases the portion of the constraint for which $C_1 < \bar{I}_1$ and $C_2 > \bar{I}_2$, pertaining to net savers. Conceptually, these results are due to the fact that an increase in the interest rate decreases the present value of future, or period two, income and increases the future value of present, or period one, income. Effectively, the reward for saving or the price of borrowing increases. As a result, some individuals who were net borrowers at interest rate $\bar{r}_1$ become net savers at the higher interest rate, $\bar{r}_2$. Assuming this is the case for the individual we are analyzing, the optimal consumption level of C_1 decreases from $C_{1,1}^*$ to $C_{1,2}^*$ and the corresponding level of saving increases from S_1^* to the level

$$S_2^* = \bar{I}_1 - C_{1,2}^*,$$

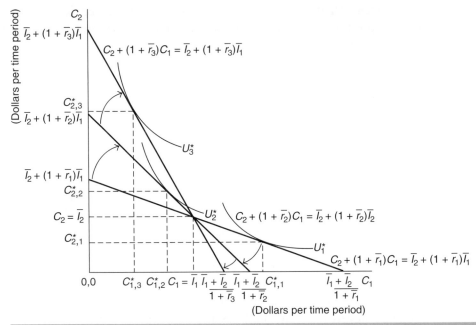

FIGURE 22.10 Total Effects Resulting from an Increase in the Interest Rate for an Individual Who Changes from a Net Borrower to a Net Saver

FIGURE 22.11 Savings Curve for an Individual Who Acts as Either a Net Borrower or a Net Saver Depending on the Level of the Interest Rate

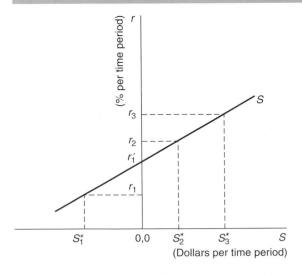

where $S_2^* > 0$. Thus, the level of saving for this individual increases from a negative value to a positive value. Finally, suppose the interest rate increases again to $\bar{r}_3$ and the budget constraint accordingly rotates clockwise, represented by the term

$$C_2 + (1 + \bar{r}_3)C_1 = I_2 + (1 + \bar{r}_3)I_1.$$

Assuming the substitution effect exceeds the income effect, the individual further decreases her consumption of C_1 to $C_{1,3}^*$ and correspondingly increases her level of saving to

$$S_3^* = \bar{I}_1 - C_{1,3}^*.$$

We have plotted these saving–interest rate combinations, (S_1^*, r_1), (S_2^*, r_2), and (S_3^*, r_3), in Figure 22.11, yielding a savings curve with a positive slope, indicating a direct relationship between S and r. Also note that this savings curve indicates that this individual dissaves, or has negative values of saving, for relatively low interest rates below r_1', where at r_1', $S = 0$, and for values of $r > r_1'$, $S > 0$. As we discussed previously and illustrated in panel (B) of Figure 22.9, there may be some relatively high interest rate at which the savings curve bends backward reflecting a negative slope, and thus an inverse relationship between the individual's level of saving and the rate of interest. For the sake of simplicity, we have omitted this possibility in Figure 22.11.

The preceding analysis has been conducted for a single individual, ultimately yielding a savings curve expressing the individual's level of saving as a function of the interest rate. More generally, we can apply this analysis to all consumers to generate a set of such savings curves, one for each individual consumer, where the exact nature of each savings curve depends on the individual's tastes and preferences regarding present versus future consumption. Once a set of such individual savings curves has been generated, we can construct an aggregated, or economywide, savings curve by horizontally summing these individual curves. This process involves selecting an interest rate, determining the corresponding level of saving for each individual, and then summing these values to obtain the corresponding level of aggregate saving. By repeating this process for several levels of the interest rate, we can construct an aggregate savings curve. By now, you should be quite familiar with this process, and therefore it will be left to you as an exercise. The important point, however, is that this aggregate savings curve indicates, at various interest rates, the corresponding levels of saving that are available to borrowers, which in turn, ultimately provides the basis for the accumulation of capital used by firms in their production processes.

We can provide some additional insight into the important role played by the interest rate in saving and capital formation by analyzing consumer behavior with a specific mathematical example. Assume a typical consumer derives utility, U, from consuming amounts of goods and services C_1 and C_2 for time periods one and two, respectively, according to the utility function

$$U = C_{1,}^{.55}C_{2,}^{.45}.$$

The higher exponent associated with C_1, 0.55, compared with that for C_2, 0.45, reflects this individual's tastes for present rather than future consumption. This individual is subject to the intertemporal budget constraint discussed earlier, or

$$C_2 + (1 + \bar{r}_1)C_1 = \bar{I}_2 + (1 + \bar{r}_1)\bar{I}_1.$$

The goal of this individual is to determine the values of C_1 and C_2 corresponding to a maximum value for her utility subject to this constraint. We solve this problem by constructing a Lagrangian function, $\mathcal{L}$, that embodies the aforementioned utility function as the objective function and the budget constraint, solved in a manner such that it is equal to zero, as

$$\mathcal{L} = C_1^{.55}C_2^{.45} + \lambda[\bar{I}_2 + (1 + \bar{r}_1)\bar{I}_1 - C_2 - (1 + \bar{r}_1)C_1],$$

where λ is the familiar Lagrangian multiplier. The first-order conditions for this constrained utility maximization problem are

$$\frac{\partial \mathcal{L}}{\partial C_1} = 0.55C_1^{-.45}C_2^{.45} - \lambda(1 + \bar{r}_1) = 0 \qquad \textbf{(22.19)}$$

$$\frac{\partial \mathcal{L}}{\partial C_2} = 0.45C_1^{.55}C_2^{-.55} - \lambda = 0 \qquad \textbf{(22.20)}$$

$$\frac{\partial \mathcal{L}}{\partial \lambda} = \bar{I}_2 + (1 + \bar{r}_1)\bar{I}_1 - C_2 - (1 + \bar{r}_1)C_1 = 0. \qquad \textbf{(22.21)}$$

Rearranging equations (2.19) and (22.20), and dividing the modified version of equation (22.19) by the modified version of equation (22.20) yields

$$\frac{0.55C_1^{-.45}C_2^{.45}}{0.45C_1^{.55}C_2^{-.55}} = \frac{\lambda(1 + \bar{r}_1)}{\lambda},$$

or

$$\frac{1.22C_2}{C_1} = 1 + \bar{r}_1,$$

representing the necessary condition for a constrained utility maximum. We can solve this equation for C_2 as

$$C_2 = 0.8196(1 + \bar{r}_1)C_1, \qquad \textbf{(22.22)}$$

and substituting this expression for C_2 into equation (22.21) yields

$$\bar{I}_2 + (1 + \bar{r}_1)\bar{I}_1 - 0.8196(1 + \bar{r}_1)C_1 - (1 + \bar{r}_1)C_1 = 0,$$

or

$$\bar{I}_2 + (1 + \bar{r}_1)\bar{I}_1 - 1.8196(1 + \bar{r}_1)C_1 = 0.$$

Solving this equation for C_1 and allowing r to vary yields

$$C_1 = \frac{1}{1.8196(1 + r)}[(1 + r)\bar{I}_1 + \bar{I}_2],$$

or

$$C_1 = 0.5496\left(\bar{I}_1 + \frac{\bar{I}_2}{1+r}\right). \tag{22.23}$$

This equation expresses the individual's consumption of goods and services in period one, C_1, in terms of the interest rate, r, and therefore represents the individual's demand for C_1 curve. Also observe from equation (22.23) that the relationship between C_1 and r is clearly inverse for this example.

Since saving is the difference between the individual's income and consumption in period one, or

$$S = \bar{I}_1 - C_1,$$

then by substituting the expression for C_1 from equation (22.23) into the above generalized equation for saving, we obtain the individual's savings curve as

$$S = \bar{I}_1 - 0.5496\left(\bar{I}_1 + \frac{\bar{I}_2}{1+r}\right),$$

or

$$S = 0.4504\bar{I}_1 - \frac{0.5496\bar{I}_2}{1+r}. \tag{22.24}$$

The relationship between saving, S, and the interest rate, r, in this expression is clearly direct.

For specified values of I_1, I_2, and r, we can compute the optimal values for C_1, C_2, and S from these demand for C_1 and savings curves. For example, if $I_1 = I_2 = \$20,000$ and $r = 10\%$, then the value for consumption in period one is

$$C_1^* = 0.5496\left(20,000 + \frac{20,000}{1+0.10}\right) = \$20,984.73.$$

By substituting these values for I_1, I_2, and r into the savings curve expressed in equation (22.24), the level of saving is

$$S^* = 0.4504(20,000) - \frac{0.5496(20,000)}{1+0.10} = \$-984.73.$$

At this interest rate, 10 percent, the individual acts as a net borrower, spending a greater amount on consumption in period one than her income in that period, and thus dissaves \$984.73 in period one. We obtain the value for consumption in period two, C_2, by substituting $C_1 = \$20,984.73$ into equation (22.22) yielding

$$C_2^* = 0.8196(1+0.10)(20,984.72) = \$18,918.98,$$

indicating this individual spends less than her income in period two for consumption in that period.

Now suppose the interest rate increases to $r = 30\%$ while I_1 and I_2 remain constant at \$20,000. In this case we compute C_1 as

$$C_1^{*\prime} = 0.5496\left(20{,}000 + \frac{20{,}000}{1 + 0.30}\right) = \$19{,}447.38$$

and obtain S as

$$S^{*\prime} = 0.4504(20{,}000) - 0.5496\left(\frac{20{,}000}{1 + 0.30}\right) = \$552.62,$$

indicating that at this higher interest rate, 30 percent, this individual acts as a net saver. The individual's consumption in period two when $r = 30\%$ is

$$C_2^{*\prime} = 0.8196(1 + 0.30)(19{,}447.38) = \$20{,}720.79.$$

Again, we should emphasize that individuals acting either directly or indirectly as net savers ultimately provide the pool of funds from which capital inputs are financed and therefore establish the basis for the supply of capital.

22.4   DEMAND FOR CAPITAL

Using a specific example, we derived a firm's demand for capital curve for the case of more than one variable input in Section 20.3 of Chapter 20, where this curve is represented by equation (20.18). However, we based this derivation on the implicit assumption that the firm purchases and uses this capital in only one time period, or alternatively, that the firm rents its capital for the time period under analysis. Realistically, many firms purchase their capital inputs. Moreover, these inputs contribute to the firm's production of output and level of profit, not only in the present time period, but in future time periods as well. As a result, the dimension of time becomes very important in analyzing a firm's demand for capital. Specifically, when a firm purchases capital in the present time period, the price it pays for this input depends on the discounted contributions to production and profit in future time periods, as well as the present period, attributed to this input. Once we introduce the dimension of time into our analysis, additional complications such as depreciation of the capital input and changes in its price over time need to be taken into account.

22.4.1   Discounted Profit Stream

We can address all these considerations by constructing a multiperiod profit maximization model for a firm, incorporating the fact that a capital input contributes to a firm's profits for more than just the time period in which it is initially purchased. Over a period of several years, a firm expects to earn a stream of profits, where we will designate the level of profit for each year, t, as π_t. If this firm expects to operate indefinitely, then this stream extends forever into the future, and thus $t = 0, 1, 2, \ldots, \infty$ time periods; the expected profit for each of these time periods is $\pi_0, \pi_1, \pi_2, \ldots, \pi_\infty$, respectively. Designating $t = 0$ as the present time period, then we must discount the future profits for periods $t = 1, 2, \ldots, \infty$, to determine their present value. Thus, the present value, PV_0, of this stream of future profits, along with the firm's profit in the present year, is

$$PV_0 = \pi_0 + \frac{\pi_1}{(1+r)^1} + \frac{\pi_2}{(1+r)^2} + \ldots + \frac{\pi_\infty}{(1+r)^\infty}.$$

This process is simply an application of the present value formula discussed in Section 22.2.2, where we can express this equation for PV_0 more concisely as

$$PV_0 = \sum_{t=0}^{\infty} \frac{\pi_t}{(1+r)^t}. \tag{22.25}$$

The firm's profit in any time period t is the difference between its total revenue, TR_t, and its total cost, $LRTC_t$, for that time period. Since all inputs are assumed to be variable over time, we will interpret these profits as constituting long-run profits, or

$$LR\pi_t = TR_t - LRTC_t. \tag{22.26}$$

The firm's total revenue for any time period is the value of its sales, equal to the price of its output, $\overline{P}_t$, multiplied by the quantity of output sold, Q_t, or

$$TR_t = \overline{P}_t Q_t, \tag{22.27}$$

where we have fixed this price at some specified level for this time period on the assumption that the firm operates as a perfect competitor in its output market. Although it has been convention throughout this text to place a subscript on predetermined variables, we will not add such a subscript on P_t for the sake of clarity. The level of output a firm produces and sells in period t is represented by its production function

$$Q_t = f(K_t, L_t), \tag{22.28}$$

where we are assuming that the firm produces its output using inputs capital, K_t, and labor, L_t, treating both as variable. Therefore, we can express the firm's total revenue in terms of the inputs it uses as

$$TR_t = \overline{P}_t f(K_t, L_t).$$

A firm's long-run total cost in time period t is the summation of its expenditures on the two inputs, capital and labor. The capital input generally possesses some degree of durability over several time periods. Thus, in any particular time period, the firm possesses some capital that it purchased in previous periods. We should note that any expenditure on capital in this particular time period is for the addition of new capital known as **investment**, I, more generally defined as *the change in a firm's level of capital for a given time period*. Symbolically, this investment in period t is

$$I_t = \frac{\Delta K_t}{\Delta t},$$

or if $\Delta t = 1$ year, then

$$I_t = \Delta K_t.$$

Therefore, a firm's expenditure on new capital, or investment, in period t is $\overline{P}_{K,t}\, I_t$, where the price of capital in this period, $\overline{P}_{K,t}$, is predetermined as is the price of labor, $\overline{P}_{L,t}$, in perfectly competitive input markets. Note, however, that although these input prices are predetermined for any particular time period, it is indeed possible for them to change across time periods due to changing market conditions. The firm's long-run total cost function for period t is

$$LRTC_t = \overline{P}_{K,t} I_t + \overline{P}_{L,t} L.$$

We can substitute this expression for $LRTC_t$, along with the expression for TR_t from equation (22.27) into equation (22.26), to represent the long-run profit function as

$$LR\pi_t = \overline{P}_t Q_t - (\overline{P}_{K,t} I_t + \overline{P}_{L,t} L_t).$$

Substituting the expression for Q_t from the production function, equation (22.28), yields

$$LR\pi_t = \overline{P}_t\, f(K_t, L_t) - \overline{P}_{K,t} I_t - \overline{P}_{L,t} L_t.$$

Finally, by substituting this expression for $LR\pi_t$ into equation (22.25), we can express the present value, PV_0, of a firm's stream of future profits as

$$PV_0 = \sum_{t=0}^{\infty} \frac{\overline{P}_t\, f(K_t, L_t) - \overline{P}_{K,t} I_t - \overline{P}_{L,t} L_t}{(1+r)^t}. \tag{22.29}$$

22.4.2 Capital Constraint

Before proceeding further, it is necessary for us to incorporate an additional complication associated with capital in a multiperiod model; that is, over time, it tends to wear out, or depreciate. As a result, the amount by which a firm's capital changes over time is, in part, affected by this rate of depreciation, D. More broadly, we can represent the process by which a firm's amount of capital changes over time by the equation

$$K_{t+1} = K_t + I_t - DK_t, \tag{22.30}$$

or

$$K_{t+1} = I_t + (1 - D)K_t.$$

This expression indicates that the amount of capital available for use by a firm in period $t + 1$ equals its amount of capital in the preceding period, t, plus its investment in period t, less the depreciation rate multiplied by the amount of capital in period t. Technically, the term I_t represents the firm's gross investment, or addition to its capital stock, that does not begin depreciating until the next time period. The term DK_t represents the amount of capital possessed in period t that wears out over this period. Accordingly, equation (22.30) represents the constraint by which we determine the firm's amount of capital available for use in period $t + 1$, and since $t = 0, 1, 2, \ldots, \infty$, a different such constraint exists for each respective $t + 1$ period.

22.4.3   Constrained Maximization of Discounted Profit Stream

In this case, the goal of the firm is to determine the optimal values of its decision variables K_t, L_t, and I_t. These are the values corresponding to a maximum value for the firm's objective function, consisting of its discounted profit stream, PV_0, as shown in equation (22.29), subject to the set of capital formation constraints represented by equation (22.30) and expressed such that each constraint is equal to zero. We solve this problem by constructing a Lagrangian function of the form

$$\mathcal{L} = PV_0 + \sum_{t=0}^{\infty} \lambda_t [I_t + (1 - D)K_t - K_{t+1}],$$

or

$$\mathcal{L} = \sum_{t=0}^{\infty} \frac{\overline{P}_t f(K_t, L_t) - \overline{P}_{K,t} I_t - \overline{P}_{L,t} L_t}{(1 + r)^t} + \sum_{t=0}^{\infty} \lambda_t [I_t + (1 - D)K_t - K_{t+1}].$$

The first-order conditions are

$$\frac{\partial \mathcal{L}}{\partial K_t} = \frac{1}{(1 + r)^t} \left[\overline{P}_t \frac{\partial f(K_t, L_t)}{\partial K_t} \right] + \lambda_t (1 - D) - \lambda_{t-1} = 0 \tag{22.31}$$

$$\frac{\partial \mathcal{L}}{\partial L_t} = \frac{1}{(1 + r)^t} \left[\overline{P}_t \frac{\partial f(K_t, L_t)}{\partial L_t} - \overline{P}_{L,t} \right] = 0 \tag{22.32}$$

$$\frac{\partial \mathcal{L}}{\partial I_t} = \frac{-\overline{P}_{K,t}}{(1 + r)^t} + \lambda_t = 0 \tag{22.33}$$

$$\frac{\partial \mathcal{L}}{\partial \lambda_t} = I_t + (1 - D)K_t - K_{t+1} = 0. \tag{22.34}$$

Some explanation is necessary regarding the λ_{t-1} term in equation (22.31). The λ term in this Lagrangian function indicates the amount by which the objective function, the discounted profit stream, PV_0, changes due to a one-unit change in the constraint, caused in this case by a change in K_t. This amount of capital in period t depends on the level of investment in period $t - 1$, or I_{t-1}, and on the amount of depreciation associated with the level of capital in that period, K_{t-1}. Thus, we represent the level of capital in period t as

$$K_t = I_{t-1} + (1 - D)K_{t-1}.$$

Since K_t changes according to events in period $t - 1$, the term λ_{t-1} is the change in the objective function, PV_0, due to a change in K_t, expressed as

$$\lambda_{t-1} = \frac{\partial PV_0}{\partial [I_{t-1} + (1 - D)K_{t-1} - K_t]}.$$

Note that a change in K_t affects the amount of capital in period $t + 1$ and therefore

$$\lambda_{t-1} = \frac{\partial K_{t+1}}{\partial K_t},$$

as well.

We can solve the set of first-order conditions for this problem simultaneously to obtain optimal values for K_t, L_t, I_t, and λ_t. However, we will focus on K_t since our objective is to develop a firm's demand for capital function. Solving equation (22.33) for λ_t yields

$$\lambda_t = \frac{\overline{P}_{K,t}}{(1 + r)^t},$$

which we can lag one period to express λ_{t-1} as

$$\lambda_{t-1} = \frac{\overline{P}_{K,t-1}}{(1 + r)^{t-1}}.$$

Substituting these expressions for λ_t and λ_{t-1} into equation (22.31) yields

$$\frac{1}{(1 + r)^t}\left[\overline{P}_t\,\frac{\partial f(K_t, L_t)}{\partial K_t}\right] + \frac{\overline{P}_{K,t}(1 - D)}{(1 + r)^t} - \frac{\overline{P}_{K,t-1}}{(1 + r)^{t-1}} = 0$$

which, after multiplying all terms by $(1 + r)^t$, we can express as

$$\overline{P}_t\,\frac{\partial f(K_t, L_t)}{\partial K_t} + \overline{P}_{K,t}(1 - D) - \frac{\overline{P}_{K,t-1}}{(1 + r)^{-1}} = 0 \qquad \textbf{(22.35)}$$

The term, $\partial f(K_t, L_t)/\partial K_t$, is the marginal product of capital in period t, $MP_{K,t}$, and after rearranging terms, equation (22.35) is

$$\overline{P}_t MP_{K,t} = \frac{\overline{P}_{K,t-1}}{(1 + r)^{-1}} - \overline{P}_{K,t}(1 - D)$$

$$= (1 + r)\overline{P}_{K,t-1} - \overline{P}_{K,t} + D\overline{P}_{K,t}$$

$$= \overline{P}_{K,t-1} + r\overline{P}_{K,t-1} - \overline{P}_{K,t} + D\overline{P}_{K,t},$$

or finally

$$\overline{P}_t MP_{K,t} = r\overline{P}_{K,t-1} + D\overline{P}_{K,t} - (\overline{P}_{K,t} - \overline{P}_{K,t-1}). \qquad \textbf{(22.36)}$$

The term on the left-hand side of equation (22.36) represents the change in a firm's total revenue in period t due to a change in the amount of capital it uses in that period. We can also interpret this term as the value of the marginal product of capital, $VMP_{K,t}$, that is inversely related to the amount of capital employed by the firm due to the law of diminishing marginal productivity. The group of terms on the right-hand side of this equation represents the change in a firm's cost in period t due to a change in the amount of capital it uses in that period. Thus, we can interpret these terms collectively as the firm's marginal expense of the capital input, $MEI_{K,t}$. More specifically, this $MEI_{K,t}$ term represents the rental rate, or user cost, of capital, consisting of the opportunity cost of holding an amount of capital from period $t - 1$ to period t, $r\overline{P}_{K,t-1}$, plus the depreciation charge associated with this amount of capital, $D\overline{P}_{K,t}$, less any appreciation in the price of this capital over the time period from $t - 1$ to t, $\overline{P}_{K,t} - \overline{P}_{K,t-1}$.

Optimally, a firm employs units of capital in period t to the point where the extra revenue is equal to the extra cost from doing so, or where $VMP_{K,t} = MEI_{K,t}$. As a result, the present value of the firm's profit stream, PV_0, is maximized. We can use this $VMP_{K,t} = MEI_{K,t}$ relationship to develop a firm's demand for capital function. For example, assume PV_0 is maximized when the firm employs, say $K_{t,1}^*$ units of capital for which $VMP_{K,t,1} = MEI_{K,t,1}$. Now, if $MEI_{K,t}$ rises to level $MEI_{K,t,2}$, then at $K_{t,1}$, $VMP_{K,t,1} < MEI_{K,t,2}$. Now, to maximize PV_0 the firm will decrease the amount of capital it employs to level $K_{t,2}^*$ causing the $VMP_{K,t}$ to rise until $VMP_{K,t,2} = MEI_{K,t,2}$. Since the rental rate of capital is equal to $MEI_{K,t}$, we can use this relationship between $VMP_{K,t}$ and $MEI_{K,t}$ to establish the basis for a firm's demand for capital function, which expresses the optimal quantities of capital demanded, K_t, for different levels of the rental rate. This relationship between K_t and the rental rate is inverse for the reasons we have discussed. In addition, we can observe in equation (22.36) that the rental rate of capital, or the $MEI_{K,t}$, is directly related to the interest rate, r. As a result, we can express this demand for capital function in terms of the interest rate, where this relationship is also inverse, since an increase in r causes an increase in the rental rate of capital. Thus, a firm's demand for capital curve is

$$K_t^d = K_t^d(r, \overline{P}_{K,t,1}, \overline{P}_{K,t-1,1}),$$

where the prices of capital, $\overline{P}_{K,t,1}$ and $\overline{P}_{K,t-1,1}$ in periods t and $t - 1$, respectively, have been fixed at specified levels and included in this function since they also affect the rental rate of capital.

The broader market demand curve for capital in period t is obtained by the familiar process of horizontally summing individual firms' demand for capital curves. We can express this market demand for capital in period t in terms of the interest rate, or alternatively, in terms of the rental rate of capital, represented by the term on the right-hand side of equation (22.36). Ultimately, it is this market demand for capital that interacts with the supply of savings curve to determine the market rate of interest and the rental rate of capital. In closing, we should note that capital markets and interest rate determination are extremely complex and somewhat controversial subjects of analysis to which entire textbooks have been devoted. As a result, we have developed the analysis in this chapter with the intent of providing you with only a basic introduction to these very complex topics.

22.5   SUMMARY

Our focus in this chapter has been on analyzing capital markets, which primarily involves developing market supply and demand curves for these types of inputs. Implicit in our development is the fact that the interaction of these supply and demand curves in their respective markets ultimately determines the equilibrium values of such key variables as the price of capital, the interest rate, and the equilibrium quantities of capital inputs supplied and demanded. The key topics discussed in this chapter are briefly outlined as follows.

- An interest rate is the ratio of a per annum payment generated by an asset to the value of that asset, or alternatively, we can interpret it as the per annum growth rate in the value of an asset. An interest rate can be expressed in either real or nominal terms.
- The future value of an asset or payment is the value of a present asset or payment in terms of what it is worth in some future time period.
- The present value of an asset or payment is the value of a future asset or payment in terms of what it is worth in the present time period.
- The supply of funds for the accumulation of capital is provided by those consumers who choose to defer some of their consumption from the present time period to future time periods.
- We determine the optimal levels of an individual's consumption in the present and future time periods by solving a constrained utility maximization model that embodies an intertemporal utility function, along with an intertemporal budget constraint, containing these consumption levels as decision variables.
- The impact of a change in the interest rate on an individual's constrained utility maximization solution for present and future consumption levels depends on the associated substitution and income effects and also on whether the individual is a net borrower or a net saver.
- A savings curve expresses the level of saving explicitly in terms of the interest rate. It also represents the supply of funds available for capital accumulation.
- We can determine the optimal amount of capital purchased by a firm by constructing a constrained profit maximization model that embodies the firm's discounted future profit stream as the objective function and an intertemporal capital formation equation as the constraint.
- Investment is the change in a firm's level of capital for a given time period.
- We generate a demand for capital curve from the optimization process, where this curve expresses the quantity of capital demanded in terms of either the interest rate or the rental rate of capital.

KEY TERMS

- discounting, page 583
- future value of an asset or payment, page 582
- interest rate, page 579
- investment, page 607
- nominal interest rate, page 579
- present value of an asset or payment, page 582
- real interest rate, page 579

EXERCISES

22.1 Suppose your rich uncle tells you he will give you $100,000 in one lump sum three years from now. Ignoring tax considerations and assuming the interest rate is 20 percent, what is this amount worth today?

22.2 A bond has a face, or par, value of $10,000 that is paid to the owner at the time the bond matures. The bond also generates annual coupon, or income, payments equal to $400 per year. If the bond has two years to maturity and the interest rate is 5 percent, what is the price of the bond?

22.3 Assume the average price level in constant dollars for 1998 is 1.90 and for 1999 it is 2.05. Now, assuming expected inflation equals actual inflation and that the real interest rate is 4 percent, what is the nominal interest rate lenders will charge to borrowers? Explain the rationale underlying your computation.

22.4 Assume an individual derives utility from consuming goods and services in two periods according to the utility function

$$U = C_1^{1/2} C_2^{1/2},$$

where U represents utility, and C_1 and C_2 represent the individual's consumption in time periods one and two, respectively. Furthermore, this individual is subject to the intertemporal budget constraint

$$C_2 + (1 + \bar{r}_1)C_1 = \bar{I}_2 + (1 + \bar{r}_1)\bar{I}_1,$$

where r is the interest rate, and I_1 and I_2 represent the individual's income received in periods one and two, respectively.

a. If $r = 10\%$ and $\bar{I}_1 = \bar{I}_2 = \$1000$, what are the optimal levels of C_1 and C_2?

b. Is this individual a net saver or a net borrower in this situation? What is the value of her saving?

22.5 Refer to the information given in Exercise 22.4.

a. If r increases to 20 percent and income for the two periods remains the same, what are the optimal levels of C_1 and C_2?

b. Is the individual now a net saver or a net borrower?

22.6 Again, refer to the information in Exercise 22.4. Plot the savings curve for this individual. What does the slope of this curve indicate?

22.7 An individual derives utility from consuming goods and services in two time periods. Furthermore, his income for the two time periods is fixed. Assume the individual is a net saver and that the income effect exceeds the substitution effect associated with a change in the interest rate. Illustrate the savings curve for this individual. What does the slope of this curve indicate?

22.8 Refer to Real-World Application 22.1. Using the same tax information provided in that application, rework the results assuming the interest rate is 10 percent, the lotto amount is $1,000,000, and that it can be paid annually for two years, or received as a lump sum. Compare the results for the two alternative options available to the lottery winner.

CHAPTER 23

General Equilibrium Analysis in an Exchange Economy

23.1 INTRODUCTION

In the preceding chapters, our primary focus was on attaining equilibrium as it relates to individual consumers, firms, and markets. Specifically, in Chapter 4 we demonstrated that an individual consumer achieves his goal of constrained utility maximization by purchasing and consuming the combination of goods for which his marginal rate of substitution for two goods is equal to the ratio of their prices. Similarly, we showed in Chapter 10 that a firm selects a combination of inputs that minimizes the cost of producing a specified level of output. Specifically, the firm employs a combination of inputs for which the marginal rate of technical substitution equals the ratio of the input prices. We also showed in previous chapters that a firm achieves its goal of profit maximization by producing that level of output for which the marginal cost associated with the last unit of output produced equals the marginal revenue it receives from the last unit sold. This profit-maximizing condition holds true regardless of the market structure within which the firm operates. In addition, in Chapter 14 we demonstrated that a perfectly competitive market for a good achieves equilibrium when the quantity supplied of the good at a particular price is equal to the quantity demanded at that same price. This concept of market equilibrium was also a recurring theme in Chapters 20, 21, and 22 where our focus was on labor and capital markets.

Although we have given the concept of equilibrium considerable attention, our discussion has been exclusively relegated to individual markets operating in isolation. Technically, the type of economic analysis we have conducted thus far is known as **partial equilibrium analysis**, or *the isolated examination of equilibrium in individual markets, and for individual consumers and firms comprising those markets*. Yet, if we examine these markets from a broader perspective, we can easily demonstrate that markets for goods and services, as well as individual consumers and firms in an economy, do not operate in isolation. Rather, they are highly interdependent since events that affect one market or economic agent ultimately influence the economic performance of other markets and agents.

We have demonstrated this concept in Figure 23.1 using the circular flow model from your principles of microeconomics course. In this model we depict two general markets—the input market where resources such as labor and capital are

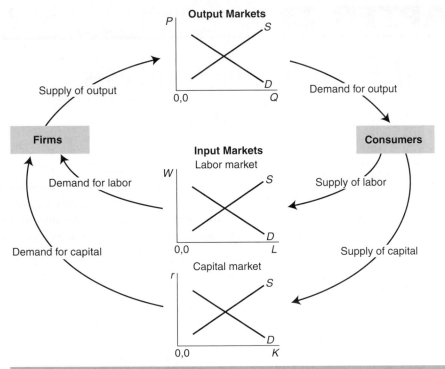

FIGURE 23.1 Circular Flow Diagram

bought and sold, and the output markets where final goods and services are bought and sold. We also specify two distinct types of economic agents in the circular flow diagram, consumers and firms. The actions of all economic agents, as well as the reactions in the input and output markets, are closely linked because individual consumers buy goods and services in the output markets and sell their labor and capital resources in the input markets. At the same time, firms supply goods and services to the output markets, and buy resources such as labor and capital from input markets. Firms use these inputs to produce the goods and services they supply to the output market. It is through this constant interaction among the various economic agents that equilibrium is established in both output and input markets.

In a distinct departure from the type of analysis we previously used in this text, our focus in this chapter is on **general equilibrium analysis**, or *the process by which all markets, and all consumers and firms comprising those markets, simultaneously attain equilibrium.* For the sake of clarity, we will initially analyze the attainment of equilibrium by consumers in the absence of production, integrating many of the topics we developed in previous chapters. In the following chapter we will extend this analysis to incorporate the behavior of firms as well. Therefore, if you cannot readily recall the fundamental concepts related to consumer, firm, and market equilibrium, we highly recommend that you review these topics before proceeding in this chapter.

23.2   INITIAL ENDOWMENT IN AN EXCHANGE ECONOMY

General equilibrium analysis, by its very nature, is complex. This is due to the fact that it focuses on the simultaneous attainment of equilibrium in all markets and by all consumers and firms in an economy. Given this complexity, we will make several simplifying assumptions in the general equilibrium models developed in this chapter. In particular, we will assume that there are only two consumers in the economy, denoted A and B, and only two goods, X and Y, that are available in fixed amounts. We will also assume that there is no actual production in the economy. Rather, the consumers receive an **initial endowment**, defined as *the particular allocation of goods consumers are assumed to possess before they engage in any exchange of these goods*. We denote the initial endowments of goods X and Y to consumers A and B as (X_0^A, Y_0^A) and (X_0^B, Y_0^B), respectively.

Using the same graphical framework employed in Chapters 3 and 4 to illustrate consumers' indifference curves, we have illustrated each consumer's initial endowment of goods X and Y in Figure 23.2. The initial endowment of goods X and Y consumer A receives, denoted (X_0^A, Y_0^A), is shown in the first graph in panel (A) of Figure 23.2. In this graph we measure the quantity of good X consumer A receives, X^A, on the horizontal axis, and the quantity of good Y consumer A receives, Y^A, on the vertical axis. The origin in this graph, denoted 0^A, indicates a combination of zero units of good X and zero units of good Y for consumer A. Similarly, in the second graph in panel (A) of Figure 23.2, we have illustrated consumer B's initial endowment of goods, denoted (X_0^B, Y_0^B). In this graph the quantity of good X that consumer B receives, X^B, is measured along the horizontal axis, and the quantity of good Y he receives, Y^B, is measured along the vertical axis. The origin, denoted 0^B, represents a combination of zero units of good X and zero units of good Y for consumer B. Since we assume there are only two consumers, the total fixed amount of good X available in the economy, denoted X^T, is computed as the sum of each consumer's initial endowment of good X; thus

$$X^T = X_0^A + X_0^B,$$

and the total fixed amount of good Y present in the economy, denoted Y^T, is computed as

$$Y^T = Y_0^A + Y_0^B.$$

In the following section, we will use the concepts of an initial endowment and the total quantities of the goods available in the economy to develop a diagrammatic representation of the process of exchange between two consumers.

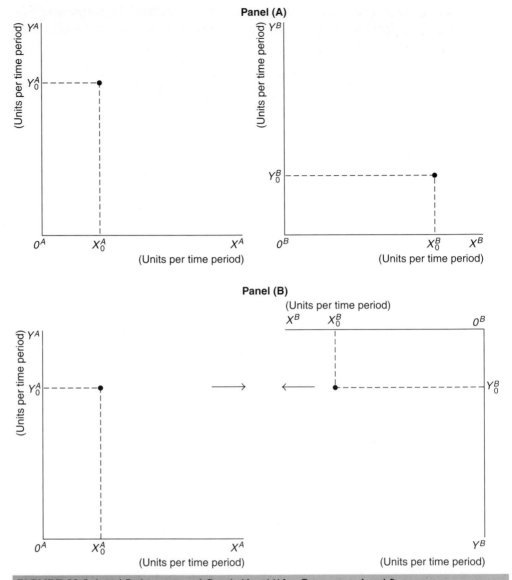

FIGURE 23.2 Initial Endowments of Goods X and Y for Consumers A and B

23.3 EDGEWORTH BOX IN AN EXCHANGE ECONOMY

Graphically, we can use a box to represent the two-consumer, two-goods, simple exchange economy described earlier. Specifically, we construct this box by first rotating the graph pertaining to consumer B in panel (A) of Figure 23.2 by 180 degrees, as we have shown in the second graph in panel (B), and then sliding the graphs for consumers A and B together to create the box shown in Figure 23.3. This figure, known as

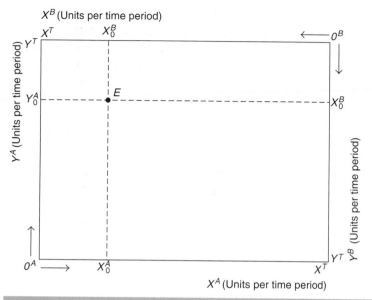

FIGURE 23.3 Edgeworth Box with Initial Endowments of Goods *X* and *Y* for Consumers *A* and *B*

an **Edgeworth box**, is *a rectangle containing all of the feasible combinations of two goods, X and Y, available in the economy that can be distributed between two consumers, where the length of the box measures the total amount of good X available in the economy and the height of the box measures the total amount of good Y available.*

The Edgeworth box depicted in Figure 23.3 illustrates the total amounts of both good X and good Y, denoted X^T and Y^T, respectively, available to the two consumers, A and B. Each point within the box or on its perimeter represents a feasible combination of goods X and Y that can be allocated between consumers A and B. By construction, the quantity of good X consumer A receives, denoted X^A, is measured along the bottom of the Edgeworth box, while the amount of good Y consumer A receives, denoted Y^A, is measured along the left-hand side of the box. The point at which the bottom and left-hand sides of the Edgeworth box intersect represents consumer A's origin, denoted 0^A. This origin represents an allocation of zero units of good X and zero units of good Y to consumer A. We indicate increases in consumption of good X by consumer A as rightward movements along the bottom of the Edgeworth box, and increases in consumption of good Y by individual A are indicated as upward movements along the left-hand side of the box. Temporarily ignoring the top and right-hand sides of the Edgeworth box, we can see that the bottom and left-hand sides essentially replicate the horizontal and vertical axes of the two-dimensional graphs in goods space we used extensively throughout Chapters 3 and 4 in the development of consumer theory.

The Edgeworth box in Figure 23.3 also simultaneously illustrates the allocation of goods X and Y to consumer B. Specifically, we measure the quantity of good X available to consumer B, X^B, along the top of the Edgeworth box, while the number of units of good Y available to consumer B, Y^B, are measured along the right-hand side of the box. The point at which the top and right-hand sides of the Edgeworth box intersect represents consumer B's origin, denoted 0^B, where this point indicates an allocation of zero units of good X and zero units of good Y to consumer B. From consumer B's perspective, increases in his consumption of good X are indicated by leftward movements from 0^B along the top of the Edgeworth box, while we indicate greater levels of consumption of good Y by consumer B by downward movements from 0^B along the right-hand side of the box. Temporarily ignoring the bottom and left-hand sides of the Edgeworth box, we can observe that the top and right-hand side of the box replicate, respectively, the horizontal and vertical axes of the two-dimensional graphs in goods space, rotated 180 degrees.

Recall that the specific dimensions of an Edgeworth box are determined by the total fixed quantities of goods X and Y available in the economy. The greater the amount of good X available in the economy, the longer will be the Edgeworth box, and the greater the amount of good Y in the economy, the greater is the height of the box. In Figure 23.3, we have denoted the initial endowment of goods X and Y in the economy as point E, specifically indicating an initial endowment of X_0^A units of good X and Y_0^A units of good Y to consumer A, and X_0^B units of good X and Y_0^B units of good Y to consumer B. We can easily verify in this figure that the sum of the initial endowments of good X to consumers A and B, X_0^A and X_0^B, respectively, is equal to the total amount of good X in the economy, or

$$X_0^A + X_0^B = X^T.$$

Similarly, the sum of the initial endowments of good Y to consumers A and B, Y_0^A and Y_0^B, respectively, is equal to the total amount of good Y available in the economy; therefore

$$Y_0^A + Y_0^B = Y^T.$$

Alternatively, if we know the value of one consumer's initial endowment, along with the total amounts of each good available in the economy, then we can compute the initial endowment of the other consumer as simply the differences between the total amount of each good and the respective initial endowment of each good available to the first consumer. For example, if we know the total amounts of goods X and Y in the economy, X^T and Y^T, along with consumer A's initial endowment, (X_0^A, Y_0^A), then consumer B's initial endowment of good X is computed as

$$X_0^B = X^T - X_0^A,$$

and consumer B's initial endowment of good Y is

$$Y_0^B = Y^T - Y_0^A.$$

These relationships hold true for all feasible allocations of goods X and Y to consumers A and B, not just for their initial endowments.

23.4   EXCHANGE IN THE EDGEWORTH BOX

Just as we used two-dimensional graphs, measuring the quantity of good X on the horizontal axis and the quantity of good Y on the vertical axis, to illustrate an individual consumer's preference orderings with indifference curves in Chapters 3 and 4, we can use the Edgeworth box to simultaneously plot the indifference curves for two consumers. In Figure 23.4 we have illustrated a strictly convex indifference curve mapping for consumers A and B. From consumer A's perspective, the indifference curves are plotted in the conventional manner. Each indifference curve indicates all of the possible combinations of goods X and Y that yield a particular level of utility, where the level of utility consumer A receives increases along each successively higher indifference curve. Thus, for the four indifference curves pertaining to consumer A plotted in Figure 23.4, $U_0^A < U_1^A < U_2^A < U_3^A$. We have also plotted four indifference curves for consumer B in this figure. However, since consumer B's origin is located at the upper right-hand corner of the Edgeworth box, each successively lower indifference curve, when moving in a southwesternly direction relative to consumer B's origin, 0^B,

FIGURE 23.4 Edgeworth Box Containing Indifference Curves and Initial Endowments for Consumers A and B

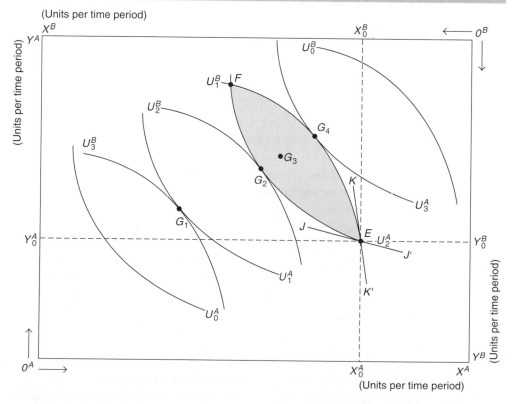

indicates a higher level of utility for consumer B. Thus, for the four indifference curves plotted in this figure for consumer B, $U_0^B < U_1^B < U_2^B < U_3^B$.

In the Edgeworth box illustrated in Figure 23.4, we assume the initial endowment of goods X and Y occurs at point E, where consumers A and B each receive an initial endowment, denoted (X_0^A, Y_0^A) and (X_0^B, Y_0^B), respectively. Consumer A's initial endowment contains a relatively large portion of good X compared to her endowment of good Y, while consumer B's initial endowment has a relatively small amount of good X and a large amount of good Y. Given the skewed distribution of goods X and Y between consumers A and B, and the knowledge that no additional production of either good is possible, it seems logical that the two consumers may be able to engage in some exchange of one good for the other and achieve a different allocation yielding a higher level of utility to one or both of the consumers. For us to determine if this is possible, recall the concept of the marginal rate of substitution defined in Section 3.4.1 of Chapter 3. This is the rate at which an individual is willing to substitute units of one good for units of another, while maintaining the same level of utility. We should also recall that we can measure a consumer's marginal rate of substitution at a particular combination of two goods by evaluating the negative of the slope of a line drawn tangent to the consumer's indifference curve at that combination.

We can apply this analysis to the two consumers depicted in Figure 23.4 by sketching lines tangent to each consumer's indifference curve at the initial endowment of goods indicated at point E. In the case of consumer A, we have drawn the line segment JJ' tangent to her indifference curve, U_2^A, at her initial endowment of X_0^A units of good X and Y_0^A units of good Y. Similarly, the line KK' is drawn tangent to consumer B's indifference curve, U_1^B, at his initial endowment of X_0^B units of good X and Y_0^B units of good Y. We can observe that JJ', the line segment drawn tangent to consumer A's indifference curve at the initial endowment, is flatter than KK', the line segment drawn tangent to consumer B's indifference curve. Therefore, we can readily infer from this graphical analysis that at their respective initial endowments, consumer A's marginal rate of substitution of good X for good Y is less than that for consumer B.

How can we use this information regarding the relative values of the consumers' marginal rates of substitution? Since consumer B's marginal rate of substitution is greater than consumer A's, then consumer B, whose initial endowment contains a relatively sparse amount of good X and a large amount of good Y, is willing to give up many more units of good Y than consumer A, to receive an additional unit of good X, while maintaining the same level of utility. Conversely, consumer A, whose initial endowment contains a relatively large number of units of good X, along with a small allocation of good Y, is willing to give up many more units of good X to receive an additional unit of good Y, while maintaining the same level of utility, than will consumer B. Thus, by engaging in exchange, leading to allocations of goods X and Y that are different from their initial endowments, one or both of these consumers can increase their utility.

In general, one or both consumers have the potential for increasing their level of utility, while not decreasing the utility of either consumer, by engaging in exchange, as long as their marginal rates of substitution are not equal at any given allocation of goods X and Y. Referring to the two consumers depicted in the Edgeworth box in Figure 23.4, exchange between consumers A and B that leads to an allocation of goods X and Y lying within the shaded area between indifference curves U_2^A and U_1^B constitutes mutually beneficial trade. This means that both consumers are better off with a combination of goods lying in this shaded area and thus receive a higher level of utility than when consuming their initial endowments. Recall from Section 3.5.1 in Chapter 3, that an important characteristic associated with indifference curves is that the indifference curve mapping is everywhere dense, and thus every point in goods space, constituting a unique combination of goods X and Y, must lie on an indifference curve. Although we have not drawn any indifference curves strictly within the shaded region in Figure 23.4, an infinite number of indifference curves exist in that area for both consumers A and B, representing higher levels of utility for each consumer. For example, suppose consumer A trades some of her good X to consumer B in exchange for additional units of good Y, such that the two consumers ultimately settle on an allocation of goods corresponding to, say point G_3 in Figure 23.4. It is now possible for us to draw an indifference curve for consumer A containing the point G_3 that clearly lies above U_2^A, the indifference curve containing consumer A's initial endowment. Similarly, we can draw another indifference curve for consumer B containing the new allocation of goods represented by point G_3. This indifference curve lies beneath U_1^B and therefore corresponds to a higher level of utility than U_1^B, the indifference curve containing consumer B's initial endowment. We have depicted this situation in Figure 23.5, which essentially contains all of the information presented in Figure 23.4, with the addition of consumer A's new indifference curve $U_2^{A\prime}$ that lies above U_2^A, indicating $U_2^{A\prime} > U_2^A$. In addition, this figure contains consumer B's new indifference curve $U_1^{B\prime}$ that lies below U_1^B, thereby indicating $U_1^{B\prime} > U_1^B$. The two new indifference curves for consumers A and B, $U_2^{A\prime}$ and $U_1^{B\prime}$, respectively, are tangent at point G_3, corresponding to the new allocations of goods X and Y, (X_3^A, Y_3^A) and (X_3^B, Y_3^B), to consumers A and B, respectively. Since these indifference curves are tangent at point G_3, both consumers' marginal rates of substitution are equal at this new allocation of goods.

Depending on the relative negotiating skills of each consumer, however, it is also possible for trade to take place that results in an increase in utility by only one consumer, while the other consumer's level of utility remains constant. For example, if consumer A is the more skilled negotiator, she can convince consumer B to trade away units of good Y to her in exchange for additional units of good X, ultimately agreeing to the goods allocation indicated by point G_4 in Figure 23.4. In this case, consumer A's level of utility increases, since this combination of goods lies on a higher level indifference curve than the one associated with her initial endowment. Specifically, point G_4 lies on consumer A's U_3^A indifference curve, while her initial endowment, (X_0^A, Y_0^A), lies on the relatively lower indifference curve, U_2^A. However, this new allocation of goods at G_4 leaves consumer B's utility unchanged since both point E, representing his initial endowment, and point G_4 lie on his U_1^B indifference curve. We can also note in Figures 23.4 and 23.5 that at point G_4, consumer A's indifference curve, U_3^A, and consumer B's indifference curve, U_1^B, are tangent, indicating that the

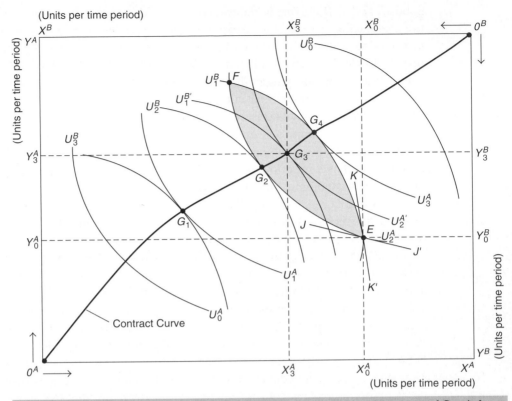

FIGURE 23.5 Edgeworth Box Containing Initial Endowments and New Allocations of Goods for Consumers A and B, along with the Contract Curve

two consumers' marginal rates of substitution are equal at this allocation of goods. Therefore, neither consumer has any further opportunity to exchange goods and increase his or her utility without decreasing the utility that the other consumer receives.

Alternatively, suppose consumer B is the better negotiator and is able to convince consumer A to relinquish units of good X to him in exchange for additional units of good Y, so that the new allocation of goods is represented by point G_2 in Figure 23.4. In this situation, consumer B increases his level of utility because the new combination of goods lies on consumer B's U_2^B indifference curve, representing a higher level of utility than that pertaining to his initial endowment at point E on his U_1^B indifference curve. Consumer A's utility is left unchanged because the new allocation of goods, represented by point G_2, as well as her initial goods endowment at point E lie on the same indifference curve, U_2^A. In Figures 23.4 and 23.5 at point G_2, the two consumers' indifference curves are also tangent, thereby indicating that their marginal rates of substitution are equal at this allocation of goods.

23.5   CONTRACT CURVE

In the previous section, we demonstrated that one or both consumers have the potential for increasing their utility by engaging in exchange, if their marginal rates of substitution are not equal to each other for some given allocation of goods. However, once equality between the consumers' marginal rates of substitution is achieved—specifically when the consumers' indifference curves are tangent at a particular combination of goods within the Edgeworth box—the consumers cease trading, since any movements from such an allocation of goods result in at least one of the consumers becoming worse off. In general, we say goods combinations such as these are **Pareto optimal**, or **efficient**, defined as *an allocation of goods where no one consumer can be made better off without making another consumer worse off.* In Figure 23.5, we have illustrated several Pareto optimal allocations of goods X and Y at which consumer A's marginal rate of substitution is equal to that for consumer B. Specifically, at each of the goods allocations we have denoted as G_1, G_2, G_3 and G_4, in Figure 23.5, the two consumers' indifference curves comprising the pairs U_1^A and U_3^B, U_2^A and U_2^B, $U_2^{A\prime}$ and $U_1^{B\prime}$, along with U_3^A and U_1^B, respectively, are tangent to each other. Hence, $MRS_1^A = MRS_1^B$ at G_1, $MRS_2^A = MRS_2^B$ at G_2, $MRS_3^A = MRS_3^B$ at G_3, and $MRS_4^A = MRS_4^B$ at G_4. Clearly, goods allocations such as G_1, G_2, G_3, and G_4 are Pareto optimal since movement away from any one of these goods combinations, in an effort to make one consumer better off, results in a decrease in the other consumer's utility. For example, movement from allocation G_2 to G_1 in the Edgeworth box depicted in Figure 23.5 results in an increase in consumer B's utility from U_2^B to U_3^B and a simultaneous decrease in consumer A's utility from U_2^A to U_1^A.

In general, we say that allocations of goods in an Edgeworth box where the consumers' marginal rates of substitution are equal lie on a **contract curve**, or *the set of allocations of goods within an Edgeworth box that are Pareto optimal.* Specifically, in Figure 23.5, we have designated the contract curve as the curve passing through consumer A's origin, 0^A, the Pareto optimal allocations, G_1, G_2, G_3, and G_4, and consumer B's origin, 0^B. An infinite number of other allocations of goods also lie on the contract curve, where these allocations are determined at the points of tangency for consumer A's and consumer B's infinite number of indifference curves.

What will happen to the consumers' levels of utility as we move from one Pareto optimal allocation on the contract curve to another? Referring once again to the contract curve in Figure 23.5, we can observe that movement from one point on the contract curve, such as G_3, to another point on the contract curve, say G_4, results in an increase in consumer A's utility, from $U_2^{A\prime}$ to U_3^A. However, this increase comes only at the expense of consumer B's utility, which necessarily declines from $U_1^{B\prime}$ to U_1^B. Note that points lying off the contract curve are not Pareto optimal. Therefore, movement from a goods allocation that does not lie on the contract curve to one that does results in an increase in utility for at least one consumer, without reducing the utility of the other. For example, in Figure 23.5 observe that movement from an allocation of goods not lying on the contract curve, such as at point F, to a Pareto optimal point, such as G_2 that does lie on the contract curve, results in an increase in consumer B's level of utility from U_1^B to U_2^B, while leaving consumer A's level of utility unchanged at U_2^A. Therefore, point F, as well as other points not lying on the contract curve, cannot represent Pareto optimal, or efficient, allocations of goods because further exchanges are possible between consumers A and B that can result in a higher level of utility for one individual, without reducing the utility received by the other.

23.6 CONSUMER EXCHANGE UNDER COMPETITIVELY DETERMINED GOODS PRICES

In the previous sections, we demonstrated how two consumers can achieve a Pareto optimal distribution of goods in an economy purely through the process of exchange. Ultimately, the particular Pareto optimal allocation the two consumers agree upon depends largely on the relative negotiating skills of each consumer, where logically, the better negotiator benefits more from the exchange process. As shown in our previous analysis, the consumers attained a Pareto optimal allocation of goods without any knowledge of the prices of the two goods being exchanged. Yet it is a well-established fact that prices, in particular relative prices, of goods play an important role in determining the best allocation of goods in an economy. In Section 4.3.1 of Chapter 4 we demonstrated, from a partial equilibrium perspective, the necessary condition for a constrained utility maximum. Recall that this necessary condition states that an individual operating in a perfectly competitive market consumes a combination of two goods for which his marginal rate of substitution between these goods is equal to the ratio of their prices. Also recall that, given the fact that the goods prices are competitively determined, all consumers in the economy face the same prices for the goods they purchase and consume. In mathematical terms

$$MRS = \frac{P_X}{P_Y}$$

at the utility-maximizing combination of goods X and Y for a typical consumer. However, if an individual consumes some combination of goods X and Y for which

$$MRS \neq \frac{P_X}{P_Y},$$

then by allocating his income differently and purchasing an alternative combination for which his *MRS* for goods X and Y is equal to P_X/P_Y, he can receive a higher level of utility while not exceeding his budget constraint. We can also analyze a consumer's constrained utility-maximizing, or optimal, combination of goods graphically. Recall from Chapter 4 that at an optimal combination of goods, the consumer's indifference curve corresponding to his maximum level of utility is tangent to his budget constraint. This tangency necessarily implies that at the optimal consumption combination, the slope of the indifference curve, measured as the negative of the consumer's marginal rate of substitution, equals the slope of the budget constraint, or

$$-MRS = \frac{-P_X}{P_Y}.$$

After multiplying both sides of the above equation by negative one, we obtain the familiar necessary condition for a constrained utility maximum as

$$MRS = \frac{P_X}{P_Y}.$$

This condition holds true for all consumers who achieve the maximum utility possible, given their levels of income and the competitively determined prices of the goods they are purchasing and consuming.

   This necessary condition for a constrained utility maximum also holds true for two consumers exchanging goods on the basis of their competitively determined relative prices. We can demonstrate this statement with an Edgeworth box, as depicted in Figure 23.6, for individuals A and B who both consume goods X and Y. Two indifference

FIGURE 23.6 Consumer Equilibrium under Competitively Determined Goods Prices

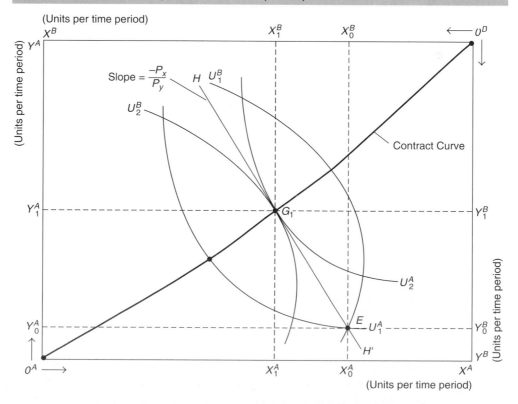

curves are shown for consumer A, specifically U_1^A and U_2^A, where $U_2^A > U_1^A$, and two indifference curves are shown for consumer B, U_1^B and U_2^B, where $U_2^B > U_1^B$. The initial endowment, labeled point E, indicates that consumer A's initial allocation of goods X and Y is X_0^A and Y_0^A, respectively, while consumer B's initial allocation of goods X and Y is X_0^B and Y_0^B, respectively. Note that we have also included the line HH' in this figure. We refer to it as the price line, since the slope of this line reflects the negative of the ratio of the prices both consumers pay for goods X and Y. By observing the Edgeworth box in Figure 23.6, it should be clear that the initial endowment is not Pareto optimal. Specifically, if consumer A exchanges $(X_0^A - X_1^A) = (X_1^B - X_0^B)$ units of good X with consumer B, in return for $(Y_1^A - Y_0^A) = (Y_0^B - Y_1^B)$ units of good Y, both consumers achieve higher levels of utility at the new allocation of goods denoted by point G_1.

Consumer A receives U_2^A level of utility at G_1, an amount greater than the U_1^A level of utility she receives at her initial endowment represented by point E. Furthermore, at the goods allocation G_1, consumer B receives a U_2^B level of utility, an amount greater than the U_1^B level of utility he receives at his initial endowment, also point E. In Figure 23.6, the rate at which consumers A and B exchange goods X and Y is equal to the slope of the price line, HH'. Specifically, the slope of this price line is Δ rise/Δ run, and thus between points E and G_1 we compute the slope of HH' as

$$\frac{(Y_1^A - Y_0^A)}{(X_0^A - X_1^A)}.$$

This value is also equal to the slope of consumer A's U_2^A indifference curve at the goods combination represented by point G_1, as well as the slope of consumer B's U_2^B indifference curve at that same point. Therefore, the rates at which the two consumers are willing to exchange goods X and Y at point G_1 are equal, or

$$MRS_1^A = MRS_1^B.$$

These marginal rates of substitution for the two consumers are also equal to the ratio of the prices of goods X and Y, P_X/P_Y. Also note that since the consumers' indifference curves are tangent to one another at point G_1, this allocation of goods must also be Pareto optimal and thus lie on the contract curve passing through points 0^A, G_1, and 0^B.

Observe in Figure 23.6 that at the new allocation of goods for consumers A and B, represented by point G_1, there is neither an excess supply nor an excess demand for either good. Recall that when the consumers engage in exchange in accordance with the relative prices of goods X and Y, the quantity of good X consumer A trades to consumer B, $(X_0^A - X_1^A)$, is equal to the quantity of good X consumer B demands, $(X_1^B - X_0^B)$. Similarly, the quantity of good Y consumer B trades to consumer A, $(Y_0^B - Y_1^B)$, is equal to the quantity of good Y consumer A demands, $(Y_1^A - Y_0^A)$. Therefore, after consumers A and B exchange their goods, according to the competitively determined relative prices of goods X and Y, the markets for goods X and Y are in equilibrium, since there exists no excess supply or excess demand for either good.

This result demonstrates that an extremely important outcome is associated with competitively determined equilibria. Specifically, an allocation of goods that is a competitive equilibrium is also Pareto optimal, or efficient, since at such an allocation of goods

$$MRS^A = \frac{P_X}{P_Y} \quad \text{and} \quad MRS^B = \frac{P_X}{P_Y},$$

and therefore

$$MRS^A = MRS^B.$$

REAL-WORLD APPLICATION 23.1

The Effect of Transportation Costs on International Trade Patterns

When we analyze exchange between two consumers within the context of an Edgeworth box, we assume that the process of trading goods is costless, which means that the participants encounter no transportation or transaction costs. In the real world, however, the exchange of goods between individuals or countries, especially those separated geographically, do generate transportation costs. These costs can often be significant, especially when measured relative to the value of the good or service being traded. Therefore, shipping costs can have a very large influence on the type of goods being sold internationally as well as the volume of trade between nations. Real-world data reflecting the flow of goods between countries also support this hypothesis.[1] For example, the United States and Canada serve as each other's largest trading partner, while Hong Kong is the largest export market for both China and Taiwan. Similarly, most European Union (EU) member nations ship the majority of their exports to other EU countries, both because of their proximity to one another and favorable trade agreements.

Historically, the volume of goods traded among countries has grown significantly over the past 50 years, partly as a result of techno-

logical advances that have made it easier and cheaper to transport products abroad. In particular, the invention and use of shipping containers has greatly facilitated the movement of large quantities of goods from trucks to cargo ships, and once in their destination port, back onto trucks or railcars. The use of containers has drastically reduced firms' shipping costs since far fewer longshoremen are needed to transfer goods onto ships. Containerization has also decreased the amount of pilferage that can take place. Another factor that has helped to expedite the movement of goods and services, both domestically and internationally, is the deregulation of the transportation industry. In the United States, regulations facing air, rail, and road carriers regarding the types of goods they can haul, where they can transport them, and the prices they can charge have been greatly reduced. This has increased competition in the shipping industry and given firms the ability to better coordinate multiple modes of transport between origination and destination points, resulting in greater efficiency and lower shipping costs. Undoubtedly, such reductions in transportation costs will foster an even greater volume of trade among nations in the future and lead to a more efficient allocation of resources worldwide.

[1] *The Economist*, November 15, 1997, pp. 85–87.

This important result is known as the **First Theorem of Welfare Economics**, which states that *an allocation of goods that is a competitive equilibrium must also be a Pareto optimal allocation of goods*. This result holds true as long as each consumer's preferences and indifference curves follow the assumptions underlying rational consumer choice described in Chapter 3, each consumer's utility is unaffected by the consumption choices of the other consumer, and the consumers incur no transactions costs when they exchange goods. In other words, it is not possible to deviate from a competitively determined allocation of goods, such as the one we represent by the point G_1 in Figure 23.6, without reducing the utility of at least one consumer. This result underscores one of the most economically desirable characteristics of perfectly competitive markets, described by Adam Smith's invisible hand process and discussed in previous chapters. Specifically, it is the ability of perfectly competitive markets to efficiently allocate resources to their most desired uses, based solely on information regarding consumers' preferences, incomes, and the relative prices of the goods being bought and sold. A second related outcome, known as the **Second Theorem of Welfare Economics**, states that *there exists a set of goods prices such that each Pareto optimal goods allocation lying on the contract curve is also a competitive equilibrium*. This result also requires that all consumers' preferences and indifference curves follow the assumptions underlying rational consumer choice described in Chapter 3. We will focus on the implications associated with these important theorems in the following chapter.

23.7 UTILITY POSSIBILITIES FRONTIER

We can present the information conveyed in the Edgeworth box regarding the set of Pareto optimal goods allocations comprising the contract curve in a somewhat different manner. Rather than plotting the Pareto optimal allocations in goods space, we can plot these efficient allocations in utility space, indicating the level of utility each consumer receives at every Pareto optimal goods allocation lying on the contract curve. By doing so, we can derive a curve known as a **utility possibilities frontier**, or *a set of points measuring the combinations of utility levels attainable for two consumers corresponding to allocations of goods lying on the contract curve*.

Any point on the utility possibilities frontier corresponds to a Pareto optimal, or efficient, allocation of goods that lies on the contract curve, while any point lying beneath the utility possibilities frontier corresponds to a goods allocation that is not Pareto optimal, or efficient. Any point that lies above the utility possibilities frontier corresponds to an allocation of goods lying outside of the Edgeworth box; therefore, the associated levels of utility are unattainable to the consumers, given the total quantities of goods available in the economy. A combination of utility levels associated with such a point could only be achieved if the total allocation of goods in the economy were sufficiently increased, thereby causing the utility possibilities frontier to shift to the right.

We can derive a utility possibilities frontier directly from an Edgeworth box. This process is illustrated in panels (A) and (B) of Figure 23.7, where in panel (A) we have

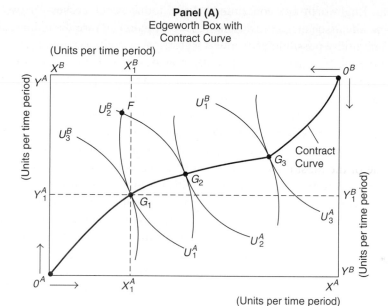

Panel (A)
Edgeworth Box with
Contract Curve

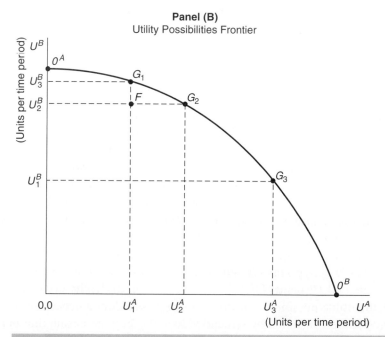

Panel (B)
Utility Possibilities Frontier

FIGURE 23.7 Derivation of Utility Possibilities Frontier from Contract Curve

shown an Edgeworth box containing several indifference curves for two consumers, along with the associated contract curve, and in panel (B) we have illustrated the corresponding utility possibilities frontier. Referring initially to panel (A), we have illustrated three indifference curves for consumer A, where $U_1^A < U_2^A < U_3^A$, and three indifference curves are shown for consumer B, where $U_1^B < U_2^B < U_3^B$. All of these indifference curves are strictly convex and indicate increasing levels of utility the farther away they are from the respective consumer's origin. We have indicated the points of tangency between consumer A's and consumer B's indifference curves by the goods allocations at points G_1, G_2, and G_3. These three points, along with each consumer's respective origin, 0^A and 0^B, lie on the contract curve, which is also shown in panel (A).

When constructing the utility possibilities frontier, we must focus on the level of utility each consumer receives at every point indicated on the contract curve. Beginning with consumer A's origin, 0^A, it is clear to us that since consumer A receives zero units of good X and zero units of good Y, her utility associated with this allocation of goods is zero. Since consumer A receives zero units of both goods, then consumer B must be the sole recipient of these goods, and therefore, consumer B achieves his highest level of utility at this allocation of goods. Hence, consumer A's origin, 0^A, in the Edgeworth box we have depicted in panel (A) of Figure 23.7 must correspond to the point 0^A, the vertical intercept of the utility possibilities frontier, shown in panel (B). Similarly, when consumer B's allocation of goods is represented by the point 0^B in the Edgeworth box in panel (A), he receives zero utility since he is consuming zero units of good X and zero units of good Y. Conversely, at this point consumer A receives her greatest level of utility, since she is consuming the total amount of goods X and Y available in the economy. This goods allocation corresponds to the point 0^B, the horizontal intercept of the utility possibilities frontier in panel (B).

We can easily determine the levels of utility each consumer receives from the remaining points indicated on the contract curve from the labels identifying each indifference curve. Specifically, at the goods allocation represented by point G_1 in panel (A), consumer A receives U_1^A level of utility from consuming the goods combination (X_1^A, Y_1^A), while consumer B, who is the recipient of a comparatively much greater allocation of goods X and Y, (X_1^B, Y_1^B), receives a relatively higher level of utility, designated U_3^B, where $U_3^B > U_1^A$. We can plot the associated utility combination, (U_1^A, U_3^B), as a point on the utility possibilities frontier in panel (B). Similarly, the utility combinations associated with points G_2 and G_3 on the contract curve are plotted in panel (B) as the points (U_2^A, U_2^B) and (U_3^A, U_1^B), respectively, on the utility possibilities frontier. In general, the utility possibilities frontier is negatively sloped because as greater quantities of goods are consumed by one individual, thereby increasing that person's utility, fewer goods remain for the other individual, thus lowering his level of utility.

The goods allocation at point F in the Edgeworth box, associated with a level of utility U_1^A for consumer A and U_2^B for consumer B, is represented in panel (B) also as point F, lying strictly beneath the utility possibilities frontier. This result follows because this goods combination does not represent a Pareto optimal allocation of goods since it does not lie on the contract curve. More generally, any point, such as F, that lies beneath the utility possibilities frontier represents a goods allocation that is not Pareto optimal. By reallocating the goods combination represented by point F in the Edgeworth box, it is possible to increase one or both consumers' utility. For example, reallocations exist such that consumers A and B can achieve the utility levels associated with points G_1, G_2, or any of the infinite number of points lying between G_1 and G_2 on the utility possibilities frontier.

From a social perspective, a point lying on the utility possibilities frontier is preferred to one that lies below the frontier because it represents a greater total level of utility for all consumers in the economy. However, it is impossible to determine which point on the utility possibilities frontier represents the most desirable combination of utilities for the two consumers. To do so, we need additional information concerning society's preferences regarding the distribution of goods in the economy, a topic we will discuss in the next chapter.

23.8 SUMMARY

Our primary focus in this chapter was on developing a simplified general equilibrium model of exchange between consumers. We relied on the necessary equilibrium conditions for consumers established in previous chapters, as well as concepts and graphics introduced in this chapter to develop this exchange model. An especially important outcome we underscored in this chapter is the efficiency of perfectly competitive markets in allocating goods in an exchange economy. The major concepts covered in this chapter are summarized as follows.

- Partial equilibrium analysis examines equilibrium in individual markets, and for individual consumers and firms comprising those markets.
- General equilibrium analysis examines the process by which equilibrium is simultaneously attained in all markets, as well as for all consumers and firms comprising those markets.
- An Edgeworth box is a rectangle containing all of the feasible combinations of two goods available in the economy that can be distributed between two consumers.
- A Pareto optimal, or efficient, combination of goods is one in which no one consumer can be made better off without making another consumer worse off. At any Pareto optimal allocation of goods, the consumers' marginal rates of substitution for two goods are equal.
- The contract curve is the set of allocations of goods within an Edgeworth box that are Pareto optimal.
- If consumers A and B exchange goods X and Y in accordance with their competitively determined relative prices, P_X/P_Y, a Pareto optimal distribution of goods exists, where $MRS^A = MRS^B = P_X/P_Y$.
- The First Theorem of Welfare Economics states that an allocation of goods corresponding to a competitive equilibrium must also be a Pareto optimal allocation of goods.

- The Second Theorem of Welfare Economics states that there exists a set of goods prices such that each Pareto optimal goods allocation lying on the contract curve is also a competitive equilibrium.
- The utility possibilities frontier is a set of points measuring the combinations of utility levels attainable for two consumers corresponding to Pareto optimal allocations of goods that lie on the contract curve.

KEY TERMS

- contract curve, page 625
- Edgeworth box, page 619
- First Theorem of Welfare Economics, page 630
- general equilibrium analysis, page 616

- initial endowment, page 617
- Pareto optimal, or efficient, page 625
- partial equilibrium analysis, page 615

- Second Theorem of Welfare Economics, page 630
- utility possibilities frontier, page 630

EXERCISES

23.1 Distinguish between partial equilibrium analysis and general equilibrium analysis.

23.2 Is it possible for an initial endowment of goods to also be Pareto optimal? If so, illustrate such a situation using an Edgeworth box diagram containing indifference curves and a contract curve. Accurately label all lines, points, and axes.

23.3 Assume there are two consumers in the economy, Samantha and Matt, and two goods, steak and lobster. Construct an Edgeworth box containing an initial endowment that is not Pareto optimal. Illustrate and explain the process by which the consumers can achieve a Pareto optimal allocation of goods when they do not know the prices of the goods.

23.4 Assume there are two consumers in the economy, Olga and Allene, and two goods, X and Y. Construct an Edgeworth box containing an initial endowment that is not Pareto optimal. Illustrate and explain the process by which the consumers can achieve a Pareto optimal allocation of goods when they are aware of the prices of the goods.

23.5 How would transportation costs incurred in the exchange of goods affect the attainment of general equilibrium in an exchange economy?

23.6 Assume an economy is characterized by two consumers, Steve and Jan, and two goods, cheeseburgers and onion rings. Jan's initial endowment contains 1 cheeseburger and 5 onion rings. Steve's initial endowment contains 2 cheeseburgers and 3 onion rings.
   a. Construct the Edgeworth box for this economy.
   b. Indicate each consumer's initial endowment in the Edgeworth box.

23.7 Assume there are two consumers in the economy, consumer A and consumer B, and two goods, X and Y. Consumer A's initial endowment contains 3 units of good X and 4 units of good Y. Consumer B's initial endowment contains 5 units of good X and 3 units of good Y. At her initial endowment, consumer A's marginal rate of substitution of good X for good Y is 4. At his initial endowment, consumer B's marginal rate of substitution is 2.

a. Construct the Edgeworth box for this economy.

b. Indicate each consumer's initial endowment.

c. Is this allocation of goods Pareto optimal? Explain your response.

d. Does this allocation of goods lie on the contract curve? Explain your response.

23.8 Assume an economy characterized by two consumers, A and B, and two goods, X and Y. The price of good X is \$8 and the price of good Y is \$2. Consumer A purchases 2 units of good X and 5 units of good Y. Her marginal rate of substitution of good X for good Y at her goods combination is 2. Consumer B purchases 3 units of good X and 2 units of good Y. His marginal rate of substitution at his goods combination is 6.

a. Is consumer A maximizing her utility when she purchases 2 units of good X and 5 units of good Y? Explain your response.

b. Is consumer B maximizing his utility when he purchases 3 units of good X and 2 units of good Y? Explain your response.

c. Is this allocation of goods purchased by the consumers Pareto optimal? Explain your response.

d. Is this allocation of goods purchased by the consumers a competitive equilibrium? Explain your response.

e. Can either consumer reallocate his or her spending on goods X and Y and increase his or her utility? If so, what should each consumer do?

CHAPTER 24

General Equilibrium Analysis in an Economy with Production and Exchange

24.1 INTRODUCTION

In the previous chapter we developed the concept of general equilibrium under the assumption that two individuals comprising a simplified economy each receive an initial endowment of goods they can choose to exchange with one another. We also assumed that together these initial endowments constitute the total amount of goods available in the economy, and since we also assumed that no production takes place, this total amount of goods is necessarily fixed. In the real world, however, the production of goods in an economy is not fixed. Therefore, in an effort to make our general equilibrium analysis more realistic, we will now modify our former simplistic model of the economy to include the production of goods.

Specifically, we will assume that two inputs, capital and labor, are available in the economy in fixed quantities, and are used to produce the same two goods, X and Y, as in our previous exchange analysis. However, rather than assuming that consumers are given an initial endowment of goods, we will assume that firms receive fixed initial supplies of the two inputs. Once again we will use the Edgeworth box to analyze the attainment of general equilibrium, except now our analysis pertains to a production-based economy. Once this is accomplished, we will devote the remainder of this chapter to examining the concepts of production efficiency, the efficiency of a competitive production equilibrium, and the inefficiency created by monopoly power in a market.

24.2 EDGEWORTH BOX IN A PRODUCTION ECONOMY

The Edgeworth box we used to develop the pure exchange analysis in the previous chapter must be modified before we can use it to depict the process of general equilibrium in a simplified production economy. Specifically, an **Edgeworth production box** is *a rectangle containing all feasible combinations of two inputs, labor and capital, available in the economy that can be used in the production of two goods, where the length of the box measures the total amount of labor input available in the economy, and the height of the box measures the total amount of capital available.* The Edgeworth production box in Figure 24.1 illustrates the total amounts of labor and capital, denoted L^T and K^T, respectively, available for use in the production of goods X and Y. Each

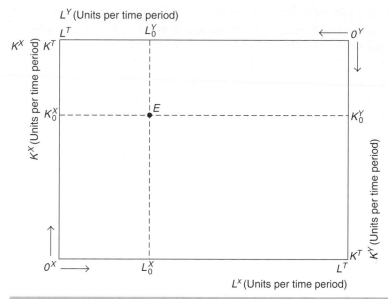

FIGURE 24.1 Edgeworth Production Box with Initial Allocation of Capital and Labor Inputs Used to Produce Goods X and Y

point lying in the Edgeworth production box, inclusive of its perimeter, represents a feasible combination of labor and capital inputs that can be used in the production of either good X, good Y, or some combination of both goods.

We construct the Edgeworth production box in a manner similar to the Edgeworth box developed in the previous chapter. The Edgeworth production box measures the quantity of labor input used in the production of good X, L^X, from left to right along the bottom of the box. The quantity of the capital input used in the production of good X, K^X, is measured from bottom to top along the left-hand side of the box. The point at which these two perpendicular sides of the Edgeworth production box intersect represents the origin, denoted 0^X, with respect to the use of inputs in the production of good X. This origin represents an input combination where zero units of labor and zero units of capital are allocated to the production of good X. We represent increases in the use of labor in the production of good X by rightward movements from 0^X, while increases in the use of capital in the production of this good are indicated by upward movements along the left-hand side of the Edgeworth production box from the good X origin, 0^X. Temporarily ignoring the top and right-hand sides of the Edgeworth production box, we can recognize that the remaining bottom and left-hand sides of the box replicate, respectively, the horizontal and vertical axes of the two-dimensional graphs in input space used throughout Chapters 9 and 10 to develop long-run production theory.

The Edgeworth production box also simultaneously measures the allocation of inputs for use in the production of good Y. In particular, we measure the quantity of labor used in the production of good Y, L^Y, along the top of the box, while the number of units of capital used in the production of good Y, K^Y, is measured along the right-hand side of the box. The point at which these two perpendicular sides of the Edgeworth production box intersect represents the origin, denoted 0^Y, with respect to the use of inputs in the production of good Y. This origin represents an input combination where zero units of labor and zero units of capital are allocated to the production of good Y. Note that we represent increases in the use of labor in the production of good Y by leftward movements along the top of the Edgeworth production box away from the relevant origin, 0^Y. Increases in the use of capital in the production of good Y are shown by downward movements along the right-hand side of the box away from the good Y origin, 0^Y. Temporarily ignoring the bottom and left-hand sides of the Edgeworth production box, we can recognize that the remaining top and right-hand sides replicate the horizontal and vertical axes of the two-dimensional graphs in input space, rotated 180 degrees.

Earlier we mentioned that the particular dimensions of an Edgeworth production box are determined by the total fixed quantities of the inputs, labor and capital, available in the economy. Therefore, the more labor available in the economy, the greater is the length of the box, and the more capital, the greater is the height of the box. The total amount of labor available in the economy, L^T, is equal to the sum of the number of units of labor used in the production of good X, L^X, and the number of units of labor used in the production of good Y, L^Y. Similarly, the total amount of capital available, K^T, is equal to the sum of the number of units of capital used in the production of good X, K^X, and the number of units of capital used in the production of good Y, K^Y. Therefore, given some initial distribution of labor and capital in the economy, as we have depicted as point E in Figure 24.1, L_0^X units of labor are used in the production of good X and L_0^Y units of labor are used in the production of good Y, or

$$L^T = L_0^X + L_0^Y.$$

Similarly, K_0^X units of capital are used in the production of good X, and K_0^Y units of capital are used in the production of good Y, or

$$K^T = K_0^X + K_0^Y.$$

These relationships also hold true for all other allocations of labor and capital in the Edgeworth production box. Any allocation of labor used in the production of goods X and Y for which

$$(L^X + L^Y) < L^T$$

indicates that there is some unemployment of labor in the economy. Similarly, any allocation of capital used in the production of goods X and Y for which

$$(K^X + K^Y) < K^T$$

indicates that there is unemployment of capital.

24.3   PRODUCTION IN THE EDGEWORTH BOX

In Chapters 9 and 10 we used two-dimensional graphs, measuring the quantity of the labor input on the horizontal axis and the quantity of the capital input on the vertical axis, to illustrate a firm's production capabilities with respect to a single output. However, we can use an Edgeworth production box to demonstrate the simultaneous production of two goods, such as X and Y, in an economy, given fixed amounts of labor and capital. Specifically, within the Edgeworth production box, we can plot isoquant mappings for each good illustrating the allocation of inputs used in the production of these two goods, as well as the associated levels of output of each good. In Figure 24.2 we have illustrated strictly convex isoquant mappings for goods X and Y.

From the perspective of the production of good X, we can see that the isoquants are plotted in the conventional manner, where each isoquant indicates all of the alternative combinations of labor and capital capable of producing a particular level of good X, Q^X. The level of output produced increases along each successively higher isoquant. Therefore, in Figure 24.2 we have plotted four isoquants, Q_0^X, Q_1^X. Q_2^X, and

FIGURE 24.2 Edgeworth Production Box Containing Isoquants and Initial Allocation of Capital and Labor Inputs Used to Produce Goods X and Y

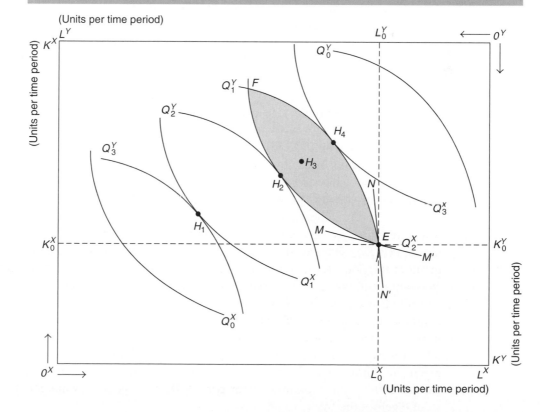

Q_3^X, indicating four different levels of good X, where $Q_0^X < Q_1^X < Q_2^X < Q_3^X$. We have also illustrated four isoquants for good Y in this figure. However, since the origin for good Y is located in the upper right-hand corner of the Edgeworth production box, an isoquant mapping for good Y must demonstrate higher levels of output for each successively lower plotted isoquant moving in a southwesternly direction relative to the origin for good Y, 0^Y. Thus, regarding these four isoquants, $Q_0^Y < Q_1^Y < Q_2^Y < Q_3^Y$.

Let's initially assume that the fixed supplies of labor and capital are allocated to the production of goods X and Y as indicated by point E in Figure 24.2. This allocation corresponds to the input combinations, (L_0^X, K_0^X), used in the production of good X, and (L_0^Y, K_0^Y), used in the production of good Y. At this initial allocation of inputs, Q_2^X units of good X are produced along with Q_1^Y units of good Y. A closer inspection of the initial allocations of labor and capital between the production of goods X and Y reveals, for the case illustrated, that relatively more labor than capital is used to produce good X and relatively more capital than labor is used to produce good Y.

Since the amounts of capital and labor in this economy available to produce goods X and Y are fixed at particular levels, the quantities of these goods produced are limited. Thus, given this scarcity of inputs, it is in our interest to determine whether the input allocations used to produce the goods X and Y are **technically efficient**, defined as *input allocations for which the output of one good cannot be increased without decreasing the output of another good*. To determine whether an input allocation, such as that represented as point E in Figure 24.2, is technically efficient, we must evaluate the marginal rate of technical substitution for each good produced at this point. Recall from Section 9.4 of Chapter 9 that the marginal rate of technical substitution, or *MRTS*, measures the rate at which one input can be substituted for another input in a production process while producing some constant level of output. Also recall that we can measure this marginal rate of technical substitution as the negative of the slope of a line drawn tangent to an isoquant. Therefore, by sketching a line tangent to each isoquant at the initial input allocations indicated at point E, we can evaluate the marginal rates of technical substitution between units of labor and units of capital used in the production of each good.

In the case of good X, we have drawn the line MM' tangent to the Q_2^X isoquant at the initial input combination (L_0^X, K_0^X) as shown in Figure 24.2. Similarly, we have drawn the line NN' tangent to the Q_1^Y isoquant for good Y at the initial input combination (L_0^Y, K_0^Y). Observe that the slope of the line MM' drawn tangent to the Q_2^X isoquant at the point E is flatter than the slope of NN', the line drawn tangent to the Q_1^Y isoquant at this same initial input allocation. Since the marginal rate of technical substitution is measured as the negative of the slope of the isoquant at a particular input combination, we can readily infer from this graphical analysis that at the respective initial input allocations for each good, the marginal rate of technical substitution of labor for capital in the production of good X is less than that for good Y. As a result, given the initial input allocations, it is easier to substitute units of labor for units of capital in the production process for good Y than for good X, while maintaining constant levels of the two outputs.

This outcome seems reasonable, given the relatively large amount of capital in the initial input allocation used to produce good Y, (L_0^Y, K_0^Y). After substituting some units of labor for units of capital in this situation, there is still a sufficient amount of capital with which labor can work. Conversely, in the production of good X, where the initial input allocation, (L_0^X, K_0^X), contains a relatively large number of units of labor along with a small amount of capital, it is relatively easy to substitute units of capital for units of labor, while still producing a constant level of output. Therefore, given the relative ease with which labor can be substituted for capital in the production of good Y, and the ease with which capital can be substituted for labor in the production of good X, it seems logical that a feasible alternative allocation of labor and capital can be determined that might result in an increase in the level of output of one or both of these goods in the economy.

In general, we base this line of reasoning on the fact that more efficient mixes of the inputs can be used in the production process of the two goods. Thus, if the marginal rates of technical substitution for each good are not equal at an input allocation, the potential exists for increasing the level of production of one or both goods, while not decreasing the production of either good, by altering the allocation of inputs in an economy. We can observe in the Edgeworth production box shown in Figure 24.2 that an alternative allocation of labor and capital represented by any of the input combinations lying strictly in the shaded region results in an increase in the level of production of both goods. Recall that every point lying within the Edgeworth production box or on its perimeter constitutes a feasible input combination that lies on some isoquant. Therefore, it is possible for us to sketch two isoquants—one for good X and one for good Y—through any point lying in the shaded region in Figure 24.2, representing higher levels of output for each good than those levels generated using the initial input combinations indicated by point E.

For example, shifting units of labor from the production of good X to the production of good Y, and simultaneously reallocating units of capital from the production of good Y to the production of good X, results in a new input allocation, such as the one shown as H_3 in Figure 24.2. We can sketch an isoquant for good X through this new allocation of inputs, H_3, which represents a higher level of production than Q_2^X, the output level of good X associated with the initial input allocation at point E. Similarly, we can draw an additional isoquant for good Y that also contains the input allocation depicted by point H_3. This new isoquant lies beneath the Q_1^Y isoquant and therefore corresponds to a higher level of output than that associated with Q_1^Y, the isoquant on which the initial input combination is located.

We have illustrated this new isoquant mapping in Figure 24.3. This figure contains all of the information presented in Figure 24.2, along with the new isoquants for goods X and Y. Note that $Q_2^{X\prime}$ lies above Q_2^X, indicating $Q_2^{X\prime} > Q_2^X$, and $Q_1^{Y\prime}$ lies beneath Q_1^Y, indicating $Q_1^{Y\prime} > Q_1^Y$. We can observe that the two new isoquants for goods X and Y, $Q_2^{X\prime}$ and $Q_1^{Y\prime}$, respectively, are tangent at the point H_3, corresponding to new labor and capital allocations of (L_3^X, K_3^X) and (L_3^Y, K_3^Y) for goods X and Y, respectively. Since these isoquants are tangent at this point, the marginal rates of

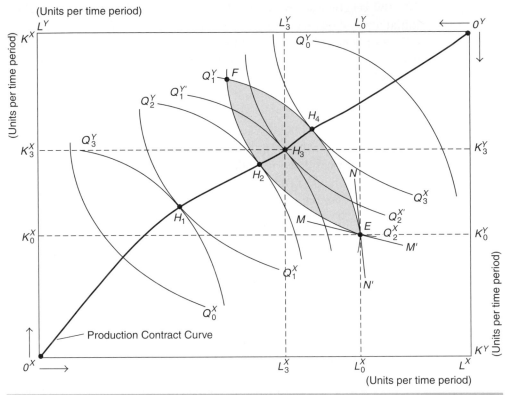

FIGURE 24.3 Edgeworth Production Box Containing Both Initial and New Input Allocations for Goods X and Y, along with Production Contract Curve

technical substitution for the production of both goods are equal at this particular distribution of labor and capital in the economy.

We previously mentioned that it is also possible to redistribute the initial input allocation in our example so that the level of production of only one of the two goods increases, while production of the other remains unchanged. For example, we can move a relatively small number of units of labor from the production of good X to the production of good Y while also redistributing a relatively large number of units of capital from the production of good Y to the production of good X. In Figures 24.2 and 24.3, we represent this reallocation of inputs in the economy as a movement from the initial combination of labor and capital, point E, to one such as point H_4. This change results in a higher level of production of good X, as indicated by the fact that the new input combination associated with point H_4 lies on a higher isoquant, Q_3^X, than the one previously attained, Q_2^X, using the original input allocation (L_0^X, K_0^X). This new distribution of inputs leaves the level of production of good Y unchanged, since point G_4 lies on the same isoquant for good Y, Q_1^Y. Observe in Figures 24.2 and 24.3 that at point H_4, the isoquant for good X, Q_3^X, and the isoquant for good Y, Q_1^Y, are tangent. This indicates that the marginal rates of technical substitution for the production of each good are equal at this distribution of inputs.

Finally, it is also possible to reallocate the initial distribution of inputs so that only the production of good Y increases, while the production of good X remains unchanged. This result is accomplished by switching a relatively large number of units of labor from the production of good X to the production of good Y, while also transferring a somewhat smaller number of units of capital from the production of good Y to the production of good X. Ultimately, this reallocation achieves an input combination that we represent as point H_2 in Figures 24.2 and 24.3. At this input allocation, the level of output associated with the isoquant for good Y is Q_2^Y, a greater amount than the Q_1^Y level of output represented by the isoquant for good Y containing the initial input allocation, point E. In this case, the production of good X remains unchanged because the new distribution of labor and capital, represented by point H_2, lies on Q_2^X, the same isoquant pertaining to the initial input allocation represented by point E. It is also important to note in Figures 24.2 and 24.3 that, at the labor and capital combination indicated by point H_2 in each figure, the Q_2^X isoquant for good X and the Q_2^Y isoquant for good Y are tangent, indicating that the marginal rates of technical substitution for the production of both goods are equal at this allocation of inputs.

24.4   PRODUCTION CONTRACT CURVE

In the previous section, we demonstrated that if an allocation of inputs, such as labor and capital, is efficient, then it is not possible to reallocate these inputs in a manner enabling an increase in the production of one good without reducing the production of another. Alternatively, if the marginal rates of technical substitution for the production of each good are not equal at a particular allocation of inputs in the economy, then we can redistribute the fixed quantities of labor and capital so as to produce greater amounts of both goods or a greater amount of one of the goods without simultaneously experiencing a reduction in the production level of the other. In summary, once the marginal rates of technical substitution are equalized at a particular input allocation, no net gain in the production of output can be achieved by redistributing the resources between the production of the goods. In Figure 24.3 we have indicated several efficient allocations of labor and capital, where the marginal rate of technical substitution for the production of good X is equal to the marginal rate of technical substitution for the production of good Y. Specifically, at the labor and capital allocations we have depicted as points H_1, H_2, H_3, and H_4 in Figure 24.3, the isoquants representing alternative levels of production of goods X and Y are tangent. Hence, $MRTS_1^X = MRTS_1^Y$ at H_1, $MRTS_2^X = MRTS_2^Y$ at H_2, $MRTS_3^X = MRTS_3^Y$ at H_3, and $MRTS_4^X = MRTS_4^Y$ at H_4. Clearly, the input allocations represented at the points H_1, H_2, H_3, and H_4 are efficient from a production perspective since movement away from any one of these input combinations, in an effort to increase production of one good, results in a decrease in production of the other good. For example, movement from point H_2 to H_1 results in an increase in the production of good Y from Q_2^Y to Q_3^Y but a simultaneous decrease in the production of good X from Q_2^X to Q_1^X.

In general, the input allocations in an Edgeworth production box for which the marginal rates of technical substitution pertaining to the production of two goods are equal lie on a **production contract curve**, or *a set of input allocations within an Edgeworth production box that are efficient*. Specifically, in Figure 24.3, we have designated the production contract curve as the curve passing through the origin for good X, 0^X, the efficient input combinations represented by the points H_1, H_2, H_3, and H_4, and the good Y origin, 0^Y. An infinite number of other allocations of labor and capital also lie on the production contract curve, determined by the infinite number of points of tangency between isoquants plotted in the Edgeworth production box. Referring once again to the production contract curve shown in Figure 24.3, movement from one point on the curve, for example H_3, to another point on the curve, say H_4, results in an increase in the level of production of good X from $Q_2^{X'}$ to Q_3^X, accompanied by a decrease in the amount of good Y produced from $Q_1^{Y'}$ to Q_1^Y. Input allocations not lying on the production contract curve are not efficient since movement away from such an allocation to one represented by a point on the production contract curve results in an increase in the level of production of at least one of the two goods, without reducing production of the other. For example, movement from an input allocation not lying on the production contract curve, such as point F in Figure 24.3, to an efficient allocation, such as H_2 on the production contract curve, results in an increase in the production of good Y from Q_1^Y to Q_2^Y, while leaving the production of good X unchanged at Q_2^X units. Therefore, input allocations such as points F and E in Figure 24.3, as well as any other input combinations not lying on the production contract curve, cannot represent efficient allocations of inputs. This conclusion follows, because at these points it is possible to redistribute the finite amounts of capital and labor available in the economy to produce a greater combined number of units of goods X and Y.

24.5 PRODUCTION WITH COMPETITIVELY DETERMINED INPUT PRICES

In the previous section, we used the Edgeworth production box to demonstrate how efficient production of two goods in an economy can be achieved. We showed this result by redistributing the fixed supplies of inputs used to produce the goods to the point where the marginal rates of technical substitution for producing both goods are equal. Note that in that analysis we used no information regarding the prices of the two inputs, capital and labor, used to produce the two goods, X and Y. However, input prices, in particular relative input prices, play a crucial role in determining the types and quantities of goods produced in an economy. As discussed in Chapter 10, we derived from a partial equilibrium perspective the necessary condition for a constrained cost minimum for a firm operating in a perfectly competitive input market. This condition states that a firm employs a combination of capital and labor for which the marginal rate of technical substitution between these inputs is equal to the ratio of their prices. It follows that if a firm uses some combination of labor and capital for which this equality does not hold true, then by purchasing and using a different input combination, it is possible for this firm to reduce its production costs while still producing the same predetermined level of output.

From a graphical perspective, when a firm purchases and uses a combination of inputs that minimizes its costs of production subject to its production constraint, the isoquant representing the firm's predetermined level of output is tangent to the isocost equation corresponding to its minimum cost for producing this level of output. This tangency necessarily implies that, at the optimal combination of labor and capital, the slope of the relevant isoquant, which we measure as the negative of the marginal rate of technical substitution, equals the slope of the isocost equation, or

$$-MRTS = \frac{-P_L}{P_K}.$$

After multiplying both sides of this equation by negative one, we obtain the familiar necessary condition for a constrained cost minimum as

$$MRTS = \frac{P_L}{P_K}.$$

We can use an Edgeworth production box to demonstrate that the necessary condition for a constrained cost minimum simultaneously holds true for two firms choosing to employ optimal combinations of inputs, provided the prices of these inputs are determined in perfectly competitive markets. In Figure 24.4 we have illustrated an Edgeworth production box for two goods, X and Y, that are produced using capital and labor. This figure contains two isoquants for good X, Q_1^X and Q_2^X, where $Q_2^X > Q_1^X$, along with two isoquants for good Y, Q_1^Y and Q_2^Y, where $Q_2^Y > Q_1^Y$. At the initial allocation of inputs, labeled point E, L_0^X units of labor and K_0^X units of capital are used to produce Q_1^X units of good X, while at the same time L_0^Y units of labor and K_0^Y units of capital are used to produce Q_1^Y units of good Y. Also included in this figure is the line RR' which we refer to as the input price line since the slope of this line reflects the negative of the ratio of the competitively determined prices of labor and capital, or $-P_L/P_K$. Observe in Figure 24.4 that the initial allocations of labor and capital are not efficient since at this input allocation $MRTS^X < P_L/P_K$ and $MRTS^Y > P_L/P_K$. Hence, $MRTS^X < MRTS^Y$, implying that this allocation of inputs does not lie on the production contract curve. Thus, by reallocating $(L_0^X - L_1^X) = (L_1^Y - L_0^Y)$ units of labor from the production of good X to the production of good Y, and $(K_1^X - K_0^X) = (K_0^Y - K_1^Y)$ units of capital from the production of good Y to the production of good X, greater amounts of both goods can be produced in the economy. We have indicated this new allocation of inputs by point H_1. At H_1 the rate at which labor and capital can be exchanged in the production of goods X and Y is equal to the slope of the input price line, RR'. Specifically, the slope of the input price line is measured as Δ rise/Δ run; thus, between points E and H_1 we compute the slope of RR' as $(K_1^X - K_0^X)/(L_0^X - L_1^X)$. This value is also equal to the slope of the Q_2^X isoquant for good X at the combination

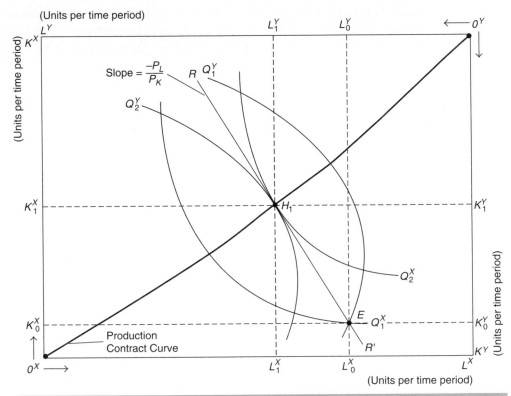

FIGURE 24.4 Production Equilibrium under Competitively Determined Input Prices

of inputs represented by H_1, as well as the slope of the Q_2^Y isoquant for good Y at this same point. Therefore, it is clear that the rates at which labor and capital can be substituted in the production of goods X and Y at H_1 are equal, or $MRTS^X = MRTS^Y$, where these rates are also equal to the ratio of the competitively determined input prices, P_L/P_K. Since the isoquants for the two goods are tangent to one another at H_1, this allocation of inputs must also be efficient and thus lie on the production contract curve passing through the points 0^X, H_1, and 0^Y.

Also observe in Figure 24.4 that at the new distribution of labor and capital between the production of goods X and Y, indicated by H_1, there is neither an excess supply nor an excess demand for either input. Recall that when these inputs are redistributed from the initial allocations in accordance with their competitively determined relative prices, the quantity of labor redistributed from the production of good X, $(L_0^X - L_1^X)$, is equal to the additional amount of labor used to increase the production of good Y, $(L_1^Y - L_0^Y)$. Similarly, the quantity of capital traded away from the production of good Y and subsequently used in the production of good X, $(K_0^Y - K_1^Y)$, is equal to the additional quantity of capital used to increase the production of good X, $(K_1^X - K_0^X)$. Therefore, after the labor and capital inputs are redistributed, the markets for labor and capital are in equilibrium, since there exists no excess supply or excess demand for either input. This result demonstrates that an allocation of inputs pertaining to a competitively determined equilibrium is also efficient since at such an allocation, it follows that

$$MRTS^X = \frac{P_L}{P_K}$$

and

$$MRTS^Y = \frac{P_L}{P_K},$$

and therefore,

$$MRTS^X = MRTS^Y.$$

As a result, it is not possible to deviate from a competitively determined distribution of inputs, such as that represented by point H_1 in Figure 24.4, without reducing the level of production of at least one of the goods. This result indicates, once again, the ability of perfectly competitive markets to allocate resources to their most efficient uses.

24.6 PRODUCTION POSSIBILITIES FRONTIER

Using the information contained in the Edgeworth production box, we can plot the efficient input combinations in goods space to indicate the quantities of goods X and Y associated with every point on the production contract curve. By doing so, we can derive a curve with which you should be familiar from your principles of microeconomics course. Specifically, this curve is the **production possibilities frontier**, defined as *a set of points measuring the combinations of two goods that can be simultaneously produced, corresponding to allocations of labor and capital lying on a production contract curve.* Each point on the production possibilities frontier represents the maximum quantities of two goods that can be simultaneously produced when the fixed levels of inputs available in the economy are used efficiently. Therefore, any point on this production possibilities frontier corresponds to an efficient allocation of inputs lying on the production contract curve. Conversely, any point beneath the production possibilities frontier corresponds to an inefficient allocation of inputs. Such an input allocation does not lie on the production contract curve, since by reallocating resources it is possible to increase the production of one or both goods, thus moving the economy to a combination of outputs where the production of goods is maximized. Any point that lies above the production possibilities frontier is associated with an allocation of inputs that lies outside of the Edgeworth production box. Therefore, in this situation, the associated production levels of goods are not attainable given the fixed amounts of inputs available in the economy. A combination of goods associated with such a point can only be achieved by a sufficient increase in the total allocation of inputs in the economy, thereby causing the production possibilities frontier to shift to the right.

The process by which we derive the production possibilities frontier from the Edgeworth production box is illustrated in panels (A) and (B) of Figure 24.5. In this figure, panel (A) contains an Edgeworth production box in which we have plotted several isoquants for two goods, X and Y, along with the associated production contract curve. The corresponding production possibilities frontier is shown in panel (B). Referring initially to panel (A), we have illustrated three isoquants for good X, represented by Q_1^X, Q_2^X, and Q_3^X, where $Q_1^X < Q_2^X < Q_3^X$, and three isoquants for good Y, represented by Q_1^Y, Q_2^Y, and Q_3^Y, where $Q_1^Y < Q_2^Y < Q_3^Y$. These isoquants are all strictly convex and indicate increasing levels of output as they lie farther away from the origin of the respective good. We have indicated the points of tangency between the isoquants for good X and good Y by the input combinations at the points H_1, H_2, and H_3, showing that these three points, along with the origin for each good, 0^X and 0^Y, lie on the production contract curve.

To construct the production possibilities frontier, it is necessary for us to focus on the amount of each good produced at each point on the production contract curve. Beginning with the origin for good X, 0^X, it is clear that since zero units of labor and zero units of capital are allocated to the production of good X, no units of this good are being produced with this allocation of inputs. However, when no inputs are being used in the production of good X, it is possible to allocate all labor and capital available in the economy solely to the production of good Y, and to generate the maximum quantity of good Y that can be produced. Therefore, the origin for good X, 0^X, in the Edgeworth production box in panel (A) of Figure 24.5 must correspond to the point 0^A, the vertical intercept of the production possibilities frontier, shown in panel (B). Similarly, the point 0^Y, the origin for good Y in the Edgeworth production box, corresponds to the use of zero units of labor and capital in the production of good Y, indicating that zero units of good Y are produced. At this combination of inputs, the maximum amount of good X is produced, since all inputs available in the economy are being used to produce good X. Thus, this input combination corresponds to the point 0^Y in panel (B), the horizontal intercept of the production possibilities frontier. We can easily determine the production levels of goods X and Y corresponding to the remaining efficient combinations of capital and labor lying on the production contract curve from the labels identifying each isoquant. Specifically, at the input allocation represented by point H_1 in panel (A) of Figure 24.5, Q_1^X units of good X are produced using the input combination (L_1^X, K_1^X), while a much greater allocation of both labor and capital, (L_1^Y, K_1^Y), is used to produce Q_3^Y units of good Y. As a result, the quantity of good Y produced at this point is much greater than the quantity of good X, or $Q_3^Y > Q_1^X$. We have plotted the associated output combination, (Q_1^X, Q_3^Y), as a point on the production possibilities frontier in panel (B) of Figure 24.5. Similarly, the output combinations associated with points H_2 and H_3 on the production contract curve are plotted in panel (B) as the points (Q_2^X, Q_2^Y) and (Q_3^X, Q_1^Y), respectively, on the production possibilities frontier.

In general, the production possibilities frontier possesses a negative slope because as greater amounts of inputs are used in the production of one good, thereby increas-

Panel (A)
Edgeworth Production Box with
Production Contract Curve

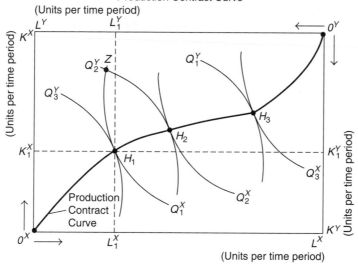

Panel (B)
Production Possibilities Frontier

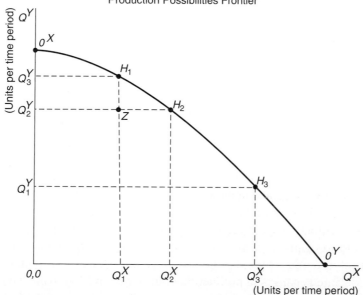

FIGURE 24.5 Derivation of Production Possibilities Frontier from Production Contract Curve

ing the quantity of this good produced, fewer inputs remain to be used in the production of the other good, thus necessarily causing its level of production to decline. Alternatively stated, the negative of the slope of the production possibilities frontier, which we also know as the **marginal rate of transformation**, denoted **MRT**, *measures the rate at which the production of one good must be reduced to release enough labor and capital to produce an additional unit of another good.* Typically, we draw the production possibilities frontier concave with respect to its origin. This shape indicates that the marginal rate of transformation increases, in absolute value terms, as additional units of the good plotted on the horizontal axis are produced in place of the good plotted on the vertical axis. For example, observe in panel (B) of Figure 24.5 that, as the production of good Y is reduced from Q_3^Y to Q_2^Y, the production of good X increases from Q_1^X to Q_2^X. These results reflect a movement from left to right along the production possibilities frontier from the output combination represented by point H_1 to the one we designate as point H_2. This movement results in an increase in the absolute value of the marginal rate of transformation. This indicates that there is a higher cost associated with the production of additional units of good X, in terms of foregone units of good Y, at point H_2 than at point H_1 along the production possibilities frontier.

In panel (B) of Figure 24.5, we have plotted the input allocation designated by point Z in the Edgeworth production box, associated with Q_1^X units of good X and Q_2^Y units of good Y, as a point lying strictly beneath the production possibilities frontier. This input combination is not efficient inasmuch as it does not lie on the production contract curve and therefore at point Z, $MRTS^X > MRTS^Y$. By allocating labor and capital differently, it is possible to increase the production of one or both goods to generate the output levels associated with points H_1, H_2, or any of the infinite number of points lying between H_1 and H_2 on the production possibilities frontier. For example, it is possible to reduce the amount of labor used in the production of good Y and transfer it to the production of good X, while simultaneously reducing the amount of capital used in the production of good X and transferring it to the production of good Y. By doing so, it is possible to redistribute the inputs available in the economy so that $MRTS^X = MRTS^Y$. We have demonstrated this process in panel (A) of Figure 24.5 as movement from the input allocation designated by point Z to point H_2, lying on the production contract curve. By reallocating inputs in this manner, it is possible to increase the level of production of good X from Q_1^X to Q_2^X, while still producing the original level of output of good Y, Q_2^Y. We have represented this reallocation of inputs and the associated changes in production of goods X and Y in panel (B) of Figure 24.5 as movement from the inefficient combination of outputs designated by point Z, lying beneath the production possibilities frontier, to the efficient combination of outputs represented by point H_2 that lies on the production possibilities frontier.

From a social perspective, a point on the production possibilities frontier is preferable to one that lies beneath it. This conclusion follows because any point lying on the production possibilities frontier represents a greater combination of outputs that can be produced via the efficient allocation of scarce resources in the economy than does

a point lying beneath the frontier. However, it is impossible for us to discern which point on the curve represents the most desirable combination of goods from an overall social perspective. To make such a determination, we need additional information concerning society's preferences regarding the mix of goods desired in the economy.

24.7   DETERMINATION OF GENERAL EQUILIBRIUM OF PRODUCTION AND EXCHANGE

In the previous chapter, we demonstrated that for a given initial endowment of two goods, X and Y, two consumers, A and B, can determine a Pareto optimal allocation of these goods merely by engaging in exchange until their marginal rates of substitution between the two goods are equal, or

$$MRS^A = MRS^B.$$

We also showed that if the consumers exchange the goods in accordance with their relative prices, P_X/P_Y, a Pareto optimal outcome can once again be achieved. In this chapter, our focus has been on the production of the two goods, X and Y, using fixed quantities of labor and capital. We have demonstrated that an efficient allocation of inputs exists when the units of capital and labor available in the economy are distributed between the production of goods X and Y such that

$$MRTS^X = MRTS^Y.$$

Furthermore, an efficient allocation of labor and capital can also be achieved when the inputs are exchanged on the basis of their relative prices, P_L/P_K. Finally, we derived the production possibilities frontier by transferring the output levels associated with the efficient input combinations from the Edgeworth production box to a graph in output space. Each point on the production possibilities frontier represents the maximum quantities of the two goods that can be produced using the fixed levels of inputs available in the economy. Yet, even though we can determine the set of efficient input allocations in the economy, along with the maximum quantities of outputs associated with each efficient input combination, we cannot determine which output combination, or point on the production possibilities frontier, represents society's most desired combination of outputs. However, we can determine an efficient mix of outputs at which the economy is in general equilibrium. We will demonstrate this result by bringing together the Pareto optimal condition established when equilibrium is achieved via pure exchange among consumers, $MRS^A = MRS^B$, with the efficiency condition that prevails when equilibrium is established in input markets, $MRTS^X = MRTS^Y$.

In Chapter 23, we defined the concept of general equilibrium as the process by which simultaneous equilibrium is attained in all output and input markets and for all consumers and firms comprising those markets. We can demonstrate this process using the two necessary conditions. The first pertains to a Pareto optimal distribution of goods for two consumers and for two goods, such as X and Y. The second is for the attainment of an efficient allocation of labor and capital used in producing the two goods.

For general equilibrium to be established, the equilibrium conditions for c̶ sumer exchange and production must hold simultaneously, or

$$MRS^A = MRS^B$$

and

$$MRTS^X = MRTS^Y,$$

where any such allocation of inputs yielding equal marginal rates of technical substitution is associated with a particular efficient output combination lying on the production possibilities frontier. Recall that the negative of the slope of a line drawn tangent to any point on the production possibilities frontier measures the rate at which units of one good can be transformed into a unit of the other good by reallocating resources, where this rate is known as the marginal rate of transformation, or *MRT*. From a consumption perspective, for a particular efficient combination of goods lying on the production possibilities frontier to be Pareto optimal, the rate at which one good can be transformed into the other must also be equal to the rate at which the consumers are willing to substitute the two goods for each other. Therefore, at any combination of goods constituting general equilibrium in an economy, not only will

$$MRS^A = MRS^B$$

and

$$MRTS^X = MRTS^Y$$

but

$$MRS^A = MRS^B = MRT.$$

At such a combination, the finite quantities of labor and capital available in the economy are efficiently used in the production of goods X and Y, and the total quantities of these goods are distributed between consumers A and B such that one consumer cannot be made better off without reducing the utility received by the other. Therefore, we can also state that any combination of goods for which a consumer's marginal rate of substitution does not equal the marginal rate of transformation cannot represent a Pareto optimal allocation. In this situation, there exists some way to better allocate the finite labor and capital inputs in the economy so as to produce an alternative mix of goods X and Y that will make at least one consumer happier, while not reducing the utility received by the other.

For example, suppose that at a particular goods combination, consumer A's marginal rate of substitution of good X for good Y is equal to one, showing that he is willing to give up one unit of good Y to receive an additional unit of good X and still maintain the same level of utility. Also suppose, at the goods combination currently produced, that the marginal rate of transformation between goods X and Y is 3, indicating that in order to produce an additional unit of good X, three units of good Y must be foregone. Thus, by reducing the production of X by one unit, 3 additional units of good Y can be produced, which will in turn increase the consumer's utility

since he can receive 3 units of good Y in exchange for giving up a unit of good X. For an efficient allocation of goods to be Pareto optimal, not only must the consumers' marginal rates of substitution equal each other, but they must also equal the marginal rate of transformation between the two goods.

By bringing together the consumption-oriented Edgeworth box with the production possibilities frontier, we can illustrate the concept of general equilibrium for a simplified two-consumer, two-goods, two-input economy. By reviewing the Edgeworth box depicted in the previous chapter in Figure 23.6, and the Edgeworth production box, along with the associated production possibilities frontier illustrated, respectively, in panels (A) and (B) of Figure 24.5, we can observe that they share common variables, namely, the output level of good X and the output level of good Y. These variables provide the necessary linkages by which we can demonstrate the concept of general equilibrium. Specifically, in Figure 24.6 a production possibilities frontier is shown for the two goods X and Y, where we have selected for analysis the goods combination (X_1, Y_1) from the infinite number of efficient goods allocations lying on the

FIGURE 24.6 Production Possibilities Frontier, Edgeworth Box, and General Equilibrium for Production and Consumption

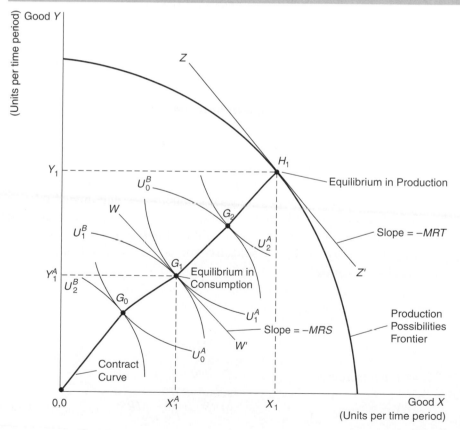

production possibilities frontier. Given any efficient allocation of goods, we can construct a corresponding Edgeworth box with dimensions determined by the total quantities of goods X and Y produced in the economy. In Figure 24.6, we have illustrated an Edgeworth box for the present case, where X_1 units of good X and Y_1 units of good Y are produced in the economy. Note that we have constructed it within the interior of the production possibilities frontier; thus, the dimensions of this Edgeworth box are consistent with the quantities of both goods produced. Specifically, it is X_1 units in length and Y_1 units high. Within this Edgeworth box, we have plotted indifference curve mappings for consumers A and B, along with the contract curve, indicating the set of Pareto optimal goods allocations between these consumers.

While the three goods combinations, G_0, G_1, and G_2, lying on the contract curve all represent Pareto optimal allocations of goods, only G_1 represents a general equilibrium outcome in the economy. This result occurs because only at this goods allocation is the marginal rate of substitution for consumers A and B—measured as the negative of the slope of the line WW' drawn tangent to the consumers' indifference curves at point G_1—equal to the marginal rate of transformation for goods X and Y—measured as the negative of the slope of the line ZZ' drawn tangent to the production possibilities frontier at the output combination (X_1, Y_1). Therefore, since

$$MRS^A = MRS^B = MRT$$

at the efficient output combination (X_1, Y_1), general equilibrium is achieved at this point. At this output combination, consumer A receives X_1^A units of good X, Y_1^A units of good Y, and achieves a level of utility equal to U_1^A, while consumer B receives $(X_1 - X_1^A)$ units of good X, $(Y_1 - Y_1^A)$ units of good Y, and achieves U_1^B level of utility.

24.7.1 General Equilibrium and the Efficiency of Perfect Competition

The previous section demonstrated, from a theoretical perspective, that general equilibrium can be achieved in an economy through the process of exchange. We can now show that general equilibrium in an economy can be achieved when all goods and inputs are traded on the basis of their competitively determined relative prices. Recall from Section 23.6 in Chapter 23 that this outcome leads to a Pareto optimal allocation of goods because the necessary condition for a competitively determined consumer equilibrium, $MRS = P_X/P_Y$, holds true for each consumer. Hence

$$MRS^A = \frac{P_X}{P_Y}$$

and

$$MRS^B = \frac{P_X}{P_Y},$$

and therefore

$$MRS^A = \frac{P_X}{P_Y} = MRS^B.$$

The marginal rates of substitution for the two consumers are equal at the competitively determined consumer equilibrium, thereby indicating that this outcome is Pareto optimal. We also demonstrated this result graphically in the previous chapter in Figure 23.6 where you can observe that the indifference curves for each consumer are tangent to a line possessing a slope reflecting the competitively determined relative prices of the two goods.

From a production perspective, we demonstrated in Section 24.5 that an efficient allocation of labor and capital can be achieved if these inputs are distributed between the production of goods X and Y in accordance with their competitively determined relative input prices, represented by the ratio P_L/P_K. This occurs because the necessary condition for a constrained cost minimum, $MRTS = P_L/P_K$, holds true for all producers in the economy. Therefore, given the production of two goods, X and Y, in the simplified general equilibrium model of the economy, it must be true that

$$MRTS^X = \frac{P_L}{P_K}$$

and

$$MRTS^Y = \frac{P_L}{P_K},$$

and hence

$$MRTS^X = MRTS^Y,$$

at the competitively determined production equilibrium. Recall that this equality of marginal rates of technical substitution for the two goods is necessary for an input combination to be efficient and, accordingly, for it to lie on the production contract curve. We demonstrated this result in Figure 24.4 where the isoquants for each good were shown to be tangent to a line possessing a slope reflecting the relative prices of the two inputs, capital and labor. Also observe in panels (A) and (B) of Figure 24.5 that these efficient input combinations that lie on the production contract curve, as well as on particular isoquants, can be represented by points lying on the production possibilities frontier.

As we saw earlier, all of the points lying on the production possibilities frontier represent alternative combinations of the maximum levels of goods X and Y that can be simultaneously produced when all resources in the economy are used efficiently. Given that the quantities of inputs available in the economy are fixed, then for an additional unit of one good to be produced, some amount of the other good must be foregone. As a result, we can also interpret the marginal rate of transformation as measuring the marginal cost of producing one good relative to the marginal cost of producing the other, or alternatively stated

$$MRT = \frac{MC_X}{MC_Y}.$$

Graphically, we measure this tradeoff in goods production by the negative of the slope of a line drawn tangent to the production possibilities frontier. We showed in the previous section that an efficient outcome in the production of two goods in the simplified general equilibrium model can be achieved if the consumers' marginal rate of substitution for goods X and Y is equal to the marginal rate of transformation for these goods, or

$$MRS^A = MRS^B = MRT.$$

A competitive market can achieve this result because perfectly competitive firms produce that level of output where the price, or marginal revenue, associated with the last unit of each good produced is equal to its marginal cost. Thus, in this two-goods case

$$MR_X = P_X = MC_X$$

and

$$MR_Y = P_Y = MC_Y.$$

Since we have defined the marginal rate of transformation as the ratio of the marginal cost of producing each good, then we can express the output efficiency condition as

$$MRT = \frac{MC_X}{MC_Y} = \frac{P_X}{P_Y}.$$

Moreover, since $MRS = P_X/P_Y$ with perfect competition, then for this market structure

$$MRS = MRT.$$

This result was illustrated graphically in Figure 24.6. However, we can now say that the negative of the slopes of the tangent lines WW' and ZZ' represent the ratio of the competitively determined prices of goods X and Y, P_X/P_Y. This result indicates that a general equilibrium outcome, representing the efficient use of resources in producing the Pareto optimal levels of goods, can be achieved in a perfectly competitive market, with resources being allocated to their most highly desired uses.

24.7.2 Monopoly Power and Economic Inefficiency

In the previous section, we demonstrated the ability of perfectly competitive markets to efficiently allocate inputs and goods in an economy to achieve general equilibrium, in an effort to underscore perhaps one of the most desired features of this type of market structure. By contrast, a monopolistic market structure, or more broadly, a market structure characterized by some degree of monopoly power, does not possess the same ability to efficiently allocate scarce resources to the production of those goods most desired in the economy. Recall from Chapter 15 that, unlike a perfectly competitive firm that acts as a price taker and therefore determines its profit-maximizing level of output where $P = MR = MC$, a monopolist charges a price that exceeds its marginal revenue. Since this firm determines its profit-maximizing level of output where $MR = MC$, the price it charges is also in excess of its marginal cost of production. As a result, the efficiency condition for production we developed in the previous section, specifically

$$MRT = \frac{MC_X}{MC_Y} = \frac{P_X}{P_Y},$$

does not hold true if one of the goods is produced in a monopolistic market, since in this case

$$\frac{MC_X}{MC_Y} \neq \frac{P_X}{P_Y}.$$

Recall that consumers exchange goods for the purpose of achieving the result $MRS^A = MRS^B = P_X/P_Y$. Then, since $MRT = MC_X/MC_Y \neq P_X/P_Y$, when one of the goods is produced in a monopolistic market, the general equilibrium efficiency outcome for consumption and production cannot be achieved because $MRS^A = MRS^B \neq MRT$. This result is manifested in the market by a misallocation of resources associated with the production of a less desired combination of outputs than that which prevails when the output market is perfectly competitive.

As an example, consider an economy where two goods, X and Y, are produced by firms operating in different types of market structures. Assume that good X is produced in a monopolized market, thus $P_X > MC_X$, while good Y is produced in a perfectly competitive market, hence $P_Y = MC_Y$. Because we measure the marginal rate of transformation between the two goods, X and Y, as the ratio of their marginal costs, or $MRT = MC_X/MC_Y$, then

$$\left(MRT = \frac{MC_X}{MC_Y} \right) < \frac{P_X}{P_Y}.$$

Furthermore, the Pareto optimal distribution of goods is determined by the condition

$$MRS^A = MRS^B = \frac{P_X}{P_Y},$$

and given the monopoly power in the market for good X, enabling the producer of this good to restrict its output and sell the good at a price exceeding its marginal cost, then it follows that

$$\left(MRT = \frac{MC_X}{MC_Y} \right) < \left(\frac{P_X}{P_Y} = MRS^A = MRS^B \right)$$

This result indicates that the rate at which producers are capable of transforming units of good Y into units of good X in the economy is less than the rate at which consumers A and B are willing to substitute units of good X for units of good Y. Clearly, labor and capital resources are misallocated in the economy, since too few units of good X and too many units of good Y are being produced owing to the presence of monopoly power in the market for good X. Both consumers can be made better off if labor and capital resources are shifted so as to increase the production of good X and decrease the production of good Y until

$$MRT = MRS^A = MRS^B,$$

thus achieving general equilibrium in the economy.

We can extend the concept of monopoly power to input markets, since any form of noncompetitive behavior in input markets also results in a misallocation of resources in the economy. Recall from Chapters 20 and 21 that both monopoly and monopsony power in input markets cause a distortion of the prices paid to inputs, leading to different marginal rates of technical substitution for the goods produced in the economy, or in the two-goods general equilibrium model

$$MRTS^X \neq MRTS^Y.$$

This inequality reflects the production of an inefficient combination of outputs that does not lie on the production possibilities frontier. We can also use the general equilibrium model developed in this chapter to analyze other sources of inefficiency in an economy. Some of these sources are the incomplete information on the part of buyers or sellers, the impact of externalities, and the inadequate provision of public goods. However, we will reserve these additional topics for economics textbooks devoted to the study of public choice.

24.8 SUMMARY

In this chapter we modified the two-consumer, two-goods exchange model developed in the previous chapter to include production. We then used the Edgeworth production box to illustrate the concept of general equilibrium in an economy with both production and exchange. In addition, we contrasted the efficiencies of a perfectly competitive market structure in allocating resources and goods to where they are most highly valued with the inefficiencies associated with markets characterized by some degree of monopoly power. These and the other major topics discussed in this chapter are as follows.

- An Edgeworth production box is a rectangle containing all feasible combinations of two inputs, labor and capital, available in an economy that can be used in the production of two goods.
- A technically efficient input allocation is one for which the output of one good cannot be increased without decreasing the output of another good. At an efficient input combination, the marginal rates of technical substitution for producing the goods are equal.
- A production contract curve is the set of efficient input allocations within an Edgeworth production box.

- If capital and labor are allocated in the production of two goods in accordance with their competitively determined relative prices, then it is possible to attain an efficient distribution of inputs.
- The production possibilities frontier is a set of points measuring the combinations of two goods that can be simultaneously produced, corresponding to allocations of labor and capital that lie on the production contract curve.
- The marginal rate of transformation measures the rate at which the production of one good must be reduced in order to release enough inputs, usually labor and capital, to produce an additional unit of another good.
- Assuming goods X and Y, along with consumers A and B, we find that general equilibrium in an economy is attained where $MRS^A = MRS^B$, $MRTS^X = MRTS^Y$, and $MRS^A = MRS^B = MRT$.
- General equilibrium can be attained in an economy characterized by perfectly competitive input and output markets.
- Monopoly power in input or output markets distorts the prices of either goods and/or inputs such that these inputs and outputs are not efficiently allocated.

KEY TERMS

- Edgeworth production box, page 636
- marginal rate of transformation, page 650
- production contract curve, page 644
- production possibilities frontier, page 647
- technically efficient, page 640

EXERCISES

24.1 Using an Edgeworth production box containing isoquants and a production contract curve, derive the associated production possibilities frontier.

24.2 Discuss the significance of the attainment of general equilibrium in an economy characterized by perfectly competitive input and output markets.

24.3 State the various conditions that must simultaneously hold true in perfectly competitive input and output markets for general equilibrium to be established in an cconomy.

24.4 State the efficiency conditions that must hold true for the following outcomes.
   a. An allocation of inputs that lies on the production contract curve.
   b. A Pareto optimal allocation of goods that lies on the contract curve.
   c. An allocation of goods that lies on the utility possibilities frontier.

24.5 Provide two alternative explanations of what the slope of the production possibilities frontier measures.

24.6 Can general equilibrium in production and consumption be established in an economy with monopolized output markets? Explain your response using the necessary conditions for establishing a general equilibrium in an economy.

24.7 Provide real-world examples of two output markets—one that is characterized by monopoly power and one that is not. Discuss the manner in which capital and labor inputs are allocated in these markets. Can general equilibrium be attained in these markets?

24.8 Assume that all markets in an economy have achieved competitive equilibrium and that the prices of goods X and Y are \$20 and \$10, respectively.

a. Determine the value(s) of the marginal rate(s) of substitution between two goods, X and Y, for two consumers A and B.

b. Determine the value of the marginal rate of transformation between goods X and Y.

Glossary

Allocative Efficiency The flow of resources to their most highly valued uses.

Average Fixed Cost (AFC) A firm's fixed cost per unit of output produced.

Average Product of an Input (AP) The amount of output produced per unit of an input used in a production process, while holding all other inputs constant.

Average Revenue (AR) The value of a firm's sales, or total revenue, per unit of output it sells.

Average Total Cost (ATC) A firm's short-run total cost per unit of output produced.

Average Variable Cost (AVC) A firm's variable cost per unit of output produced.

Bandwagon Effect A condition that exists when some individuals' quantities demanded of a good are directly dependent on other individuals' consumption levels of that good.

Barrier to Entry A factor that restricts the number of firms operating in a particular market.

Budget Equation The set of combinations of goods and services an individual is able to purchase, given a predetermined level of money income and predetermined prices of the goods, where her expenditure on these goods exactly equals her income.

Budget Set The set of combinations of goods that are affordable to a consumer, given predetermined levels of the prices of the goods and income.

Cardinal Utility A method of measuring utility that is based on the assumption that a consumer has the ability to accurately evaluate the amount of utility he derives from consuming a particular combination of goods and services, and assign an actual (cardinal) number to it.

Cartel A group of firms that, through some type of explicit agreement, collude to jointly determine the values of strategic variables such as price and output.

Certainty A condition that exists when an individual has access to perfect information regarding the occurrence of a particular outcome.

Compensated Demand Curve A curve that expresses the optimal consumption level, or quantity demanded, of a good in terms of its own price while holding the prices of other goods and utility constant.

Compensated Demand Function A function that expresses the optimal consumption level, or quantity demanded, of a good in terms of its own price, the prices of other goods, and utility.

Condition of Fixed Proportions A characteristic of some production processes where it is possible to produce a given level of output from a finite number of input ratios.

Condition of Variable Proportions A characteristic of some production processes where it is possible to produce a given level of output from an infinite number of input ratios.

Conjectural Variation How one firm thinks another will react to its own adjustments in some strategic variable.

Constant Cost Industry An industry in which input prices do not vary with changes in the demand for the inputs.

Constant Output Demand for an Input Curve A curve that expresses the quantity of an input demanded as a function of its own price, holding output and all other determinants of this input constant.

Constant Returns to Scale A result reflecting the fact that a firm neither gains nor loses production efficiency as it proportionally expands or reduces its use of inputs.

Constant Sum Game A game for which the sum of the payoffs to all players in the game is a constant value for all possible strategy combinations.

Constrained Optimization The process of maximizing or minimizing some objective function subject to the limitations imposed by some predetermined factors affecting the values of the decision variables in that function.

Consumer Surplus The difference between the value consumers place on each unit of a good and the price they actually pay for that unit, summed over all units purchased.

Contract Curve The set of allocations of goods within an Edgeworth box that are Pareto optimal.

Cost Function A function that expresses a firm's costs in terms of the output it produces, along with other determinants.

Critical Value A value in the domain of a function at which the first derivative of the function is equal to zero.

Cross-Price Demand Curve A curve that expresses the quantity demanded of a good in terms of the price of another good, while holding its own price and money income constant.

Cross-Price Elasticity of Demand The percentage change in the quantity demanded of a good resulting from a percentage change in the price of another good.

Deadweight Loss The loss of consumer and producer surplus due to output restriction.

Decreasing Returns to Scale A result reflecting the fact that a firm experiences decreases in its production efficiency as it proportionately expands its use of inputs.

Degree of Homogeneity The degree n if $\delta^n Q = f(\delta K, \delta L)$, where δ represents some scale factor.

Demand Function A function that expresses the optimal consumption level of a good, or the quantity demanded of a good, in terms of the prices of all the goods and money income in the constrained utility maximization problem.

Dependent, or Objective, Variable A variable designated to be explained and/or predicted.

Discounting The determination of the present value of a stream of future payments.

Diseconomies of Scale A production situation for which an increase in the use of inputs, in either a proportionate or disproportionate manner, results in higher per unit costs of production.

Dominant Strategy A strategy that consistently optimizes a player's payoff in a game, regardless of the strategies chosen by the other players in the game.

Dynamic Efficiency Technological progress.

Economies of Scale A production situation for which an increase in inputs, either in a proportionate or disproportionate manner, results in lower per unit costs of production.

Economies of Scope A situation where a firm achieves lower per unit costs of production by producing multiple outputs rather than by producing only one good or service.

Edgeworth Box A rectangle containing all of the feasible combinations of two goods, X and Y, available in the economy that can be distributed between two consumers, where the length of the box measures the total amount of good X available in the economy and the height of the box measures the total amount of good Y available.

Edgeworth Production Box A rectangle containing all feasible combinations of two inputs, labor and capital, available in the economy that can be used in the production of two goods, where the length of the box measures the total amount of labor input available in the economy and the height of the box measures the total amount of capital available.

Elastic Own-Price Demand A result indicating that some percentage change in the price of a good results in a greater percentage change, in the opposite direction, of the quantity demanded of that good.

Elasticity A measure that indicates the degree of responsiveness between two variables, regardless of the units of measurement.

Elasticity of Substitution The ratio of the percentage change in the capital–labor ratio to the percentage change in the marginal rate of technical substitution between two inputs, holding output constant.

Engel Curve A curve that expresses the optimal consumption levels of a good for different levels of income, while holding the prices of all goods constant.

Equilibrium Condition A condition for which the quantity supplied of a good is equal to its quantity demanded.

Equilibrium Price A stable price that can be maintained in the absence of changes in the underlying determinants of the market own-price supply and demand curves.

Excess Capacity The difference between the perfectly competitive level of output and that for a monopolistically competitive firm in long-run equilibrium.

Expansion Path A set of input combinations corresponding to constrained cost minimization solutions for different predetermined levels of output, while holding input prices constant.

Expected Utility Function A function that measures the expected utility of a set of possible outcomes as the sum of the products of the utility received from each outcome multiplied by its respective probability of occurrence.

Expected Value, or Mean Value The summation of the products of each value of a variable and its corresponding probability of occurrence.

Expenditure Function A function that expresses a consumer's expenditure in terms of the prices of goods and his level of utility.

Explicit Cost A component of a firm's cost associated with the nonowner-supplied inputs used in its production process.

Fair Game A game for which the cost of playing is equal to the expected value of the game.

First Theorem of Welfare Economics An allocation of goods that is a competitive equilibrium must also be a Pareto optimal allocation of goods.

Fixed Cost (FC) The cost associated with the fixed input(s) a firm uses in its production process.

Fixed Input An input for which the quantity used cannot be changed during the time period under consideration.

Future Value of an Asset or Payment (FV) The value of a present asset or payment in terms of what it is worth in some future time period.

Game Any situation in which two or more participants, or players, directly compete to make optimal strategic decisions.

Game Theory A mathematically based framework for modeling optimal decision making under conditions of strategic interactions among players in a game.

General Equilibrium Analysis The process by which all markets, and all consumers and firms comprising those markets, simultaneously attain equilibrium.

Giffen Good An inferior good for which the income effect dominates the substitution effect.

Gross Complements Two goods for which the quantity demanded of one good varies inversely with the price of the other good, while

holding its own price and money income constant.

Gross Substitutes Two goods for which the quantity demanded of one good varies directly with the price of the other good, while holding its own price and money income constant.

Higher-Order Derivative The derivative of a derivative.

Implicit Cost The cost associated with those inputs supplied by the owners to their firm.

Income Consumption Curve A set of combinations of goods corresponding to constrained utility maximum solutions for different levels of money income, while holding the prices of the goods constant.

Income Effect The impact that a change in the price of a good has on the quantity demanded of that good due strictly to the resulting change in real income, or purchasing power.

Income Elasticity The percentage change in the quantity demanded of a good resulting from a percentage change in money income.

Increasing Cost Industry An industry for which input prices vary directly with changes in the demand for the inputs.

Increasing Returns to Scale A result where a firm experiences increases in production efficiency as it proportionally increases its inputs.

Independent, or Decision, Variable A variable that provides the basis for explanation and/or prediction of some dependent variable.

Indifference Curve A set of combinations of two goods that yield the same level of utility.

Individual's Own-Price Demand Curve A curve that expresses an individual's optimal consumption level, or quantity demanded, of a good in terms of its own price, while holding other prices and money income constant.

Inelastic Own-Price Demand A result indicating that some percentage change in the price of a good results in a smaller corresponding percentage change in the quantity demanded of that good, in the opposite direction.

Inferior Good A good for which the optimal consumption level varies inversely with income.

Initial Endowment A particular allocation of goods consumers are assumed to possess before they engage in any exchange of these goods.

Input A resource that a firm uses in its production process for the purpose of creating a good or service.

Interest Rate The ratio of the payment per annum generated by an asset to the value of that asset.

Investment The change in a firm's level of capital for a given time period.

Isocost Equation An equation that represents the set of all input combinations that a firm is able to purchase for a particular level of expenditure on inputs and a given set of input prices.

Isoquant A set of input combinations that can be used to produce a given level of output.

Labor Supply Curve A curve that expresses the quantity of labor supplied as a function of its own price, *ceteris paribus*.

Lagrangian Function A function used in solving constrained optimization problems, which comprises the objective function plus a created variable, λ, multiplied by the constraint expressed in standard form.

Law of Diminishing Marginal Productivity of an Input A result indicating that as additional units of an input are used in a production process, while holding all other inputs constant, the resulting increments to output, or total product, become successively smaller.

Law of Diminishing Marginal Utility A result indicating that as additional units of a good are consumed, while holding the consumption of all other goods constant, the resulting increments in utility become successively smaller.

Long-Run A period of time during which none of a firm's inputs remain fixed, or alternatively, all of a firm's inputs are treated as variable.

Long-Run Average Cost (LRAC) A firm's long-run total cost divided by the level of output produced.

Long-Run Elasticity of Supply A measure of the ratio of the percentage change in the market quantity supplied of a good in the long run to a percentage change in its own price.

Long-Run Marginal Cost (LRMC) The change in long-run total cost due to a change in a firm's production of output.

Long-Run Market, or Industry, Supply Curve (LRS) A curve that comprises the set of quantity-price combinations that constitute long-run equilibria in a perfectly competitive market.

Long-Run Perfectly Competitive Equilibrium A situation for which a perfectly competitive firm produces a level of output corresponding to its minimum long-run average cost and zero profit.

Long-Run Total Cost Function (LRTC) A function that expresses a firm's minimum costs in terms of the level of output it produces, while holding input prices constant at some specified levels.

Marginal Expense of an Input (MEI) The change in total cost due to a change in the amount of an input employed, holding all other inputs constant.

Marginal Function The first derivative of a total function.

Marginal Product of an Input (MP) The change in the production of output, or total product, due to a change in the amount of an input used in a production process, while holding all other inputs constant.

Marginal Rate of Substitution (MRS) The rate at which a consumer is willing to substitute one good for another within her utility function, while receiving the same level of utility.

Marginal Rate of Technical Substitution (MRTS) The rate at which one input can be substituted for the other in a production process, while producing some constant level of output.

Marginal Rate of Transformation (MRT) The rate at which the production of one good must be reduced to release enough labor and capital to produce an additional unit of another good.

Marginal Revenue (MR) The change in total revenue resulting from a change in the quantity of a good sold.

Marginal Revenue Product of an Input (MRP) The change in total revenue due to a change in the amount of that input used, holding all other inputs constant.

Marginal Utility of a Good (MU) The change in utility resulting from a change in the amount of a good consumed, while holding consumption of all other goods constant.

Market An aggregation of actual or potential buyers and sellers of a good or service who, through their interactions, determine the equilibrium price and quantity of that good or service being bought and sold.

Market Own-Price Demand Curve The aggregation of individual own-price demand curves.

Market Period or Immediate Run A period of time during which all of a firm's inputs remain fixed.

Market Structure The number and size distribution of buyers and sellers operating in a market.

Maximin Strategy A strategy that maximizes the minimum gain a player can earn in a game.

Minimax Strategy A strategy that minimizes the maximum loss a player can earn in a game.

Mixed Strategies A process that requires a player to select each of his strategies a particular percentage of the time so that the player's payoffs are equal regardless of the strategies chosen by his rivals.

Model A formal framework that expresses relationships among certain facts.

Monopolistic Competition A market structure consisting of a large number of firms selling slightly differentiated products.

Monopoly A market structure consisting of a single seller of a good.

Monopoly Power The ability to influence the price of a product.

Monopsony A market structure in which a single firm acts as the sole purchaser of an input.

Multivariate Function A function containing more than one independent variable.

Nash Equilibrium An outcome in a game where each player selects the strategy that optimizes her payoff, given the strategies chosen by the other players.

Net Complements Two goods for which the quantity demanded of one good varies inversely with the price of the other good, while holding its own price and utility constant.

Net Substitutes Two goods for which the quantity demanded of one good varies directly with the price of the other good, while holding its own price and utility constant.

Nominal Interest Rate A per annum percentage expressing a future payment in "current" dollar terms.

Normal Good A good for which the optimal consumption level varies directly with money income.

Oligopoly A market structure generally consisting of a few sellers of a good, where each seller accounts for a significant portion of the marketwide sales.

Ordinal Utility A measure of utility where individuals are only required to rank consumption bundles from best to worst, on the basis of the amount of utility received.

Output Effect The effect of a change in the price of an input on the quantity demanded of that input, due strictly to the resulting change in the profit-maximizing level of output.

Own-Price Elasticity of Demand The ratio of the percentage change in the quantity demanded of a good to the percentage change in the price of that good.

Pareto Optimal, or Efficient An allocation of goods where no one consumer can be made better off without making another consumer worse off.

Partial Derivative The change in a dependent variable in a function resulting from an infinitesimally small change in an independent variable, while holding all other independent variables constant.

Partial Equilibrium Analysis The isolated examination of equilibrium in individual markets, and for individual consumers and firms comprising those markets.

Partial Slope The change in the dependent variable in a function due to a change in any one of the independent variables, while holding all other independent variables constant.

Payoff The return a player in a game receives from selecting a particular strategy, contingent on the strategies chosen by the other players in the game.

Perfectly Competitive Market A market in which there are a large number of insignificantly small buyers and sellers of a homogeneous good or service.

Players Rational decision makers having the goal of selecting the strategy that yields the best payoff, given the strategies available to the other players in a game.

Positive Monotonic Transformation A transformation of a function, such as U, into another function $V(U)$, where $V(U_1) > V(U_0)$ whenever $U_1 > U_0$.

Present Value of an Asset or Payment (PV) The value of a future asset or payment in terms of what it is worth in the present time period.

Price Consumption Curve A set of combinations of two goods corresponding to constrained utility maximization solutions for different prices of one good, while holding the price of the other good and money income constant.

Price Discrimination The charging of different price to marginal cost ratios for different units of a good that are of the same grade and quality, once an equilibrium price is established.

Producer Surplus The difference between the price a producer receives from selling each unit of a good and the marginal cost associated with producing each respective unit, summed over all units sold.

Product Group A set of heterogeneous but closely related goods.

Production Contract Curve A set of input allocations within an Edgeworth production box that are efficient.

Production Efficiency Production of a given level of output in the least costly manner and producing that level of output that corresponds to a minimum value of long run average cost.

Production Externality Either a negative or beneficial side effect associated with the production of a good or service by one firm that affects at least one other firm's production, and therefore generates uncompensated costs or benefits to the affected firm(s).

Production Function A function that shows the maximum quantity of a good or service that can be produced from various combinations of inputs, while holding technology constant at some predetermined state.

Production Possibilities Frontier A set of points measuring the combinations of two goods that can be simultaneously produced, corresponding to allocations of labor and capital lying on a production contract curve.

Proportional Own-Price Demand Curve A set of quantity–price combinations representing the proportion of the total product group quantity demanded at each price attributed to one firm within the group.

Rational Consumer A consumer who uses all prevailing information available to choose among various goods and services with the explicit goal of maximizing her utility.

Reaction Function A function that expresses one firm's profit-maximizing level of output in terms of the output sold by another firm.

Real Interest Rate A per annum percentage expressing a future payment in terms of the goods and services that can be purchased with this payment in the present time period.

Repeated Game A game that is played over and over again, where each player has complete knowledge of the strategies previously chosen by each of his rivals.

Ridge Lines for Indifference Curve Mapping Sets of goods combinations for which the marginal utility of one of the goods is equal to zero.

Ridge Lines for Isoquant Mapping Sets of input combinations for which the marginal product of one of the inputs is equal to zero.

Risk A situation that exists when perfect information is unavailable to a decision maker but the probabilities associated with all outcomes are known.

Risk-Averse Describes an individual for whom the expected utility she receives from the outcome associated with a risky choice is less than the utility she receives from a certain outcome, which is equal to the expected or mean outcome associated with the risky choice.

Risk-Neutral Describes an individual for whom the expected utility he receives from the outcome associated with a risky choice is precisely equal to the utility he receives from an outcome with certainty, which is equal to the expected or mean outcome associated with the risky choice.

Risk-Preferring Describes an individual for whom the expected utility he receives from the outcome associated with a risky choice is greater than the utility he receives from an outcome with certainty, which is equal to the expected or mean outcome associated with the risky choice.

Risk Premium The amount of money an individual is willing to forego in order to make him indifferent between a risky investment and one with a certain return.

Saddle Point A solution to a game in which players follow maximin and minimax strategies and no player has an incentive to change its strategy, given the strategies chosen by each of the other players in the game.

Second Theorem of Welfare Economics A theorem stating a set of goods prices exists such that each Pareto optimal goods allocation lying on a contract curve is also a competitive equilibrium.

Sequential Game A game in which the order of the players' participation is prespecified prior to the start of the game.

Short-Run A period of time during which at least one of a firm's inputs is treated as fixed.

Short-Run Elasticity of Supply The ratio of the percentage change in the quantity supplied of a good, in the short run, to the percentage change in its own price.

Short-Run Marginal Cost (SRMC) The change in a firm's short-run total cost due to a change in its production of output.

Short-Run Market Supply Curve A curve that expresses the quantity supplied of a good by all firms in a market explicitly in terms of its price, holding all other determinants constant.

Short-Run Total Cost Function (SRTC) A function that expresses a firm's costs in terms of its production of output, holding constant the level of at least one input, as well as the prices of all inputs.

Slutsky Equation The mathematical decomposition of the total effect of a change in the price of a good on the quantity demanded of that good, into the summation of the subsequent substitution and income effects.

Snob Effect An effect reflecting the fact that some individuals' quantities demanded of a good are inversely related to other individuals' consumption levels of that good.

Social Cost A cost that includes a firm's private production costs plus any costs or minus any benefits generated by its production externality.

Stage I Area of Production That range of production for which increases in the use of a variable input cause increases in its average product.

Stage II Area of Production That range of production for which increases in the use of a variable input cause decreases in its average product, while values of its associated marginal product remain nonnegative.

Stage III Area of Production That range of production for which use of a variable input corresponds to negative values for its marginal product.

State of Technology Society's pool of knowledge concerning the industrial arts.

Strategies The set of all alternative choices available to all the players in a game.

Substitution Effect The impact that a change in the price of a good has on the quantity demanded of that good due to the resulting change in relative prices, while holding utility constant.

Technically Efficient Input allocations for which the output of one good cannot be increased without decreasing the output of another.

Tit-for-Tat A strategy in which players in a repeated game immediately reward their rivals for cooperative behavior or penalize them for noncooperative behavior in the subsequent round of the game.

Total Derivative The change in the dependent variable in a function due to an infinitesimally small change in an independent variable, where all independent variables are allowed to vary.

Total Product Curve (TP) A curve that expresses the maximum quantity of output, or total product, produced by a firm explicitly as a function of one input, while holding all other inputs and technology constant at some specified levels.

Total Revenue (TR) The total value of consumers' expenditures associated with the sale of a good.

Uncertainty A situation in which a decision maker does not possess perfect information nor any probabilities associated with the occurrence of a specific outcome.

Unit Elastic Own-Price Demand An own-price elasticity value indicating that some percentage change in the price of a good results in an equivalent percentage change in the quantity demanded of that good in the opposite direction.

Univariate Function A function containing one independent variable.

Util A unit of measure for the amount of satisfaction an individual receives from consuming goods and services.

Utility The satisfaction an individual receives from consuming goods and services.

Utility Curve A curve that expresses a consumer's utility in terms of his consumption level of a good, while holding his consumption levels of all other goods constant.

Utility Function A function that expresses a consumer's level of utility in terms of the amounts of goods and services she consumes.

Utility Possibilities Frontier A set of points measuring the combinations of utility levels attainable for two consumers corresponding to allocations of goods lying on the contract curve.

Value of the Marginal Product of an Input (VMP) The change in total revenue due to a change in the amount of an input used in a production process, holding the output price and all other inputs constant.

Variable Cost (VC) A firm's cost associated with the variable input(s) it uses in its production process.

Variable Input An input for which the quantity used can be changed during the time period under consideration.

Variance A measure of the dispersion of a random variable about its mean, or expected value.

X-Efficiency A condition in which a firm's management is able to minimize the cost associated with producing each level of output.

Index